TRUTH UNCHANGED, UNCHANGING

A Selection of Articles from The Bible League Quarterly 1912 – 82

"Thy Word is Truth"
(John 17.17)

The Bible League, Larkhill House, 4 Godwyn Close, Abingdon OX14 1BU.

1984

Contents

Contents Continued

FOREWORD

The Bible League came into existence as a result of C. H. Spurgeon's noble fight for the fundamentals of our Faith during the 'Down Grade' controversy of 1887-1892. In the latter part of the eighteenth century rationalism swept across Germany and in Spurgeon's day it was beginning to make its presence felt in England. A great deal of scholarship and theological activity was being concentrated upon an attempt to discredit the Bible. As a result, college professors and ministers were denying the doctrines of verbal inspiration and inerrancy, claiming that the Bible was like all other books, subject to the infirmities of humanity, error included. 'The Higher Criticism', as Professor Eichhorn had called it, was really an all-out attack upon God's Word and historic Christianity. Spurgeon saw it for what it was: one of the greatest evils ever to have infested the Church. He sounded an alarm which shook the evangelical world, and then withdrew from his denomination on the grounds that he could have no fellowship with unscriptural 'down grade' doctrines. After his death the Bible League was formed to continue his faithful and militant witness to the truth.

The trend and development of 'downgradism' continued; but, under the auspices of the Bible League, some scholars and theologians, who were committed to a belief in Scripture as word for word God-given, began aggressively to expose the arbitrary assumptions, illogical arguments, and false conclusions of the Higher Criticism. Their outstanding contributions appeared in 'The Bible League Quarterly' and many of them now re-appear in this volume.

Today the anti-inerrancy approach to the Bible is widespread; and sadly even evangelical Protestants are losing their vision of what truth is and faltering in their fidelity to it. In our Bible Colleges concessions are being made to liberal scholarship with regard to the authorship, date, interpretation, and the underlying text of biblical books. In our churches many now appear to believe in the continuance of revelation through 'charismatic gifts', thus jettisoning the cardinal doctrine of Scripture's completeness, sufficiency and finality. And even in those quarters where the full inspiration of the Bible is recognized there is a strong reluctance to obey it in a separated stand from organized apostasy. The Trustees of the Bible League hope and pray that the articles in this book will lead many to a deeper appreciation of God's written Word and to a more vigorous defence of the 'truth unchanged, unchanging.'

We owe a very special debt of gratitude to our esteemed Editor, Mr. S. M. Houghton. For a number of years he has rendered an invaluable service to the work of the Bible League as Editor of its Quarterly. He has now spent many hours in the arduous task of preparing this volume for publication. His untiring efforts in the cause of God and Truth are deeply appreciated and we take this opportunity of expressing to him our united and most sincere thanks.

May God Almighty bless these pages to the establishing of sound scriptural doctrine among His people

Malcolm H. Watts
Chairman of the Bible League Trust

CHARLES HADDON SPURGEON
(1834-1892)

INTRODUCTION

The present century is moving steadily—or some would say unsteadily—to its close. Its chequered history makes far from pleasant reading. Wars and rumours of wars, famines, pestilences, social unrest and much else have marked its course. Remarkable developments have taken place in the world scene. Scientific progress has been amazing. Conquests have extended into outer space. The moon has known the tread of man's foot. Satellites have been launched into space. Improvements in communications have gone far to change the pattern of everyday life. On the other hand, by and large, tension has been greatly heightened among men. Tragically, there has been obvious deterioration—and of necessity we speak particularly of Britain—in matters moral and spiritual. Degradation has come in apace. We here make no attempt to apportion blame; we simply state the fact of the matter. In national life departure from ancient Christian standards has shown clear acceleration. Religious revival has seemed far away.

This does not imply that true Christians are dismal pessimists. But events during the present century have underlined the great biblical truth that the unbelieving world retains its ancient and unchanging character. The apostle John in his First Epistle writes, 'We know . . . the whole world lieth in wickedness' (5.19). We know it also by experience, by observation, and by the records which the world itself publishes of its doings. Salvation involves 'deliverance from this present evil world according to the will of God and our Father' (Gal. 1.4): and that will is to be paramount in the life of the Christian.

The Christian has a responsibility to fulfil. The Lord Jesus Himself, as John's Gospel reminds us (7.7), testified of the world that its works were evil. Hatred, contempt, opposition on the world's part may be the result of our testimony. But testimony to the truth is the Christian's responsibility. In this he follows his Lord and Master, come weal, come woe. As a unit in a Christian community and fellowship, he is to bear his testimony and demonstrate the saving power of godliness.

Regretfully, however, we all of us discover that among those who bear the Christian name are deep-seated divisions. Dis-union marks the Church as well as the world. It has been so during the 'running' centuries. We grant that during the Middle Ages, as far as Western Europe was concerned, there appeared to be a considerable degree of unity. The Church of the West professed allegiance to a 'holy Father' known to all as 'the Pope'. Groups of believers here and there held aloof and were savagely persecuted. In the Sixteenth Century came the break-up of Western Christendom. 'Truth sprang out of the earth and righteousness looked down from heaven'(Psa. 85.11). Great doctrines of Scripture, long replaced by the traditions of men, came to light. Protests against error multiplied. Truth was, as it were, born again. In the centuries that followed the Reformation, despite intervals of decadence and decline, there were periods when believers, earnestly desiring a 'closer walk with God', were granted the experience delightfully described at the close of the Old Testament: 'Unto you that fear my Name shall the Sun of righteousness arise, with healing in His wings' (Mal. 4.2). Their path became as 'the shining light, that shineth more and more unto the perfect day' (Prov. 4.18). Individually, many of them could say:

'So purer light shall mark the road
That leads me to the Lamb!'

Within the church of God at large, however, darkness and light seemed to be often in conflict. It was so in the Nineteenth Century when faithful ministers of God's Word found themselves in direct conflict with men who openly challenged the inspiration, authority and infallibility of that Word, introduced 'pernicious heresies', substituted a theory of 'the Origin of Species' in place of the plain teaching of Scripture, and, in sum, aimed at replacing the age-old beliefs of the Christian by the findings of a modern age.

It was at such a time that the so-called Downgrade Controversy produced a stir in the evangelical camp, beginning about 1887. Charles Haddon Spurgeon raised the standard of Christian orthodoxy and expressed grave concern about doctrinal and practical departures from 'the faith once delivered to the saints'. In the course of the ensuing battle, Spurgeon died, but the fight continued.

Proverbially unity is strength, and a group of men, including both Anglicans and Nonconformists, decided in May, 1892, to found the Bible League and to pursue the aim set out at the head of every issue of its Quarterly from that day to this. The reason for the long-continued fight is tremendously serious. Not only is the integrity of the Scriptures involved, and on that integrity the salvation of our souls hinges, but the personal testimony of the Lord Jesus Christ Himself is under attack if men query the truth of His sayings, and urge, as not a few do, that He shared in ideas of his day long refuted. It is impossible for His true disciples to hold at one and the same time the view that He was God's only begotten Son, one with the Father and the Holy Spirit, and yet that as Son of man He was in error concerning the nature of Old Testament Scripture, and a propagator of that error. Undeniably He taught that Old Testament Scripture was the very Word of God, true, unbreakable, and utterly reliable. Apostles held and taught precisely the same doctrine. '*All* Scripture', wrote Paul, 'is given by inspiration of God' (2 Tim. 3.16).

But, says the Modernist, that is not so. Thereby he denies what the New Testament declares. He mis-interprets and misuses Paul's statement that, 'being found in fashion as a man, he (Christ) emptied himself' (Phil. 2.8). He asserts that among the human limitations that the Son of God assumed on 'being found in fashion as a man' was that of ignorance on many matters including the origin of Old Testament Scripture, and the reception of ideas which belonged to mistakes of His own time. But the words 'emptied himself' imply no such thing. It is the responsibility and blessedness of every believer to hold tenaciously to the declaration that the Lord Jesus Christ is 'the way, the truth and the life'. His coming in faith to 'the Father' ('by Me' John 14.6): is directly involved and explicitly stated in these particular words.

The Bible League Quarterly

As already stated the Bible League dates from May, 1892. But at first its publications were scanty. Its testimony to Scripture truth was given, for the most part, in public meetings, and it will interest our readers to know that, as the League grew in numerical strength, these came to number several hundreds a year held in various parts of Great Britain. It was 1912, however, before the League's Quarterly began to appear in anything like its present form. Of the first 45 issues there is no trace, and No. 46 (dated July, 1912) is tattered and incomplete. Its price was one penny, its length some twelve pages. From 1918, however, there is hardly a break in the series up to the present day and the present trustees of the Bible League have been happy to commission the Editor to make a selection from the entire run of magazines from 1912 to the present day, that is to say, a period of seventy years. In making the selection the Editor has reported to the trustees that he has been spoiled for choice, so many and so valuable are the articles, the consequence being that not a few considered suitable for reprinting have been by-passed. But it deserves mention that, if God will, the Bible League reaches its Centenary in 1992 and a second volume of reprints may then be a possibility. Not one of us knows what a day (or a year) may bring forth. The chief thing we know is that after 'a little while', He 'that shall come will come and will not tarry' (Heb. 10.37), a promise linked with the exercise of patience, the doing of the will of God and the receiving of 'the promise'.

The thoughts of many Christians will doubtless be exercised with the fact that two millenniums terminate in the year 2,000, and probably many people will be asking whether there is any outstanding religious significance in that date. We are no prophets of the future beyond what Scripture reveals. We assuredly know that Christ will some day return in glory, bringing all the holy angels with Him and the spirits of just men made perfect (at which time also will take place the resurrection of the just); living saints will be caught up to meet Him in the air and thereafter to be for ever with the Lord. But we know, too, that the Father has 'put times and seasons in His own power' (Acts 1.7). Scripture itself ends with the glad tidings, 'Surely I come quickly. Amen'; and with the glad response of the faithful, 'Even so, come, Lord Jesus' (Rev. 22.28). What could we wish more?

We are saved to serve, even as it is written in the chapter of the Book of Revelation just quoted (v.3). Members of the Bible League during the present Century realize, we trust, that prayer for, and support of the League belongs to that service. We ask them also to seek God's blessing on the sale and reading of the book. The Bible League has issued pamphlets and booklets from time to time, but it has never previously engaged in the publishing of a book, and the plain truth is that our venture much needs the backing of our members. We are certain that, judged by present-day standards, the book will be considered very good value in relation to its cost. It is substantial, varied in content, and, we believe, thoroughly biblical and fitted to confirm believers in their most holy faith.

A Request Repeated

We repeat our request to members of the Bible League to do what in them lies to make the book known in these days, marked as they are on every hand by neglect of Scripture, by unbelief, and by public repudiation of many truths which to the believer are more precious than life. A valued subscriber has recently written to us as follows:

'The witness of the Quarterly was never more necessary than it is today. I can think of no journal in this country which so consistently maintains a high doctrine of Scripture—the doctrine to which Scripture itself testifies—together with everything in Christian faith and life which is based on that doctrine. The original purpose of the Bible League is very simply and plainly worded, and the Quarterly continues single-mindedly to give effect to that purpose. Long may it do so!'

S. M. Houghton

CHARLOTTE ELLIOTT
(1789-1871)
authoress of

'Just as I am, without one plea
But that Thy blood was shed for me,
And that Thou bidd'st me come to Thee,
O Lamb of God, I come!'

Section One

The Origin and Aims of the Bible League

Contents: Section One

The Origin and Aims of the Bible League

The Bible League: its Origin and its Aims

By S. M. Houghton

We take heed to the biblical warning that it is not good to inquire why former days were better than present days, if such indeed be the case. But we do not interpret this Scripture to mean that we are not to look at foundations; and it is certainly good to consider whether an institution continues to maintain the aims of its founders. Some churches, alas, now preach a gospel, if 'gospel' it can be called, which is radically different from that of their basic documents; and it is amazingly common for men who pay lip homage to the value of Scripture to speak anything but scripturally in their public utterances. As a famed hymn reminds us, 'decay' almost invariably follows 'change'. Certain it is that if we depart from biblical doctrine, precept and practice, we shall depart from blessing also, and shall know little but 'trouble and darkness, and dimness of anguish'.

The aims of the Bible League are proclaimed in every issue of its Quarterly. They are:
(1) A belief in the inspiration and sole sufficiency of the Holy Scriptures as the Word of God.
(2) The promotion of the reverent study of the Scriptures.
(3) Resistance to the varied attacks made upon the Scriptures.

Linked with these aims is the further (historical) statement that the Bible League was founded on May 3rd, 1892.

It is somewhat unusual for an association thus to announce with every issue of its literature the date, complete to the day, of its foundation, but there is an importance about the period of time thus precisely defined which invites and merits investigation.

Charles Haddon Spurgeon

Of necessity we begin with a warm-hearted reference to the ministry of Charles Haddon Spurgeon which terminated at the end of January, 1892, with his death at Mentone, at the age of 57. All men who know anything of the impact which that ministry made on Victorian England and who are competent to assess its significance in the 2,000-years-old history of the Christian Church, cannot but confess, if they are men of sound historical judgment, that it was one of the greatest and most fruitful of ministries since apostolic days. Spurgeon was a 'chosen vessel' unto Christ of no mean calibre. His remarkable gifts and skills, his powers of concentration in his God-given task, the variety of his activities within the kingdom of God, and much else, constitute him an amazing phenomenon in the Christian Church. For thirty-six years with unwavering and undiminishing zeal and faithfulness he preached the gospel of the grace of God in London and throughout Britain. Thousands crowded to his preaching services; scores of thousands gave close attention to his written ministry. To adapt a famous and ancient encomium: 'Here was a preacher! when comes such another!'

It is not the man that we praise, but his Lord and Master whose goodness and mercy conferred such a gift on Britain's capital city and sustained him in a ministry of vast extent and depth for so long a period. The fact that the 62 volumes of his week-by-week printed sermons are being reprinted is testimony to the continuing value of a preaching pastorate which, of its kind, is virtually without parallel in the long annals of the Church. Our estimate may, to some, appear exaggerated, but a forty-years' knowledge of the value of Spurgeon's printed ministry permits the writer to utter his settled verdict. He is not unwilling to defend it.

But what connection has Spurgeon, it may be asked, with the Bible League, which did not come into existence until his ministry had run its course? To answer the query it is needful to make reference to the controversy which troubled Spurgeon's closing years and which, indeed, undoubtedly hastened his death. It is known as The Downgrade. The title indicates its nature. Its history in its fulness has yet to be written, but in outline it has received recurring mention during the present century. The most recent and the most informative account of The Downgrade is to be found in Iain Murray's *The Forgotten Spurgeon* (Banner of Truth Trust, 1966) which devotes four chapters to the sad story. Here we can only mention the chief matters of contention.

The Downgrade

By the middle of the 1880's Spurgeon had become convinced that within the Protestant Churches of Britain a marked decline had set in. Whereas in the earlier part of his ministry places of worship were in general well attended, and by and large the gospel was preached and the Scriptures believed, in the days of his later ministry the case was far different. The Metropolitan Tabernacle where he himself ministered maintained its vast congregation but in many areas change and decay were all too evident. Spurgeon's magazine, *The Sword and the Trowel,* pronounced as follows on the matter in August, 1887: 'Attendance at places of worship is declining and reverence for holy things is vanishing. We solemnly believe this to be largely attributable to the scepticism which has flashed from the pulpit and spread among the people . . . In meeting-houses holding a thousand or twelve hundred or fifteen hundred, places once packed to the ceiling with ardent hearers, how small the numbers now!'

'The scepticism which has flashed from the pulpit and spread among the people'! This was the pernicious evil which Spurgeon diagnosed, and which in his later sermons he smote hip and thigh. The volumes of *The Sword and the Trowel* and of the *Metropolitan Tabernacle Pulpit* from 1887 and onwards (until early 1892) manifest the grief which struck at the heart of this Mr. Valiant-for-Truth. He found widespread evidence, both within and outside his own Baptist denomination, that perilous times had come. 'A chasm is opening,' he wrote, 'between the men who believe their Bibles and the men who are prepared for an advance upon Scripture . . . Inspiration and speculation cannot long abide in peace. Compromise there can be none. We cannot hold the inspiration of the Word and yet reject it; we cannot believe in the atonement and deny it; we cannot hold the doctrine of the fall and yet talk of the evolution of spiritual life from human nature; we cannot recognize the punishment of the impenitent and yet indulge "the larger hope". One way or the other we must go; decision is the virtue of the hour.' And again: 'Those who hold evangelical doctrine are in open alliance with those who call the fall a fable, who deny the personality of the Holy Ghost, who call justification by faith immoral, and hold that there is another probation after death . . . It is our solemn conviction that where there can be no real spiritual communion there should be no pretence of fellowship. Fellowship with known and vital error is participation in sin.' And again: 'Let us see to it that we set forth our Lord Jesus Christ as the infallible Teacher through His inspired Word. I do not understand that loyalty to Christ which is accompanied by indifference to His words. How can we reverence His person if His own words and those of His apostles are treated with disrespect? Unless we receive Christ's words we cannot receive Christ; and unless we receive His apostles' words we do not receive Christ; for John says, 'He that knoweth God, heareth us: he that is not of God heareth not us. Hereby know we the spirit of truth and the spirit of error.'

And we add one further word of Spurgeonic protest: 'There are now two parties in the religious world . . . The party everywhere apparent has a faith fashioned for the present century—perhaps we ought rather to say, for the present month. The 16th-century gospel it derides, and that indeed of every period except the present most enlightened era. It will have no creed because it can have none: it is continually on the move: it is not what it was yesterday, and it will not be tomorrow what it is today. Its shout is for "liberty", its delight is invention, its element is change. On the other hand there still survive . . . a few whom these superior persons call "fossils": that is to say, there are believers in the Lord Jesus Christ who consider that the true gospel is no new gospel, but is the same yesterday, today, and for ever. These do not believe in "advanced views", but judge that that view of truth which saved a soul in the 2nd century will save a soul now, and that a form of teaching which was unknown till the last few years is of very dubious value, and is in all probability "another gospel, which is not another".' 'When a text from the Word has been peculiarly precious to the heart of a Christian man, he will hear its authenticity impugned, the translation disputed, or its gospel reference denied. He will not travel far on the dark continent of modern thought before he will find the efficacy of prayer debated, the operation of divine providence questioned, and the special love of God denied. He will find himself to be a stranger in a strange land when he begins to speak of his experience, and of the ways of God to men.'

We have quoted Spurgeon at some length on these matters because 20th-century evangelicals do not always realize the nature of the religious modernism, now termed liberalism, which came into vogue towards the end of the last century, and which regarded Scripture in radically different fashion from all that had preceded it. The Word was fallible; the Christ was fallible; folklore and myth belonged to much of the sacred books; 'bloody theology' was primitive and out-moded; old things were passing away; new things must prevail in a world of education, enlightenment and bonhomie in which every man was free to regard as truth that which was right in his own eyes. We can but claim that events since the days of The Downgrade have justified Spurgeon to the hilt in the protest which he raised.

It needs to be added that Spurgeon's protest was raised not only on doctrinal grounds, but also because of the foolish, nonsensical and fatuous introduction into Church life of the jollities of the secular world—comic songs, humorous recitations, dramatic performances, in short what Archibald G. Brown rightly termed 'the devil's mission of amusements'. The 1889 volume of *The Sword and the Trowel* includes an extract from an American tract entitled 'Ecclesiastical Amusements' in which the author pours righteous scorn on all such things, whether intended as entertainment for Church-goers or methods of raising money for Church purposes. Such developments went hand in hand with the doctrinal heresies which characterised The Downgrade.

A Bible League is mooted

The death of Spurgeon on January 31st, 1892, caused the deepest grief in the evangelical camp. It had the effect of giving added force to the protests he had raised and the warnings he had given at such cost to himself during the closing years of his life. On February 11th the mortal remains, brought back to England from Mentone, were interred at West Norwood Cemetery, London. The following day an article appeared in the magazine *Word and Work,* edited by the Rev. John Urquhart, under the title, 'What is to be done?' It was written doubtless well before the date of publication, but accorded well with the disturbed and distressed thoughts of evangelicals who were lamenting the death of their standard-bearer in chief.

The article drew particular attention to the dishonour done to the Lord in the writings and utterances of many professed preachers of the gospel. 'We, who have had so many sad surprises, have had to endure one more. The authority of Jesus is calmly surrendered. There are some who are ready to admit and to proclaim that, as regards any knowledge of what was the Word of God and what was not, He who was "God manifest in the flesh" was merely a man of that time! As an authority on the nature and origin of Scripture, He, who proclaimed Himself greater than Solomon, must now be admitted to be less than Wellhausen! The time has come for action.' This said, and more to the same effect, the editor invited his readers to send in their comments and suggestions.

A week later, in the next issue, it was stated that some readers, while welcoming the article, considered that the proposed title—Bible Defence League—was inappropriate. The editor also amplified his views and, to give edge to his suggestions, he said that Christian brethren had been too long separated by party walls and that the new dangers to the faith rendered union essential. Handley Moule, then Principal of Ridley Hall, Cambridge, wrote favourably of the enterprise. He had been much tossed about in his mind, and for a time tempted to cast in his lot with the 'new theology', but he realized that he could not be loyal to his Master and adopt a different view of Holy Scripture from that of his Master. 'As for myself,' he wrote, 'I pray to my Master and Lord, and I trust Him to hold me now firm to the end, after many a struggle about it, in His opinion of the Holy Scriptures. I wish to enter into the rest and peace of the Bible as He abode in it. Therefore I accept His yoke of the Bible as He accepted it. I wish to feel what He felt, that living incitement to the lifelong study of the Bible, which is bound up vitally with a firm persuasion that the Bible is supernatural.'

Another interested person was Prebendary H. W. Webb-Peploe, although in writing to *Word and Work* he expressed the view that 'the number of societies and leagues already existing seems almost to preclude the success of another . . . But go forward, slack not, and the great God of the Bible defend

His own Word through the humble efforts of His servants'. W. Fuller Gooch wrote from West Norwood with the departure of Spurgeon still very much in mind. 'It may indeed be questioned,' he wrote, 'whether another has been seen since the days of the great apostle of the Gentiles who has had so world-wide and all-round an influence as he wielded. But Mr. Spurgeon's God still lives, his Master and ours still abides, and the omnipotent Spirit of grace, by whom alone he was made mighty, is still with us.' His letter concluded with a plea for special prayer meetings in London and the provinces, that the proposed League might be established.

Pastor James Stephens of Highgate Road Chapel, Kentish Town, wrote guardedly. He favoured the proposal but wished to know in more detail what exactly was in view before according it his full committal. Gavin Kirkham, the Secretary of the Open-Air Mission, wrote to say that, in his view, there were enough Societies in existence already, and that even though he agreed heartily with the defence of the Bible, it was inexpedient to start another. But Frank Cockrem of the same Mission wrote only a week later to promise his support. James Ormiston, editor of the *British Protestant,* wrote from Clifton in the same strain as Pastor James Stephens. The Secretary of the Evangelical Alliance wrote sympathetically but disapprovingly. The attitude of *The Christian* was interesting. It commented that it was as unnecessary to found a League in defence of the Bible as one to defend the sun against fogs, clouds and mists. All true Christians, it claimed, constituted *de facto* a Bible League.

While matters were thus being ventilated, the editor of *Word and Work* continued to supply evidence of further alarming departures from evangelical landmarks. The British Weekly had published a letter by James S. Candlish, son of a famed Scottish Free Church leader and a Professor of Theology in the Glasgow Free Church College, in which he frankly stated his modernism and his belief that in both Testaments there were 'doubtful books' for which inspiration could not properly be claimed (e.g. Ecclesiastes). The editor also reported his disappointment that he had not received the support expected from the Christian Evidence Society whose leading member had intimated that he saw no need for a Bible League 'as there was no real danger, the present assault (on the Word) being merely a harmless fashion of theological thought which would soon pass'. *Word and Work* thereupon accused the Christian Evidence Society of gross neglect of duty. It commented that erring Christian leaders in the 'nineties were adopting the teachings of Tom Paine and Charles Bradlaugh of former days, and that it was high time evangelicals rallied to the defence of the truth.

By April, 1892, plans to form a Bible League were well under way. Two lists of names were compiled: one which included Handley Moule, Archibald G. Brown, Fuller Gooch, James Ormiston, John Wilkinson (of Mildmay), Newman Hall, George Williams (of the Y.M.C.A.), and others of lesser note; these were deeply interested but could not promise active support as 'they had already as much to do as they could manage'. A second list contained the names of men able to form a Council. These included Prebendary Webb-Peploe, William Cuff, Frank Cockrem, F. E. Marsh, and several others. About the same time F. E. Marsh arranged a three-days Conference at Sunderland, County Durham—he was minister there—the speakers including Dr. E. W. Bullinger of Trinitarian Bible Society fame, John Urquhart of Weston-super-Mare (editor of *Word and Work*), Henry Varley (evangelist), and C. Russell Hurditch (indefatigable worker with Open Brethren and editor of five magazines in succession which 'changed their character and style according to the needs of the day').

The Bible League is inaugurated

And so we reach May 3rd, 1892, on which day the inaugural meeting of the Bible League took place. It was held in the Council Chamber, Exeter Hall, Strand, London, and was convened by John Urquhart. General Sir Robert Phayre, K.C.B., presided. Pastor William Cuff, one of Spurgeon's men, was selected to move the resolution that all who 'believed in the verbal inspiration and infallibility of the entire Bible as originally given' should be invited to found the Bible League. This was seconded by John Urquhart and unanimously approved.

The aims of the League were declared to be:

(1) To organize conferences in various parts of the country . . . and to create a public opinion which

will have a powerful effect on the issues of the struggle.

(2) To arrange for lectures by capable and reliable men.

(3) To recommend and supply books adapted to the needs of the time.

(4) To encourage the formation of classes for the study of the Bible and its evidences.

(5) To offer prizes and to prepare papers for Sunday School examinations, with a view to fostering doctrinal instruction, and of counteracting in a measure the present extreme tendency to emphasize merely the historical element in the Scriptures.

At the same time a brief explanatory statement was attached to the resolution above-mentioned which said: 'Verbal inspiration: this phrase is not intended to suggest any **theory** of inspiration, but merely to define its **result.** The "words" are claimed as God's words by the Scripture itself in 1 Cor. 2: 13, "Which things also we speak, not in the words which man's wisdom teacheth, but which the Holy Ghost teacheth".'

The first elected President of the Bible League was W. H. Seagram, while the list of Vice-Presidents included the names of Handley Moule, Charles Spurgeon, General Phayre, and Fuller Gooch. John Urquhart was made Honorary Secretary. The number on the Council was nineteen. We know little concerning W. H. Seagram but the following obituary notice which in later days appeared in *The Christian* is of interest: 'He was a joyous happy believer, ever engaged in the quest of souls. The story of his conversion is striking. He was brought to the Lord at a gospel meeting in Exeter Hall over thirty years ago. While still utterly indifferent he was "button-holed" by a young worker who could never afterwards be identified, and was at first indignant, but finally agreed to see what the meeting was like. There the Lord met him and on the following day he found peace. He ever remained a "button-holer" of others for the Lord, and this to such purpose that for at least twenty years continuously he is known to have led at least one person to Christ every day. In train or restaurant, in public or in private, wherever he went, among waitresses or cabmen, clubmen or servants, he seized every opportunity of speaking to others about Christ, and he was wont to say that he never found lack of openings. When he was convicted of sin, a copy of *Safety, Certainty and Enjoyment* was given to him, and was used to lead him into the light. Thereafter he circulated thousands of that tract and was ever after an enthusiastic supporter of Bible and tract distribution, as well as of evangelistic effort and of clear testimony to the Word of God.'

'Work for the day is coming'

Thus then it was that the Bible League came into existence. Its further history we do not at present propose to trace. Through the 78 years of its testimony it has been enabled to maintain without flinching its raison d'être. Presidents, Council members, and editors have come and gone. The League has experienced to the full the vicissitudes incidental to all human societies. But by the grace of God it holds on its way and carries on its witness in an unbelieving and ever-changing world, the witness that Holy Scripture is God's Word which:

'. . . floateth like a banner
Before God's host unfurled;
It shineth like a beacon
Above the darkling world;
It is the chart and compass
That, o'er life's surging sea,
'Mid mists and rocks and quicksands,
Still guides, O Christ, to Thee.'

If there was need for a Bible League in 1892 there is a ten-fold need for its testimony today. Spurgeon's days saw apostasy as a trickle; by the time of the Bible League's foundation it had become a stream; shortly it expanded to a river, and today it has become a veritable ocean of unbelief. For the most of men the ancient landmarks have disappeared from sight. Life upon earth has become a voyage on an uncharted ocean in a cockle-shell boat 'tossed to and fro, and carried about with every wind of doctrine'. Never before in human history has the 'sleight of men, and cunning craftiness, whereby they lie in wait to deceive' (Eph. 4: 14) been so greatly in evidence. 'Evil men and seducers wax worse and worse, deceiving and being deceived' (2 Tim. 3: 13). The faithful evangelical can hardly avoid being a prophet of gloom. At the same time, however, he alone possesses the secret of gladness. He walks by faith and not by sight. He knows that the darkest hour usually precedes the dawn, and that the sovereign Lord of life is never perplexed and nonplussed by the world situation. The Lord always knows what He will do. The believer knows that ultimate and complete victory belongs to the One who died on Calvary and rose again in the power of an endless life. All power even now is His in heaven and on earth. By faith the Christian looks to Him; in faith he holds forth the Word of life to those who are perishing and bids them 'look and live'.

To all 'believers in Jesus' the Bible League holds out a supporting hand. It sounds a 'Sursum Corda' (lift up your hearts). It proclaims the coming again of the Lord of glory.

'The name of Jesus yet shall ring
Through earth and heaven above;
And all His ransomed people know
The Sabbath of His love.'

Testimony to Him in this present evil world is not in vain. 'Light is sown for the righteous and gladness for the upright in heart' (Psa. 97: 11).

'Work for the Day is coming!
Made for the saints of light;
Off with the garments dreary,
On with the armour bright.

'Soon will the strife be ending,
Soon all our toils below;
Not to the dark we're tending,
But to the Day we go.'

Psalm 119.105
'Thy Word is a lamp unto my feet and a light unto my path'.

Spurgeon and some of his Predecessors

By R. Wright Hay

Paul never forgot the sight he had of Jesus. On this he based the validity of his own apostleship, for he says, 'Have I not seen Jesus Christ the Lord?' 'It pleased God to reveal His Son in me.' Conversion meant to Saul of Tarsus the endowment of a tremendous power. 'The years of his ministry threw the Gospel of Christ with conquering force into the heart of the world, shattered old systems, and established everywhere those organisations called 'churches,' which have been multiplying ever since, and which are destined to work a moral revolution in the world.' When giving an account of himself before Agrippa, it was to this he pointed: 'At mid-day, O king, I saw in the way a light from heaven, above the brightness of the sun, shining round about me, and them which journeyed with me. And when we were all fallen to the earth, I heard a voice speaking unto me, and saying in the Hebrew tongue, Saul, Saul, why persecutest thou me? it is hard for thee to kick against the pricks. And I said, who art Thou, Lord? And He said, I am Jesus whom thou persecutest. But rise, and stand upon thy feet; for I have appeared unto thee for this purpose, to make thee a minister and a witness both of these things which thou hast seen, and of those things in the which I will appear unto thee; delivering thee from the people, and from the Gentiles, unto whom now I send thee, to open their eyes, and to turn them from darkness to light, and from the power of Satan unto God, that they may receive forgiveness of sins, and inheritance among them which are sanctified by faith that is in me. Whereupon, O king Agrippa, I was not disobedient unto the heavenly vision.'

If we look to the human originators of other great movements in the Church of Christ, we find behind them all the fact of similar change. It was so in the case of Luther, who, on that memorable day, when, to gain an indulgence which the Pope had promised to everyone who should on his knees climb Pilate's stairs, he was crawling up the steps, he was arrested as he thought, by a mighty voice, crying, 'The just shall live by faith.' That was not only the creating word in the heart of Luther—the decisive period in his own life—it was also the birthday of the great Reformation.

Whence came the mighty influence of Thomas Chalmers in his later years? We quote a biographer's record: 'Sometime ere leaving Kilmany, a remarkable change took place in his character and deportment. Partly through the circumstance of his being requested to write on the 'Evidences of Christianity' for the Edinburgh Encyclopaedia, his mind was deeply and permanently affected by what with Scottish reserve has been described as 'vital Christianity.' He felt that his preaching had hitherto been a sham. With characteristic determination, he sought in the Scriptures a new foundation for faith and ministry. Ceasing to be an 'Ape of Epictetus,' he became for the first time a preacher of Christ crucified. Those who heard him have told us that we have no idea of the miracle which issued in his addressing himself to the 'old Evangelism of the Puritans and the Reformers, much more than a change in character and deportment—a new creation of the man is here exemplified.' He 'laid about him like a man inspired.' He spoke with the freshness and fervour of one to whom all things had become new. His eye seemed to see the invisible. His body trembled and panted under the burden of a present God.'

Apart from the great fact of conversion, the future of Chalmers, Luther, and Paul would have been like their past. Paul would have lived and died a Pharisee, Luther a monk, Chalmers a respectable scholarly, 'moderate' divine and parish minister. It would have been the same with Mr. Spurgeon without the experience of sovereign grace which he himself has so fervently narrated. He thus speaks of the day, the circumstances, the means, and the fact of his conversion: 'I sometimes think I might have been in darkness and despair now, had it not been for the goodness of God in sending a snow-storm one Sunday morning when I was going to a place of worship. When I could go no further, I turned down a court and came to a little Primitive Methodist chapel. In that chapel there might be a dozen or fifteen people. The minister did not come that morning, snowed up I suppose. A poor man, a shoemaker, a tailor, or something of that sort, went up into the pulpit to preach. The text was, "Look unto Me, and be ye saved, all the ends of the earth." There was, I thought, a glimpse of hope for me in text. When he had managed to spin out ten minutes or so, he was at the length of his tether. Then he looked at me under the gallery, and I dare say with so few present he knew me to be a stranger. He then said, "Young man, you look very miserable." Well, I did; but I had not been accustomed to have remarks made on my personal appearance from the pulpit before. However, it was a good blow struck. He continued: "And you will always be miserable, miserable in life and miserable in death, if you do not obey my text. But if you obey now, this moment, you will be saved." Then he shouted, as only a Primitive Methodist can: "Young man, look to Jesus Christ!" There and then the cloud was gone, the darkness had rolled away, and that moment I saw the Sun; and I could have risen that moment and sung with the most enthusiastic of them of the precious blood of Christ, and the simple faith which looks alone to Him. O, that somebody had told me that before: "Trust Jesus, and you shall be saved." It was no doubt wisely ordered, and I must for ever say—

'E'er since by faith I saw the stream
Thy wounds supplied for me,
Redeeming love has been my theme,
And shall for ever be.'

The influence of his conversion is manifest in the text which he selected when he preached his first sermon at the age of sixteen years. He thus refers to that memorable occasion in a sermon preached in 1872, from the text, 'Unto you therefore which believe, He is precious' (1. Pet. 2. 7). 'Emotions,' he says, 'may well be stirred in the preacher, if not in the hearer, by the memories awakened by this passage. For I remember well that more than twenty-two years ago, the first attempted sermon that I ever made was from this text. I had been asked to walk out to the little village of Teversham, some little distance from the town of Cambridge, in which I lived, to accompany a young man whom I supposed to be the preacher for the evening, and on the way, I said to him, that I trusted God would bless him in his labours. "Oh dear," said he, "I never preached in my life. I never thought of doing such a thing; I was asked to walk with you, and I sincerely hope that God will bless you in your preaching." "Nay," said I, "but I never preached, and I don't know that I could do anything of the sort." We walked together till we came to the place, my inmost soul being all in a tremble as to what would happen. When we found the congregation assembled, and no one else there to speak of Jesus, though I was only sixteen years of age, as I found that I was expected to preach, I did preach, and this was the text.'

The vital connection between the conversion of the predecessors of Spurgeon we have named and their view of Holy Scripture is seen in the case of Paul in a single utterance of the apostle: "All Scripture is given by inspiration of God (literally, is God-breathed) and is profitable for doctrine, for reproof, for correction, for instruction in righteousness, that the man of God may be perfect, throughly furnished unto all good works" (2 Tim. 3. 16, 17).

In the case of Luther that connection is seen in his challenge and declaration before the Emperor and a vast assemblage of the princes and prelates of Germany in 1521: 'Let me be refuted and convinced by the testimony of the Scriptures, or by the clearest arguments; otherwise I cannot and will not recant; for it is neither safe nor expedient to act against conscience. Here I take my stand; I can do no otherwise, so help me God. Amen.'

In the case of Dr. Chalmers the connection is seen in his words regarding the coming again of the Lord Jesus Christ: 'Of this I am satisfied, that the next coming of Christ will be a coming, not in final judgment, but a coming to usher in the Millennium. I utterly despair of the universal prevalence of Christianity as the result of a missionary process. I look for its conclusive establishment through a widening passage of desolations and judgments, with the demolition of our civil and ecclesiastical structures. "Overturn, Overturn, Overturn," is the watchword of our coming Lord.

'I desire to cherish a more habitual and practical faith than heretofore in that coming which even the first Christians were called to hope for with all earnestness, even though many centuries were to elapse ere the hope could be realised; and how much more we who are so much nearer this great fulfilment than at the time when we believed!' (*Sabbath Readings*, Vol. 1., page 311.)

The significance of the citation here of the words of Ezekiel's prophecy (chapter 21., verse 27) as Divinely authoritative cannot be exaggerated when it is remembered that Chalmers was reared in the Church of Scotland a century ago and that the formulated Creed of Presbyterianism to this day can scarcely be said to sponsor Chalmers' view of the Lord's coming. The scholarly theologian was by his conversion carried beyond the creed of his Church to the Word of God. That was henceforth to him so truly inspired that its *words* determined his belief.

Then coming to Spurgeon, what could be more explicit than the following extracts:

'The inspiration of the Bible is verbal inspiration. In some cases it must have been only verbal; in every case it must have been mainly so. The human mind is not able to understand and to express all the thoughts of God, they are too sublime; and therefore God gave to the prophets the very language which they were to give forth—language of which they themselves could not see the full far-reaching meaning. They rejoiced in the testimony of the Spirit within them, but they were not free from the necessity to search, and to search diligently, if they would for themselves derive benefit from the divine revelation. I know not how this is, but the fact is clearly stated in 1 Pet. 1.10—"Searching what . . . the Spirit of Christ which was in them did testify." How diligently then we ought to search the inspired writings and listen to the saving word.'

'I would as soon dream of blaspheming my Maker, as of questioning the infallibility of His word.'

'We have a faith to preach, and we are sent forth with a message from God.'

'We stand in a very solemn position, and ours should be the position of old Micaiah, who said, "As the Lord my God liveth, before whom I stand, whatsoever the Lord saith unto me that will I speak." '

'Our business is to preach Jesus Christ.'

'There will be no uncertain sound from us as to the doctrine of the Atonement. We cannot leave the blood out of our ministry, or the life of it will be gone: for we may say of our ministry, "the blood is the life thereof." The proper substitution of Christ, the vicarious sacrifice of Christ on behalf of His people, that they might live through Him, this we must publish till we die.'

'One man abiding in the truth has more weight in His witness than millions under the power of the father of lies.'

'What have I or any other Christian man to do with the spirit of the age? The Spirit which is in us, by which we ought to speak, is the Spirit of God, and not the spirit of the age.'

'Does it run thus: "Go ye into all the world and adapt the gospel to every creature?" I find it not so written. Our standing orders are to preach the gospel, the gospel, the same gospel to every creature, thoughtful or thoughtless, philosophical or ignorant, civilised or uncivilised. *Semper idem* is the motto which the gospel may write above her temples. There let it stand. She cannot alter. For her to alter were death to truth, and treason to Christ.'

'I mean to preach it as a man who is absolutely sure.'

'You remenber, when they condemned Leighton because he did not speak according to the times, he replied, "If all of you are speaking for the times, let one poor brother speak for eternity." '

Spurgeon's antagonism to all the endeavours of professed ministers of Christ to ignore, suppress, belittle, or modify the doctrine of the Atonement was due to his unflinching devotion to the 'Faith once for all delivered to the saints' AS HE FOUND IT SET FORTH IN THE WRITTEN ORACLES OF GOD.

Spurgeon's contention for the Faith illuminated the motto of the well-known seventeenth-century controversialist: 'Not peace, but TRUTH,' and was instigated by the Scripture, 'The wisdom that is from above is *first pure,* THEN peaceable' (James 3.17).

My Personal Knowledge of Spurgeon

By Arthur G. Edgerton

I count it an unspeakable honour to be invited to tell you something of what I remember of that mighty man of God, C. H. Spurgeon, whom we were proud to call leader, and who is venerated beyond all words.

There are those here this morning who knew Spurgeon well, and they are perhaps ready to say to me: 'Tell us what we knew before; but, paint the prospect from thy door.' That I shall try to do.

My message, I believe, is from God, and is to be found in the 26th chapter of Jeremiah and the second verse: 'Thus saith the Lord; Stand in the court of the Lord's house, and speak unto all the cities of Judah, which come to worship in the Lord's house, all the words that I command thee to speak unto them; *diminish not a word.*'

I want to say, this morning, that in relation to the *Bible* Spurgeon obeyed that direction; he did 'not diminish a word.' And in relation to the *doctrines* of the Holy Scriptures he did not 'diminish a word.' And in the last great stand he took, for the *defence of the faith,* he did not soften a syllable, or withdraw a sentence; he did not 'diminish a word.' This Society exists for the maintenance of the doctrine that the Holy Scriptures, as they came from Almighty God, are verbally (I use that word with deliberation) and infallibly inspired. 'Oh,' says somebody, 'what about the many variations?' Some professor shakes the documents, with their various readings before our eyes. These make no difference to the doctrine of verbal inspiration. I do not suppose that when Adam looked at the Tree of Life in the Garden of Eden, and saw its thousand leaves glistening in the sunlight, and waving in the wind, he doubted for a moment, but that *each* of those leaves belonged to the Tree. The variations in readings, and so on, make no difference whatsoever to the fact that the Word is verbally inspired; and these different renderings of the original are fresh glancings of the leaves of the Tree of Life; and fresh facets of the jewels of Revealed Truth.

I hold in my hand a rather worn copy—of a book entitled, *The Greatest Fight in the World.* It contains the last Pastors' College Conference address that Spurgeon delivered—on the 21st April, 1891, and I have a note on the flyleaf—made about the time,—'This address occupied in delivery one hour and fifty odd minutes.' It has as its banner, the infallibility of the Word of God; and the first part of it, is all concentrated upon that one truth.

Spurgeon says in his manifesto, spoken in the hearing of over five hundred brethren (and he was speaking within two months of the illness which proved to be fatal): 'TO US THE PLENARY VERBAL INSPIRATION OF HOLY SCRIPTURE IS FACT, NOT HYPOTHESIS.' And again, he writes a month later, of the Bible (in the *Sword and Trowel,* May, 1891, page 215): 'It is a MARVELLOUS Book. Believe its every word and syllable, and entertain no shadow of doubt about the inspiration of every jot and tittle, and you shall find that each word'—(this is remarkable)—'will be required, and verified in the various stages of your spiritual career.'

Let us remember that these are the words of a man who had a vast, and—shall I say?—restless intellect. I do not mean, of course, one that was not at peace, but, a mind that was always mightily moving; I heard his brother, James Spurgeon, say, that C. H. Spurgeon had a memory as 'capacious as a barn and as tenacious as a vice.' Remember, that the man who taught us, his students, to believe, not only in the inspiration of the Bible, but in its *verbal* inspiration, was a man who spoke to the whole world; a man who was the author of at least one hundred volumes, and whose discourses were scattered far and wide like leaves of the tree for the healing of the nations.

Spurgeon derived his marvellous power in preaching from the Word itself. We have heard a great deal about his gifts; his voice, for example. What a marvellous voice it was! I am reminded of a description of George Jacques Danton. His biographer says: 'His voice was a good symbol of his mind, for there was heard in it not only the deep tone of a multitude, but that quality which comes from the mingling of many parts—the noise of waters or of leaves';*but I think that in recent Celebrations, the fact that he laid such stress upon Holy Scripture, has been lost sight of*—and, that the

Divine authority of Scripture, even down to the thread, and the border, of the holy garment of God's Word, was a primary article of Spurgeon's faith.

About this time last year I was in Rouen Cathedral. It was in the afternoon, when the autumn light was beginning to wane. As the guide was passing with us through one of the cloisters, he brought us to some very beautiful miniature statuary. But there was one figure, the face of which we could not see. Then the guide took from his pocket a small mirror, and turned it on to the statue that stood in a recess; and catching the light, the glass revealed a face of wondrous beauty.

So Spurgeon turned his powerful Spirit-controlled mind upon the phrases, and apparently casual expressions of God's Word, and capturing heaven's light—he shewed rare beauty in the very words of Scripture. Not only did he take the great multitude through the broad aisles, and spaces of the Book, but he also shewed its minute loveliness, and manifold truth. Therefore, we can say of him as a preacher what Milton said of Shakespeare: '*Thou in our wonder and astonishment hast built thyself a livelong monument.*'

Spurgeon 'did not diminish a word' of Holy Scripture. Here we have this mighty man of God, without any hesitation or apology, taking his stand on the very same basis as that of the Bible League. One of our textbooks, at College, was *The Plenary Inspiration of Holy Scripture,* by Dr. L. Gaussen, of Geneva. And not long before his great ministry at the Tabernacle came to an end, Spurgeon had that book reprinted. There is no doubt whatever that his position was *exactly* that of the Bible League.

I pass on to speak of the fact that Spurgeon 'did not diminish a word,' as to the *doctrines* of the Bible. At that time the 'larger hope' was prevalent. Tennyson, with his poems, and Canon Farrar, with his preaching, had popularised it more or less. Baldwin Brown in Nonconformity, and others, were advocating such theories. But these ideas made no difference to Spurgeon; and you do not need to be told that his sermons are as full of the truths of the Gospel as the rainbow is of the hues inherent in the rays of the sun. Spurgeon's testimony was not an arc, it was a globe; full-orbed and conspicuous, shining in the sky of his world-wide ministry. There was no note missing in the music of The Message that sounded from the Tabernacle pulpit. I remember hearing Mr. Sankey say, as he stood in that pulpit, that, whenever any religious controversy arose on the other side of the water, they always looked towards the Metropolitan Tabernacle, as to a lighthouse, to see what its witness would be.

I had the privilege of hearing Spurgeon preach and lecture some forty times; and I can vividly recall some of those sermons.

I recall one Sunday morning how he came into his pulpit with the awe of God resting upon him, and took as his text, 'My God! My God! why hast Thou forsaken me?' And then the same night he preached from the words: 'And ye . . . shall leave Me alone, and yet I am not alone, for the Father is with Me.' May I say, in passing, that Spurgeon never allowed you to feel that he was 'a great man.' When I went into his little room one day to speak to him, I left feeling that my student life and opening ministry, were all-important to *him.* His word, as I left, was, 'Give my love to your father'; just as Nelson when dying, sent a message to the father of a young cadet, when that young man appeared upon the last scene with a message from Hardy.

I have met some eminent people since those days; and sometimes they have made you feel that they were '*much taller*' than *you* were; but *never* Charles Haddon Spurgeon! When he came into the pulpit, it was nearly always with his eyes averted, as though he would not look at the mighty crowd lest his heart be elated. On a particular Sunday morning he preached from 'Therefore doth My Father love Me, because I lay down My life that I might take it again.' He said, "The Queen" (Queen Victoria was of course on the throne then) 'loves her son; but, if it should be the case that the Prince had saved someone from a watery grave, how she would love him all the more because of *what he had done.*' And then he went on to say: 'Down from the cliffs of heaven, the Son of God had dived into the boiling sea of our iniquity, and with strong swimmer strokes brought us to our place of safety.' Therefore 'did His Father love Him' because 'He had laid down His life, that He might take it again.'

Well do I remember one Sunday morning, when he preached about the leper who *came* to Jesus. It is described in Matthew's Gospel; just after the Sermon on the Mount. Many were *brought* to the

Lord, like the paralysed man on the bed; but *this* leper came. And in the course of his sermon, Spurgeon stood out at the end of the platform, with outstretched finger, and said: 'There may be someone who has come here this morning, and, you do not know *why* you are here. You have been swept in on the crowd. If there is no other finger to point you to Jesus this one shall do it.' On the following Thursday he pulled out a piece of blue paper from his pocket, and said, 'This week I have had a great sorrow' (I think it was the death of Canon Liddon), 'but I have also had a great joy.' It appeared that what he had described on the previous Sunday morning had actually occurred. A poor girl, who had been out all night, had been borne into the Tabernacle on the crowd, and she had written, 'Dear Sir, while you were preaching (I do not know what the text was); but, I looked to Jesus; and by the time you get this I shall be on my way home to my Mother.' 'That,' added Spurgeon, with deep feeling, 'shews me the repentance is true.'

I must draw these fragmentary memories to a close, but I should like to say, that these sermons of Spurgeon's were uttered after the manner of Isaiah, 'The voice said, Cry.' Men who have been in the Army, will remember the note of 'The Last Post.' Sir, there was always the echo of 'The Last Post' in Spurgeon's voice. That note is missing to-day, the note of the urgency of concern for lost souls. The sound of that high clear voice is still with me; you felt as you heard him the stimulus of his heart in yours, and his pulsating love for Christ; you felt, 'I must go out and do something.'

Dear Spurgeon!—

'Thou hast thy record in the monarch's hall
And on the waters of the far-flung sea
And where the mighty mountain shadows fall,
The Alpine hamlet keeps a thought of thee.'

And, beloved friends, he 'did not diminish a word' of his *protest* against the Modernism of his day. It has been said that the 'Down Grade' protest was due to his failing health, or some ignoble reason has been assigned. What a contemptuous measure to take of such a man of God! To hearsay! Or to a desire for prominence!! Why, I heard him say, in College, in a moment of confidence to us, 'Brethren, they say I have done it for gain. What have I to gain? I have everything to lose.' In my judgment the finest thing C. H. S. ever did was to follow the example of the great German reformer, who said, 'Here I stand, I can do no other. So help me, God!' He significantly said: 'I can bear anything rather than an accusing conscience.' He foresaw what is happening in these days; and, as I said nearly twenty years ago in Bloomsbury Chapel, Spurgeon flung himself in the way of the runaway horses. You may say he was knocked down, but at any rate, he bravely bore his faithful testimony. And he said (you may find it in *The Sword and Trowel*, May, 1891, for yourselves) not many weeks before he was taken ill: *'If I had to bear my testimony over again I would not soften a syllable. I would rather add emphasis to it.'*

In the words of Archibald Brown, spoken over his open grave in Norwood cemetery, we can adoringly say, 'We praise God for him; and by the blood of the Everlasting Covenant, hope and expect to praise God with him.'

Defence of the Gospel in Spurgeon's Day and Now

By Dr. T. T. Shields, of Toronto

I count it a peculiar privilege to speak under the auspices of a Society which is set for the defence of the Gospel. Mr. Spurgeon in his day observed and frequently remarked upon the tendency on the part of many of the Lord's people to desire to take a neutral position in respect to matters then at issue. He said in effect that on the one side there was to be found Mr. White, and on the other side Dr. Black who believed the opposite; and between the two a Mr. Whitey-Black who believed both and neither. I think you will agree that that strange colour, 'whitey-black,' has become very popular in religious circles in our day.

The Chairman has referred to a movement that has taken strong hold of the popular imagination in this country and is not wholly unknown in mine. The Oxford Group Movement, to those to whose mental vision the Word of God sharply divides asunder the soul and the spirit, is both significant and symptomatic of the prevailing religious temper. You may be a Protestant or a Roman Catholic; an Evangelical or an Anglo-Catholic; a Supernaturalist or an Anti-supernaturalist; a Creationist or an Evolutionist; a Fundamentalist or a Modernist; or a composite of all of them; and without changing your opinion or your convictions you may become a full-fledged member of the Oxford Group.

That fact in itself is a revelation of the anti-Christian character of that movement. I have no hesitation whatever in so describing it. It is just as anti-Christian as Christian Science, and some wag in the United States said that Christian Science was like a guinea-pig, because it was neither a guinea nor a pig. The Oxford Group Movement is but a positive expression of that psychological operation, that is all. In its very heart it is utterly anti-Christian and will be recognised in due time, I am sure, by all lovers of the Word of God as such.

But I refer to it, not to deal with it, for that is beyond my province this afternoon, but merely to say that its extraordinary popularity is itself an indication of the religious trend of the day. The inventors, with their *penchant* for combinations—the inventors of a composite Pentateuch, have furnished us with a synthetic religion which is about as nutritious for our souls as loaves of sawdust would be for our bodies, destitute utterly of any element of the heavenly manna, and is a thing that is from below and not from above.

Now Spurgeon in his day found it necessary to make clear distinctions between things that differed, and to state positively his convictions. Notwithstanding, many of the celebrations in honour of the Centenary of his birth have entirely ignored that which I venture to believe was chiefly characteristic of the man, namely, that which has been called the 'Down-Grade Controversy.' It is a mistake to suppose that that controversy was an incident in his great career. It was rather the culmination and climax of the testimony of his whole life. Spurgeon was always a controversialist, as every 'convictionist'—if I may coin the word—must in the nature of things be. If you have a conviction in respect to the truth, then you cannot possibly allow that which is in its very nature and essence entirely opposed to it,—you cannot allow that that also is true. Truth is always intolerant, utterly intolerant of error. The multiplication table is the most intolerant thing in the world. And surely there must be some law, some standard to which our religious views may be brought, some scale in which our opinions may be weighed, that we may know whether they are true or not.

I might speak of the verbal inspiration of Scripture to you and I have little doubt that most of you would breathe a fervent 'Amen' to anything I might say. You know there are people who love to hear other people say exactly what they believe. If you want to get a reputation for being a great man, a man of keen discernment and even of great scholarship, all you have to do is publicly to sanction the veriest platitudes, make yourself the apostle of the obvious, and resolve never to say anything in any audience until you are sure everybody believes it; and everybody will go away and say, 'He is a great man, he believes just as I do.' I may say something here and now which you do not believe, and I may say something that will challenge your thought, and possibly I may stumble upon some idea with which you will not quite agree; I hope I shall not incur your displeasure, but rather stir up your minds and inspire you to do a little thinking on the subject.

My dear Friends, the attitude, the defensive and the offensive attitude which C. H. Spurgeon assumed on the great principle for the advocacy and conservation of which this Bible League, as I understand it, exists, that offensive attitude is just as necessary to-day as it was in Spurgeon's day. Indeed I think it is far more necessary. I greatly fear there has been no improvement in religious conditions since the late Eighties and the early Nineties. Evangelical principles are at a greater discount to-day than they were in Spurgeon's day. If it be true that the departure from the truth in that day was worthy to be called 'Down-gradism,' I think we might well call it to-day 'Tobogganism.' Did you ever see a toboggan when it shoots down at the rate of sixty miles an hour?

If the anti-Evangelical movement travelled in a coach-and-four in Spurgon's day, it hops about from place to place in our day by aeroplane. If the enemies of the truth used rifles then, they use machine guns now. I have re-read Spurgeon's articles on the Down-Grade controversy, and I have marvelled at their moderation and their mildness. It did not seem to me that there was anything in them that was at all offensive, and why they should have stirred up such bitterness would be difficult to understand were we not thoroughly aware of the seriousness of the issues that were involved. Things have greatly changed since Spurgeon's day. In that day he saw individual Modernists as isolated units. Now they have become a trained and disciplined army, and the Modernists whom he observed privately practising their goose-stepping about their own barracks, are now thundering at the gates of Paris and air-raiding London. Indeed there is a true analogy between the tactics of the Germanic powers in the Great War and that of the Modernists, or Modernism. The departments of propaganda, of espionage, their prison camps with their tortures, their aeroplanes, their submarines, every kind of deception that Hell itself can devise, is now employed by the armies of Modernism wherewith to oppose the Gospel.

We may indeed frankly recognise that this movement which we are attempting to combat and against which this organisation is chiefly arrayed, is not a dilution of Christianity but an absolute denial of it. It is not a modification of the Gospel, but the deliberate murder of it. It involves the crucifixion of the Son of God afresh and the putting of Him to open shame. I greatly fear that there are comparatively few Evangelicals who have awakened to the seriousness of the present situation. They seem to think that it is still possible to be on good terms with the enemy, to live in association with the enemies of Christ. Let us frankly admit, dear friends,—I say no new thing—everybody who has thought at all about it must recognise that the Bible of the Modernist is not God's Bible at all; it is another one. The God of the Modernist is not the God and Father of our Lord Jesus Christ. He would not make a decent schoolmaster, so small, so insignificant, so remote is He. I do not know who He is, or whether there be a God at all or not. I could more easily be an orthodox Roman Catholic than I could be a Modernist. I have a great deal more fellowship with the Roman Catholics who, in spite of their superstition, may some of them get through the darkness to God, than I have with a baptized pagan who calls himself a Baptist. There is no greater enemy of the Gospel of Jesus Christ anywhere in the world than a man like Harry Emerson Fosdick, and you have them in your country, plenty of them. Do not charge me with uncharity. I recognise them, I identify them as the enemies of Jesus Christ. I say the Christ of the Modernist is not the Christ of the Bible at all; the salvation of the Modernist is not the salvation that comes to us by the grace of God; the Heaven of the Modernist is not the city which hath foundations, 'whose builder and maker is God.' And as for the Hell of the Modernist, it is a special one that they have created in order that they may deal with Fundamentalists, and to which they would consign us all.

I tell you, my dear friends, this Down-Grade controversy is far more than a controversy. It is war, cruel, bloody war to the death. It is nothing less than that. Unless you recognise that and are prepared to face the consequences of it, I beg of you, have nothing to do with it. I say there is a thousandfold more reason for not only defending the faith but for contending for it, and taking the offensive against Modernism everywhere, than there was in the days of C. H. Spurgeon.

Since his day Modernism has dug itself in. In his day it skirmished about in the open on the surface. Now you find it in entrenched positions. If has dug itself in, I say, to editorial and professional chairs; into administrative positions; in augmentation and sustentation departments; it has dug itself in everywhere, and to-day we face an army that is firmly entrenched everywhere. I talk to men of different denominations, from India, China, Japan, the United States and Canada, from the Antipodes and from Great Britain, and I have learned what the Bible teaches, that Beelzebub is never divided against himself, and that long before the Allies discovered the necessity for it on the war-swept plains of Europe, during the 1914-18 war, Beelzebub learned the necessity for unity of command. Our Lord Jesus Christ never expected to drive a wedge between Pilate and Herod. He knew very well the enemy would close his ranks and present a united front against Him.

Has it ever struck you as being singular that in His day there were two religious sects that, so far as their own personal views were concerned, were as the poles asunder? The Pharisees and the Sadducees had nothing in common. The Pharisees were the orthodox Supernaturalists of their day, and the Sadducees were the Rationalists, the Naturalists of their day. But when the Incarnate Word came into contact with them, a dead orthodoxy having to choose between a vital spirituality and a cold rationalism, preferred the cold rationalism to the vital spirituality, joined hands in a campaign against the Incarnate Word and brought Him at last to the Cross.

You have the same thing to-day. Great multitudes of people profess an intellectual adherence to the great evangelical principle that the Bible is the Word of God—they have it in their heads and none of it in their hearts—and between that and a vital, aggressive godliness that has not only the form but the power, they always choose the Modernist, and in any great religious assembly you will see the Pharisees and the Sadducees joining hands and voting for the crucifixion of the Holy Book.

It is the same thing. Why are we so slow to recognise it? The battle is on and we must fight it with all vigour in our day as Spurgeon did in his day.

So then, dear friends, I want you to consider some reasons why we now should enlist in the same warfare in which the great Spurgeon drew his sword.

My first reason is this: I know no other way of being loyal to Christ. After all, Modernism is something vastly more than an academic dissection and appraisal of the value of a particular Book. It is something more than an examination, and on the basis of that examination a rejection and repudiation of a Book for its alleged inaccuracies in respect to matters of science and history and for the unethicalness of its precepts and programme. That is not what Modernism is about. I know the inwardness of the thing. I have been amazed sometimes when I have observed with what care, with what perseverance, with what great industry this opposition to the truth is pursued, and I have sometimes asked myself what is it inspires the man. What does he hope to gain by it? Who is back of all this? I have seen men, even-tempered, mild-mannered, apparently naturally amiable men, become ferocious in this conflict, forgetting and failing to exemplify in any degree even the ordinary courtesies of life. What is the explanation of it? (A voice: "The Devil.") Our brother is right, for just as surely as the Bible is inspired from above, Modernism and all its works is inspired from below. There is no doubt about it. If once that be admitted, then our duty is clear. We are to resist the devil, and not invite him to lunch and make him a member of our club, much less confer upon him the degree of Doctor of Divinity!

But what is it all aimed at? At the person of Christ! It does not make any difference where you begin, from Genesis to Revelation, the Modernist at last lays his protest at the feet of Christ. Christ's knowledge is discounted; His veracity is impugned; His infallibility is denied; and His Deity utterly repudiated. You cannot be a Modernist and believe on the Lord Jesus Christ. It is useless to speak of these men as amiable gentlemen, as fine Christian characters. The man who denies the Deity of Christ and repudiates His authority, I do not care if he is Dean of St. Paul's, he is not a Christian and never was.

Surely there is a *sine qua non* of Christian faith, there must be an irreducible minimum somewhere, and all this is directed against the person of Christ. How then can I as one who has been bought with

His precious blood be loyal to Him to whom I owe everything for time and Eternity, how can I be loyal to Him and be silent in circumstances like these? Can a wife be loyal to her husband if she allows without protest his honour to be dragged in the mire? It is not only the written Word, it is still the Word Incarnate, for in every trial of this written Word the Living Word is put on trial; when the Word Incarnate is on trial before the modern Sanhedrin, and even the secular arm is invoked to give effect to the wicked will of a faithless religion, the man who for fear of consequences will withhold his testimony, is guilty of Peter's sin—denying his Lord. Surely the man who would, for fear of the loss of certain emoluments, or in the hope of gaining some temporal reward, dare to aid and abet the cause of those who would bring Jesus Christ again to the Cross, that man is treading in the footsteps of Judas Iscariot. It is a serious business we are engaged in. I have greatly misunderstood the religion of Christ if it does not in the last analysis consist of vital union with the living Saviour. I cannot be in union with Him and be disloyal to Him at the same time. I cannot be loyal without protesting, to the last drop of my blood if I must, against those who are the enemies of the truth of Christ.

Let me say further, we must needs take up this defensive attitude for the health of our own souls. I met a lady of great discernment, a cultured woman, in Los Angeles, some years ago, and she said, "Mr Shields, I find that for my own soul's sake I have to fight every day of my life for the truth that saved me." Of course we must. There is no other attitude. The religion of Christ never commends to us a negative attitude. It is not a system of mere negation. It always leads us to the adoption of a positive attitude. How are we to cleave to that which is good? By abhorring that which is evil. How are we to avoid being overcome with evil, to meet the positiveness, the aggressiveness of evil? By overcoming evil with good. That is how! Never a neutral position. There can be no neutral position for the moral man where moral issues are concerned. It is a simple impossibility.

Talk to your physician. We hear a lot about various germ-theories and about hygienic rules of life, and all the rest of it. We are very careful when we go abroad lest we should take into our system some deadly bacillus that will multiply and bring us down to death. That is all to the good, I have nothing to say against it. But any physician will tell you that when you have done your utmost, you do take in the germs, you cannot escape tuberculosis and many other germs. You cannot get away from them. Why is it some of us are here in health and strength to-day, exposed perhaps in some place in some circumstances to certain conditions which have brought others to the sanatorium, and by and by to the grave? The physician will tell you you have a certain immunity, there is a certain physical resistance, your exuberant health antagonises this thing, fights against it and throws it off. Unless there be that physical resistance that is always at war with everything that would injure the body, you will not live very long.

My dear friends, there must be an analogy to that in our spiritual nature. The new man which after God is created in righteousness and true holiness, that new life that comes from God, should ever be opposed to everything that is alien to God, so that we should deliberately cultivate an inherent antagonism to everything that is alien to Jesus Christ. 'Beware,' said the Apostle, 'lest any man spoil you through philosophy and vain deceit, after the tradition of men, after the rudiments of the world, and not after Christ.' Beware of everything that is not after Christ. If you take that principle it will make you a warrior from this minute, fighting against that which would take the crown of Deity from His wounded brow.

And then another thing. There is a distinct advantage to any man who takes a definite position. My first pastorship was in a little village at a little village church of about 100 members. I made a solemn vow to the Lord on a very simple matter, that I would never under any circumstances anywhere be pastor of a church for 24 hours that dishonoured the Lord by holding bazaars and tea-meetings and all that sort of thing for the purpose of raising money. I promised the Lord that I would face that thing wherever I found it, and if I could not overcome it I would get out, but I would never for a minute be a party to it. I had not been long in my pastorate before some good sisters wanted to have what they called 'some doings'—what kind of doings they were I forget now. But I quietly said, 'I am under a solemn vow to the Lord, and the moment you initiate that movement, that moment you become pastorless.' 'Oh, but Pastor!' I said, 'There is no discussion about it. I am no Pope, I am no priest; you can have it if you like, but I am master of my own course under God, and if you have that, you cannot have me.' 'Well then,' they said, 'we will not have that.' I said, 'Thank you.'

The Oxford Group Movement came to Toronto. Some of their leaders to my certain knowledge had letters of introduction to me. I think I can say without immodesty that the place where I preach is not the least conspicuous of the places in Toronto. There are a few places that are less widely known and perhaps somewhat smaller. They came, a team of them, two or three times. Not one of them ever called on me, not one of them ever asked for entrance to my pulpit, not one of them ever presented a letter of introduction. Why? Can you tell me? Why did not they come? Because they said, 'It is no use.' A lady said to me last week, 'I told Dr. Buchman I was coming to see you.' I said, 'That would not mean anything to him, he has never heard of me.' She replied, 'Oh, hasn't he? He said, "You will do something for the Group if you win him." '

My point is simply this. We save ourselves from many temptations if we put the flag to the top of the mast and announce to the whole world exactly where we stand. You have made your decision in advance of the overture and the overture never comes, and you go sweetly on your way in respect of many of these things. The minister who thinks he is going to avoid difficulty by being diplomatic is likely to find himself greatly entangled after a while. I tried diplomacy for a long time. I used to be the champion conciliator of the Baptist denomination in Canada, and if ever they had a Church row they sent for me. If ever there were differences to be composed I was asked to preside at a Council. I have done it often and there is a place for legitimate compromise. But in respect to this matter I tried it too, on Boards and Committees, behind closed doors where our discussions could never possibly reach the public ear. I did exactly what the statesmen of Great Britain did in the summer of 1914, exhausted every possibility of diplomacy, and when they reached the end of it they declared war. There was nothing else to do. So I screwed up my fountain pen and resigned from the diplomatic corps and joined the army. There was nothing else to do under the circumstances, and so far as I can see there is no prospect of my being demobilised until the Lord comes, or any of the rest of you for that matter. It is a real warfare.

Then, my dear friends, we need to take this defensive attitude for the sake of the uninstructed among us, lest the unwary should be beguiled. Let no one make any mistake, this Bible League, the members that compose it, not one of them has any doubt as to the battle.

I used to have a deacon who was a bookman, he was not a bookworm exactly, but he read everything. He was a well-informed man. At one time he was in London, looking through a book warehouse. He had come to see about buying books, and he saw a man wheeling whole truckloads of well-bound books to a deep hole in the floor and then upsetting them, and they were going down into the basement. The books looked to be well-bound, and it seemed a great waste to be treating good books like that, so he said to the man who was showing him round, "What are those books? They seem to be all alike." The man said, "They are, we have thousands of them, they are dead." "What are they?" The answer was, "Colenso on the Pentateuch." That same afternoon he went to the British and Foreign Bible Society and saw the shelves stocked with Bibles in all the languages of the earth, and there was not one dead book among them. Of course, we have no doubt about that. The Bible does not need us to defend it. That is not why we take up this attitude. It is because of those who may be led astray. It is for the sake of the blind that we would rob them of their blind guides lest both should fall into the ditch. That is our reason.

You know that shrewd adversary, before he launched this campaign of Modernism, destroyed very largely in our churches the teaching ministry. Ah, what an important consideration that is! The preacher who expounds the Word of God week after week, year after year, until his people are thoroughly indoctrinated, until they are inoculated with what Spurgeon called "Bibline," until the truth of the Bible gets into the very blood, so fortifies his congregation that all these heresies will not 'take'—the people throw it off. But we have had one or two generations of typical preachers who have aimed at expertness in economics. If we had stuck to our business; if preachers had been content just to preach the Gospel, we and they would have made the greatest contribution possible, not only to individual salvation, but to public, national welfare and international relationships too; the Biblical Gospel is the basis of everything. It is because of ignorance of this that so many people are so easily deceived. Take, for instance, this matter of Oxford Groupism. Is it not amazing! There is one useful thing about it. I have noticed it has been welcomed in the most pronounced Modernistic churches, because most of them are ecclesiastical cemeteries and they want a stir of some kind, movement of some kind. They say, "If the Oxford Group can justify our existence, come along, brethren, because we are about at the end of our tether." There is not anything in the world, I think, that has more effectively the last year or so advertised the spiritual bankruptcy of Modernism than the Oxford Group. It would never be welcomed if it were not that people have put aside the Bible and the Gospel.

Therefore, for the sake of the multitudes to whom the first principles of the Gospel are strange, for the sake of a generation that is arising that knows nothing about the Bible except to reject it and scoff at it, we need to be on the defensive and to begin over again teaching the very alphabet of Evangelical Faith.

We need to be on the defensive because we ought to identify the enemy. Perhaps you do not believe in that. Do you? Perhaps he had a reason for it that I have never quite been able to discern, but very humbly I would venture to say that if Spurgeon made one mistake in that Down-Grade controversy, it would appear to me that his mistake was in his not actually naming the men. He did not do it, and they said it was not fair. If you do not name anybody, they say, 'Oh well, he deals in generalities.' If you name them, they say, 'He indulges in personalities.' So as they say on the other side of the water, they 'get you going or coming or both.' After all, I do not see why the Modernist should be ashamed of his Modernism. If I were a Modernist I would not object to anybody charging me with it. That is what I am doing all the time, anyhow. Is there any value in it? Yes, sir. We had a certain English brother come to our country (Canada) and I named him. I told him at once what would happen to him, and after two or three years he returned to England. Why? Because I had named him and there were not twenty pulpits in Canada that were open to him. The Modernists said, "We had better get somebody that is not identified,"—not that they repented, but they did not want *him,* and he had to go.

I think it is eminently fair that when Nathan has told his trouble, he should just look straight into David's eyes and say, "Thou art the man"!

A distinguished lawyer told me that he heard Joseph Parker and C. H. Spurgeon preach on one Sunday, Parker in the morning and Spurgeon in the evening, and there was a great congregation for both. In the morning Dr. Parker spoke with his usual air as though to say—you must not think that you are everything, there is a vast congregation outside to whom I am addressing myself. It was all good and wonderful, and my friend was impressed with the greatness of the preacher and the brilliance of his oration. He said, 'I went to hear Spurgeon at night. There was a far bigger crowd of people of course. Presently he came in. For a few minutes I was conscious of the crowd, but from the moment that man announced his text, he got me, and within five minutes I had lost all consciousness of the Tabernacle, or the person on either side of me, and of Spurgeon himself, and God the Holy Ghost was talking to my heart and conscience.' That is preaching, brethren. That is the kind of preaching we ought to aim at. Sometimes we have to draw a bow at a venture in this country, possibly if I knew where he was I would deliberately aim that way, so that there should be no mistake about the man. I do not mind naming Dr. T. Reaveley Glover and Fosdick, and the whole crowd of enemies of the Gospel, as occasion requires.

It is a cruel warfare. You must be prepared for all the exigencies of war. Do not allow yourselves to be persuaded that you can oppose people on this issue and be good friends with them. You say —of course you can be a gentleman, you do not need to break friendships on an issue like this. An issue like what? An issue which will make all the difference between light and darkness, between Heaven and Hell, between God and the Devil. You cannot touch an issue like that and be friends with the men who deny the Faith. Mark my words, try as much as you like, if you do not wear a uniform nobody will know which side you belong to. Get into the King's uniform and you will soon find whether your friendships will be disturbed or not. They are bound to be. There is no trick known to the worst enemy in war—I say it advisedly—to which Modernism and Modernists will not descend.

I was a member of the Board of Governors of a certain University for a number of years. On one occasion I had to make a speech before that Board in protest against certain courses. The Registrar got a Chartered Stenographer and every word that I uttered was recorded. The next time I went to that meeting I found a storm was on. I deliberately went a little late in order to avoid the necessity of social intercourse because relations were sadly strained, and when the Minute of the last meeting relating to the matter that had produced the uproar was read, I recognised at once my own phraseology and recognised that there was not one word in that which purported to be a verbatim account of what I had said that was not mine. But by the deletion of every modifying clause, every qualifying adjective, and by the elimination of all my negatives, by using my words, they had made me say exactly the opposite of what I had said. I knew I was in the company of a lot of crooks, and from that moment I said, "Gentlemen, I will discuss these matters with you when I have two stenographers that will take an exact account and when every word shall be checked one against another; otherwise, you can talk until to-morrow morning and I have nothing to say. I will make my answer in the presence of witnesses." They knew I could talk to a couple of thousand people any time I liked, and so they said, "We will have no stenographic report at all."

Then in a Convention man after man got up to make a speech. A man that repudiates the authority of Scripture, mocks at the precious blood, an Englishman, got up and said, "I stand with C. H. Spurgeon on the Atonement." The Chancellor of that University got up and read from Dr. Orr. I had two Parliamentary stenographers taking down every word, Hansard men. I happen to remember it because it cost me 600 dollars for that one session, which lasted from ten in the morning until half-past two the next morning. And when I had that report and I put it down beside that from which they claimed to be quoting, I saw at once that the speeches in that Convention had all been, so to speak, by one man. Spurgeon's sermons and Dr. Orr's, every quotation had been treated in the same way, and by taking part of a sentence here and part of a sentence there, and piecing them together, they had made Dr. Orr and Spurgeon and everybody else say the very opposite to what they had said. They had put a lie into the lips of truth, and my dear friends, you will get it here. I have had it.

The devil is back of Modernism and the devil never showed you any kindness yet and he will not in this warfare.

I must close with this one word. There are great compensations. After all, in the war the Bible becomes a new book. I never knew the Bible until I went to battle on its behalf. I did not know what the Acts of the Apostles meant until I walked in their footsteps; then I was able to understand the book. I venture the affirmation that no man can ever understand the Acts of the Apostles merely in the study. He has got to be out on the battlefield, then it will speak to him its full message.

Then also you will have close personal fellowship with Christ. That is a great thing. The Hebrew children found an intimacy in converse with the Son of God in the furnace that they had never known before. Daniel was no stranger to the ministry of angels, but there was one angel with him he had no acquaintance with until he went into the den of lions. Do you know, the furnace and the den of lions are the Divine Teacher's training college, where He is training men to be officers in His army, where they have the advantage of the special personal instruction of the Son of God. And best of all, as we put the principles and precepts and promises of God's Holy Word to the test, seeking very clear methods to honour our Lord Jesus Christ and to serve the highest interests of souls for whom He died, we shall enjoy a fruitfulness in our ministry that can be had in no other way.

I had some people, uninstructed for awhile, who thought I was unduly controversial, and some men who never had a convert, used to say, 'Preach the Gospel.' Well I did, and one night I remember we had an enormous audience, and it was a fighting speech—anything I have said to-day would be of the homeopathic order in comparison—it was a bit of real militancy, I can assure you, but we were standing for the Book. When it was over I just said, "Now we have thus spoken because we have a Saviour for whom we would die if need be. How many of you will receive Jesus Christ as the sinner's

Saviour?" Without any further appeal that night I recall eighteen walked down to the platform, most of them men. They said, 'If Jesus means all that to a believer, I want Him.'

Oh, the comradeship of the saints! Some pastors are troubled because they have churches they cannot trust, people who betray them, people who break their hearts. We all know something about that. But get into the furnace, get out into the place where the battle is raging, where men face difficulties with you, and by and by you will have people that would die for you as they would die for their Lord. There is a comradeship known in warfare which we can know nowhere else and I have not said a new thing to you. The Bible was born in controversy; every apostolic preacher was a defender of the faith; all down through the history of the Church the martyr fires have been kindled because there were men who would rather die than surrender this truth.

Remember there is a world of truth in that old saying which is scriptural in principle though it is not Scripture—'The blood of the martyrs is the seed of the Church.' When you and I are ready to shed our blood, to lay down our lives if need be, we shall see the Church prospering again and thousands will be enquiring their way to Zion with their faces thitherward, and God the Lord shall be honoured and glorified. May He bless His Word!

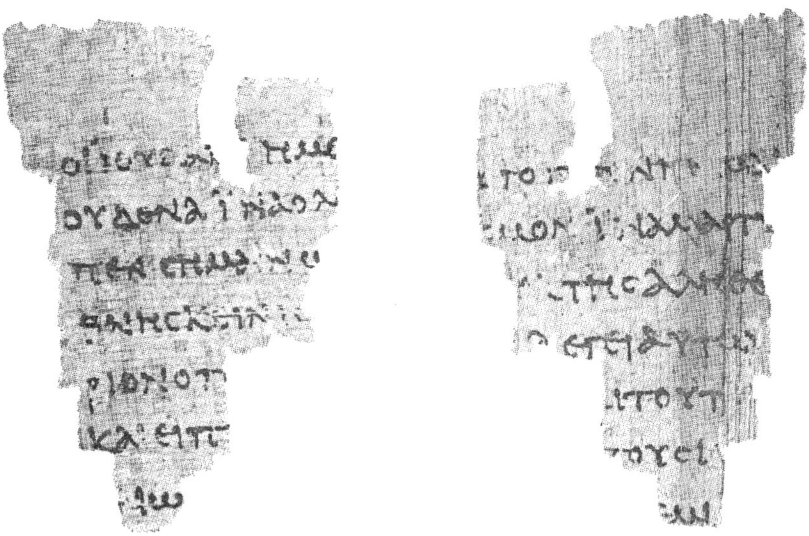

THE OLDEST NEW TESTAMENT MANUSCRIPT IN EXISTENCE
A fragment of S. John's Gospel, A.D. 140

(from John chapter 18)

Spurgeon's Testimony and that of the Bible League

By R. Wright Hay

When the news of Spurgeon's death reached India I, as a missionary working in Eastern Bengal, had an immediate deep sense of personal bereavement. This sense was voiced by a friend who said, 'Everything seems edged with black, except the Bible.' The exception made by my friend commended itself to me even more deeply than my consciousness of loss in Spurgeon's being taken from us; for one was moved reverently to bow before the Author of Holy Scripture, whom Spurgeon believed in and loved and honoured and served, and to say in the words of Scripture: 'The crown is fallen from our head,' but 'Thou, Lord, remainest.'

You will be enabled to understand the nature of my sense of bereavement through Spurgeon's being taken from us when I tell you that for some years before his death I had been working as a missionary among students and educated men in the educational capital (as it was at that time) of Eastern Bengal—among such men as my beloved son in the faith, Bimal Ananda Nag (present on the platform), whom it is such a joy to have associated with us in our Bible League testimony to-day.

In ministering the Gospel to such men I was made familiar from the beginning of my work with the fact that in the minds of many educated Bengalis there was lodged a prejudice against the Gospel due to the printed utterances of avowed unbelievers which had been brought within their reach by the activities of an anti-Christian agency. Such men would quote Tom Paine's *Age of Reason,* Colonel Ingersoll's *The Mistakes of Moses,* and certain utterances of Charles Bradlaugh, as against the truth of the Bible. But for some little time before Spurgeon's death the same type of man who had quoted avowed infidels against the Word of God had taken to quoting utterances, to the same practical effect, from the writings of British doctors of divinity.

To bring home to you the situation in its relation to the death of Spurgeon, I may mention that, on my first furlough from India, I took occasion to call on one of those doctors of divinity and to tell him of the difficulty put in my way by his book on the Bible as I sought to evangelise educated Indians, Hindus, Brahmos, and Mohammedans. He said to me, 'I am surprised and sorry that you should have thought it necessary or expedient in your preaching of the Gospel in Bengal to introduce any theory of inspiration.' My reply to him was, 'Dr. So-and-So, I did not introduce any theory of inspiration in my preaching of the Gospel, but I found to my distress, and in a measure to my discomfiture, that *the theory of inspiration which you had introduced* was being used by unconverted men against the good news which I knew to be God's one message of salvation to them as it had been to me personally.'

That was the position. Spurgeon stood for the verbal inspiration of Holy Scripture, and the Modernistic attack upon the Christian revelation was based upon the abandonment of the historic Christian faith in the Bible as verbally inspired.

As we realised our loss in the withdrawal of a specially conspicuous and powerful exponent not only of the whole body of saving truth, but also and primarily of the basic fact of the inspiration of the Scriptures from which alone the knowledge of that body of truth can be derived, we were constrained to pray that in the absence of this one outstanding exponent of the historic doctrine, who commanded the ear of thinking people in all parts of the world, there might, if it pleased the Lord, be brought into existence a collective testimony to the same effect borne by believers standing where Spurgeon stood in relation to the Divine Authority of Holy Scripture.

C. H. Spurgeon died on 31st January, 1892. The Bible League was founded on 3rd May in the same year; and I believe that my wife and I were the first to join the League from abroad. We saw in the news of the establishment of the League an answer to fervent prayer, which gladdened our hearts and strengthened our hands not only to preach but also to defend the Gospel.

The need for a specific testimony to the quality of Holy Scripture in relation to the evangelisation of the world may be seen the more vividly if I mention a remark made by the Modernist Principal of a theological college in London. I had occasion to see this Principal because of the tragic communication that had been made to me of the effect upon the faith of a young lady, a candidate for missionary service, of his manner of presenting the *Kenosis* theory in connection with the subject of the testimony of the Lord Jesus Christ to the Divine authority of the Old Testament.

When this candidate for missionary service, entirely unacquainted beforehand with this rationalistic theory regarding our Lord and Holy Scripture, personally inquired of the Principal, after he had delivered a lecture in her hearing, as to how such a view of the limited knowledge of Him whom she had been accustomed to regard as God Incarnate could be reconciled with faith in Christ's Deity, the Principal put to her the question, "Do you think that Jesus knew about chloroform?" The student replied, "I cannot imagine His ever having used chloroform." The Principal said, 'My question is, Do you think that He knew about it?—because, frankly, if I had to think He did know about it, I could not believe in Him, seeing that He kept it a secret.'

On securing an interview with the man who dealt in this heartless manner with a comparatively young believer, staggered by the strange doctrine which she unexpectedly encountered on the threshold of her training for missionary work, I first of all ascertained that what had been reported to me was an accurate statement of what had passed between this missionary student and himself, and I said to him, 'To be consistent, sir, you ought to be an atheist, for, clearly, an omniscient God knew all about chloroform before it was discovered by Sir James Simpson.' This led to a discussion, in the course of which the Principal remarked, 'Mr. Wright Hay, I am prepared to admit that the work of evangelisation is easier on your view of the Bible than it is on mine.' My reply was, 'You have conceded all that I contend for in making that acknowledgment, for no view of the Bible can be true which militates against the taking effect in any hearer of the Gospel of the divine purpose that men should be saved through the preaching of the Gospel according to the Scriptures.' With that we parted.

It may perhaps be helpful if at this point I give an instance of the misrepresentation of the doctrine of verbal inspiration which is found in so many utterances of the Modernistic school. In a book published by the Student Christian Movement, avowedly for theological students, the author makes the statement that according to the doctrine of verbal inspiration the writers of Scripture were merely automatic pens. I wrote to the author of this book soon after its publication and courteously inquired as to what accepted exponent of the historic doctrine of verbal inspiration he would cite in support of his statement that believers in verbal inspiration regard the human writers of the Bible as being merely automatic pens. A fortnight passed without my receiving any reply, and I therefore repeated my inquiry and sent it to the author of the book by registered post. I then received the reply, 'I had no special exponent of the doctrine in mind, but in my opinion the doctrine can mean nothing else.' My reply was, 'It is surely due to the students who read your book, looking to you for guidance on a matter of fact as to the historic doctrine of Verbal Inspiration, that you should hasten to make a public announcement that what you ought to have said in describing the doctrine as you did was that this description was based entirely on your personal opinion of what the doctrine must mean.' I am not aware that any such announcement was made. And it is wrong and unspeakably sad that there should be such deliberate misrepresentation of what the Church of God has thought and believed and taught and contended for in regard to the Holy Scriptures from the days of the Apostles, as in the statement that I have quoted.

As showing the close connection between faith in the verbal inspiration of Holy Scripture and the full presentation of saving truth, it is significant that the author whom I have just referred to, when President of the National Federation of Free Churches, on being approached with a suggestion that a simultaneous mission should be arranged among the Free Churches of the land, replied, it was reported, 'If what you mean is an evangelistic mission, my view is that we are not yet ready for it. We must first of all know where we are.'

I remember that on my quoting those words to Dr. Dixon, then pastor of the Metropolitan Tabernacle, Dr. Dixon said, 'The theologian who does not know where he is, is theologically lost'! He certainly has lost the message of salvation.

The sense that C. H. Spurgeon had of the vital importance of the fact of verbal inspiration of Holy Scripture is exemplified in his having not only used as a textbook in his college the *Theopneustia* of Dr. Gaussen, of Geneva, but in his also having made the book available for general reading when it had passed out of print, by bringing out a new edition of this classic on the subject with which it deals, which he did in 1888. In the preface of that edition, written by Spurgeon himself, we read, 'The turning point of the battle between those who hold the faith once for all delivered to the saints and their opponents lies in the true and real inspiration of the Holy Scriptures. If we have in the Word of God no infallible standard of truth we are at sea without a compass and no danger from rough weather without can be equal to this loss within. "If the foundations be destroyed what can the righteous do?" And this is a foundation loss of the worst kind. When a man falls into an error, but reverently conceives that he finds what he believes in his Bible, he is on a very different footing from the man who says that he judges by his own moral consciousness or some other unreliable standard and declares that if the Bible contradicts him he would sooner renounce Scripture than change his opinions. We can have a measure of fellowship with a mistaken friend who is willing to bow before the teaching of Scripture, if he can be made to understand it; but we must part company with the errorist who overrides prophets and apostles and practically regards his own inspiration as superior to theirs. We fear'—and I ask you to note how tragically the great preacher's fear is being justified in what is taking place within the professing Church to-day—'We fear that such a man will before long prove himself to be an enemy of the Cross of Christ, *all the more dangerous because he will profess loyalty to the Lord whom he dishonours.'*

In regard to the book itself Spurgeon says, 'In this work the author proves himself a master of holy argument,' and again, 'It is a delight to turn from the dreamings of the new school to the certainties of the Word of God. Gaussen charms us as he proclaims the divine veracity of Scripture. Did the reader ever notice the grand utterances of Chalmers, Haldane and Carson, to the same effect? These noble men fought against the theories of inspiration which in their day were only covert attacks upon the fact of inspiration, and truly they warred a good warfare. Men who are not worthy to loose the latchet of their shoes would do well to study and accept what these great teachers had to say. If they will not do so we can only mourn for them and pray to God to convert them.'

I may be permitted to say that I came to know of C. H. Spurgeon as a preacher in my boyhood through the fact that my mother received and read one of his sermons every week. She had been converted in Australia, and after her conversion she read a sermon by Spurgeon published as an advertisement in a newspaper circulating in the Bush. This was so helpful to her that when she brought her three boys to her native Scotland and set up a home for herself and them in St. Andrews, although a convinced Presbyterian, she, after listening to the preaching in each of the Presbyterian Churches in the Ancient City, settled at what was then called an Independent Chapel, because there only did she hear the Scriptural Gospel clearly preached, and she wished her boys to hear that, and only that. This, in addition to her practice of regularly reading a sermon by Spurgeon, was part of the fruit of his ministry as it was exercised over her mind and heart at the Antipodes. And I thank God for the godly wisdom given to my mother through the Word preached in the Metropolitan Tabernacle.

It is not to be wondered at that on my first visit to London I made a point of going to the Tabernacle to hear Spurgeon. During the service that Lord's Day morning a child in the top gallery of the great building, filled with some six thousand people, uttered a short, sharp cry. Spurgeon, engaged in prayer at the time—in what in those days was called the 'long prayer'—immediately took that child into the arms of his interest, his love, his intercession. He prayed for the child. I was impressed by the fact that this preacher was so at home with the Author of the Bible that when engaged in the solemn and absorbing exercise of praying with and praying for a great congregation, he could emulate the example of his Lord, who said, "Suffer the little children to come unto Me," and immediately give his attention to that babe as though for the moment it alone engaged his thought.

It seems fitting to mention a beautiful sequel to this significant incident. Years after the time to which I refer I had the privilege of speaking at the annual meeting of the Stockwell Orphanage—

Spurgeon's Orphanage—and Mr. Thomas Spurgeon, at that time pastor of the Metropolitan Tabernacle Church, was in the chair. As illustrating Spurgeon's interest in and love for children, I mentioned the incident of the child crying while he prayed and being prayed for by him because of its crying. At the close of my address Mr. Thomas Spurgeon said to the meeting, 'I am glad to be able to carry that touching story a stage further. Just the other day I had the joy of receiving into membership in our church at the Tabernacle that child, grown to be a young man. He was never allowed to be ignorant of or to forget that when he was but a babe the great preacher publicly prayed for him. This deepened his interest in the preacher's ministry, and in course of time he found the Lord and is now a member of the church of which my father was for so long the honoured pastor.' Surely we have here an instance of the absolute truth of our Saviour's word—'Whatsoever ye shall ask, believing, ye shall receive.'

I have another memory of Spurgeon which it is quite relevant I should mention. Returning from the West Coast of Africa, where I began my missionary work, I was invited to address Spurgeon's students one Friday afternoon, with the President of the College himself in the chair. I had a very simple story to tell of the tragic condition of the people in the Cameroons and of the manifested power of the Gospel to meet their need and to lift individual souls into the family of God through the new birth which the Holy Spirit brings about, as it pleases Him, wherever the Gospel of redemption by the blood of Christ and the forgiveness of sins is preached. The great preacher was deeply moved at the thought both of the need of unevangelised people and of the demonstrated suitability to the case of all the unevangelised millions of mankind of that Gospel which it was his delight to preach. I have never been able to forget—nor would I wish to—how the great preacher was melted to tears as he listened to the young missionary's simple story. What a heart he had—how thoroughly evangelized! At the first Pastors' College Conference following on the occasion I have just referred to, I was privileged to speak, and I remember, as we moved from the ante-room to the platform, Spurgeon put his hand on my shoulder and said, 'Urge the men to go out.' One has rejoiced times without number to think of the fruit from Spurgeon's own Biblical evangelism that has appeared in different parts of the world in evangelistic work carried on by his students.

Surely the test of the presentation of thought regarding matters of revelation and in regard to the salvation of man, as to whether it is of God or merely according to the natural workings of the human mind is this: Is the Lord Jesus Christ loved by souls as a result of what is spoken? In this connexion I would close with a touching incident. A little girl from a Hindu home attended for the first time a mission day school. In that school, whatever else the girls were taught, prominence was given to the telling of the good news of the love of the Lord Jesus Christ in coming to seek and save that which was lost. The Gospel message was absolutely new to this little girl, and at the close of school that day she came to the missionary lady in charge of the school and said, 'Memsahib, that was a beautiful story you told us this morning. I never heard it before. Would you please tell it to me again?' And the missionary lady, with her congregation of one, again briefly told of the love of God's Son in dying for sinners. The Hindu child was intensely interested and she said, 'I am sure that no one at home has heard this story. I want to tell them as I go home now, and I want to be sure that I tell it right. Will you please tell it to me again?' And again the story was told. Shortly after, the child, having even then reluctantly left the school, as the missionary lady passed through a room leading to the street she came upon this child kneeling by a bench (the children in the school had been asked to kneel while prayer was offered at the beginning and close of school), and as the child heard footsteps, still kneeling she turned and saw that it was the lady who had told her the wonderful story, and she beckoned to her to come over, and she said, 'Memsahib, I feel I would like to say something to Jesus, but I don't know if He would like to hear me say it.' And the missionary said, 'Tell me what you thought of saying, and I will tell you if I think the Lord Jesus would like to hear you say it.' And the child said, 'I thought of saying, "Jesus, how could You do it? How could You do it? Was it just love? And if so, won't You make me love You?"' And the lady encouraged the child so to pour out her heart to the Saviour, and she did, saying at the suggestion of the missionary, 'Lord Jesus, how could You do it? How could You do it? Was it just love? And if so, won't You make me love You?'

And we know that the gracious answer to such a prayer was assured by the faithfulness of Him Who had appointed that that child should hear that day the Word through hearing which faith comes—the faith which worketh by love. May the Gospel message, familiar to us because of our possession of the verbally inspired Scriptures, affect our hearts as deeply as that Hindu child's heart was affected; and in love to our great God and Saviour Jesus Christ may we seek to make known 'the common salvation' and to contend for the Faith once for all delivered to the saints, and to say from the heart with Spurgeon, 'I would as soon dream of blaspheming my Maker as of questioning the infallibility of His Word.'

C. H. Spurgeon in his early twenties.

The Secret and the Source of the Power in Spurgeon's Sermons

By Rev. Bimal Ananda Nag

The name and fame of Charles Haddon Spurgeon had travelled to India before I became a Christian. I heard of him not from Christian missionaries or from other Christians, but from non-Christian young men who had been to England for University degrees or training in their professional careers as barristers-at-law. They used to come and tell me that it was such a privilege to hear C. H. Spurgeon that they felt while present at his services—and some of them had the privilege of personal conversation with him,—that to be with him or to hear him was 'to feel the presence of God.'

Now, such a statement from non-Christian young men naturally encouraged me somehow to get hold of some of his sermons, and the first that I read was a sermon entitled, 'Is it nothing to you?' I read it very carefully, and I remember coming to this passage: 'Is there one here heavy of heart? Are there not many here conscious of fault, Are you wrong? Would you be right? Are you guilty; would you be forgiven? Then the Cross for you, Jesus for you. Turn aside and look at Him, look till your eyes are full of tears, look till you brush those tears away and see it all; Jesus as Saviour suffering in my stead; I am forgiven; my Father has adopted me; I am His child; I am glad. Oh, guilty ones, there is something in Christ for you, for He died, the Just for the unjust, to bring us to God.'

I cannot say to-night to what extent those words, in addition to the title of the sermon, "Is it nothing to you?"—to what extent those words created in me an inclination to know of this Jesus. But that it did work in me I have not the slightest doubt. I continued to read some of his other sermons, and when I became a Christian I heard a good deal more of Charles Haddon Spurgeon. I heard of him as 'the prince of preachers'; I heard that thousands flocked to hear him. I often asked myself the question, what was the attractive power in him? I have asked myself that question even today. And I have asked, "What went they out to see?" Did they want to see an orator? Orators were to be found in those days in the House of Commons. Did they go to hear a learned man or a philosopher? The learned men were to be found in the university halls. What went they out to hear? A preacher of the Gospel, whose message met the deepest needs of human souls. For I believe deep down in every human heart, though man has lost God he has not lost the consciousness that God is, he has not lost the longing for God, and because Charles Haddon Spurgeon encouraged those longings, fed those longings, people gave up their work, gave up their play, and flocked round to hear him. Even to-day, wherever the Gospel is faithfully preached, wherever the preacher distributes the Bread of Life faithfully, the people will come and hear him. It is only when in the name of bread, so-called preachers give a stone, when in the name of an egg or a fish they give a scorpion—it is then that men do not come to hear.

As I was listening to Dr. Shields speaking I was thinking of my own country, full of intelligent men, civilised men, but still blind enough to worship idols; and I say to myself, Why are they continuing to worship idols while we rejoice in Jesus Christ? The answer has been to me—those idol worshippers in the very depths of their hearts want to find a God whom they can see, whom they can hear, whom they can touch, and because we Christians have not presented to them effectively our Lord Jesus Christ, who alone can satisfy those longings, they are still deep down in idolatry. To-night, celebrating the Centenary of Charles Haddon Spurgeon, if we will make up our minds to carry the message of Jesus Christ to these people who, in the depths of their hearts are unconsciously, unknowingly, longing for Christ,—that will be a real celebration of this centenary.

I have heard of the Oxford Group Movement since I reached this country. Some friends have been anxious that I should go and be with them. If they have made any stir in this country it is because people unconsciously desire a Friend and a God just as Jesus Christ is, but because in the churches in this city Christ probably is not faithfully presented these people go astray. Charles Haddon Spurgeon faithfully preached Christ.

One of the tests of the faithfulness of his preaching, of his sermons, as of all sermons, lies in the test of translation. You know, in India the translation of the Bible into the Indian vernaculars is very often unfavourably criticised by the literary men in India. They say that the language is not good. But the Bible, being the Word of God, even if the translation is not good it does not lose its power when it approaches a sinner. It is the same power of God for salvation. Mrs. Spurgeon, I think, or it may have been Mrs. James Spurgeon, desired that some of the sermons of Charles Haddon Spurgeon should be translated into Bengali and circulated. I need hardly tell you that when I was consulted, I said this sermon, 'Is it nothing to you?' should take the very first place, and it is there in that collection of his sermons. About twenty were printed and circulated. I translated some of them. I do not claim any literary excellence for anything that was done by me; I am also prepared to admit that probably literary excellence does not belong to the work of the other friends, but the power has been there, for we have received testimonies from different quarters saying how helpful the sermons of Mr. Spurgeon so translated and distributed have been.

Sir, in India there is a natural tendency, inclination, to believe in inerrant Scripture, for their mentality is this. Hindus speak of their Scriptures, of their Gita, as inerrant; the Mohammedans speak of their Koran as the inerrant Scripture; they cannot understand how there can be any religion on the face of the earth if God has not given an inerrant Scripture. Theirs are spurious claims; I need not go into the evidence of that. But all spurious claims denote the existence of a real one somewhere; and that is the Bible.

Someone, just pulling a leaf from a plant on one occasion, asked me, "Can you tell me who has made these markings on this leaf?" I said, "God"; and do you think God, who has taken such pains to mark this one leaf, would easily let us down with an errant Scripture: No! I therefore, friends, fully believe, rejoice to believe, in the plenary inspiration of the Bible. I am using the word plenary rather than verbal inspiration—I believe in it fully, but I do not use the term, for if the inspiration is not in the words where can the inspiration stand? When I say I will speak here to-night at 7 o'clock, if those words do not mean what I say, where is my meaning? It is according to my thought that I have breathed those words. Equally God means what He hath said, every word being true. If there is no verbal inspiration there can be no inspiration at all, and I am not prepared to concede to them, by using the phrase "verbal inspiration," that any other kind of inspiration was possible.

Now then, they say, 'Still, it is the inspiration of thought.' A Principal of a theological college was discussing this very question with me while driving his motor car, and I said to him, 'If your words are true then you are making Christianity the indicative mood and the present tense of the verb To Think.' He said, 'What do you mean?' It comes to mean this: What I think is Christianity to me, what he thinks is Christianity to him, what they think is Christianity to them—everybody according to his own thought, no one according to the thought of Christ. That is what Christianity is reduced to if the inspiration lies in the thought alone, because who is to find out the exact thought apart from the words?

I do not know how many of you know the name of Dr. Rabindranath Tagore, our great poet of Bengal, a poet who has been given the Nobel Prize for his literary excellence. He is a great thinker, a great philosopher. One day I was travelling with him in a railway carriage, and we entered into a conversation about Modernism, and I asked him what he thought of Modernism. He is not a Christian, mind you; he belongs to a reformed movement of Brahmoism. He said, 'I welcome Modernism.' I said, 'Why?' He said, 'If Modernism is a success in England, Christianity is dead and Brahmoism is established.' I thought he was right. Indian minds are most logical.

There are people who come and tell us some parts of the Bible are inspired and other parts are not. I have often been asked by the students amongst whom I work, 'Sir, if you Christians think some parts of the Bible are not inspired, how do you know that the parts on which you rely to-day you will not reject as uninspired to-morrow?' That theory takes away the whole Bible from us.

When I come to consider the attitude ot Charles Haddon Spurgeon I cannot help thinking that a Baptist by conviction must be a believer in the plenary inspiration of the Bible, for his doctrine on Baptism depends on the verbal inspiration of the Word. ('Yes.') He is not a Baptist if he does not stress the full inspiration of the word 'baptism', if he does not accept verbal inspiration in such a passage as 'He that believeth and is baptized'—believing first, being baptized afterwards. All these things are evidences of verbal inspiration, and I do not know how anyone can consistently be a Baptist who does not believe in the verbal inspiration of the Bible.

In India you have so to speak as to indicate even the verbal inspiration of prepositions. Shall I give you an illustration? If a young Indian student comes and tells me, 'I believe Jesus,' does he mean anything in the nature of saving faith? He does not. We have to insist, 'Friend; you must believe *in* Jesus or *on* Jesus.' These prepositions are inspired prepositions. They have profound meaning in themselves.

Having been known to be a believer in the plenary inspiration of the Bible, some of my friends, particularly the learned Christian friends, some of the Principals of the Christian colleges in Calcutta, and some of the ministers, have been most anxious to secure that I should 'see the light'—that is, to see that I should have this my faith destroyed. When Dr. George Adam Smith visited Calcutta, I received many invitations to lunch with him and to discuss such matters with him. I was very glad indeed to have such discussions. Before I say what I put to him, I would like to say how he talked about the Atonement. In his sermon in the church on a Sunday morning, his description was this: 'God permitted this death of Jesus Christ as an example to the people of what sin meant.' Oh, the pain I had! When we came together I said, 'Dr. Smith, if you were a worker amongst Indian students here, you would have to face this question: "If you do not believe in the verbal inspiration of the Bible, what justification have you for believing, say, in the Ten Commandments?" There might be a hundred-and-one arguments given by these students against the observance of the Ten Commandments. I say to them, "God has commanded and therefore they must be obeyed"; and they accept it. What would you say? What do you say?' I further gave him that argument that if you admit there are mistakes, how do you know that the very thing you believe to-day would not be considered by you as a mistake some other day.

He was good enough, sincere enough, to tell me, 'Mr. Nag, I have not considered this question from this point of view, but I will, and I hope to be able to write on this subject.' He promised to send me the article. I have not yet received it though several years have passed. I do not blame him; such matters are little matters to trouble him.

I will tell you of another instance. This was an elderly man, coming in contact with the missionary who made a name in India as a great scholar. This man, a missionary of the Bramo Somaj, the reformed movement, was discussing with him the divinity of Christ, and the missionary said to me, 'I cannot make any impression upon him.' I was not surprised, for when has an unbeliever helped a man to believe in Jesus Christ? He said, 'He seems to have a great affection for you'—he and I were together, before my conversion; in the Brahmo Somaj he was my teacher. The Christian missionary said, 'I will ask him to see you.' I agreed and he came. How could a youngster who had been under his instruction enter into a personal discussion with such a man. I took a volume of Spurgeon's sermons. I opened this very sermon from the volume of 1881, and I read this sermon. I said, 'Let me read something—it has been very, very helpful to me.' Before I finished this sermon he took away his chair from behind him and knelt down and said, 'Pray,' and he began to pray to the Lord Jesus Christ himself.

As to the power of the Bible even in that heathen country, I will give you one instance, and probably I will conclude with that. In this case the man was a city magistrate. At the end of one of my meetings he said to me, 'Mr. Nag, is there any book with the help of which I can study all the passages in the Bible on the subject of sin?' I said, 'Yes, and I have such a book, and I will bring it to you to-morrow morning.' I took to him Young's Concordance. It took us some months to go through the passages, and while reading together—and we used to read almost every day—it seemed to me he was a most hard-hearted man; I found no response from him. At last he was transferred from Calcutta, where I was, and though I corresponded now and again there was no further response towards Christ. Some years later I received a letter from his wife. She wrote to me, 'Probably you do not know that my husband is seriously ill and there is no hope of his life. We are here for his treatment. It is his desire that you should come and see him and pray for him.' I went, and I not only prayed with him, but I arranged to visit him every morning and pray for him. At the end of my prayer every morning—he was very weak indeed; he could hardly speak audibly—he used to whisper these words, 'Lord Jesus, make me and keep me Thine own.' Day after day that prayer went up, until I had to leave this city to fulfil a previous engagement, and when I was leaving his wife said to me, 'If you must go, go; but will you promise to come if you receive any telegram from me?' I said, 'Most certainly.' He was lying on his back, very weak, but with great effort he put his hands together in the Indian fashion and said to me, 'We will meet Yonder.' I received a telegram and I hastened there, but it was too late; he had gone. I have often asked myself, was not that a glorious salvation through the use of the Word of God? Is not he a soul who must be welcomed by Jesus Christ Himself as His very own? 'Him that cometh to Me I will in no wise cast out.'

My dear friends, I have told you something of the secret, something of the source, of the power of Charles Haddon Spurgeon. The last thing I want to tell you is this, that his sermons were soaked in power because they were soaked in prayer. Without it he never delivered a single sermon; you can read it from his sermons, which really are the biography of his inner life. Therefore he spoke with power. The Lord Jesus Christ has Himself said, 'Abide in Me and I in you. If ye abide in Me and My words—My words—abide in you, ye shall ask what ye will and it shall be done unto you.' The Lord fulfilled His promise in the life of Charles Haddon Spurgeon. He is gone, but the same Lord liveth. The same blessing is for us who can claim it. May God lead us into that blessing!

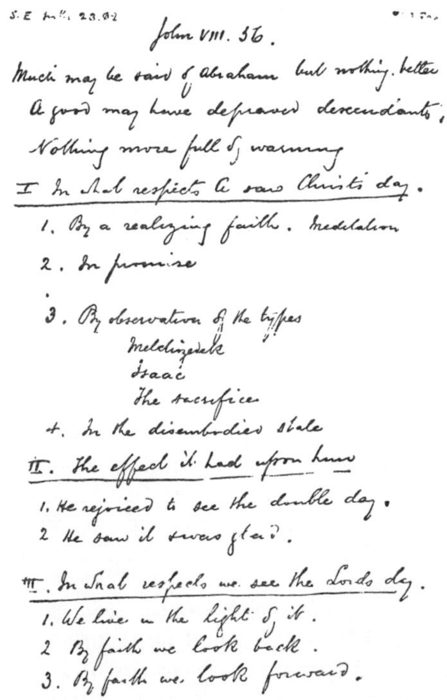
John VIII. 56.
Much may be said of Abraham but nothing better
A good man may have depraved descendants,
Nothing more full of warning
I In what respects he saw Christ's day.
1. By a realizing faith. Meditation
2. In promise
3. By observation of the types
Melchizedek
Isaac
The sacrifice
4. In the disembodied state
II. The effect it had upon him
1. He rejoiced to see the double day.
2 He saw it & was glad.
III. In what respects we see the Lord's day.
1. We live in the light of it.
2 By faith we look back.
3. By faith we look forward.

IV. The Effect it has upon us.

We are glad.

(The notes from which C. H. Spurgeon preached a sermon on John 8.56: No. IV was on reverse side of paper)

Spurgeon: the Man, his Message and his Ministry

By Dr. T. T. Sheilds

I think I shall be correct in saying that the Centenary of the birth of Charles Haddon Spurgeon has, in some way, been observed throughout the whole of Christendom. For months past nearly every evangelical publication has contained some reference to Spurgeon, while not a few have published special Spurgeon Centenary editions. Nor has the recognition of the centenary of Spurgeon's birth been confined to evangelical papers and institutions, for many whose theological positions are widely removed from Spurgeon's have acknowledged the world's debt to his incomparable ministry. In addition to these tributes, new lives of Spurgeon have been written, and new interpretations of the man and his message have been published. Thus in books and magazines and weekly journals the fascinating story of Spurgeon's life and ministry has been retold. This, of itself, must have accomplished great good.

To some of us to be uninformed respecting the unique ministry of C. H. Spurgeon would seem to be inexcusable ignorance of the greatest evangelical force the world has known in many centuries. We must not, however, be too harsh in our judgments in this respect, for it must be remembered that the religious world of our day is radically different from that of forty or fifty years ago.

Spurgeon died in eighteen hundred and ninety-two, forty-eight years ago, but even now his voice is still greatly missed; and his memory, to a great multitude, is still fresh and fragrant.

The whole world of Evangelical Christianity may say of Spurgeon: he is not dead, but speaketh; the echo of the music of his matchless voice can still be heard. The influence of his beautifully symmetrical Christian character, the fruits of his incomparably effective ministry, and the power of the glorious gospel he proclaimed, still abide.

Notwithstanding, since Spurgeon's day, a new generation has arisen to which the great things which he taught have not been ministered. In the realm of theological authority a new Pharaoh has arisen which knows not our Joseph. It is well, therefore, that the whole story should be retold, that the alluring romance of this great figure should be proclaimed afresh as a humbling challenge to a vainglorious generation, and as an inspiration to great multitudes of people who do not esteem as a strange thing the great things of God's law.

I shall refrain from mentioning the details of the inspiringly familiar story of the circumstances of Spurgeon's life, or of his unprecedentedly fruitful ministry. I propose, rather, humbly and gratefully to record my own simple tribute to his greatness, and my own appraisal of his unique place in Christian history; with some attempt to set forth my own view of the philosophy of his life and work. This I shall do by speaking of Spurgeon on this occasion as a Bible preacher.

One cannot, with any hope of accuracy, analyse the Spurgeon phenomenon without recognising *his apparent precocity*. Perhaps it would not be an exaggeration to say that his place in religious history is comparable to that of Pitt the Younger in the history of this country, for it would probably be correct to say that, by the time he was twenty-one years of age, C. H. Spurgeon was the most conspicuous figure in the evangelical world.

How is his youthful pre-eminence to be accounted for? That he was a man of uncommon mental capacity I think is generally conceded. He was, by nature, cast in an unusual mould. Moreover, his remarkable native powers had been highly developed, and thoroughly disciplined, at a very early age. Diminutive, theoretical, educational technicians have had the audacity to speak of Spurgeon as 'uneducated.' As well might some miniature hot-house shrub, could it become vocal, describe the giant oak of the forest that had braved a thousand storms as 'uncultivated' because it had not been pampered and petted in its little hot-house pot.

Education consists essentially in developing and disciplining and directing to the highest degree, and to the noblest purpose, a man's natural capacities. The average youthful mind needs, for such development, the direction of an intellectual senior, and the reinforcement and regulation of another's will. Hence the value of the regimen of college and university life. But here and there is found a man possessed of such native qualities that he becomes in himself both student and faculty, and therefore makes more progress in a year than most men would in four or five, and is found to be as mentally mature at twenty-one as the average man would be at twice his age. And in all departments of human activity and progress, history has chiefly been made by men of just such independent, personal resourcefulness and power.

By what criteria shall we appraise Spurgeon's intellect? One scarcely knows whether to be amused or indignant at the presumptuous attempts of certain religious Lilliputians to estimate the dimensions and potentialities of this intellectual sun through the medium of their sixpenny spy glass! I will make a confession: when Dr. T. Reavely Glover made his inexcusably vulgar attack upon the memory of this mighty man of God, my temper outran my judgment. I planned a reply which should reach every Baptist minister in the English-speaking world. I had an initial thirty thousand envelopes made and printed for the job. Then I cooled down. I thought I saw the great and magnanimous Spurgeon smiling. I remembered a Spurgeon story of a minister who called to see Spurgeon, and told him he was in great trouble. He had a member of his church who was strongly opposed to his ministry. He said that he always sat in the front seat, and as soon as the minister announced his text, this man put his fingers in his ears, and so continued to the end of the sermon. Having told his story, he asked Spurgeon if he did not think that was a terrible situation, and enquired what he would do in like circumstances; to which Spurgeon replied, 'I think I should ask the Lord to send a fly to light upon his nose.' The man saw the humour of the situation, and found relief in a hearty laugh.

That was characteristic of the attitude of our hero. He ever refused to exercise his mind with trivialities. Remembering this, I felt that the vulgar attack made upon Spurgeon's memory was not worth a reply. Of one thing one may be sure, that by the time the centenary of the birth of some of these critics rolls round, there will be nobody to celebrate it, for the reason that the world will have forgotten that they ever lived.

It is difficult to measure the intellectual stature of Spurgeon. I venture humbly the opinion that for native mental capacity and power of absorption; for rational vigour; for analytical acumen; for analogical acquisitiveness; for poetic insight and imagination; for philosophical comprehensiveness; for prophetic vision, and compass, and perspective; for fearless inquisitiveness and power of courageous exploration; for heroic abandonment to the consequences of knowledge, for daring intimacy with truth—in many centuries, few minds have equalled, and none have excelled, that of C. H. Spurgeon.

But when all this has been recognised and acknowledged, there still remains the wonder of Spurgeon's ability as a youth to describe nearly every conceivable phase of human experience, and to play upon every element of human emotional, intellectual, and volitional life as upon a harp of a thousand strings. When but a youth I recall laying down a volume of Spurgeon's sermons, and enquiring of myself, whence and how did this youth of twenty-one acquire so intimate a knowledge of the whole gamut of human experience? And one day I found a satisfactory solution of the phenomenon, and in the discovery I thought, and still think, I discerned the explanation of the depth, and breadth, and height, the wealth of content, the timeless character, the enlarging compass and abiding fruitfulness of Spurgeon's ministry. Here it is: *'O how love I Thy law! It is my meditation all the day. Thou through Thy commandments hast made me wiser than mine enemies: for they are ever with me. I have more understanding than all my teachers: for Thy testimonies are my meditation. I understand more than the ancients, because I keep Thy precepts.'* (Psa. 119: 97-100).

But no estimate of Spurgeon's intellectual qualities can be even approximately correct which does not take account of the quality of his spiritual life and endowments. Challenging as the statement may be, belief is less an exercise of the understanding than an attitude of will: 'If any man will do his will, he shall know of the doctrine, whether if be of God.' 'Holding faith, and a good conscience; which some having put away, concerning faith have made shipwreck.' In the First Epistle to Timothy, three times within the compass of three short chapters, conscience is linked with faith, Paul insisting that 'faith unfeigned' is inseparable from 'love out of a pure heart, and a good conscience'; and that whoever thrusts from him a good conscience, inevitably 'makes shipwreck concerning the faith'; and that the full Christian revelation, 'the mystery of the faith,' is not to be held by any peculiarity of intellectual aptitude, but 'in a pure conscience.' In Paul's view, therefore, if the woof of a man's belief is intellectual, its warp is moral. While religious belief is sometimes regarded as though it were a fabric woven in reason's loom of material called facts, the truth is, that it is not a mere manufacture at all, but a cultivated growth; which, while rising out of the surface soil of the intellectual, is yet rooted in the subsoil of conscience and the moral nature.

Hence there is a mutually complementary and reciprocal relation between what a man is and what he believes, between what he believes and what he is. A conscience drugged with dereliction will inevitably befog the understanding with unbelief. A man's view of the Bible must, in the nature of the case, be affected by his relationship to the Person the Bible enshrines. Spurgeon's crystal-clear view of the doctrines of grace, and of the Bible as their authoritative source, was the natural result of his personal intimacy with Jesus Christ our Lord. Thus a person of superior piety, though of mediocre mental capacity and attainments, may have a clearer understanding of divine truth than the greatest intellectual religious theorist.

Somewhere I read a Spurgeon story the source of which I am unable to recall. I once related it to Thomas Spurgeon, who said that he had never heard it before, but that it bore the stamp of truth because it was so like his father. One summer afternoon Spurgeon called on Rev. Arthur Mursell and asked him to accompany him on an excursion into the woods. Mursell himself, according to the story, is reported to have related the incident. On this particular occasion, for some reason, he was somewhat disinclined to respond to Spurgeon's suggestion, but, being pressed, he said, 'I will go on one condition, that you will not talk "good" to me.'

Relating the experience, as I recall, Mursell is reported to have said that he thought he discerned something like a shadow pass over Spurgeon's countenance. It cleared in a moment, and he replied, 'All right, then, I will not cast my pearls before—but there, put on your hat and come along.' Mursell said they went into the woods, and all that afternoon Spurgeon was the perfect gentleman, and a most considerate companion, seeming especially careful to respect the wishes of his friend. But Mursell said, 'It was not Spurgeon.' There was something unnatural about his whole demeanour. At last, as they sat on a log together in the woods, Mursell put his hand on Spurgeon's knee and said, 'Forgive me, friend, I have made you uncomfortable. Let us talk about the Beloved.' Instantly Spurgeon's whole aspect changed, and smiling radiantly, he said, 'Thank you; I shall feel more comfortable.' 'Never,' said Mursell, 'in his loftiest flights of oratory had I heard Spurgeon discourse more eloquently on the glories of the Lord Jesus Christ than there in the woods.'

Again I remember to have read, but where I have been unable to recall, that Spurgeon, who was not given to boasting, and who was humbly reticent so far as his own spiritual attainments were concerned, remarked to some friends that he believed that during his waking moments, over a period of twenty years, he had not been unconscious of the presence of Christ. Ah, that is the meaning of such great sayings as this: 'And truly our fellowship is with the Father, and with His Son Jesus Christ.' I believe Spurgeon's personal relationship to Christ, his unbroken communion with Him, his passionate love for the Master, is the truest explanation of his spiritualized intellectuality, and his intellectualized spirituality—the only possible explanation, indeed, of his attitude toward the Bible and the essential doctrines of the gospel of grace.

I propose to try to give you some idea of the development of Spurgeon's view of the Bible, and of that system of truth which he conceived the gospel of Christ to comprehend.

We hear much from our critics about their growth in knowledge, and their progressive acquaintance with facts; much, too, by implication, to our disadvantage, of the handicap of a 'static' mind. But within the realm of any man's knowledge there are certain factual elements which never change; there are facts which never cease to be facts. The multiplication table, in principle, cannot wholly be ignored even by an Einstein. The greatest of all composers, whoever he may be, or may have been, never escaped nor can escape from the harmonious bondage of the musical scale; while not even a Shakespeare himself could dispense with the alphabet.

Is there no analogy here to elements of spiritual knowledge? May not a spiritual babe know some things from which he will never depart, though he should become a spiritual Methuselah? Why should Christian men boast of their release from the thraldom of 'revelation'? It is one of the chief glories of Spurgeon and his ministry that while there was undoubtedly a progression in knowledge, and enlargement of view, in the essentials of his faith, he was to the end of his ministry what he had been at the beginning. And the Scripture adequately explains this fact: 'They went out from us, but they were not of us; for if they had been of us, they would no doubt have continued with us: but they went out, that they might be made manifest that they were not all of us. But ye have an unction from the Holy One, and ye know all things. I have not written unto you because ye know not the truth, but because ye know it, and that no lie is of the truth. Who is a liar but he that denieth that Jesus is the Christ? He is anti-christ, that denieth the Father and the Son. Whosoever denieth the Son, the same hath not the Father: but he that acknowledgeth the Son hath the Father also. Let that therefore abide in you, which ye have heard from the beginning. If that which ye have heard from the beginning shall remain in you, ye also shall continue in the Son, and in the Father. And this is the promise that he hath promised us, even eternal life. These things have I written unto you concerning them that seduce you. But the anointing which ye have received of Him abideth in you, and ye need not that any man teach you: but as the same anointing teacheth you of all things, and is truth, and is no lie, and even as it hath taught you, ye shall abide in Him. And now, little children, abide in Him; that, when He shall appear, we may have confidence, and not be ashamed before Him at His coming.' (1 John 2: 19-28).

In many respects the truest indications of the quality of a man's inner self are given in his spontaneous utterances. Sermons are not, or ought not, to be impromptu expressions, but considered presentations of truth. Notwithstanding, the necessity of weekly output injects into the weekly product elements of spontaneity. The preacher who is constantly before the public is more likely to express his heart than his head in his regular pulpit deliveries.

Let us hear then a little of Spurgeon's view of the Bible as expressed in a sermon preached in 1855, at Exeter Hall, when he was three months short of his majority. The text of the sermon was, 'I have written to him the great things of My law, but they were counted as a strange thing' (Hosea 8: 12):

> 'First, then, concerning this book, who is THE AUTHOR? The text says that it is God. "I have written to him the great things of My law." Here lies my Bible—who wrote it? I open it, and I find it consists of a series of tracts. The first five tracts were written by a man called Moses. I turn on and I find others. Sometimes I see David is the penman, at other times, Solomon. Here I read Micah, Amos, then Hosea. As I turn further on, to the more luminous pages of the New Testament, I see Matthew, Mark, Luke, and John, Paul, Peter, James, and others; but when I shut up the book, I ask myself who is the author of it? Do these men jointly claim the authorship? Are they the compositors of this massive volume? Do they between themselves divide the honour? Our holy religion answers, No! This volume is the writing of the living God: each letter was penned with an Almighty finger; each word in it dropped from the everlasting lips, each sentence was dictated by the Holy Spirit. Albeit, that Moses was employed to write his histories with his fiery pen, God guided that pen. It may be that David touched his harp and let sweet Psalms of melody drop from his fingers, but God moved his hands over the living strings of his golden harp. It may be that Solomon sang Canticles of love, or gave forth words of consummate wisdom, but God directed his lips, and made the Preacher eloquent. If I follow the thundering Nahum when his horses plough the waters, or Habakkuk, when he sees the tents of Cushan in affliction; if I read Malachi, when the earth is burning like an oven; if I turn to the smooth page of John, who tells of love, or the rugged fiery chapters of Peter, who speaks of the fire devouring God's enemies; if I turn to Jude, who launches forth anathemas upon the foes of God, everywhere I find God speaking: it is God's voice, not man's; the words are God's words, the words of the Eternal, the Invisible, the Almighty, the Jehovah of this earth. This Bible is God's Bible; and when I see it, I seem to hear a voice springing

up from it, saying, 'I am the book of God: man, read me. I am God's writing: open my leaf, for I was penned by God; read it, for he is my author, and you will see him visible and manifest everywhere. "I have written to him the great things of my law." '

That is surely a pretty strong assumption of the verbal inspiration of Scripture.

In the same sermon he speaks of the authority of the Scriptures after this fashion:

"First, my friends, stand over this volume, and admire *its authority*. This is no common book. It is not the sayings of the sages of Greece; here are not the utterances of philosophers of past ages. If these words were written by man, we might reject them; but oh, let me think the solemn thought—that this book is God's handwriting, that these are God's words. Let me look at its date; it is dated from the hills of heaven. Let me look at its letters; they flash glory on my eye. Let me read the chapters: they are big with meaning and mysteries unknown. Let me turn over the prophecies: they are pregnant with unthought-of wonders. Oh, book of books! And wast thou written by my God? Then will I bow before thee. Thou book of vast authority, thou art a proclamation from the Emperor of Heaven; far be it from me to exercise my reason in contradicting thee. Reason! thy place is to stand and find out what this volume means, not to tell what this book ought to say. Come thou, my reason, my intellect, sit thou down and listen, for these words are the very words of God. I do not know how to enlarge on this thought. Oh! if you could ever remember that this Bible was actually and really written by God! Oh! if ye had been let into the secret chambers of heaven, if ye had beheld God grasping his pen and writing down these letters, then surely ye would respect them. But they are just as much God's hand-writing as if you had seen God write them."

It would surely be difficult to find a stronger statement than that. Again he speaks of its truthfulness:

'Then, since God wrote it, mark *its truthfulness*. If I had written it, there would be worms of critics who would at once swarm on it, and would cover it with their evil spawn; had I written it, there would be men who would pull it to pieces at once, and perhaps quite right too. But this is the Word of God; come, search, ye critics, and find a flaw; examine it from its Genesis to its Revelation, and find an error. This is a vein of pure gold, unalloyed by quartz, or any earthy substance. This is a star without a speck; a sun without a blot; a light without darkness; a moon without its paleness; a glory without a dimness. O Bible! it cannot be said of any other book, that it is perfect and pure; but of thee we can declare all wisdom is gathered up in thee, without a particle of folly. This is the judge that ends the strife where wit and reason fail. This is the book untainted by any error; but is pure, unalloyed, perfect truth. Why? Because God wrote it . . . . Strange that there should be men so vile as to use the penknife of Jehoiakim, to cut passages of the Word, because they are unpalatable. Oh, ye who dislike certain portions of the Holy Writ, rest assured that your taste is corrupt, and that God will not stay for your little opinion. Your dislike is the very reason why God wrote it, because you ought not to be suited; you have no right to be pleased. God wrote what you do not like; he wrote the truth. Oh! let us bend in reverence before it, for God inspired it. It is pure truth. Here from this fountain gushes *aqua vitae*—'the water of life,'—without a single particle of earth; here from this sun cometh forth rays of radiance, without the mixture of darkness. Blessed Bible; thou art all truth.'

There is no room there for the modernistic idea that the Bible contains certain elements of truth, but with a large admixture of error. All this which I have quoted from a young man not yet twenty-one!

But now let me quote from two sermons preached in the year 1887: the first, in March of that year, and just thirty-two years and a few days later than the sermon from which I have just quoted; the second quotation is from a sermon but a few days earlier in the same year:

'Notice, that our Lord believed in the *divinity of Scripture*. He says, "How then shall the scriptures be fulfilled?" But if the Scriptures are only the writings of men, there is no necessity that they should be fulfilled. If they are merely the fallible utterances of good men, I see no particular necessity that they should be fulfilled. Our Lord Jesus Christ insisted upon it that the Scriptures must be fulfilled, and the reason was, that they are not the word of man, but the Word of God. The Scriptures were evidently the Word of God to our Lord Jesus Christ. He never trifles with them, nor differs from them, nor predicts that they will vanish away. It is he that saith, "Think not that I am come to destroy the law, or the prophets: I am not come to destroy, but to fulfil. For verily I say unto you, Till heaven and earth pass, one jot or one tittle shall in no wise pass from the law, till all be fulfilled."

'He believed in the divine origin of the Scriptures, and also in their *infallibility*. "How then shall the Scriptures be fulfilled, that thus it must be?" He does not hint that the Scriptures might be a little mistaken. He does not argue, "I will bring the twelve legions of angels down to deliver myself, and it is no matter to me that then the Scriptures will be made void." Oh, no! the Scriptures must be true, and they must be fulfilled, and therefore he must be betrayed into the hands of men. He settles it as a matter of necessity that Scripture must infallibly be verified, even to its jots and tittles.

'See, brethren, the *priceless worth* of Scripture in the estimation of our Lord. In effect he says, I will die rather than any Scripture shall be unfulfilled. I will go to the cross rather than any one word of God should not be carried out. The prophet Zechariah has written, "Awake, O sword, against my shepherd, and against the man that is my fellow, saith the Lord of hosts: smite the shepherd, and the sheep shall be scattered abroad." The fulfilment of that prophecy fell due that night, and the Son of God was prepared to be smitten as the Shepherd of the sheep, rather than the word of the Father should fall to the ground. "Skin for skin, yea, all that a man hath will he give for his life"; but Jesus would give his life for the Scriptures. Brethren, it were worth while for the whole church to die rather than any truth of Scripture should be given up. Let all our thousands be consumed upon the altar as one great holocaust sooner than the Scripture should be dishonoured. The Word of the Lord must live and prevail whether we die or not. Our Lord teaches us to prize it beyond liberty or life . . . .

'And then, if I may trouble you to look at the text again, you will notice that the word, "it," is in italics; and so is the word "as." Let me read the text again: "When ye received the word of God which ye heard of us, ye received not the word of men." You see I have left out the 'it' and the 'as' because they are not really there, though they are correctly added by the translators as giving the meaning of the apostle. Verbally they are not in the text. I take the sentence out of its connection, and say *that these Thessalonians received not the word of men*. And I like them for that. Oh, but there were very learned men in those days! When Paul was on the earth, and a little before his day, some of the greatest natural minds that ever existed were in Greece teaching the people. Yet the Thessalonians were in such a state, that they received not the word of men. They did not hearken to Plato, or accept Socrates, for there was a something about them which made them hunger for more than the philosophers could bring them. God's elect are of that mind. You may know the Lord's sheep by the fact that "a stranger will they not follow: for they know not the voice of strangers." They will not receive the word of man; it is too light, too chaffy, too frothy for them. You may put it before them in the daintiest guise, illustrate it with poetry, and prove it by the fictions of science, but they cannot feed on such wind. They receive not the word of men; they will not have it; they want something more substantial.

'To come back to our translation: *they received not the gospel as the word of men*. In these days there are some who receive the gospel, but they receive it as the word of men. This is their spirit—"Yes, I know that such is the view that is held by Mr. Black; but there is another view held by Dr. White; and another view is upheld by Professor Gray. All these different 'views' are supposed to be very much upon a par." Beloved friends, this is not our way; there is the truth of God, and there is a lie; and I want you always to feel that there is a solemn difference between the true and the false, and that no lie is of the truth. "Believe not every spirit, but try the spirits whether they are of God." If one says, "Yes," and the other says, "No," it cannot be that they are both true. Salvation is of grace, or else of man: it cannot be a joint-stock-company affair. There is truth, and there is error; and these are opposite the one to the other. Do not indulge yourselves in the folly with which so many are duped—that truth may be error and error may be truth; that black is white, and white is black, and that there is a whity-brown that goes in between, which is, perhaps, the best of the whole lot.

'There is an essential difference between man's word and God's word, and it is fatal to mistake the one for the other. If you receive even the gospel as the word of man you cannot get the blessing out of it; for the sweetness of the gospel lies in the confidence of our heart that this is the word of God. You fall back upon Holy Scripture in the grief of an aching heart; but you cannot rest, however soft the pillow of the promise may seem to be, till you can surely say, "I know that it is of God." If you have even the shadow of a doubt about it, comfort oozes out. The life of comfort flies before doubt, even as love is said to fly out at the window when want comes in at the door. Prick the heart—ay, with but a needle's point—and life will go; and prick the heart of faith—ay, even with the smallest doubt, and the life of you is gone! The joy of faith, and the strength of faith, yea, and the life of faith, are gone when you distrust the word of the Lord!'

Let me go on now two years farther to May, 1889, only three years before his death. Here we have a strong statement respecting the verbal inspiration of Scripture:

'Looking at the text, does it not strike you as a marvel of condescension, that Jehovah, the Infinite, should use words? He has arranged for us, in his wisdom, this way of communicating with one another; but as for himself, he is pure spirit and boundless: shall we contract his glorious thoughts into the narrow channel of sound, and ear, and nerve? Must the eternal mind use human words? The glorious Jehovah spake worlds. The heavens and the earth were the utterances of his lips. To him it seems more in accordance with his nature to speak tempests and thunders, than to stoop to the humble vowels and consonants of a creature of the dust. Will he in very deed communicate with man in man's own way? Yes, he stoops to speak to us by words. We bless the Lord for verbal inspiration, of which we can say, "I have esteemed the words of thy mouth more than my necessary food." I do not know of any other inspiration, neither am I able to conceive of any which can be of true service to us. We need a plain revelation upon which we can exercise faith. If the Lord had spoken to us by a method in which his meaning was infallible, but his words were questionable, we should have been rather puzzled than edified; for it is a task indeed to separate the true sense from the doubtful words. We should always be afraid that the prophet or apostle had not, after all given us the divine sense: it is easy to hear and to repeat words; but it is not easy to convey the meaning of another into perfectly independent words of your own: the meaning easily evaporates. But we believe that holy men of old, though using their own language, were led by the Spirit of God to use words which were also the words of God. The Divine Spirit so operated upon the spirit of the inspired writer, that he wrote the words of the Lord, and we, therefore, treasure up every one of them. To us, "every word of God is pure," and withal full of soul nutriment. "Man doth not live by bread only, but by every word that proceedeth out of the mouth of the Lord doth man live." We can heartily declare with the Psalmist, "Thou art my portion, O Lord: I have said that I would keep thy words."

'Our condescending God is so well pleased to speak to us by words, that he has even deigned to call his only-begotten Son, "The Word." "The Word was made flesh, and dwelt among us." The Lord useth words, not with reluctance, but with pleasure; and he would have us think highly of them, too, as he said to Israel by Moses, "Therefore shall ye lay up these my words in your heart and in your soul."

'We believe that we have the words of God preserved for us in the Scriptures. We are exceedingly grateful that it is so. If we had not the words of the Lord thus recorded we should have felt that we lived in an evil time, since neither voice nor oracle is heard to-day. I say, we should have fallen upon evil days if the words that God spake of old had not been recorded under his superintendence. With this Book before us, what the Lord spake two thousand years ago he virtually speaks now: for "He will not call back his words" (Isaiah 31.2). His word abideth for ever; for it was spoken, not for one occasion, but for all ages. The Word of the Lord is so instinct with everlasting life and eternal freshness, that it is as vocal and forceful in the heart of the saint to-day as it was to the ear of Abraham when he heard it in Canaan; or to the mind of Moses in the desert; or to David when he sang it to his harp. I thank God that many of us know what it is to hear the divine word re-spoken in our souls! By the Holy Ghost the words of Scripture come to us with a present inspiration: not only has the Book been inspired, *it is* inspired. This Book is more than paper and ink, it talks with us. Was not that the promise, "When thou awakest, it shall talk with thee"? We open the Book with this prayer, "Speak, Lord; for thy servant heareth"; and we often close it with this feeling, "Here am I; for thou didst call me." As surely as if the promise had never been uttered before, but had been spoken out of the excellent glory for the first time, the Lord has made Holy Scripture to be his direct word to our heart and conscience. I say not this of you all, but I can say it assuredly of many here present. May the Holy Spirit at this hour speak to you yet again.'

I need give you but one quotation in support of the principle of the equal inspiration of the Old and New Testaments. This also is of the year 1889:

'Above all, do not drop into the semi-blasphemy of some, who think the New Testament vastly superior to the Old. I would not err by saying that in the Old Testament you have more of the bullion of truth than in the New, for therein I should be falling into the evil which I condemn; but this I will say, that they are of equal authority, and that they cast such light upon each other that we could not spare either of them. "What therefore God hath joined together, let not man put asunder." In the whole Book, from Genesis to Revelation, the words of Jehovah are found, and they are always pure words.

'Neither is it right for any to say, "Thus spake Christ himself, but such-and-such a teaching is Pauline." Nay, it is not Pauline; if it be here recorded, it is of the Holy Ghost. Whether the Holy Ghost speaketh by Isaiah, or Jeremiah, or John, or James, or Paul, the authority is still the same. Even concerning Jesus Christ our Lord this is true; for he says of himself, "The word which ye hear is not mine, but the Father's, which sent me." In this matter he puts himself upon the level of others who were as the mouth of God. He says again, "For I have not spoken of myself; but the Father which sent me, he gave me a commandment, what I should say, and what I should speak." We accept the words of the apostles as the words of the Lord, remembering what John said, "We are of God; he that knoweth God heareth us; he that is not of God heareth not us. Hereby know we the spirit of truth, and the spirit of error" (1 John 4:6). A solemn judgment is thus pronounced upon those who would set the Spirit of Jesus against the Spirit which dwelt in the apostles. The words of the Lord are not affected in their value by the medium through which they came. Revealed truth is all of the same quality even when the portions of it are not of the same weight of metal.'

Here is a quotation on this subject respecting the fulness of inspiration of the entire Bible, without admixture of error:

'It is also a book pure in the sense of truth, *being without admixture of error.* I do not hesitate to say that I believe that there is no mistake whatever in the original Holy Scriptures from beginning to end. There may be, and there are, mistakes of translation; for translators are not inspired; but even the historical facts are correct. Doubt has been cast upon them here and there, and at times with great show of reason—doubt which it has been impossible to meet for a season; but only give space enough, and search enough, and the stones buried in the earth cry out to confirm each letter of Scripture. Old manuscripts, coins, and inscriptions, are on the side of the Book, and against it there are nothing but theories, and the fact that many an event in history has no other record but that which the Book affords us. The Book has been of late in the furnace of criticism; but much of that furnace has grown cold from the fact that the criticism is beneath contempt. "The words of the Lord are pure words": there is not an error of any sort in the whole compass of them. These words come from him who can make no mistake, and who can have no wish to deceive his creatures. If I did not believe in the infallibility of the Book, I would rather be without it. If I am to judge the Book, it is no judge of me. If I am to sift it, like the heap on the threshing-floor, and lay this aside and only accept that, according to my own judgment, then I have no guidance whatever, unless I have conceit enough to trust to my own heart. The new theory denies infallibility to the words of God, but practically imputes it to the judgments of men; at least, this is all the infallibility which they can get at. I protest that I will rather risk my soul with a guide inspired from heaven, than with the differing leaders who arise from the earth at the call of "modern thought." '

But once more: in February, 1889, Spurgeon professed his own faith in contrast with the attitude of those who deny the unique inspiration of Scripture:

'These were not a critical, sceptical people. They trembled at the Word, and did not sit down on the throne of usurped infallibility, and call the Scriptures to their bar. There are men abroad nowadays—I grieve to say some of them in the ministry—who take the Bible, not that it may judge them, but that they may judge it. Their judgment weighs in its balances the wisdom of God himself. They talk exceedingly proudly, and their arrogancy exalteth itself. O friends, I know not how you feel about the prevailing scepticism of the age, but I am heart-sick of it! I shun the place where I am likely to hear the utterances of men who do not tremble at God's word. I turn away from the multitude of books which advocate doubt and error. The evil is too painful for me. If I could be content to be an Ishmaelite, and have my hand against every man, I might seek this company, for here I find every faculty of my being called to warfare; but as I love peace, it sickens and saddens me to meet with the enemies of my soul. If I knew that my mother's name would be defamed in certain company, I would keep out of it; if I knew that my father's character would be trailed in the mire, I would travel far not to hear a sound so offensive. I could wish to be deaf and blind, rather than hear or read the modern falsehoods which, at this time, so often wound my spirit.

'I feel more and more a tenderness for the truth of God of the same sort as I would feel for the good name of my wife or my mother. I wish the modern revilers would have some compassion upon us, old believers, to whom their talk is such torture. They might keep their doubts for home consumption. When a man was going to swear, a wise person bade him wait till he was further away from the town, so that nobody might hear him; for it might cause grief to a Christian ear. When a man has anything to say against the eternal truth of God let him speak it to those who love to hear it—to his mates and admirers. But as for us, we are determined we will not be tortured by this kind of thing; we cannot endure it; and we will not remain among those who bespatter us with it. "Oh, but surely you are open to conviction?" they say. We are open to no conviction that shall be contrary to the truth that has saved us from going down to the pit. We are open to no conviction that shall rob us of our eternal hope, and of our glorying in the cross of our Lord Jesus Christ. We do not deliberate, for we have decided. To be for ever holding the truth of God, as though it might yet turn out to be a lie, were to lose all the comfort of it. To be for ever prepared to desert our Lord and Master, to follow some brand-new philosopher, would be perpetual disloyalty. Nay, we have not come thus far at a guess. We have known our Lord and his truth for these forty years, and it is not may-be-or-may-be-not with us now. We neither speculate, nor hesitate; but we know whom we have believed, and by his grace we will cleave to him in life and in death.'

And again:

'I have largely told you what these tremblers are not; and I must now tell you a little of what these people are. They are people who do believe that there is a Word of God. There are plenty of persons who profess and call themselves Christians, and yet do not believe that this sacred book is the very Word of God. Say that it is inspired, and they answer, "So is the Koran, and so are the Vedas." They talk after this fashion: "This is the religious book of the ancient Hebrew nation. A very respectable book it is, but infallible, certainly not: the very Word of God, certainly not." Well, then, we distinctly part company with such talkers. We can have no sort of fellowship with them in any measure or degree with regard to the things of God. They are to us as heathen men and publicans. If we are to come under the head of those that tremble at God's Word, we must believe that there is a Word of the Lord to tremble at, as we do most assuredly believe, let others talk as they may.'

These quotations are surely sufficient to establish the fact that from the beginning of his ministry, to the end, Spurgeon never for a moment wavered in his conviction that the Bible is the very Word of God. It is surely folly to talk of honouring Spurgeon's memory while dishonouring the Book he so consistently revered.

I have taken so much time to establish this principle which is so indispensable to any fair estimate of Spurgeon's ministry, that I have left myself no time in which to discuss at length the inplications of the position. To Spurgeon, the Bible was the supreme court of appeal. So ought it to be with us. Differ as we may in some of our interpretations of what the Holy Book contains, if we are one in our readiness to accept the decisions of the Book as being the final authority upon any subject with which it deals, there is hope of ultimate agreement. But Bible-believers can find nothing in common with those who either deny, or debase, or despise, or even condescendingly compliment, the Bible.

One man may live in a house that has more and larger windows than his neighbour's, and thus may enjoy more sunshine; but the light in each dwelling in such case would be derived from the same source. So, with our varying capacities of perception and reception there will be varying opinions upon many matters. But such light as shines is the light of the Orb of day. But if all the windows be shuttered, and the day be excluded, and tapers of human wisdom be substituted for the sun of divine revelation, the light that is in us must be darkness—and then how great is that darkness!

I have already said that Spurgeon's view of truth was determined largely by his personal intimacy with the Lord Jesus; and of course it is equally true that his knowledge of the Lord of the Word was communicated through the Word of the Lord. Spurgeon was a systematic theologian. He ever viewed truth relatively.

Dr. Joseph Parker was himself one of the greatest preachers of his day—perhaps second in popularity only to Spurgeon himself. And, in the main, he was true to the principles of the gospel. Yet the two men were poles apart in their mental outlook. Parker was a brilliant preacher, but his sermons were devoid of system. I do not mean that they were homiletically defective, but rather that they were without doctrinal order and relation. Someone, I think it was Carlyle, somewhere describes certain editors as editing their papers after the manner of upsetting a cartload of coals. Parker preached after the manner of emptying a casket of jewels; but they were of all sorts, and sizes, and qualities.

Spurgeon, on the other hand, was keenly logical and analytical; and viewed one truth in relation to another. His conviction of divine inspiration and authority of the Scriptures inevitably made him a Trinitarian, involving belief in the essential Deity of Jesus Christ. Every doctrine he preached was the inevitable corollary of that major premise. The death of Incarnate Deity could be no accident. Hence it was purposeful, adequate, and determinative. An acceptance of the involved principles of substitution and expiation was logically inevitable; and that view of the eternally pre-determined redemptive purpose of the Incarnation made him a Calvinist.

The word, Calvinism, he defines in the preface to the first volume of his sermons:

'The word Calvinism, is frequently used here as the short word which embraces that part of divine truth which teaches that salvation is by grace alone.'

So then his theological system of grace, as he conceived it, was based upon his conviction of the Deity of Christ. The truths of total depravity, effectual calling, and final perseverance, inhered in the truth of the sovereign immutability of the Saviour he adored.

May I at this point, without offence, call attention to the difference between the abiding residues of these two ministries? It was but a short time after Parker's death that his pulpit became the centre from which was disseminated a radical new theology. On the other hand, through varying fortunes, in the forty-two years which have passed since Spurgeon's death, while none of his successors would presume to claim equality with him, the message of the Metropolitan Tabernacle pulpit has continued to be that of the gospel of salvation by grace.

Surely it would be idle to contend that David's sling and stone were no factor in his victory over Goliath, but that that great triumph was to be attributed exclusively to the personality of the shepherd-lad without any relation to the instrumentality he employed. And would it not be folly, while recognising Spurgeon's greatness, and desiring that the same abounding fruitfulness should characterise our ministries, to agree to discard, or delete, or emasculate, the gospel he preached?

Let us hear for a moment something from his last great conference address. Thus he spoke:

'After preaching the gospel for forty years, and after printing the sermons I have preached for more than six-and-thirty years, reaching now to the number of twenty-two hundred in weekly succession, I am fairly entitled to speak about the fulness and richness of the Bible, as a preacher's book. Brethren, it is inexhaustible. No question about freshness will arise if we keep closely to the text of the sacred volume. There can be no difficulty as to finding themes totally distinct from those we have handled before; the variety is as infinite as the fulness. A long life will only suffice us to skirt the shores of this great continent of light. In the forty years of my own ministry I have only touched the hem of the garment of divine truth; but what virtue has flowed out of it! The Word is like its Author, infinite, immeasurable, without end. If you were ordained to be a preacher throughout eternity, you would have before you a theme equal to everlasting demands. Brothers, shall we each have a pulpit somewhere amidst the spheres? Shall we have a parish of millions of leagues? Shall we have voices so strengthened as to reach attentive constellations? Shall we be witnesses for the Lord of grace to myriads of worlds which will be wonder-struck when they hear of the incarnate God? Shall we be surrounded by pure intelligences enquiring and searching into the mystery of God manifest in the flesh? Will the unfallen worlds desire to be instructed in the glorious gospel of the blessed God? and will each one of us have his own tale to tell of our experience of infinite love? I think so, since the Lord has saved us "to the intent that now unto the principalities and powers in heavenly places might be known by the church the manifold wisdom of God." If such be the case, our Bibles will suffice for ages to come for new themes every morning, and for fresh songs and discourses world without end.'

Further he added in respect to the Scriptures:

'We are resolved, then, to use more fully than ever what God has provided for us in this Book, *for we are sure of its inspiration*. Let me say that over again. WE ARE SURE OF ITS INSPIRATION. You will notice that attacks are frequently made as against verbal inspiration. The form chosen is a mere pretext. Verbal inspiration is the verbal form of the assault, but the attack is really aimed at inspiration itself. You will not read far in the essay before you will find that the gentleman who started with contesting a theory of inspiration which none of us ever held, winds up by showing his hand, and that hand wages war with inspiration itself. There is the true point. We care little for any theory of inspiration; in fact, we have none. To us the plenary verbal inspiration of Holy Scripture is fact and not hypothesis. It is a pity to theorise upon a subject which is deeply mysterious, and makes a demand upon faith rather than fancy. Believe in the inspiration of Scripture, and believe it in the most intense sense. You will not believe in a truer and fuller inspiration than really exists. No one is likely to err in that direction, even if error be possible. If you adopt theories which pare off a portion here, and deny authority to a passage there, you will at last have no inspiration left, worthy of the name.'

As to the relation of Spurgeon's belief in, and his use of, the Bible as the Word of God, he has this to say:

'To-day it is still the self-same mighty Word of God that it was in the hands of our Lord Jesus. How it strengthens us when we remember the many conquests of souls which we have achieved through the sword of the Spirit! Have any of you known or heard of such a thing as conversion wrought by any other doctrine than that which is in the Word? I should like to have a catalogue of conversions wrought by modern theology. I would subscribe for a copy of such a work. I will not say what I might do with it after I had read it; but I would, at least, increase its sale by one copy, just to see what progressive divinity pretends to have done. Conversions through the doctrines of universal restitution! Conversions through the doctrine of doubtful inspiration! Conversions to the love of God, and to faith in his Christ, by hearing that the death of the Saviour was only the consummation of a grand example, but not a substitutionary sacrifice! Conversions by a gospel out of which all the gospel has been drained! They say, "Wonders will never cease"; but such wonders will never begin. Let them report changes of heart so wrought, and give us an opportunity of testing them; and then, perchance, we may consider whether it is worth our while to leave that Word which we have tried in hundreds, and, some of us here, in many thousands of cases, and have always found effectual for salvation. We know why they sneer at conversions. These are grapes which such foxes cannot reach, and therefore they are sour. As we believe in the new birth, and expect to see it in thousands of cases, we shall adhere to that Word of truth by which the Holy Spirit works regeneration. In a word, in our warfare we shall keep to the old weapon of the sword of the Spirit, until we can find a better. "There is none like that; give it me," is at present our verdict.'

Perhaps I ought explicitly to state something which everything I have said thus far implies. When all allowance has been made for his natural qualities, augmented by divine illumination, when we have recognised his personal devotion to Christ, his surrender of heart and intellect to the inspired Word, and the resultant wisdom and skill in its continual employment, we must, at the same time, recognise that his ministry of power was a ministry of the Holy Spirit. I have viewed with a holy covetousness the spiritual frame which enabled the Apostle Paul to write to the Romans, 'And I am sure that, when I come unto you, I shall come in the fulness of the blessing of the gospel of Christ.' Surely that is an example of the daring of faith! Can anyone other than an apostle speak after that manner? But here is a quotation from a sermon preached two days before C. H. Spurgeon was twenty-one, on the text, 'The power of the Holy Ghost':

'It is concerning the power of the Holy Ghost that I shall speak this morning; and may you have a practical exemplification of that attribute in your own hearts, when you shall feel that the influence of the Holy Ghost is being poured out upon me, so that I am speaking the words of the living God to your souls, and bestowed upon you when you are feeling the effects of it in your own spirits.'

What a daring thing was that for any man to say, particularly a youth of twenty-one years! We have all known superficial emotionalists who have attributed their psychic activities to the operation of the Holy Ghost. But we have seen these religious ebullitions quickly subside, and leave their subjects in a condition of apathetic deflation. But listen to Spurgeon speaking at a date thirty-three years removed from the date of the daring utterance I have quoted. Speaking of the Spirit and the wind, he says:

'The Spirit of God works differently at different times, according to the necessity of the case, and according to His own will; for He bloweth *as* He listeth as well as *where* He listeth. Sometimes I have almost trembled to pray for the power of the Holy Spirit. I remember a brother praying that we might be filled with the Spirit of God; and I, being very young then, yet ventured to ask him whether he knew what he meant; and he looked at me with astonishment when I said, "Where He comes He is the Spirit of judgment, and the Spirit of burning." It is a blessing, no doubt, to be filled with the Spirit; but who may abide the day of His coming? Like the Lord Jesus, He is as refining fire, and like fuller's soap. We might have had the Spirit much more copiously had we been able to bear the wondrous work within us.'

And here is another saying:

'When you hear the Scriptures, and read the Word, the Spirit of God speaks to you. It is well to hear the Spirit whisper in the ear of conscience when He brings home the truth, and makes the mind to feel its power. Sweetest of all is it when the newly-opened ear hears the Spirit of God speak to it its own peculiar "still small voice." Then it is sweetly true, "thou hearest the sound thereof." My dear hearers, do you know anything about this? Has the Spirit of God so wrought with thee that thou hast recognised the sound thereof? It is a manifest work: hast thou felt it?'

And in this same sermon is a biographical passage descriptive of Spurgeon himself as a mystery:

'The man that lives near to God is a mystery, more or less, at all times. He is not all he desires to be, nor all he hopes to be, but he is far beyond what he ever expected to be. Strange impulses move him at times, so that he does things which he cannot himself account for. He feels that he is bound to do them, and he does them, and has the warrant of having done rightly in the result of what he does. I am sure that every child of God who walks in the light of his countenance, will understand what I mean when I say, that we are moved in singular ways; so moved, that we ourselves hardly know how; but so moved that Wisdom is justified of all her children. Strange is the power of the Holy Spirit over the heart of the regenerate; and this is made manifest in the singular changes of which they are the subjects. God's own people know what it is to sound the deeps, and outsoar the heights. Up, up, up, where the callow lightnings first spread their wings, we mount in ecstasy; and then down we go, down into the abysses where sea-monsters have their dens: such strange beings are we when under the highest power. The wind sighing through the trees, or singing amid the chords of an AEolian harp, is not more strange than the experience of a genuine child of God. I know what it is to run before Ahab's chariot with Elijah, and I am afraid I know what it is to faint under the juniper, and need to be awakened that I may partake of food, that I may go forty days in the strength thereof. The Christian man does not understand himself, but his varying experiences go to make up that sickness of self and fondness of Christ which is so desirable.

'I will give you two words you cannot explain, just to show the mystery of our manhood. "Spirituality": now, then, turn to your dictionaries, and see whether they define it. You know what it is: you cannot tell me, and I shall not tell you, because I cannot. There is another word—"unction." You know what it is. If you hear a sermon that has none of it you know what the absence of it is; but when an unction rests upon the Word, can you tell me what it is? I cannot tell you; but I pray that I may have that unction myself. Of course, the ungodly make jests upon the expression, because it has no meaning to them. Yet the children of God delight in it.'

Thus we have seen that toward the close of his ministry Spurgeon laid the same emphasis, and placed the same dependence upon, the power of the Holy Ghost, that he did in the beginning. In his last conference address he spoke of the Holy Spirit as the strength upon which believers must rely. Here are a few sentences:

'Remember, next, that the Holy Ghost will never set His seal to falsehood. Never! If what you preach is not the truth God will not own it. See ye well to this. What is more, the Holy Ghost never sets His signature to a blank. That would be unwise on the part of man, and the Holy Lord will not perpetrate such a folly. If we do not speak clear doctrine with plainness of speech, the Holy Ghost will not put His signature to our empty prating. If you do not come out distinctly with Christ and Him crucified, we may say farewell to true success.'

Thus, from the beginning to the end of his ministry the Scriptures were Spurgeon's supreme authority; Christ crucified and risen at once his constant theme and continuous experience; and the Holy Ghost the only power adequate for Christian living and gospel labour.

I say, therefore, my brethren, if we are to exercise fruitful ministries, comparable to that of Charles Haddon Spurgeon, only as we breathe his atmosphere, as Daniel did, with windows open really toward the heavenly Jerusalem; as we nourish our souls, as he did, upon food from the King's table; as we employ his weapons, preaching the same gospel in demonstration of the Spirit and of power, shall we in any measure emulate him. There is no substitute for these things.

For myself, this is my confession of faith with respect to the Bible: If this building were large enough to hold all the Biblical scholars of the world; and if they should all unite to tell me that the story of the Deluge is unhistoric; that Moses did not write the Pentateuch; that the book of Jonah is not historically true, I would believe Christ's naked word before the contrary judgment of all the scholarship of the world, and stake the interests of my soul for time and for eternity upon the unsupported word of my absolutely infallible Lord; and, if need be, be a fool for Christ's sake. And I then should be much less a fool for His sake, than the contrary attitude would make me for the sake of agreement with a 'scholarship' falsely so-called. For though I speak for the purpose of emphasis, I am convinced that the body of thought which is worthiest the high and honourable title of 'scholarship,' and which represents the findings of disciplined intellectual powers in co-operation with spiritually enlightened and penetrating understandings, will always be found to be in agreement with the word of Him who is Incarnate Truth.

When we thus approach the Bible as being instinct with the personality and authority of the Lord

Jesus Christ, what a world of intellectual and spiritual treasure it becomes to us! We have walked with Him among the flowers of Eden; and where first the shadow of the curse fell athwart the path of sinful man. We have seen Him walk the waves of the shoreless sea of judgment; and, in the patriarchs' tents, in the voice of angels, we have heard the Word which was in the beginning with God. In the tabernacle of the wilderness, with its crimson ritual, and in all the forty miraculous years, we have heard Him speaking in righteousness, mighty to save. We have followed Him with Joshua in His triumphal progress into Canaan's promised land; we have found Him sitting among Israel's judges; and in the fields of Boaz, near to Bethlehem. we have heard His whispered promise of the marriage of the Lamb. Where, indeed, have we not found Him? Is there a scripture path untrodden by His feet? Is there a valley which has not echoed with His voice? Is there a mountain which has not been transfigured by His presence?—'The voice of My beloved: behold, he cometh leaping upon the mountains, skipping upon the hills. My beloved is like a roe or a young hart: behold, he standeth behind our wall, he looketh forth at the windows, shewing himself through the lattice. My beloved spake, and said unto me, Rise up, my love, my fair one, and come away. For, lo, the winter is past, the rain is over and gone; the flowers appear on the earth; the time of the singing of birds is come, and the voice of the turtle is heard in our land; the fig tree putteth forth her green figs, and the vines with the tender grapes give a good smell. Arise, my love, my fair one, and come away.' And we have followed Him—through historical wildernesses, and biographical mountain solitudes, and through genealogical deserts, only to find that the wilderness and the solitary place are made glad for Him; and in His presence the desert rejoices and blossoms as the rose. In psalmist's melodies, in words of transcendent wisdom; in pregnant type, and glowing symbol; in wheels that are dreadful; in chariots of fire; in seraphic visions of enraptured spirits of prophets, priests and kings, we have seen and heard the form and voice of our beloved; until, at last, He has come to us from out the grave, being declared to be the Son of God with power, according to the spirit of holiness, by the resurrection from the dead, and with perfect knowledge of both worlds, He has joined us on the Emmaus road; where with burning hearts we have heard Him, beginning at Moses and all the prophets, expound unto us in all the Scriptures the things concerning Himself.

Therefore by the illumination of His presence in its pages; by the seal of His authority upon all its principles, and precepts, and promises; by His own invariable assumption of the Scriptures' infallibility, there is wrought into our deepest spiritual consciousness the unwavering conviction that the Bible is the Word of God that liveth and abideth for ever!

'Should all the forms that men devise
   Assault my faith with treacherous art,
I'd call them vanity and lies
   And bind the gospel to my heart.'

Spurgeon's Secession from The Baptist Union

By E. J. Poole-Connor

(*Introductory Note.* The publication of Dr. Payne's *Short History of the Baptist Union* has again brought the subject of C. H. Spurgeon's resignation from that body before the Christian community. As the matter is of far wider significance than that of any mere denominational difference, we insert in the present number of the *Quarterly* some extracts from our volume on *Evangelicalism in England* which give details of that event. We have judged it to be helpful to our readers to include some preliminary mention of the steady departure from faith in the Holy Scriptures which prepared the way for the still larger surrender of evangelical doctrine against which Spurgeon so powerfully lifted up his voice).

During the 19th Century theology in Germany, at that period exercising great sway in England, became increasingly averse to the supernatural, and growingly addicted to the application of higher critical methods to the study of Scripture. Its earlier conclusions were relatively modest. Dr. T. K. Cheyne assigns a foremost place amongst his *Founders of Old Testament Criticism* to J. G. Eichhorn (1752-1827), professor of Oriental languages at Göttingen, who was apparently desirous to avoid instilling doubt concerning the trustworthiness of Scripture in his students' minds. His theory was that the miraculous element in Israelitish records was due to oriental habits of thought, which 'seizes upon the ultimate results, and ignores the intermediate processes'. His successors were far less squeamish, and later in the century Julius Wellhausen (born 1844) applied the evolutionary hypothesis to the Scriptures in such a way as wholly to recast the nature of their contents, and to assign to them an authorship largely unknown.

These views found ready acceptance in most English theological colleges, and strongly affected the outlook of the next generation. 'The idea of Evolution' says Dr. A. C. Underwood, in his *History of the Baptists,* 'was the principal, though not the sole, agent in bringing about the abandonment of the assumptions of the older theology. Biblical criticism was largely the application of the evolutionary hypothesis to the sacred writings. It created a new historical sense—perhaps the most original and distinctive feature of the 19th-century mentality'. Meanwhile, religious writers, not otherwise unorthodox, were preparing the way for the dethronement of Scripture by setting up a new claimant to authority: the intuitive ability of man to recognize truth. Amongst these was Dr. R. W. Dale (1829-1895), of Birmingham, whose work on the Atonement, for example, is accepted in most Evangelical circles. But in his volume *The Living Christ and the Four Gospels,* in which he broached the theory that it is rather personal experience of Christ which supports belief in Scripture than that Scripture is the ground of faith in Christ, he remarks, 'Whether the writers of the New Testament are infallible or not is a question which rarely occurs to me. Somehow, when they tell me a truth I know it for myself. The truth is mine and not merely theirs'. He therefore accepted the reliability of the Four Gospels not only on historical and critical grounds, but because they commended themselves to his inward verifying faculty. After recounting the story they contain he exclaims, 'It transcends human invention! It *must* be true!' The weakness of his position was that others professing to exercise precisely the same innate ability declared that much in the Gospels was not only uncertain, but palpably fictitious.

Dr. Joseph Parker, as his *Ecce Deus* and other works show, was a devout believer in such basic doctrines of the Christian faith as the Deity of Christ, His virgin-birth, the vicarious nature of His atonement, and the future punishment of sin; but he, too, suggested that there might be a higher authority than the Written Word. In the volume above cited he says, 'There is one remarkable saying of Christ's which prepares us for ever-widening revelations of His purpose in relation to man. He said, 'I have many things to say unto you, but you cannot bear them now . . . but when He, the Spirit of Truth is come, He will guide you into all truth" . . . The plan of revelation hinted that man should become more and more independent of the scribe, and more and more dependent on the Spirit.

Writing is a human contrivance, but thinking is a divine operation. The scribe for the child, the Spirit for the man'. Yet principles such as these, which substituted for an infallible Bible an alleged infallible ability to recognize truth, set men's feet upon a slope as facile as the descent to Avernus. So rapid was the pace that by the time Spurgeon had reached his early fifties (1887) the threat to Evangelicalism could no longer be ignored. He sounded a vigorous alarm; and his so doing marked his entry upon the last and not least important stage of his great career.

This phase of Spurgeon's services to Evangelicalism is as variously regarded as is the character of Oliver Cromwell or the execution of Mary, Queen of Scots. The most favourable accounts are found in the biographies of Dr. W. Y. Fullerton, Dr. J. C. Carlile, and other of his friends and former students, and in Dr. A. C. Underwood's *History of the Baptists,* published in 1947. The majority of Encyclopaedias and Biographical Dictionaries dismiss the subject with some such statement as that 'in his later life Spurgeon's suspicions of the orthodoxy of his Baptist brethren led him to break with a section of his own denomination'. References of a more detailed kind are usually reactions according to type. There is that of the Free-Churchman who judges every situation by its relation to intellectual liberty. Silvester Horne's comment is of this nature. 'Such was Spurgeon's influence and popularity', he says in his *History of the Free Churches,* 'that when he began to suggest publicly that some ministers with whom he was associated in the Baptist Union were heretical, an atmosphere of suspicion was created, and when he took the extreme step of severing his connection with the Union a very painful controversy was precipitated. The Baptist Union, however, showed itself not unworthy of the heritage of liberty which had descended upon it, and even its unmeasured affection and reverence for its greatest preacher did not make it waver from its trust, nor prevail upon it to hedge the ministry with illiberal restrictions'.

There is the version of the Modernist, who is convinced that no good thing can come out of Nazareth. Dr. Reaveley Glover, Public Orator of Cambridge University, and President of the Baptist Union, was a sample of the latter. In the course of a series of articles on Nonconformity in *The Times* of 1932, he said 'It is no strange thing, unhappily, that great men will at last prefer the homage and tattle of admirers to the challenge of independent minds . . . In 1887 . . . Spurgeon launched his 'Down-grade Controversy'. Baptists, he said—people told him so and he believed it—were abandoning the Bible and the Evangelical faith, and "going down-hill at breakneck speed". The Baptist Union Council quietly asked for proof, and begged him to see old friends, but nothing served. The Council then gravely voted that as no evidence was forthcoming, the charges should not have been made. Moderate enough, one would think. Spurgeon flung out of the Union, and to the day of his death carried on a jihad against it. The man was ill . . . gout, conscience, and Satan make queer alliances in us all'. Dr. Glover's articles were marred by other wholly inexcusable personalities.

Finally, there is the restrained and decorous presentation of the case for the Baptist Union, in which deference is shown to the memory of Spurgeon, but a steady claim is made for the propriety of the Union's action. An example of this is found in chapter nine of Sir James Marchant's biography of Dr. John Clifford. Here the main insistence is upon what is described as 'Spurgeon's failure to produce evidence, as the Council understood evidence', of any heterodoxy in the Union; and upon the Council's being prevented from taking action by Spurgeon's 'withholding the names of those whom he accused'. It enters a plea for the Council's desire for peace, and for its concern to preserve 'liberty of prophesying'; it also strongly affirms that the motion commonly known as the 'vote of censure' upon Spurgeon was not intended so to be understood. Finally, it describes the Baptist Assembly of April, 1888, in which that denomination finally rejected Spurgeon's appeal to put its house in order, as one in which the 'greatest harmony prevailed, doxologies crowning the sudden peace'; the author even going so far as to add that had Spurgeon been present 'he would have received a rapturous and tumultuous welcome'; a picture singularly at variance with that of an eye-witness recorded later in these pages.

A further noticeable feature of most allusions to Spurgeon's protest is the tendency to dwell upon relatively small details in such a way as to divert attention from the major issue. Even those biographers who view the matter in its larger aspect occasionally do this. 'If Dr. Shakespeare, say, had been Secretary', says Dr. Fullerton, 'I venture to think that the Down-grade controversy would have taken a different direction'. 'Unfortunately', says Dr. Carlile, 'Spurgeon's articles . . . appeared at the time described in journalistic circles as "the silly season", when editors run short of interesting copy . . . and numbers of irresponsible writers added fuel to the fire'. 'There is no telling how the controversy might have gone if Spurgeon had been in health or the Secretary had supplied to the Council the information he had supplied to Mr. Spurgeon', he says elsewhere; adding 'It would not be easy to find a controversy of such magnitude so badly handled'.

Observations of the kind might be multiplied; and all tend to imply that there was no substantial ground for Spurgeon's anxiety; that there was no such drift from orthodoxy as he alleged; that it all really resolved itself into a matter of bad management. The truth is that the very reverse was the case. 'Spurgeon'—as the last-named writer himself says—'had plenty of evidence for his statements; there were the utterances of well-known men which had been published in the pages of the *Christian World,* the *Independent,* the *Freeman,* the *British Weekly,* and the *Baptist.* Reference to the files of these journals for 1887 and 1888 can still be made, and will provide ample proof of Spurgeon's general charge'.[2] Dr. Underwood's account of the matter in his *History of the Baptists* confirms that of Dr. Carlile. 'Many wrote to Spurgeon', he says, 'pleading with him to do something to stem the tide of what they called "Modern Thought". They saw no future for a Christianity that was not pledged to the inspiration of Scripture, a substitutionary view of the Atonement, and the old-fashioned doctrine of future rewards and punishments'; clear evidence that it was these doctrines that were being assailed.

As to the broader situation, Dr. Carlile is quite explicit. 'Age-worn traditions' he says 'were passing away as the failing light in a winter sky . . . The records of the book of Genesis became the subject of fierce controversy. Doubt as to the value of the historical narratives spread from the Old Testament to the New. The Deity of Christ and the sacrificial nature of His death were denied . . . It was impossible for the clash of contending views indefinitely to be postponed'.[3] 'It is a plain and literal fact', said a leading article in the *Christian World* for November, 1887, 'that those who share the opinions which Mr. Spurgeon condemns constitute a very large majority of all thinking Christian people'. It was a case of 'To your tents, O Israel!' The hour of partition between Evangelicalism and Modernism had as surely struck as four centuries earlier it had sounded for the separation of Protestantism from Romanism; and it was as clearly written by the Moving Finger that Spurgeon should lift his voice against the one as it was that Luther should protest against the other. Tetzel or no Tetzel: Baptist Union or no Baptist Union; in both cases the collision between two systems of thought was bound to come. 'The "Down-grade" controversy', to quote Dr. Carlile again, 'was no squabble between Spurgeon and the Union. It was one of those inevitable thought-conflicts which reappear in history, when opposing ideas can no longer refuse battle'.

But as in the Oxford Movement men of marked personality left their indelible impress upon the character of their Church so was it in the modernizing of the Free Churches. In the case of the struggle between Evangelicalism and Modernism in the Baptist Union the leadership of the forces of Liberalism was vested in a man of high integrity, great mental gifts and commanding influence. Without some knowledge of Dr. John Clifford, and some understanding of his theological sympathies, there is no possible clue to the Daedalian labyrinth which Baptist policy during the period of the Down-grade controversy presents to the modern student.

John Clifford was born at Sawley, a village nine miles from Derby, on October 16th, 1836. He came of Puritan stock, his father being an upright, somewhat severe Calvinist and Chartist, his mother a woman of prayer, who remained a gentle memory to her son throughout his long life . . . In due course he began to preach with such acceptance that in 1855 he entered the Midland Baptist College to be trained in the regular ministry. While there he was brought into contact with influences which began to shape his later theological bent. The Secretary of the College introduced him to his brother, Thomas Goadby, who became Principal of the College after Clifford left, and who was strongly of the Modernist school. 'It is interesting to note', says Sir James Marchant 'in view of Clifford's later attitude toward modern theological thought . . . that he made long notes of Principal Goadby's conversation concerning the urgent necessity for the readjustment of theological belief'[4]. Yet he was greatly impressed by Spurgeon's presentation of the Gospel. 'I was one of a group that travelled from Leicester to Wellingborough to see, hear, and study the new planet that had appeared in the Free Church heaven', he says. 'Where lay the secret of his amazing power? Was it his doctrine? Hardly, for that was only fresh in that it blended most daringly teachings that theologians had set over one against another. Was it his voice? All agreed that it was an organ of exquisite sweetness and strength, and that his mastery over it, however acquired, was unquestionably complete. It was always musical and never harsh, not even in its loudest tones, and in its quietest and lowest modulations always easily heard. Was it his fine and faultless elocution, his felicitous choice of language, his clear, logical arrangement of his material? No, it was in his transparent and dominating purpose to bring men to God by the Gospel of Christ that his strength lay... In a living, burning, reality in a preaching of the Gospel with tremendous force, was the secret of his power. So completely was I absorbed in what he said that I had to postpone all consideration of how he said it till the sermon was ended'; and although at a crucial moment he became Spurgeon's greatest opponent, he remained his friend and admirer all his life.

Before leaving college Clifford was invited to the pastorate of Praed Street Baptist Church, Paddington. He continued as pastor of this congregation, which a year or two later migrated to a new place of worship in Westbourne Park, for the remainder of his life. As his personality developed, and his activities took a wider range, he was seen to be a man of great kindliness of heart, possessed by a veritable passion for what he believed to be righteousness and truth; little interested in Scripture prophecy, but intensely concerned to 'build Jerusalem in England's green and pleasant land'; a great social reformer; an ardent politician of the Radical-Liberal type; so capable on the platform as to be frequently urged to enter Parliament. He was from his youth, he said, filled with a 'keen desire to see men imbued with the spirit of the Gospel, responsible to the call of Christ, delivered from their oppressive surroundings, free to live the lives of men and not merely of animals'. His devotion to Christ and belief in His atoning work for men never wavered; and when his public activities made him a national figure, consulted by statesmen, and created a Companion of Honour by the King, he remained a humble, self-critical man.

Nevertheless, it was with him as it was with the leaders of the Oxford Movement. To a high moral character and devotion of spirit he added views which in the end were wholly subversive of the older Evangelicalism. He early surrendered faith in the inerrancy of Scripture, and gradually but surely ranged himself with the 'Broad School' of Nonconformist belief. His biographer makes frequent reference to his theology as being 'too liberal for many a sincere Baptist to appreciate'; and quotes Dr. Blomfield (a Baptist President and College Principal, who accepted practically all the alleged 'assured results' of Higher Criticism) as saying 'I sympathized intensely with his broad interpretation of Evangelicalism, his appreciation of the work of Biblical criticism, his resolute opposition to blind conservatism'.

Dr. Clifford became Vice-President of the Baptist Union in 1887, and President in 1888: and for various reasons had frequently to take the President's place during the year of his vice-presidency. This dynamic, complex figure was therefore leader of the Baptist body during the eventful 'Down-grade' controversial years; and Sir James Marchant leaves his readers in no doubt as to the extent of his influence upon their counsels. He brought to their discussions the widest tolerance of the views against which Spurgeon protested; they were to him no more than the necessary 'adjustment of theological belief'. His ideas of doctrinal soundness were so flexible and so optimistic that at the very moment when Modernism was daily increasing its hold of the Baptist ministry he declared that in his opinion it was 'sounder than it had been for the last twenty or thirty years', and the famous Resolution in which the crowded assembly declared, by two thousand votes to seven,[5] that the Baptist body was Evangelical to the core was the triumph of his ability to impose his delusion upon others. Henceforth the Baptist denomination was committed to the principle that there could be the widest departure from the older Evangelical faith without the least charge of heterodoxy being laid against it. We turn now to details.

It was sometime during the summer of 1887 that Dr. Booth, secretary of the Baptist Union, first struck flint and steel. He approached Spurgeon for advice. He was alarmed at the public utterances of some members of the Baptist Union Council, and felt that they should be called to account, but could find no machinery in the Union by which this could be done. He was also concerned at the character of the teaching being given in some of the Baptist colleges. He gave the names, and extracts from the sermons and speeches, of those about whom he was unhappy.[6] Spurgeon, who had for some time been similarly concerned, thought that the best course would be to invite the Baptist Union to issue a declaration clearly stating the beliefs of the denomination. To this the Council objected, on the ground that any form of creed was undesirable, as it came between a man and his God. Spurgeon replied that the 'objection to a creed is a very pleasant way of concealing objection to discipline, and a desire for latitudinarianism'.

But Spurgeon was aware that far wider issues were at stake. While apostasy from earlier standards might be showing itself in the Baptist denomination, it was still more marked outside its borders. Attention was called to this in an article from his pen which appeared in the *Sword and Trowel* of August, 1887. 'Read those papers which represent the Broad School of Dissent', he wrote, 'and ask yourself: How much further will they go? . . . . The Atonement is scouted, the inspiration of Scripture is denied, the punishment of sin is turned into a fiction and the Resurrection into a myth . . . It now becomes a serious question how far those who abide by the truth once delivered unto the saints should fraternize with those who have turned to another Gospel'.

The article, and others which followed, caused an extraordinary commotion. Everyone leapt into the fray. Reactions of the most diverse nature were excited. Many confirmed the necessity for Spurgeon's protest; others charged him with gross exaggeration, or with sowing discord amongst brethren. Some, affecting to attribute his article to the depression of ill-health, advised him to take a long rest. Others, again, found in the subject a source of merriment. A month later Spurgeon returned to the charge: 'We have received abundant proofs', he wrote, 'that our alarm was none too soon. Letters from all quarters declare that the case of the church at this present is worse than we thought it to be . . .A chasm is opening . . . Let us take our places, not in anger nor in the spirit of suspicion or division, but in watchfulness and resolve'.

To those who charged Spurgeon with 'sour pessimism', he replied: 'We are denounced as gloomy. Well, well! The day was when we were censured for being wickedly humorous, and many were the floggings we received for our unseemly jests. So the world's opinion changes. A half a farthing would be an extravagant price to pay for its verdict one way or another . . . Our amiable critics will possibly be pleased to know that they will not find us bathing in vinegar, nor covering our swollen foot with wormwood, nor even drinking quinine with our vegetables; but will find us rejoicing in the Lord, and buckling on our harness for the war with as much confidence as if all men were on our side'.

A still further article in the *Sword and Trowel,* entitled 'The Case Proved', contained quotations confirmatory of the position he had taken up. One was from Dr. David Brown, Principal of the Free Church College, Aberdeen, who had just contributed a paper to *The Christian Age* entitled 'Scepticism in Ministers'. In it Dr. Brown referred to those who 'are expected to preach the faith of orthodox Christendom . . . yet neither hold nor teach that faith, but do their best to undermine the sacred records of it', and added: 'I should not have said so much were it not that all our churches were honeycombed with this mischievous tendency to minimize all those features of the Gospel the natural man cannot receive'. Not less to the point was a quotation from a current number of the *Christian World,* one of Spurgeon's most outspoken antagonists. So far from denying the prevalence of 'modern thought', its Editor exulted in it, and taunted those who endeavoured to conceal the facts. 'Modern thought', he said, 'is in Mr. Spurgeon's eyes a deadly cobra; in ours it is the glory of the century. It discards many of the doctrines dear to Mr. Spurgeon and his school, not only as untrue and unscriptural, but as in the strictest sense immoral . . . It is not so irrational as to pin its faith to verbal inspiration, nor so idolatrous as to make its acceptance of a true Trinity cover polytheism'.

In November, Dr. Clifford entered the lists with an article in the *Pall Mall Gazette,* which his friend W. T. Stead then edited. It was a semi-official pronouncement in which the Doctor, wearing the rosiest of rose-coloured spectacles, declared, in effect, that Spurgeon's statements were unproved, and in his belief, unprovable; that the Baptist ministry was sounder than ever; and that nothing had been shed but 'metaphysical conceptions of medieval philosophy'. Sir James Marchant describes the article as 'a "delaying action" of an advance guard'.

In October, 1887, Spurgeon, finding that no headway could be made, withdrew from the Baptist Union. His letter of resignation was in the following terms: 'Dear Friend, I beg to intimate to you, as Secretary of the Baptist Union, that I must withdraw from that Society. I do this with the utmost regret, but I have no choice. The reasons are set forth in the *Sword and Trowel* for November, and I trust you will excuse my repeating them here. I beg you not to send anyone to me to ask for a reconsideration. I fear I have considered too long already. Certainly every hour of the day impresses upon me the conviction that I am moving none too soon. I wish to add that no personal pique or ill-will in the least degree has operated upon me. I have personally received more respect than I desire. It is on the highest grounds alone that I take this step, and you know that I have delayed it because I hoped for better things. Yours always heartily, C. H. Spurgeon'.[7]

The crisis called the Council of the Union together in December, eighty out of its one hundred members being present. It was evidently a very confused gathering. Dr. Angus submitted a declaration of Evangelical faith; others thought that Spurgeon should be interviewed; others again insisted that he had brought no specific charges which would justify action; some declared that his statement concerning Dr. Booth's confidential communications was untrue, upon which James Spurgeon rose and left the assembly. He reported later that it was 'a horrible meeting'. Spurgeon wrote to Dr. Booth to say that he felt that he must now hand over to the Council the letters which had passed between them; but Dr. Booth replied that his correspondence with Spurgeon was not official but confidential; and that Spurgeon could not in honour use it. His hands were therefore bound. 'Spurgeon was never righted', writes Dr. Carlile; 'the impression still remains in many quarters that he made charges which could not be substantiated, and that when called upon to produce the evidence he resigned and ran away. Nothing could be further from the truth. Spurgeon could have produced Dr. Booths's letters. I think he should have done so'. It was not the first time that a man has suffered for his magnanimity.

Spurgeon, whose health was beginning to fail, and who had been away at Mentone, could not receive a deputation from the Union until January, 1888, when Dr. Culross, Dr. Clifford, and Dr. Booth met him at the Metropolitan Tabernacle. But it was much too late to seek for reunion, Evangelical soundness being capable of such diverse interpretation. The Council of the Union therefore met again on 15th January and passed a resolution accepting his resignation, and added 'that the Council recognizes the gravity of the charges which Mr. Spurgeon has brought against the Union . . . It considers that the public and general manner in which they have been made reflects on the whole body, and exposes to suspicion brethren who love the truth as dearly as he does. And as Mr. Spurgeon declines to give the names of those to whom he intended them to apply, and the evidence supporting them, those charges, in the judgment of the Council, ought not to have been made'.[8]

Thus did many Evangelical members of the Council consent to fiddle while Rome was burning. There is a sense in which the least blameworthy of those present was Dr. Clifford himself. In voting against Spurgeon he was acting according to his profound conviction. But others present were under no such illusion as he. They were one with Spurgeon in his beliefs, and shared his alarm at the departure of some of their brethren from them; they were as cognizant as was he of the wider defection outside their ranks. Yet for any trace of concern for the perils which threatened their own denomination, or the Christian church in general, the resolution to which they agreed may be scanned in vain; and upon a technicality which Dr. Fullerton has declared to be worthy of a pettifogging lawyer or a peevish woman, the one watchman who sounded the alarm was told, in terms as feeble as the policy which dictated it, that 'the charges ought not to have been made'.

At the Baptist Assembly, held during the same month in the City Temple, a resolution prepared by the Council was proposed and carried. It affirmed the Evangelical character of the Baptist Union, in general terms, and declared that 'there is no need of additional tests of membership, as the Council and the Assembly have ample powers to deal with any church or person who may not hold Evangelical doctrine'. The resolution was moved by Charles Williams and seconded by James Spurgeon, and it speedily became evident that what some expected to be an instrument of peace was regarded by others as a gage of battle. Its terms could be diversely construed, and it was clear that it would largely depend upon the interpretation put upon it by the mover and seconder whether its passing would be thought favourable to Spurgeon or otherwise. The Assembly was evidently prepared to vote for it or against it on this understanding. Even those appointed to speak to the motion represented widely differing points of view. Charles Williams was the advocate of advanced theology and hostile to Spurgeon; James Spurgeon stood more for his brother's conservative position. The former lost no time in making it clear that he moved the resolution as one which defended liberal theology and repudiated Spurgeon's protest. So strongly did he speak to that effect that James Spurgeon's first word on rising was that he seconded the motion but not the mover's speech. The presentation of his point of view was to no purpose. The sails of the Assembly were by this time spread to a powerful gale. The work of Dr. Clifford had been wholly effective. The new theology was to be stamped as genuine Evangelicalism; Spurgeon's interpretation of it was to be triumphantly rejected. 'I was present at the City Temple', wrote the late Henry Oakley, 'when the motion was moved, seconded, and carried. Possibly the City Temple was as full as it could be. I was there very early, but found only a "standing seat" in the aisle of the back gallery. I listened to the speeches. The only one of which I have any distinct remembrance was that of Mr. Charles Williams. He quoted Tennyson in favour of a liberal theology and in justification of doubt. The moment of voting came. Only those in the area were qualified to vote as members of the assembly. When the motion of censure was put a forest of hands went up. "Against", called the chairman, Dr. Clifford. I did not see any hands, but history records that there were seven. Without any announcement of numbers the vast assembly broke into tumultuous cheering, and cheering and cheering yet. From some of the older men their pent-up hostility found vent; from many of the younger men wild resistance of "any obscurantist trammels", as they said, broke loose. It was a strange scene. I viewed it almost with tears. I stood near a "Spurgeon's man", whom I knew very well. Mr. Spurgeon had welcomed him from a very lowly position. He went wild almost with delight at this censure of his great and generous master. I say it was a strange scene, that that vast assembly should be so outrageously delighted at the condemnation of the greatest, noblest, and grandest leader of their faith'.[9]

Part of the price which Spurgeon had to pay for fidelity to conviction was that, as he said, like Garibaldi, he became a stranger amongst his own people; but he was cheered by the affectionate support given him by Evangelicals of other denominations. The Evangelical Alliance was prominent in this. 'Never shall we forget', writes Robert Shindler, 'the first meeting called by the Alliance for testimony to the fundamental truths of the gospel, which was held in Exeter Hall. The reception given by the audience to Mr. Spurgeon when he rose to speak was overpowering in its fervour and heartiness. We occupied a seat on the platform near enough to witness the powerful emotions that agitated him, and the tears that streamed down his cheeks as he listened to the previous speakers; and though only a very few of his Baptist brethren were present, there was not wanting such a display of sympathy as must have cheered and comforted his heart'.[10] He was even led to hope for some closer fellowship with like-minded Christians which should transcend denominationalism. In the concluding paragraph of the four articles on the 'Down Grade' he expressed the hope that 'the day would come when, in a larger communion than any sect can offer, all those who are one in Christ may be able to blend in manifest unity'. But his own day was drawing to a close. In the spring of 1891 he showed signs of growing weakness. On 17th May he commenced the service at the Tabernacle, but could not preach. His last sermon there was on the morning of 7th June. On the Friday he was stricken down. After a temporary recovery he was taken in October to Mentone, in the south of France. Loving messages of good will and hopes for his recovery came to him from all quarters of the globe; not the least affectionate being from Dr. Clifford. He held a few informal services, some in his bedroom. At such a gathering on 17th January, 1892, he asked for the hymn 'The Sands of Time are Sinking', of which the last verse runs:

'I've wrestled on towards heaven
'Gainst storm and wind and tide,
Now, like a weary traveller
That leaneth on his guide,
Amid the shades of evening
While sinks life's lingering sand,
I hail the glory dawning
In Immanuel's land'.

On the following Tuesday he became unconscious, and on Sunday, 31st January, 1892, he passed to be with Christ. Doubtless, as Dr. Carlile quotes from Bunyan, the trumpets sounded for him on the other side. 'He was my master and my friend', says Dr. Fullerton; 'I stand at the salute'. Many whose knowledge was less personal echo his concluding words.

The tide which Spurgeon sought in vain to stem swept steadily outward. The tolerance of advanced views in the Baptist churches reached its climax in 1925 when, as already noted, Dr. T. Reaveley Glover was elected to the presidency of their Union. The event was a landmark in the progress of Modernism in Dissent.

[1] The irony of the situation, so far as Sir James Marchant's volume is concerned, is that his defence of the Baptist Union is based upon the plea that there was no evidence of any such heterodoxy in Baptist ranks as Spurgeon affirmed. Yet within a year of its publication the Baptist body set about electing to their Presidency, by an overwhelming vote, Dr. Reaveley Glover, a Modernist whose references to Scripture were outrageous, who denied the sacrificial element in the death of Christ, and whose views on Justification were those of the Church of Rome.

[2] *C. H. Spurgeon; an Interpretative Biography,* page 249.

[3] *Ibid.,* page 242.

[4] *Dr. John Clifford,* by Sir James Marchant, LL.D., page 27. The details of Dr. Clifford's life and views are taken from this volume.

[5] Marchant's *Clifford,* page 162.

[6] Carlile's *Spurgeon,* page 246.

[7] Dr. Glover's statement that Spurgeon 'flung out of the Union' seems scarcely to accord with this mild communication.

[8] Carlile's *Spurgeon,* page 251.

[9] *The Witness,* edited by Rev. Henry Oakley, May, 1934. Mr. Oakley's first-hand evidence shows clearly that the resolution in question was taken by the Assembly as one which censured Spurgeon, and that it was on this understanding they voted in favour of it. But what is commonly known as the 'resolution of censure' was that previously passed by the Council and reported to the Assembly.

[10] *From the Usher's Desk to the Tabernacle Pulpit,* by Rev. R. Shindler, page 274.

'Dinna forget Spurgeon'

By S. M. Houghton

[There are two main reasons for including the following article in *The Quarterly.* In the first place we wish to encourage readers to acquire volumes of Spurgeon's sermons and to appreciate them. In the second place, several years ago we read through the first Minute Book of the Bible League Council (period 1892 et seq.) and discovered that Spurgeon's stand for truth in the days of the Downgrade Controversy (1887-1892) and his efforts to stem the swelling tide of Modernism were potent factors in the founding of the League. His death in January, 1892, acted as a spur to the founding fathers. Hence the title of this article—its source of origin is mentioned in its pages—might well be regarded (out of context) as of historical importance.]

To the best of my recollection it was the year 1930 when I first appreciated the value of the work of Charles Haddon Spurgeon, and the knowledge came through the reading of several of his sermons in the thick Metropolitan Pulpit volumes.

I acquired them in Manchester. In that somewhat grimy city two or three second-hand bookshops adorned its Oxford Road, and in the doorway of one of them, attracting the eye of the passer-by, and not least mine, were shelves on which I found my never-to-be-forgotten treasure. I hardly suppose that their price was above a shilling a volume. Home they came, and before long I had tasted their sweet. To change the figure, it was not long before they gripped me like a magnet. There are sermons and sermons. Some go well into print, others appear pale and cadaverous. Some are fit but for the fire, others are like burnished gold. Spurgeon's, I found, belonged to the burnished class. I had so far come across nothing of their kind comparable to them. Philpot I knew, and Whitefield I knew, but these! I had sampled the cream of Scottish sermons in the three volumes of *The Free Church Pulpit:* sermons and lectures by eminent Scottish divines (published in 1852), and good they were, but these! They seemed nonpareil.

The Spurgeonic sermons, like Daniel's fourth beast 'diverse from all the others'—readers will forgive the uncouth comparison—possessed outstanding characteristics. They were expository, and Bible-based; certainly not without application; doctrinal without being dry; practical without being excessively so; experimental without being sentimental or flabby. The more I read them the more I was impressed by their balance, by their freshness, by their apt illustrations of spiritual truth almost after the manner of Gurnall, indeed by their perfect 'technique', if such a term may be allowed me. I could supply illustrative examples without end, but must forbear to do so. At the same time I was captivated—I use the word deliberately—by the sheer beauty of their language, by their sturdiness of expression, by their charming diction. Like Dan Chaucer, they seemed to be 'a well of English undefiled.' No matter what the date of the volume into which I dipped my bucket—for before long I had obtained many more volumes than the Manchester three—the result was the same. Whether 1862, 1882, or 1902, or whatever, their quality remained unimpaired. It amazed me that sixty-two volumes of sermons, throughout their entire range, could maintain, on average, such a standard of excellence. Here was pulpit genius indeed. I noted the difference, of course, between sermons of the New Park Street Pulpit volumes and those, say, of the 'eighties; again, between sermons revised by the master-preacher himself (up to his death in 1892) and the later 25 annual sermon volumes which, though well edited, lacked 'the touch of a vanished hand'. Yet 'the sound of a voice that was still' remained. All in all, their quality was superb. I became a Spurgeon lover, as too did my wife. We must have read at least a thousand of the sermons aloud together.

Long after 1930 I came across the tribute paid by Robertson Nicoll to Spurgeon. For certain reasons—and I think they are well-founded—I had learned not to value too highly any commendation of a work from the pen of the editor of *The British Weekly,* but in this particular case I was wholeheartedly with him. His tribute runs thus:

'The influence of Spurgeon was not of those that have passed, or that can pass away like a dream. Even yet, people will explain his popularity by his voice, his humour, by his oratory, and the like. But the continued life and power of his printed sermons show that his oratory, noble as it was, was not the first thing. Our firm belief is that these sermons will continue to be studied with growing interest and wonder; that they will untimately be accepted as incomparably the greatest contribution to the literature of experimental Christianity that has been made in this century, and that their message will go on transforming and quickening lives after all other sermons of the period are forgotten.' (Tribute printed at end of Sermon 2572, published in 1898.)

I read sermons aloud to my wife so that we might enjoy them simultaneously. In this way we derived increased benefit. On reflection I see that there are three chief ways of 'tasting' a sermon—the first, and doubtless the best, is to hear it delivered by the living voice of its author; a second is to read it in cold print; a third, and I would claim that it is the second-best, is to read it, or to hear it read, aloud. If the reader is sufficiently skilled, something of the fervour and urgency of the preacher himself may be recaptured. I discovered by the experiment that the sermons had a penetrating quality which reached to heart and mind and conscience. One such occasion I shall never forget.

Three or four of my wife's relations—not parents or sisters or brother—happened to be with us in our home, and I read to them. The sermon I selected—and I do not think that I had read it previously—was on Amos 4:12, 'Prepare to meet thy God, O Israel' (No. 923, dated 27 March, 1870). Spurgeon's preface—his prefaces are often sermons in miniature in themselves, and strikingly original—was followed by mention of the 'divers tones' in which such words might be spoken, as for example to Adam in paradise, to the believer engaged in private devotions, to saints going up to the house of the Lord, to believers meeting God in the disembodied state. From such a delightful theme, cunningly worked out, the sermon next moved to a consideration of 'Prepare to meet thy God' as 'words of caution to the vast majority of men': to the dying who know not the Lord, to the ungodly who have set God's law at defiance. This concluded Part 1 of the sermon. Part 2 spoke the same five words as 'heavy tidings to the ungodly.' And here by means of italicized words and phrases the sinner was told about God's message 'for THEE, . . . for YOU, YOU, YOU must meet YOUR God . . . a God of *unblinded omniscience, infinite discernment, unsullied holiness, insulted mercy, everlasting truth, omnipotent power'*—six or eight lines of print on each phrase. Then came Part 3, entitled 'a weighty precept'—'prepare to meet thy God.' With all the skill of which he was such a pulpit-master, Spurgeon wrote his text, so to speak—and I tremble even now as I write the words—on his hearers' hearts, five or six thousand of them, listening doubtless as though the world was not, and as though eternity was nigh. They, they, they were to meet God! He warned them of their need of the Advocate, the Daysman, Jesus Christ the righteous, the one Saviour in the whole universe of being. He urged their own unrighteousness upon their inmost consciences to show them the peril in which they stood before the bar of infinite justice and the judgment throne of God. Finally, in what must have been a burst of surpassing eloquence of the most exalted kind, he spoke these words—Gospel application at its tremendous best:

'Perhaps ere another Sabbath's bell shall ring, some of you now listening to my voice will be in the land of spirits and have passed the solemn test—weighed in the balances and found wanting. If it be so, and it were hard for any man here to prophesy that it shall not be so, for where several thousands are met together, the very chances of mortality, as men call them, go to make us fear it. The fact of this subject bring thrust upon me, makes me feel as though a prophetic impulse were in it. Then, if it be so, you and I, whoever you may be, fated for death this week, stand in a peculiar relationship to each other.

'I may be gazing straight into those eyes which shall never look upon me again till we meet at the judgment-bar, and if I be not faithful to your soul, you may rise up amidst that throng and say, "I strayed into that Tabernacle, and I listened to you, but you played with your theme, you were not in earnest, and so I was lost."

'SO THEN I WILL BE IN EARNEST. I conjure thee by the living God, escape from the wrath to come! As the Lord liveth, there is but a step between thee and death! Flee for thy life! Look not behind thee! Turn thy whole soul to Jesus! A crucified Saviour waits for a lost sinner, willing to receive him, willing to receive him now!

'Now thou canst not look me in the face in the next world, and say I did not speak to thee earnestly. O that the glance which we exchange at this moment may be succeeded in that tremendous day by a glance of recognition in which there shall be the soft emotions of gratitude and affection, as thou and I shall say to each other there, "Blessed be God we met on that hallowed Sabbath day, for now we shall meet for ever before the throne of Him that liveth and was dead, and is alive for evermore, and hath the keys of hell and of death." God bless you, every one of you, richly, for Jesus' sake. Amen.'

There is a reference in these words to the fact that on the Saturday evening before the morning on which the sermon was preached, Spurgeon was, as he says, sitting in his study 'about eight o'clock, revolving in my mind a subject for this hour's discourse' when there came 'a knock at my door and I was earnestly entreated by a father to hasten to the deathbed of his dear girl. I wanted much my time for preparation, but as the dear one was in such a case, and had long been a constant hearer of the Word in the Tabernacle, I felt it my duty to go whether I could prepare a sermon or not . . . I see my sermons in sick rooms often, and I come to think of preaching sermons in a different light from what many do.'

My quotations are somewhat lengthy, but they are more than worthy of my present use. I read the sermon, or rather, most of it. Facing me as we sat together were, as I have explained, uncles and aunts of my wife, four of them, all elderly, and one only of them had confessed the Name of the Lord in believer's baptism. Born and bred among Strict Baptists they had heard the Word times without number, but in the strict and biblical sense they yet remained outside the Church of God. Lifelong attenders upon the means of grace, for one reason or another, they had not come to the point of confessing the Lord in any public way. Their lives were, to public view and to private knowledge, all that could be desired, upright, homeloving, generous, kind; and yet . . . ! My heart felt for them as I read the sermon. The words were indeed searching, and though I am not esteemed in any visible sense an emotional man, the moment came when I was too much charged with inward emotion to continue my reading. The final paragraphs had to be read by another. The room, the company, the occasion, the text, the discourse, are engraven upon the tablets of memory. Truth is masterful! truth is sublime! and thank God, truth is saving!

Week by week the sermon reading continued. The discourses were nutritious, enlivening, soul-stirring, never dull. It is a temptation to quote paragraphs and sentences from them at length. But I must restrain my steeds as they champ at their bits, lest they carry me far off course.

My Scottish friends may be interested to know that Spurgeon was responsible for my first journey north of the Cheviots and even into 'Caledonia stern and wild'. I had been reading a sermon to my wife, but cannot now recall the text or even the nature of the discourse, but in the course of it Spurgeon remarked that he thought the canniness of the Scots was probably due, at least in part, to the fact that the Book of Proverbs played such a prominent part in their system of education, and doubtless in the instruction of their youth in church and home alike. Previously I had been disinclined to visit Scotland, for I am somewhat of a stay-at-home, a tribute to the high success of my late wife's management, but the preacher's words caused me to say, 'Then we must go to see that wonderful country.' My wife kept me to my pledge, and very pleasant we found the trip to be.

I soon fell into the practice of separating my duplicate sermon volumes into their component parts, fifty-two in number, so as to distribute sermons far and wide. Occasionally friends have told me by letter about blessings they have brought to them. As I write I recall the case of a friend resident in Cheshire to whom I sent a sermon (No. 1257-8) on the text, 'Jesus said unto them, If God were your Father, ye would love me.' The title of the discourse was 'Love to Jesus the great test'. He was enraptured with the sermon—I choose the word deliberately—took its message to heart, and although I must have sent it to him twenty or twenty-five years ago (how speedily time flies!), I received from him this message: 'A Christian friend has typed me a copy of that wonderful sermon of Spurgeon which you so kindly sent me some time ago, and when I am well (he is an invalid) I will have some photostat copies made and send one to you.' Previously—he writes once a year—he had asked me for any other duplicate copies of the sermon that I might possess but I could not oblige him. At one time I could supply sermons to friends on a substantial range of texts. I think of an Anglican clergyman who pressed me hard in this way. But my hundred duplicate volumes became depleted and by now they have shrunk almost to nothing. I trust they have served the Lord's purpose. To my widowed step-mother, a Methodist, not much older than myself, I recall giving a sermon on the subject of the Lord's Supper. That, too, was maybe eighteen years ago, and I may claim that from that time she too became a Spurgeon lover. She read and re-read the sermon until, had it belonged to the world of the clothier, it would have been described as completely threadbare.

I freely confess that, after forty years and more, my early enthusiasm for the sermons has never waned. I do not read today anything like as many as formerly, but they remain my favourite reading, in the sermonic department, and are as good to me as a square meal to the famished. If on a journey, especially by train, I usually carry one or two in my breast-pocket. I well remember once finding myself in London with an odd hour to occupy. Nearby was an Anglican Church with ever-open hospitality. I entered, found a seat, and with much profit and pleasure read a sermon on Judges 11:35, 'I have opened my mouth unto the Lord, and I cannot go back' (Vol. 23, No. 1341). It met my soul's need at that particular time, and was as a substantial meal. Indeed it seems to me that the Christian reader might well be encouraged to turn to the sermons in words that belong to the auctioneer's repertoire as he urges bargains upon his audience, 'You cannot go wrong.' I accept that some find the sermons so different from those to which they have long become accustomed to listen, that they have difficulty in getting an appetite for them. One or two have described them to me as 'flowery.' I do not consider the term justified, but I do accept that a man has a right to state his own reactions, and the enthusiast has to consider them. Possibly the late 20th-century reader would find that to enjoy the sermons one needs nowadays something of an 'acquired taste.' The form in which they present divine truth is not that of many a pulpit to-day, but it can never be said that their language is outdated except in such matters as 'thou' and 'thee.' Basically their language is true Anglo-Saxon refined by the Latin and other elements which in Mediaeval times were grafted upon it. The thousands who hung upon Spurgeon's lips for thirty-six years did not complain of floweriness, obscurity, high-falutin propensities, or aught else. They listened to a servant of the Lord speaking out his heart and mind and soul in a language which they could well understand, from the costermonger of the streets to the aristocrats of the highest circles in the land. And to the ends of the earth the printed discourses were blown to the nations like thistledown, not to sow the earth with noxious growth, but to spread the wisdom from above, and the 'fruit of righteousness which is sown in peace of them that make peace.' 'Dinna forget Spurgeon' was the parting cry of the wife of the Scottish highlander as her husband went to market; and to the weekly pamphlet brought home from the book stall many owed, under God, their soul's nutriment.

I recall only one now distant occasion when a sermon was abused, and I must be blamed to the extent of being the sermon's donor. A young man of my acquaintance, a novice in the ministry of the Word, had been invited to 'take a service'. He had consented. His sermon, which I heard, sounded suspiciously unlike what one would have expected to be his normal manner of speech, for after all, a man in the pulpit is not expected to speak in a language entirely at variance with his everyday utterance. I was set a-wondering. Ere long I realized what was happening. He was repeating the sermon of Spurgeon as though it were his own, or at least, a substantial part of it. To make the mention of the incident complete I must add that the young man, though not by any means unintelligent, in this case bewrayed himself. He went on unthinkingly until he made reference to a happening in the United States—it was either in Colorado or California—which must have been dated about 1865 or 1870, but the foolish young fellow gave it as though it were an event of his own day and time. If he has long forgotten the discrepancy, I have not, but I never charged him with the fault, for I had not invited him to 'take the service'.

One domestic incident I must mention. It arose through the reading of the sermons with my wife. It dates from December 1931. We already had one son and a second was expected. The latter received his name sermon-wise. The particular sermon in this case was about one of the Johns of the New Testament, whether the Baptist or the Apostle I do not remember. My wife had earlier expressed the desire that, if the second child proved to be a boy, he should be named John. Apparently I had different thoughts, though after this long lapse of time I fail to remember where my own choice lay. But the sermon gave me a change of mind. John was the sermon's theme, John therefore was in my thoughts, and ere I finished the reading, or it may have been a few minutes afterwards, I was led to say, 'I agree, if it is a boy, his name must be John.' And John it was!

I came to value all Spurgeon's writings, though none of them occupied the same place in my heart as did the sermons. His 'Treasury of David' is excellent reading on the Psalms. Spurgeon's own comments followed by the quotations which he appends from a vast variety of authors I have invariably found good and useful. Then, too, all the volumes of *The Sword and the Trowel,* the monthly magazine which Spurgeon launched in 1866, have their strong appeal. They furnish sermons not found in the Metropolitan Tabernacle Pulpit volumes, and articles of biographical, historical and theological value. Their book reviews, mostly from the editor's own pen, are pungent, sometimes amusing, and never dull. One review in particular I call to mind; I imagine it to be unique of its kind. The reviewer found himself reading a certain book favourably, but ere long he found disagreeable Romish tendencies, which he terms 'the smell of Roman candles.' As he read on he encountered more such noxious odours, and in sheer revolt he flung the book into the corner of the room. Later, relenting, he went to recover it, found its back broken, and picked it up muttering 'served it right'. There the review ended!

Spurgeon's four-volume autobiographical volumes were sheer delight, particularly the first pair of volumes. Much improved in presentation, trimmed and suitably augmented, they add their substantial quota to the Book List published by the Banner of Truth Trust, and supply much information about their subject not to be found elsewhere. The re-publication of the Metropolitan Tabernacle Pulpit volumes by Pilgrim Publications in U.S.A. and by The Banner of Truth Trust in Britain is a notable event in the realm of truth. God speed the sale! Now that the feast is spread, may many hearken to the call!

I cannot but commend that which I find to be good, and I cannot but rejoice in a ministerial career which has meant, and still means, so much to me. When I reflect on Spurgeon's career, his humble beginnings, his lack of a university education, his impact on the nation and the Church of God, his magnificent contribution to the interests of the Kingdom of God, I am compelled to say, 'Here was a Caesar; when comes there such another!' And one word I would add for the encouragement of any obscure mother or other person who may be entrusted by God with the so-important work of rearing children. Spurgeon was never ashamed to confess that he had learned not a little of his theology from 'the old cook', Mary King, a person who, when a sermon was of little worth, warmed her theological faculties in the same way as did a hen scratching over a heap of rubbish. 'I do believe' says the Autobiography, 'that I learnt more from her than I should have learned from any six doctors of divinity of the sort we have nowadays. The cook of Newmarket was a godly experienced woman, from whom I learned far more than I did from the minister of the chapel we attended.' Doubtless had the power to confer D.Ds. been Spurgeon's she would have received one, for, said he, 'so many D.Ds. are fiddle-de-dees.' But I close on a biblical note befitting the theme: 'Unto you which believe, there is honour' (1 Peter 2:7).

The Bible League and What it stands for.

By Prebendary H. E. Fox, M.A.

I like to think of the Bible League not merely as a Society or Association, though these names have good thoughts of fellowship and co-operation connected with them.

The word "League" suggests something stronger; it represents a closer union, as brotherhood is closer than fellowship. What is the bond? It is described in the old apostolic phrase, 'the unity of the Spirit in the bond of peace,' and that can only be realized fully by a common faith in the Bible itself and in Him whom it reveals. Think how this Book binds Christians together. We may differ in many ways; it is inevitable that we should, where there are diversities of gifts and administrations, but in the great essentials which the Word of God has revealed, and in the Word which reveals them, Christians who accept that authority are knit together, and that not only in England, but all over the world wherever the Bible is honoured and loved by people of every kindred and language and race. Only where the Bible is unknown or disregarded come separation, strife and confusion. Every missionary will tell you how the Book and its message draw men both to God and to one another. This morning one from Africa told me of black men, offered by the Government work for which they might have earned £3 a month, yet refusing it in order that they might go as God's messengers to their own people and teach them what that Book had taught them, and willing moreover to accept a salary not a quarter of the Government offer. And when the missionary said, "You know what you will have to meet: you will be despised, hated, or even ill-treated by your own people, and even the white men may laugh at you," the men replied, 'We know all that, but we must carry God's message to our people.' Are not your hearts drawn to those men? And is it not because the Bible has been to them what it is to you? Thus through the Bible we are in fellowship with Christians all over the world. And not only so, we are in fellowship also with the saints who have entered into their rest. Think of the Bible lovers of the old days. Read the history of the Churches and of the nations; you will find that all through the past the men who have been of the greatest good to their fellow men have been men who knew the Bible, believed the Bible and acted on Bible lines. We may go back to what we call the early Fathers, and read what they said, from Chrysostom and Augustine to later ages, and we shall see that it was from the Bible there came the knowledge of God, it was the Bible that made them what they were, and it was the Bible that linked the long chain together and to us. We are their heirs, and are put in trust with the heritage they have left us.

I was reading on Sunday evening a book by one of our latter day Bible students, whom I knew and loved well, and with whose writings I often refresh myself, Bishop Ryle of Liverpool. The subject was the one on which I am now speaking. He quotes the testimony of some of our great English divines as to what they believed the Bible to be. I think the best thing I can do this afternoon, instead of giving you more of my own thoughts, is to read to you what three or four of these great men have written.

John Jewel, who died in 1571, after he had been driven from his bishopric by Queen Mary, and to whom we owe one of the ablest defences of the Protestant Church against Popery, says: 'The words of the Lord are pure words, as the silver tried in a furnace of earth refined seven times. There is no sentence, no clause, no word, no syllable, no letter, but it is written for thy instruction; there is not one jot but it is sealed and signed with the blood of the Lamb.'

My next reference comes from a writer in the generation which followed. Few English divines have a higher repute for sound and sober judgment than Richard Hooker, and though his views are not always those of many of our modern teachers, that is to their misfortune and not from his error. He writes: 'We have received, not the spirit of the world, but the Spirit which is of God: which things also we speak, not in words which man's wisdom teacheth, but which the Holy Ghost doth teach. This is that which the Prophets mean by those books written full within and without; which books were so often delivered them to eat, not because God fed them with ink and paper, but to teach us, that so often as He employed them in this heavenly work, they neither spake nor wrote any word of their own, but uttered syllable by syllable as the Spirit put it in their mouths.'

Nearly a hundred years later came the writings of John Owen, Dean of Christ Church, Oxford, one of the most learned of our Puritan Fathers, too little read by modern students, though his books are a storehouse of Biblical exposition and spiritual experience. Owen writes: ' "Holy men of God spake as they were moved by the Holy Ghost." When the word was thus brought to them it was not left to their own understandings, wisdom, minds, memories, to order, dispose, and give it out; but they were borne, actuated, carried out by the Holy Spirit, to speak, deliver, and write all that and nothing but that—to very tittles—that was so brought to them. They invented not words themselves, suited to the things they had learned, but only expressed the word that they received. Though their mind and understanding were used in the choice of words (whence arise all the differences in their manner of expression), yet they were so guided that their words were not their own, but immediately supplied to them. Not only the doctrine they taught was the word of truth—truth itself—but the words whereby they taught it were words of truth from God Himself.'

Let me give you one more quotation. It comes from a great Scotsman, who in his day influenced Christian thought in this country, as well as in his own, more than most men. His Commentary on the Epistle to the Romans, his Discourses on Astronomy, and his book on Christian Evidence deserve far more attention than is claimed by the shallow thinking and crude indefiniteness that make up so much of the religious literature of these days. This is what Thomas Chalmers, who died in 1847, thought about the Bible: "We believe that in the composition of that record (i.e., the Bible) men not only thought as they were inspired, but spake as they were moved by the Holy Ghost. But our argument for the absolute perfection of Holy Writ is invulnerable beyond the reach even of those who have attempted to trace with geographical precision the line which separates the miraculous from the natural; and tell us when it was that Apostles wrote the words which the Spirit prompted them, and when it was that they wrote the words which the Spirit permitted them.

'To the result, in my humble apprehension, it positively matters not. Did they speak the words that the Spirit prompted—these words were therefore the best. Did they speak the words that the Spirit permitted—it was because these words were the best. The optimism of the Bible is alike secured in both these ways; and the sanction of the Spirit extended, both in respect of sentiments and of sayings, to every clause of it. In either way they effectively are the words of the Spirit; and God through the Bible is not presenting truths through the medium of others' language. He in effect has made it His own language; and God, through His Bible, is speaking to us.'

It is an honour to follow such great men, and it is a sacred duty to pass on to our children the truths so precious to them and to ourselves. As our fathers lived through dark days and drew their strength from the Word of God, so should we do in the sad times through which we pass. Some of us are not without our experience of sorrow. We have had our days of perplexity and grief. We have sat by the bedside and watched the shadow coming over some dear face. We have been stricken by pain, and have had cruel disappointments and doubts. What helped us most? Was it not our Father's Word, that gave us strength as well as comfort, and brought a message of power as well as of peace? And shall we not expect the same help in our present troubles? Whither shall England turn with more hope than to the Word of our God? We shall find there much about these dark days; much of counsel and comfort, caution for watching, courage for duty, patience in waiting, and above all hopes that far outstrip the world's furthest imaginations. We cannot be pessimists who study a Bible that teaches optimism. The sadness and misery, the madness and agony which are tearing human hearts to-day, are Bible signs of a coming transformation when all the former things will have passed away and a glory be revealed far beyond men's conception. Our King must reign till He hath put all enemies under His feet. So true faith can look through the darkness and expect the coming dawn. It is His own Word, which assures us—'When these things begin to come to pass, then look up and lift up your heads, for your redemption draweth nigh.'

The Need for the Witness of the Bible League

By W. Fuller Gooch

Mr. President and Christian friends and fellow-believers in the Holy Word of God, it gives me special pleasure to rise on this platform this afternoon because this is the twenty-fifth anniversary of the Bible League in the interests of which we are met together. A quarter of a century is no mean part of a man's life or of a Society's work, and it is right for us on an occasion like this to celebrate such a fact, as that for twenty-five years the work of this Society has been maintained, and that in closest manifest connection with the Spirit of God. My mind, while on this platform, has been going back to the beginning of that period of twenty-five years. I hold in my hand here to-day a copy of the first annual report of the Bible League. It is a small contribution you might say, as you look at it, but it is exceedingly interesting. I have been looking through the list of names which were enrolled as the first friends and, in part, the founders of this work. My heart has been touched by noting those who have passed away. I knew them all intimately well, and as I think of them I rejoice in the thought that they are with God—'with Christ, which is far better.' But we remember their work in connection with the formation of this Society. Then I just note that the Bible League was inaugurated at a meeting held in the Council Chamber of Exeter Hall, on Tuesday, May 3rd, 1892, presided over by General Sir Robert Phayre, K.C.B. I was present at that meeting, and I remember well that though the numbers were but few, there was a spirit of prayer and of deep humiliation before God, and a note of sincerest conviction that the time had come when something should be done to withstand the attacks which the Higher Criticism at that time was making on the veracity of the Holy Scriptures. That was a meeting deeply suffused by the Spirit of God, and out of that little gathering in a room dear to the memory of many of us here to-day, sprang an effort in which, we rejoice to know, there has been constant evidence that God has been sustaining it.

As we look back upon these twenty-five years of the League's history, two questions properly suggest themselves to us. In the first place, has the League done the work to which it gave itself? Has it earned the right to live? Has it proved such a weapon, such an instrument, as it was intended to be? I venture to say that those who know the League's work best will have no hesitation in answering, 'Yes,' to that question. It has had difficulties—great difficulties—and has had little support financially, and of course it does not uphold a popular cause; but, nevertheless, if you read carefully the twenty-five annual reports, from the one I hold in my hand, which was the first, down to the brief statement made to-day, you will feel that the Society has amply justified and vindicated its position and existence.

Then comes the second question, and it is a question in these days of the multiplication of societies which is of very great interest and importance: Is there still need for the existence and the work of the Bible League? A survey of the past twenty-five years shows that great progress has been made in the world's history in material and—in some respects—in mental and spiritual spheres. But I do not hesitate to say that the most observant and the most thoughtful man of to-day will admit that a survey of the past twenty-five years shows a very serious retrogression in relation to spiritual affairs, and especially in relation to the position which the Word of God holds in our land—in the nation as a nation, in the church as a church, in the homes and families of the people, and in many individual hearts. The Word of God has not the power nor has it the place to-day in the church, in the world, and in our own country, that it had years ago, and that it ought to have; and that, if we are to see what our deepest hearts are seeking of God, it must have. I know that this is a very serious thing to say, but I do not feel that I need apologise for saying it, for facts prove it. As we look around to-day, God stands for less in the estimation of the people than He did in former days. Straws show the way in which the wind blows, and as one looks on society to-day one finds that the reverence for God which once existed is not—to put it mildly—so manifest as it has been in times past. Why, one feels saddened to the heart by illustrations of the truth of this!

I was reading in the *Times* last week the report of the application by a family for the overthrow of a legacy to the Secular Society, and I was astonished and saddened to find that it had been decided that our constitution is not based on the Christian religion, and that efforts made by a body like the Secular Society to annihilate the name of God and destroy Christian literature out of existence can not only be looked upon as legal but can be sustained by the highest court. I do not enter into the general question of freedom of thought. I would wish for that, on right lines, as much as anyone. I am out for freedom of conviction for all, but there is a limit when the name of God and the value of Christianity are set aside. I noticed to-day, in relation to another case being pleaded in our law courts, that the idea was received with 'laughter' when an artist, on giving his opinion concerning the question as to whether Romney was or was not the painter of a disputed picture, said, 'If God Almighty were to tell me he was, I would contradict Him.' Statements like that only indicate the trend of popular thought. They show the need of a trumpet blast being continually given. I mention these things—and, of course, one could easily add to them—simply to show that we are not living in times when we can afford to let the Word of God and its maintenance slip. We are living in days when every effort to uphold the banner of the absolute truthfulness of the Word of God from Genesis to Revelation should be sustained. The witness of our League is still needed.

What has the Higher Criticism, as it is called—what has it done, what has it brought to pass? We remember twenty-five years ago what great promises it gave to us. It promised us assured results that would place Christianity on a firmer basis than before. It promised us a revised Bible that we might read with confidence and assurance of faith. The Polychrome Bible was to displace our Bibles, and we were to find in it a wealth of new revelation. The *Encyclopaedia Biblica* was to give us such information about the truths and facts of Scripture that we should settle at once controversies which had divided us for years. Where is it to-day? You had better ask the second-hand booksellers. At any rate the Higher Critics have given us—and I speak advisedly—fallacies instead of facts, failures instead of fulfilments, free thought instead of firm foothold on revelation, the foolishness of this world instead of the fulness of grace and truth that are in Christ Jesus, flights of fancy instead of faith's firm anchorage within the veil. Many of you know that we can bring forward names of those who were then among the Higher Critics themselves, but who admit now that their past conclusions were baseless, and their promises untrustworthy as well as unfulfilled. Modern thought has not strengthened faith; it has weakened faith among all classes of society, and the effect is seen in the uncertainty and shiftiness of the humanised religion which is so generally prevalent.

The Bible League stands for the full inspiration, for the infallibility, for the sole sufficiency of the Bible as the Word of God. All through its history it has stood for that position, and I am very much mistaken if it means to recede from it one iota. We are told that we are obsolete, old-fashioned, we are charged with obscurantism, with being opposed to progress, with setting ourselves as steel against what is new, and that in a new age. But we are not setting ourselves against that which is new as long as it does not contradict the old. Our Lord said that the wise householder, instructed to the kingdom of God, brings forth out of his treasure things *new* and *old.* We believe that the Lord has yet more light and truth to break forth from His Word. Many of us feel that we are only at the margin of that great river which comes down from the throne of God and the Lamb. We are longing for the new, and for clearer and fuller light, if it is on the foundation God has laid. But the new of modern speculation, of modern belief, of rationalistic theory, we fling out to the wind. We stand or fall by what the Lord God hath said.

We are charged with a refusal to adapt ourselves to the age in which we live. One of the master-works on the reconstruction of the Bible, and the reconstruction of religion to meet a reconstructed Bible, has as its opening sentences: 'A modern thinker has said that the most disastrous thing that can happen in the spiritual life of any age is that it should not be responsive to the thought of its age.' Then the author goes on to say that 'that disastrous thing has happened.' Is it so? Is it true that the teaching of the Word of God for which our fathers have stood, to which the apostles testified, which our Lord endorsed as being true in relation to *all* that the prophets had spoken—is it true that that is contrary to the thought of the age? Yes, undoubtedly! Then so much the worse for the age! The question is this: what does the Bible say about the age into which we were introduced by the Gospel of our Lord Jesus Christ? It characterises it as an evil age. All through it warns us to expect its closing period to be one of apostasy from the faith, and a setting up, in the place of God's revelation, of human thoughts and devices. That has come to pass in the fact that the age will not tolerate apostolic teaching. A large proportion of the religion of the age makes Christ to be a fallible teacher. The fact that such a state of things has come to pass only strengthens our faith in the Word of God. We feel all the more sure that by standing in the old paths and asking for the old apostolic-taught truths we are standing where God would have us stand and receiving His blessing.

Beloved friends, this age is an age that growingly has no place for God. It has no reverence for the Christ of the Scriptures—a 'Christ' of the twentieth century it may admit, but the Christ of the Bible it will not receive. We, therefore, refuse to listen to the voice of the age save so far as the age will receive the testimony which God by His revelation sent for its benefit until Christ should return again. We are charged with traditionalism. Well, sir, there are two kinds of tradition. Thirteen times is the Greek word *paradosis* translated "tradition"; ten times we are warned against it, ten times we are told of the tradition of the elders, of the fathers, of the Jews, of men as misleading and evil; three times we are told of traditions which were according to the Word God had given, and therefore to be received. When it comes to tradition that is based on the Word and that maintains the Word, are we not right in valuing it? Is there nothing in the fact that for nearly two thousand years there has been an unbroken succession of firm believers in the full inspiration of the Word of God? Is it nothing that for nearly two thousand years multitudes have died rather than depart from the faith 'once for all delivered to the saints'? Is there nothing in the fact that the Bible has been the one rule of faith and practice for all the holiest and best of every section of the Christian Church? Were it not that the Holy Ghost set His seal upon the Book, could this have happened? The power of the Holy Ghost has maintained in the Church from Pentecost unbroken testimony to the integrity of its faith.

I close by making this statement. There are three things which are essential to a healthy spiritual life and to a successful Christian testimony. They are these: certainty, fixity, spirituality. You cannot have a healthy spiritual life with uncertainty. Everywhere the New Testament and the Old alike contemplate Christians and believers as settled—that is the apostolic phrase. Our blessed Lord said that every true-hearted believer was a wise man because he dug deep and built his house upon the foundation of the rock—certainty. In the Old Testament we are told that the Lord hath written excellent things, that 'He might make us know the certainty of the words of truth' (Prov. 22. 20,21). The Gospel of Luke tells us of one who looked at all the facts that were around him in relation to Christ that we might know 'the certainty of the things wherein we are instructed.'

I remember Dr. Andrew Bonar (whose name ever abides as a sweet savour among those who reverence and love the Truth), saying that 'the articles of our creed are not articles of doubt but of faith. We are teachers of what we have learned out of the one great volume by the enlightenment of the Holy Spirit. We were not born to be the sport of uncertainties or the children of conjectures, still less had we been born again to be so.' But the Higher Criticism gives us nothing but uncertainties. The theories of one year are thrown over by the next year sets in. You have no certainty if you build on human thought or on human devices. Where are the great men of the Higher Criticism?—Baur, Eichhorn, Wellhausen, Vatke? They have started theories, but their theories to a large extent have been given up, and wherever their theories have been taken up by spiritually-minded men it has been to the detriment of those men. How did Baur become what he was in the criticism of the New Testament Scriptures? We are told that he, at the beginning of his career, was an earnest evangelical believer, but he became infected by Straussian teaching, and lost his faith in evangelicalism. He lost his faith, and what was the result? He lost all confidence. When his own wife was dying he had to send for an evangelical pastor to pray with her because he could not pray with her himself. Uncertainties deaden the life and unsettle the faith.

Equally so is the higher Criticism the enemy of *fixity*. There you have no fixity. You are constantly being shifted from one position to another. Does the mariner crossing the sea guide his path by the wandering meteors that flit across the sky? No, he fastens his eye upon the pole-star, his compass is ruled thereby, he takes his latitude and longtitude from the fixity of things. If we are travellers to eternity we must have something fixed to travel by. Our pole-star is the Holy Ghost-given revelation of God. Follow that, and you will have fixity, and life eternal.

And then *spirituality.* We need that to guide us which is not of the flesh but of the spirit. How much we need to-day to be sure that what we receive is of God! The Bereans were more noble than the Thessalonians because, even though the apostles taught it, they would not receive apostolic teaching as such, but for themselves 'searched the Scriptures daily, whether those things were so.' And so with us. We must be careful to-day that all is of the Spirit of God. Subtle influences are at work, even where you least look for them. I took up a book last week—one of the most recently-published books—written by an evangelical author, and I read, 'The Old Testament is not the ground of our faith in Jesus. We believe in Him on other and different grounds.' That is one of the most dangerous statements that can be made. Why, sir, every day my faith in the Lord Jesus Christ is strengthened by the study of the Old Testament revelation. I would willingly die in the faith of the Christ as revealed in the Old Testament studied in the light of the New, even if I had no other ground of confidence whatever. Leviticus and Hebrews alike are God-sent revelations of His Son. The New Testament gives us Jesus the Christ of God, and the Old Testament shows us Jesus in its light.

Let us not sit at the feet of a man, let us not honour men, let us ever be looking beyond the man, whoever he may be, to the living Word of the living God. In the last verses of the first chapter of the first epistle of Peter you have the 'word' spoken of in two aspects—the word 'which liveth and abideth for ever,'—the word which is incorruptible, the word which can never pass away, and the word 'which by the gospel is preached unto you.' Peter speaks of *logos,* the personal Christ, as the Word; and also of *rhema,* the written Word. There is our anchorage. There must we stand firm and hold fast. Christ the personal Word for our trust, and the written Word for our unerring guide. Let us take Augustine's creed—I do not know a better:—

The whole Christ for our salvation,
The whole Bible for our staff,
The whole Church for our fellowship,
The whole world for our parish.

May God help the Bible League to carry on its work in love as well as in truth, and always in the power of His Spirit!

SPURGEON PREACHING IN HACKNEY FIELDS.

Earnest Contention for the Faith

By R. Wright Hay

THE EPISTLE OF JUDE 20-25.

The ordering hand of the Divine Author of Holy Scripture can very easily be seen even in the arrangement of the books of our Bible. We see its working, for instance, when, after being led by the Holy Spirit, through the Epistle to the Hebrews, into the Holy of Holies, which is the true home of every believer in the Lord Jesus Christ, in the book immediately following we are led by James, a brother of the Lord, through this present world, and are shown the law from heaven for life on earth, by which faith's steps are to be directed.

Similarly we see God's ordering hand in the fact that, in the Epistle of Jude, another brother of the Lord conducts the believer through the perils and the perplexities of the last days, right into the vestibule of that glory for the revelation of which it is our privilege expectantly and prayerfully to wait. Jude's Epistle closes with a reference to this glory before the presence of which the Church is to be presented faultless with exceeding joy. And from thence we pass to the Book of the Revelation, which gives inspired details of the glory, and of the judgments decreed upon the world's vaunted civilisation.

It is surely of the Lord's grace that in this Epistle, which appeals specially to those of us who have it laid upon our hearts to engage in contention for the faith which was once for all delivered unto the saints, prominence should be given to the coming again of the Lord, and that we pass immediately into the Book of the Revelation, in which the Lord repeatedly says, 'Surely, I come quickly.' Also, that Jude should carry us back to Enoch's prophecy of the Lord's return, the first of which we know.

Of Enoch himself we have three mentions in God's Word, and from these we may learn what our attitude should be while we contend as commanded. In Genesis we are twice told that Enoch 'walked with God,' and in the Epistle to the Hebrews we read that 'before he was translated he had this testimony, that he pleased God.' Walking with God and pleasing God are fundamental in all true contention for the faith.

It becomes us to note how Jude's letter opens. He says: 'When I gave all diligence to write unto you of the common salvation, it was needful for me to write unto you, and exhort you that ye should earnestly contend for the faith which was once delivered unto the saints.' 'The faith' undoubtedly is the whole body of revealed truth; that which God purposes man should believe. It is only here that we have the expression, 'THE COMMON SALVATION,' and I am bound by this Scripture to recognise that, in God's purpose, the salvation which is mine belongs to others. I must see to it that The Faith—the great body of revealed truth, by which alone salvation can come—is preserved intact, in order that others may be saved. It was as Jude was writing about the common salvation that the Holy Ghost impelled him to exhort others who had been saved by grace through faith that they should 'earnestly contend for the faith.' In Luke 13.24 we have the words of the Lord Jesus: 'Strive to enter in at the strait gate'—contend (literally *agonise*) to enter in at the strait gate. Here we have the same word taken by the Holy Spirit and emphasised—'*Epi-agonise* for the faith.' All saved people are enjoined to be more in earnest in regard to the maintenance of the faith once delivered to the saints than they were about their own salvation before they knew the Lord Jesus Christ and trusted in Him.

Then note, 'But ye, beloved, building up yourselves on your most holy faith, praying in the Holy Ghost, keep yourselves in the love of God, looking for the mercy of our Lord Jesus Christ unto eternal life.' While earnestly contending, we should build up OURSELVES. We are very apt in our contention on behalf of the truth to concentrate on the pulling down of strongholds (and there is arduous work to be done in that direction), but the Holy Spirit here exhorts us in our contention to see to it that we are building up ourselves on our most holy faith, becoming more and more Christlike every day, increasing in the knowledge of God, experiencing more and more deeply the truth we already know by the revelation of the Holy Spirit. Also, 'praying in the Holy Ghost.' Is there any Scripture which leads us more deeply into the meaning of prayer than this expression? In the Epistle to the Romans we are introduced to the great truth that the Holy Spirit prays in us. Here we are shown that it is the privilege and solemn duty of the believer to enter into such communion with the indwelling Holy Ghost that he shall pray in Him. We need to be constantly praying *that we may pray,* praying for grace so to walk in the Spirit that our praying shall always be 'in the Holy Ghost.'

The next item in the manifold exhortation is—'Keep yourselves in the love of God.' In this Epistle a holy hatred is shown to be part of our contention for the faith—'hating even the garment spotted by the flesh.' But we cannot exercise that hatred unless we are always dwelling in the sphere of the Divine love—'Keep yourselves in the love of God.' In Christ we are loved by God, even as God loves His Eternal Son, and the Lord Jesus says, 'Abide in Me,' 'Continue ye in My love.' It ought not to mean an effort on the part of those who have been redeemed by the precious blood of Christ to keep themselves in the love of God. Rather, a believer should find it difficult to step for a moment out of the love of God. Satan is constantly showing us that which we cannot have without going outside the circle which the love of God revealed in His Holy Word draws around us. Keeping ourselves in the love of God means a refusing to be enticed out of the place into which God in His grace has brought us.

In the days when faction fights in Scotland were of frequent occurrence, it is recorded that on a certain occasion the heavy cannonading of the insurgents by the garrison of Edinburgh Castle made such fissures in the rock on which the castle is built that the well upon which the garrison depended for its life was emptied of its water, and the garrison had to capitulate. We have to guard against the loss of spirituality of mind while we contend for the faith. And we are safeguarded against all possible loss of this sort as we keep ourselves in the love of God, abiding in Christ, praying in the Holy Ghost, building ourselves up on our most holy faith.

As the letter begins with mention of the 'common salvation,' in connection with which contention for the faith once delivered to the saints is necessary, it practically ends with the exhortation to the believer, who is keeping himself in the love of God and looking for the mercy of the Lord Jesus at His coming, to stretch out his hand even into a flaming fire, to snatch the perishing from sin and death. Here is self-sacrificing service for the salvation of others;—'others save with fear, pulling them out of the fire.' It is not a pleasant thing to put one's hand into the fire. But we must be willing to have our hands scorched, to suffer pain, to incur the risk of being hurt and marred in the service of God for the salvation of men.

In verse 11 we have an impressive warning—'Woe unto them! For they have gone in the way of Cain, and ran greedily after the error of Balaam for reward, and perished in the gain-saying of Korah.' Here we have—(1) *Selfwill in religion.* Cain was not an irreligious man, but whereas God required blood in the offering brought to Him, he elected to bring an offering of flowers and fruit. (2) *Self-seeking in religion.* Balaam was a religious man, but for the sake of reward he willed to propagate error. (3) *Self-assertion in religion.* Korah presumed to assert his right to the priesthood. We have all three around us to-day, and we must guard against their intrusion into our own hearts and lives. God's will, not self-will; God's glory not our own advantage; self denial, not self-assertion—these must dominate our witness and our work. And the Epistle assures us that God is able to keep us from stumbling in our walk with Him, to enable us to walk worthy of our high calling through all the perils and temptations, and difficulties of these critical days, and to present us faultless before the presence of His glory with exceeding joy.

The Bible League Trust

By S. M. Houghton

In January, 1971, when we published an article entitled 'The Bible League: its Origin and Aims', we described the circumstances in which the Bible League came into existence in 1892, and explained the one aim of the League as being 'To promote the reverent study of the Holy Scriptures, and to resist the varied attacks made upon their inspiration, infallibility, and sole sufficiency as the Word of God'. Our readers will have noted that this aim is stated in every issue of the Quarterly. It will also have been noted that, as evidenced by the spread of articles in the Quarterly, we hold that the 'reverent study of the Holy Scriptures' includes liberty to expound biblical Doctrine and all else on which Scripture pronounces. Church History and Biography, Theology, biblical Archaeology and kindred topics have also found a place in our pages.

For a considerable time after its inauguration the League did not produce a magazine. It issued a variety of leaflets, but some 25 years passed before a magazine comparable in size and content to the present Quarterly was supplied to members. Unhappily virtually all early issues have been lost. Three issues of the years 1918 and 1919 survive, but thereafter the League's set of the Quarterlies is all but complete, only one or two issues being missing. Present-day readers may be interested to know the titles of the major articles printed during 1918-19 —Further Evidence on the Virgin Birth, Evolution or Cataclysm - Which?, Earliest Christianity, The Unity of the Pentateuch, The Higher Criticism of Isaiah, The Higher Criticism and the Decline of Evangelical Religion, The Wiles and Darts of the Devil, The Last Six Months of our Lord's Ministry, The Missionary Outlook in the Far East, Science and Christ, Why did Balaam's Ass speak? Spiritism, and Let the Bible Speak for Itself. We do not doubt that there is complete unity between the mind and aims of Bible League Council and members sixty years ago and their successors today. Nevertheless time brings its changes.

Some years ago the League Council felt it desirable that it should seek registration by the Charity Commission under the terms of The Charities Act (of Parliament) of 1960. Several advantages would result therefrom. Registration involves the drawing up of a Trust Deed stating the aims and constitution of the registered body. When its terms have been agreed upon by the League Council and accepted by the Charity Commission, both parties then share responsibility for the faithful carrying out of the Deed. The benefits to the registered body are chiefly financial and legal. The Charity Commission leaves the registered body entirely free to manage its own affairs in accordance with its Trust Deed.

We mention the matter primarily to inform Bible League members and subscribers that the League now possesses a Doctrinal Basis. Somewhat surprisingly, in the 1892 beginning it was not so. But the League's Council holds that in present days of widespread apostasy from the Christian Faith, and the willingness of very many in days of Ecumenicity to regard many of the fundamental truths of Christianity as optional and indefinite, it is not only desirable but essential to give clear definition to the main truths of 'the faith once delivered to the saints'. These truths we hold dear, and with God's help we intend to maintain them, 'come wind, come weather'. We find them in the Scriptures -

Truth unchanged, unchanging,
The light of our dark sky.

Upon life's pathway they shed the light of the truth which comes from God and which shines on from age to age. Heaven and earth will pass away, but the Word which proceeds from divine lips will never pass away. Satanic forces continually endeavour to quench the light; in every age it has been assailed; it has been required of Christians that 'they loved not their lives unto the death'. The Devil's agents hate the truth of God. As members of the kingdom of darkness they gnaw their tongues with pain when they learn that truth flourishes. And we do not doubt that the conflict between light and darkness, truth and error, will carry on to the end of the age.

The Doctrinal Basis of the Bible League

The Doctrinal Basis of the Bible League, as now reconstituted, reads as follows:

1. The personal unity of the Father, the Son, and the Holy Spirit in the Godhead.
2. The sovereignty of God in creation, providence, revelation, redemption, and final judgment.
3. The divine inspiration, inerrancy, and sufficiency of Holy Scripture, and its supreme authority in all matters of faith and practice.
4. The total depravity of human nature in consequence of the fall in Adam.
5. The Incarnation, through Virgin Birth by the Holy Spirit, of the Son of God, His sinless life, His atoning work on Calvary, His bodily resurrection from the dead, His sole mediatorial intercession, and His endless reign.
6. The justification of the repentant sinner by grace through faith alone, and his eternal security.
7. The work of the Holy Spirit as essential to new birth and sanctification.
8. The personal return of the Lord Jesus Christ in glory, the resurrection of the body, the judgment of the world by Christ, the eternal blessedness of the righteous and the eternal punishment of the wicked.

Our members will note that certain important matters which are involved in church membership are not included in this Declaration of Doctrine, for the Bible League is not linked with church membership as such. We hold that the truths defined in our Basis belong to the historic Christian Faith and have been held, and held forth, by true believers since the days of the apostles. Indeed, the Testaments both Old and New proclaim ONE TRUTH, valid from the foundation of the world. Peter, moved by the Holy Ghost, asserted that 'God hath spoken by the mouth of all His holy prophets since the world began' (Acts 3.21). With the gracious and powerful enabling of the Spirit we shall continue to uphold and proclaim that truth.

God's Word shall stand,
His truth prevail,
And not one jot or tittle fail.

C. H. Spurgeon
8.1.1892
(from the last photograph taken at Mentone)

Section Two

Scripture: Its Inspiration, Authority, and Infallibility

Contents: Section Two

Scripture: Its Inspiration, Authority, and Infallibility

The Authority of the Bible as Related to its Inspiration

by Principal A. McCaig

The Bible League stands emphatically for the Full Inspiration and Absolute Authority of the Word of God—the Scriptures of the Old and New Testament. With that position I am in the heartiest accord. It is many years since I publicly declared my conviction that a denial of the Full Inspiration of the Bible lay at the foundation of all the departures from the Faith which we were then mourning. And as the years have passed this conviction has grown: there has been an accumulation of evidence in support of it. It is, alas! a common thing nowadays to repudiate the Authority of the Word and substitute some other authority (which is not another) in its place. It is not possible to uphold the Authority if the Full Inspiration of the Word is denied. The course of present-day thought is proving that conclusively.

I desire, then, to speak a little about the question of Authority as related to Inspiration.

We believe that the Word of God is Infallibly Authoritative, and we believe that the Fulness of Authority rests upon the Fulness of Inspiration.

This Inspiration is usually called Plenary and Verbal. This does not mean *Mechanical Dictation,* as our opponents continually assert or insinuate. We do not pretend to explain the *how,* but simply insist upon the *fact.* If we wish a word that suggests the nature of the Inspiration, we should instead of 'Mechanical' use the term Dynamical, indicating the living power in the inspired man by which he was enabled to give forth the Divine message: while the human faculties were used they were all under Divine control. Plenary, of course, equals Full, and it is less technical to use the Anglo-Saxon term. It is an Inspiration extending to the *words* as well as to the *thoughts,* covering all Scripture in all its parts: the Old Testament as well as the New; the Historical as well as the Doctrinal and Ethical; the Law as well as the Prophets; the Chronicles as well as the Psalms; the Epistles as well as the Gospels. It is the Inspiration of the Writings as well as that of the Writers. The Inspiration of the Writers is for us only of value as we are assured of the Inspiration of the Writings. The opposite contention is a favourite one today, viz., that we ought not to speak of the Inspiration of the Writings but of the men. We do believe that the holy men of old were Inspired, but we believe equally that their Writings partook of that quality. The product of these men's Inspiration is the Sacred Book, and that Product is Inspired.

So the Inspiration extending to every part of the Book is the same in kind and degree in every part of it. That does not mean that every part of it is of equal value: there comes in the distinction between Revelation and Inspiration. There is the difference between human opinion, the result of human thought and research conveyed accurately by means of Inspiration, and Divine Truth communicated to the mind of the Seer by Revelation, and conveyed infallibly to us by Inspiration.

Based then upon that Full Inspiration is the Infallible Authority of the Word of God. It remains the Only and All-sufficient Guide in all matters of Faith and Practice.

What is the doctrine or theory of Inspiration held by those who reject the old idea? Nobody knows. I think it is high time that it should be formulated, that we should know where we are on this important subject. It used to be held that only the thoughts were Inspired: not the words. And to-day, when objection is taken to Verbal Inspiration, it is implied that the objector holds the Inspiration of the thoughts. But this is not really so. It has been shown repeatedly that most of the objections against the Inspiration of the *words* tell equally against the thoughts (since the thoughts can only be apprehended through the words); but to-day you will find, in most cases, it is the Inspiration in any real sense as attaching to the thoughts that is repudiated.

Some used to hold that there were degrees in Inspiration: some parts being more surely inspired than others. But is it so to-day? Some of the very portions which used to be held most fully Inspired are now denied to have that quality. The ideas of Inspiration entertained by those who have given up the old position are vague in the extreme. And just because so little stress is laid upon the Inspiration, there is a setting aside of the Authority of the Word. Professor Haering, who finds the Authority in the

Revelation of God in Christ, and seems to narrow that down to the testimony of the Consciousness of Christ only in relation to the most essential things of the Faith, makes the confession that 'on account of the altered conception of Authority, the problem of Inspiration has now retired completely into the background.' And truly it is in the background that our modern theologians keep it. It is for the Bible League to bring this great truth to the front and keep it there.

Believing in the Full Inspiration we do not need to alter the conception of Authority. We cannot find Authority in our own Inner Consciousness; the Inner Consciousness has too often led men astray to have any claim to such a position. Some of the vilest deeds have been approved by the Consciousness of the doers. The Christian Consciousness as a whole is by many set in the place of the Word; but that is also an unsatisfactory position. In so far as the Christian Consciousness is able to give a sound judgment and afford any true guidance, it has been formed and *informed* by the Word,and surely it is unwise to trust the effect rather than the cause: to repair to the stream when we have access to the Fountain. Besides, how can the decision of the general Christian Consciousness be formulated so as to become authoritative for the individual? The Authority of Christ, say many, is the great matter; but how are we to know the Authority of Christ save through His Word? It is just because we have such a high regard for the Authority of Christ that we give such reverence to His Word. Because we yield allegiance to the King, we bow to His Will as expressed in His Word.

II. My second point is that The INFALLIBLE AUTHORITY of the Word, based upon the FULL INSPIRATION, has been the *doctrine of the Church from the beginning*. The doctrine of the Church has ever been that the Scriptures constituted the Authoritative Rule for Faith and Practice. Whatever difference there may have been as to details of Inspiration, the Authority of the Word was unquestioned.

No one, I think, will dispute the truth of this assertion as far as it relates to Protestant Churches; but we are to-day often met with the contention that this idea of the Infallible Authority of the Bible is due to a Protestant mistake. It is granted that the doctrine has always been the Protestant doctrine; but they say now it was introduced by the Protestants at the Reformation as a new doctrine. When they were led to give up the idea of an Infallible Pope and an Infallible Church, they felt the need of some substitute, and so they conceived this idea of an Infallible Book. Now I maintain that this is a misconception of the Protestant position, and it is also a misconception of the Roman Catholic position. Give even Rome her due. The Roman Church held to the Authority of the Holy Scriptures as really as did the Protestants. It is true the Romanist added to the Scripture tradition; but that Church held to the Authority of Scripture. The difference between the Romanist and the Protestant was as to the Interpretation of the Authority. The Romanist said that the Church, the Pope could alone interpret it; the Protestant held that the Bible was its own Interpreter, that any spiritually-illuminated soul could from it know God's will concerning himself.

It is equally a mistaken conception which is put forth in the same quarters, viz., that while the Romanist looks to an Infallible Pope or Church, and the Protestant to an Infallible Book, we must correct both mistakes and look to the Authority of Christ. Now we maintain that both Romanist and Protestant upheld the Authority of Christ. He was held to be SUPREME in His Church. The truth might be obscured in the Romish system by other doctrines of the Church, and in practice doubtless that Supremacy was much impaired; but both alike claimed to be ruled by Christ. But, again, it was a matter of interpretation. How is the Authority of Christ to be expressed? The Romanist said, through the Pope and the Church as interpreting the Scriptures. The Protestant said, 'Nay, the Authority of Christ is expressed in the Scriptures and can be known by any believing soul.'

Before the Reformation, as after, the Scriptures held sway over the people of God. From the earliest times they were the standard of appeal in all controversy. (Of course, we know that during the Middle Ages and the supremacy of the Papacy, the Word was little known by the people and seldom appealed to, and the great glory of the Reformation was the putting the Bible into the hands of the people, and calling its voice Inspired; but even then the Church of Rome held sway over men because it claimed to rule in Christ's name; the Pope ruled as vicegerent of Christ, as the interpreter of His

Statute Book.) All the great leaders of the early Church sought to expound the Scriptures. And for Athanasius and Augustine, for Jerome and Chrysostom, for Clement and Origen, for Cyprian and Tertullian, for Ignatius and Polycarp the Scripture was 'the Judge to end the strife.'

And equally the great heretics recognized the Authority of Scripture, and sought to have it on their side. Individual books for their theories they might set aside as not belonging to Scripture; but whatever was held to belong to Scripture was decisive, although they might give a different interpretation of it than did the Orthodox.

III. Not only is the doctrine of the Supreme Authority of the Word, as founded upon its FULL INSPIRATION, the doctrine of Protestants and of the Church back to the earliest times, but it is undoubtedly that of the Apostles. The INFALLIBLE AUTHORITY of the Word based upon its FULL INSPIRATION *is the doctrine of the Apostles.*

Of course, we are not committing the anachronism of saying that the Apostles had the Scriptures as we have them; but the difference was not so great as is sometimes thought. They certainly had the Old Testament as we have it, and there can be no question that they appealed constantly to its Authority. As to the New Testament, its equivalent was found in the Inspired utterances of the Apostles. These Apostles had the Teaching of the Lord, which they held Authoritative, and they regarded their own utterances as Authoritative and binding upon the Church. Their Authority rested upon their Inspiration. It is unnecessary to elaborate this. The simple reading of the New Testament makes it clear. In reading the Acts of the Apostles, we are constantly struck by the fact that the Apostolic utterances have this ring of Authority, there is no thought of appealing from it: there is never any question of the oughtness of it. And it is always felt that these men are full of the Spirit of God, and the believers obey them because they are conscious of the fact that these men are speaking in the name of God: that God is speaking through them. So in the Epistles you always find this tone of Authority. The writers may reason, may exhort, may advise; but there is ever the ground tone of command. Look at Paul's Epistles and you always find that in the doctrinal parts he does not speak as one giving his opinion of some aspect of Divine truth, but as one whose heart is full of the Divine message, and who is conscious that what he says is nothing other than the truth of God, the truth which it behoves his readers to know, and the truth which they ought to receive, and it is at their soul's peril if they do not receive it. Then in the practical parts (so called to distinguish them from the purely doctrinal, though as a matter of fact all Paul's doctrine is practical) the exhortations which he gives are not in the nature of kindly advice, but they are definite commands; the imperative may sometimes be softened in form, but it is always there: and these commands are just as binding as the decalogue. Sometimes Paul puts the matter categorically, as to the Corinthians—'If any man think himself to be a prophet, or spiritual, let him acknowledge that the things that I write unto you are the commandments of the Lord.' And to the Thessalonians—'Now we command you, brethren, in the name of our Lord Jesus . . For even when we were with you this we commanded you . . . . And if any man obey not our word by this epistle note that man.' It is simply inconceivable that the most honoured preacher of the present day would speak in that fashion to his flock. But Paul's authoritative tone was not resented by the true believers. They knew that he was speaking in the name of the Lord, by the Spirit of the Lord, with all the Authority of the Lord behind him. The more spiritual a man was, the more readily he acknowledged the Apostle's Authority. The same phenomena appear in the Epistles of John and James and Peter. And we have Peter specifically placing the teaching of the Apostles on the same level as to Inspiration and Authority as the Old Testament—'That ye may be mindful of the words which were spoken before by the holy prophets, and of the commandment of us the apostles of the Lord and Saviour.' And, again, he speaks of the wisdom with which his beloved brother Paul had written—'As also in all his epistles, speaking in them of these things; in which are some things which are hard to be understood, which they that are unlearned and unstable wrest, as they do also *the other Scriptures* unto their own destruction.' I need only add a reminder of the solemn words at the close of the Book of Revelation (chapter 22. 18, 19)—'If any man,' &c. Which words, though not applying as some have thought to the whole of the New Testament, undoubtedly claim Full Authority and Inspiration for the Book of Revelation.

By the way the emphasis there is on the very *words* of the book, only in the words can the truth be enshrined. This is Verbal Inspiration surely. And so in Paul's great definition of Inspiration (1. Corinthians 2. 13)—'Which things we speak (there you have the thoughts, the substance of the message, the truth itself) not in the words which man's wisdom teacheth, but which the Holy Ghost teacheth'—there you have the medium through which the truth is conveyed, and that is as much from the Holy Spirit as the truth itself. That is what we mean by Verbal Inspiration. But there is nothing mechanical in that. We believe that the working of the Spirit in the man left him free to write in his own style, using words of his own vocabulary, but so directing, prompting and controlling, that the right words were chosen by which the truth was correctly, infallibly conveyed. We are often reminded that the treasure is in an earthen vessel; and that therefore, it is argued, we may expect flaws, mistakes, &c., in the human element of the Word. But surely an earthen does not mean an imperfect vessel. The vessel may be a very humble one, but that does not hinder it from being a whole vessel, without any leak, so that it may contain and safely convey the precious liquid which is put in it. But Paul, in using the metaphor of the earthen vessel, is not speaking about the Inspiration of the Word at all: he is speaking of his own human weakness in contrast to the precious treasure of the Gospel which he had to preach. And in any case, the result of the consideration is not to make us question the reliability of the message, but to lead us adoringly to see that the excellency of the power is of God and not of men.

As to the Apostles' belief in the Full Inspiration and Authority of the Old Testament there is little need to speak. No one can deny that they ever appealed to it as Supreme, as the recognized Standard, as the Oracles of God. The oft-quoted words of 2 Timothy 3.16 give Paul's definition of the Inspiration which belongs to the Old Testament. 'All Scripture is God-breathed': I care not what translation be adopted. The new and favourite rendering, 'Every Scripture inspired of God (God-breathed) is also profitable,' I believe is not well warranted: the context as well as the Greek usage of the New Testament supports the old rendering; for the *graphe* is equivalent to a proper noun and needs not the article, the absence of which is made the reason for the new translation. But even if we allow that translation and read, 'Every Scripture inspired of God is also profitable,' you are still bound to take it as referring to the Old Testament Scriptures mentioned in the previous verse—the Holy Scriptures, the *hiera grammata,* in which Timothy had been instructed. Another passage of great importance is 1 Peter 1. 11—'Searching what or what manner of time the Spirit of Christ which was in them did signify, when it testified beforehand the sufferings of Christ and the after glories.' Undoubtedly the important matter here is the great Messianic truth—the thought of Salvation through the Suffering and glorified Christ; but the passage indicates how essential the Inspiration of the words was for the conveyance of that thought. The prophets themselves did not understand the thought—had to ponder their own God-given message in order to learn God's great idea of the coming Salvation; but if they did not understand the thought, how could they have used words that would correctly express the thought, unless these words had been suggested by the Holy Spirit? So here you have undoubtedly the Divine Inspiration of both thoughts and words—Plenary and Verbal. One more important passage may be mentioned—2 Peter 1. 19-21. Because of the voice heard in the holy mount, Peter says, 'We hold more sure the prophetic Word.' Instead of the Revelation of the New Dispensation setting aside the Old, as some would argue, Peter says the Old is thereby confirmed. Here, then, we have the *Confirmation* of the Old Revelation by the New. Then he goes on to say, 'Whereunto ye do well that ye take heed as unto a light shining in a dark place': there you have the *Illumination* which the Word gives, and the Illumination comes from an *Authoritative* Word. 'Whereunto ye do well that ye take heed.' It is not one light among many: it is a light—the only light—shining in a dark place, and if we heed it not, surely there is no morning for us. Then we have the assurance, 'For no prophecy of the Scripture is of any private interpretation.' I do not need to tell you Bible students that the meaning is not the Roman Catholic or High Church one, that the private individual is not to presume to interpret the Scripture, but must be guided by Church or priest. No, it means that the prophecy is not of one's own unloosing, it was not the outcome of the individual prophet's cogitation or speculation, it is not the fruit of private, individual reasoning at all. This sets aside all naturalistic explanations of

Inspiration. It is not a human movement of the mind, but contrariwise—'The prophecy came not at any time by the will of man: but holy men of God spake as they were moved by the Holy Ghost.' The Revised Version has it, 'But men spake from God, being moved (or borne along) by the Holy Ghost.' There you have Divine *Revelation*—the truth coming not by the will of man, but directly from God; and there too you have the Fulness of *Inspiration*—'*spake* as they were *borne along*': words and thoughts under the guidance and control of the Mighty Spirit.

IV. My last point is that The INFALLIBLE AUTHORITY of the Word, based upon its FULL INSPIRATION, is the doctrine of Christ HIMSELF.

It seems strange to me that anyone should question this: and I certainly do not feel that there is any need to prove it. We have only to point to the uniform representation in the Gospels of Christ's attitude to the Old Testament, remembering that there is no dispute as to the fact that the Bible that Christ had was the same as our Old Testament, according to the threefold division of the Jews—the Law, the Prophets and the Hagiographa. Undoubtedly He ever appealed to its authority, quoted from all the divisions of it, treated every part as equally authoritative, proved great doctrines by individual statements, rested arguments upon single phrases and words and letters, declared that every jot and tittle must stand till fulfilled, and emphatically declared of the whole—'The Scripture cannot be broken.'

Now for all Christians surely the Authority of Christ on this matter ought to be decisive. But just here appears to-day the most baleful effect of the modern notions. *The Authority of Christ Himself is impugned.* As against the Authority of the Word they assure us that they place the Authority of Christ; but when we advance the Authority of Christ in support of the Old Testament they tell us that His Authority does not extend to that subject. And we soon find that His Authority is repudiated on many other points as well. The repudiation began at this point. The Higher Critics, met by His general endorsement of the old belief, had either to confess their theory mistaken or set aside Christ's Authority on the matter. One of the crucial instances is the question of the authorship of the 110th Psalm. The Higher Criticism declares that the Psalm could not have been written by David, was most likely written in the time of the Maccabees. But Christ not only attributes it to David, but His whole argument rests upon the Davidic authorship: it is not a question of the supposed conventional attribution of all the Psalms to David and so citing a particular one as his. But if David did not write the Psalm there is no point in Christ's question—'If David called Him Lord, how is He then His Son?' The puzzled Pharisees had no answer, but the Higher Critic, had he been present, could easily have overthrown Christ's contention. I am very sorry to see in the utterance from the Moderator's Chair of the English Presbyterian Synod an endorsement of the Higher Critics' position. Mr. Gillie is reported to have said: 'I can remember when . . . . to deny that David wrote the 110th Psalm was to impugn the authority and with it the Divinity of our Lord. We no longer think so.' But we maintain that this is impugning the Authority of our Lord. They distinctly say that He is not to be taken as an Authority upon matters of Old Testament criticism. In the same way His references to the words of Moses do not prove that we have any words of Moses; His allusions to Abraham and Isaac and Jacob, to Elijah and Daniel and Jonah do not prove that these were real personages; His quotations from the history do not establish the truth of the history. If that is not impugning His Authority I do not know what it is. It is futile to say that Christ refers to such matters just as a preacher might refer to a character of Shakespeare or Dickens without implying the reality of these personages. It is easy, but we have not time, to show the fallacy of this contention: I only mention one consideration. Speaking of Nineveh, Christ says, 'The men of Nineveh shall rise up in judgment with this generation, and shall condemn it because they repented at the preaching of Jonah.' How could fictitious characters, mere literary creations, rise in the judgment with actual men and women?

It is the fashion now in books written under the influence of the Higher Criticism to speak of the early history of Israel as 'tradition.' I think we are warranted in protesting against this question-begging use of the word 'tradition,' which is technically used of the opposite of reliable history. But it serves their purpose to represent the sure word as tradition, and so to undermine its Authority. Christ said to the Scribes of His day: 'Ye have made the Word of God of none effect by your traditions'; but the Scribes of our day have turned the Word of God itself into traditions' And yet the so-called 'moderate' Higher Critics assure us that we have Inspiration in these traditional legends, myths, mistaken representations, &c., and solemnly declare that there is no reason why the Spirit of God should not convey spiritual truth by means of these old stories, whether they represent actual fact or not. I think when such assertions are made it is well to remind ourselves that God is the 'God *of Truth*,' the 'God *who cannot lie*'; Jesus Christ is '*the Truth*'; the Holy Spirit is the '*Spirit of Truth*'; the Word of God is 'the *Scripture of Truth*'; 'The sum of Thy Word is truth.' The object of the Spirit is to lead into all the Truth; the object of Christ is to make us to know the Truth and so make us free. The object of the Scriptures is to lead us to believe the Truth. And we need more than the assertion of the Critics to make us believe that myth, legend, falsehood, and mistaken conceptions may as well be the vehicle of spiritual Truth under the guidance of the Spirit as Truth itself, and, for this is the chief point, that these false and foolish things should by men inspired be treated as true.

But not only is the Authority of Christ impugned as to the Old Testament. It is impugned in regard to many other matters. His statements as to Demonology, Angelology, Eschatology, and other subjects are no longer to be considered as Authoritative. He was a child of His time: He was subject o human limitations. Now I submit that, apart even from the question of His full Divinity (and I entirely object to the justifying of these contentions upon the ground of any doctrine of Kenosis), Jesus Christ, considered as God's great Prophet, the Head of the New Dispensation, anointed by the Spirit of God without measure, must surely have been qualified to pronounce upon such subjects which so closely concern the matter of His Redeeming work.

But my contention now is that those who appeal from the Authority of the Word to the Authority of Christ really do not yield full Authority to Christ, and I maintain that it is only as we believe in the Full Inspiration and Absolute Authority of the Word of God, that we can fully uphold the Absolute Authority of Christ. The Word for us is Authoritative because it expresses the Authority of Christ. Its Authority rests upon its Full Inspiration, and that Inspiration is the Inspiration of the Spirit of Christ. We cannot put the two conceptions in opposition. It is because we bow to the Authority and follow the example of Christ that we acknowledge the Authority of His Word, given through His Prophets and Apostles Inspired by His Spirit, and so I wish all success to this Bible League, which stands for 'the Word of God and the testimony of Jesus Christ.'

He that is down needs fear no fall,
  He that is low no pride;
He that is humble ever shall
  Have God to be his guide.

I am content with what I have,
  Little be it or much;
And, Lord, contentment still I crave
  Because Thou savest such.

Fulness to such a burden is
  That go on pilgrimage;
Here little, and hereafter bliss
  Is best from age to age.
    (*John Bunyan,* 1684)

The Internal Proof of Inspiration

by Prebendary Webb-Peploe

No higher honour can be conferred upon a man than to be allowed to set forth what he knows to be the truth, and what he has found to be sufficient for every possible need. And when that truth is given directly by the revelation of God, that man stands upon the highest possible level that can be known by humanity here upon earth. While there are to-day a large number of persons, claiming to themselves particular gifts of intellect and wisdom, who are saying that the basis upon which we Christians take our stand is not a solid or a sufficient one, it is enough for us to stand before the world and prove, as we are commissioned to prove, the grandeur and the dignity of believing in the Lord Jesus Christ as being Himself the Way, the Truth, and the Life; and as One who can bring men to know God as the Father, and can seal to their souls the gifts from God.

As we testify to our faith, our testimony must be, I humbly think, rather upon the positive than upon the mere negative or contradictory side. It is well that in the syllabus for the objects of this Bible League's existence we are told to place first the all-sufficiency of Scripture, and to be satisfied with the statement that we make, because the Scripture has proved itself to be sufficient. The second part of our principles and purposes is to resist the attacks of those who venture to deny the truth of what we affirm. What then do we affirm? We have to go forth realizing that that which we claim to be a direct revelation from Almighty God includes the whole of the Bible—from Gen. 1 to Rev. 22—and showing by character, by conduct, and by testimony, which none can resist, that the Bible is indeed the Word that comes from God, and that it is sufficient for every possible need of man.

Now is it to be so? You and I claim that we belong to the Lord Jesus Christ, and that He Himself is the very centre and power of everything for us. Christ is 'all, and in all,' as Paul says in Colossians 3. 11. 'For me to live is Christ,' he says in Philippians 1.21. 'I can do all things through Christ which strengtheneth me,' he says in Philippians 4.13. 'I can do all things *in* Christ' is the Greek. And then he goes on to say in the 19th verse, speaking from his own personal experience, 'MY God shall supply all YOUR need according to His riches in glory by Christ Jesus.'

The one object of our lives should be to show that Christ is a living personality and is a revelation of power from God sufficient for every possible need. And what are we told in regard to this matter? If you take up any of the writings of the older people who have stood before the world for the power of the gospel, you will hear them say (and I will only quote the words of one that I love to think of, Pascal, that great French writer, and he shall show us what he had found, and what I think every truly enlightened person has found) that 'Jesus Christ is the centre of everything and the object of everything; and he who does not know Him knows nothing of the orders of the world, and nothing of himself.' Now if we take up this interesting statement, as a condensation of all the statements which could be put forth by Christian people, we are at once brought into the closest relation with the Lord Jesus Christ; and the enquiry may be heard, 'Well, and what does HE say, then, concerning the Scriptures?' The Lord Jesus Christ says concerning the Scriptures, 'Search the Scriptures,' (John 5.39) or, as the Greek there is, 'Dig down into the Scriptures,' meaning the Old Testament books.

Did then the Lord Jesus believe in the Inspiration of the Old Testament? Did He affirm positively that it comes from God, and that it really is to be taken as being sufficient? Let us take the words of one of the most learned and deeply-faithful students of Scripture in our generation. He tells us, after a most careful calculation, that the Lord Jesus Christ Himself directly speaks from or quotes out of the Pentateuch—the most disputed books of the whole Bible—no fewer than 66 times; that out of the Psalms He quotes 36 times; that out of the book of the Prophet Isaiah He quotes 40 times; and that out of the Book of Daniel (that disputed, that mythological book, as it is said to be) He quotes no fewer than 22 times.

If that is true concerning the Lord Jesus Christ—and I think I may say that oneself has practically confirmed it—then He is either the most terrible impostor that ever trod this earth, or He is to be accepted as the fountain of authority, by all who profess to believe in Him, with regard to all that is contained in the Old Testament Scriptures.

Now let us take one of the attacks of the present day. A small book was forwarded to me about a fortnight ago by the author, with a kindly expression of his wish that I would criticize it, or affirm my belief in it. He himself is a so-called preacher of the gospel on the borders of this City of London, holding a most important position, and to be addressed as 'the Rev.,' with certain titles after his name, showing that he has a University education, and that he should be a man of high position. Yet he can deliberately send out these pages, and his idea is to start with this enquiry—'Has Jesus Christ lived on earth?' Then he puts forth an essay seeking to show that 'Jesus Christ was not the second Person of the Godhead, once incarnated, nor a man on earth who became deified, but that the gospels are simply an aspect of God, His Ideal Love, experienced, personified and dramatized by the early Church.'

Toward the end of the book he says, 'The conclusion to which we are driven is that there was no man Jesus.' That is the teaching of the present day, and with what pain and shame we have to confess this fact! We have to ask ourselves whether we can prove to our own satisfaction, and that of those who carefully watch our lives, that Jesus Christ is not only a reality in His historical personality, but that that Christ of God, who is taken as the power of God unto salvation by the true believers, and the true Christians, of all Churches and denominations, is in Himself such a living power that it is impossible for men to resist it, when they see Him exemplified in His followers.

What, then, have we humble Christians to offer to the world? We have the Lord Jesus Christ, as being to us the Way, the Truth, and the Life; and I would ask you to take up the Bible with that idea in your mind, and then to give yourselves to such a study—positively, not merely now contradicting those who heretically put forth their views, but positively—taking the teaching and enquiring, 'Is this satisfactory to my soul? I have a right by grace to deem myself sufficiently intelligent to judge of this Book called the Bible, and what do I find?'

I find in the Old Testament Scriptures that the following words occur in the numbers that I would briefly mention. In the very first chapter of Gensis you have the expression, 'God said,' no less than 10 times. Then later on you discover this fact, that there are found the expressions, 'The Lord spake,' or 'God spake,' or 'Thus saith the Lord,' no fewer than 501 times in the Pentateuch, 292 times in the historical books, and 1,111 times in the prophetical books, making a total of 1,904 times in the thirty-nine books of the Old Testament; and this is, of course, a declaration that 'God Almighty,' as He is called, or 'The Lord Jehovah,' as He is otherwise called, actually spake the words that follow. I have not had time to verify—I am waiting for an opportunity to count, or I would like to have any other man who would take the trouble to count and let me know the result—how large a proportion of those thirty-nine books are in this way declared to be the absolute words of 'the High and Holy One who inhabiteth eternity.' The 'Almighty God' is, of course, the same to us as 'Jehovah the Lord.' We only know the distinction between the two with regard to their meaning and their application to Creation or Salvation. But if you have the declaration 1,904 times,—and in many instances the subsequent utterances as given from the mouth of the Lord would extend to two, three, four, or even five chapters, or any number of verses—you will come, I believe, to this conclusion, that perhaps five-eighths, or even more, of the Old Testament is declared to be the actual utterance of God Himself. More than 200 times in Ezekiel alone you have the expression, 'Thus saith the Lord God.'

Then when you come to the New Testament you have the declaration of which you have heard that God Himself is speaking, that He is the One who speaks through the Lord Jesus Christ, or His Apostles; and the Apostle Peter will tell you that, 'We have a more sure word of prophecy,' 'For the prophecy came not in old time by the will of man; but holy men of God spake as they were moved by the Holy Ghost.' And, to confirm the Apostles, you have the words of our blessed Saviour (besides those already quoted to you), 'Ye do err, not knowing the Scriptures' (Matthew 22.29).

Now putting all these and other such things together, we come to this conclusion, it seems, that man is evidently a being capable of appreciating the beyond, the Divine, the everlasting, or we might almost say the Infinite; and that it was never in the thought of the Almighty Being who called man into existence so to create him with the possibility and power of realizing and enjoying things attaching to the Deity, without making provision for the supply of his desire. Yet nowhere else can any revelation be found that in any way corresponds to the infinite possibility of man's thought *except in this Book*; and in the pages of this Book we have all that satisfies, all that can be required to fulfil the desire of the heart of man, all that shall really link him on to the Deity. And at last we come to this enquiry, Who are they among the whole race descended from Adam and Eve who are found to be the noblest, the highest, the most truly corresponding to our expectations of what is Divine, omniscient, absolutely universally true? Who are they that correspond to those claims that we can put forward? Who are the closest and the most obedient to the revelations that are found in this Book? Surely they are those who most humbly believe in its absolute Inspiration of God.

But in conclusion let me ask if you have ever pondered the INTERNAL evidence? Are there not many today who have set themselves to honest, earnest, faithful, patient study of that kind, and have said at last, 'This is the one complete revelation, and I have to take its teaching'?

I will say for myself, in my own humble personality, that this is the chief proof of the Divine Inspiration of the whole Bible. In my early days, some forty years ago, I received a book from America which did not completely satisfy me, on 'The Baptism of the Holy Spirit'; and for six months, in my country home, I gave myself to the study of the Holy Ghost; and I found to my delight at last that the internal evidence on that one subject, though it did not bring me to accept the book that had been sent me, brought me to accept *The* Book, i.e., The Bible, as God's own Word (in the original) from cover to cover.

Taking the twenty-seven books of the New Testament, I found that it satisfied me completely as to the impossibility of its being a forgery, or 'a make-up,' by any human wisdom, simply on the ground of what it says about the Holy Spirit of God. The word *pneuma* ('spirit') occurs 385 times in the twenty-seven books of the New Testament. Of these 153 have—in our translation—a capital 'S,' and clearly belong to the Spirit of God; 133 are doubtful and have a small 's,' and may be taken either way; 89 times we find the expression, 'the Holy Ghost' (*to pneuma Agion*), and 4 times we find 'Holy Spirit.'

Now taking them all, and putting them together, and studying the words in the original, I found that there are certain occasions on which the article is used, in the Greek, and others in which it is not. Sometimes, as for instance, in Luke 4:1, you have the two together: 'Jesus, being full of (the) Holy Ghost, returned from Jordan, and was led by *the* Spirit into the wilderness,' the article being absent in the Greek in the first case. I began to make close enquiry, and I marked in my own old Bible, that still stands by me, every single case where the article was given *and* every case where it was *not* given. I found at last that there was a full and complete explanation of the fact in that, wherever in the Greek 'the PERSON' of the Holy Ghost is mentioned the article is given; and wherever His 'QUALITIES' or His 'GIFTS' to men are mentioned, the article is left out. And when that principle occurs in the twenty-seven books from so many different authors, I ask you, was it feasible for that to be by trickery, or brought about by forgery, or by design of human intellect? It could only be by a clear and definite revelation of the purpose of God. And what is that purpose? As we have said, that the Person should be realized in His majestic personality and power; and that the gifts should be recognized as those things that proceed from Him.

Let us take one more remarkable feature of Revelation. Only lately was I struck with the fact that sometimes the Apostles will mention the words 'Jesus Christ,' and at other times they will mention 'Christ Jesus'; and at last when I was reading Philippians 1.1, I realized that the Apostle mentions them both in one sentence, 'The servants of Jesus Christ, to all the saints in Christ Jesus,' and so again in Eph. 1.1 and in quite a few other passages, and I asked, what is the meaning of this change! I then pondered the different passages in which the titles occur, and I found to my own satisfaction—I cannot say what you will feel—that it was absolutely clear that when the Holy Spirit would have us work upward from the work of the Saviour Jesus to the throne of God, He speaks of the Saviour as Jesus Christ. Whenever He wants us to think of the gift of God from above coming down to be a blessing to men, in bringing the Deity into touch with humanity, He says, 'Christ Jesus.' This distinction is carried on accurately and absolutely through the whole of the books. Could any man or men invent such thoughts as these? It is clear that the Holy Spirit pervades every single part of the Book; and from Genesis 1 to Revelation 22 if only we could have the original, we might see, I believe and still hold firmly to, the fact that there is actual verbal inspiration, and that every word proceeds direct from God.

It came to my province on a certain occasion in the Church Congress, a year or two ago, to speak; and I happened to mention, again and again, the Bible as "The Word of God." Then some time afterwards, last year, I received a kindly note, and with it a large magazine, and outside was written, 'With affectionate remembrance from the Rev. T. A. Lacey,' who is known to some of us as a great writer and upholder, from the doctrinal point of view of the English Church Union, and other societies, of extreme High Church teachings. What does he do? He writes a long article of several pages upon myself, and says that nobody could ever have thought that I should be so foolish, for it was so different from what he expected of me, and yet I had done it, and so he is constrained to rebuke me for saying that 'The Bible is the Word of God.' He says that eighty-six times—I think that is the number—the expression 'Word of God' is found in the whole of the books of the Bible, and that not in one of them, *he* thinks, except in one doubtful reference, can it be said that the writer meant to apply the words to the Scriptures. Therefore it was not wise, or right, that I should put forward my declaration, or speak of 'The Bible' as 'The Word of God.' Where, then, does that school of thought profess to find the *complete* Word of God? Why, it is not enough for them that God should have spoken, as He has, in this Book, and that He has ordered the Book to be closed, and that the man should suffer who dared to add to it (Revelation 22. 18); but they must hold to the value of Tradition, and they must have the priest as the revealer of the Word of God, and that therefore we are to look to human beings now to give to us the Word of God just as much as they look to the Scriptures. Alas! for that school of thought and for the Roman Catholics also. (I do *not* speak bitterly; I would speak tenderly and with love.) Surely *we* cannot admit that either in Tradition, or in the words of a priest, we have any real Divine Authority or substitution for the Scriptures.

I do not know whether any of you have ever heard of the Abbé Migue. He presses forward this fact, that he had been called upon to make a library of the literature of the Church that was equal in authority to the Scriptures, and which is now known under the title of 'Tradition,' I believe; and he had brought out 'in beautiful form,' he says himself, 'the productions of the Fathers of the Latin School in 222 large volumes, and of the Greek in 169.' Add these together, and then say what value Tradition can have for us; especially when, as he allows, he has not been able at all to do justice to the Fathers, as there are many, many more to be edited yet. The Roman Church will tell you that no man can be really intelligent, or hope for full salvation, unless he has taken fully into notice the Tradition of the Early Church, and we ask: Where are we? Is there one of us who would like to have to study 222 large folio volumes of the Latin Fathers and 169 big volumes of the Greek Fathers, and then feel that we had not got half over the ground, and that therefore we were still in the dark with regard to the real force and power of Tradition? I humbly think that we Protestant Christians, enlightened by the privileges and blessings given to us through the Reformation, have a better stand, a more joyful stand, and it is this. I will take out my little volume, my beloved Bible, that has been my treasure for fifty-three years. It is getting so brown that I can hardly read it, but at the same time it is a great joy to my heart; and I will say with all humility that I do not think it can be possible for the highest and most learned critic in the world to make me doubt, after what I have been learning from the internal evidence of the Bible, that that Book proceeds from Almighty God in every single portion of it, and contains in itself everything that man could require to enlighten him on earth, to comfort him in dying, and to assure him of an everlasting welcome into the eternal kingdom of our Lord and Saviour Jesus Christ.

The Possibility of Miracle

By E. K. Simpson

Among all the sickly exotics reared in the hot-house of modern culture there seems to be none on which present-day votaries of novelty set greater store than that specimen of the 'sensitive plant' called 'little faith,' which recoils with such marked antipathy from the miraculous. Strange to say, it is not the mere worldling who dotes on this particular oddity. There are actually professors of divinity in our midst who, eager to be abreast of Harnack and his compeers, do not scruple to sport the grotesque sprig in their buttonholes, that they may have the satisfaction of being in the 'latest fashion.' To simple souls it would appear that a state of mind suspended *in vacuo* betwixt faith and unbelief, one that blends profession of fealty to Christ with a rooted distrust of miracle, and an incurable suspicion of any narrative in which the supernatural finds a place, itself verges on the miraculous. That is an uncommonly queer frame of mind which thus blends faith and unbelief in equal proportions, and lets them play hide-and-seek through the entire circuit of religious truth. Assuredly, an armistice patched up between such deadly foes, like those painful exhibitions of seeming amity known as 'happy families,' must turn out a miserable sham one day or other.

Doubtless, various circumstances have tended in recent years to foster that violent prejudice which displays itself in the current claptrap that 'miracles are impossible.' A too exclusive study of physical science has much to answer for on this score. The rigorous reign of law which scientific men remark in their own domain they are apt to transfer to every other province of thought. How many make a fetish of the laws of nature, and then seat it on the throne of the universe in the room of the Living God! Sir Isaac Newton's name is revered by all scientists, and it is much to be wished that they would learn sounder doctrine from his sage observation: 'God governs all things by means of the laws He has ordained, *except when He sees good to act otherwise.*' Precisely! Those laws are inflexible only because, and only so long as, He wills they should be so. Every man who names Him 'the Infinite' concedes that proposition; for what is infinite but *unbounded*? Limited monarchies are excellent institutions in the sphere of human infirmity, but the Lord of lords is not a Sovereign by courtesy. Rightly has Milton uttered the sentiment that 'He made His laws to bind *us*, not Himself.' *He* 'sits on no precarious throne,' but as final Arbiter in heaven and earth and hell, and has power to effect whatsoever does not involve a contradiction in terms. Much of that suspicion of the miraculous which is so rife to-day is begotten of very grovelling notions of the majesty and glory of the Most High. Some of our religious teachers have such a wizened, poverty-stricken idea of God, they obviously conceive of such a stunted, abortive Deity, that it is not surprising that they stagger at the mention of miracles, and pronounce them contraband articles! To these belittlers of the One and Only Potentate, as to their lineal ancestor, the ancient Sadducee, there needs to be addressed the old rebuke: 'Ye do err, not knowing the Scriptures, nor the *power of God.*' Creation spread abroad its banners at Jehovah's nod, and at His nod those banners shall be furled. To shackle the Almighty in the trammels of natural law is nothing short of constructive blasphemy. Who will have the face to post up a notice prohibiting Him from working miracles within the pale of natural law, 'by order of scientific thought'? We seem to hear the sublime rejoinder: 'Who would set the thorns and briars in array against ME? I would pass through them, I would burn them together.' (Isa. 27.4).

The Lord's self-revelation through the medium of His Word, where it is honestly accepted, cannot but dash these starveling notions of the Godhead to atoms. Let the Deist frame to himself, if he will, an absentee Deity standing inertly aloof from His works; let the Pantheist swamp the nebulous vanity he worships in the circumambient universe; but be it ours to adore an effectual Omnipotence, a Supreme Being who holds the clue of all the complex maze in His steadfast grasp, and 'worketh all things according to the counsel of His own holy will.' He has not abdicated liberty of action, or covenanted never to vary His modes of operation. Is it not preposterous to conceive that the range of the Divine activities is more circumscribed than that of man? Is there no impiety in reducing the Most High to the level of a retainer or satellite in His own cosmos, in deeming Him powerless to dispense with His own appointments? Human wills are free to divert and intercept the course of events; and shall we be persuaded that God has tied Himself irrevocably to a stereotyped order, to rubrics as tyrannous and hide-bound as the edicts of the Medes and Persians? At this very hour we see considerations affecting the public weal overriding legal enactments in our own land. In face of a great emergency half the nations of Europe are suspending some of their most time-honoured institutions without scruple. And shall a pedantic regard for the stated course of nature deter the Lord of all from exerting His saving might? Here is a world out of square, a planet manifestly gone astray from its proper moral orbit. Is not that a signal emergency in the Divine administration? Must not an occasion which warranted the Son of God in leaving the bosom of the Father and assuming our nature have been one that taxed all the resources of moral government to the breaking-point? Undoubtedly. And does not that crowning miracle of grace Divine go far to accredit all the other miracles of Scripture? Is not the unique occasion worthy of unique interpositions? And are not these subordinate marvels part of the equipage attendant on that surpassing wonder; are they not the unearthly gems that glisten in the lustrous diadem of the Crucified? Some glimpses of the 'excellent glory' must perforce flash out through the disguise He wore, and awe the dazzled beholders. Even when it pleased Him to travel incognito, the royalty of the Saviour could not be hid! Nay, in the very hiding of His power there surely lay a greater wonder than in its exercise. Not that He should have come down from the cross, but that He stayed there—that, I ween, was the marvel!

By far the most specious objection urged by quibblers at miracle is that it clashes with the 'uniformity of nature.' Now, if by nature he meant the sum-total of physical forces at work within the material system that environs us, we fully grant its fixity. For we hold that all real miracles are nothing less than the hand of the Lord God omnipotent reaching down from above to displace the ordinary phenomena of the natural sphere by extraordinary phenomena. They do therefore contravene every-day experience, they do run counter to standing usage. But we flatly deny that the beaten path of natural law is the single possible track of the Divine energies, and we challenge opponents to show that it is incapable of modification. For the wisest and most beneficent ends Providence has ordained a settled constitution of things in this nether sphere, with a minimum of infraction or deviation. Were it not for that constitution man could not build on the future as he is constantly doing, and no farmer could sow his crops with any confidence of reaping a harvest. Human activities would be paralyzed if the manufacturer could no longer rely on the stability of the processes of which he avails himself, or the chemist on the fixed properties of his elements and compounds. What use could men make of steam or electricity if their action were fickle and inconstant from day to day? How could insurance companies issue policies or financiers frame budgets, if the law of averages were not fairly stable even in the realm of human actions? But, unlike the law of causality, what is termed the 'uniformity of nature' is not a necessary principle. A sane mind cannot conceive of an effect without a cause, but we can readily suppose the laws of nature to have been other than they actually are. Henry Drummond defined them as 'ascertained working sequences' in the natural sphere. Why then should not nature's ordinary time-table be sometimes for good and sufficient reasons readjusted, even as railway time-tables are subject to modification, and 'valid until further notice'? It is pre-eminently fitting that physical laws, which in themselves are not ends but means, *should* bend to redemptive purposes. For this universe is not a vast self-moved automaton, as some men fancy, but a creation upheld by its Creator to subserve grand moral designs till that day dawns when it shall be folded up like a threadbare vesture.

It is experience, and experience alone, that teaches us to trust in the constancy of nature to her established statutes. We expect day to succeed night, not because we can discern any intrinsic necessity that the sun should rise, or rather the earth revolve, but because we have never known the event to fail. But the moment we infer that it *cannot* be otherwise, we erect our experience into the rule of all experience—a preposterous generalization. No amount of experience can demonstrate the immutability of the prevailing sequences of nature; it would be premature for an experience that had ransacked the profoundest recesses of God's universe to attempt that! We have no right to make the local the standard of the universal. That is but to repeat the error of the Siamese prince alluded to by Hume who, never having seen ice, scouted the Dutch ambassador's story that in his native land men were sometimes able to walk on solid water. No doubt the youthful Israelite who had been born in the wilderness was disposed to regard the daily manna that fell round about the camp as the most conventional phenomenon in the world. To him it must have seemed part and parcel of the 'uniformity of nature'; for, to the best of his knowledge, it was an ordinance unfailing as the dews of heaven or the recurring phases of the moon. Wherein then lay his mistake? Why, in making his infinitesimal experience the guage and measure of all experience, in presuming that to be necessary which was merely provisional. His fallacy was exposed the very day when the manna ceased, and the host was left dependent on the old corn of the land. Such incidents in the history of Israel, written for *our* learning, if we have the docility that submits to be taught, are adapted to convince us that there may be cogent reasons in the vast economy of the Divine administration for a distinct breach of the stated routine of nature, and that Omniscience alone is judge when such extraordinary interventions are seasonable. One main purpose served by such events would seem to be to confute the scientific bigotry that calls God's free agency in question. As Eustace Conder has well remarked: 'Miracles reveal Him not as a sublime hypothesis requisite to complete our theory of the universe.'—which, I take it, is about the creed of Sir Oliver Lodge—'but as a *Living Presence.* They show us the hand upon the helm of the universe'; in short, that its glorious Ruler is no lay-figure, but, in Paul's great phrase, the 'God who quickeneth all things,' and 'in whom we live and move and have our being.'

Even, however, if we grant the uniformity of nature to be as constant as you please, the problem is only shelved, not solved. For the old difficulty reappears the moment we cast our gaze backward to the beginning of the present order of things. 'To create nature,' said Sir Thomas Browne, 'is as great a miracle as to transcend her'; yet the only alternative to the miracle of creation is the Aristotelian postulate that the existing system, or at any rate its material embryo, dates from all eternity. And the sceptic of the miraculous who shrinks from the extreme position that the sun has always risen and set, and the earth always brought forth the green herb, even as at this day, is still confronted with miracle when he strives to account for the genesis of life. It avails him nothing to screen himself behind that most elastic term 'evolution'; for on *any* scheme of evolution there must have been crises when something became something else, and surely that is the biggest miracle conceivable!

An illustration will make my meaning clear. It seems to gratify a section of our present-day theologians to say to the tadpole, 'Thou art my father,' and to the ape, 'Thou hast brought me forth.' Well, tastes differ; and for my part I prefer the old pedigree, 'son of Adam, who was the son of God!' (Luke 3:38). But let us allow for the moment the correctness of the bestial genealogy wherein a topsy-turvy materialism glories. Then the advance of humanity from the toadlet to the Titan, from the slimy to the sublime, has presumably been marked by successive stages. True, one of the most favourite axioms of this school is that nature exhibits no 'solutions of continuity.' There must have been, however, some auspicious hour when man's early prototype cast its brutish slough, some crucial birthpang when the parental baboon burst the barriers of the beast, began to babble some boorish brogue, and so ultimately budded into the ecclesiastical bigwig of the twentieth century. Now I ask whether such a transmutation as that is not flatly 'miraculous.' Assuredly it constitutes an infraction of the 'common course and constitution of nature' visible around us! Nothing in the least degree approximating to such a metamorphosis meets our gaze in the physical realm, as we behold it. The fact is, the creation of the first man cannot but involve a miracle; if not a miracle of creation, then a miracle of conservation; for no infant of the human race exposed to the mercy of the elements as a fenceless and untended foundling could possibly survive the ordeal. All genuine creation is *anomalous,* and no amount of pressure will squeeze it within the rigid grooves of any 'law of uniformity.'

Our world rests on a supernatural basis: that truth stares us in the face, which way soever we turn. The hand of the Lord founded it of old, and it is by His edict that it continues to be. God Himself is the Miracle of Miracles, and the long and short of the matter is that disbelief in the supernatural is at root disbelief in *Him.* A tacit denial of His Omnipotence underlies the insinuations of scepticism. No one has put this more forcibly than the Unitarian Channing, and we cannot do better than conclude with his own admirable statement of the case. In default of books we are compelled to quote the substance of it from memory. He remarks that to the consistent theist it is just as easy to conceive of God as using miraculous action as non-miraculous. He has undoubtedly instituted an established order of the universe, and will not depart from His usual method of working without good and sufficient reason for such deviation. But, though there is thus a presumption against what we reckon the abnormal, we must remember that the order of the universe is a means, not an end, and like all other means must give way when the end can best be promoted without it. For it is the mark of a weak mind to make an idol of order and method, to cling to established forms when they clog instead of advancing the end sought. We may be confident that Divine wisdom *will* depart from its accustomed process of working whenever that is requisite to secure the grand aims it has in view.

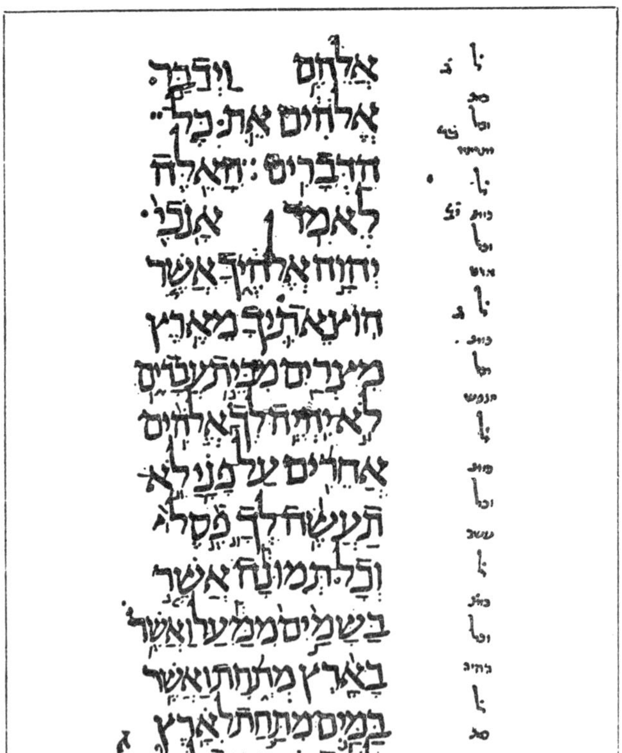

HEBREW MS. (Exod. xx. 1-5)—Written earlier than A.D. 916.

The Proof of Miracles

By E. K. Simpson

Having made some reflections in a previous article on the *possibility* of miracles, we feel that it is advisable to add a word or two respecting their *proof*; for many, like Huxley himself, who do not challenge their abstract possibility, reject all actual instances of their occurrence as inadequately attested. No intelligent theist can dispute that a power competent to the performance of miracles exists; but it is open to him to cavil at every alleged example of its exercise. Now to meet this particular form of incredulity it is not enough to argue that 'the things which are impossible with men are possible with God.' For that proposition may be admitted in the abstract, and yet specific cases of miracle be pronounced incredible. Manifestly this phase of the argument relates to the question of *testimony*. Can miraculous events be sustained by such cogent evidence that disbelief in them becomes unreasonable scepticism? Or, to put the matter in another way, can things antecedently improbable be proved to be true?

Miracles are confessedly rare events in the economy of the universe; that is to say, they fall under the observation of comparatively few eye-witnesses, and the remainder of the human race has to accept them upon testimony. Now everybody is in the habit of trusting his memory in regard to all important occurrences that have come within the circle of his personal observation. But as the range of our personal observation is of necessity very limited, we naturally draw upon the experience of others for its enlargement. In fact, testimony is simply another man's memory supplementing our own. All authentic history is founded on some one's recollection of the past; and we may remark here that faith in testimony is instinctive, whenever the character of the witness is such as to lend weight to his evidence. All our courts of law rely on this means of verifying facts; and sentences are passed on criminals every day without the least demur or misgiving, on the strength of the evidence forthcoming against them. If the confidence universally reposed in the statements of 'credible witnesses' be rash and unfounded, the sooner we radically revise our canons of jurisprudence the better; and, instead of judging with an eye to the honesty and competency of the witness, juries must in future weigh evidence solely in the balances of antecedent probability, or, in other words, by ingenious guesswork. Of course, if this principle be adopted, it will follow that we can be certain of none but probable events; and inasmuch as our knowledge of what is probable is anything but exhaustive, once having discredited the value of testimony, we shall find our catalogue of ascertained facts dwindling to a very modest compass.

As is well known, the first writer of any note to deny that the reality of miraculous events could be substantiated by testimony was the sceptic David Hume. The celebrity of his argument rather than its intrinsic value entitles it to some attention. The gist of the whole contention lies in the allegation that there is always more likelihood that the witnesses of a supposed miracle should have been deceived than that such a 'violation of the laws of nature,' in contradiction to universal experience, should have taken place. Seeing that this bit of sophistry forms a favourite text with unbelievers, and still crops up in almost all discussions of the subject, we shall reconnoitre it in some detail.

There are two points in which Hume gains an unfair advantage by mis-statement of the case; and we propose to range our criticism under these two heads. In the first place there is crafty dealing involved in his definition of miracle as a *violation* of natural law. Prof. Huxley had the candour to own the inaccuracy of this description. What then is a miracle? To that query it is certainly not easy to supply a satisfactory answer, partly because the term is so often used in a loose and popular sense, as when we speak of conversion or of recovery from a dangerous illness as a 'miracle.' Properly speaking, we think it may be defined as a *visible* prodigy or 'sign' transcending the range of human power or the effects of natural agency, and therefore (since every event must have an adequate cause) attributable to a superhuman agent, to a cause above the natural sphere. Setting the vexed question of diabolical miracles on one side, it may be said to be an immediate interposition of Divine power in the outward world, the 'finger of God,' as our Lord Himself styles it, made palpable to the senses. Miracles are *sensible* signs of God's presence and working; and for that reason 'transubstantiation' is no miracle at all; for after all the priest's conjuring no perceptible change in the elements is effected!

But it by no means ensues from this definition that miracles 'violate' natural law, any more than the raising of one's arm ruptures the law of gravitation. On the contrary, the law of gravitation acts just as usual, but is counteracted and overcome by an exertion of will. And all true miracle in like manner is a display of supernatural energy controlling natural law, or, it may be, in some cases co-operating with it. Observe that Biblical miracles are not merely unaccountable puzzles to be placed on a par with the mysteries of the divining-rod or the phenomena of hypnotism; for they exhibit the manifested presence and power of God. The notion nowadays widely propagated that they are wrought by virtue of some higher or occult law unknown to us robs them of their unique glory, and debases them—at least, such is the writer's opinion—to the level of vulgar magic, which excites our wonder only so long as we remain in ignorance of the secret, a knowledge of which would divest the performance of all its mystery. It may not be practicable to fix the border-line of the humanly possible; but such events as Elijah's ascent to heaven, or the reanimation of the dead body of Lazarus, or the stilling of a tempest-swept lake by a bare word, absolutely surpass the bounds of human agency; and we must either reject the narratives blankly as so much idle romancing, or else receive the record with the reverence befitting the 'finger of God' beheld at work.

But a scrutiny of Hume's argument discloses a further piece of sharp practice on his part, which cannot be allowed to pass unchallenged. Fair play is a jewel; and we really cannot give him leave to shuffle the cards as he pleases before he begins his game. Do you notice how he does it? Why, by slily whisking all testimony extant in favour of miracles into the waste-paper basket, and then labelling the remainder 'universal experience'! Nay, friend Hume, adept as you are in legerdemain, that ruse will not pass muster! We maintain that the witness forthcoming in support of the miraculous forms an integral part of 'universal experience,' and that it must not be put out of court, or cavalierly brushed aside, just because it clashes with your prejudices. Granted that there is a presumption against every exceptional event, owing to its very rarity, and that the more rare it is, the stronger becomes that presumption; still, let the witnesses be heard. Suppressing evidence is every whit as bad as packing juries! Besides, very surprising things do happen now and then. How many scores of unexpected and startling facts all of us have been induced to believe on the strength of testimony in which we have learned to place full confidence! All depends on the good character of the parties testifying, on their known veracity, and on the clearness and concurrence of their evidence. *Le vrai n'est pas toujours vraisemblable,* as Boileau wittily puts it. Truth does not always look like truth; but a candid examination may convince a man of the reality of things quite at variance with general experience; nay, quite unprecedented. Else how could anything happening for the first time ever be authenticated at all? Wireless telegraphy sounded fabulous enough to most of us, when first announced in the press. Why does everybody credit it now? Is it because we have all fathomed its mode of operation, or subjected the matter to the test of personal experiment? Nothing of the sort! But the facts are by this time notorious; and so we accept the voice of general testimony, even though it flies in the face of antecedent probabilities. Of course, the comparison halts in some respects; nevertheless, it holds in the main point. For the New Testament miracles were matters of common fame throughout all the region where they had been wrought; so much so that Peter could challenge the mixed multitude on the day of Pentecost to gainsay his appeal to them. So patent were the facts that the Pharisees themselves could not rebut the evidence; all that their invention, edged with keenest malice, could devise was to ascribe them to Satanic agency. In fact, our Scriptures hold the field; their witness, published close to the time and place concerned, stood uncontroverted in the very citadel of their enemies—enemies exasperated moreover to the utmost pitch of hatred, and who would have given anything to crush the new sect by exposing their falsehood.

Touching the greatest miracle of all, the resurrection of Jesus, Paul could appeal in a written document, largely occupied with the confutation of certain false brethren who were most eager to seize any occasion against him, to 500 *eye-witnesses,* the most of whom were still alive; and thousands more were ready to lay down their lives in maintenance of its truth, as many of them actually did. If such testimony as that is not conclusive, pray, what is? Indeed, Henry Rogers has neatly turned the tables on Hume at this point, in his once celebrated book, *The Eclipse of Faith,* by remarking that the principle of universal experience is one that extends to the world of *mind* as well as *matter.* He argues with much force that the falsehood of testimony, borne at such cost and with such zeal and unanimity by such diverse parties, to the New Testament miracles, would be much the bigger miracle of the two! The sceptic gains nothing after all by substituting a *moral* miracle for a *physical* one.

Nor does Hume take the least account of the *setting* of the Biblical miracles, of the sublime truths with which they are interwoven, and which many of them so beautifully image forth. It is sorry work dissecting these ethereal wonders with the rude scalpel of criticism, irrespective of the doctrines they confirm, and not seldom embody in the most graphic shape. They are the credentials of heavenly tidings, the superscription of a Divine commission. To be sure, Paley exaggerated their import when he made them the all-in-all of the Christian evidences, and thereby provoked such a violent reaction that the danger now is that they should be slurred over, and their significance weakly disparaged, where it is not denied outright. But the attempt to oust the supernatural from the Bible leaves us nothing save the covers. Miracles are inwoven with its very texture. Inspiration is one and prophecy another; and the Incarnation and Resurrection constitute main pillars in the edifice of the faith. The Scriptural miracles in general (and this is their vindication) promote loftier ends than themselves. They are the birthpangs of a new creation destined to repair the ravages sin has made in the old. They have their exits and their entrances, their appropriate groupings and appointed times. When the purposes of Divine grace take some decisive step forward, they appear as harbingers of the brightening day. It was so when Moses led up Israel from the house of bondage; it was so when the prophetical order was commissioned to spiritualize Judaism; it was so when He to whom both Moses and the prophets bore witness came to fulfil all that they had foreshadowed, and when the glorious company of His apostles marched forth, clad in invisible armour, to rout a deriding world, mustered in fell antagonism to the truth as it is in Jesus. John Foster quaintly likened the miraculous to the great bell of the universe tolled to call together the congregation to listen to God's sermon. Rather would I picture them as engines of war in the Lord's arsenal kept in reserve for critical campaigns in the long-drawn conflict between darkness and light.

Does anyone ask: how shall we distinguish the true from the false wonder? By certain broad characteristics, we reply, which part them asunder. The true court scrutiny; the false evade it, even when professing the contrary. The true are wrought without elaborate preparation or strenuous effort; the false wear that spasmodic, gaudy, theatrical air which characterizes, for instance, the lying wonders palmed off by the Church of Rome on her facile devotees. The pretended miracles of the apocryphal gospels resemble fairy tales in respect of whimsicality and childishness, whereas the authentic miracle never forfeits its celestial dignity and grace. Nor is it performed without rhyme or reason, like the idiotic freaks fathered on Mahomet, but grafts itself congenially on the order of nature. Aaron's rod budded and the cursed fig-tree withered *after their kind,* like members of the vegetable kingdom. Finally, the counterfeit article almost invariably betrays symptoms of quackery or yields signs of collusion; but the Biblical miracles are eminently straightforward and above-board. Of that the Tishbite gave a fine example when he drenched the altar on Carmel with twelve buckets of water,—probably salt-water, after such an intense drought,—that no lurking suspicion of fraud might suggest itself to the spectators. Heaven's miracles, in short, defy competition, and carry God's own autograph stamped upon them, no less than His blue canopy overhead, and His green ocean folding us round.

Just one more observation by way of caution. There is an economy observed in the use of special expedients like these. They are never wrought for the mere gratification of Paul Prys. The natural order constitutes the rule of God's working in the physical realm, and a breach will not be made in it wantonly or without good reason. In the childhood of Christianity miracles played an important and essential part. Thomas Fuller styles them not inaptly the swaddling-bands of the infant Church. Until the completion of the Canon of Scripture the balance of evidence that the new faith was indeed of heavenly lineage and final authority needed to be thus redressed. Miracles served to mitigate the sovereign contempt with which the haughty Roman naturally viewed a Judean superstition, and to thaw the polite incredulity which the subtilising Greek felt for so unphilosophical a creed. Having accomplished their peculiar ministry for the time then present, they were withdrawn. Many excellent people crave to have these signs and wonders back again, because they deem that if the modern Church possessed the miraculous gifts of former days, the world would straightway fall at her feet, and the most inveterate of Christ's foes be disarmed of all enmity against His unique claims. Yet with what sullen apathy was the witness of our Lord's own miracles despised by multitudes who beheld them, to their own perdition! To how many they proved a veritable savour of death! Let us not forget that the desperate perversity of the human heart rebuffed the most signal wonders ever wrought for its conviction; and let those who sigh for portents and prodigies as things pregnant with irresistible spiritual power bethink them that He Who knew what was in man has pronounced a very different judgment, declaring them the idols of an adulterous generation, and protesting that they who believe not Moses and the Prophets would not be persuaded, though one should rise from the dead for their reproof and admonition.

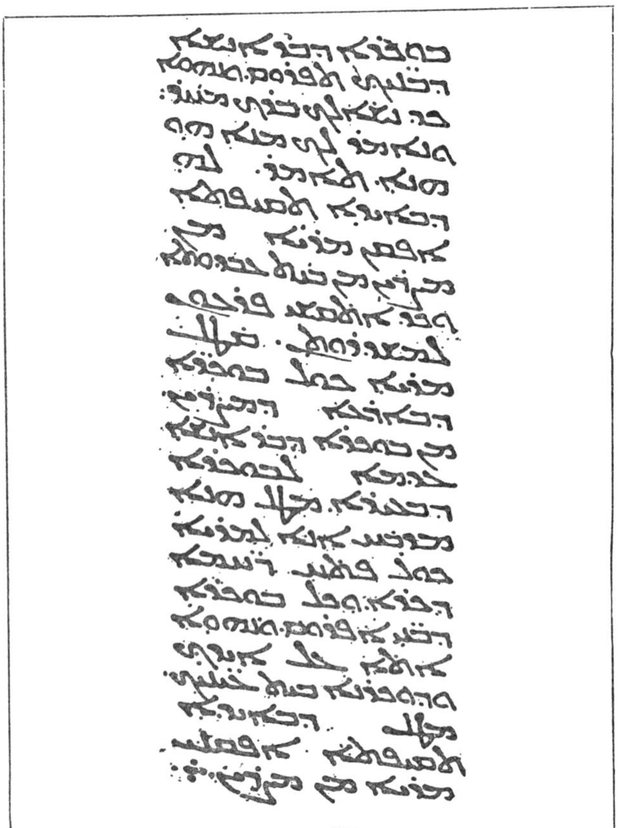

SYRIAC MS. (Exod. xiii. 14-16)—A.D. 464.

The Final Authority of the Bible

By Dr. G. Campbell Morgan

I am announced to speak on 'The Final Authority of the Bible.' When a subject is chosen for a man—and I did not choose this subject—he always labours under the difficulty at least of being not quite sure what was in the minds of those who chose the subject for him. However, he may be comforted by the knowledge that his audience has no more idea than he has himself as to what was in the minds of those who gave him his subject. With these preliminary words, you will let me define what I mean by accepting this subject. I am proposing to-day to address this company of Christian men and women, students of the Holy Writings, not in proof of the final authority of the Bible, but rather along the line of considering the finality of authority. I do propose, however, to conclude with some few words along one line of evidence in proof of that selfsame final authority of the Scriptures.

Another difficulty confronts me in an assembly like this. Perhaps I may say it is not the kind of assembly that I have been most accustomed to address on such subjects. It is almost a work of supererogation to talk to you about the final authority of the Bible, and perhaps I rather like having audiences not in such perfect accord with my conceptions as this audience is. Yet it is good for us to consider anew the foundations of our belief, and to ask ourselves what are the things that we do hold with all our mind and heart, and to which we give ourselves entirely. Therefore, I think, in approaching such a subject as this, it is of importance that we remind ourselves of the nature of the Bible, and I will say concerning it at once—that we may emphasize it for a moment or two—that when we approach the subject of its final authority we are bound to recognize that the Bible is Christocentric, that the final fact of the Written Word is the Living Word, and that we have no right to speak of the authority of any part of it save as that part contributes to the final exposition of the authority which is vested in Christ Himself.

I remind you of those words that you have so often heard, the words of Augustine, that Christ is latent in the Old Testament and patent in the New. If I may take so clear a statement as that, and attempt to express it for a moment or two in another way, I think it is important that we should ever remember that in the Scriptures of the Old Testament we have the writings that reveal human need and promise Divine supply; but in those writings we never reach the revelation of supply, whereas in the writings of the New Testament we have the record of how God supplied that need which is so clearly revealed in the writings of the Old Testament.

It has been my lot in life to come in close association with the Jewish people, not from the Christian standpoint, but from the educational standpoint, and I am perfectly sure that every devout Jew—non-Christian—would agree with me when I say that the sum total of the value of the writings of the Old Testament is that a need is revealed. There is a sense in which undoubtedly there was a supply, for we believe the history of the Old Testament as it is written, and that God did in very deed provide for His people the whole system of ceremonial and worship which was suggestive and symbolic, and directed their thought to the finality of things; yet the very language I am employing proves the matter of finality. We find in the Old Testament it is always pointing on. For myself—and I simply submit it to you as being somewhat suggestive—I always think of the Old Testament as in three departments, not strictly the departments of the Hebrew Bible, but in the first place the Pentateuch and the Torah, or the Law; then the historical books, ending with Ezra and Nehemiah; and the rest, the devotional and prophetic literature. Then I think of the whole, and having studied the whole in the quiet of my own soul, I should say that in the earliest part of it I hear perpetually the sigh of humanity after a priest, but the priest is never found. I turn to the history of Israel from its fall, to monarchy from theocracy, and I say this very carefully, because there is another modern theory that there was a gradual rise until you come to the monarchy, but the Bible account of the monarchy is this: "They have not rejected thee, but they have rejected Me, that I should not reign over them," so said God to Samuel, and I cannot see a rise in it; now I say that the period of history from the fall to monarchy away to the return from captivity under Ezra and Nehemiah is all a history which reveals humanity's need for a king, a final and central authority; but the king is never found. Then when I take all the rest of the writings—God-breathed writings, finding the soul as no other literature can find the soul—I nevertheless am conscious all through of what I may venture to describe as humanity's quest for the prophet, answered in divers manners, by which God spake to the fathers through the prophets, but with no final voice, no Logos, no Word of God which is perfect, and final, and all-inclusive; they are all broken parts. I put down the literature, feeling that I have a revelation of a need, and upon all the literature rests the light of a Divine thought and a Divine promise and a Divine intention; but if I have none other than the Old Testament, I have writings that are incomparable with any other in their revelation of the supreme necessity and agony of the human soul, and yet the answer is not there, and it is not found anywhere there. Of course, you and I can find it there as we read back in the light of the Christian fulfilment, and that is the meaning of typology, and the proper place of typology in all our study—we go back, and in the light of fulfilment we see the wonderful significance of it all; but as a literature there is no full and final authority in the Old Testament. On the other hand, when I turn to the New, if I am asked to destroy the Old, there is no authority at all in the New, for the New is absolutely dependent on the Old for its history and philosophy and religion and reference from beginning to end.

But, to go back to what I was saying, I need not stay for a moment to argue that the New is the religion of Christ. Just take the simplest test. Take the first four pamphlets; what are they but the history of Christ? Take the epistles, what are they but the interpretation of the Christ and His Church by men who had come into union with Christ by the Holy Spirit? And when you take the last book of the Bible, which you and I are not afraid of, but which many people are, what is it but the unfolding of Jesus Christ? That is how it opens, and He is its subject, unveiled in the glory of His Person, in the matchless grace of His relation with His people, in all the august majesty of His dealing with the world. It is the unveiling of Christ from beginning to end.

> 'Christ! I am Christ's! and let the name suffice you,
> Ay, for me too He greatly hath sufficed.
>
> Christ is the end, for Christ was the beginning,
> Christ, the beginning, for the end is Christ.'

Now, if that be so, and I am sure it is granted, for I have been but leading you along the line of your own conviction, then if we come to speak of the final authority of the Bible we must remember that it is found in Christ, and to that accordingly I turn. And, speaking first of all of what the Bible reveals progressively in a true sense toward Christ, central in Christ, and by development and teaching in all the writings following His historical presence, I want to refer to things concerning which the Bible speaks with authority (for there are things of which it says nothing authoritatively; there are things concerning which it has no Divine message, there are things to which it refers, to which it alludes, never inaccurately, as I shall venture to declare, but on which it is never specific). We are told—it is a subject constantly discussed—that we have outgrown the Bible scientifically, that we have outgrown the Bible philosophically, that we have outgrown the Bible theologically.

Now, if I argued these three things I should carry you with me some of the way and then drop you very suddenly. I should say, first of all, the Bible never professes to be a scientific text-book. There I carry you; but I should affirm that there is no discrepancy between any ascertained fact of science and what the Bible really says; and I should urge young people always when they investigate for themselves to follow two principles—first of all, to distinguish carefully between the ascertained facts of science and the hypotheses of scientific investigators; and I should also dare to ask them to discriminate carefully between what the Bible says and what some of its best friends say that it says. If you will follow those discriminating lines, I should affirm that there is no discrepancy between the ascertained facts of science and the Biblical allusions and references to matters scientific.

Then I am told we have outgrown the Bible philosophically. I always ask young people to remember that you cannot in fairness put Biblical philosophy in comparison with any other methods of philosophy, and that is not to speak disparagingly of other methods. I realize that they may be mainly true in their method and intention. I think you will agree with me when I say that philosophy is the history of attempts to find answers to one question, and that one question is Pilate's, 'What is truth?' I always quarrel with the people who say that that was said jestingly. Pilate was not jesting when he was asking that question; he was up against a big thing, and he felt the power of that Personality dominating him. Now what is truth? Away back from Anaxagoras, in the first ages of philosophical investigation, through the comparatively decadent or dead millenniums, down to the last three hundred years of philosophy, it is based on that "What is truth?" The only really philosophical books in the Bible, as you know, are Job, Ecclesiastes and Proverbs, and if I dare say so, I should put the Epistle of James in the same category. What have you there? The Bible philosophy—I may be right or wrong—does not start with a question; it starts with an affirmation: God is. It makes a second affirmation: All wisdom is in God. Then follows a deduction: The fear of the Lord is the beginning of wisdom. I am not at all sure that we have outgrown that. I am not at all sure that the one system of philosophy which asks the question, "What is truth?" will not find itself singing the anthem with which the Hebrew started: 'God is, and all wisdom is in Him, and we know wisdom as we fear the Lord.' So I am not at all sure we have outgrown Bible philosophy.

Then I am told that we have outgrown the Bible theologically. That is where I may not carry you. I say you have no systematic theology in the Bible. You have the elements from which you can make a system of theology, but you have truth, which is more than systematic theology, which in the last analysis may be the human theory about systematic truth.

In the Bible everything is centralised in Christ. What are the things on which it claims to speak with authority? For myself I cover the ground for a moment by saying that in the Bible you have Christ, the final word about God; secondly, Christ, the final word about man; thirdly, Christ, the final word about morality; and, fourthly, Christ, the final word about salvation or redemption. Under these four headings, I should say, you have the whole Biblical message as it is finally centralised and expressed in Christ Himself, and we do claim that the Bible is final in its authority upon all those subjects.

Christ is the final word about God. Now, is it reverent, is it proper even to attempt to ask what the Bible says in Christ about God? Well, with reverence and with reticence, I should say that Christ is the exegesis of God, and that is a Bible quotation, as you know perfectly well. 'No man hath seen God at any time; the only begotten Son, which is in the bosom of the Father, He hath *exegeted* Him.' And if you ask me for the exposition of the exegesis, or the exegesis of the Incarnate Word of God concerning Himself, I should not hesitate to say that you have it right there immediately, the full and final revelation, all the rays of the Bible combining until it flashes in the central white revelation of two words, 'We beheld His glory, the glory as of the only begotten of the Father, full of *grace and truth.*' That is the Biblical message concerning God—truth: holiness which makes no compromise with sin; grace: compassion that stops at no cost in order to regain and ransom the sinner. I pray that that may be heard with the reverence with which I attempt to say it, knowing how inadequate it is, and yet that is what the Bible finally says about God.

There are many other things—true things—about God that we may know apart from the Biblical revelation. We may know something of His might, something of His wisdom, something of His beauty; but apart from the Biblical revelation we know nothing either of His holiness or of His compassion. The very word of which holiness is a translation in the great Old Testament Scriptures is a word that stood—apart from the Hebrew people, the people of God—for separation; but it had no moral signification until it gained it through this religion and this Divine revelation. The separation of gods, according to the conception of men, apart from Jehovah, was the separation of being, and power, and dignity; it was not moral. There emerged into human thought and history the conviction and the conception as the result of revelation that God's separation is that of holiness. And there is no conception of compassion anywhere else. So I say, leaving the great theme there, quite inadequately dealt with, suggestively only, that the Bible says of God, 'Full of grace and full of truth,' and the supreme revelation of the Bible concerning God is how these two facts of God are inter-related in themselves and in their activity. The ultimate unveiling is the Cross, where holiness is the central passion, and love the overwhelming power. I submit to you to-day that the Bible is final in authority about God. Beyond that nothing has been suggested that can satisfy the human intellect if the human intellect will approach it reverently. Nothing has been suggested that could appeal to the human heart so as to gain the heart; nothing has been suggested that could constrain and inspire the human will except that revelation of God.

When I turn to the next of these things I find in Christ a final and authoritative revelation concerning man. And what do I see of man in Christ? My method now is not that of reference to His teaching, it is that of reference to Himself. With all reverence, and with apologies to some on this platform, I speak of Him for a moment as Jesus, thinking only of Him in the realm of His manhood. What do I see at last in that Man? I see that Man ideally as like God, and that is only to go back to the beginning of your Bible—man made in the likeness, in the image of God, a limited revelation of the illimitable mystery and majesty Divine. I am speaking of man ideally. Christ has declared that man is like God, and therefore He has declared that experimentally man only realizes himself in the life of fellowship with God. I take the teaching of the whole Bible, beginning with all the poetic accuracy and majesty of Genesis, and proceeding through the wonderful history of humanity along one certain line as it is traced for me, until at last I stand in the presence of this one Man, and I say that the Bible declares these things concerning man through Jesus Christ.

For a moment let us ask what other view of man there is for us. There is only one other view possible, and it is—forgive me if I put it bluntly—that man is the king of the beasts. There is no other view. Say if you like that he is an animal, it is the same thing; he is certainly the king, but he is only that, and therefore he is bestial. God compels humanity to prove that by working out its own philosophies when it declines His ideal of humanity, and we are doing it to-day. Do not let us be blind to the things in the midst of which we are living. While you and I are sitting here a death-grapple in the darkness is going on between the superman and God's ideal of humanity. It is the thing that we are face to face with. The superman is a beast, and nothing more. I feel as though I need cleansing for putting that thought in comparison with Christ, yet there He emerges before us in all the dignity of His manhood, revealing to us what was in the mind of Deity according to our own Holy Writings when God did say, 'Let us make man in our own image and after our own likeness.'

Then I turn to the question of morality. What does the Bible teach concerning morality? What is Christ's conception of morality?—and that is the Biblical conception from beginning to end. He insists upon the centrality of the spiritual to all human life. Or in another way, let me say that He declares that morality is rooted in religion, that there is no sanction sufficiently powerful to make man behave as he ought to his fellow-man other than that which tells him to recognize himself as under the reign and rule of God. And then what? Mark the inclusiveness of it. According to Jesus Christ, morality is being in right relation with God in life. 'Thou shalt love the Lord thy God with all thy heart, and with all thy soul, and with all thy mind. This is the first and great commandment. And the second is like unto it'—the child of it, the corollary of it, the consequence, there is no escape—'Thou shalt love thy neighbour as thyself.' But you never know that law apart from the first, and that conception of man's duty to his neighbours never did emerge in history apart from revelation; and when the law of revelation is refused, that passes away again, and the neighbour, if he be weak and poor, can be bludgeoned to death to make way for the march of the proud and the arrogant. That is where we are to-day. Christ has given us that conception of morality as rooted in right relation with God, and consequently as bearing its flower and fruit in all right relationships with our fellow-man.

Apart from that, what have you? You have laws based on convenience, and they are always in conflict, and they break down. Out of that false conception of morality comes that most pernicious saying that we use very often quite carelessly—I mean that we do not stop to think what we are saying—'When in Rome, do as Rome does.' That is utterly disloyal and immoral according to the

Biblical standard; it is not immoral according to any other standard. Of course, when in Rome you must do as Rome does, because Rome is making its laws of convenience to suit its situation. That applies also to London, or England, or Germany, or anywhere else. That is why all human laws are always breaking down. But our Lord says, 'The final throne is one throne, the final law is one law, the final King is one King, and you cannot behave as you ought to do in London or Rome save as you are behaving as you would behave in heaven where the throne is.' I believe that is the moral ideal of the Bible. It begins in the Old Testament. It is as clear there in certain regards as it is in the New. Not from the Decalogue would I quote the principle of morality—the Decalogue is an application of the principle. The principle is here: 'Hear, O Israel: the Lord our God is one Lord: and thou shalt love the Lord thy God with all thine heart, and with all thy soul, and with all thy might.' That is the principle of morality in the Old Testament, and it emerges in all clarity in the Person of the Christ and in His teaching.

I come to the last of these four things for a moment. In the Bible we find in Christ—now here one can hardly say the final authority, and yet one says it with more emphasis than anywhere else—the final authority concerning human salvation. For, remember, here the voice of the Christ is the only voice that proclaims that possible. Here we are out of the realm of comparison; there is no competition. Others will speak much to us of God; others will speak to us of man; others will speak to us of morality, but over all the ruin and wreckage of human life, born of its misconceptions of God, born of its misunderstandings, born of its false standards of morality, over all the sounding, sobbing sea of human sorrow, there is no voice sounds of redemption but the voice of Christ; and the voice of this Biblical literature therefore as authority is final because it is without competition and without comparison. Consequently, the proof as to whether that authority is authority or no must be pragmatic or practical. We at once ask whether the thing that is said concerning the possibility of human regeneration and redemption and renewal is true, and there I am not going to insult your intelligence by arguing. I could turn this Cannon Street Hall into a testimony meeting, and could have the witnesses here all over the building speaking with definiteness of the power of this great gospel.

'I ask them whence their victory came;
They, with united breath,
Ascribe their conquest to the Lamb,
Their triumph to His death.'

The final value of the Bible is this: beyond its doctrine of God; beyond its doctrine of man; beyond its ethical standard, it is sounding out ransom and redemption, it is an evangel, it is that from first to last. If this were the time and place I would be prepared to argue—you all know it—that the idea of the Gospel emerges from the beginning of your Bible, and the sound continues and grows in volume until it is central in Christ, and the last anthem is in the apocalyptic literature with which our Bible closes.

Now in conclusion for a moment. You may say, 'How would you prove the finality of the authority of the Bible in all these things?' There are many lines of proof which I do not propose to follow. Let me name one or two. When you put into comparison the Biblical revelation of these matters as we have it in Christ with every other attempt to deal with them, you will find immediately how the Bible has taken up everything that is true in every other system of thought, and gone beyond it and fulfilled it, and it stands alone.

Again, this, I think, is to be borne in mind, that all development along the line of application through these centuries of the Christian era is found to be for ever true to the germ and the norm of truth in Christ, and wherever it departs it destroys itself and comes back again to the very things He said, and the things He was, and to the revelation of Him that you have in the Bible.

I should say again that the proof of the final authority of the Bible is to be found in the effects which it has produced in the lives of men. That I am not going to follow.

Now, as I close, let me stress one thing, which is this, that to me the finality of the authority of the Bible is demonstrated by the response that it gains from the soul of man himself. I pray you ponder that for yourselves. You may say that is a very insecure foundation. I am not so sure of its insecurity. I am greatly impressed as I read again and again—the more I read it the greater it becomes—that simple statement of Matthew concerning our Lord, after He had delivered what we call the Sermon on the Mount. Was there ever so inapt a name for such an utterance? Of course, I am assuming that it is not a composite record. It is altogether too marvellous for any editing. It is the manifesto of a king. Now, Matthew records in the simple, artless way that characterises all these utterances, 'The multitudes were astonished at His teaching, for He taught them as one having authority.' That is not the amazing part of the declaration to me, but what follows, 'and not as the scribes.' That is the thing that arrests me, because the scribes were the authoritative teachers. The one thing that marked the scribes was the note of authority. They were official teachers, and to them men came when they needed an application of the Law. They asked the scribe to set a Torah, or Law, or to say how it applied. Then listen: 'He taught them as one having authority, and not as the scribes'—which does not mean that the scribes had no authority, but which does mean that His authority was of a different kind. Now, I am not going to say that there was no dignity in the way our Lord said things: I believe there was. I am at war myself with all pictures of Jesus I have ever seen, especially with those pictures of Him that represent Him as weak and anaemic. I think He was gloriously beautiful in His humanity. Ah, yes, a face more marred than any other face, but a beautiful face may be marred with the lines of sorrow, and I think there must have been an almost irresistible grace and dignity about the way in which He said things. Yet that was not the impression He made, it was the impression of the thing He said, and the human soul, listening to Him, answered, 'Yes, yes, that is so.'

Now, I am submitting to you as Christian men and women, for a moment, to test what I am saying by going back at your leisure to that very Sermon on the Mount and listening to it without any prejudice. Can you quarrel with it anywhere? Is there any point at which you take any exception, when you have freed your mind of all prejudice, to anything Jesus said? Oh, yes, there is one thing you can say, and there is only one, in criticism of Christ's ideals in the Sermon on the Mount. What is that? That they are not practical, that you cannot obey them. You will say that if you are honest. There is a good deal of jugglery with the Sermon on the Mount which is of the nature of blasphemy. I am tired of hearing men praise it. I am told to preach it, and not the 'Green Hill.' My answer is, 'You do not know the Sermon on the Mount, or you would be driven to the Green Hill.' The Sermon on the Mount will scorch and shame you, and yet, where will you quarrel with it? Only there—that you cannot live up to it!

Pardon a reminiscence: I am going back a generation. When I was a young man, beginning my ministry in Birmingham, a man said to me, 'You know, my quarrel with your Master is that He is so utterly unreasonable.' 'What do you mean?' I replied. 'I will tell you,' said he. 'Confucius says, "Be just to your enemies." I can do that. Your Master says, "Love your enemies." I cannot do that; it is unreasonable.' Does anyone want to quarrel with that man? Do you find it easy to do it to-day? Did you ever know how high above the snowline is the ethical standard of Jesus as you know it now? I put my hand on my lips and say, 'If that is His ideal, I am unclean.' But He is right. I said to that man long ago, 'I see your point, but supposing you could, supposing there is some way by which you could learn to love your enemies?' 'Then,' said he, 'you have solved all your problems in this world.' He was wrong; you cannot quarrel with Christ's ethical ideal. I am not going over His points; you go over them, and think of them. Think of His revelation of God. When we really can reach it, when man really stands in the presence of God revealed in Christ, I do not say that necessarily he yields, but he consents. The human soul knows, and the human soul is compelled to say, 'My Lord and my God.' I am not dealing now with the problem of the human will, but the soul of man consents to the final authority of truth concerning God as it has been revealed in Christ.

Not to labour this or detain you, it is true concerning man; it is true concerning the moral standards of Christ; it is true concerning salvation.

Let me say this as I conclude—and I will speak for myself and for none other—that revelation concerning God and man and morality and salvation that I have in Christ, I have in Christ in my whole Bible, and in the moment in which I find some part of that Bible being destroyed, as I follow the line of destruction through, I find finally it strikes at Christ who is at the heart of the Bible. And that is the terror of it to my soul, and yet that is the joy and comfort of it to my soul, because He abides faithful, unharmed, while tempests sweep around Him. I know that that revelation will abide and emerge from all conflict concerning it into the place of God's full and final revelation of Himself to man, of man to man, of the law of love to man, of His way of salvation to man, until the hour shall come when again the Incarnate Word shall appear and seal the authority of the Written Word, and make sure work in righteousness of all the purposes of our God.

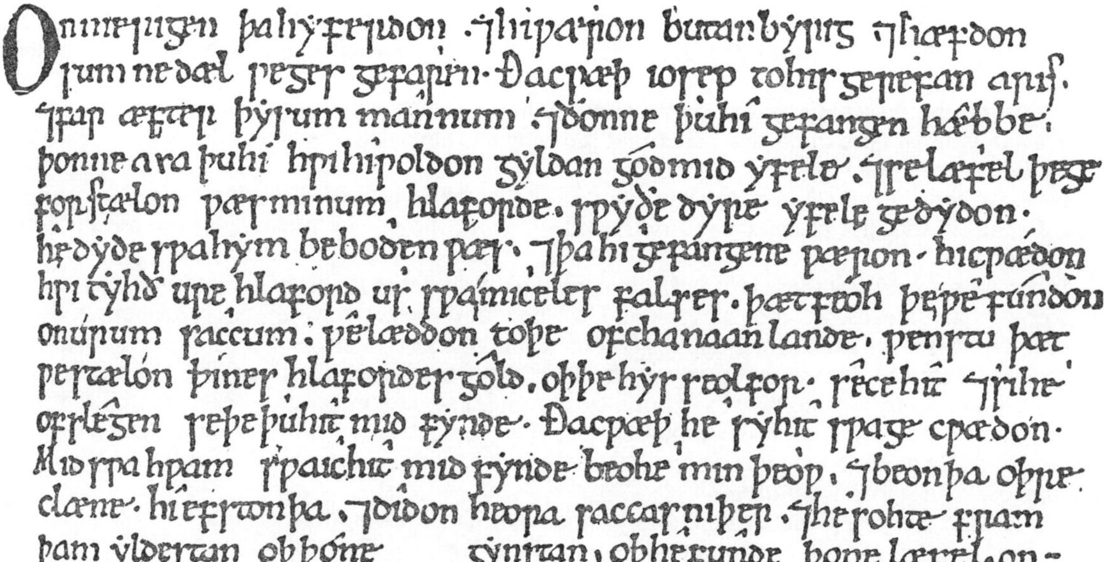

THE PENTATEUCH, &c., in Anglo-Saxon (Gen. xliv. 3-12)—Early Eleventh century.

Verbal Inspiration

By J. P. Wiles

Jude, a servant of Jesus Christ, found it needful in writing to those who were sanctified by God the Father, and preserved in Jesus Christ, and called, to exhort them that they should earnestly contend for the faith which was once delivered unto the saints. If it was needful then, how needful it must be now! My spirit was grieved, and my heart depressed, to read certain things recently in a well-known evangelical magazine with a wide circulation.

After plainly and truthfully stating that God holds Himself responsible for the truth of every part of the Bible, so that we may commit ourselves without reserve to its word, the writer goes on to say:—

> 'Verbal inspiration is not a biblical term; we may, therefore, have the less regret in laying it aside. Undoubted emphasis is laid, in Scripture, upon the *ipsissima verba*, the literal terms, of prophetic discourse or apostolic narration; as, for example—"I have given unto them the words which Thou gavest Me" (John 17.8; "We speak not in words which man's wisdom teacheth, but which the Holy Ghost teacheth" (1 Cor. 11.13); "Write: for these words are true and faithful" (Rev. 21.5). But to conclude from passages such as these that the inspiration of the Spirit is conveyed in words rather than in thought and feeling would be to press unduly the language of Scripture.'

Further on the writer says:—

> 'A prophet receives the inspiration of the Almighty with pain and distress; in confused and tumbling words he gives it utterance. Yet those stammering accents have upon them the seal of God.'

Why God should set His seal on stammering, tumbling, confused words I cannot conceive. Such a statement is subversive of all real belief that the prophets have delivered to us the 'words which the Holy Ghost teacheth.'

I want to speak to you then on the important truth that 'all Scripture is given by inspiration of God'; and I shall, in the first place, speak briefly and simply of the precise meaning of the term 'Verbal Inspiration.'

When we are told that there is in a certain newspaper a verbatim report of a statesman's speech, we all know what it means. What do we look for? We look for the exact words that were spoken. A report that does not give the exact words spoken is not a verbatim report.'Verbatim' is a Latin adverb, and we very commonly use the word verbally in precisely the same sense. Thus verbal inspiration means inspiration given by God to man in definite words; and the word 'inspiration' denotes that action of the Spirit of God on the heart, the mind, the soul of his servants by which He communicated to them the message He would have them deliver. My method of dealing further with this subject will be this: I shall show from Holy Scripture—

1. That the law was given by verbal inspiration as I have defined it.
2. That prophecy was given by verbal inspiration as I have defined it.
3. That the Gospel of God was given by verbal inspiration as I have defined it.

If that be the case, how dare we lay aside this term? And how can we say that it is not biblical when we remember that the first syllable of 'verbal' simply means 'word,' as in the term 'verbatim'? In present-day English 'verb' denotes a certain part of speech; but its original sense is 'word'; and hence a verbally inspired message is a message which the inspirer has given in his own words. He does not give men feelings and ideas and then leave them to stammer out his message in their own confused words; that was not God's way of giving to us the 'living oracles' which were committed to the Jews of old and delivered to us through Christ and His apostles.

I have now to prove from Scripture that the law was given by verbal inspiration, that is, in words which were spoken or given by the Spirit of God. For this purpose, let us turn to the seventh chapter of the Book of Numbers. In the last verse of this long chapter, which tells us of the dedication of the brazen altar, we read: 'And when Moses was gone into the tabernacle of the congregation to speak with Him, then he heard the voice of One speaking unto him from off the mercy seat that was upon the ark of testimony, from between the two cherubim: and He spake unto him.' That was not only verbal, but vocal. Moses heard the voice of One speaking to him from off the mercy seat. Whose voice was it? Who fills the mercy seat? How can we doubt that God Himself spoke with audible voice to Moses? And this is exactly in keeping with the fact, the wondrous fact, that when Israel stood at the foot of the mountain from which the law was given, the mountain which burned with fire unto the midst of heaven, the Lord spake unto them out of the midst of the fire, and declared unto them the covenant which He commanded them to observe, even the ten commandments. If that was not verbal, I do not know what is. And as we read in Deuteronomy, Moses afterwards reminded the people that the Lord had spoken to them out of the midst of the fire. 'Only take heed to thyself,' said he, 'and keep thy soul diligently, lest thou forget the things that thine eyes have seen; specially the day that thou stoodest before the Lord thy God in Horeb, when the Lord said unto me, Gather me the people together, and I will make them hear My words . . . . And the Lord spake unto you out of the midst of the fire: ye heard the voice of the words, but saw no similitude; only ye heard a voice' (Deut. 4.9-12). It is monstrous, yes, monstrous, in the face of such a testimony, to say that the law of God was not given by verbal inspiration; it was at times more than verbal; it was vocal. God spake in a voice of thunder, and was heard by the whole nation of Israel: 'I am Jehovah thy God; thou shalt have no other gods before Me,' and so on. If we admit that God gave Moses certain thoughts, and then told him to write out a law for the people, where do we stand? The law was given by verbal, and, as I have said, more than verbal inspiration. It was not that God just impressed certain words on the mind of Moses: He spake those words with a voice from heaven, and from the midst of the fire, the smoke, the clouds, the darkness.

Now I ask you people, acquainted with English as your mother tongue, what reason have we for laying aside the term 'Verbal Inspiration'? It is admirably fitted to express and to define both the thought and the reality of the thing. I will not dwell further on that, though it would be easy to do so; for the Lord spake face to face with Moses repeatedly, and Moses often heard His voice. But let us come to the question of prophecy.

Prophecy was given to the prophets, and through the prophets, by the spoken words of the eternal God. I will take one illustration, which from time to time has powerfully struck my own mind. Hannah prayed for a son. God gave her a son, and when she had weaned the child she took him to Eli, at Shiloh, and left him there to serve the Lord in His Tabernacle. One evening Eli and Samuel had both laid them down to rest.

'Hushed was the evening hymn;
  The temple courts were dark;
The lamp was burning dim
  Before the sacred ark;
When suddenly a voice divine
Rang through the silence of the shrine.'

Samuel did not know whose voice it was. He had never heard it before: for we are told that 'Samuel did not yet know the Lord, neither was the word of the Lord yet revealed to him.' But so real—or, if I may use a philosophical expression, such an objective reality—was that voice, that Samuel three times mistook it for the well-known voice of Eli. 'Thou calledst me,' he said to Eli. 'I called not,' was the answer; 'lie down again.' Again God called, and the child said to Eli, 'Here am I, for thou didst call me.' 'I called not, my son; lie down again.' Then came the voice yet again. 'Thou didst call me,' said the child. And at length Eli perceived that the Lord had called him. A fourth time the Lord called, 'Samuel, Samuel.' And thus began the ministry of one of the earliest and greatest of the Prophets of God. Was not that verbal, vocal? What mean the men that question verbal inspiration and profess to be servants of Jesus Christ and preachers of His Gospel? Thus it was in the beginning, and thus it was all along the line of the Prophets. 'Yea, and all the prophets from Samuel and those that follow after, as many as have spoken,' have likewise received from God the very words which they were to speak. Sometimes, it is true, the Lord may have moved one of His servants to write certain words without actually speaking to him by a voice, but the words thus written were always the words of God. God pleased Himself as to the precise method in which He conveyed His inspiration; but the point I want to bring before you, and before all to whom this message shall come, is that God undoubtedly did often communicate his mind in an audible voice. Moses heard that awful holy voice, and happily for him it came from the mercy seat. Samuel heard it, and the first communication granted to him consisted of only one word: 'Samuel.' How could that be other than verbal? We could not have more conclusive proof that the words of God were definitely given to His servants that they might be definitely handed on to others. The oracles of God were always given to the prophets by verbal inspiration; and even where it was not vocal we may be sure that they were the very words of God. God led the men to use these words. Inspiration was the gift of divine words to divinely chosen men.

I have a few more words to say about the Prophets. I know not precisely how often they use the words, 'Thus saith the Lord.' But it has been well said that 'The Bible uniformly teaches the doctrine of verbal inspiration. It never in a single instance says that the thoughts of the writers were inspired, or that these writers had a "concept." The Scriptures are called "The Oracles of God" (Rom. 3.2); "The Word of God" (Luke 8.11); "The Word of the Lord" (Acts 13.48); "The Word of Life" (Phil. 2.16); "The Word of Christ" (Col. 3.16); "The Word of Truth" (Eph. 1.13); "The Word of Faith" (Rom. 10.8); and by these and similar statements they declare, *more than two thousand times,* that the words are God-breathed, are inspired.'

We know indeed that God could cause men's minds to be filled with the words He intended them to speak without addressing an audible voice to them; but we also know that in certain cases he did use an audible voice, and therefore we are certainly justified in affirming that the Oracles of God were given to us by verbal inspiration. Look at dying David, and listen to his testimony: 'The Spirit of the Lord spake by me and His word was in my tongue': (2 Sam. 23.2) His word, not my word. It is most dangerous to depart from this truth. We need to stand firm for it. Now let us come to the Gospel.

The text in which we shall find a proof and an illustration of the blessed fact that the Gospel of the grace of God was given in God's own words, by God's own voice from heaven, is Matt. 3.17: 'And lo, a voice from heaven, saying, This is my beloved Son, in whom I am well pleased.' What word is there here that God did not speak? 'This is,' saith God; 'My,' saith the Father; 'beloved,' saith the Father; 'Son,' saith the Father. Why shrink ye from calling that verbal inspiration? And was not the occasion worthy of it? If God would send His own beloved Son into this world to save His enemy—man, was it not fit that He should talk about it from heaven? And He did: 'This is my beloved Son, in whom I am well pleased.'

Again, go with me to the holy mount, where Christ met with Moses and Elijah. There the same voice tells the same truth in the same words with an addition, and a sweet addition too. We read, 'While he yet spake, behold, a bright cloud overshadowed them: and behold a voice out of the cloud, which said, This is my beloved Son, in whom I am well pleased; hear ye Him.' Now if the voice of the Father spake that truth then, did not the voice of the Father speak it by the mouth of Isaiah? 'Behold my servant, whom I uphold; mine elect, in whom my soul delighteth; I have put my Spirit upon him: he shall bring forth judgment to the Gentiles.' (Isa. 42.1). Who dares to say that those syllables of Isaiah were not syllables uttered by the mouth of Almighty God? I care not to prove, I could not prove, that Isaiah heard a voice with the outward ear; but knowing that his mind was moved by the Spirit of God to utter those precious words, I contend that he received his message by verbal inspiration. Our eternal salvation hangs on this. Once let slip this fact that God gave His own words to His Prophets and Apostles, and where are we drifting to? I tell you, it grieved me to the heart to see these things in a magazine of evangelical stamp. I have been informed that those who manage the magazine have no intention, no desire to give up the precious truth that the Bible from cover to cover is the inspired Word of God, which we may trust everywhere as a revelation of divine truth; and that their intent is merely to lay aside the term 'verbal inspiration' because some Christians cannot see their way to use it, and consider that it 'implies a theory of the mode of inspiration' which cannot be fully sustained: but my contention is that it accurately sets forth a truth revealed in the Bible itself, and is an 'ancient landmark' that must not be 'removed.' To let it go is the first, and in some cases the second, step to giving up the truth for which it stands. In the present day it is needful to retain terms hitherto used in the expression of sound doctrine.

Many British theologians and teachers have for a long time been trying to Christianise terms invented by godless German scholars; and I will now digress to tell you how this has come about.

Some years ago a German writer, Julius Wellhausen, who openly denied the inspiration of the Bible, and rejected the very idea of a divine revelation, wrote a book called the *History of Israel,* wherein he manufactured a fresh history instead of that which we have in the Book of God. This work remained in its native German, and was therefore unknown to most English readers until a certain Scotch Professor of Divinity, Robertson Smith, afterwards Librarian in the University Library at Cambridge, where I have seen him in my younger days, translated it into English, and so introduced to this country Wellhausen's infidel theories. These were embraced by many professedly orthodox preachers in Scotland and England, who nevertheless claimed to hold fast the doctrines of Christianity. When news of this reached Wellhausen, he said: 'I knew the Bible was a fraud; but I never dreamed of making God Almighty a partner to the fraud, as these men do.' What a rebuke for British Doctors of Divinity from the mouth of a German infidel!

I do not accuse the Editor of the magazine from which I have quoted of consenting to the teaching of an ungodly man like Wellhausen; but I am sure that the spreading influence of German unbelief is affecting the minds of many who have hitherto stood firm for the great truths of the Gospel.

Many years ago Bishop Waterland, a learned divine in the Established Church, wrote a treatise on the Athanasian Creed, when men began to talk about doing away with it. In that treatise he wittily and wisely said: 'So long as there are Arians in England (that is, those that deny the Godhead of Christ), we shall want the Athanasian Creed; and when there are no Arians among us, nobody will want to get rid of it.' In like manner we may now say, while there are men among us who are undermining the authority of God's Word, we shall want the term Verbal Inspiration, and when there are none such, nobody will want to part with it.

There is another instance of God's use of audible words of which I wish to remind you. Our Lord Jesus, shortly before He suffered, went up to Jerusalem to keep the Passover, and entered the city in triumph amid shouts of Hosanna. On that occasion, as He stood among the multitude, He prayed aloud, 'Father, glorify Thy name.' And we read, 'Then came there a voice from heaven, saying, I have both glorified it and will glorify it again.' Were those words imparted secretly to the mind of Jesus Christ? Not so, the people heard them, and some said, 'It thundered'; others said, 'An angel spake to Him'; but He said, 'This voice came not because of Me, but for your sakes.' How can we banish the thought, the fact, of verbal inspiration after such things as that, and why should we? It is a valuable term, and it may encourage and confirm us in our belief in Holy Scripture, and help us to realize the infinite importance of the daily and prayerful reading thereof. Whenever you open this Holy Book to read therein, remember that you are about to read the words of your Creator, your Judge, your Father, your Redeemer, your Sanctifier.

I have spoken very plainly because of the vast importance of the subject under consideration. If by pleasing God I offend man, I do not mind whom I offend. Even if my words inflict a wound, please remember that it is written, 'Faithful are the wounds of a friend; but the kisses of an enemy are deceitful.'

I conclude with two quotations which express my mind so beautifully and forcibly that I feel I cannot do better than read them to you. The first is this:—

> 'Let this, then, be our attitude, to tell it out to the wide world that the blessed Bible, the "Holy Scriptures" of both Testaments, are the product of the "Breath of God," who made heaven and earth, and "breathed" into man his soul; the product of that divine "Breath" that regenerates, illuminates and sanctifies the soul; that they are "God-breathed Scriptures," whose "words" are the "words of God." Tell it to the Church in her seminaries, universities and colleges, from her pulpits, and in her Sunday Schools and Bible Classes; and sound it in every convention, conference

and assembly, that our conception and estimate of the Scriptures must be no lower and no less than were the high conception and estimate of our Lord and His Apostles; that what they regarded as the "Breath of God," we must so regard in opposition to every breath of man that dares to breathe otherwise. Say, with the immortal Athanasius, who knew how to read Greek better than the scholars of our own times: "O, my child, not only the ancient, but the new Scriptures are God-breathed, as Paul saith, Every Scripture is God-breathed." Say to the rising ministry, "Speak as the Oracles of God speak," the words that "God hath spoken," the words that Christ has sealed. Be at least as decent as Balaam, who said, "I cannot go beyond the commandment of the Lord, to do either good or bad of mine own mind; but what the Lord saith, that will I speak." Tell every reader and hearer of the word, that what Moses saith and David saith, and Isaiah, Peter, Paul, John, and the Scripture saith, is what "God saith." Tell it to the dying saint, when his last pulse quivers at the wrist, and friends are weeping by his bed, and Science has exhausted in vain all her poor resources, that God, who breathed the Scriptures, cannot lie; that Jesus is a Rock, and that the "firm foundation" laid in the word for faith can never disappoint our trust. To every question of exposition or of criticism, return the answer, "What saith the Scripture?" "How readest thou?" "It is written!" And cease to deride the most sacred, age-established, and time-honoured tradition that the Apostolic Church has left us. With this attitude such days will revisit the Church as were in the beginning; and God, honoured in His word, will no longer restrain the Spirit, but open the windows of heaven, and pour upon His Church a blessing so great that there will not be room to receive it. God hasten the day!"*

My second quotation is from the Second Epistle of Peter: 'For we have not followed cunningly devised fables, when we made known unto you the power and coming of our Lord Jesus Christ, but were eye-witnesses of His majesty. For He received from God the Father honour and glory, when there came such a voice to Him from the excellent glory, This is My beloved Son, in Whom I am well pleased. And this voice which came from heaven we heard, when we were with Him in the holy mount.'

When we trust the words of God we have something to build upon: for heaven and earth shall pass away, but His words shall not pass away.

Ah, my dear friends, think of this matter! It is profitable for your present instruction, and it concerns your eternal salvation. He that believeth the Scriptures with a heart which God has broken and which God is teaching is wise unto salvation; and how can you, why need you, be wiser than that? God give you that wisdom if you lack it, and give you more of it if you have it, and grant me the same favour, for His name's sake. Amen.

* Quoted from 'The Fundamentals' (Vol. 7), published in U. S. A.

Say, Christian, wouldst thou thrive
  In knowledge of thy Lord?
Against no Scripture ever strive,
  But tremble at His Word.

Revere the sacred page;
  To injure any part
Betrays, with blind and feeble rage,
  A hard and haughty heart.

If aught there dark appear,
  Bewail thy want of sight;
No imperfection can be there,
  For all God's words are right.

The Scriptures and the Lord
  Bear one tremendous name;
The written and the incarnate Word
  In all things are the same.

(Joseph Hart)

The Unity of the Bible a Proof of its Inspiration

By R. Wright Hay

Will you try to imagine yourselves opening the Bible for the first time, knowing nothing about the Lord Jesus Christ? Perhaps I ought to put it: Will you try to imagine yourselves in the place of someone opening the Bible for the first time, knowing nothing about the Lord Jesus Christ? Try to imagine such an one opening the Bible at the beginning of the New Testament. The first sentence of the New Testament begins thus: 'The book of the generation of Jesus Christ.' Now we are so constituted as that the one who for the first time reads these words, not knowing about Jesus Christ, if he is reading thoughtfully, is bound to ask a question: 'What kind of a person is this?' There is nothing in the language to relate Jesus Christ to the past. The one who is reading these words for the first time, and only beginning to learn about the Lord Jesus Christ, if he were reading thoughtfully, would relate Him to the present and ask, 'What kind of a person is this?'

Now something must happen before any one of us can begin to get to know what kind of a person another is. That person must speak; either by lip or by sign the person must utter himself, otherwise one cannot begin to get to know what kind of person he is. And I ask you to note this. The first reader of the New Testament, engaged by the question raised by the first half of the first sentence of the first chapter of the first Gospel, as he goes on reading this Gospel, encounters the fullest record of the speech of the Lord Jesus Christ on earth that we have in any single book of the New Testament. And we may take as the keynote of the first Gospel, in this view of it—because it is possible to look at the Gospel from various points of view—the word in chap. 5. 2: 'He opened His mouth.' And you begin to get the answer to your question, 'What kind of a person is Jesus Christ?' by noting what He is recorded in the first Gospel to have said. And when the one who is beginning to learn about Jesus Christ from the New Testament has concluded his careful reading of the first of the four Gospels he has travelled a very long way in the direction of the answer which the Bible contains to the question, 'What kind of a person is He?'

But then we have a proverb, 'Actions speak louder than words'; and it is needful to note what a person does as well as what a person says if we would know what kind of a person he is. And it is a very impressive fact that the moment one who is reading the New Testament for the first time passes out of the copious record of the speech of the Lord in Matthew, he comes into the much briefer, but singularly vivid, record of His deeds in the Gospel according to Mark. And we may safely take as the key word of the Gospel according to Mark, in this view of it, the words of testimony that are recorded in chap. 7. 37: 'He hath done all things well.' And when the one who is reading the New Testament for the first time, and beginning to learn about the Lord Jesus Christ, has added to his reading of Matthew the reading of Mark, he has almost reached the conclusive answer to the question, 'What kind of a person is Jesus Christ?'—almost, but not quite.

There is something about every one of us, even those of the least impressive personality, that counts for quite as much as speech and conduct in the revelation of character. You probably have known people who had not very much to say, and who could not do very much, who nevertheless exercised a great influence. I can recall an elderly invalid lady of my student days, who kept open house for students, that she might do them spiritual good—a woman of few words, and, as an invalid, confined to her couch, not able to do much. But from that couch there streamed out an influence over the University, the impress of which is upon scores of men to this day—this poor man who is addressing you included. And it is a very impressive fact that when the first reader of the New Testament, in quest of instruction as to what manner of person Jesus Christ is, has passed through the record of His speech by Matthew and the record of His doings by Mark, he comes immediately into the Gospel according to Luke, which is distinguished by this—it shows us the influence that the Lord Jesus Christ exercised over different types of people. And the key word of the third Gospel, in this view of it, may be found in chap. 6. 19, 'There went virtue out of Him.' And when His words have been studied, and His deeds, and His influence, the first reader *knows* what kind of a person Jesus Christ is. He does not jot down data and draw inferences; but he knows without a shadow of question what kind of a person Jesus Christ is.

And by this time—and, indeed, long before this point—another question has become insistent in the mind of the thoughtful reader for the first time, and that question is, 'Who is He?' because it is possible to know what kind of a person a person is, and not fully to know who he is. But the one who has become acquainted with the quality of the person of Jesus Christ wants, with an intensity of desire that cannot be surpassed in regard to any other subject, to know without a shadow of doubt who He is. And surely it is impressive and instructive to note that the moment the reader learning about Jesus Christ passes into the fourth Gospel, he receives on the very threshold of it a categorical answer to the question, 'Who is He?', for there we read, 'In the beginning was the Word, and the Word was with God, and the Word was God . . . . And the Word was made flesh, and dwelt among us (and we beheld His glory, the glory as of the only begotten of the Father), full of grace and truth.'

And as the reader and inquirer pursues his way through the fourth Gospel, remembering what he learned from the speech of Jesus Christ recorded by Matthew, he comes upon this in John 7. 46: 'Never man spake like this man.' And pursuing his way through the Gospel further, remembering what he learned about Jesus Christ from the study of His deeds recorded by Mark, he comes upon John 15. 24: 'I did the works which none other man did.' And already, in this fourth Gospel, remembering what was learned about the influence of Jesus Christ from the Gospel according to Luke, he has encountered these words in John 12. 32: 'I, if I be lifted up from the earth, will draw'—that is, influence, 'will draw all unto Me.' And accordingly in the fourth Gospel, which opens with the categorical declaration of the Godhead of the Man Christ Jesus, we have His speech, His conduct, His influence, declared to be absolutely unique.

Is there no suggestion here of the organic unity of the four Gospels? Is it not impressively clear that we have only one Gospel in four parts? The four Books hold together as a flower holds together: they are an organic unity. A watch is a unity, but it is a mechanical unity; it consists of different parts making one thing, but put together from without. A flower, as I have just suggested, is an organic unity. It is made up of different parts, but it is put together from within. A little child can pick an exquisitely beautiful flower to pieces in a moment, and then not all the scientists in the world can ever put it together again. It is an expression of life, put together from within. And one cannot study these four Gospels along the line of meditation that we are now in a simple way pursuing, without becoming impressed by the fact that the four Gospels are an organic unity, a record put together, not by collusion between man and man, but put together from within—the mind of God expressing itself in the record so that the revelation of the Lord Jesus Christ may be given by the Holy Ghost to man.

Then before the enquirer concludes the reading of this fourth section of the one Gospel he receives the answer to another question, which one would think must many times have presented itself to his mind, as he has sought the answer to the first question and the answer to the second—the question: 'Why such a record of such a Person?' The answer is given in John 20. 31: 'These (things) are written that ye might believe that Jesus is the Christ, the Son of God, and that, believing, ye might have life through His name.' You remember His words: 'I am come that they might have life.' Again and again I have been used by the Spirit of God to draw the attention of eager Mohammedans, Hindus and Brahmos to the Person of the Lord Jesus Christ by saying to them: 'You young men are so religious as that you could put to shame many of my fellow countrymen, but I want to tell you this—the Lord Jesus Christ, as far as we have His words recorded, never once used the word religion; He never claimed to be the founder of a religion. But He did say, "I am come THAT MEN MIGHT HAVE LIFE." ' This distinguishes Him from all the so-called religious leaders of men. And I cannot but pause for a moment to act the part of an evangelist and say this: Christ died for the ungodly, that the ungodly, believing in Him, might be forgiven and live. Have we received God's free gift of eternal life in Jesus Christ His Son? If there is one here who has not yet done that, then I beg that one by the grace of God to do it now. As many as receive Him, to them gives He the power, the right, the privilege, to become the children of God.

But you have noticed that the imagined first reader of the Bible has only got half way through the first sentence of the New Testament. We must note how that sentence concludes. After the mention of the ineffable name 'Jesus Christ,' we read: 'the Son of David, the son of Abraham.' We are so constituted as that anyone for the first time reading these words must wish to know what is to be known about David and about Abraham. And in order to get this knowledge the reader must go back to the Old Testament. There is an organic connection between the first sentence of the New Testament and the earlier Scriptures. It meets us there, on the very surface. We cannot fully understand the first sentence of the New Testament without making ourselves acquainted with the content of the Old Testament. Recognising this link, and the significance of it in relation to our subject, let me briefly present to you some of the evidence of the unity of the Old Testament.

If I were to ask any one of you—I think I may venture to say—to which Book of the Old Testament would you go if you wished to read a chapter which looks as though it belonged to the New Testament, I am sure I would get at once the answer, The Book of the prophet Isaiah. The prophecy in Isaiah 53 is couched largely in the language of history: 'He was wounded for our transgressions, He was bruised for our iniquities: the chastisement of our peace was upon Him, and with His stripes we are healed.' We think of that chapter as belonging to the New Testament—and it really does. But what I particularly want you to notice with me now is this—and let me at this point say there is one sense in which I believe we Christians ought to read the Bible as we would read any other book; only one sense! There are many senses in which we cannot read the Bible as we would read any other book, but there is one sense in which I feel sure we ought to, and it is this: we ought to read the Bible from beginning to end. We ought to be always reading the Bible as an entity, working our way from the first verse of Genesis to the last verse of the Book of the Revelation. And if we treat the Book of the prophet Isaiah on this principle, not confining our attention to that wonderful 53rd chapter because it is so full of precious, saving truth, we will find something very significant in the opening verse of the Book. The first verse of the Book of the prophet Isaiah reads: 'The vision of Isaiah the son of Amoz, which he saw concerning Judah and Jerusalem in the days of Uzziah, Jotham, Ahaz, and Hezekiah, kings of Judah.' Anyone reading that verse for the first time—reading it thoughtfully—whatever else he might not be moved to desire to know, would certainly ask the question, 'What about Uzziah, Jotham, Ahaz, and Hezekiah kings of Judah?' And in order to reach the knowledge that he is in quest of he would have to read the Books of Kings and Chronicles. There is an organic connection between the Books of Kings and Chronicles and this evangelical Book of the prophet Isaiah. You cannot fully understand the first sentence of Isaiah without making yourself acquainted with the Books of Kings and Chronicles. Just recognize the significance of this single fact in connection with this subject of the unity of the Bible.

If I were to ask any Bible student to which of the earliest Books of the Bible must we go if we would find the fullest presentation of Christ in type anywhere to be found in the Scriptures, I know the answer would immediately be, 'The Book of Leviticus.' And it is so. One cannot understand the state of heart and mind of the critics who to-day discount the Book of Leviticus as having very little, if any, devotional value. There is no Book in the Bible that more frequently claims to consist of the direct speech of God than the Book of Leviticus. I would like you young people to test the accuracy of that statement by searching the Bible. You will find it to be true. The Book of Leviticus, more frequently than any other Book in the Bible, claims to consist of the direct speech of God; and when you study that Book you find Christ typically presented, so that those of us who know Him by the Holy Spirit's teaching through the New Testament get to know Him better through the study of Leviticus.

But how does the Book of Leviticus open? and I ask you to remember we found our way to this Book from the New Testament because of the wonderfully full presentation of Christ in it in type. Having come to it in quest of Christ, we note how the Book opens. 'The Lord called unto Moses and spake unto him out of the tabernacle of the congregation.' Anyone reading these words for the first time, reading them thoughtfully, would be impelled to ask, 'Who was Moses?' and 'What was the tabernacle of the congregation?' And in order to get the answer to these two questions the reader has to move back into the Book of Exodus. There he learns about Moses. There he learns about the tabernacle of the congregation. But how does the Book of Exodus open? We have seen the organic connection between Exodus and Leviticus, and Exodus opens with these words: 'These are the names of the children of Israel which came into Egypt.' Anyone reading these words for the first time, reading thoughtfully, would be impelled to ask, 'Who was Israel?' and he might also be curious to know, What about his children coming into Egypt? And it is necessary to go back to Genesis in order to get the information desired—an organic connection between Genesis and Exodus. And when one opens the Bible at its first verse he is at a point beyond which the mind cannot travel: 'In the beginning God . . . . ' No room for any earlier Book than Genesis! On the very first sentence of Genesis there is the stamp of unchallengeable evidence that it is the beginning of the oracles of God. No room for an earlier thing than that which took place in the beginning. So that upon the very surface of the Bible, as we are privileged to look at it together, there is abundant proof of its organic unity.

Now I ask you to note with me one very impressive link between the Old Testament and the New. The central Book of the Pentateuch is Leviticus; the central chapter of the Book of Leviticus is chapter 14. That chapter contains a word which, each time the reader meets it, obliges him to ask a question. It occurs first in verse 4. There we read: 'Then shall the priest command to take for him that is to be cleansed two birds, alive and clean, and cedar wood, and scarlet, and hyssop.' Now, the first-time reader of that verse might ask several questions. If he is reading thoughtfully, he *must* ask one: 'Scarlet'—'Scarlet what?' Scarlet is a colour. We cannot think of a colour apart from something to which the colour attaches; and we are so constituted as that the thoughtful reader, coming upon that word 'scarlet' for the first time, must ask, 'Scarlet what?' And five times in this chapter that question is raised.

Now I want to make a statement behind which there lies the experience of many years of close study of the Word of God; and it is this: Every question which the Bible *inevitably* raises, the Bible answers. I can remember the time when I began to search the Bible for the answer to the question, 'Scarlet what?' five times raised in that one chapter. And it was a revelation to me to discover that the answer is not given in the Old Testament. You have to travel into the New Testament to get the answer to that insistent question. And there is only one passage in the New Testament where the answer is found. The answer to this question, raised five times in the central chapter of the central book of the Pentateuch is found in Heb. 9. 19, where we read: 'When Moses had spoken every precept to all the people concerning the law, he took the blood of calves and of goats, with water, and scarlet wool, and hyssop . . .' 'Scarlet wool!' the only place in the Bible where the question raised in Leviticus five times in that central chapter, is answered—an organic connection between the Old Testament and the New, an organic connection between Leviticus and Hebrews, an impressive proof of the unity of the Bible. And the moment we come upon that word 'wool' the mind is carried back to the evangelical chapter in Isaiah, and especially to the words, 'He was led as a lamb to the slaughter; and as a sheep before her shearers'—that is where the "wool" comes in—'as a sheep before her shearers is dumb, so opened He not His mouth.' And our mind is carried back to the beginning of the Gospel according to John, in which the Godhead of the Man Christ Jesus is explicitly declared and we recall the words of one described by God's Son as 'more than a prophet,' when He said: 'Behold the Lamb of God, which taketh away the sin of the world.' Also we remember that in the Book of the Revelation the 'Lamb as it had been slain' is seen 'in the midst of the throne' alive for evermore. And this impressive illustration of the organic unity of the two parts of the Bible, the Old and New Testaments, is sanctified by the Holy Ghost to the concentration of thought not only on the personality of the God Man, but also on the fact of His substitutionary, expiatory sufferings and death for sinners. And we begin to realize how true it is, that these Scriptures in their entirety, Old Testament as well as New, are able to make us wise unto salvation, through faith which is in Christ Jesus.

But now, in a few concluding sentences, let me ask you to note what we have come to, in having been obliged to travel from Leviticus to Hebrews for the answer to a specific question. What have we come to? Before we note the answer to that question, I would recall to your minds our Lord's manner of speaking of the Old Testament after His Resurrection. We have His words in Luke 24. 44: 'These are the words which I spake unto you while I was yet with you, that all things must be fulfilled which were written in the Law of Moses and in the Prophets and in the Psalms concerning Me.' The Law of Moses—the Prophets—the Psalms—the three divisions of the Old Testament: the three divisions recognized by the Jews to this day; the three divisions of the Old Testament, consisting of just the Books that we have, not one more or one less. Even the Higher Critics allow that to be true. With the Old Testament (which, by God's grace, we have in our own tongue) before Him, the Lord Jesus spoke of three divisions—the Law of Moses, the Prophets, and the Psalms.

Bearing that in mind, let us note in the Epistle to the Hebrews what is said in regard to each of these three divisions of the Old Testament. We have come to chapter 9 of the Epistle for the only answer which the Bible gives to that question raised by the 14th chapter of Leviticus, and in this chapter, in which we have found that answer, we read in verses 6 and 7: 'When these things were thus ordained, the priests went always into the first tabernacle, accomplishing the service of God. But into the second went the high priest alone once every year, not without blood, which he offered for himself and for the errors of the people.' The reference here is to the Law of Moses, but notice what immediately follows: 'The Holy Ghost this signifying, that the way into the holiest of all was not yet made manifest.' The passage refers to the Law of Moses (to Exodus and Leviticus), but the authorship of it is attributed to the Holy Ghost, for we are not told what Moses meant, but what the Holy Ghost meant—profoundly significant in connection with our subject, the unity of the Bible a proof of its inspiration. Here we are down at the deepest root of the fact of the unity of the Bible, ITS DIVINE AUTHORSHIP. The Holy Ghost is declared to be the author of the Law of Moses, the first section of the Old Testament.

In the immediately succeeding chapter—Heb. 10. 16,17—we read: 'This is the covenant that I will make with them after these days, saith the Lord, I will put My laws into their hearts, and in their minds will I write them; And their sins and iniquities will I remember no more.' The quotation is from the second division of the Old Testament, 'the Prophets,' specifically from the Book of the prophet Jeremiah; but the speaker is declared to be the Holy Ghost, for we read in verse 15: 'The Holy Ghost is a witness to us, for after that HE had said before,' and then the words are quoted which we find in the Book of the prophet Jeremiah. These words are the speech of God the Holy Ghost. The authorship of the second division of the Old Testament is here attributed to the Holy Ghost.

And earlier in this Epistle—Heb. 3. 7—we have the third division of the Old Testament, 'the Psalms,' referred to in the words, 'The Holy Ghost saith, To-day if ye will hear His voice, Harden not your hearts'—the words of the Psalmist attributed to the Holy Ghost. You note the significance of the fact, that in this part of the New Testament, to which we are obliged to come to receive the answer—and the only answer to be found in the Bible—to the question raised in the Book of Leviticus, we come upon this disclosure to us of the authorship of the Old Testament: it is declared to be the word of the Holy Ghost. And then let me ask you to note the functions of authorship that are here attributed to the Holy Spirit. Here, in chapter 3, the Holy Ghost 'saith'; in chapter 9 the Holy Ghost 'signifies,' in chapter 10 the Holy Ghost 'is a Witness to us'—the Bible the speech of the Holy Ghost, the Bible containing the mind of the Holy Ghost who has a meaning in every part of it; and the Holy Ghost a witness to the individual believer as to what His meaning is.

You are reading a book by a favourite human author, and you come upon a passage in it which you cannot fully understand. How glad you would be if you could go to the author, and take his book and point to the specific passage, saying to him, 'Please tell me exactly what you mean there.' There are very few human authors in relation to whom any of us enjoy such a privilege. But the Author of this Book is accessible in His grace to every one of us; and not only may we come to Him and ask Him to witness to our spirit as to what this and that word means—we *must* do so if we would understand that which is written. Needless to say, what is true of the Old Testament is true also of the New Testament. Our Lord Himself teaches us that what is written is SPOKEN BY THE SPIRIT—'He that hath an ear let him hear what the Spirit is saying unto the churches' (Rev.2. 7,11,17,29; 3. 6,13,22).

Let us cleave to the Scriptures as attested by Christ that we may cleave to the Christ to whom the Scriptures testify.

The Authority of the Bible

By A. H. Finn

What is 'the Bible'? There is, first, a collection of ancient works by Jewish writers on a variety of subjects—historical, poetic, philosophic—by a variety of authors in various different ages, written in Hebrew and Chaldea. To these have been added a collection of memoirs and letters, most of these also by Jewish writers, but in Greek. How comes it that any idea of Authority could be attached to such a collection? We should not dream of putting together the works of a number of classical writers—say Homer, Thucydides, Herodotus, Plato, Aristotle, Virgil, Tacitus, Livy, Cicero, and Marcus Aurelius—and claiming any authority for such a medley as that. Why then should we do so for the collection we call 'the Bible?'

The only possible answer is that there is an essential difference of nature between the Scriptural writings and those of the classical authors. The classical works, however brilliant and profound, have never claimed to be and have never been considered as anything but human. The Scriptures from the first have claimed to be and adown the ages have been accepted as God's messages conveying the mind of God to mankind, God's Word, not man's. If that claim is justified and that acceptance not illusory, then that collection of writings must have an authority which cannot possibly attach to any merely human literature.

That claim to Divine authority has been disputed by numberless opponents from the first rise of Christianity down to the present time. Nowadays, however, it is assailed, not by unbelievers, but by many who claim to be Christians and even Christian clergy, and that in two quite distinct directions, the critical and the ecclesiastical.

(1) *The Critical.*—With infinite pains and a well-nigh microscopical examination of words, phrases, and other literary features, modern critics have by slow degrees built up a theory which, if true, would seriously affect our estimate of the Old Testament. They claim to have shown that much which has been believed to be exceedingly ancient is in reality of comparatively recent origin. Hence what appears to be contemporary history is in fact quite unreliable. Parts are alleged to be sheer myth and legend; parts to have some small foundation in facts, but so 'idealised' as to be altogether misleading; while other parts are so compounded of contradictory accounts as to leave it uncertain which of them, if either, is actually true. Poetry as well as history, such as Jacob's blessing, the Song of Moses, the Psalms, and the later parts of Isaiah, is brought down to a much later age than it appears to belong to. Even the prophetic writings, to which for the most part critics are willing to give a good deal of credence, are considerably discounted by assertions that they are chiefly, if not entirely, to be regarded as referring to their immediate circumstances. They are stripped of all predictions of a distant future, except some which are looked on as expressing lofty hopes never to be fulfilled. Jonah is a romance or a parable, while Daniel is an amalgam of imaginary history and apocalyptic dreams.

All this resolves itself into a denial of the truth of a very large part of the Old Testament, besides a contention that, as we now have it, the contents have been so manipulated and rearranged as to convey a totally false impression. Clearly if this be established, there would be little room for attributing to it any authority at all. Who could rely on such a mixture of fact and fiction? If the Scriptures be not true, to depend on them is but to trust in a bruised reed 'on which if a man lean, it will go into his hand and pierce it.'

Fully to examine this theory and expose its many weaknesses would require a lengthy treatise, but there are one or two considerations which deserve notice. The most important is that the critics persist in treating all these works as merely human productions. Indeed they do not extend to them as much credence as is usually given to secular documents. The possibility of Divine guidance is left completely out of sight. The frequent assertions in the law that 'the Lord said unto Moses,' and those in the Prophets, 'Thus saith the Lord,' are invariably disregarded, and the instructions or predictions are estimated solely by considering whether the unaided human agent could have uttered them. Thus, the 'minute specialisation' of the sacrificial laws in Leviticus, and the 'elaborately organised civil community' legislated for in Deuteronomy are supposed to prove that both of these must be the outcome of a long process of development, and therefore belong to much later ages than the laws of Exodus 23. That hardly allows much for the foresight of even a human lawgiver and certainly takes no notice of any possibility that these could have been God's laws.

This deliberate refusal to recognise any Divine element is in reality a one-sided treatment of the evidence, judging it according to a preconceived idea that the writings are only to be considered as human productions and nothing more. It is indeed a mere begging of the main question, Is the Bible God's Word or man's?

Another important point is that the critical reasonings are often based on what are no more than arbitrary assumptions. There are, for instance, incidental notices in the earlier histories of matters implying the existence of the injunctions alleged to be of late origin. These notices are either asserted to be later interpolations of which there is no proof, or else they are said to refer to matters which were in use without any previous legislation, the laws being afterwards drawn up to codify 'pre-existing practice.' It is obvious that some such assertions have to be made if the theory that much of the Law was of post-Exilic origin is to be maintained. None the less they are mere assertions devoid of proof.

The kind of criticism which has thus been used to discredit the greater part of the Old Testament has now been extended to the New Testament as well. Here, too, much of the contents are pronounced unreliable. The narratives of the virgin Birth, of most of the miracles, and of the Resurrection and Ascension are dismissed as 'legendary,' imaginations of too enthusiastic followers eager to swell the fame of their Leader. Most of the discourses in the Fourth Gospel are rejected as not the utterances of Christ. The teachings of our Lord Himself, the Apostles, and the Book of Revelation about the 'Last Things' are dismissed almost contemptuously as mere echoes of Jewish apocalyptic dreams, and those borrowed from heathen sources. Paul's teaching about the Resurrection of the dead is affirmed to be inconsistent and unsatisfactory, and his sacramental doctrine only the pagan mysteries in disguise. His belief in the pre-existence of Christ and John's about the Eternal Word are said to be only reproductions of Rabbinic speculations about the 'Memra' or Greek philosophising about the 'Logos.' Several of the Epistles are rejected as spurious or of late origin. It is a sadly fragmentary New Testament that is left us.

As in the case of the Old Testament criticism so also in that of the New there is a marked reluctance to admit any Divine element. The Gospels are treated as simply human productions, with a large element of possible error or self-deception, as well as later accretions and editorial insertions. The Epistles are looked upon as the expression of the writer's opinions, dealing only with matters of immediate interest. The possibility that both Evangelists and Apostles were inspired or guided by the Holy Spirit is utterly ignored. That the wonderful works attributed to our Lord were possible to Him because He was the Word 'by whom all things were created' is left out of sight. Since unquestionably they were impossible for man to accomplish, it is taken for granted that they never were performed, and therefore the circumstantial accounts of them in the Gospels are no better than so much fiction. Yet if these narratives are only the imaginations of too credulous disciples, how is it that they have left untouched so large a portion of His life? The apocryphal gospels indeed relate marvels about His childhood and youth, but the canonical Gospels pass over nine-tenths of His history in almost unbroken silence. Their reticence is significant.

Just as there are arbitrary assumptions as to interpolations, glosses, editorial comments in the Old Testament criticism, so there are the like as regards the Gospels. One specimen may be sufficient. Mark, now somewhat dogmatically asserted to be the earliest Gospel, records our Lord's utterance mentioning the two miraculous feedings of the multitude. The critics set this down as an editorial insertion. Why? Not on grounds of style or MS. evidence but simply because they assume that such an incident could not have occurred more than once; therefore the two accounts must be 'duplicate narratives,' and therefore some officious editor invented the saying which our Lord could not have uttered.

There are, then, good reasons (only a few have been mentioned) for doubting the soundness of the critical theories. Certainly if they were true the authority of the Bible as a whole would be entirely gone.

(2) *The Ecclesiastical.*—The line taken in this direction is very different. It is not disputed that the Bible has some authority, but it is contended that there is a higher authority, that of the Church. It is argued that the Church determined the Canon of the Scriptures and is their Interpreter. Therefore, it is maintained that the authority of the Church must be superior to that of the Scriptures which we only receive on the Church's decision, and must understand according to the Church's interpretation.

It is no doubt true that the Christian Church was in existence before any of the New Testament books were written. It is also true that the Canon of the New Testament was not finally and formally settled till well on in the fourth century. Yet that does not mean, as a preacher recently put it, that the Church was without a Bible for 300 years. From the very first, the books of the Old Testament were 'the Scriptures' of the Apostles and the Apostolic Church. The witness of Papias and Justin Martyr shows that the Gospels were accepted as authoritative early in the second century. What may be called the 'first Christian Bible,' the ancient Syriac Version known as the Peshitto, which probably dates back to about A.D. 150, contains nearly the whole of our New Testament. So does the old Latin Version, not much later in date. The Muratorian Fragment and the quotations in Irenaeus, Tertullian, and Clement of Alexandria support this evidence, and it would be fairly safe to say that by the year A.D. 200 by far the greater part of the New Testament was accepted as Scripture.

There were, it is true, some doubts as to whether a few of the books now included, such as the 2nd Epistle of Peter, the 2nd and 3rd of John, and that of Jude, should be so received or not. There were other books, such as the Apocryphal Gospels or the Acts of Paul and Thecla (condemned by Tertullian as a forgery), which were rejected as spurious, while there were a few, like the Clementine Epistles actually found in the Alexandrine Codex, or the 'Shepherd of Hermas' and the 'Epistle of Barnabas' in the Sinaitic which for a time were deemed almost worthy of inclusion.

It is not then as if there were for a long time a large number of books which might or might not be Scripture, and that the Church in some sort of arbitrary way picked out some for acceptance and discarded the rest. Long before there was any sort of formal decision the bulk of the New Testament was received by the whole body of Christians and received as of Divine authority. The most that was ever decided by Church Councils was in regard to a few books about which there had been some hesitation. On what grounds were those decisions arrived at? Considering what books were accepted and what were rejected, there can hardly be any question that only those were accepted which were believed to be of Apostolic origin. The Councils did not of their own initiative decide 'This is Scripture, and that is not.' They were guided solely by consideration of the previous beliefs, just as the Council of Nicaea did not select from a number of philosophical theories just what they happened to approve, but ascertained what doctrines had been held from the first and embodied them in the Creed.

It is therefore misleading to assert that the Church 'selected the canonical books' and that thus 'the Church herself confers authority on the Bible.' It would be more correct to say that the Church received those books as authoritative which had Apostolic authority behind them.

What, then, of the claim that the Church is the interpreter of the Bible, and therefore, as the Church of Rome claims, has authority over it?

It has been argued that 'There is no historical justification for the idea that they (the Christian Scriptures) were specially provided by God for the edification of the *idiotes* or private man.' It might fairly be retorted that there is no greater justification for the idea that they were specially provided by God to be the property of the Church. But there is more than this.

The Old Testament Scriptures were certainly believed to be for the edification of the individual. What says the first Psalm? That man is declared blessed whose 'delight is in the Law of the Lord; and in His Law he doth meditate day and night.' So Psalm 19. 7: 'The Law of the Lord is perfect, restoring the soul: the Testimony of the Lord is sure, making wise the simple'; while Psalm 119 elaborates similar thoughts at great length. If Habakkuk was to make the vision plain in order that 'he who readeth may run' (2: 2) it is clear that it was intended to affect the conduct of individuals. Our Lord by thrice answering the Tempter with 'It is written' showed that the contents of Deuteronomy were meant to be known and acted on by each and all. When He reproved the Scribes and Pharisees for 'making the word of God of none effect through your tradition' (Mark 7: 13), not only was it in reference to a command affecting everyone, but He was condemning the interpretation put on it by the then authorities of the Jewish Church. When He reproached the two disciples on the way to Emmaus with being 'slow of heart to believe all that the prophets have spoken' (Luke 24:25), He took it for granted that the prophetic writings would be familiar to them. The Ethiopian eunuch would hardly have been studying the book of Isaiah on his journey unless he believed that it was intended for his edification. Clearest of all is Paul's introduction to Timothy when he lays it down that 'the holy Scriptures . . . are able to make thee wise unto salvation,' and adds that every God-inspired Scripture is profitable 'that the man of God may be complete, furnished completely unto every good work' (2 Tim. 3: 15-20). What does all this refer to if it be not the edification of the 'private man'? If then the Old Testament Scriptures were to be better known to, studied by, acted on by the faithful in general, can it be supposed for a moment that the Christian Scriptures, with all the wealth of our Lord's teaching and example and the heaven-inspired wisdom of the Apostles, were not equally intended for the guidance and edification of every one?

Sometimes reference is made to 2 Peter 1:20, 'No prophecy of the Scripture is of private interpretation,' as though that precluded the private man from interpreting. But the Greek word here is not the noun '*idiotes.*' It is an adjective '*idias*,' which means 'its own,' *i.e.*, special, or peculiar to itself. The next verse explains this by giving the reason that no prophecy came by the will of man: it was the over-mastering urge of the Holy Spirit which moved men of God to utter the prophecies. The true force of the passage then is, Since all prophecy is from the Holy Spirit, not from the individual prophets, every part must be consistent with all the rest, and therefore no single prophecy is to be interpreted as though it stood alone and unrelated. Its meaning must be determined by the general trend of all prophecy. Scripture must be interpreted by Scripture.

That the Church is in some sense the interpreter of the Scripture is a sort of half truth. The living body of Christians has handed down from generation to generation the Apostolic teaching as to the essentials of the Christian faith, and no individual Christian or body of Christians has any right to challenge that. Here is precisely the presumption of those who call themselves Modernists, since they claim to set aside the consensus of Christian teaching from the Apostles downwards in such vital matters as the Godhead of our Lord, and the three Persons of the Trinity in Unity, and to substitute a teaching of their own.

Yet this claim that the Christian Church has faithfully preserved the true meaning of Holy Scripture does not in the least imply that the Church has any independent authority to override the Scriptures, to affix, for instance, some new meaning to the teaching, or has any unwritten tradition differing from and equally binding with what is written. What reasons are there then for concluding that the Bible is in very deed the Word of God?

In the first place, there are the claims made by the Scriptures themselves: both Old and New Testaments profess to be Divine, not human. Those claims are corroborated by various facts about the Bible. There is the amazing character of the whole volume. Made up of a great many writings by a considerable number of authors of different classes and dispositions, living in widely separated ages and circumstances, and dealing with a great variety of subjects, it yet displays throughout a wondrous unity of design and purpose. That purpose and design, too, is a Divine one, nothing less than the working out of God's plan for the redemption of mankind and the whole creation. There is, again, the character of the teaching, so high, so pure, so confidently secure in its unfolding of Divine mysteries. There is the astounding effect it has actually produced on the minds and hearts and lives of men of all races, ranks, and conditions through many a long age. There is its career, triumphant over the bitterest opposition of foes; cavilled at and assailed by men of brilliant intellect; perverted and misrepresented sometimes by those of its own household; twice in the world's history threatened with utter destruction by the might of Syria and Rome; yet surviving through all unconquered and unconquerable. Let those who are able account for all this by any possible theory of human authorship.

Yet have we something still more secure on which to depend: 'God, Who at sundry times and in divers manners spake in time past unto the Fathers by the Prophets, hath in these last days spoken unto us by His Son.' Beyond question the Old Testament was the original Bible of the Christian Church, but it is a gross mis-statement to try to account for that by merely saying 'this the Church received with the traditional reverence of the Jews.' It was much more than that. The Church received the Old Testament as endorsed by the express testimony and approval of her Lord. He it was Who declared that He came to fulfil the Law and the Prophets; Who said, 'the Scripture cannot be broken,' and 'these are they which testify of Me.' He constantly quoted them as of authority; refuted His opponents, Sadducee or Pharisee, out of them; and uttered one of His dying words from the cross 'that the Scripture might be fulfilled,' while two more of the seven were quoted from the Psalms. The 'traditional reverence of the Jews' would have had little weight with the Gentile world: the authority of the Christ is sufficient for all.

But is not the Church also of Divine origin?

Certainly! The Lord Himself declared that He would build it upon the Rock, which is the Rock of Ages, His own Deity. It was so builded 'upon the foundation of the Apostles and Prophets, Jesus Christ Himself being the chief Corner Stone' (Eph. 2: 20). As a living Temple, 'a spiritual House' (1 Peter 2: 5), the Body and Bride of Christ, its birth-day was the descent of the Holy Spirit at Pentecost.

Yet that in no way detracts from the independent Divine authority of Scripture. Just as the Jewish race had the advantage in that 'to them were committed the oracles of God' (Rom. 3: 20), so the Christian Church has been entrusted with the honour of being the Divinely constituted 'keeper and witness' of the oracles, both Old and New. The Church and the Bible must never be looked on as rivals. They are complementary, and each bears witness of the other. Both are of God, and the only authority of either is derived from God. In its being 'God's Word written' is the one true Authority of the Bible.

The Spirit breathes upon the Word,
And brings the truth to sight;
Precepts and promises afford
A sanctifying light.

A glory gilds the sacred page,
Majestic, like the sun:
It gives a light to every age;
It gives, but borrows none.

The hand that gave it still supplies
The gracious light and heat:
Its truths upon the nations rise;
They rise, but never set.

Let everlasting thanks be Thine
For such a bright display
As makes a world of darkness shine
With beams of heavenly day.

My soul rejoices to pursue
The steps of Him I love,
Till glory breaks upon my view
In brighter worlds above.
(*William Cowper,* 1779)

The Witness of Christ to the Old Testament

By J. P. Wiles

When I received notice of the objects of this day's meetings, to promote Christian Faith in the Bible and Biblical Faith in Christ, it reminded me of a stereoscopic view, one of those views which consist of two parts that melt into one as you look at them through the proper medium, and give you a startling impression of reality and solidity: the one part was Christian Faith in the Bible, and the other was Biblical Faith in Christ. They combine in one when seen in the light of the Holy Spirit. The longer I consider the matter, the more clearly do I perceive that this is the case. Faith in the Bible and Faith in our Lord Jesus Christ are one inseparable reality, the work of God in the heart of man.

And yet when I remember that our Lord Himself said, 'To this end was I born, and for this cause came I into this world, that I should bear witness unto the truth,' I see that His personal testimony to the truth of the Scriptures is an all-important branch of the subject which now claims our attention.

Before I attempt to speak of it, let me remind you that the authority of our Lord's testimony is not only established by the dignity of His own Person, though that would be infinitely sufficient: it is confirmed by the witness of his Father. Thus the man who refuses to believe the word of Christ insults the Eternal Father; and let such a man know that he shall certainly answer for it, either with bitter repentance at the throne of grace, or with everlasting confusion before the throne of judgment.

The Father's testimony to his dear Son reaches us from heaven, spoken in His own Person as truly as were the ten commandments from the burning mountain.

It comes to us from the banks of Jordan: 'This is My beloved Son, in Whom I am well pleased.' It comes to us from the excellent glory on the holy mount: 'This is My beloved Son; hear ye Him.' It comes to us again from heaven in direct answer to Christ's own prayer, 'Father, glorify Thy name': 'I have both glorified it, and will glorify it again.' And what did that second glorification consist in? In the approaching death of the great Redeemer, the only Saviour of lost mankind; in his atoning sacrifice, which was to fill heaven with the eternal praise of His ransomed flock. The Apostle John might well say at a later date, 'He that denieth the Son denieth the Father.'

We come now to consider the witness of Jesus Christ the Son of God to the inspiration, truth, and authority of Holy Scripture, the Scripture which during His life on earth He had in His own holy hands.

The subject is so great that it is hard to know where to begin and where to end. It reminds me of the stream that issued from the mystic temple which Ezekiel saw in vision. Whatever the primary meaning of that vision may be, the river may serve us a a picture of the testimony borne by God's Word Incarnate to God's Word written. It rises at God's mercy-seat, and it flows through the wilderness of this fallen world; it transforms a sea of death into a sea of life; its waters nourish trees whose leaves are for the healing of the nations, and under whose shadow Christ's fishermen catch men in the net of the Gospel, thus filling with ransomed souls that city whose builder and maker is God.

Yes: the testimony of Jesus Christ is a thing of vital importance. It is the foundation of the present kingdom of God on earth and of the future kingdom of God in heaven. It is not such a simple matter as certain men who despise us for insisting on it seem to think. The more they despise us, the more cause we have to thank God for our position here today.

As I have said, it is difficult to know where to begin and where to end; but we will endeavour to solve that difficulty by taking our stand at three successive points on the bank of the mighty stream of Christ's testimony to the truth of His Father's word. There let us listen, and love, and worship; and as we do so, may Paul's words take possession of our hearts: 'Without controversy great is the mystery of godliness; God was manifested in the flesh, justified in the Spirit, seen of angels, preached unto the Gentiles, believed on in the world, received up in glory' (1 Tim. 3: 16).

1. Let us first go to Gethsemane, and listen to Him there. He is surrounded by His would-be murderers, and has been tortured by the unclean kiss of Judas. Peter has taken the sword in his Master's defence: but what saith Christ? 'Thinkest thou that I cannot now pray to My Father, and He

shall immediately give Me more than twelve legions of angels? BUT HOW THEN SHALL THE SCRIPTURES BE FULFILLED THAT THUS IT MUST BE?' And He passes meekly on to the scourge, the cross, the grave, in order that the Scriptures may not be broken!

2. Let us next go to meet Him on the road to Emmaus. The cross is now behind Him, and His Father's throne in front; but He has a few hours still to spare for communion with His sorrowing disciples. How does He spend these precious hours? Does He bring them the slightest hint that the instruction which He has previously given them was imperfect or needs a supplement? No! He says, 'These are the words which I said unto you while I was yet with you.' He thus identifies the words of the risen Christ with those which He spoke while He was despised and rejected of men, a Christ who had laid aside His glory without losing aught of His Godhead. And later in that same day we find him returning in the evening to Jerusalem and saying, 'Thus it is written, and thus it behoved the Christ to suffer, and to rise from the dead the third day. And ye are witnesses of these things.' And we know by the example that His apostles have set us that they bore steadfast witness, steadfast and, at times, indignant witness, to the truth of His words and against all adulteration of His Gospel. We find one of them saying, 'If any man preach any other gospel, let him be accursed.'

3. But let us go further along the banks of this stream of truth and love. Christ's testimony to His Father's word did not cease when He ascended through the clouds from Olivet. Ten days afterwards He sent down the promise of the Father, fitting the apostles to preach to all nations of the world all things that are written in the Scriptures, and nothing outside them; and He still bears witness by sending out His servants to preach His gospel and by confirming their message with signs following.

What is civilization but a by-product of missionary effort? Missionaries do not go forth to spread civilization; it would not be worth the while. They do not want civilized heathen; they want saved souls: and the Lord is always bearing witness to His word whensoever and wheresoever it is preached. Consider an historic incident, which has occurred repeatedly. A man who is ready to lay down his life in Christ's service goes to an island in the ocean where he is surrounded by savages and devoured in some cannibal orgy, but not before he has preached the gospel to them. Fifty years later another preacher follows up the labours of the first; and, instead of witnessing the bloody deeds of cannibals, he shares in the Christian worship of their sons. What can explain this but the heavenly fact that Christ still bears witness to the word of His grace?

And for such transformations we need not go to the far Pacific. Let us consider our own spiritual history. What were we, you and I, fellow-believer, before we were born again? Let Paul answer: 'And you hath He quickened, who were dead in trespasses and sins; wherein in time past ye walked, according to the course of this world, according to the prince of the power of the air, the spirit that now worketh in the children of disobedience: among whom we all had our conversation in times past in the lusts of our flesh; and were by nature the children of wrath, even as others.'(Eph. 2. 1-3). And what has happened since? Let James reply: 'Of His own will begat He us by the word of truth' (James 1:18). And thus we carry about the witness of Christ in our hearts, and manifest it in our lives.

I have referred to one important fact which, before concluding, I ask you to remember with special care, and which, I fear, has not been made sufficiently prominent by present-day defenders of the truth. It is this: that after Christ had risen from the dead He altered nothing that He had said during the days of His humiliation. I say humiliation, not 'kenosis,' because I regard the latter word as the exclusive property of the sceptics who invented it, hoping to prove by it that when Christ laid aside His glory to be found in fashion as a man He voluntarily submitted for a time to the loss of some of the attributes of Godhead, and therefore could and did make mistakes as to historic facts. A more foolish and a more impious conception one can hardly imagine. Paul, writing to the Philippians, says that Christ emptied Himself, meaning, as the context shows, that 'He took upon Him the form of a servant and was found in fashion as a man,' not that He parted with His omniscience.

If what I have said should seem lacking in logical precision, my apology, in the oldest sense of that word, is this: I am very glad to have escaped from the Arctic Regions of logic and to have stretched my wings in the light and warmth of the Sun of Righteousness. Christ has no need of logic; for He cannot lie. I commend Him to you as the Truth.

I love this Book, and hope to die on it. When I enter another world I shall find that the Scriptures were truer than I thought they were. In language of unrivalled simplicity and grandeur they tell of the origin and end of all things, of the work of the Creator and the government of the Most High, of the sin of man and the salvation of God, of the ultimate downfall of the mystical Babylon and the everlasting glory of the Church of Christ, of New Heavens and a New Earth wherein dwelleth righteousness.

Some twenty years ago, when sickness compelled me to spend a Sunday in bed instead of going to my pulpit, the thought struck me that Tennyson's "Ode to Roman Virgil" might serve as a model for an Ode to the Holy Bible. As I lay there I endeavoured to carry out the plan; and this was the result:

Holy Bible, thou that tellest
  Of the sky's blue arches wrapped in fire;
Babel falling, Zion rising
  Fresh and young from nature's funeral pyre:

Thou that tell'st how night and chaos
  Fled, when light its Author's bidding heard;
All the mystery of creation
  Often shrouding in a lonely word:

Lordlier in thy lowly language
  Than the epics which the nations praise;
Treasures of unearthly wisdom
  Flashing forth from many a mystic phrase:

Record of the life unfallen,
  Sinless Adam tending Eden's bowers;
Record of the great transgression,
  Woeful ending of those golden hours:

Charter of the future, glorying
  In the righteousness again to be;
Heaven and earth anew created,
  Saints triumphant on the glassy sea:

Thou that seest nature's Maker
  Riding on the wings of nature's wind;
Thou majestic in thy gladness
  At the love of God to humankind:

Only light of all the ages,
  Star of dawn to earth's benighted shore;
Radiance of the eternal morning
  Whose exhaustless Sun shall set no more:

I believe thee, Holy Bible,
  I have loved thee since my day began;
Herald of the sweetest tidings
  Ever welcomed by the soul of man.

Inspiration and Variation

The importance of the study of quotations from the Old Testament in the New Testament, in regard to the living and continuous inspiration of Holy Scripture.

By Dr. C. H. Waller

In dealing with quotations from the Old Testament, the ordinary habit of the English student of the New Testament is to compare the two passages in his own Bible, Authorised or Revised. That is, he compares the New Testament in English, as translated from the Greek, with the Old Testament in English, as translated from the present Hebrew. If they agree, there is no further question. If they differ, the careful student will seek to have the difference accounted for as best he may. But it seems an axiom that the citation in the New Testament should agree with the Old Testament, substantially, in the place referred to. Otherwise, some sort of apology or explanation is demanded from the New Testament for presuming to differ from the more ancient portion of the Bible.

The position of the learned reader is not very different. He has, however, the advantage of knowing that, the Old Testament being in Hebrew, and the New Testament in Greek, there are some slight difficulties in the way of exact quotation from a book written in one language into a book written in another. He is, moreover, aware that there is a Greek version of the Old Testament called the Septuagint, which, if the Canonical Books of it are bound in one volume with a Greek Testament, makes a Greek Bible. In this, so much of the New Testament reproduces the very words and phrases of the Old Testament that the agreement is closer than it is in our English version. Such a Bible is a most interesting companion, as I can testify from the constant use of it for more than forty years.

But even in the use of this volume, it takes a long time for the student who knows Hebrew to get rid of the habit of requiring the Greek New Testament (and, of course, the Greek Old Testament also) to apologise, as it were, and account for its presuming to differ from the Old Testament as we know it, whether in the present Hebrew or as translated in our English version. It is not only in quotations from the Old Testament that the New Testament will show differences from what we understand to be the original Hebrew. The reader of the Greek Bible soon begins to see a fresh set of difficulties arising from the fact that his Old Testament in Greek tells the stories and reports the words in language which more or less differs from the Hebrew and from his English Bible. Neither Greek nor Hebrew will ever quite displace the English from that position in his mind which lies nearest to his memory in the daily use of the Holy Book.

I think this describes the average reader's position pretty fairly, whether he is learned or unlearned in the sacred languages of the Bible.

Let me now refer to a fact with which all are supposed to be familiar, but which must seriously affect our mental attitude towards New Testament quotations, if we are to get at the truth of the matter. *The Hebrew Bible, as it existed in the time of our Lord and His Apostles, was a book of consonants without written vowels.* There are no vowels, as we make them, in the Hebrew written alphabet. There are three or four letters which, for the sake of making what I say clear to any who do not happen to read Hebrew, I may call, A, H, V or W, and Y, which, in some cases, can stand as vowels, but the sound attached to them may be that of any vowel you please, from A to U. And to see them written, and evidently requiring a vowel, does not tell you what particular sound is to go with them, unless you know what the whole word is. The result is that when you have before you a book, printed as all Hebrew books used to be written, and, in fact, as all Hebrew books, except the Bible and its paraphrases or Targums, are usually printed now, the process of reading, as we know it, is reversed. In English, we spell first and read afterwards. In unpointed Hebrew, you have to read first and spell afterwards. When you know what the sentence means, you can read it. Until you can do so, you are as little able to read as King Belshazzar and his guests could make sense of the handwriting on the wall, before Daniel came. Daniel knew what it meant, and so he could read it. *When he had read it, everyone could see that he had read it right*; and as the fact that he was able to understand it was what enabled him to read it, there was no ground for disputing his interpretation.

To return to our quotations. We are now in a position to appreciate the full force of our Lord's reply to the lawyer who asked Him, 'What must I do to inherit eternal life?' (Luke 10.) The reply was: 'What is *written* in the law? How *readest* thou?'—two distinct questions. First, 'What is your written text?' Secondly, 'How do you read it? What sense do you make of it, and what vowels do you use?' The answer is familiar. But the passage, which is cited several times in the Gospels, familiar as it is, illustrates how differences arise in quoting from one language into another. The first commandment is an order to 'Love the Lord, the God of Israel, with all the heart and with all the soul,'—and all of a third something which has been the means of introducing no less than four Greek words into the verse as it appears here and there in the New Testament: *mind* (in Greek, *dianoia*); *sunesis, understanding; dunamis, ability;* and *ischus, strength*—all representing some aspect of the single Hebrew word *m'od*—all that exuberance of vital energy, which in different persons takes such variety of forms.

In order to bring what I am saying into a moderate compass, let me now mention two principles that appear in all New Testament citations from Scripture by our Lord and His Apostles; and then let me mention some of the ways in which these principles are carried out.

(I.) As to the principles first. We find absolute adherence and obedience to the written text: 'Think not that I am come to destroy the law or the prophets. I came not to destroy, but to fulfil. For verily I say unto you, Till heaven and earth pass, one jot or one tittle shall in no wise pass from the Law, till all things are done' (that is, until what is ordered is obeyed, and what has been said is come to pass). That 'jots and tittles' are the smallest portions of the *written text* is clear. They are not vowels, although in Greek *jot* is *iota*, and *iota* in Greek is a vowel. In Hebrew, *jot* is *yod* or *y*, and may carry any vowel you please from alpha to omega. And in repeating this saying in Luke (chapter 16.), our Lord speaks of tittles only: 'It is easier for heaven and earth to pass than one tittle of the law to fail.' The tittle is the small horn or tip by which similar consonants are distinguished in written or printed Hebrew.

These sayings as to the absolute authority of the true written text, wherever it is preserved (perhaps no-where on earth in absolute perfection), run obviously on the same line with the common forms of quotation, 'It is written,' or 'As it is written,' 'It hath been said' (i.e., commanded; Greek, *eiretai*), 'That it might be fulfilled which was spoken of the Lord by the prophet,' and, more rarely, but most significantly, 'Then was fulfilled,' in cases where nothing further is needed to exhaust the thing spoken. We may contrast the other phrase, 'In them is being fulfilled what was spoken by the prophet Esaias,' and 'This day has this Scripture been fulfilled in your ears.' 'Did ye never read in the Scriptures?' is another variation of the same thing. All such appeals alike point to a written text, and all are alike final. Even if they imply, as the last of them does, in one place at least, a special way of reading (Matt. 21:16), the thing as cited is not open to dispute. From what is 'written' there is no appeal. This is the first principle.

(II.) But the question, 'How readest thou?' appears at first sight to introduce a second principle of such latitude that the first is almost destroyed. We are obliged to remind ourselves at this point that the written text of the Old Testament had not then, and that the printed text has not now, any vowels attached to it which are of the same authority as the consonants. However awkward the fact may seem, a fact it is, and must be faced, at whatever cost of inconvenience, and even seeming risk. The jots and tittles of the written or printed text of the Old Testament in Hebrew, so far as correctly ascertained, have direct Divine sanction. The vowels, as we have them, rest on the tradition of the Jews—a tradition collected and elaborated in writing between the third and seventh centuries of the Christian era, after the rejection of the Messiah. Must this reading of the Hebrew, therefore, be set aside as worthless? By no means. GOD HAS MADE THE JEWS TRUSTEES OF THE DIVINE ORACLES. His gifts and call to them are irrevocable. But we need not forget that their vowel-pointing of the Hebrew Scriptures has, as yet, received generally no express Divine sanction.

How, then, does our second principle work out? In other words, what is written being clear, what answer have we to the question, 'How readest thou?' Our only safe answer to this question lies in the most careful observation of the manner in which our Lord and His Apostles have, in fact, answered it, and in noticing how far they have, in fact, authorised any particular reading of the Old Testament Scriptures.

Error on our Lord's part is *unthinkable.* Between Him and the Holy Spirit working in the Apostles the New Testament is well guarded from it; and thus we need not fear to place the most absolute confidence in the handling of the Old Testament which we find in the New Testament. In the most accurate and careful study of the quotations we shall find our only certain answer to the second question which concerns what is written in the law—the inevitable query, 'How readest Thou?'

How, then, did our Lord and His Apostles vocalise or vowel the written consonants of the Old Testament?

First, we can note two or three lines on which they worked, and then illustrate them by some examples.

(*a*) We find them making use of the Greek version known as that of the LXX.,* not , indeed, invariably, but, in Matthew, for example, about fourteen times out of twenty-eight. The exact proportion would differ probably in different books. Stephen's apology before the Sanhedrin would probably show a larger use of Septuagint readings than any other portion of equal length. There is an obvious reason for this. He was on his trial as a Hellenist, and would be expected to stand by his own authorised version. Perhaps Matthew, as writing more especially for Jews, and not specially for Hellenists, might show more deviation from the Greek than any other writer. It is noticeable that the Epistles to the Hebrews, by which, of course, those of Peter and James and Jude are intended, as well as the one attributed to Paul by Peter himself, by no means avoid the version of the LXX.; and the fact that these Epistles are especially directed to the Dispersion, who used the Septuagint, must not be pressed to outweigh the other fact, that this version is to a great extent authorised and apostolically sealed by its employment in the New Testament upon so large a scale. I do not mean to say that its authority can be affirmed to outweigh all other possible readings of the Hebrew, where the LXX. differs from the Jewish traditional Hebrew text as now read in Israel. But this version, authorised by the Jews themselves for general use before Christ came, is yet further authorised for Christians by its use in the New Testament.

There is also this further pertinent inquiry:—How many English Churchmen can answer it? From the time of the Apostles until this day there has been a Greek Church accepting the Canonical Scriptures of the Old Testament, and reading them in the Greek tongue. Has that Church as a body ever received and authorised any version of the Old Testament for general use in preference to the LXX., and if so, under what circumstances?

However, the Gospel of Matthew uses the LXX. as often as any other form for quotations from the Old Testament.

(*b*) But, in other cases, not only in the Gospel of Matthew, but in other New Testament writings, we find independent translations from the Hebrew of the Old Testament, where it seemed desirable.

(*c*) In other cases, again, we find both the above methods combined. In Matt. 13:35 we find one-half of a verse cited verbatim from the LXX., and the other independently translated.

(*d*) Sometimes a paraphrase, rather than a translation of the passage cited, appears. Matt. 2:6 and 5:44 Rabbinical.

(*e*) Many quotations can only be verified by *combining* words and phrases from different passages of the Old Testament, either in the LXX. version, or partly in the LXX. and partly in the Hebrew literally rendered.

(*f*) Occasionally, we find traces of the Targum, or Aramaic (Chaldee or Syriac) paraphrase then in use. ('Eli, Eli, Lama Sabachthani' is a case in point.)

In all cases, however, the Apostles, under the guidance of the Holy Spirit and the Lord Himself, too, are found to have exercised the most absolute discretion, both in citation and interpretation of the written text, so far as is consistent with faithful adherence to its authority. In one case only is there anything approaching to a contradiction of the law, and this is carefully shown to be only a stricter approach to its full recognition. The sentences in Matt. 5., introduced by 'Ye heard (were taught) that

* The Septuagint

it was said to the ancients,' are references, *not to the Bible, but to the Catechism*—a different thing altogether. It ought to be a sufficient evidence of this fact to note that in no other passage of the New Testament except this fifth chapter of Matthew, are citations from the Old Testament thus adduced, and never in an appeal to its authority. The attempt to set the Church above the Bible on the basis of our Lord's correction of a faulty Catechism can only recoil upon the heads of those who are so ill-advised as to make it.

Let me finally illustrate the above methods by quotations selected from the pages of the first Gospel.

(*a*) 1. Matt. 1:22— 'That it might be fulfilled which was spoken of the Lord through the Prophet, Behold *the virgin* (*Parthenos* with the definite article) shall conceive,' etc.

How much depends on the precise form of this citation I need not say. But it was no small matter for the Evangelist Matthew to be able, as he clearly was, to appeal to an unquestioned Jewish version of Isaiah, in support of the fact, which his Gospel may well have been the first published writing to make generally known, that such a prediction as this had been given and literally fulfilled.

I offer the following opinion on the facts attending this prophecy. Isaiah had two sons, whose names were both significant: Shear-Jashub (in Hebrew meaning, 'A remnant shall return'), who was by some years the older, for he was meeting King Ahaz with his father before the other was born; and Maher-Shalal-Hash-Baz, the child whose birth was to be the sign of the 'speedy spoliation' of Samaria and Damascus. This second sign was the one which Ahaz did not ask; and, perhaps for this very reason, it was not at first illustrated in the miraculous way which, we now see, the prophecy about it implied. The facts seem to have been thus. Isaiah was just about to take him a second wife. Referring to her, the prophet said to Ahaz: 'Behold, this maiden' (for she was not yet married) 'will conceive and bear a son, and they will call his name Immanuel' ('God is with us'), 'as will presently appear by the utter downfall of the enemies who now terrify us.' Ahaz took little or no heed to what was said to him. The marriage was consummated, and the first child of it was named in a second way, Maher-Shalal-Hash-Baz. The 'speedy spoliation' of Damascus and Samaria illustrated this name well, and showed that as yet *God* was *with Judah*. Thus the whole thing passed off for the time. 'Behold I and the children that God hath given me are for signs and wonders' is the saying that sums it up as far as Isaiah was concerned. Whether he or any one else suspected a remainder in the prophecy does not appear. I am disposed to think not. But by all means see Romans 9. 27,28, and the reproduction there of the names of both Isaiah's sons. It will be easily seen now how the word 'Almah' in Isaiah 7 may have been rendered *parthenos* in the Septuagint version, without the idea presenting itself to any one that this translation might some day occasion a difficulty. At least, the translation was made without prejudice. And when for the first time it appeared publicly in the writing of Matthew that the words had been fulfilled by one becoming a mother in her virginity, we can imagine the amazement with which the coincidence was received. How any one can suppose that this announcement was delayed till the fact was past proving, or that it went untested by any appeal to competent testimony, I am at a loss to imagine. The fact that Matthew begins with this story, and ends with the common explanation of the resurrection which vanished before the beginnings of Church history, is one of the best grounds for believing, what was long since established,—that HIS WAS THE FIRST GOSPEL, and was published within a few years of the Ascension, and in the Greek tongue.

But my point is that the very first appeal to the Old Testament in Matthew is made to the LXX., where it, so to say, begs a question which has often been disputed in the Hebrew, and this a question involving the first article of belief respecting the Manhood of the Lord Jesus. How this illustrates the living inspiration of the Old Testament in the first of all versions I need not stay to remark.

The above is a signal instance of the adoption of the LXX. version in a matter of the first importance, where the Hebrew is not necessarily conclusive, and where the Greek translation would in all probability have been different, if the translator had realised that, in the intention of the Divine Author, the text meant exactly what it said.

Other passages in Matthew, where the Septuagint version is followed in a noticeable way, are:—

(*a*) 2. The reference to Isaiah 6., 'By hearing ye shall hear,' etc. The passage is referred to also in Mark 4.12, Luke 8.10, John 12.40, Acts 28.26, Hebrews 5.11. In Romans 11.8 it seems to be combined in the mind of Paul with Isaiah 29. 10. But in the two places where the citation is most fully given—in Matthew and the Acts—the Septuagint version is very closely followed. [It should be observed, by the way, that the reference to the Holy Ghost as the Author of the passage in Acts 28 is not to be taken as though the Third Person of the Trinity had appeared or spoken in the *vision* recorded in Isaiah 6., as some commentators have most strangely supposed. In that passage, it is the word spoken *by*, not *to*, Isaiah; that is to say, the word written or spoken 'to the fathers' that is ascribed to the Holy Ghost, not the word as Isaiah heard it when he saw the glory of the Saviour (John 12.41). The citation in Acts 28, is on the same line with those in Hebrews 3.7, 9.8, 10.15.]

There is no special difference between the Hebrew as read by the Jews, in this place, and the LXX. as given by the Evangelists and Apostles.

(*a*) 3. In Matthew 4.16, however, the LXX., as we now have it, is followed in a most remarkable deviation from the Hebrew. This is an omission of the verbs and nominatives of the sentence, which I may exhibit by translating the passage (as I understand it) from the Hebrew, and italicising those words which appear in the Gospel, premising that they also represent the LXX. version very fairly.

'The First brought contempt to *the land of Zebulon and the land of Nephthalim.*'

'And the Last brought glory *by the way of the sea, beyond Jordan, Galilee*' (or to Galilee, the circle) '*of the nations.*'

'*The people,*' etc. (the remainder of the passage is the same, in substance, in Hebrew, LXX., and New Testament, and calls for no special comment in this connection).

I have no doubt that 'the First' and 'the Last' in this passage are the well-known names of our Lord in Isaiah, and not adverbs, as our version, following the Jews, has made them. I suspect the prophecy really points to the first and second Advents. For obvious reasons, this was not a topic to be discussed by Matthew for the Jews in this connexion. I am not in a position to say whether the Septuagint, as we have it, may have been affected by the quotation in Matthew, as the fourteenth Psalm has been by the citation in Romans 3. All I remark is that we have here a citation in the Gospel where the Hebrew (as we have it) is treated in a very unusual way, deserving the most careful attention, and demanding the strongest sense of the inspiration of the Scriptures in order to accept it. Were the writings implicated here purely and simply human, I confess that I should not know how to justify a quotation of this sort. It may, however, be placed in the same category with the reading from Isaiah in Luke 4.18,19.

Thus far for deviation from the Hebrew in favour of the LXX., and generally for the following of the Septuagint in quotations. One deeply interesting example appears in Matt. 21.16, from Psalm 8.2: 'Thou hast perfected praise.'

(*b*) Now as to *independent translation.* A good and simple instance is in Matt. 8.17: 'Himself took our infirmities and bare our sicknesses.' This is an application of the Hebrew, perfectly legitimate, but by no means obvious. And the LXX. gives us no help in this place. We can only refer it to the Holy Ghost, there being no Greek version with which we are acquainted, of that date, except the LXX. Of course, it is impossible to assert that no other Greek versions of particular books existed. But, so far as our knowledge goes, here is an independent translation of the Hebrew, based on an Evangelical interpretation, for which Matthew is, humanly, responsible.

(*c*) The next instance I mention is a case where both methods appear in the same citation. In Matt. 13.35, 'I will open my mouth in parables,' is word for word from the LXX. of Psalm 78.2. But the next clause is independently translated from the Hebrew. It so happens that the LXX. rendering in this place is particularly precise: 'I will utter problems, or riddles, from the beginning,' i.e., things that have been riddles from the first, or dark sayings. But the Evangelist, knowing from his Master's teaching exactly what was intended, says plainly: 'I will blurt out things that have been kept secret from the foundation of the world.' What sort of things he means we see when we note the position of the sentence in the Gospel, between the parable of the tares and the interpretation of it. The fact that this world is peopled partly by the children of the wicked one, distinguishable and yet inseparable from those whom the Creator placed in it at the first, when properly considered, is the key to some of the profoundest doctrinal difficulties that have ever vexed the people of God. I pass on to

(*d*) *The combination of passages* from different parts of the Old Testament into a single sentence is another noticeable feature. In the citation from Isaiah 42. in Matthew 12.18-20, we have some Septuagint, but broken by independent rendering of particular clauses, and then a short phrase from the Hebrew of Habakkuk 1.4, 'Judgment unto victory,' and then a verse from the Septuagint verbatim, apparently for the purpose of showing exactly where the quotation ends. In Matthew 21.5 we have a *combination* from Isaiah 62.11 (Septuagint) and Zechariah 9.10, which, however, is really Jeremiah's (see Matthew 27.9), with some independent translation. The whole is introduced by the phrase, 'That which was spoken (ordered) through the prophet.' We have here combination, exact quotation, independent translation, and modification, all exhibited in the one instance.

Other citations in Matthew will be found to illustrate these several principles in different degrees. It may be said, upon the whole, that the most important citations are in every way the clearest. Such are the first-named, from Isaiah 7., concerning 'the virgin,' and two of the latest in the course of our Lord's ministry, the one from the 110th and the other from the 118th Psalm. These concern the acceptance of our Lord as the Messiah, and His twofold nature, as God and Man. In both the LXX. version is cited verbatim. It was known to the Jews of Palestine and to all foreigners. Thus, we may say, it was the one form of the Old Testament acknowledged by all, and accessible to all alike.

Facts like these need but little comment. There are not a few of the same kind within reach of thoughtful students, and worthy of more discriminating attention than they commonly receive. Such attention will very soon convince the candid reader that the theory of careless and unverified quotation is contrary to the obvious facts of the case. It is little short of a disgrace to modern scholarship that the writers of the New Testament and of the Greek Scriptures should first of all be charged with error for deviating in their translations and citations from a critical text of the Hebrew, which (when they wrote) had no existence, and, secondly, charged with quoting the Scriptures carelessly and from memory, in the face of such facts as are here adduced, and which are but a handful, taken at random from the pages where they abound. The traces of human diligence and Divine guidance are alike everywhere manifest. The moral is plain. The translation and citation of the Old Testament Scriptures by our Lord and His apostles was made in such a way as to show that the Word of God is alive. It was always presented with such deliberate precision that we can say without doubt of every citation: 'As the Holy Ghost saith,' and 'This is the finger of God.'

Lord, Thy Word abideth,
And our footsteps guideth;
Who its truth believeth
Light and joy receiveth.

When our foes are near us,
Then Thy Word doth cheer us,
Word of consolation,
Message of salvation.

When the storms are o'er us,
And dark clouds before us,
Then its light directeth,
And our way protecteth.

Who can tell the pleasure,
Who recount the treasure,
By Thy Word imparted
To the simple-hearted?

Word of mercy, giving
Succour to the living;
Word of life, supplying
Comfort to the dying!

Oh, that we discerning
Its most holy learning,
Lord, may love and fear Thee,
Evermore be near Thee!

(*Henry Williams Baker,* 1861)

Verbal Inspiration Considered

By Dr. Basil F. C. Atkinson

In an age of shallow thinking and unreasoned vagueness the expression 'verbal inspiration' has at least one great merit. It is definite and its meaning unmistakeable.

The theological mind of to-day, inclined to shrink from dogma, is ready to concede the expression 'inspiration' to the Scriptures and to very many other writings, sacred and secular, besides. In exactly the same way it is ready to concede the expression 'atonement' to the central fact of the Christian faith. But it shrinks from any further definition, preferring to leave itself free to range over a whole realm of fancy and settle, if it settles at all, in some convenient self-erected shelter of the imagination, in which it hopes to be out of the sound of the convicting call of the Spirit of God. There is also another simple explanation of modern vagueness. In the day-time outlines are sharp and clear because they are seen in the light; in darkness, even only of degree, all is hazy, indefinite and blurred. And so, when the light of revelation floods any fact or any God-given idea, that fact or that idea is seen to stand out clearly in the shape that it in reality possesses. All of this is missed by those that walk in darkness.

However that may be, we are surrounded to-day by a smoke-screen of vicious thought that speaks of Atonement and of Inspiration, but refuses to define either. Try to define, and you are told that you are dealing with theory and not with fact. Thus the doctrine of verbal inspiration is looked upon as a theory of inspiration, just as the doctrine of substitutionary or propitiatory atonement is looked upon as a theory of atonement, and incidentally in both cases as a discarded theory at that. Those who concede the expressions, 'inspiration' and 'atonement,' suppose they are recognising the Biblical facts. We who believe know that this is not the case. We know that if we abandon the doctrine of substitutionary atonement or of verbal inspiration, we abandon in both cases not a theory which may be replaced by another of equal value, but a fact of revelation.

May I reiterate that in the matter of the acceptance or refusal of the doctrine of verbal inspiration, what is at stake is not a theory of inspiration, but the fact? In other words, if the Scriptures are not verbally inspired, they are not inspired at all. To say that they are is merely to confuse the issue and to make use of language which is ambiguous. Owing to the ambiguity of human language and to the constant change that is going on in the value and meaning of words, this confusion frequently takes place, and here incidentally is our first great argument for the truth of verbal inspiration. Eternal thoughts, breathed out from the mind of God, surely must be expressed in eternal language, language that will ensure the conveyance of the thoughts in their purity to the minds they are intended to reach. This must still be true, even if the language used be human language.

The truth of verbal inspiration is frequently emphasized in Scripture, but the depth of its meaning is never perhaps anywhere brought out to a greater extent than by the use of the expression, 'the Word of God,' to refer both to Christ, the Living Word, and to the Bible, the Written Word. A close parallelism is implied, and a little study will show that a close parallelism is the fact. The origin of the Scriptures may be regarded as parallel to the incarnation of our Lord Jesus Christ. The beginning of all was the action of the Holy Spirit upon a human instrument, and here at the outset was where the miracle lay. The conception of our Lord Jesus Christ was the primary miracle of the incarnation. This hidden action of the Holy Spirit united two natures in One Person. This action was of necessity secret. The fact was known to the human instrument alone—except incidentally by revelation—and the meaning of the fact had to be conveyed even to her by revelation. So with the human authors of the written Word. In their hearts and minds a secret action of the Holy Spirit took place, a fact that could be known only to their own spirits, and this action was the germ and guarantee of the two elements united in perfection in Holy Scripture. The Living Word was in a perfectly unequivocal sense the Child of Mary. 'Man, of the substance of His mother.' And as the Living Word was, in being made of a woman, guarded against all taint of sin, so has the Written Word been guarded against the intrusion of error.

As regards the writers of Holy Scripture, their whole intellectual and moral heredity and environment were in the hands of God, and so were their spiritual life and spiritual experience. They were—for they must have been—prepared instruments, just as Mary was a prepared instrument. And the Scripture is intrinsically theirs, the limitations of expression theirs, the peculiarities of grammar or diction theirs.

This fact is seized upon as a handle by those who deny the Divine origin of the Scriptures. But one might as well say that because the Lord Jesus Christ was the Son of Mary He was therefore not the Son of God. We are painfully familiar with the futile evasions of the hour. Jesus was Son of God as we are all sons of God, but to a greater degree. The Bible is of Divine origin, as many other books are of Divine origin, but to a greater degree. The influence of the Spirit on the incarnation of Jesus did not procure supernatural conception, but ensured high moral character in the Son of Mary naturally begotten. Similarly the *thoughts* of the writers of Scripture were inspired by their pious contact with God, so as to insure a high moral character to the work they produced. All this is merely trifling with language, the paying of lip-service with denial of true inspiration in the heart. No, the incarnation of our Lord Jesus Christ was due to Divine action, a powerful, clear-cut Divine intervention in human affairs, and so was the giving to man of God's Word in the Bible. The Lord Jesus Christ was God's revelation to men, and so is the Bible which bears witness to Him.

In the case of the Living Word the Divine nature interacted with the human throughout the whole Person, spirit, soul and body. It is the simple unequivocal truth to say of the leper, and of many another otherwise hopeless sufferer also, that he was touched by the Divine hand. The Divine nature did not cease where the body began. And so with the Scriptures. The Divine nature does not come short of that part of them that we can see and hear. If we say it does, we break the implied parallelism between the Living and the Written Words. And that part of them is nothing more nor less than what we call THE WORDS. If the hand that touched the leper was not Divine, then Jesus was not God. If the word that is heard or read is not God-breathed, then no inspiration attaches to the Scriptures at all.

Of what practical use to us is this truth of verbal inspiration? We have not the autographs of the original writers. We have confused the original text—practically always, it is true, in an inessential manner, but still in many places. This is made a frequent handle of attack upon the original inspiration and proves besides a puzzling difficulty to many. Let us carry our parallelism a step further—though it must be clearly understood that here it holds good only partially and only in some respects. We have not in any visible or material sense with us on the earth, the Person of our Lord Jesus Christ. 'The Body of our Lord Jesus Christ is in heaven and not here.' Yet in a real sense we have Him, the Living Word. Leaving aside for a moment the profound fact of the presence and action of the Holy Spirit—a fact that is of course intimately concerned with the whole problem—let us ask ourselves in what sense does the world at the moment have the Living Word of God, with what contact does it come in touch with Him? The answer is of course overwhelming in the sense of responsibility which it brings, but in our hearts we all know it. The world has and sees the Living Word in the body of those who have been created anew in Him, in the lives and persons of the regenerate individuals who believe in and love and follow Him, being indwelt by the Holy Spirit. A single generation knew the Living Word Himself, as present to sight and sense. Countless generations have had to be content as regards sight and sense, with a manifestation of Him through imperfect instruments. The Holy Spirit is constantly presenting the Living Word to the world in and through these imperfect instruments who abide in Him, and who provide the only means, the only channels, by which He can be brought into direct contact with the world. But this could not by any possibility be the case if the perfect Living Word had not at one time tabernacled in the world, leaving saved men and women 'an example, that' they 'should follow in His steps.' 'As the Father hath sent Me, even so send I you.' The essential foundation of the manifestation of Christ in His own is the perfect Living Word, Himself once manifested among men by miraculous incarnation, whom having not seen believers love, and who says, 'Because I live ye shall live also.' Further, because of this living foundation, the Holy Spirit is enabled to use these imperfect human instruments in order to present the Living Word to the world, and does so with success and convicting power.

The realisation of these facts makes the vexed question of the imperfect translations and imperfect texts to my mind much simpler. Just as the Spirit uses with success imperfect media for the manifestation in testimony and life of the Living Word, so He can and does use with success imperfect renderings of the perfect written Word. And the imperfections of the human representations of the Living Word are far greater than those of the written representations of the original written Word. Just as the presentation of the Living Word through imperfect living instruments stands as a fact on the foundation of the manifestation of the original perfect Living Word, visible and immediately audible on the earth, so it is with the presentation of the written Word. There could be no text or translation at all if there were not the original writings to copy or translate. And the fact that these texts and translations are Spirit-used to make contact with the hearts of men and make sinners wise unto salvation is to my mind explicable only on the ground that their original was perfect as the Living Word was perfect. In the case of the reflexions of the Living Word, while the Spirit acts, it is true, miraculously upon them, yet He never repeats the single initial miracle that brought down to earth the eternal original Living Word, nor is His action upon them directed towards making them flawlessly perfect representations of the life and character of the Living Word during this present age. So with the written Word. The Spirit does not renew the original miraculous output of power that brought the written Word down to earth. He does by the exercise of His functions of control see to it that there are available on earth representations and reflexions of the original written Word, which if imperfect, are yet perfectly adequate for His purpose and use. And how comparatively minute those imperfections are is a cause of thankfulness and praise for the providential superintendence and control of the Spirit of God.

What have we then in our English Bible? We have a representation of the original written Word of God, not flawless in every detail of text or translation, but usable and used by the Spirit, and perfectly adequate to convey to us the meaning of the original Word; very much more adequately reflecting the original than most of us, alas! in our lives reflect the original Living Word.

We have not the original text. But neither have we our Lord Jesus in the flesh.

Some are troubled because of the confusion that has sometimes arisen in the case of the particles and other little words. We do not know if the original text had an 'and' here or a 'but' there. We do not know, for example, in three instances in the account of the Gadarene miracle whether the original says 'herd' or 'herd of pigs.' The meaning is not obscured in the slightest by the uncertainty, so that it does not matter to our faith or work and witness which the original said. Similarly, to speak with reverence, we do not know particularly the several physical features of our Lord. But this lack of knowledge does not affect in the least our knowledge of Himself, or our love and witness and work for Him. In that sense these things do not matter. But that does not mean that they did not matter once. We cannot imagine that every detail of our adorable Lord's person was not absolutely perfect in itself, and also absolutely perfect for the purposes for which He took hold of the body that had been prepared for Him. We may be sure that all such details, though we have lost the knowledge of them, carried their full weight in the great redemptive purpose of God. They did matter then. So with the words of Scripture, Gods's words, the minute details. We may have lost the knowledge of them, but they did once matter. Each one fulfilled its small—or important—part in the one perfect utterance, the one perfect revelation, the one final expression of the mind of God in the language of man.

Then there comes in the great principle that God does not perform supernaturally for man what He had already given him natural power to do for himself. Man can copy, and man can translate. Therefore God does not do these things miraculously for Him. The original language was not an END in itself, it was a perfect means towards an end, the end being the realisation by the spirit of man of the thoughts and intentions of the mind and heart of God, and the receiving of faith as His gift.

If we had to-day the original perfect text—as indeed we have, buried in the various versions—most of us would not understand it. Human language is constantly changing. The only way to preserve the meaning of the Word of God at all to the mass of people is by constant translation, and revision of translation, from language to language. And the confusion of text is a boon in the sense that it has driven thousands to minute study of the text, a study that when undertaken reverently has never been otherwise than amply rewarded in the spiritual field. There are of course many places where the sense is affected. Take the passage in Rev. 1. 5. Are we to read 'washed us from our sins' or 'loosed us from our sins.' Both ideas are thoroughly scriptural. But who of us that has studied the uses and occurrences of the word *louo* 'to wash' in the New Testament does not feel convinced that *luo* 'to loose' is the right reading in this instance? The text is recoverable under the guidance of the Spirit in instance after instance.

Finally, have we lost it for ever? Shall we never know for certain whether 'washed' or 'loosed' is right? Shall we never know about the little 'ands' and 'buts' and 'thes'? Have we lost the Person of our blessed Lord for ever? God forbid. Are we not to gaze on His glorified form for ever, rejoicing in the perfect image of the Godhead? And so with the written Word. 'For ever O Lord, Thy Word is settled in heaven.' We have only to wait, and we shall possess, I hope and believe, for ever a glorified Bible. Difference of language will be nothing to us then. Shall we not be able to revel in the perfect text and the fulness of its meaning, as our hearts burn within us listening to the Perfect Expounder as did the two on the road to Emmaus. Certainly we shall have no less there than they had. Broken study will be taken up and carried to perfection in the place where no doubt or doubter can enter, and the Word of God in all the perfection of its individual words will be ours to rejoice in for eternity.

SPECIMEN OF THE WYCLIFFE BIBLE (1382)
(Gospel of John 1.1-5)

"Thy Word is Truth"

By E. K. Simpson

An indestructible craving for certainty is implanted within the human breast. *May-bes* and *peradventures* are betrayals of confusion and weakness; but *verily, verily* is an announcement of power, a word for the King's lips. It has indeed become the fashion lately in many quarters to applaud Lessing's sentiment, borrowed from Fontenelle and echoed by Goethe, that the quest after truth is to be preferred to its possession. But such a notion is quite unnatural, not to say morbid, and begotten of the artificial refinement of a sceptical age. It is not the genuine explorer, needing sustenance for his journey, but the mere amateur sportsman, who is more enamoured of the chase than the quarry. Granting that the mind, in certain moods and by way of pastime, may please itself with the silvery haze of ambiguity, or be lulled by 'dreams that wave before the half-shut eye'; yet no sooner is it summoned back to the world of earnest waking realities, in which suspense of judgment finds no place, than it longs for an environment of daylight. The moment we want full assurance of our whereabouts the gloaming forfeits its charm for us. And the strength of this innate yearning for certainty may be gauged by the fact that the majority of those who spurn an infallible revelation pay homage to an infallible expert, or bow at the domestic shrine of their own infallible selves.

Now this is a world brimful of gracious provisions for human needs. God has adjusted the light of day to the mechanism of man's eye, and furnished a treasury of sweet sounds to gratify man's ear, and prepared a globe teeming with physical marvels for man's inquisitive intellect to explore, and charged with motive-forces whose laws man may ascertain, and bend to his will. Surely then there is a presumption in favour of the view that He will also bestow on a creature who is a moral agent an authoritative directory of His will.

We believe that the Lord has never left Himself altogether without witness among the sons of men. We discern traces of a primitive revelation in ethnic tradition—for example, in the almost universal rite of animal sacrifice. We believe moreover that conscience is His inward monitor; and although its compass-needle, under the disturbing influence of sin, has been deflected from its primeval polarity, yet it ever tends, when released from counter-currents, to revert to the true north. We hold that 'natural light' (to use the old-fashioned term) suffices to discover the existence of God and the truth of human accountability. Yet its glimmering ray shines much too dimly to illumine an understanding clouded by transgression, or to yield relief from that darkling sense of guilt to the incubus of which all false religions owe their ascendancy over their dupes. The most illustrious of ancient moral speculators, Plato himself, owns the need of some heavenly tidings to authenticate his conjectures regarding Divine things.

For philosophy, with all her lofty pretensions, but mocks the hopes she awakens. Her solutions of the moral riddle of this universe blink the issue. They are obtained by a careful elimination of some of the main factors in the problem, and in particular of that most refractory and 'irrational' term in all its formulae, to wit, *sin*. Only Omniscience can grapple with the nucleus of all the other ills that flesh is heir to. *Gospel* she knows none. What, in fact, is her record, in so far as she affects to replace religion, but a long catalogue of ambitious errors, a huge aggregate of rash reasonings interspersed with rueful recantations? Philosophy cannot slake our inextinguishable soul-thirst.

There is only one revelation extant which really responds to this passionate cry of the human heart for religious truth. Its unique characteristics attest its unique origin. This unearthly oracle speaks with conscious authority, and 'not as the Scribes.' It indites no apologies for its wonders, and condescends to few explanations of its mysteries. It betrays no tokens of hesitancy, and claims universal acceptance for its message; baffles curiosity, but searches the reins. Both its wrath and its compassion well up from deeper fountains than human genius can tap. It has, in the words of an unbeliever (Hazlitt), 'a power to excite awe and admiration, and to rivet sympathy,' that are without parallel elsewhere. The epithet 'holy,' so inappropriate to any other volume, fits this one well. The Book possesses many styles. All manner of fruits 'pleasant to the sight and good for food' flourish in this garden of the Lord.

There are sections which may be described as the response of quickened souls to foregoing revelations. Job's perturbations of spirit, or the wise man's soliloquies, or the Psalmist's sobs merging in songs, do not always give us full-orbed presentations of truth. Sometimes they resemble pictures of an object taken from an oblique angle, or veiled in a half-light. But they are true to the conditions of their production under the oversight and prompting of the Spirit of God; and the analogy of faith supplies a corrective of the more partial aspects of truth they may, taken severally, unfold. These varied samples of sanctified experience under trial have their indispensable use and place in Holy Writ. They convey most precious, most essential, instruction, that could be imparted so suitably in no other way. Without them the great medicine-chest of the soul would be incomplete.

It may suffice here to notice two or three features which differentiate the Bible from all productions of purely human thought, and thus evince the veracity of its claim to be Divine.

Remark (1) *its theocentric point of view.*

How wide is the contrast in this respect between the Scriptures and human literature in general! Here is a volume which pleads throughout the cause of God against man. All the inspired writers manifest a jealousy for the Lord's honour, not for their own; of that they are sublimely careless. Their zeal for the glory of Jehovah never flags; to vindicate His dealings forms the master-passion of their souls. In Gilfillan's phrase, 'the Hebrew prophets have God vertical overhead.' When Paul exclaims, 'Let God be true and every man a liar,' he breathes the very spirit that animates all the sacred penmen.

Nor is this all. Whether consciously or unconsciously, the inspired writers survey human history from a Divine standpoint, as those who have been introduced into the council-chamber of heaven. Their 'philosophy of history' centres in redemption. The importance of events is rated according to their relation to that crowning purpose of the God of all grace whereby 'many sons are to be brought unto glory.' That is not a human, but a Divine horizon, the outlook of One who 'seeth the end from the beginning,' and is the Alpha and Omega of His creation; such a view of man's destiny as we might expect Milton's 'regent of the sun,' the mighty archangel Uriel, to take from his central station, that pinnacle far above 'the smoke and stir of this dim spot called Earth.' But how unnatural the phenomenon on the hypothesis that these Scriptures are mere products of this planet. In that case we may justly ask by what spiritual aeroplane these Jewish visionaries contrived to attain that serene altitude, from whence the glitter of empires, the pomp of kings, the din of battle, the ensigns of victory, and all those fleeting splendours which dilate the hearts of the sons of pride, dwindle to the insignificance of shooting-stars, visible for an instant, then vanished for ever. That is not man's way of writing his own history, but rather the panorama as it is scanned by Him before whom 'the nations are counted as less than nothing and vanity, who sitteth upon the circle of the earth, and the inhabitants thereof are as grasshoppers.'

(2) Another proof of the Divinity of the Book may be drawn from its *portraiture of the Divine character.* Man cannot by searching find out God; what we know of Him we know by His self-disclosure. Much might be said on this theme; but one remark must suffice. It is no abstract Godhead, sphered in a veil of light too refulgent for mortal vision to behold, that meets our view, but One Who clothes Himself with all pure human emotions. What overtures of loving-kindness temper the severity of the earlier Dispensation! Even on the very birthday of the Law, and beneath the shadow of the Mount that burned with fire, we hear a voice proclaiming the Lord to be 'merciful and gracious, long suffering and abundant in goodness and truth, forgiving iniquity, transgression and sin.' Awful holiness is the burden of the Old Testament delineation of Deity; yet there are wistful pleadings with rebellious Israel in the prophetic rolls of unspeakable tenderness, yearnings as of a forbearing Father's heart over some graceless child. The heart of the Eternal is laid bare in these *His confidences.* How beautifully they accord with the mind that was in Christ Jesus, and with His teachings concerning the Father! Ah, the style of love Divine is not to be counterfeited any more than the Shekinah glory. These chords can only be struck by One hand.

Need we add that the supreme disclosure of the Divine character greets us in the work of redemption? That betrothal-kiss of justice and mercy, that 'peace with honour' consummated at

Calvary, is radiant with a moral loveliness which no other scene can rival. Even as the seal allies with the impression, so does God's grand remedy for sin answer to man's sore disease; and the volume that so perfectly diagnoses his case, and prescribes the sovereign antidote, carries the watermark of truth inwoven with it. But who dare say that that work is 'after the manner of men'?

We next signalize, as another striking characteristic of the Word, (3) *its humbling view of human nature.* It exalts the Lord, but abases man, insisting that he is a truant from his Maker, a defaulter whose place is not the bench, but the bar. Now, as old John Trapp puts it, man is naturally a 'self-ascribing creature.' And in this age, flushed with the pride of its mechanical inventions, many, no doubt, would aver that his brilliant achievements fully justify his clamorous vaunts. It remains to be seen how far the exhibition of human depravity on a colossal scale which we are, alas! witnessing to-day may moderate his paeans of self-congratulation. Assuredly blushes rather than crowings befit a civilization which has *lost caste* even in the eyes of the savage world.

Now on this head the Old Book runs counter to the drift of human nature. Far from displaying any of the common fables of hero-worship or of national prejudice, it paints mankind, including the Jew, in darkest colours, and does not labour to excuse its best friends. Moses indites no apology for Jacob or his brother Aaron, or for his own act of homicide. No one can allege that David's transgressions are whitewashed, or Solomon's apostasy condoned. Which of the Evangelists palliates Peter's denial of his Master, or pleads extenuating circumstances in behalf of the apostles, when all forsook Him and fled? They do not even, in common with the generality of keen partizans, launch out into stinging invectives against their persecutors, or brand with scorn and infamy the basest of all conceivable traitors. Pagan soothsayers *rhapsodize;* but the judicial calmness of naked truth never deserts these prophets. The hand that holds the pencil of the Holy Ghost does not tremble. The Bible is beyond comparison the *sanest* of books, as well as the most straightforward.

By their plain-spoken denunciations of sin the Scriptures come into sharp conflict with the programme of 'modern thought'; for one of its leading aims is at all costs to patch up the damaged credit of human nature. Almost all present-day 'looseners of the faith' lay themselves out to champion the cause of the wrong-doer. Like the wicked servant in the parable, the unregenerate heart naturally espouses the side of man against his Maker, arraigning the adjudications of Divine justice as partial or austere, and complaining moodily of the harsh measure dealt out to frail humanity. Cartloads of modern literature harp on this string. But how it jars with the tenor of God's Word! How indelibly does that stain the purple of human pride; how relentlessly it pricks the bubble of self-righteousness, that 'much ado about nothing'; how magisterially it shuts up the whole human race 'under sin'! Were the accusation made by a fellow-sinner merely, such a wholesale indictment of mankind might well be taxed with misanthropy. It beseems none except the commissioned mouthpieces of the wronged and injured Jehovah, before whom all alike stand guilty, and whose standard of perfect rectitude cannot brook readjustment, like the sliding-scales of earthly jurisprudence. This Book sets our sins in the all-searching light of God's countenance, beneath the Röntgen rays of immaculate purity. Wondrous is its anatomy of human nature, its commendation of the *truth about himself* to every man's conscience, the photograph which it holds up to our gaze, that ugly but undeniable likeness. Such 'terrible sagacity,' such an exhaustive knowledge of what is in man bears the hall-mark of man's Creator, of One whose sure insight 'understands his thought afar off.' Would we learn the truth about God or about man? Then this Book must be our preceptor and our umpire.

There is a way of shelving, but not solving, the difficulties attaching to inspiration with which we are but too familiar. Its catchword runs: 'The Bible *contains* the word of God'—that is to say, in a state of diffusion. According to this theory, inspiration resembles an intermittent spring, now active, now quiescent. It concedes a spasmodic Divine afflatus, waxing and waning by turns. Sometimes the writers are wafted above themselves into the realm of pure truth; sometimes they are left without supervision to their own unaided resources. This notion sounds very specious, but it creates embarrassments more puzzling than any it removes. Keeping the promise of infallibility to the ear, it breaks it to the heart. It protests that we have an anchor of the soul, sure and steadfast; only, most unfortunately, several strands of the cable are rotten (how many is uncertain!), and will not bear the slightest strain. The casket of jewels Heaven has consigned to us includes some gems of the first water, of absolutely priceless worth; but by a sad mischance it has been tampered with on the road, and the real Kohinoors are now so cunningly interchanged with paste that none save specialists can detect the dexterous fraud. Hence (such is the moral drawn) it behoves us to hang on the lips, and walk in the leading-strings, of the *pontifices maximi* of criticism, who hold a monopoly of that novel Urim and Thummim which enables those initiated into its secrets without fail to discriminate between the prophet and the puppet, between the pinchbeck of the Jewish 'old-curiosity shop' and the sterling ware of heaven! These professors of spiritual second-sight can tell us to a nicety, by virtue of that sixth sense of theirs not granted to us babes and sucklings, where the invisible seams in the patchwork quilt of the Old Testament run; though ordinary eyes, minutely studying the fabric for these 2,000 years past, have stupidly deemed it all of a piece. Heretofore Protestantism has taken its Magna Charta straight, as it were, from the Lord's own hands; but henceforth we are to exchange the Divine signet stamped upon it for the guarantee of a sacred college of detectives, who are so kind as to certify that the charter of our faith is largely a forged document, but, for our reassurance, add that the deceit was piously meant, and that enough of the purport of the whole can be recovered to content all reasonable minds. Our oracular clairvoyants will issue rescripts from time to time, informing us how much of our spiritual title-deeds we must relinquish, and how much we may retain, if we would be ecclesiastically genteel and not incur the fatal stigma of lagging behind the times! Our modest province consists in saying ditto to *their* revelations!

Surely of all flimsy pretexts for the erection of a tribunal to dictate the contents of belief this hierarchy of Higher Critical popelings sets up the flimsiest. It revives the *a priori* methods of the schoolmen; for at its base lie the dogmas of anti-supernaturalism. It shapes its data to square with its day-dreams. Eagerly credulous of whatever seems to favour these, it adopts a whimsically petulant tone towards all evidence that sustains the catholic faith of the past. It complacently frames lines of partition and conjunction of its own, for which not a tittle of external evidence exists. Our divines have turned *diviners,* and, spider-like, spin their fantastic cobwebs from within themselves. Yet what real criterion can those who have abandoned the ground of testimony produce for winnowing the precious from the vile in that loose heap of chips and shavings to which they boast they have reduced the bulk of the Old Testament? Assuming for argument's sake that their alchemy has succeeded in resolving the amorphous conglomerate into something like its component elements, how are they going to extract and isolate the precious ore? What talisman has the critic capable of identifying the bullion and the base metal? He proclaims that his critical shears have slit what former ages took for 'garments of glory and of beauty' into a thousand shreds and patches. On what principle then am I to select my spiritual wardrobe from this motley rag-fair which he parades before my eyes? It has to be owned that that will mainly depend on my 'selective affinities.' For a religious creed divested of its authority soon exhales into a volatile sentiment, a subjective question of taste. *My* 'resultant text' may find its place among *your errata,* or *your* fine wheat be rated by me drossy chaff! Nor will the critic's own particular mete-wand serve our turn. That may faithfully reflect the unconscious but fixed bias which he fondly entitles a 'scientific' judgment; but his certificate cannot be reckoned final. The surety needs a surer surety to be its voucher. God alone can be Sponsor for Himself. In sooth, if his contentions hold, we urgently require a new revelation to determine for us the precise extent and area of the old! Meanwhile all is in a state of 'hodge-podge,' and we must live from hand to mouth on scraps benevolently dropped from our dons' 'high table'! In certain parts of America the woodpecker is known by the name of *sapsucker.* We beg the honest woodpecker's pardon for the liberty we take in applying the term *spiritual sapsuckers* to those who drain the Church's vitality nowadays by preying on its very pith and marrow, the lifegiving Word of the Lord.

The exponents of this school of thought (if thought that can be called whose prime aliment is suspicion) owe us some explanation of the glaring moral anomaly they ask us to accept. Uncommonly cogent proof would be requisite to accredit a notion so preposterous as the amalgamation of true

Divine revelation with a litter of 'old wives' fables.' We can understand the total rejection of the Scriptures as one vast imposture; but this coalescence of light and darkness, this dovetailing of God's truth and man's fraud together, strikes us as a singularly grotesque conception. Would it be worthy of human wisdom? Suppose that Sir Isaac Newton intends to bequeath to posterity that magnificent legacy of astronomical truth which is embodied in his *Principia*. Will he let his monumental work be interleaved with lying fables of astrology, or grafted on those false systems he means it to supersede? Certainly not: that would be egregious folly. Yet we are invited to believe that Divine wisdom rich in infinite resources, has chosen to stultify its sole written message to mankind by incorporating it with a tissue of myths and fairytales, and that inextricably; for Biblical doctrine and history interpenetrate one another, and the nexus cannot be dissolved without mangling both. We ask: Is it credible that God has left His tapestry-work of true revelation thus intertangled with a trammelling web of fancy embroidery for latter-day connoisseurs to unravel and mend; or given us a Bible 'in the block' for modern carvers to chisel into shapeliness?

Nor is this all. There are tougher morsels yet to task our powers of digestion. For the New Testament, which the more moderate critics profess to reverence, most emphatically ratifies the Old. Christ Himself has set His own endorsement upon it likewise. There is no disputing these facts. And so, to save their leaning-tower of rationalism from toppling over and crushing them beneath its ruins, 'devout criticism' does not recoil from impeaching either the Lord's sincerity or else His intelligence. On the one hand we encounter the monstrous assumption that He was an adept in its own pet art of 'accommodation.' It would seem that, instead of exposing the jumble of falsehoods which had for centuries been taking God's name in vain, instead of sweeping them unceremoniously into the limbo of oblivion by a kind of collusion with the father of lies (whose works we thought He came to destroy), Jesus chose to rivet on the necks of His disciples for two millenniums longer the grievous yoke of a simulated authority. What sober understanding can swallow that crazy figment?: Hearken to His own words, ye blind guides, '*If it were not so, I would have told you*.' Nor is the case one whit mended by the alternative suggestion that the Lord was Himself deceived. O shameless imputation! The Chief of prophets gulled by sham prophecy! The depths of Satan overtasking the penetration of his great Unmasker! The Divine Thought-reader, before whose piercing scrutiny the inner man of the heart, stripped of all disguises, stood crystally transparent, the dupe of spurious parchments purporting to be His Father's word! He to whose majestic intuition all later 'heirs of fame' have borne willing or unwilling homage, unable to detect the flash notes in the portfolio of the Hebrew Scriptures from genuine drafts on the bank of heaven! Nay truly! We should be loth to credit that 'hard saying' either. Reverence forbids, love forbids, faith forbids, reason forbids. Dissent from Him Who is the Ipse Dixit of Creation, and disparagement of His awards, must of necessity spell delusion. 'Truth,' says John Milton, 'came once into the world with her Divine Master, and was a perfect shape most glorious to look upon.' And every heart that throbs in unison with the Saviour's will echo the words of Dr. John Arrowsmith, the Puritan Master of Trinity, Cambridge, concerning that record on which Jesus sets His unchallengeable imprimatur: 'Verity of verities: all is Verity.' For *no lie is of the truth*, but of the old serpent, that arch-pretender and earliest professor of subtleties, whose *forte* is fiction and his native tongue deceit.

The sad fact is that the capacity for recognizing truth may be forfeited by abuse. And in this day of nebulous sentiments in lieu of heartfelt convictions multitudes have fallen into that melancholy plight through paltering with all manner of insincerities and compromises. Long familiarity with glimmering moonshine has rendered the genial beams of the sun repellent to their diseased vision. The very glow and intensity of God's revelation rebukes (and therefore offends) the frigid neutrality of these 'children of the twilight.' Yet to the genuine truth-seeker that note of certainty is its glory. Here is a platform of granite amid quagmires, a solid foothold for sinking feet. Certainly it would be an error on the right side to follow John Foster's council, and, if needs be, believe God's Word and *nothing beside*! For no other records ray out such a 'self-evidencing light' of veracity as the Bible, and the sturdiest generations, those that knew how to die for truth, have loved it best. The life of the Church must have become mournfully enfeebled, before she could hobnob with its disembowellers as amicably as at this day, alas! she is doing. Howbeit Truth rests a queen and an immortal; nor shall this deathless virgin perish whilst God lives to keep vigil over her who is His ward. She may be thrust out of the sanctuary and raved at and reviled, may even 'fall in the street' but she cannot be slain. Ere now, like the Christ who is her glorious namesake, she has suffered many things at the hands of her tormentors, has been gagged and baited and scourged and impaled; but never annihilated. If in some dire hour of 'darkness that might be felt' she has seemed to yield up the ghost, it was only a trance that befell her; the eyelids of the morning have seen her revive 'as one awaketh from slumber, like a mighty man that shouteth by reason of wine.' Reader, be of good cheer; 'the end is not yet.' We are not arrived yet at the fifth act of the drama. The usurping dynasty of falsehood hath a term, a *finis* assigned to it. When the harvest is ripe, and all that is combustible shall be consumed, the tares are doomed to blaze; but the Word of the Lord, which is not tinder, but asbestos, endureth scatheless for ever. O proscribed, scorned, slandered, pilloried, derided Truth of God, what a jubilee shall be thine in that blest day of restitution, which is yet to dawn, when thy wrongs shall all be righted, and thou shalt enjoy thy coronation and sit enthroned for ever; in that day when a sentence without appeal or revocation shall chase into outer darkness 'whosoever loveth and maketh a lie'!

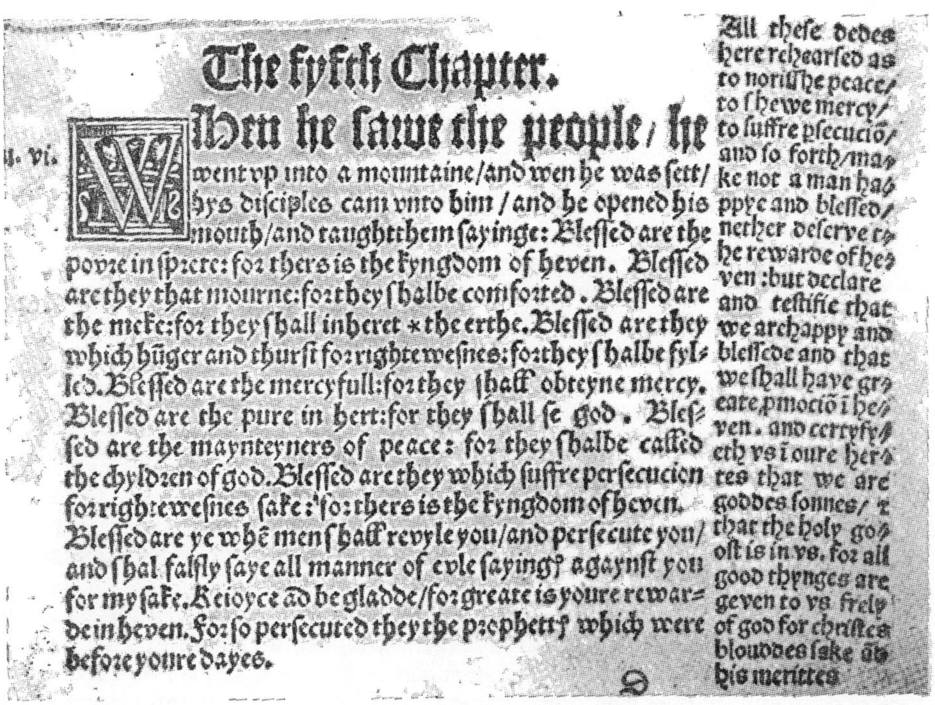
The fyfth Chapter.

When he sawe the people / he
went vp into a mountaine/and wen he was sett/
hys disciples cam vnto him / and he opened his
mouth/and taught them sayinge: Blessed are the
povre in sprete: for thers is the kyngdom of heven. Blessed
are they that mourne: for they shalbe comforted. Blessed are
the meke: for they shall inheret the erthe. Blessed are they
which hunger and thurst for rightewesnes: for they shalbe fyl-
led. Blessed are the mercyfull: for they shall obteyne mercy.
Blessed are the pure in hert: for they shall se god. Bles-
sed are the maynteyners of peace: for they shalbe called
the chyldren of god. Blessed are they which suffre persecucion
for rightewesnes sake: for thers is the kyngdom of heven.
Blessed are ye when men shall revyle you/and persecute you/
and shal falsly saye all manner of evle sayings agaynst you
for my sake. Reioyce and be gladde/for greate is youre rewar-
de in heven. For so persecuted they the prophetts which were
before youre dayes.

All these dedes here rehearsed as to norisshe peace/ to shewe mercy/ to suffre persecucion/ and so forth/make not a man happye and blessed/ nether deserve the rewarde of heven: but declare and testifie that we are happy and blessede and that we shall have greate promocion in heven. and certyfyeth vs in oure hertes that we are goddes sonnes/ and that the holy gost is in vs. for all good thynges are geven to vs frely of god for christes bloudes sake and his merittes

Tyndale's New Testament—A.D. 1525
(Matthew 5)

On Reading the Bible

(Extracts from George Müller's Autobiography,
selected by P. J. Wiseman)

HOW TO KNOW THE WILL OF GOD.

I never remember in all my Christian course, a period now of sixty-nine years and four months, that I ever SINCERELY and PATIENTLY sought to know the will of God by the *teaching of the Holy Ghost,* through the instrumentality of the *Word of God,* but I have been ALWAYS directed rightly. But if honesty of heart and uprightness before God were lacking, or if I did not *patiently* wait upon God for instruction, or if I preferred the counsel of my fellow men to the declarations of *the Word of the living God,* I made great mistakes.

ADVICE ON BIBLE STUDY.

If any one should ask me how he may read the Scriptures most profitably, I would advise him, that:

Above all he should seek to have it settled in his own mind that God alone, by His Spirit, can teach him, and that therefore, as God will be enquired of for his blessings, it becomes him to seek God's blessing previous to, and whilst reading.

He should have it, moreover, settled in his mind, that although the Holy Spirit is the *best* and *sufficient* teacher, yet that this teacher does not always teach immediately when we desire it, and that, therefore, we may have to entreat Him again and again for the explanation of certain passages; but that He will surely teach us at last, if indeed we are seeking for light prayerfully, patiently, and with a view to the glory of God.

It is of immense importance for the understanding of the Word of God, to read it in course, so that we may read every day a portion of the Old and a portion of the New Testament, going on where we previously left off. This is important—(1) Because it throws light upon the connection; and a different course, according to which one *habitually* selects particular chapters, will make it utterly impossible ever to understand much of the Scriptures. (2) Whilst we are in the body, we need a change even in spiritual things; and this change the Lord has graciously provided in the great variety which is to be found in His Word. (3) It tends to the glory of God; for the leaving out of some chapters here and there, is practically saying, that certain portions are better than others; or, that there are certain parts of revealed truth unprofitable, or unnecessary. (4) It may keep us, by the blessing of God, from erroneous views, as in reading thus regularly through the Scriptures we are led to see the meaning of the whole, and also kept from laying too much stress upon certain favourite views. (5) The Scriptures contain the whole revealed will of God, and therefore we ought to seek to read, from time to time, through the whole of that revealed will. There are many believers, I fear, who have not read even once through the whole of the Scriptures; and yet in a few months, by reading only a few chapters every day, they might accomplish it.

It is also of the greatest importance to meditate on what we read, so that perhaps a small portion of that which we have read, or, if we have time, the whole may be meditated upon, in the course of the day. Or a small portion of a book, or an epistle, or a gospel, through which we go regularly for meditation, may be considered every day without, however, suffering oneself to be brought into bondage by this plan.

Learned commentaries I have found to store the head with many notions, and often also with the truth of God; but when the Spirit teaches, through the instrumentality of prayer and meditation, the heart is affected. The former kind of knowledge generally puffs up, and is often renounced when another kind of commentary gives a different opinion, and often is also found good for nothing, when it is to be carried out into practice. The latter kind of knowledge generally humbles, gives joy, leads us nearer to God, and is not easily reasoned away; and having been obtained from God, and thus having entered into the heart, and become our own, is also generally carried out. If the enquirer after truth does not understand the Hebrew and Greek languages, so as to be able to compare the common translation with the original, he may concerning several passages get light by an improved rendering, provided that he can be sure that the translator was a truly spiritual person.

FURTHER LIGHT ON GOD'S WORD.

I will mention some points which God then began to show me: that the Word of God alone is our standard of judgment in spiritual things; that it can be explained only by the Holy Spirit; and that in our day, as well as in former times, He is the teacher of His people. The result of this was, that the first evening that I shut myself in my room, to give myself to prayer and meditation over the Scriptures, I learned more in a few hours than I had done over a period of several months previously. But the particular difference was that I received real strength for my soul in doing so. I now began to try by the test of the Scriptures the things which I had learnt and seen, and found that only those principles which stood the test were really of value.

HOW TO BE CONSTANTLY IN THE LORD.

While I was staying at Nailsworth,* it pleased the Lord to teach me a truth, irrespective of human instrumentality, as far as I know, the benefit of which I have not lost though more than forty years have since passed away. The point is this: I saw more clearly than ever, that the first great and primary business to which I ought to attend every day was, to have my soul happy in the Lord. The first thing to be concerned about was not, how much I might serve the Lord, how I might glorify the Lord; but how I might get my soul into a happy state, and how my inner man might be nourished. For I might seek to set the truth before the unconverted, I might seek to benefit believers, I might seek to relieve the distressed, I might in other ways seek to behave myself as it becomes a child of God in this world; and yet, not being happy in the Lord, and not being nourished and strengthened in my inner man day by day, all this might not be attended to in a right spirit. Before this time my practice had been, at least for ten years previously, as an habitual thing, to give myself to prayer, after having dressed in the morning.

Now I saw, that the most important thing I had to do was to give myself to the reading of the Word of God and to meditation on it, that thus my heart might be comforted, encouraged, warned, reproved, instructed; and that thus, whilst meditating, my heart might be brought into experimental communion with the Lord. I began, therefore, to meditate on the New Testament, from the beginning, early in the morning. The first thing I did, after having asked in a few words the Lord's blessing upon His precious Word, was to begin to meditate on the Word of God, searching, as it were, into every verse, to get blessing out of it; not for the sake of the public ministry of the Word; not for the sake of preaching on what I had meditated upon; but for the sake of obtaining food for my own soul. The result I have found to be almost invariably this, that after a very few minutes my soul has been led to confession, or to thanksgiving, or to intercession, or to supplication; so that though I did not, as it were, give myself to prayer, but to meditation, yet it turned almost immediately more or less into prayer. When thus I have been for a while making confession, or intercession, or supplication, or have given thanks, I go on to the next words or verse, turning all, as I go on, into prayer for myself or others, as the Word may lead to it; but still continually keeping before me, that food for my own soul is the object of my meditation.

The result is this, that there is always a good deal of confession, thanksgiving, supplication or intercession mingled with my meditation, and that my inner man almost invariably is even sensibly nourished and strengthened, and that by breakfast time, with rare exceptions, I am in a peaceful if not happy state of heart. Thus also the Lord is pleased to communicate unto me that which, very soon after, I have found to become food for other believers, though it was not for the sake of the public ministry of the Word that I gave myself to meditation, but for the profit of my own inner man.

The difference then between my former practice and my present one is this. Formerly, when I arose, I began to pray as soon as possible, and generally spent all my time till breakfast in prayer, or

*Gloucestershire

almost all the time. At all events, I almost invariably began with prayer, except when I felt my soul to be more than usually barren, in which case I read the Word of God for food, or for refreshment, or for a revival and renewal of my inner man, before I gave myself to prayer. But what was the result? I often spent a quarter of an hour, or even half an hour on my knees, before being conscious to myself of having derived comfort, encouragement, humbling of soul, etc.; and often, after having suffered much from wandering of mind for the first ten minutes, or a quarter of an hour, or even half an hour, I only then began really to pray. I scarcely ever suffer now in this way. For my heart, being nourished by the truth, being brought into experimental fellowship with God, I speak to my Father, and to my Friend (vile though I am, and unworthy of it!) about the things that He has brought before me in His precious Word.

It often astonishes me that I did not sooner see this. In no book did I ever read about it. No public ministry ever brought the matter before me. No private intercourse with a brother stirred me up to this matter. And yet now, since God has taught me this point, it is as plain to me as anything, that the first thing that the child of God has to do morning by morning is to obtain food for his inner man. As the outer man is not fit for work for any length of time, except we take food, and as this is one of the first things we do in the morning, so it should be with the inner man. We should take food for that, as every one must allow. Now what is the food for the inner man? Not prayer, but the Word of God; and here again not the simple reading of the Word of God, so that it only passes through our minds, just as water runs through a pipe, but considering what we read, pondering over it, and applying it to our hearts.

When we pray we speak to God. Now prayer, in order to be continued for any length of time in any other than a formal manner, requires, generally speaking, a measure of strength or godly desire, and the season, therefore, when this exercise of the soul can be most effectually performed, is, after the inner man has been nourished by meditation on the Word of God, where we find our Father speaking to us, to encourage us, to comfort us, to instruct us, to humble us, to reprove us. We may therefore profitably meditate, with God's blessing, though we are ever so weak spiritually; nay, the weaker we are, the more we need meditation for the strengthening of our inner man. There is thus far less to be feared from wandering of mind, than if we give ourselves to prayer, without having had previously time for meditation.

I dwell so particularly on this point because of the immense spiritual profit and refreshment I am conscious of having derived from it myself, and I affectionately and solemnly beseech all my fellow-believers to ponder this matter. By the blessing of God I ascribe to this mode the help and strength which I have had from God to pass in peace through deeper trials in various ways than I had ever had before; and after having now above forty years tried this way, I can most fully, in the fear of God, commend it. How different when the soul is refreshed and made happy early in the morning, from what it is when, without spiritual preparation, the service, the trials, and the temptations of the day come upon one!

HOW FAITH MAY BE STRENGTHENED.

This leads me to the following important point. You ask, 'How may I, a true believer, have my faith strengthened?' The answer is this: 'Every good gift and every perfect gift is from above, and cometh down from the Father of lights, with whom is no variableness, neither shadow of turning' (James 1. 17). As the increase of faith is a good gift, it must come from God, and therefore He ought to be asked for this blessing.

The following means, however, ought to be used:—

(1) The careful reading of the Word of God, combined with meditation on it. Through reading of the Word of God, and especially through meditating on the Word of God, the believer becomes more and more acquainted with the nature and character of God, and thus sees more and more, besides His holiness and justice, what a kind, loving, gracious, merciful, mighty, wise and faithful Being He is, and therefore, in poverty, affliction of body, bereavement in his family, difficulty in his service, want

of a situation or employment, he will repose upon the ability of God to help him, because he has not only learned from His Word that He is of almighty power and infinite wisdom, but he has also seen instance upon instance in the Holy Scriptures in which His almighty power and infinite wisdom have been actually exercised in helping and delivering His people; and he will repose upon the willingness of God to help him, because he has not only learned from the Scriptures what a kind, good, merciful, gracious, and faithful Being God is, but because he has also seen in the Word of God, how in a great variety of instances He has proved Himself to be so. And the consideration of this, if God has become known to us through prayer and meditation on His own Word, will lead us, in general at least, with a measure of confidence to rely upon Him: and thus meditation on the Word of God will be one special means to strengthen our faith.

(2) As with reference to the growth of every grace of the Spirit, it is of the utmost importance that we seek to maintain an upright heart and good conscience, and therefore, do not knowingly and habitually indulge in those things that are contrary to the mind of God, so it is also particularly the case with reference to the growth in faith. How can I possibly continue to act in faith upon God, concerning anything, if I am habitually grieving Him, and seek to detract from the glory and honour of Him in whom I profess to trust, upon whom I profess to depend? All my confidence towards God, all my leaning upon Him in the hour of trial, will be gone, if I have a guilty conscience, and do not seek to put away this guilty conscience, but still continue to do the things which are contrary to the mind of God. And if, in any particular instance, I cannot trust in God, because of the guilty conscience, then my faith is weakened by that instance of distrust; for faith with every fresh trial in it, either increases by trusting God, and thus getting help, or it decreases by not trusting HIm; and then there is less and less power of looking simply and directly to Him, and a habit of self-dependence is begotten or encouraged. One or the other of these will always be the case in each particular instance. Either we trust in God, and in that case we neither trust in ourselves, nor in our fellow-men, nor in circumstances, nor in anything besides; or we do trust in one or more of these, and in that case we do not trust in God.

Day by day the manna fell;
Oh, to learn this lesson well!
Still, by constant mercy fed,
Give me, Lord, my daily bread.

'Day by day,' the promise reads;
Daily strength for daily needs;
Cast foreboding fears away,
Take the manna of to-day.

Lord, my times are in Thy hand;
All my sanguine hopes have planned
To Thy wisdom I resign,
And would make Thy purpose mine.

Thou my daily task shalt give,
Day by day to Thee I live;
So shall added years fulfil
Not my own, my Father's will.

Oh, to live with mind subdued,
Yet elate with gratitude;
Strong in faith, exempt from care,
By the energy of prayer.

(*Josiah Conder,* 1836)

The Trustworthiness of the New Testament*

By Sir Wm. Ramsay

I propose to speak, not about the Old Testament, but about the New Testament. In regard to the Old Testament, I cannot claim to speak with knowledge. I do not know the languages in which the Old Testament is written, but one thing I can say: you have only to read in comparison a translation of the history made by important Arab historians in the Middle Ages and the translation of the historical Books of the Old Testament, and any person who dispassionately studies and compares, as far as he can through translations, these two classes of documents, must be struck with the extraordinary difference. In the Arab historians, though they rank as historians among the Critics, you are struck with the fact that there are six pages of rubbish to one page of rational history, whereas when you are reading the historical Books of the Old Testament, any person with the historical sense feels he is standing on historical ground.

They talk about Abraham as a myth. Now, any person who possesses the psychological sense, who has accustomed himself to the discrimination of mythology and history, knows that when he is dealing with Abraham, he is dealing with a real man—a real personality. Anyone who studies mythology properly, who has any rational conception of what legend is, must recognize that Abraham is a real character, a true man—in touching him you are in contact with actual life. I can imagine a better case made out against the historicity of Jacob, because in Jacob you feel you are dealing with one who is typical of the race, but in Abraham you are not dealing with the typical Jew, but with a wider, a more representative character than the Jewish, and it is altogether out of keeping with any sound judgment about history and myth to imagine that a people would describe itself as originating from a person who is so totally different in character from itself. Jacob, on the other hand, might be treated as a typical Jew, and you might make out a case to show that he exhibits the characteristic features of the future Jewish nation at the beginning of its history, but it would be after all special pleading, because Abraham carries Jacob with him. You cannot imagine that the older generation is historical and the newer generation is merely mythological.

But I come to the New Testament, where I can feel that I am in contact with the original words of the original language, and where I have been able to stand on the ground where so much of the history has been transacted. Now, what one always wants to test at the present time is this question: Is the New Testament a true record, or did it grow up gradually through human agency step by step in a sort of process of accretion of legend and story and half-remembered history and myth through several generations, finally assuming the form in which we have it before us? Did it grow up in that way through human agency in a mist of fable and legend and untruth? It would be a remarkable thing that the religion of moral values, the one religion which out of sight beyond all others values moral principles, which founds itself on the belief in truth, which teaches the duty of truth in a way that no other religion does—it would be an astounding thing that this religion should grow up in that process of fable and legend and untruth. You cannot get the true out of the untrue.

Now, the more I live—and I say, the *more* I live, not the longer I live, because one may live a long time and yet be living very little, and at another time in a short period one may live a great deal, and most of us have been living a great deal in the last nine or ten months—the more I live, the more I feel that the New Testament is a unique Book, standing apart from all other literature. Judging of it from the point of view of the historical student—the quality in it that most strikes me is its perfect sanity. It is so full of common-sense, so sane in its judgments, so well balanced in its statements with regard to the world and the conduct of man. Its outlook on life is so healthy, so invigorating, and at the same time, judged as literature, it is such a perfect expression of its own thought and gives us such a perfect expression of the facts that it records that you can press to the uttermost any sentence or any

*An address at the Annual Meeting of the *Bible League (1915) immediately after the publication of his book, The Bearing of Recent Discovery on the Trustworthiness of the New Testament.*

paragraph, and the harder and the closer you press it in a commonsense, rational way, the more you find that it yields its truth. It is never vague, or wishy-washy, in its assertions.

I have had the opportunity of comparing this Book a great deal with another book I have been studying for a great many years, another book which at present a group of scholars is beginning to translate and comment on, upon a great scale, with a view of doing something for this world of learning and of keeping our minds occupied profitably. I compare the New Testament with that book, which is the *Geography,* written by Strabo. Strabo died at a very advanced age in the year 21 A.D. He is therefore a contemporary in the later part of his life with the early part of the life of the Saviour. He writes in a similar kind of Greek to the records of the writers of the New Testament. He is a little earlier, but he belongs to the same quarter; he was a native of the eastern part of Asia Minor, and he learnt his Greek in the same way and amongst similar surroundings to many of the writers of the New Testament. There you have an author who, towards the end of his life, set down all he had been able to learn with regard to the geography of the whole known world, and he regarded geography as closely connected with human history. He did not write geography from the point of view merely of description of rivers and mountains; he regarded the conformation of a country as closely connected with the history of the country, and as moulding the history of men who lived in it. And from many points of view Strabo is an eminent writer, and a writer who pays the utmost respect to truth, whose sole object is to set down what he had learnt about the world in which he had travelled a good deal.

But you compare his language with that of the New Testament and you feel how inferior is the expression of his thought. It is far harder to get hold of the real meaning of a sentence or the real implication of a paragraph. You cannot press Strabo, because you feel you are squeezing the language too hard. It will not hold together in the same way. Now that perfection in the expression of the New Testament strikes me more and more as I read and understand and criticise the book.

The only way to demonstrate this is to take certain passages—almost any passage whatsoever will do—and to see how you can examine the sentence word by word and phrase by phrase; and then you realize that the New Testament is unique in the compactness of its thought, in its lucidity, in its fulness of meaning and vivid truthfulness of expression throughout every sentence.

Now, that is not the character merely of one or two of the Books that compose the New Testament—it belongs in different ways to all alike. At present I would like to direct your attention to one particular passage which has been more criticised and more trampled upon amd more derided and laughed at and ridiculed than any other passage in the New Testament—that is the first four verses of the second chapter of the Gospel of Luke, stating that all the world should be taxed, i.e., a world census made. The word rendered 'world' does not really mean world in our sense; it means the 'civilised world,' and it is practically equivalent in this passage and in contemporary usage to the Roman Empire—the civilized Empire. This was the first census which was taken while Quirinius (Cyrenius) was Governor of Syria. And everyone went up to be counted in the census: 'And Joseph also went up from Galilee, out of the city of Nazareth, into Judaea, unto the city of David, which is called Bethlehem'; and there, in Bethlehem, the child Jesus was born of a mother who lived at Nazareth.

Now that is the passage which has been subjected to such ridicule, and many of the modern historians who profess to write a life of Christ on modern principles, simply ignore it altogether, do not find it worthy even of a footnote, but begin their history: 'Jesus was born at Nazareth of humble parents.' That is quite a recognised way of beginning a Life of the Saviour by critics who think there was any Jesus at all—some regard Him as myth from beginning to end, but they are few, and hardly any of the great critics have any sympathy with that view: almost all leave some historical remnants of the Gospels. A number of statements in that passage have been regarded as incredible, altogether opposed to anything we know about the Roman Empire. It is said that there never was a census of the Roman world, that Caesar Augustus never issued any decree regarding such a subject, that Quirinius was not Governor of Syria at any time which could correspond with the circumstances recorded in the

Gospels, because Quirinius did not govern Syria until about ten years after Herod the king was dead. Even admitting, for the sake of argument, that there had been a census, they say, it would be naturally made according to the place where people lived, and people would not go up to a town to which they belonged by origin in order to be counted there—and so on.

I might run over a number of statements, each of which was regarded twenty years ago as proving with absolute certainty the absurdity of this passage. And yet there has been no place in the whole range of the New Testament where such an astonishing series of discoveries has come to prove the truth of the details as in this instance. We now know that there was in the Roman Empire a system of census taking regularly every fourteen years, and that that system was inaugurated by the Emperor Augustus, and went on for two and a half centuries, until it broke up in the gradual decay of the Empire; and we know that one of the features of such a census was that it was preceded by a proclamation issued by the Governor of the Province or by the magistrates of a free city, directing that every person should repair to his place of origin, his proper home, to be counted there—the very fact recorded by St. Luke, that all went to be taxed, everyone to his own city. The evidence for this proclamation does not reach so far back as the reign of Augustus, but we know that was the regular custom a little later, and every historian regards it as certain that this must have been the practice from the beginning, because it is vouched for in this allusion to the first census. And one great German scholar, who is not concerned at all with the study of the New Testament, regards the proclamation as a proof that this passage of Luke is a legend, because the tale had to be made to correspond with the facts. Twenty years ago the passage was a legend because it was contrary to the facts; now he says it is a legend because it is so exactly true to the facts. It has never been in my experience a characteristic of any legend that it is true to facts; legend is always vague and misty, you cannot get hold of details.

Now, let us pass over the mere facts, assuming for this present time that the facts are all, as I have said, actually true, for it would take three or four hours to give you even an outline of the course of reasoning by which it has been established,* not merely in the estimation of scholars who approached the New Testament with a mind disposed to believe, but of scholars who have no interest in the New Testament, or are actually opposed to the historicity of the New Testament, that the facts recorded here are true. But not only are they true: what I would like you to observe is that they are large historical facts. This passage presents to us world-wide administrative measures, great forces working on human society. The fact that everyone was called to go up to his own home instead of being counted in the place where he lived, is related to one of the important forces working on human history centuries before Christ, and gradually elaborating itself in the serfdom of the Middle Ages—the system which lasted in Russia down to 1860.

You are dealing here with big historical processes, not merely with niggling details. The birth of the Saviour is set before us by Luke as taking place in these circumstances owing to the interplay of great forces which were moulding human society. The mere elaboration of a system of census taking for a single country is a big thing; it requires the collaboration of a large number of persons, and the whole value is in the collection of facts. No person devises the plan of a census simply for noting that there are so many hundreds or millions of persons in the country; what you want are the facts as to the class grouping of the nation; and the future economy of the nation has to be determined by what you learn from studying the census in conjunction with other methods of the study of the human society. But in the Roman Empire you have this system applied once every fourteen years, not to one country, but to the countries of the civilised world, and you can imagine what an enormous step that is in bureaucratic government; it implies the co-ordination of a great staff of men, it implies an extraordinarily intelligent apprehension of the principles on which government should rest. And this great fact we learned for the first time from this passage; subsequently we have come to know about it from the progress of archaeological study, from what we have got out of the rubbish heaps of Egypt and the

*An account of the evidence bearing on this and on some other passages is given in the writer's book, *The Bearing of Recent Discovery on the Trustworthiness of the New Testament.*

Wycliffe before the Convocation at Oxford
(1381)

marbles of the Grecian world. That knowledge has come to us within the last twenty years. The first time that the fact of a general census of the Roman Empire was stated by any learned historian was in 1892, when three different scholars—two German and one English—all independently, and within a few months of each other, published this discovery; and then, when once this discovery was published, you find it described in the Gospel of Luke; and, finally, it was not till about ten years later that Luke's statement about making the census by calling every person to his own home was discovered to be true. That, again, was found out when documents which contained the decree as it was issued by successive prefects in Egypt at the time of each census were discovered, a decree in which the people were called upon to go for the purposes of the census to their proper homes.

To my mind, an incident like this, which sets before us big historical facts, which brings you into contact with great forces moulding human history, is marked indubitably as historic. No person would dream of saying to Roman readers that there was a census if there had not been one. Notice that it was the first census—the first of a series. When I say that, I am assuming a fact about the meaning of Greek words which is disputed by many scholars, because it is maintained by many that when Luke used the word "first" he did not mean exactly what he said, but I think in every such passage if you take it rationally, you observe that there is involved the thought of a second and a third, and in this case there is the thought of many censuses in the writer's mind.

Now this passage, then, is not the mere fancy of some inventor of pseudo-romantic fiction. That is what it has been called by some writers, because you observe how pathetic it is. You observe the pathos with which the poor mother is set over against the mighty Emperor. He issues the order; she is compelled to go at such an unsuitable time on a troublesome, difficult journey from Nazareth to Bethlehem; and there is a distinctly pathetic and romantic—you might almost call it sentimental—effect in the studied contrast between the great Emperor and Mary the mother. But the surroundings show that it is history, as it is conceived by a true historian, a historian who can look into the heart of things, who thinks always on a great scale, who knows the real forces that go to make history. Now, of course, it is perfectly correct to say that every event when rightly looked at can be conceived in this way. The forces which play through the Universe make every single man in the course of their interplay, and these same forces unmake him when his span of existence is ended, but the person who can conceive and describe the life of any one being in that way, the person who can do that, is, I think, the true historian in the highest sense, or the great poet, or the prophet.

Augustus, then, formed this great plan of world survey and world registration, extending from the Atlantic Ocean to the River Euphrates, and from the coasts of the North Sea to Mount Atlas far away in Africa; and in the course of doing this, all that he succeeded in doing was to bring about the fulfilment of a prophecy. The Saviour must be born in Bethlehem. Now I confess that, when I see the self-satisfaction and the pretentious ignorance of the critical theologians miscalling and vilifying these historical facts, I find myself saying, these are the dull and blind savants whom the modern world has accepted as learned, and to whom so many have humbly bowed down and done worship. The man who cannot see the splendour of this passage, who is insensate to its historical character and its literary power, is absolutely blind. But Luke was sensitive to the dramatic character of the episode, and in fact, many critics have distrusted him because he has such a clear perception of the dramatic aspect of the story he is writing, and the literary effect of the episodes he describes.

But now, assuming all this is true, you are brought no nearer through the mere historical truth of these details to the ultimate fact that this Jesus was the Son of God. The surrounding facts may be true, but you have not thereby proved the ultimate truth of the one thing which makes the whole passage important. And that cannot be done. On the other hand, you must always remember that the falseness of those details, the falseness of the historical surroundings, would disprove the truth that lies behind. You cannot, it seems to me, have the real truth of the Divine origin of the Saviour encompassed with a crowd of false details; yet the truth merely of those details, the truth of a census taking and the travelling of people from one place to another does not of itself prove the ultimate fact. The essential truths do not condescend to be tested by historical evidence. The real truth with regard to the Nature of Jesus exists and moves on a higher plane. You have to know it through an absolute insight into the heart of human life and the Divine Nature. That insight comes to a man, or is granted to him, or is forced upon him, as the completion of his experience in this world; it proves itself to the soul of man. He must be able to see it for himself and to recognize the truth for himself; and when he sees it, he knows that it is the one truth, the one ultimate truth, in a world of half-truths, a world of preparation, a world in which he is being moulded and fashioned and hammered into a condition in which he is fit to see the truth himself.

And this knowledge cannot be proved by mere verbal argument, just as little as it can be proved by the truth of historical stories. It cannot be proved because it has not sprung from any more fundamental principle. You prove a thing by showing it originates from a deeper truth that lies behind it. But this is the ultimate truth of all; this is the fountain from which all other truths flow; this is the guarantee of all other truth. There is nothing true without God, and there is nothing true except the Divine power of the infinite variety of His manifestations. So no one can make mere historical investigation and historical proof take the place of faith. Faith is the power which enables you to distinguish the truth in the world, and it is not my purpose to suggest that you can put history in the place of faith. The more you see of the world, the more you recognize that the ultimate power of the world is the power of faith. The Christian religion is a matter of living, it is not a matter of mere intellectual knowledge—'the just shall live by faith.'

Still, it is really valuable to have the proof of the truth of the surroundings, these concomitants of the ultimate fact, because the falsehood of them would justly throw discredit upon the statement which is connected with them.

Furthermore, I should like to emphasize the importance of this episode, the story of the Birth of Jesus, as it is told by Matthew and by Luke. You do not have it even alluded to in Mark. It is mentioned by John only in that expression that 'the Word was made Flesh and dwelt among us.' Everything is contained in that verse; but it is expressed on the lofty plane of John's view of the universe. He looks straight at the Divine Nature in a degree that no other writer of the New Testament does. Paul occasionally rises to the same level of perfect communion with the Divine Nature, but John lives on it throughout the Gospel. Every sentence is written on the same level of sympathy with the Divine Power and the Divine Will. He had lived in contact with the Divine Nature, and he saw nothing else. John then in that one verse alludes to this matter in his own special style. Mark does not allude to it at all. Matthew and Luke describe it from different points of view, take it in different aspects, and especially Matthew describes one or two incidents which Luke altogether omits. The story of the Wise Men and their visit to Bethlehem is told not by Luke but only by Matthew. The Wise Men express to us the attitude which the wisdom of the East, the accumulated wisdom of the older world, occupied to the expected Coming of the Divine Saviour. The coming of the Divine Power to save man was looked for, was expected, and at the proper time, in the fulness of the times, the star arose. In one of the earlier parts of the Bible you find 'the stars in their courses fought against Sisera.' The powers of the Universe—to put this in modern fashion—the powers of the Universe were associated with the struggle that took place in the Plain of Esdraelon—all the powers which the Divine Will moves in the world were concerned in that battle in which Sisera was defeated. And so to the Asiatic mind, and from the peculiar point of view of the Asiatic, whatever the reason was, some particular star at a particular time, when it rose in the phases of its motion through the heavens, heralded to them the Coming of the Saviour, the Coming of Him who was to be born King of the Jews. But that was not the point of view from which Luke recorded this event. Luke, with his Western mind and his Greek way of looking at life, saw in the incident the play of great forces which were moulding history, and he describes it from that point of view. No Asiatic, brought up in the Asiatic way, looking at things from the Asiatic point of view, would look at it in that way. Luke sets it before us in the European fashion. But that does not prove that he was ignorant of or rejected the story of the Wise Men. It did not suit his special plan, it was not in accordance with his conception of the way in which human history develops.

And so, if you study this passage from every point of view, and take the different writers, each in accordance with his own conception of life, and of the relation of God to man, you see why each person expresses it in his own fashion, and yet all work together to give you a complete picture of the mightiest event in human history.

BIBLIA
The Bible/that
is, the holy Scripture of the
Olde and New Testament, faith-
fully and truly translated out
of Douche and Latyn
in to Englishe.
M.D.XXXV.

S. Paul. II. Tessa. III.
Praie for vs, that the worde of God maye
haue fre passage, and be glorified. &c.
S. paul Col. III.
Let the worde of Christ dwell in you plen-
teously in all wysdome &c.
Josue I.
Let not the boke of this lawe departe
out of thy mouth, but exercyse thyselfe
therin daye and nighte &c.

These are the lawes that thou shalt laye before them.

Title-page to Part 1 from Coverdale's Translation
of the Bible, 1535.

Textual Criticism

An Historical Note

By S. E. McNair, Brazil

Those who have followed the history of Textual Criticism during the last 60 years will know that until the end of the last century, or later, there were two schools of thought in the field, each confident of final victory, and assured that its case only needed to be clearly stated to win the approval of the studious.

In the so-called 'Critical' (Neologian?) School are found such illustrious names as Griesbach, Lachmann, Tregelles, Tischendorf, Hort, von Soden and Nestle. In the 'Traditional' School were Scrivener, Burgon, Birks, Field, Miller and Hoskier. It may be remarked that all the critical New Testament Texts printed during the last 60 years have been edited by members of the newer School. The older School persistently asserted that very much more preliminary investigation was necessary before the 'original Greek' could be rediscovered.

Anyone, even though but slightly acquainted with the subject, may wonder how it was that critical Greek Texts could be published by Griesbach, Lachmann, Tregelles, Tischendorf (in eight editions, all different), Alford, Hort, von Soden and Nestle, but not one by the Masters of the older School? The explanation is simple. The Traditional School insisted that ALL the critical material available—Manuscripts, Versions, Lectionaries, Fathers, etc.—well over 5,000 items in all, needed to be examined, while the Critical School considered that it had discovered a short cut to reach the desired end: merely to consult 4 or 5 of the oldest extant MSS., all of them admittedly belonging to the same family, and to ignore all contrary evidence.

In case anyone should challenge such an extraordinary statement as the above, I will give it in the very words of the famous scholar Constantine Tischendorf, copied from his *Narrative of the Discovery of the Sinaitic Manuscript.*

'Learned men have again and again attempted to clear the sacred text from these extraneous elements. But we have at last hit upon a better plan even than this, which is to set aside this *textus receptus* altogether, and to construct a fresh text, derived immediately from the most ancient and authoritative sources [still extant]. This is undoubtedly the right course to take, for in this way only can we secure a text approximating as closely as possible to that which came from the Apostles.'

This paragraph was written nearly a century ago, but I have not been able to hear of any modern scholar who has protested against it. I have added the words in [ ] as 'the most ancient and authoritative sources' can only be consulted in so far as they are still extant.

Whether the critical editors since Tischendorf's time ever read the pamphlet quoted above, I do not know, but only too evidently they have all followed his advice.

Hoskier comments on the 'new style' adopted by all the recent editors, as follows: 'There is no doubt that Hort chooses the short cut to "get there" by electing to adopt B readings in cases of doubt. It is not the royal road; in fact it is the disloyal road, when we consider how many witnesses he has to put aside. But it has a dangerous fascination for scholars. It is ingenious and ingenuous but it will never solve our problems.

'Thus in a variety of three or more readings . . . Hort almost invariably fell back upon B, even when quite alone, so that we know what to expect. It is otherwise with *von Soden's* text. One does not know what to expect, and it (his text) ends frequently by getting muddled and not following any document.'

But let us consider just what Tischendorf's amazing paragraph imports. It is proposed to throw overboard all the textual scholarship of all the centuries, to forget the thousands of priceless manuscripts available before the invention of printing (but no doubt burnt wholesale soon afterwards) and limit ourselves to a mere fraction of the comparatively few which still survive. In effect, to consult less than half-a-dozen of the oldest uncials still extant.

It is important to remember that *both* the rival schools endorsed Dr. Hort's declaration as to the *textus receptus:* 'The fundamental Text of *late extant Greek MSS.* generally *is beyond all question identical* with the dominant Antiochian or Graeco-Syrian Text of the second half of the fourth century.'

After quoting Dr. Hort's words, Dean Burgon adds: 'We request, in passing, that the foregoing statement may be carefully noted. The Traditional Text of the New Testament—the Textus Receptus, in short—is, according to Dr. Hort, 'beyond all question the Text of the second half of the fourth century.' We shall gratefully avail ourselves of his candid admission by and by' (*Revision Revised,* p.257).

Since Tischendorf's day the later editors—Hort, Weiss, von Soden, Nestle, etc.,—have faithfully followed his advice, and practically limited their investigations to the 5 or 6 oldest uncials. As each new editor follows along the same line it seems more and more unlikely that we shall ever see a text based upon a thorough investigation of ALL the existing evidence—over 5,000 MSS., Versions, Lectionaries, Fathers.

So far as I can discover, no one is at present interested to do this, but should it ever be done, the resultant text will still not be final. It will need to be weighed against the Text (almost) universally approved by the scholarship of the whole of Christendom from the fourth to the sixteenth centuries, during which period a vastly greater preponderance of ancient MSS. was available than now, and was decisive in forming the text accepted by the whole Church during twelve hundred years.

Indeed, the modern attempt to reverse the verdict of the centuries looks very similar to re-trying a legal case 50 years after the event, and when 90% of the witnesses are dead. We know exactly what ancient manuscripts are available now, and the agreement of 5 or 6 of them is, by the Surviving School, considered final. We have no notion how many hundreds or thousands of manuscripts, scattered all over Christendom, were available during the centuries, but we do know what was the verdict based upon their evidence *and recorded in the later cursives*—and we find that it substantially agrees with the Textus Receptus. Is it wise, is it scholarly, following Tischendorf's deplorable counsel, to flout the verdict based on the whole of the ancient evidence, and cast aside the Textus Receptus as unworthy of serious attention?

If there is one thing that modern textual scholars are agreed about it is that an 'authoritative revision' of the Greek text was made at Antioch (?) about the year 350 and was re-revised about 370; that it carried such weight with it that it could permeate Christendom until the invention of printing, then to become stereotyped in what is now called the Textus Receptus.

R. G. V. Tasker wrote in the *Harvard Theological Review* of April, 1948: 'The outstanding and permanent achievement of Hort was that he showed . . . that the text underlying Erasmus' edition . . . was in fact the result of a revision, which had taken place in the fourth century, and which set the standard for the ecclesiastical text of the Byzantine empire,' and it looks as if all the modern textual critics are anxious to make Hort's 'outstanding' achievement 'permanent.' Anyway they refer, one after another, to the 'Antioch Recension,' even though so long ago as 1882 Dean Burgon proved that we owe it solely to Hort's fertile imagination, and said that there was no historical record of any such thing.

However, as the moderns (not inconvenienced by the complete absence of historical evidence) accept the phantom Antioch Recension without question, let us do the same, and draw the inevitable conclusions.

We are asked to believe that the most learned ecclesiastics of the day, bearing a vast number of the oldest MSS., many of them certainly older than either Aleph or B, met carefully and prayerfully to eliminate all verifiable errors in the Greek text as then known. Evidently they were in great measure unanimous, as the result of their labours was acceptable throughout Christendom, and prevailed for the next 10 or 12 centuries—until, at the end of the nineteenth century, Dr. Hort and his followers declared that they were all wrong. Their prayers for divine guidance had been completely unavailing, for they invariably chose the wrong manuscripts to copy. Instead of closely following the Aleph-B family they left it severely alone. May we venture to believe that they did this because they had a great number of more ancient MSS. practically agreeing amongst themselves? That hypothesis would at once account for their preference. What other will do so? Anyway we know that what they handed down to the ensuing centuries was (approximately) the Textus Receptus.

And now, at this recent date, WE CANNOT REVERSE THEIR VERDICT, simply because we have not got, and never shall have, more than a fraction of the evidence upon which their decision was founded. And even if two or three more hoary manuscripts as old as Aleph or B should yet be discovered, in substantial agreement with either of them, even that would not serve to reverse the verdict—unless it can be proved that the (unhistorical) Revision Committee of A.D. 350 had only very few MSS. of inferior quality—which is absurd, as in that case their worthless revision could never have been imposed upon the whole of Christendom.

In the above I have not referred to recent discoveries of ancient manuscripts, which modern writers tend to assume are invariably on their side of the argument. But it would be interesting to verify just how many of the masterly findings of Scrivener and Burgon have been disproved by recently discovered documents.

To take a concrete case: the words *ho ōn en tō ouranō,* 'who is in heaven,' in John 3. 13. What recently discovered MSS. will prove to us that the words are NOT found in 13 uncials, in all the cursives except one, in all the Evangelistaria, in 10 Versions and in 38 of the Fathers? The *omission* of the words (perhaps on account of their difficulty) by four uncials and one cursive is quite understandable, but that all those Fathers should have quoted what was not there, just does not make sense.

I write all the above merely as an unlearned person, but I trust as one sufficiently intelligent to use common sense, and to draw conclusions from the findings of the experts.

Through all the changing scenes of life,
In trouble and in joy,
The praises of my God shall still
My heart and tongue employ.

Of His deliverance I will boast,
Till all that are distressed
From mine example comfort take,
And charm their griefs to rest.

The hosts of God encamp around
The dwellings of the just;
Protection He affords to all
Who make His Name their trust.

Oh, make but trial of His love,
Experience will decide
How blest are they, and only they,
Who in His truth confide.

Fear Him, ye saints, and you will then
Have nothing else to fear;
Make but His service your delight;
Your wants shall be His care.
(*Tate and Brady,* 1696)

Scholarship and the Verbal Inspiration of the Bible

By Thomas Houghton

'All Scripture is given by inspiration of God, and is profitable' (2 Timothy 3. 16).
'Holy men of God spake as they were moved by the Holy Ghost' (2 Peter 1. 21).

True Evangelicals are often saddened when they read in prominent lines in their newspapers Modernist attacks on the inspiration of the Bible, and denials of the truth of its narratives. These attacks are read in every village in the land, as well as in the large cities and towns, and the faith of the people in the truth of the Bible is thus undermined. No doubt this is a fruitful cause of the growing neglect of the Bible, and the increasing indifference to public worship on the Lord's day. When these attacks on the Bible are made by prominent clergymen and ministers in the professing Church there is danger that some even of the Lord's true people may begin to wonder if they are not mistaken in regarding the Bible as the verbally inspired Word of God.

One of the things said by Modernists in regard to those who hold the plenary inspiration of the Bible is that it is a proof of lack of education. As long ago as the year 1890 the then Bishop of Liverpool (Dr. J. C. Ryle) in a Charge which he delivered on November 4th of that year said, 'No educated person, we are constantly told nowadays, can really believe supernatural religion, or the plenary inspiration of the Bible, or the possibility of miracles' (p. 7).

We might reply that our Lord and His apostles believed fully in the plenary inspiration of the Old Testament. Are we then to have the daring to say that they were 'very ignorant'?

There can be no doubt of this, that if we follow the teaching of Modernists we must repudiate the teaching of our Lord, and of the apostles, and if we do this what have we left? We are really left without a trustworthy Bible at all, and without a trustworthy Saviour. It is appalling to see where Modernism is leading.

Now we do not undervalue what is generally regarded as education, but we venture to say that a man may be greatly distinguished for his university education, and yet be wholly incapable of grasping and knowing spiritual truth. 'The natural man,' says the inspired Apostle Paul, 'receiveth not the things of the Spirit of God: for they are foolishness unto him: *neither can he know them, because they are spiritually discerned*' (1 Cor. 2.14).

Now there are a great many people who have occupied high positions in the professing Church, and who have even been educated at our universities, and yet they have believed in the verbal inspiration of the Bible. To say that 'No bishop on the bench believes it now' does not prove that the doctrine is untrue. We live in days when men who are loyal to the old truths are passed over (despite their education) when vacancies occur on the Episcopal bench. We do not suppose that, if the Apostle Paul were now alive, he would ever be chosen for a bishop. In fact we rather think he would refuse to allow himself to be placed in so compromising a position, yet we think that the apostle is generally regarded as an educated man.

To us it is a sign of spiritual degeneration that 'no bishop on the bench believes' in the verbal inspiration of the Bible. It really shows how verbally true the Bible is; for that holy Book says, 'The time will come when *they will not endure sound doctrine*' (2 Tim. 4. 3). The rejection of the verbal inspiration of the Bible does not stand alone. The doctrines of the Fall, of the Atonement, of the Virgin Birth, of the bodily resurrection, and many other foundation truths are being also rejected. Once you deny the plenary inspiration of the Bible you are in danger of denying all other truths which are revealed therein.

We think it may reassure our readers if we bring before them proofs that even within recent times there have been and are a great many people, whose education is quite equal to that of the Modernists, who have believed in the verbal and plenary inspiration of the Bible.

In the year 1863, the Archbishops and Bishops of the Church of England, in a united protest addressed to Bishop Colenso, of South Africa, said, 'All our hopes for eternity, the very foundation of our faith, our nearest and dearest consolations, are taken from us, *if one line of that Sacred Book be declared unfaithful or untrustworthy.'* (Urquhart's *Inspiration and Accuracy of the Holy Scriptures, pp. 15, 16.)*

Now it is well known that Archbishops and Bishops are generally acknowledged to be educated men. Yet, so recently as the year 1863 the whole bench of bishops declared their belief in the plenary inspiration of every line of the Scriptures.

The late Samuel Waldegrave, D.D., Bishop of Carlisle, was no doubt an educated man, yet he said, 'The Holy Ghost so directed Isaiah, Matthew, Paul, that *each word which fell from their pen was, in very truth, not theirs, but His.'* Again, he says, 'The heavenly bodies are, every one of them, the handiwork of God; and even so were the Holy Scriptures, *every jot and every tittle of them, originally given by inspiration of God.'* (*Words of Eternal Life,* pp. 42, 43.)

Hear another Bishop: The late Dr. J. C. Ryle, Bishop of Liverpool, delivered a Charge to his clergy in November, 1890. In the course of the Charge he said, 'When you read the Bible, you are not reading the unaided, self-taught composition of erring men like yourselves, *but thoughts and words* which were suggested by the eternal God. The men who were employed to indite the Scripture "spake not of themselves." They "spake as they were moved by the Holy Ghost" (2 Pet. 1. 21). He that holds a Bible in his hand should remember that he holds not the word of man, but of God. He holds a volume which *not only contains, but is, God's Word.'* (*Hold Fast,* pp. 17, 18.)

The late Bishop Handley Moule says, 'As "the Spirit of Christ in the prophets" (1 Pet. 1. 11), the Third Person is the true Author of the Scriptures.' (*Outlines of Christian Doctrine,* p. 139.)

From Bishops let us turn to Canons of the Church of England. Hear the late Canon A. R. Fausset, who was undoubtedly a great scholar. He says, 'Once for all, let me state my unhesitating conviction of the plenary and verbal inspiration of 'all Scripture,' and of Holy Scripture alone.' (*Critical and Experimental Commentary,* Vol. 3, p. 4, Preface.)

Hear the late Canon Hoare, of Tunbridge Wells. He says, 'The minds of the writers (of Scripture) were so moved by the Holy Ghost that the word written by them is to be received as the word of God.' 'The whole of the Scriptures is the Word of God . . . . We have not to search from Genesis 1 to Revelation 22 in the hope that if we are sufficiently fortunate we may find somewhere or other some scattered seeds of hidden truth; but we have Divine truth from the beginning to the end, and we may apply to the whole the words of Our Blessed Lord, "Thy Word is truth." ' Again, he says, 'If we cannot rely on Scripture as a communication from God, we have nothing to take its place; and all our present joy, as well as our future hopes, must melt away into utter ignorance respecting all that lies beyond the range of science, and utter hopelessness as to all beyond this present world.' 'If we believe in the Lord Jesus Christ, we must receive the books of Moses as inspired Scripture; and never can we abandon them till we are prepared to admit that in His own sacred teaching the Lord Himself has misled His people, or, in other and plainer words, till we cease to be believers in Jesus.' 'There will be found ultimately to be no intermediate path between receiving the whole as the Word of God, or sweeping away the whole and launching forth on a sea of scepticism, without a Bible, without a Saviour, and, as the last step, without a God.' 'The more I have studied the subject the more firmly am I brought to the deliberate and fixed conviction that the whole book, *including words* as well as thoughts, is to be received by the believer as the Word of God.'

Again, Canon Hoare says, 'I am prepared to receive the whole book as invested with infallible accuracy from God Himself, and in taking this view of the subject, I feel the great satisfaction of believing that I am in harmony with the mind of St. Paul, St. Peter, and our great Head Himself.' (*Great Principles of Divine Truth*, pp. 4, 5, 6, 16, 21, 23, 26, 30).

Hear what the late Dean Burgon said: 'You cannot dissect inspiration into substance and form. As for the thoughts being inspired, apart from the words which gave them expression, you might as well talk of a tune without notes, or a sum without figures. No such dream can abide the daylight for a moment. No such theory of inspiration is even intelligible. It is as illogical as it is worthless.' (Quoted by Bishop J. C. Ryle in *Thoughts on Higher Criticism,* p. 37.)

Hear Dr. Charles Hodge, one of the greatest and most learned theologians of the nineteenth century. He says: 'All the books of Scripture are equally inspired. All alike are infallible in what they teach.' (*Systematic Theology,* Vol. 1, p. 103.)

Hear Dr. Robert Young, a great Hebrew and Greek scholar and the author of the *Analytical Concordance* and many other learned works. He says in his preface to the *Analytical Concordance,* written in 1879: 'In sending forth the *Analytical Concordance* for the benefit of the Christian student of Holy Writ, the author trusts that as it is only the practical outcome of all his previous Biblical studies, many of his readers, lay as well as clerical, may give themselves more to the study of the Original Scriptures, which have "God for their Author, Truth without mixture of Error for their Matter, and Salvation for their End." '

Hear the late Dr. S. P. TREGELLES. Dr. Tregelles died on April 24th, 1875. He edited *A Critical Edition of the Greek New Testament* and devoted his whole life to the accomplishment of this great task. He translated *Gesenius' Hebrew and Chaldee Lexicon* and wrote many other works which indicated that he was more than a 'so-called educated person.' Yet he fully believed in the plenary and verbal inspiration of Scripture. That he was regarded as a really educated man is evidenced by the fact that 'in 1870 he was invited to join the New Testament Company of the English Revision Company; but ill-health prevented him from attending.' (*Schaff-Herzog Encyclopaedia,* Vol. 4, p. 2388.)

Here then is a man who in the eyes of his contemporaries was admittedly a scholar. What does he say of verbal inspiration? He says: 'I consider inspiration to be a fact, not a theory; a fact which makes Holy Scripture to be what it is—the *Word of God* (so termed by our Lord Himself in Mark 7.13) and not the word of man.'

'The inspiration of the whole includes, of necessity, the inspiration of the parts of that whole, and words are the *only* medium by which ideas are set forth to us.'

'The *fact* of inspiration, which we have to uphold, irrespective of all *theory*, is, that it is *plenary* in its character, so that the *ideas* are from God, though written by men, that the phraseology in which the ideas are clothed is precisely what He *intended* it should be, and that the words, as written by His inspired servants, may be rested on as fully as being the exponents of His mind and of the ideas which He wished to convey, as those of a mere human author are of *his own* sentiments.' "All Scripture is given by inspiration of God," so that everything in it, narratives, prophecies, citations, are such as He saw fit to be there; and the whole—ideas, phrases, expressions and words—was given forth exactly as was according to His mind and will.' (*Tregelles on Daniel,* pp. 275, 279, 281.)

In view of the doctrine of Modernism, that the truths of the Bible are being superseded by present-day advances in science, we print another extract from Dr. Tregelles' book on Daniel, found on p. 285. He says, 'If it be intolerance to cleave to the truth of God, then let us be intolerant. If it be bigotry to maintain that there is no development of Divine truth, but that all is complete in Holy Scripture (whether understood or not), then let us be bigots. If it be narrow-minded prejudice to deny that modern advance in science has superseded one point of Christian verity, then let us be obnoxious to these and even worse charges, rather than surrender the truth of God, rather than overlook that the true place of Christian love is to work by truth, and by upholding the plenary authority and inspiration of the Word of God.'

Hear the Testimony of a Hebrew Christian. The late David Baron, the founder of the *Hebrew Christian Testimony to Israel,* was certainly a Hebrew scholar. In the preface to his *Types, Psalms, and Prophecies,* he says, 'My chief guide has been the Hebrew Bible itself, with the letter of which I have been familiar from my childhood in the old, pious Jewish home.'

He was the author of a large number of Biblical works, including a large volume on *The Visions and Prophecies of Zechariah.* He was more therefore than a 'so-called educated person.' What does he say about inspiration? We quote the preface of his *History of Israel,* p. 6.He says, 'The Scriptures carry their own Divine seal, and the more we seek to penetrate to the wonderful inner depths which they contain, the more deeply is the conviction wrought in us *that they are not of man's origination, but are God-breathed*' (italics ours).

Hear another Converted Jew. The late Dr. Adolph Saphir was more than a 'so-called educated man.' What does he say in reference to verbal inspiration? He says, 'The inspiration of Scripture is a fact, not a theory . . . . We receive the fact, asserted by the Scriptures themselves, and abundantly confirmed by them, that, though written by men, they are of God, and *that the ideas they unfold are clothed in such words* as He, in His wisdom and love, intended, so that they may be safely and fully received as expressing His mind, and the thoughts which He purposed to convey to us for our instruction and guidance.' (*Christ and the Scriptures*, pp. 101-2.)

The late Sir Robert Anderson wrote, 'In spite of all that has been said about it, indeed, some of us believe that the Bible is the Word of God. But this only proves our want of intelligence. For, we are assured, no one believes it nowadays unless he is "a brainless idiot." ' This is another quotation showing that many Modernists regard believers in verbal inspiration as 'very ignorant,' uneducated, or even idiotic.

The quotations we have given, however, show clearly that many godly men of great educational attainments have unhesitatingly believed that the whole Bible is indeed and in truth a verbally-inspired volume. A good many of the Lord's beloved and redeemed people have not received a university education, but they have sat at Christ's feet, and heard His Word. They have been 'taught of God,' and they have as a result come unto Christ and found pardon, peace, and joy through His blood and righteousness. This is the highest and best form of education. Many of the learned ones have never been taught by the Spirit. They have never experienced His regenerating and saving power. Being destitute of spiritual eyesight, they are unable to perceive and know spiritual truths. Hence they reject 'the things of the Spirit of God' (1 Cor. 2. 14). The Lord's humble-minded and Spirit-taught people, however, need not be disturbed by this solemn fact. And if they are told that it is only so-called uneducated people who believe the verbal inspiration of Scripture, they can show from the above testimonies that this is not true. But above all the testimony of godly and learned men, we have the testimony of Our Lord and the testimony of His apostles. No one can truthfully deny that they regarded the Old Testament Scriptures—all of them from Genesis to Malachi—as the verbally-inspired Word of God. We need not therefore hesitate to take our stand with them, 'BELIEVING ALL THINGS WHICH ARE WRITTEN IN THE LAW AND IN THE PROPHETS' (Acts 24.14).

Break Thou the Bread of Life,
  Dear Lord, to me,
As Thou didst break the loaves
  Beside the sea:
Beyond the sacred page
  I seek Thee, Lord;
My Spirit pants for Thee,
  O living Word!

Thou art the Bread of Life,
  O Lord, to me,
Thy Holy Word the truth
  That saveth me;
Give me to eat and live
  With Thee above;
Teach me to love Thy Truth,
  For Thou art Love.

Oh, send Thy Spirit, Lord,
  Now unto me,
That He may touch my eyes,
  And make me see:
Show me the truth concealed
  Within Thy Word,
And in Thy Book revealed
  I see the Lord.

Bless Thou the Truth, dear Lord,
  To me—to me—
As Thou didst bless the loaves
  By Galilee:
Then shall all bondage cease,
  All fetters fall,
And I shall find my peace,
  My All in all!

(*Mary Artemisia Lathbury,* 1880)
(v. 3 by *Alexander Groves*)

An Examination of 2 Timothy 3. 16

By J. Willoughby

In the Authorised Version we read, 'All Scripture is given by inspiration of God, and is profitable . .'; in the Revised Version we read, 'Every Scripture inspired of God is also profitable . . .' The difference in the two renderings is accounted for thus: Sometimes in a sentence in Greek the verb meaning 'is' is not expressed but is understood. This is the case in the original of this passage. The word translated in the A.V., 'given by inspiration of God,' and in the R.V., 'inspired of God,' means, literally, 'God-breathed.' Those who made the A.V. thought the verb was to be understood before both the word meaning 'God-breathed' and the word meaning 'profitable.' The Revisers thought it was to be understood before only the latter. In the margin, however, they gave an alternative rendering, namely, 'Every Scripture is inspired of God, and is profitable . . .'

Now, because of the rendering in the text of the R.V. some think this passage does not prove the Divine inspiration of all the Old Testament. They think, I take it, that Paul is distinguishing between Old Testament Scriptures given supernaturally by God, and Old Testament Scriptures supposed not to be thus given. But would there have been any use whatsoever in saying, 'Every Scripture God-breathed is profitable,' if masses of Old Testament Scriptures were not God-breathed at all, and if we had no means whatsoever of knowing what were God-breathed, and what were not? Some profound Greek scholars hold that the R.V. rendering in this instance is an incorrect translation.

Providentially it is easy to show that Paul is not distinguishing between Old Testament Scriptures supernaturally given by God and Old Testament Scriptures supposed not to be thus given; for it is easy to show that he believed all the Old Testament Scriptures to have been supernaturally given by God.

Paul's Spoken Witness.

Speaking in a law-court before Felix as his judge he said, 'But this I confess unto thee that in the way which they call heresy so worship I the God of my fathers, believing all things that are written in the law and in the prophets' (Acts 24. 14). Now apostles, when speaking in law-courts before judges were given by the Spirit of God the very words they uttered (Matt. 10.19, 20; Luke 12.11, 12). Paul was in nothing behind the very chiefest of the apostles (2 Cor. 12. 11), therefore when uttering the above statement he was given the words by the Holy Spirit. Accordingly, he without hesitation, equivocation, or mental reservation, when under verbal inspiration, made the striking declaration that he believed all things written in the law and the prophets, that is, in the Old Testament Scriptures; for our next passage shows that he believed all the Old Testament Scriptures to have been written by prophets of God.

Now, since he believed all the Old Testament Scriptures to have been written by prophets of God, and since he believed all things written therein, many of which are records of long conversations, and many of which are records of the most extraordinary events, some of which took place before any human being existed on earth, I submit that he believed them all to have been supernaturally given by God.

Paul's Written Witness.

Again, writing to the Roman believers he said, 'Whatsoever things were written aforetime were written for our learning that we through patience and comfort of the Scriptures might have hope' (Rom. 15. 4). That he was speaking of 'whatsoever things were written' in the Old Testament is clear from the words, 'that we through patience and comfort of *the Scriptures* might have hope.' The Hebrew canon which is identical with our Protestant Old Testament Canon was known by the Jews in Paul's day as '*The Scriptures.*' Paul, then, asserted in the most unqualified way that in the Old Testament everything without any exception was written for the information and benefit of Christians who did not live on earth for hundreds of years after the last of the Old Testament Scriptures had been written. These Scriptures he elsewhere called 'the holy Scriptures' (Rom. 1. 2), and 'the Sacred

Letters' (2 Tim. 3. 15, lit. rendering). That he had God in his mind as the Being who caused them to be written is clear not only from the fact that he calls them 'holy Scriptures,' and 'Sacred Letters,' but also from the fact that immediately after saying, 'that we through patience and comfort of the Scriptures might have hope,' he speaks of God as the Source of *patience* and *comfort*: 'Now the God of patience and consolation grant you to be likeminded . . . ,' and in v. 13 he speaks of God as the Source of *hope*: 'Now the God of hope fill you with all joy and peace in believing . . . ', and in Eph. 1. 3, he ascribes all spiritual benefits to God.

According to the Apostle Paul, then, '*whatsoever things were written*'—whatsoever paragraphs, sentences, clauses, phrases, words, and jots—in the Old Testament were supernaturally given by God.

The Significance of 2 Tim. 3. 16.

We are now ready to consider further 2 Tim. 3. 16. For our present purpose it does not matter now whether the rendering in the A.V., or that in the R.V., is the correct one. If the former is correct, Paul manifestly means every Scripture in those Scriptures referred to in the preceding verse, namely, the 'Sacred Letters' which Timothy had known from his early days, namely, the Old Testament Scriptures. If the latter rendering were correct, Paul would not be distinguishing between Old Testament Scriptures supernaturally given by God and Old Testament Scriptures supposed not to have been thus given; for we have seen that he believed all the Old Testament Scriptures to have been thus given. He would be distinguishing between writings supernaturally given by God, including all the Old Testament writings, on the one hand, and writings not thus given, such as apocryphal, classical, and other ordinary writings, on the other hand.

As has been pointed out, the word rendered in the A.V. by 'given by inspiration of God,' and in the R.V. by 'inspired of God' means literally 'God-breathed.'

A Logical Conclusion.

Now it would be illogical to say that a certain chain is a gold chain, but that its links are not gold links. If the chain is of gold, its links are of gold; for the chain is made up of the links. Similarly it would be illogical to say that the Scriptures are God-breathed, but that the words therein are not God-breathed. If the Scriptures are God-breathed, the words therein are God-breathed; for the Scriptures are made up of the words.

The words of a speech delivered by a man, and accurately reported and published, are *man-breathed*; the words of Scripture are God-breathed.

Holy Bible, book Divine,
Precious treasure, thou art mine!
Mine, to tell me whence I came,
Mine, to teach me what I am.

Mine, to chide me when I rove,
Mine, to show a Saviour's love,
Mine art thou to guide my feet,
Mine, to judge, condemn, acquit.

Mine, to comfort in distress,
Mine, with promise sweet to bless,
Mine, to show by living faith
Man can triumph over death.

Mine, to tell of joys to come,
Mine, to show the sinner's doom;
Holy Bible, book Divine,
Precious treasure, thou art mine!

(*J. Burton*)

The Authority of Scripture*

By C. Breed

My intention is to discuss the authority of Scripture, not so much from the standpoint of controversy with the unbeliever, but rather to examine its nature for the further establishing of our confidence and hope in God. Clearly, there must be an Authority. All the thought of men through the ages has again and again come back to that fact. In any department of investigation even aside from religion and theology some ultimate standard must be reached by which we may judge, by which we may be guided; and in matters concerning our souls and the life that is to come, we are profoundly in need of an authority to guide and establish our thought, to mould our character, to direct us in the way.

False Conceptions of Authority.

This search after authority has in history tended to show itself in three ways. It has manifested itself first in the form of *Rationalism*; secondly, in the form of *Mysticism*; and thirdly, in the form of *Romanism*. These are supposed authorities, apart from what we submit is the true Authority.

According to the rationalistic system, reason is the ultimate Court of Appeal in every investigation. Both the deistic and transcendental forms of rationalism reject every supernatural revelation and believe in no source of knowledge save that which nature can give, or which may be deduced from the constitution of the mind of man. Even the dogmatic form of rationalism which admits the possibility of a supernatural revelation, and even allows that such a revelation is found in Scripture, none-the-less puts the doctrines of Scripture into a philosophic form and submits them all to the reason of man, so that reason remains supreme.

According to the system of mysticism, feeling or intuition is the ultimate Court of Appeal in all matters. Just as the rationalist regards reason as the standard, so the mystic regards feeling as the standard. Here we have two forms: a supernatural form of mysticism which teaches that the Holy Spirit enlightens the minds of all men giving them feelings and intuitions concerning the truth, and this independently of Scripture; and a natural form of mysticism which claims that man's natural religious tendencies are sufficient to guide him in the investigation of the truth. Clearly, here also there can be no such thing as revelation and inspiration in the Reformation sense of those words, and the work of the theologian can be nothing more than the interpretation of his own consciousness rather than the interpretation of Scripture.

Thirdly, there is Romanism. Here authority resides in the Church, and such authority as is allowed to Holy Scripture really leans back upon the Church and is derived from the Church. In this connection, misuse is often made of a passage from Augustine, the gist of which is to the effect that he could not believe the Gospel except on the authority of the Church. Calvin points out in his *Institutes* (Book 1, chap. 7) that this quotation from Augustine has been misunderstood. In its context, it represents Augustine's taking the position of an unbeliever, and as such he says he has no ground to believe the Gospel, except on the authority of the Church. The statement therefore meant nothing to Rome's advantage. Has Rome been a custodian of the Scriptures, and has that authorised her to interpret the Scriptures? If she has been a custodian, she has been one who has wrapped the Scriptures in a napkin and hidden them in the earth! Is the postman who brings me my letters authorised to interpret them to me?

**Footnote by the Author*: Readers will kindly observe that in this article the question of Biblical authority is treated from the believer's point of view. Consequently stress is laid on the inner work of the Spirit as the counterpart of the external authority of Scripture. The intrinsic authority of Scripture is in no way doubted.

True Biblical Authority.

Now I want to submit certain statements regarding the true conception of Biblical authority. First of all, the authority of Scripture cannot be merely an external authority; that is, an authority entirely outside my soul. Suppose the following: someone comes to me with a written book and says, 'Here is a message from the man in the moon, who demands your obedience and claims that you must conform your life to these instructions.' I should first need an answer to one or two questions. First, a proof that there *is* a man in the moon and, given that, secondly, why should I obey him? If it should be answered, as it conceivably might be answered, that obeying him is advantageous to me and disobeying him is disadvantageous to me, then it would follow that this authority would not be a sole external authority since it would depend for its force upon my personal advantages or disadvantages. In this way the Scriptures are an external authority, but they cannot be solely an external authority.

Secondly, the authority of Scripture cannot be solely an internal authority. We shall not dispute that the Scriptures witness in the consciences of the regenerate. An authority which is solely within myself, entirely subjective, renders me independent of anything external. A sole internal authority would loose me from the claims of Scripture. It would give no norm or standard of conduct, no principle that could be utilised, for there seem to be as many intuitions about the Truth as there are individual persons; and as many reasonings about the Truth as there are individual minds. No mere internal authority will satisfy the needs of the case.

And thirdly, as I see it, neither is the authority involved a combination of the external and the internal. It is not a mere harmony between my intuition and the statements of objective Scripture. If this were so, do you not see that this authority would depend in the ultimate view upon the something which brought together these two parts—the external and the internal? The authority would not reside in either, but in their coming together.

Therefore, I want to submit that in the ultimate issue the authority with which we are concerned is at one and the same time —*internal and external.* Let me read to you a statement of the Westminster Confession of Faith. Chap. 1, section 5, reads like this:

> 'We may be moved and induced by the testimony of the Church to an high and reverent esteem of the Holy Scriptures. And the heavenliness of the matter, the efficacy of the doctrine, the majesty of the style, the consent of all the parts, the scope of the whole (which is, to give all glory to God), the full discovery it makes of the only way of man's salvation, the many other incomparable excellencies, and the entire perfection thereof, are arguments whereby it doth abundantly evidence itself to be the Word of God: yet notwithstanding, our full persuasion and assurance of the infallible truth and divine authority thereof, is from the inward work of the Holy Spirit bearing witness by and with the Word in our hearts.'

Calvin, in the chapter of the *Institutes* I have already alluded to, brings out the same thing. The Holy Spirit who witnesses in the believer is the Holy Spirit who is the author of Scripture. These are not two testimonies. The inner and the outer are but the two sides of the one thing. The one authority of God is witnessed externally in the written Word, and internally by the experienced Word. This is the authority with which we deal.

Listen to the witness of the Book itself. Begin at the 7th chapter of the Gospel by John, v. 17—'If any man will do His will, he shall know of the doctrine, whether it be of God, or whether I speak of Myself.' Here observe the two sides to this knowledge: the external teaching of Christ, and the internal knowledge of the one who is willing to do His will (a sure characteristic of a renewed person). The inner witness, and the external witness are one; and only such as possess this witness *know* with certainty that God is authoritative in His Word. Turn to Corinthians, the First Epistle, and the second chapter. Passing over other passages, notice verses 14 to 16: 'But the natural man receiveth not the things of the Spirit of God: for they are foolishness unto him: neither can he know them, because they are spiritually discerned. But he that is spiritual judgeth all things, yet he himself is judged of no man. For who hath known the mind of the Lord, that he may instruct Him? But we have the mind of Christ.' Here there is a spiritual experience which makes real, to the individual concerned, the truth and revelation of God. The two sides of the one witness are present.

Turn to the 14th chapter of 1 Corinthians to notice verse 37: 'If any man think himself to be a prophet, or spiritual, let him acknowledge that the things that I write unto you are the commandments of the Lord.' Notice that the appeal is made to the *spiritual* man to acknowledge that what Paul writes constitutes the commandments of the Lord. The authority is complete where the inner experience and the outer Word are but two aspects of one Divine operation.

Once again, John in his 1st Epistle writes in chapter 5, verse 1, 'Whosoever believeth that Jesus is the Christ is born of God: and every one that loveth Him that begat loveth Him also that is begotten of Him.' Verse 4, 'For whatsoever is born of God overcometh the world: and this is the victory that overcometh the world, even our faith.' Verse 10, 'He that believeth on the Son of God hath the witness in himself: he that believeth not God hath made him a liar; because he believeth not the record that God gave of His Son. And this is the record, that God hath given to us eternal life, and this life is in His Son.' You notice the same linking of facts—born of God, faith in Christ, belief of the record.

To proceed, let me observe the nature of this authority, looking at it for the moment with special reference to Scripture in its relationship to inspiration. As I see the position I feel that the Christian Church has sometimes laid itself open to rationalistic attacks, by viewing this matter from the wrong angle. It is popularly assumed that we can prove by logic the inspiration of the Bible, and can then pass to the further belief that the Scriptures are therefore the Word of God. This seems to me a mistake. The proof of inspiration does not lie in the realm of philosophical discussion. When Paul wrote that second chapter in the First Epistle of Corinthians, he correctly asserts that he came to them not with the 'words of man's wisdom,' because he would not have their faith stand in the wisdom of men, but in the power of God. Now if faith stood in the wisdom of men, then it would be possible to prove the fact of inspiration by human wisdom; but it cannot be done. It is a notable fact that many highly intelligent people, well-versed in logic, do not believe in the inspiration of the Bible. I submit that our approach to this question must come from the other side, from the side of faith. When this witness in my soul and this witness of the Scripture are one, then by faith I am led to realize that here I have the Word of God, and believing that, I listen to its claims and find that it claims inspiration. That is the only proof of inspiration. It lies in the realm of faith, and not in the realm of human wisdom. Most Christian people if they look back in their own personal experiences will realize that they had an inner consciousness that this Scripture was God's Word speaking to them, before they knew anything at all concerning the pros and cons of inspiration. I feel therefore that this fact of authority is first witnessed in the conscience and then we can perceive that this authority on the Biblical side leans back on inspiration. All Scripture is God-breathed, but breathing is a double action—in and out. He has breathed in the appointed agents, and He has breathed out through them; and He has thus produced the supernatural marvel that we call Scripture.

Let me carry this back a further stage by pointing out that inspiration, including the canonicity of Scripture, leans back upon a Divine plan. Or, to borrow a technical word from Dr. Hodge, I will refer to the architectonic principle in Scripture. The architect is the man who designs a house before it is built, and architectonic, with reference to the Bible, means that the whole thing was conceived in the mind of God before ever a word was written. The canon of Scripture did not just happen, least of all was it conceived by any Church Council or decided in any Church Assembly. It was planned before ever a word was spoken by a human agent, and when it took its shape, stage by stage, it did so according to the eternal mind of the Everlasting God. When the Tabernacle was made it had to be made according to a pattern that was shown to Moses. There was nothing haphazard about it. When the Church of the Living God was produced and finally will be perfected, it was and is according to a pattern that He had preconceived. There was nothing of chance about it.

I think we have at least two hints regarding this particular principle of Scripture indicated for us. Let me ask your attention to them. In the second chapter of James, we have these verses (21-23): 'Was not Abraham our father justified by works, when he had offered Isaac his son upon the altar? Seest thou how faith wrought with his works, and by works was faith made perfect? And the Scripture was fulfilled which saith, Abraham believed God, and it was imputed unto him for righteousness.' In other words, according to James, when Abraham offered up his son on the altar, Scripture was fulfilled—the Scripture which said, 'he believed God and it was imputed unto him for righteousness.' Now the act of Abraham is recorded in Genesis, chap. 22, and the statement about the imputation of righteousness to him is made in Genesis, chap. 15. 6, 'And he believed in the Lord and he counted it to him for righteousness.' Hence according to James, when Abraham subsequently offered his son Isaac, he fulfilled and exemplified that statement. But when Abraham offered up his son on the altar, *not one word* of Scripture had been written. Yet in that offering, the Scripture was fulfilled which said, 'Abraham believed God, and it was imputed unto him for righteousness.' Does this mean that something called Scripture is so called even before it has been set down? If so, then the principle is established. Before it was written God had designed it, planned it. The other instance arises from Matthew 26, in relation to the woman who had anointed Christ with ointment, in v. 13, 'Wheresoever this gospel shall be preached in the whole world, there shall also this, that this woman hath done, be told for a memorial of her.' How could Christ make that assertion, unless a record of that deed was to be made, and sent to the ends of the earth and repeated in the testimony of the Gospel? So here again something is conceived before it is done, and a record is determined upon before it is made. The whole Book was in the mind of God. He has expressed His mind through the miracle of inspiration and thus established the authority of the Book. Then He completed that establishment by His internal witness in the hearts of the redeemed.

To conclude. This is the authority which stands behind the witness of the Christian Church. This is the authority which stands behind the propagation of the Gospel of God to the uttermost ends of the earth. No revival ever came out of Rationalism; no one was ever brought to the foot of the cross by Mysticism; no man was ever loosed from the fetter bonds of sin by Romanism. But *this* Authority is my authority for warning the sinner to flee from the wrath to come. This is my authority for asserting that everyone who is coming to Christ shall 'not be cast out.' This is my authority for sending the news of a Saviour's cleansing blood far and wide. And believing *that*, we cry with the Psalmist:

'Gird Thy sword upon Thy thigh, O most Mighty;
And in Thy majesty ride prosperously.' (45: 3-4)

O that the Lord would guide my
ways
To keep His statutes still:
O that my God would grant me grace
To know and do His will.

O send Thy Spirit down to write
Thy law upon my heart!
Nor let my tongue indulge deceit,
Nor act the liar's part.

Order my footsteps by Thy word,
And make my heart sincere;
Let sin have no dominion, Lord,
But keep my conscience clear.

My soul hath gone too far astray,
My feet too often slip;
Yet since I've not forgot Thy way,
Restore Thy wandering sheep.

Make me to walk in Thy commands,
'Tis a delightful road;
Nor let my head or heart or hands,
Offend against my God.
(*I. Watts*)

Are there 'Degrees' of Inspiration?

By Dr. A. Marshall

Having regard to the differences that undoubtedly exist between the various parts of Holy Scripture, it is sometimes suggested that there are 'degrees' of inspiration—that is, that one part may be more inspired than another; that inspiration may be but partial here and full there. Such cannot be the case. Inspiration is a fact, and a fact admits of no degrees. Either a thing is so or it is not so. A given writing cannot be partly inspired and partly not inspired; and if it were possible, who is to draw the line of demarcation?

But that there is a difference between, say, the book Ecclesiastes and Paul's letter to the Ephesians is undeniable. How may we account for it? The writer has found the following analogy helpful in his own mind and in speaking on the subject to others.

He has a number of maps, to be described as follows: *Map No. 1.* This is really not much of a map: it gives the limits of the area covered by a section of the particular telephone area in which the writer lives, with parts of those that are contiguous. It merely shows a number of towns and villages where there are telephone exchanges. It gives neither county boundaries nor rivers nor railways nor ground levels.

Map No. 2. This gives the omnibus routes covered by the local motor company. Again, there are no railways shown, though connecting points are indicated. Some geographical features are given, as befits the purpose for which the map is drawn; but still no county boundaries or rivers.

Map No. 3. This is a street plan of the town where the writer lives and is useful for finding his whereabouts locally. But no churches or public buildings are shown—only the general lay-out of the neighbourhood.

Map No. 4. Here is a diagrammatic map of London's underground lines—in which the River Thames is shown as following straight lines at angles. No roads are shown, no places of interest, no metropolitan borough boundaries, though within the area there are 27 of these.

Map No. 5. This indicates the bus routes of London and its suburbs; it shows parks and open spaces, but no buildings and no railways, though stations are indicated.

Map No. 6. Here we have a map of Central London, showing main thoroughfares, with underground stations printed in red, and giving principal places of interest.

The point to be emphasized is that each of these maps is perfectly accurate for the purpose for which it was drawn; no one is deceived or misled, because no reasonable person would expect to find in it that which it was not designed to give. Two or more of them could be used complementarily, and not one contradicts another. Their reliability is equal, having in mind the purpose which each was intended to serve.

So in Holy Scripture we have a number of books—66 in all, following our English reckoning. Now, 'all Scripture is God-breathed.' But the Holy Spirit had different purposes to serve in producing these books and so He chose different men, just as different men drew up those maps. Let us deal with the two books above mentioned.

Ecclesiastes was written by a man to whom God had given wisdom, so that he could look out on the world and see things as they really are 'under the sun.' There is not a single false or erroneous statement in the whole book. It is fully inspired and perfectly accurate within its limits, and must not be condemned and criticized because it does not go beyond those limits. It inculcates the fear of God as to the things of the life that now is, and in conclusion looks beyond to one that is to come. It enjoins obedience to the commands of God, and if it does not reveal how those commands can be obeyed by sinful man, that is because God's purposes had not then been fully made known.

The Epistle to the Ephesians, on the other hand, though no more inspired than Ecclesiastes, tells us more of God's ways. The writer knew the mind of God more fully. His outlook was not limited to this present life, though he recognizes its existence (chaps. 4-6); he knows of 'heavenly places' (1:3,20; 2:6; 3:10; 6:12). Whereas Solomon was not a man of faith (he is not in Hebrews 11 as his father is), but went by the things that he could see, Paul walked by faith and not by sight.

So we affirm the need for distinguishing the various purposes for which the books of Scripture were written—narrative, prediction, devotion, instruction, and so on; all are the result of holy men writing as they were moved by the Holy Spirit, and for the purpose for which they were given, are therefore utterly reliable and trustworthy.

THE GREAT BIBLE: 1539

The Authority of Scripture

By Dr. D. Martyn Lloyd-Jones

A sermon on 2 Peter 1: 19-21, preached in Westminster Chapel on 15th of December, 1946.

In the section running from the beginning of the sixteenth verse to the end of this first chapter we have what we may describe as the 'Apologetics of the Apostle Peter.' Here is a man writing a letter to help Christian people who are in difficulty, who are facing troubles and problems. He gives them the only possible advice that can be given to such people. They must know the faith and they must realize its possibilities. They must realise who they are and that to which they are called. They must realize the perfect provision that God has made for them in every respect, and then they must go on to put that into practice. Then they are assured that if they do this their lives will not be barren or unfruitful, they will not be contradicting in practice what they claim to believe, and as they approach the end of their lives they will find an abundant entrance awaiting them into the everlasting Kingdom of God. That is the message, and Peter goes on to say that he intends to repeat that message to them as long as he is alive. He then seems to imagine someone asking certain questions. 'How can we know all that? How can we know it to be true? You are asking us to do a very big thing. We can see your argument. You are telling us that because of these things we have got to stake and risk our all upon it. It isn't a claim for intellectual contemplation of truth, it is a practical message that asks a man to put it into practice and venture his all upon it. Very well, how can we be sure it is right? How can we know that you haven't been telling us cunningly devised fables?'

Apostolic Witness

Well, let us recall the first step in Peter's apologetics. It is the Apostolic witness and testimony. Ultimately our whole position is based upon that. We either accept or we reject what these first Apostles reported concerning the Person and life and the works of our Lord and Saviour Jesus Christ. Remember how Peter put it. He said 'We . . . were eyewitnesses of His majesty.' In effect he said, we saw His miracles, we beheld Him doing things that no other man had ever done before; we were with Him on the Holy Mount of Transfiguration; we saw the Divine glory and effulgence suddenly emerging from Him; we saw Him as we had never seen Him before; but beyond even that we heard a voice from heaven which came and said, 'This is My beloved Son, in whom I am well pleased.' That is the first part of his apologetics.

The Holy Scriptures

But that is not all. He goes on to mention the second great section of his apologetics. That is, of course, the Scriptures. Those are the two things on which we ultimately stand. The Apostolic witness and testimony, and the Holy Scriptures. In verses 19, 20 and 21 he deals with this second aspect. But here again there is a double argument. Let me, for the sake of clarity of thought and exposition, indicate these two arguments. First he says there are the events which have verified prophecy. That he deals with in verse 19. The other is the nature of the Scripture itself; and that is the subject with which he deals in verses 20 and 21, which we are looking at together this morning. Facts of prophecy, yes; but in addition to that, the nature of prophecy itself. And not only the nature of prophecy, but the nature of Scripture as a whole. Notice how Peter puts it—'Knowing this first, that no prophecy of the Scripture.' Prophecy is a part of Scripture, so what is true of prophecy is true of the whole of Scripture. You remember that passage out of the Second Epistle of Paul to Timothy, third chapter, in which exactly and precisely the same claim is made. Very well; then the important thing is to discover exactly and precisely what Peter means here. 'Knowing this first, that no prophecy of the Scripture is of any private interpretation. For the prophecy came not in old time by the will of man: but holy men of God spake as they were moved by the Holy Ghost.' Now the important thing here is to know exactly what the Apostle means in verse 20, and I imagine I am right when I say that there has been no single phrase of Scripture that has produced such a variety of different interpretations as this particular twentieth verse. For those who are interested in exposition, and in the elucidation of the meaning of Scripture, I do not think there can be anything that is more fascinating than to study the history of the interpretation of this twentieth verse. The twentieth verse of this chapter has figured very prominently in the great religious controversies of the centuries. It is a verse on which in a sense the great division as between Roman Catholicism and Protestantism is based. It is therefore an extremely significant and important statement.

What does 'Private Interpretation' mean?

Let me give you a hurried account of some of the main lines of interpretation which have been suggested and put forward in an attempt to explain this verse. 'Knowing this first, that no prophecy of the Scripture is of any private interpretation.' This is how it reads in the Authorised Version. Here are some of the explanations that are put forward. Let me deal with them historically. So we start with the Roman Catholic exposition, and the Roman Catholic exposition is precisely the one you would expect. They say, there of course is the statement of Scripture itself that private judgment is something which must be rigidly excluded—it is only the Church that can interpret the Scriptures. No prophecy of the Scripture is of any private interpretation! Protestantism, they say, with its claim for private judgment and for the universal priesthood of all believers is therefore once and for ever condemned completely—nothing, they say, is more dangerous than that this Book should get into the hands of the common people and that people should try to interpret and understand it themselves. There is only one safe thing to do, they say, and that is to go to the Church. The Church alone can interpret this great tradition that has come down, hence the Councils and the Cardinals and the Pope. 'No prophecy of the Scripture is of any private interpretation'; nothing can be so dangerous as that individuals should face that word and by themselves should try to understand it. As already stated, this word has played a very prominent part in the whole argument as between Roman Catholicism and the Protestant position with respect to apologetics and the whole basis of our faith. Do you believe in the Church as well as in the Word, or do you say that the Word itself is the final authority and that the Church is not absolutely necessary to the interpretation of the Word, and must herself be judged by the Word?

Another view which has been put forward is that we have a caution here against the interpretation of any particular prophecy on its own—the view which says that the only way to interpret is to interpret it in the light of the whole prophecy. No prophecy is itself of any private interpretation; in other words, be very careful, they say, that you do not take hold of just one prophecy and on one prophecy elaborate a great doctrine or a great body of doctrines. To understand prophecy aright, they say, you must take an individual prophecy and put it in the light of the whole of the other prophecies; that is the only safe thing to do.

Then there are those who have said that what it means is that the prophets themselves were not capable of understanding all that they said in their own prophecies. The prophets sometimes spoke without understanding what they said. You will find that Peter makes that actual statement in the first chapter of his first Epistle in verses 10 and 11 and there are those who would interpret this statement in that manner. They say, even the prophet himself did not always understand what he was saying. 'No prophecy . . . is of any private interpretation.'

Again there are those who have suggested that what it means is that prophecy is not its own interpretation, and does not carry its own interpretation in itself, but that it can only be understood when the events come to pass which it has prophesied and predicted. They say, therefore, that you cannot pretend to interpret prophecy until it has been fulfilled—that is what is meant by 'no private interpretation'—you must wait for the event before you seek for the meaning of the prophecy.

The last common explanation that has been put forward is that no man reading prophecy, or even the prophet himself who expresses it, is able to interpret the prophecy by his own understanding; he can only do so as he is illumined and guided by the Holy Spirit. What they say, therefore, is that no man as he is can understand prophecy—'prophecy is of no private interpretation,' you must have the illumination of the Holy Spirit upon your mind before you can see or understand or interpret it aright. Those are the common ideas that have been put forward in the past in an attempt to interpret this particular statement.

A Closer Examination

Now as we go on to look at them surely what we must feel is this—that while there are elements of truth in all these expositions apart from the Roman Catholic, surely they all seem to fail in this sense, that they take this twentieth verse by itself and fail to consider it in the light of the twenty-first verse. But verses 20 and 21 surely must be taken together. The very word 'for' at the beginning of verse 21 makes that imperative. 'Knowing this first, that no prophecy of the Scripture is of any private interpretation. *For* the prophecy came not in old time by the will of man: but holy men of God spake as they were moved by the Holy Ghost.' Very well, verse 21 surely throws a great light upon verse 20. Not only should we bear that in mind, but we must bear something else in mind. Take that word 'is' in verse 20. Now it is generally agreed that the translation 'is' is rather unfortunate at that point. It really means 'arises,' or 'originates,' or if you prefer it, 'comes into existence.' Now let us look at that word 'interpretation' for a second. If you trace this word you will find that it is sometimes translated by the word 'expounding' or 'expound' or by the word 'determination,' so that the idea we have is something like this: 'Knowing this first, that no prophecy of the Scripture, originates or arises, as the result of any private determination.' Well, I think we begin to see exactly what Peter is saying. If I may translate it a little more loosely, we can put it like this, 'Knowing this first, that no prophecy of the Scripture originates in the prophet's own understanding of things.' And when I put it like that, you will see how naturally it leads on to verse 21. 'No prophecy of the Scripture arises or originates in the prophet's own understanding of things, for the prophecy came not in old time by the will of man: but holy men of God spake as they were moved by the Holy Ghost.'

Now there, I think, we have the only reasonable, rational and satisfactory explanation of this particular verse. And of course it links up perfectly with what Peter has already been saying in verse 19: 'We have also a more sure word of prophecy; whereunto ye do well that ye take heed, as unto a light that shineth in a dark place, until the day dawn, and the day star arise in your hearts.' Why should I take heed unto this Scripture and prophecy? Why should I meditate upon it? Why should I base my life upon it? The answer is that this prophecy has already been verified by the Incarnation, and in any case prophecy is not a mere recording of the meditation and cogitation and thought and understanding and insight of man; it has not originated in any determination on man's part, it is not the expounding of man's views—'prophecy came not in old time by the will of man: but holy men of God spake as they were moved by the Holy Ghost.' In other words these two verses go together, and the statement of verse 21 is very strong and powerful. Look at it as it is translated in the Authorised Version. 'The prophecy came not in old time by the will of man.' Now that is not as strong as it ought to be; we ought to say, 'Prophecy never came,' not at any time, 'no prophecy ever came (or was brought) by the will of man, but holy men of God spake as they were moved by the Holy Ghost.'

'Driven Along'

There is one other word which I have to deal with, and then our exposition is complete. Holy men of God spake as they were 'moved' by the Holy Ghost. Now a better way, perhaps, of putting it would be, 'Men spake from God as they were moved by the Holy Ghost'; and you are familiar with the fact that the word translated 'moved' could perhaps be still better translated 'carried along' or the one which commends itself to me above all others is 'driven,' 'driven along.' The expositors are all very fond of referring us in connection with this word 'moved' to the twenty-seventh chapter of the Book of the Acts of the Apostles. We remember the story that is given there of the shipwreck of St. Paul and his companions as they were on their way to Rome. We remember the graphic way in which the story is told, how that mighty wind, Euroclydon, arose, and there was that little ship buffeted and tossed about, and the sailors and the captain of the ship were at their wits' end. First of all they lightened the ship, then they threw the cargo overboard. They did everything man could do at that time in order to save the ship, and in a very graphic way we are told that, having done all things, 'we let her drive.' Then we are told she was driven along—that is the very same word that is used here—'holy men spake from God as they were driven along by the Holy Ghost,' or by the Holy Spirit.

Here, then, is the statement which the Apostle makes—Scripture, he tells us, and prophecy in particular, must never be thought of as just a collection of the thoughts and ideas of men. This of course is absolutely vital and fundamental. The prophecy and the prediction of Scripture are not the results of human insight and human understanding. Now this can never be emphasised too much, especially during these present years. A vital part of the so-called higher criticism of the Bible is to hold a particular view about prophecy. Ah, they say, our fathers were all wrong, they thought prophecy meant foresight and foretelling; what it really means is insight. What they really believe is that what we have in the Old Testament is nothing but the writings of men who had a profound insight into life, wise men, understanding men, men who pondered the times in which they lived, men who thought and wrote and argued and reasoned, and as a result of that great process expressed their insight. Here in these writings, they say, we have insight, not foresight. Now the Apostle Peter is at great pains to point out that what we have in these records is not just the insight of men. Indeed, he goes further; he says that, in a sense, they never intended to write, they never set out to write, 'prophecy came not in old time by the will of man.' It is not man deciding to write what he thinks, it is more than that. It is not like a man writing an article in the newspaper. Very well, what is it? The great claim that is made is this, that these men were taken hold of by the Holy Spirit. The Holy Spirit came upon them and took hold of them and gave them a message, carried them along, drove them along as they wrote and put it down on record.

Not Man's Word, But God's

And that of course is exactly and precisely the claim that is made by the prophets themselves—these are the very terms that are used—'the Word of God came unto them,' or 'the Word of the Lord came unto them'—'thus saith the Lord.' They do not say 'this is what I think,' but 'thus saith the Lord.' The other phrase is, 'the burden of the Lord,' referring to the message that the Lord has put upon them, the thing that has come to them from the Lord, the constraint of the Lord that is making them write—these are their terms. And what substantiates that still further is the thing of which I have already reminded you, namely, what we are told by the Apostle Peter in his first Epistle, to the effect that there were times when the prophets themselves did not understand the things they were writing. Far from it being their own thought and idea, this is what he says: 'Of which salvation the prophets have inquired and searched diligently, who prophesied of the grace that should come unto you: searching what, or what manner of time the Spirit of Christ which was in them did signify, when it testified beforehand the sufferings of Christ, and the glory that should follow. Unto whom it was revealed, that not unto themselves, but unto us they did minister the things.' There, then, is a further proof that it was a message that was given. But we can go even beyond that. We are told definitely and specifically that these men were not only called by God through the Holy Spirit, but that sometimes they were called against their own will and against their own desire. We remember how often Jeremiah, poor Jeremiah, objects to it all. Have we recently read chapters 15 and 20 of his Book? Read them again and notice how often he says, I do not want to give that message, I know it will lead to trouble and I shall become unpopular—I shall probably be thrown into prison; but God is speaking and God has said, 'You must give it, you are bound to speak this word.' God called him against his will; he did not want to speak. Ah! how often has that been true of the prophets—this call of God, not their own will. It has been laid upon them, they have literally been driven by God the Holy Spirit, as that ship was driven in the Adriatic.

The Scriptural Doctrine of Revelation

In other words, we have set out by Peter in this very explicit manner the great New Testament and Old Testament doctrine of revelation. The claim is made here that God has been pleased in His infinite compassion and condescension to speak to men. The claim is made for this Book that it is absolutely unique, that there is no other book in the world like it. All other books are the production of man; they are the result of man's will, man's understanding, man's insight. But here is a Book which claims that it is the record of God speaking. That is the great principle of revelation, and in particular inspiration. And this is the second great fact on which we stand, and on which we decide that the whole of our life must be lived in terms of this Book. It is not human thought and understanding, and men trying to predict and prophesy what is going to happen. Here we find that God in the heavens has been pleased to make known unto men certain things that are of vital importance. The teaching of the Book, in other words, is that mankind because of sin cannot arrive at a knowledge of God, but that God in spite of that has been pleased to grant this knowledge unto man. We cannot here deal in detail with this doctrine of inspiration, but we can put it like this. The Bible teaches us that God, who is inconceivable to man, has been pleased to reveal Himself to man in two main ways. First, there is a general revelation which you get in nature and in creation and, if we like, in the process of history. But in addition to that, there are special forms of revelation. God revealed Himself sometimes in the old dispensation in what are called Theophanies—appearances amongst men. You read about the 'Angel of the Lord,' the 'Angel of God'—well, those are the Theophanies, the appearances of our Lord in human form—not incarnation but appearance. Then God sometimes revealed Himself by addressing people in words and in actions. God sometimes revealed Himself also in miracles. But above all we desire to emphasise that God has revealed Himself by speaking to certain chosen servants, and by revealing His message unto them and by enabling them to record it—that is the claim for the inspiration of the Bible. We see that God guided men like Moses. He recorded facts. The Epistle to the Hebrews tells us, 'Through faith we understand that the worlds were framed by the word of God' (11:3). Now that was a fact that was revealed by the Spirit of God unto Moses. It was not Moses' imagination or idea or discovery; it was revealed unto him, and he recorded it. Likewise with all the other facts. And so with prophecy and prediction—these are events communicated to the prophets by the Holy Spirit of God. The doctrine goes even further than that. It does not merely tell us that the man was inspired, it does not merely say that the Truth was inspired; it announces that the very recording itself was inspired. Not only was the man taken hold of, he was carried along, he was borne along. We believe that the Words of Scripture are inspired by the Holy Spirit.

Not a Mechanical Doctrine

Does that mean, says someone, that these men were but amanuenses? Does it mean that they were just taking down what God dictated to them? No, we do not believe in a mechanical doctrine of inspiration, because you cannot read the Scriptures without noting the variation in style. When we read a certain passage you know that it has been written by St. Paul; we recognise Paul as we read it. Likewise when we come to passages written by Peter, we say, 'Obviously that is Peter.' Anyone can recognise the style of John. No! personality has not been effaced. The doctrine means this, that these men were so controlled by the Holy Spirit that they were safeguarded from error; they were guided not only to a knowledge of the Truth, but in their expression of the Truth. Their own personality was given free play, but it was controlled by the Holy Spirit, and that guaranteed this ultimate result. Now this of course is one of the most amazing and miraculous things of all. We claim that it is the Word of God. Why should I believe it? asks someone—well, here is the answer. In this Book we have the only account of God that man has. What can we know about God truly except what we are told in this Book? You can reason if you like through nature and you will arrive at a Creator. You will never arrive at a Father and a loving God; you will never know God as the Father of our Lord Jesus Christ. It is only as God has revealed Himself and His character and His holiness in this Book that we really know anything about Him.

But not only that, God has here revealed His own ideas concerning man, and life, and the world. What do we make of life? Here we are told how man came into existence, how all man's troubles are the result of sin, what God has done about sin, and what God is going to do about sin. Here is a map of history. Here is a philosophy of the ages. Here we are told what is going to happen in the days that lie ahead—and that, you will remember, is Peter's immediate point here. He has been telling these people about the return of Christ, about the Second Coming. How can I know that this is going to happen? Well, my ultimate and only answer is this. I find it is stated in this Book, and I believe that this Book is not the imagination of man but God the Holy Spirit speaking through man. So this is the position: I am confronted by these inspired, authentic records, and I believe what I believe about Christ because I find it here; and I therefore believe when I am told that He is coming again. I either accept this Book and its verities, or else I base my life and view of the future upon the thoughts and ideas and insights and understandings of men. And as I am confronted by those alternatives, I say for myself that I am driven to believe this Word, which is not of man's will, but which is the product of men moved, borne along, inspired, carried along, driven and guided by the Holy Spirit. Here is a Word which in truth and in fact is the Word of God Himself. It is not private interpretation, it is not human understanding; it is God speaking. Let him who is wise hear the Word of God.

The woman ſeduced. Geneſis. 2

1.Cor 11,8.

23 Then the man ſaid, * This now is bone
of my bones, and fleſh of my fleſh. She
ſhalbe called " woman, becauſe ſhe was ta-
ken out of man.
24 * Therefore ſhal man leaue p his father
and his mother, and ſhal cleaue to his wife,
and they ſhalbe one fleſh.
25 And they were bothe naked, the man &
his wife, and were not q aſhamed.

"Or, Mannes, because ſhe cometh of man: for in Ebr. Iſh, is man, and Iſhah the woman.

Mat.19,5. mar.10,7. 1 cor.6,16. ephes 5,31.

p So that mariage requireth a greater duetie of vs towarde ȳ wiues, thē otherwiſe we are bounde to ſhewe to our parents.

q For before ſinne entred, all things were honeſt and comely.

THE SITVACION OF THE GARDEN OF EDEN.

La grand Armenie. "Or, Armenia the great.

Terre de Hauilah. "Or, land of Hauilah.

La cheute d'Euphrates. Or, the fall of Euphrates.

La cheute de Tygris. Or, the fall of Tygris

Le golfe de la mer Perſique Or, the golfe of the Perſian ſea.

GENEVA BIBLE: 1560

Holy Scripture Its Own Evidence

By Dr. Adolph Saphir

The Scripture is its own evidence. God did not leave a matter of such vital importance as the authority of Scripture to depend upon minute investigation, for which only the learned have leisure and ability; nor upon abstruse and metaphysical argument, for which the mass of mankind have no aptitude. There must be something about the Scripture obvious and tangible, to prove its authority and demonstrate its high origin. Apart from the testimony of the Spirit, without which there is no true and vital faith in the Word of God, there seem to me to be five great and simple facts in connection with Scripture, which declare distinctly and clearly its heavenly origin.

1. The Doctrine of Scripture

We find in Scripture, doctrine which man never could have discovered, and which, now that it is revealed, no man and no age can exhaust. The one fact proves that a higher than human mind is the Author of the book; the other is a sign of its infinite and eternal character.

1. *Take the idea of God, such as the Bible gives us.* So spiritual, and yet so simple. God is infinite and incomprehensible, dwelling in light inaccessible, and full of glory; high above all that is created and finite; whom the heaven of heavens cannot contain, and before whom even the angels veil their faces as they adore Him. And yet He is presented as being near unto us, even unto all that are of a broken and contrite heart; as listening unto the sighing of every humble child, and condescending to reveal Himself unto babes. How spiritual and sublime is the Scripture teaching of God! how homely and simple its revelation of the Father! Scripture reveals to us God as the great Creator of the universe, the Governor and Upholder of the world, the adorable King of angels, who obey His commandments; and at the same time we are assured, that not even a sparrow can fall to the ground without His will, and that the very hairs of our head are numbered; we are taught that we may commend to His guidance the minutest duties of our life, and expect His answer to our prayers on behalf of our daily troubles and difficulties. Scripture reveals Him as a God of holiness, justice, and truth, who is of purer eyes than to behold iniquity, and whose throne is established in verity and righteousness; and Scripture unfolds to us the mercy, the compassion, the tenderness of God—His delight in blessing, His glory in His wonderful grace. Whence this idea of God, so sublime and yet so simple, so spiritual and yet so tangible, so pure and holy, and yet so gracious and loving? Do we find anything to be compared with it among the Greeks and Romans? It has come down from above. God revealed Himself.

2. *Or take the idea of the law of God.* What the Bible teaches us concerning man is no less wonderful than the idea of God which it brings before us. What is man? As nations advance, their idea of humanity advances. While savage nations value man according to his strength, subtlety, courage, and even cruelty, civilized nations have a higher and more intellectual and moral standard of human excellence. But what is the true, the perfect idea of man? Look at the Scriptures, teaching us that man is created in God's image. And because since the Fall we do not know clearly what that means, God gives us in the law His idea of humanity; and the law teaches us that man is to love God with all his heart, and his neighbour as himself. How wonderful are the Ten Commandments! How high is the law of God, elevating man to communion in love with the Lord God! How deep—requiring truth in the inward part, the affection of the soul, the surrender of the will! how broad—taking cognizance of all our varied relationships, of all occupations, circumstances, duties; entering into all the minute detail, into all the ramifications of our earthly life! And this idea of man, existing in the original purpose of God, realized in Adam, and subsequently described in the law of Jehovah, is afterwards manifested in greater fulness and glory in the person of Jesus Christ, the second Adam. This is the second idea revealed in Scripture, above human thought and discovery, the Divine idea of man.

3. *The Bible idea of redemption.* Of sin we have no adequate conception. Scripture reveals to us the depths of sin, as offence against God and as a disease—as guilt and pollution. But as the Bible-view of

sin far transcends our thought, still more wonderful is the Bible idea of redemption! Take a beautiful vase, a masterpiece of art, and dash it to the ground, so that it is shattered into a hundred pieces. Who can restore it? Who can unite the fragments, so that the beauty and harmony of the original shall again show forth the master's skill and thought? Yet what is this compared with the Fall, when man's understanding became darkened, his heart alienated from God, his conscience burdened, his will enslaved, his imagination defiled, his soul and mind and affections corrupt; when man became dead in trespasses and sin, so that from the inmost centre of his being to the very members of his body sin reigns unto death? And then see how the idea of redemption runs from the very threshold of the Bible in Genesis to the topmost stone of the edifice in Revelation. And such redemption! Full pardon of sin, so that our souls are whiter than the snow; enemies are reconciled, and adopted as children of God; condemnation is removed, and the kingdom of heaven is opened; the heart is changed, the will set free, the mind enlightened; in short, as sin abounded unto death, grace doth much more abound unto life! Whence such a glorious thought?

4. *Man never could have conceived this.* But could man have conceived the superabundance of this grace, restoring us not merely to the lost Paradise, and to the condition of Adam before the Fall, but giving us far more than we lost and placing us far higher than man at his creation? For we are accepted in Christ, the Beloved, and by the Holy Ghost we are one with Jesus, who is the Son of God, one with the Father. Ours is not merely peace, but Christ's peace; not merely life, but Christ's life. Christ is given to us for ever, and we are members of His body, one with Him in the Spirit. Thus are we partakers of the Divine nature, and from Christ the quickening Spirit is our new life. Who could have thought of this?

5. *And then notice how Scripture reveals to us all this as a portion of the counsel of God.* Into the council chamber of eternity, into the secret purpose which God purposed in Himself, before the foundations of the world were laid, the Word of God takes us, and shows us that according to this purpose God created the world in Christ, elected Israel, sent His Son, brought in the Church, Jews and Gentiles in one body, that in the ages to come Christ and the Church should manifest His glory, and that thus His grace should be seen and adored by angels and the nations of earth. (Ephes. and Coloss.) Who could have found out this, or imagined it? A plan so vast, so grand, so beautiful, could only emanate from Him who is God, who is love; and none could have known it but the chosen ones, to whom He revealed His will. And now that it is revealed, we cannot exhaust the Scripture teaching. It is above us and beyond us. We can only exclaim, 'Oh, the depth of the riches both of the wisdom and knowledge of God! how unsearchable are His judgments, and His ways past finding out! For who hath known the mind of the Lord? or who hath been His counsellor? For of Him, and through Him, and to Him, are all things. To Him be glory for ever. Amen.'

2. The Prophecy of Scripture

Scripture contains predictions which have been fulfilled. These predictions are marvellous, both on account of their comprehensive grandeur, containing great historical outlines and principles, and on account of their circumstantial and minute detail. The one was beyond the mind of the prophets, the other beyond their calculation.

Predictions of Messiah's Life

Let us consider only one great subject of prediction, the history of the Lord Jesus Christ. The whole life of the Saviour, from His birth to His ascension and His sending forth the Spirit, may be narrated in the words of Moses and the prophets. Without referring to the four evangelists, the whole history of Christ in its great outlines, as well as its minute particulars, has been foretold by the Spirit through the Scripture.

We ask first concerning His birth. And Genesis 3 informs us, that He is to be emphatically the seed of the woman; while Isaiah teaches us that the mother of the Saviour, the great Immanuel, is to be a virgin, and that this Child thus born, this Son given unto us, is the Wonderful, the Counsellor, the mighty God, the everlasting Father, the Prince of Peace.

We inquire further, Whose Son is the Messiah to be? The Scripture points out Shem, for 'Japheth shall dwell in the tents of Shem'; and still further we are directed to Abram, and still further to Isaac (as distinguished from Ishmael), and still further to Jacob, and from among the twelve sons of Jacob, the patriarch on his deathbed singles out the tribe of Judah; out of him shall come Shiloh, and to Him shall be the gathering of the nations. But Scripture is still more definite. The son of Jesse, even David, receives the promise of the great King and Redeemer. Thus we know that the Messiah is God and man; born of a woman, even of a virgin; a Sethite; a descendant of Abraham, Isaac, and Jacob; of the tribe of Judah; of the house of David.

His Birth

Where is He to be born? Like the wise men from the east, we would naturally suppose in Jerusalem, the holy city, the city of the great King. But Micah knows differently, and points out Bethlehem Ephratah, little among the thousands of Judah: 'Out of thee shall He come forth unto Me that is to be ruler in Israel, whose goings forth have been from of old, from everlasting.'

When is He to be born? Jacob predicts the period: 'The sceptre shall not depart from Judah, nor a lawgiver from between his feet, until Shiloh come;' and Daniel more definitely speaks of seventy periods of seven which are to elapse from the going forth of the commandment to restore and build Jerusalem, before the coming of the Messiah the Prince.

Born in Bethlehem, He is to be taken into Egypt; as Hosea saith, 'I have called My Son out of Egypt.'

What is to prepare the world for His coming? What great event is to announce His advent? Isaiah and Malachi tell us it is to be a man, a messenger, 'the voice of one crying in the wilderness, Prepare ye the way of the Lord, make straight in the desert a highway for our God.'

What is to be His character? 'Behold My Servant, whom I uphold; mine Elect, in whom My soul delighteth; I have put My Spirit upon Him. He shall not cry nor lift up, nor cause His voice to be heard in the street. A bruised reed shall He not break, and the smoking flax shall He not quench.'

His Ministry

What is to be His work? 'He shall open the eyes of the blind, and the ears of the deaf shall be unstopped. The lame man shall leap as a hart, and the tongue of the dumb sing.'

What is His preaching? 'The Spirit of the Lord God is upon Him, because He hath anointed Him to preach good tidings unto the meek.' 'The Lord God hath given Me the tongue of the learned, that I should know how to speak a word in season to him that is weary; He wakeneth mine ear to hear as the learner.'

How will the people receive Him? how will the rulers and guides of the nation welcome Him? 'He is despised and rejected of men.' The builders reject the stone.

Is He to appear as Jerusalem's king? and in what manner? Zechariah tells us: 'Behold, thy King cometh unto thee: He is just, and having salvation; lowly, and riding upon an ass, and upon a colt the foal of an ass.'

His Death

What is to be the end of His life on earth? Daniel tells us He shall be 'cut off.'

Who is to deliver Him into the hands of His enemies? The Psalmist tells us, one of His friends, he that eateth bread with Him; and Zechariah states that for thirty pieces of silver He shall be betrayed.

Will His disciples stand by Him in His last sufferings? No; the Shepherd is smitten, and the sheep of the flock are scattered.

How is He to die? He is the Lamb; and is to suffer a slow, painful death, and not a bone of His body is to be broken. Moses teaches us that His blood is to be shed, and that He is to be lifted up as the serpent in the wilderness. Zechariah adds another feature of His sufferings: He is to be pierced. No other mode but that of crucifixion fulfils all these descriptions.

What further happened during His crucifixion? The twenty-second Psalm tells us: 'All they that see Me laugh Me to scorn: they shoot out the lip, they shake the head, saying, He trusted on the Lord that He would deliver Him: let Him deliver Him, seeing He delighted in Him. I am poured out like water, and all my bones are out of joint. My strength is dried up like a potsherd; My tongue cleaveth to my jaws. They part My garments among them, and cast lots upon My vesture.'

What further circumstances attend His death? 'He opened not His mouth.' 'He is brought as a lamb to the slaughter, and as a sheep before her shearers is dumb, so He openeth not His mouth.' 'He was numbered with the transgressors.'

Why did He suffer? Isaiah answers: 'He was wounded for our transgressions, He was bruised for our iniquities: the chastisement of our peace was upon Him; and by His stripes we are healed.'

Was it only man who caused His sufferings? Isaiah saith, 'It pleased Jehovah to bruise Him; He hath put Him to grief;' and Zechariah saith, 'Awake, O sword, against the Man that is mine equal; smite the Shepherd.' And in the words of David His soul is to cry, 'My God, My God, why hast Thou forsaken Me?'

His Resurrection

Is He to remain in the grave? David says, 'Thou wilt not leave my soul in hell, neither wilt Thou suffer thine Holy One to see corruption;' 'The stone which the builders refused is become the head-stone of the corner;' while Jonah's history prophesies the same; and Hosea speaks of the third day as the day of revival.

And after His resurrection? the sixty-eighth Psalm says, 'Thou hast ascended on high, Thou hast led captivity captive: Thou hast received gifts for men; yea, for the rebellious also, that the Lord God might dwell among them.' And in another Psalm it is written, 'The LORD said unto my Lord, Sit Thou at My right hand, until I make Thine enemies Thy footstool.'

The Life of Christ in Moses and the Prophets.*

The picture of the Messiah in its grand outlines was quite above the conception of Israel, and even of the prophets, at any time. Even after the fulfilment it was new to the people, different from their ideas, high above their thoughts and expectations. And as for the circumstantial fulfilment of the wonderful detail, who can explain it on natural principles?

The prophets spake of the grace of God, as the Spirit revealed unto them the sufferings of Christ and the glory that should follow. Theirs was not the insight of great minds into future history, based on their profound knowledge of the present. It was a Divine prediction of events intimately connected with the kingdom of God. It was not in accordance with the ordinary laws which govern the history of the world, but in harmony with the laws of the Divine kingdom as they had already partially become manifest, and as they were more fully to be unfolded in the future. The events which are singled out are not those which would strike man as especially important; while events which by us are regarded as the most influential are often passed over with silence. But in the great day it will be seen that prophecy throws more light on history than history on prophecy.

These considerations are sufficient to show that the Scripture prediction is essentially spiritual, and inseparably connected with its whole teaching and history. It may be added, that although the people to whom the prophecy was addressed, and even the prophets themselves, did not fully understand the things signified by the Spirit, yet the prophecy was always connected with the peculiar history, trial, and difficulty of the people at the time; so that it was a warning to the ungodly, guidance and encouragement to the God-fearing, and a new test which separated the precious from the vile. (Thus Jer. 15-19; Dan. 9, etc.).

*Gen. 3:15; 9:26, 27; 12:3; 17:20, 21; 49:8-10; Isa. 7:14; 9:6; 11:1-10; 2 Sam. 7; Micah 5:2; Dan. 9; Hos. 11:1; Isa. 40 and Mal. 3; Isa. 42; 35; 61; Isa. 53; Zech. 11:13; 12:10; 13:7; Ps. 41:9; Exod. 12:46; Ps. 22; 16; 68:18; 110:1; 118:22, 23.

As *miràcle* is the intervention of God's grace in *act, prophecy* is the intervention of God's grace in *testimony*. Both appear on the background of man's failure; both are intended by the Divine wisdom, which educates His children and rules the world, as a help and consolation to the flock, and the hardening of the wicked.

Prophecy is a Proof of the Divine Origin of Scripture

Its force is, unlike that of a miracle, not dependent on the credibility of testimony. *It is its own evidence.* It is fulfilled before the eyes of the world. The Jews, Tyre, Babylon, Nineveh, demonstrate to all who have eyes to see that we have a sure word of prophecy, and that the mouth of the Lord hath spoken. The words of the prophets find their best explanation in the actual condition of the nations and lands of which they spake; and all men may see it, that the Lord God, who alone can see the end from the beginning, hath revealed these things to His servants the prophets.

The most striking fulfilment of prophecy is seen in

The Existence of the Jewish Nation

Forty centuries have run their course since the first promise of the nation was given unto Abram. As Balaam predicted, the people dwell alone, and are not reckoned among the nations. While the ancient Egyptians, Assyrians, Chaldeans, and Romans—the mightiest nations the world ever saw—have disappeared, Israel lives, and has survived all the fearful calamities and persecutions which came upon them. Driven from their own land, dispersed among the nations, for centuries denied the privilege of possessing land, subjected to insult, robbery, and persecutions of the greatest cruelty; they still exist, numerous, energetic, in vigour of body and mind, mysterious alike in their preservation as in their isolated position. In the midst of the numerous changes which have occurred in the history of nations, Israel is the historical nation, or, as Isaiah calls his people, 'the everlasting people' (Isa. 44:7, Heb.); a witness of the sacred history recorded in Scripture, a pledge of the fulfilment of a yet greater and more glorious Theocracy. And when the metaphysical subtleties as well as the refined secularism of our age turn with aversion from all direct interference of God, whether in the past as recorded in the history, or in the future as recorded in the prophecy of Scripture, the Jews are a living sign and irrefutable evidence of the truth of the Bible. Miracle and prophecy find in them their living monuments. No wonder that the greatest philosopher of our age (Hegel) felt the Jewish history a dark and perplexing enigma. It is the miracle of History as it is the history of Miracle; its exposition is Jesus Christ, the Son of God, the Light to lighten the Gentiles, and the glory of His people Israel.

A living God, as distinguished from idols, whether the idols of heathenism or the idol of the abstract god of philosophy, appeals to this as one of His attributes, that He revealeth future things. 'Bring forth your strong reasons, saith the King of Jacob. Let them bring them forth and show us what shall happen: show the things that are to come hereafter, that we may know that ye are gods.' And again, 'Behold, the former things are come to pass, and new things do I declare; before they spring forth I tell you of them.' (Isa. 41:21-23; 45:18-21; 48:5, 14-16). Even the king of Babylon, Nebuchadnezzar, a heathen, exclaimed, 'Of a truth it is, that your God is a God of gods, and a Lord of kings, and a revealer of secrets, seeing thou couldest reveal this secret.'

Thus prophecy is declared by the Lord Himself to be a manifestation and evidence of His wonderful wisdom and infinite supremacy, as sent in order to prove to us that He is dealing with us, and also to fortify us against the claims of error. Common, unsophisticated, natural sense will receive prophecy as a sure mark of supernatural authority, and it has been only the perverse ingenuity and pseudo-spiritualism of our age, which, from the dreamy height of its speculative wisdom, has spoken with half-contemptuous vagueness of prophecy as an evidence of the truth of Scripture.

And every fulfilment of the events predicted, whether that fulfilment be recorded in Scripture itself (as the prophecy about the captivity of Babylon, Cyrus, etc.), or recorded in the annals of history (as the destruction of Jerusalem, the dispersion of the Jews, etc.), renders to us 'more sure' the word of prophecy; so that we look forward with the firm expectation that the Lord God will do nothing but make manifest the secret which He hath revealed unto His servants the prophets, while we are most fully convinced that the Scripture contains the things which the Lord hath spoken, attested as it is by the mark given by God, through Moses, for our guidance and assurance (Deut. 18:20-22).

3. The Isolated Position of the Book

Contrast the Bible with the Apocrypha. How marked is the difference! External authority sufficiently separates between the canonical books and the apocryphal writings. But who that has tasted the old good wine could mistake for it the diluted and feeble work of man? "What is the chaff to the wheat?" We need not underrate the value of the Apocrypha, especially those which belong to the period between Malachi and Matthew. The history of God's people during this interval is most interesting and valuable; the sufferings and faith of the Maccabees most edifying and encouraging. The development of doctrinal views may also be traced in the various apocryphal books. But in reading them we cannot but feel that here is the voice of man, and not that Voice which speaks to us at sundry times and in divers manners through the prophets.

What a contrast is felt between the four evangelists and the apocryphal gospels! How puerile are the miracles which tradition attributes to Him who, in all His doings, glorified and showed forth the Father!

And the writings of the apostolic Fathers, beautiful and good as they are, only set forth more brightly the marvellous peculiarity of the inspired apostolic epistles, their inexhaustible depth, their heavenly simplicity, their wonderful condensation, their transparent clearness, their universality, in short their Divine character.

It is significant, that in the Gospel of John (2) the miracle at Cana is described as the beginning of miracles which Jesus did, thus excluding all the miracles ascribed by tradition to Christ's childhood.

With reference to the apostolic Fathers, Neander has the following important remarks (*Church History*, 2, 405): 'A phenomenon, singular in its kind, is the striking difference between the writings of the apostles and those of the apostolic Fathers, who were so nearly their contemporaries. In other cases transitions are wont to be gradual, but in this instance we observe sudden change. There is no gentle graduation here, but all at once an abrupt transition from one style of language to the other, a phenomenon which should lead us to acknowledge the fact of a special agency of the Divine Spirit in the souls of the apostles, and of a new creative element in the first period.'

4. The Marvellous Preservation of the Bible

It is wonderful how this record has been preserved. The Jews have carefully watched over the letter of their sacred writings. The most accurate and diligent research has availed to discover only trifling variations in the manuscripts. And although both the Hebrew and the Greek Scriptures have often been the object of persecuting enemies, the cruelty and ingenuity of man have not been able to destroy their existence.

This is still more wonderful when we consider by whom these writings were preserved. The Jews were the conscientious guardians of the book of the Kingdom. Rome preserved the book of the Church. The Jews, who themselves rejected the Messiah of whom Moses and the prophets testify, preserve the very books which prove their unbelief, and convince the world of the Divine authority and mission of Jesus. And where is there a nation preserving carefully a record, which so repeatedly and emphatically declares that they are obstinate, ungrateful, and perverse; and which attributes all their victories and excellences, not to their natural disposition and qualities, nor to their energy and merit, but exclusively to the mercy and power of God?

Look again at the Church of Rome preserving the writings of evangelists and apostles: *that* Church preserving writings which declare that Christ hath perfected by one sacrifice them that are sanctified; that salvation is by grace, through faith, and that not of ourselves, it is the gift of God; that all believers are kings and priests unto God; that there is no mediator between God and men but the Man Christ Jesus; that Peter savoured the things that are of man, and not the things that are of God, and that, even after Pentecost, he had to be severely rebuked, and energetically resisted by Paul; that Mary is told by the Son Himself not to interfere in the concerns of His kingdom; that freely we have received and freely we are to give; that men forbidding to marry and to abstain from meats are the expected false teachers; that in the congregation we are not to pray in an unknown tongue; and that Christians are commended for subjecting even the teaching of apostles to the authority and confirmation of the Scripture!

The Jews bear unwilling witness to Jesus, and Rome has carefully preserved and transcribed her own condemnation.

5. The Catholicity of the Bible

A Book which has existed for so many centuries, has influenced so many nations, and has moulded the minds and characters of the wise and simple, the rich and poor, the civilized and the barbarian, may well be called a catholic, world-wide Book. When we hear the people in the north of Scotland sing the Psalms which David, the king of Israel, wrote so many centuries ago, while the lyrics of Greece and Rome are known only to the learned few, we may well ask, How is it that the sorrows and joys, the difficulties and doubts, the aspirations and hopes of men, so apart in time and in clime, should find expression in the same songs? When we hear our little children conclude their prayers with the Hebrew word, 'Amen'; when we hear our dying saints utter as the symbol of their victory and hope, the Hebrew words, 'Jerusalem' and 'Hallelujah,' we may well ask, Why is Hebrew the language of our soul's life, from its earliest commencement to its latest breath on earth? Scripture, the Jewish Word, is the universal Book.

The most cultivated nations bow before it, and learn as docile children from its inexhaustible pages; to the rudest tribes light and love are brought from its simple and powerful declarations. It is the guide of Edward VI, the delight of Francis Bacon, the study of Sir Isaac Newton and Pascal. While kings and philosophers find wisdom and counsel in this inspired volume, it is the companion of the artisan and merchant, the comfort of the widow, and the instructor of the unlettered and uneducated. There is no age of man when it is not suitable. It gives milk to babes, guidance to the young, strength to men, and consolation to the aged. There is no occupation or station in life in which it is not profitable and healthful. It is an armoury to those who are in battle, a storehouse to those who are lonely, a protection to all who are in peril, a rod and staff to the dying. There is no state of mind for which it is not salutary. The tone of it is joyous, but its joy does not grate on us in our most solemn moments; its tone is earnest, but this earnestness only irradiates and elevates our joy. The twenty-third Psalm is consolation at a death-bed, and yet gives expression to our most joyous and festive feelings. Wonderful Book, for all ages, all nations, all men, all times; no marvel thou hast been called Bible—The Book!

Father of mercies, in Thy Word
What endless glory shines!
For ever be Thy Name adored
For these celestial lines.

Here the Redeemer's welcome voice
Spreads heavenly peace around,
And life and everlasting joys
Attend the blissful sound.

Divine Instructor, gracious Lord,
Be Thou for ever near;
Teach me to love Thy sacred Word
And view my Saviour there.

(*Anne Steele*)

The Inspiration of The New Testament

By Alan M. Stibbs

In this exposition of the Bible passages which we are to consider there are three significant statements of our Lord which directly concern the inspiration of the New Testament writings. These statements declare what Christ Himself has promised concerning the enablement by God the Holy Spirit of apostolic insight and testimony. Let us consider them in due order.

(1) John 14:25, 26. 'These things have I spoken unto you, being yet present with you. But the Comforter, which is the Holy Ghost, whom the Father will send in my name, he shall teach you all things, and will bring all things to your remembrance whatsoever I have said unto you'. We have here *the promise of completed instruction, and of full recollection and apprehension.*

In view of His own impending departure our Lord thus indicated the manner in which the teaching, which He had given to His disciples, was to be completed and preserved. All three Persons of the Godhead would be the guarantee of further necessary help. The Father would send the Spirit in the Son's Name. The personality of the Spirit is pointedly implied by the surprising use, after a noun in the neuter, of a masculine pronoun: '*He* shall teach you'. He was to function as their Comforter or Helper. His teaching would be comprehensive and all-inclusive. In contrast to 'these things' which Christ has spoken, He would teach the disciples '*all* things'. The foundation and controlling interest of His teaching work was to be the historic revelation of God in Christ. He would recall and interpret what Jesus said, thus making its full significance completely clear and permanently available.

Our Lord thus taught that it would be the Spirit's work to complement and complete His own teaching ministry. This means that there is nothing developed in the second stage, through the inspiration and teaching of the Spirit, which has not its roots in the first stage, in the teaching of Jesus Himself. By the Spirit the apostles were to be enabled to enlarge understanding, to discover fulness, and to define application.

The promised Spirit-given grace of detailed remembrance is one of primary importance. It was needed for the permanent preservation of the foundations of the faith. Such God-given enablement had two consequences—exact report and increased apprehension. The apostles were thus made competent as witnesses. For even ordinary human experience shows that most events are fully understood only in remembrance; one effect of vivid remembrance is clearer intelligence. So the deeds and words of Jesus awaited, and were promised, accurate recollection aided by the Spirit's illumination and interpretation. This secured their full understanding and exposition.

Such a promise directly concerns the New Testament documents. It found its outstanding and intended fulfilment in their composition. First, the words of Jesus provided primary foundations of faith and germinant principles of thought. Then, the ministry of the Spirit secured their full recollection and their out-worked understanding. In this way the testimony of the apostolic records, and the insight of the apostolic interpretations, as found in the Gospels, the Acts and the Epistles, have been given a divine seal and certificate.

(2) John 16:12-15. 'I have yet many things to say unto you, but ye cannot bear them now. Howbeit when he, the Spirit of truth, is come, he will guide you into all truth: for he shall not speak of himself; but whatsoever he shall hear, that shall he speak: and he will show you things to come. He shall glorify me: for he shall receive of mine and show it unto you. All things that the Father hath are mine: therefore said I that he shall take of mine and show it unto you'. In these words is *the promise of adequate insight and of complementary foresight.* We learn that on the night before His death, the Lord declared that He still had many things to say: and that it was impossible to say them 'now'. He knew that the minds of His hearers were still unequal to it. He knew that conditions would be completely altered when the great impending events of His death and resurrection had taken place. He knew that what His disciples could not grasp 'now' they would understand afterwards. (See also John 13:7). Thus again a great promise is given of completed education and of equipment to interpret.

We are made aware by these statements that there was gradual advance in the disciples' spiritual apprehension; and that the teaching given by Jesus before His death was not all that He had to say. The necessary further revelation was given to the disciples later by the Spirit of truth. Nor did He convey it in one sudden disclosure, but rather His illumination made possible continuous advance unto understanding. Such is the implication of the promise: 'He will guide you'. By this means they were in the end to come to know 'all the truth'. The necessary revelation would be completed.

Further, it would not be any new truth that the Spirit would disclose to them, but the truth that was already implicit in what Jesus Himself had said and done. The Revised Version rendering exactly represents the original, that is, 'all *the* truth'. This means "the specific truth about the Person of Jesus, and the significance of what He said and did". Similarly 'things to come' means 'the things which are coming'; i.e. 'the unique events which are imminent and with which the last discourses of Jesus are primarily concerned, His death and resurrection' (R. V. G. Tasker). The Spirit's governing aim and interest would be to glorify Christ.

Such promises provide important witness concerning revelation granted to the apostles after Christ's death and resurrection. Just as St. John 14:26 guarantees the inspiration of the records provided by the four Gospels, so St. John 16:14 guarantees the inspiration of the interpretation and application of the truth as it is in Jesus which we find in the Epistles and the Apocalypse.

(3) John 16:25. 'These things have I spoken to you in proverbs; but the time cometh when I shall no more speak to you in proverbs, but I shall show you plainly of the Father'. In these words we find *the promise of explicit exposition, to follow figurative suggestion, and implicit indication.* Our Lord explained that His own teaching had been parabolic—given in proverbs, by figure and analogy; but promised that the Spirit would make the implied meaning plain and clear. He assured them that the coming day of His own triumph, and of the outpoured Spirit, would give to them a new freedom and fulness, both access to God in prayer (see verses 23 and 24) and in apprehension of the truth of His saving work. A change is announced in the character of the divine communications. Our Lord had not been able to speak openly and directly. The coming of the Spirit would make possible great plainness or freedom of speech. The reasons for restraint in utterance would be past. Then symbol and figure would be superseded or complemented by unveiled language. The truth given in parable would be explicitly interpreted and by the Lord Himself. The great theme of this full revelation would be the knowledge through Christ of God as Father. For this was the goal of Christ's mission, and this is life eternal, that men should personally come to know in intimate realized fellowship the one true God (John 17:3). This promise also directly refers to the intended character of the subsequent apostolic teaching. It guarantees the completion of the revelation of God in Christ by the New Testament epistles and their explicit doctrinal teaching concerning Christ's Person and Work.

Taken together, therefore, these three passages guarantee, by the Lord's own promise, the Spirit's inspiration of the content and the character of the whole New Testament. To the Spirit's work we owe the detailed historical records of the doings and teachings of Jesus which are provided for us in the four Gospels and the Acts; and to the Spirit's work we also owe the complementary explicit, authoritative, doctrinal interpretation of Christ's Person and Work which are afforded by the Epistles and the Apocalypse.

[An Address delivered at the Annual Meeting of the Bible League in October, 1960].

The Inspiration and Authority of Holy Scripture

By S. M. Houghton

The Historical Position

It is the purpose of the following article to show that throughout the long centuries of the Christian era the entire professing Church, until recent days, has confessed firm and unswerving belief in the inspiration and authority of the Holy Scriptures both of the Old and New Testaments. It is only during the past century that the age-old doctrine of inspiration has been assailed from within the Church itself. Over the years the voice of unbelief has been raised, but it has arisen from without, not from within the sacred pale. The language of internal dissent from a belief formerly held in common by all professed Christians is, chronologically speaking, a new and startling phenomenon, and it is therefore necessary to draw attention to the stark contrast between the ancient and modern situations.

First of all, we again state and stress the truth unfolded in our previous article on this same theme, that in Scripture itself the fact of inspiration is made crystal-clear. The entire Scripture is declared to be God-breathed. It is not so much that the writers of Scripture were themselves inspired, but that the word which they uttered and wrote was inspired. '*All Scripture* is given by inspiration of God' (2 Tim. 3:16). The word, and not merely the thought underlying the word, proceeded from above. There is not a shadow of doubt that Christ Himself, THE WORD OF GOD, believed this and acted upon this belief during the days of His flesh. His utterances and His behaviour were all of a piece. And the professing Church has clung tenaciously to the same belief and conviction.

The Church-Doctrine of Inspiration

The position has been excellently stated by B. B. Warfield, an American professor (of Princeton) of remarkably fine scholarship. He wrote the following in the 1890s. We quote several of his paragraphs (as they appear in his 'The Church Doctrine of Inspiration') as showing different facets of the truth:

'This church-doctrine of inspiration differs from the theories that would fain supplant it, in that it is not the invention nor the property of an individual, but the settled faith of the universal church of God; in that it is not the growth of yesterday, but the assured persuasion of the people of God from the first planting of the church until today; in that it is not a protean shape, varying its affirmations to fit every new change in the ever-shifting thought of men, but from the beginning has been the church's constant and abiding conviction as to the divinity of the Scriptures committed to her keeping . . . Surely the seeker after the truth in the matter of the inspiration of the Bible may well take this church-doctrine as his starting-point.

'The whole body of Christian literature bears witness to this fact (*i.e.* that the utterances of this Book are properly oracles of God). We may trace its stream to its source, and everywhere it is vocal with a living faith in the divine trustworthiness of the Scriptures of God in every one of their affirmations . . . This is the mighty voice of the great river of Christian thought which sweeps through the ages, freighted with blessings for men. Dr. Sanday, in his recent Bampton lectures on "Inspiration"—in which, unfortunately, he does not teach the church-doctrine—is driven to admit that not only may "testimonies to the general doctrine of inspiration" from the earliest Fathers "be multiplied to almost any extent; but that there are some which go further and point to an inspiration which might be described as *verbal*"; "nor does this idea", he adds, "come in tentatively and by degrees, but almost from the very first". He might have spared the adverb "almost". The earliest writers know no other doctrine.

'Of course the church has not failed to bring this, her vital faith in the divine trustworthiness of the Scripture word, to formal expression in her solemn creeds. The assumption of the divine authority of the scriptural teaching underlies all the credal statements of the church'. [Warfield calls particular attention to the fact that 'the Council of Trent defined it as of faith in the Church of Rome, that God is the author of Scripture—a declaration which has been repeated in our own day by the Vatican Council (*i.e.* of 1870), with such full explanations as are included in these rich words: "The church holds the books of the Old and New Testaments to be sacred and canonical, not because, having been carefully composed by mere human industry, they were afterwards approved by her authority, nor merely because they contain revelation with no admixture of error, but because, having been written by inspiration of the Holy Ghost, they have God for their author".']

(The chief, if not the only difference, between Roman Catholic and Protestant teachings in this matter is that the former include the Apocrypha in the Canon of Scripture whereas Protestants as deliberately exclude it.)

We quote Warfield on two further points:

'This church-doctrine (as above) of inspiration was the Bible doctrine before it was the church-doctrine, and is the church-doctrine only because it is the Bible doctrine.

'But, we may be reminded, the church has not held with such tenacity to all doctrines taught in the Bible. How are we to account, then, for the singular constancy of its confession of the Bible's doctrine of inspiration? . . . It is due to an instinctive feeling in the church that the trustworthiness of the Scriptures lies at the foundation of trust in the Christian system of doctrine, and is therefore fundamental to the Christian hope and life' . . . 'Adolphe Monod gives voice to no more than the common Christian conviction when he declares that, "If faith has not for its basis a testimony of God to which we must submit, as to an authority exterior to our personal judgment, and independent of it, then faith is no faith".'

We close these particular quotations with Warfield's own concluding words: 'Our effort has been to bring out clearly what seem to be three very impressive facts regarding the plenary inspiration of the Scriptures—the facts, namely, that this doctrine has always been, and is still, the church-doctrine of inspiration, as well the vital faith of the people of God as the formulated teaching of the official creeds; that it is undeniably the doctrine of inspiration held by Christ and His apostles, and commended to us as true by all the authority which we will allow to attach to their teaching; and that it is the foundation of our Christian thought and life, without which we could not, or could only with difficulty, maintain the confidence of our faith and the surety of our hope. On such grounds as these, is not this doctrine commended to us as true?'

Our extracts may be regarded perhaps as somewhat lengthy, but the basic issues are such that it is impossible to overstate their importance. The very truth of 'the only true God' and His Son Jesus Christ is at stake. Let God and Christ be true and every man a liar. C. H. Spurgeon was not guilty of exaggeration when he wrote in 1888 that 'the turning-point of the battle between those who hold the faith once delivered to the saints, and their opponents, lies in the true and real inspiration of the Holy Scriptures. This is the Thermopylae of Christendom . . . When a man falls into an error, but reverently conceives that he finds it in the Bible, he is on a very different footing from the man who says that he judges by his moral consciousness, or some other unreliable standard, and declares that if the Bible contradicts him he will sooner renounce Scripture than change his opinions. We can have a measure of fellowship with a mistaken friend who is willing to bow before the teaching of Scripture if he can be made to understand it; but we must PART COMPANY altogether with the errorist who overrides prophets and apostles, and practically regards his own inspiration as superior to theirs. We fear that such a man will before long prove himself to be an enemy of the cross of Christ, all the more dangerous because he will profess loyalty to the Lord whom he dishonours.'

So much, then, for the general point. We shall give it illustration from the early church Fathers and from the Reformation period in particular, but before we move back in time from the modern period of change (and as we would deliberately call it, apostasy), it will be appropriate to quote other notable utterances which belong to the second half of the 19th century and which illustrate the clear-cut testimony of the Christian church.

Testimonies from the late-19th century

In 1853 John William Colenso, a Cornishman, was appointed Anglican Bishop of Natal. Ten years later he had achieved notoriety by calling in question certain beliefs of the church, and in particular the authenticity of the Pentateuch as maintained in all Christian circles. His work coincided in time with the publication of Charles Darwin's *Origin of Species,* and it was widely realised that the writings of the two men constituted a serious attack on the foundations of the faith. A comparable bomb-shell was the publication of *Honest to God* a few years ago. We mention Colenso solely for the purpose of stating the official Anglican reaction to his heresies. It took the form of a united protest addressed to Colenso in 1863 by the Archbishops of Canterbury and York and the Bishops of the Church of England, in which they said: 'All our hopes for eternity, the very foundation of our faith, our nearest and dearest consolations are taken from us if one line of that Sacred Book be declared unfaithful or untrustworthy'. Would that a similar witness was heard from the same quarter today!

An outstanding High Churchman of the same period was H. P. Liddon, for twenty years Canon of St. Paul's and one of the greatest preachers of his day. In December, 1889, he preached a notable sermon on the Inspiration of the Old Testament, in which he said: 'For Christians it will be enough that our Lord Jesus Christ has set the seal of His infallible sanction on the whole of the Old Testament. He found the Hebrew canon just as we have it today, and He treated it as an authority which was above discussion—nay, more, He went out of His way, if we may reverently speak thus, to sanction not a few portions of it which our modern scepticism too eagerly rejects. When He would warn His hearers against the danger of spiritual relapse, He bade them remember Lot's wife. When He would point out how worldly engagements may blind the soul to a coming judgment, He reminds them how men ate, and drank, and married and were given in marriage, until the day when Noah entered into the ark, and the flood came and destroyed them all. When He would put His finger on a fact in past Jewish history which, by its admitted reality, would warrant belief in His own resurrection, He points to Jonah, three days and three nights in the whale's belly. When, standing on the Mount of Olives, with the Holy City at His feet, He would quote a prophecy, the fulfilment of which would mark for His followers that its impending doom had at last arrived, He desires them to flee to the mountains when they "shall see the abomination of desolation, spoken of by Daniel the prophet, standing in the holy place".

'Are we to suppose that, in these and other references to the Old Testament, our Lord was only using what are called *ad hominem* arguments, or talking down to the level of popular ignorance which He did not Himself share? Not to point out the inconsistency of this supposition with His character as a perfectly sincere religious teacher, it may be observed that, in the Sermon on the Mount, He carefully marks off those features of the popular Jewish religion which He rejects, in a manner which makes it certain that, had He not Himself believed in the historic truth of the events and the persons to which He thus refers, He must have said so. But did He then share a popular belief which our higher knowledge has shown to be popular ignorance? and was He mistaken as to the worth of those Scriptures to which He so often and so confidently appealed? There are those who profess to bear the Christian name and who do not shrink from saying as much as this; but they will find it difficult to persuade mankind that, if He could be mistaken on a matter of such strictly religious importance as this, He can be safely trusted about anything else. Yes, the trustworthiness of the Old Testament is, in fact, inseparable from the trustworthiness of the Lord Jesus Christ; and if we believe that He is the true Light of the world, we shall resolutely close our ears against any suggestions of the falshood of those Hebrew Scriptures which have received the stamp of His divine authority.'

With Spurgeon the writer can say, 'We differ widely (from Liddon) on some important points, but in this we are at one'. Here Liddon undoubtedly echoes the irrefutable testimony of the age-old church of God, and we ourselves echo his words with confident faith, saddened as we have been recently by hearing an organiser of religious education refer to the Book of Daniel as 'a fairy tale, something like Red Riding Hood', together with utterances of the same character, such as that Christ was only a child of His age, that there is no devil, and similar outright denials of biblical testimony.

Liddon's words found, too, an echo in the heart of William Ewart Gladstone, four times Prime Minister (a schoolboy is said, in all innocence, to have accredited Spurgeon with the same title to fame) and a towering statesman. About a year after the preaching of Liddon's sermon, his

Impregnable Rock of Holy Scripture was published, in which he comments as follows: 'The Scriptures, in their substantial tissue, rise far above the region of criticism, which shows no sign of being about to do anything permanent or effectual to lower their moral and spiritual grandeur, or to disguise or intercept their gigantic work'.

The Doctrine of the Fathers

We next turn to take a brief look at the doctrine of inspiration as understood by the church of the Fathers. It is not the case that any such doctrine actually received formulation during the early Christian centuries, but it is most certainly the case that all professed Christians of that time received, believed in and confessed the authority of the Word precisely because it was God-breathed, the very utterance of the all-wise and only-wise God. Heresies developed as time went on, and creeds were therefore formulated by the orthodox, but at no point was the integrity of Scripture itself called in question. Orthodox and heretic alike held to the inspired text. Contention turned, not upon the authenticity of the Word but upon the manner in which it was to be interpreted.

Allusions to inspiration in the writings of the sub-apostolic Fathers are incidental, largely because of perfect agreement on the matter among Christians. Polycarp, Bishop of Smyrna, burnt to death about A.D. 155, pronounces anathema upon the man who turns from the Word, in the words, 'He is the first-born of Satan, whoever perverts the oracles of the Lord to suit his own passions'. Papias, a contemporary of Polycarp, similarly styles the Synoptic Gospels the 'Oracles of the Lord'. Justin Martyr, one of the earliest of church apologists, says, 'We must not suppose that the language (*i.e.* of Scripture) proceeds from the men who are inspired, but from the divine Word which moves them. Their work is to announce that which the Holy Spirit, descending upon them, purposes through them to teach those who wish to learn the true religion'.

The pupil of Polycarp, Irenaeus, Bishop of Lyons, speaks with greater fullness and clarity on the theme of inspiration. He assures us that 'the Scriptures are perfect inasmuch as they were uttered by the Word of God and His Spirit, though we lack the knowledge of their mysteries'. 'No small punishment', he continues, 'will be his who adds to, or takes from, the Scripture'. The connection of its parts may seem perplexing or even tantalizing, but 'all Scripture, as it has been given to us by God, will be found to be harmonious'.

Prominent in the African Church in the early Third century was Tertullian, a native of Carthage, a lawyer, and a man of ready pen. He was the first theologian of the church to write in Latin, and it has been claimed that 'he created the language of Western theology'. He was rigorous and unbending in his proclamation of the full inspiration of Old and New Testaments. Whether he is writing for the heathen, the heretics, or the orthodox he never wavers in expounding the integrity and authenticity of the Word. Scripture is to him 'the food of his faith, the spring of his hope, and the bulwark of his trust'. 'Happy is that church', he wrote, 'which combines the Law and the Prophets with the writings of the evangelists and apostles, and draws her faith from them.'

Precisely similar in sentiment is the slightly later Cyprian, Bishop of Carthage (d. 258). To him the two Testaments are 'the foundation of our hope, the bulwark of our faith, the support of our hearts, the guide of our path, the safeguard of our salvation'. Time and again in his writings he stresses that 'the Holy Spirit spoke in the law and in the gospel, by prophets, apostles and evangelists: by Him the prophets were quickened to a knowledge of the future'.

We select Clement (d. about 215), a catechist, and Origen, a pupil of Clement (d. about 254), to represent the eminent Church of Alexandria. Clement's testimony runs: 'The foundations of our faith rest on no insecure basis, for we have received them from God through the Scriptures . . . of which not one tittle shall pass away without being accomplished, for the mouth of the Lord, the Holy Spirit, spoke it; and we have believed on Him through His voice; and he that believeth on the Word knoweth that the thing is true, for the Word is truth; but he that believeth not on Him that speaketh disbelieveth God, for he disbelieveth that which hath been spoken by the Holy Spirit for our salvation'.

Origen's principal work—he was 'a very fertile author'—is entitled *Principles,* and in it there is a very clear exhibition of his views on inspiration. To him 'the records of the Gospels are oracles of the Lord, pure oracles, as silver purified in the fire (Psa. 12:6), and with a meaning in their minutest details; while they are without error, inasmuch as we believe that they were accurately written by the co-operation of the Holy Spirit'. He does not hesitate to say that the Christian receives the words of Paul as the words of God, equally valid with other parts of Scripture. 'All the sacred volumes', he says, 'breathe the spirit of fullness, and there is nothing, whether in the Law or in the Prophets, in the evangelists or in the apostles, which does not descend from the fullness of the divine Majesty'.

There is a large degree of sameness about the testimonies of the Fathers which have been quoted, but this in itself is illustrative of the express point which we are making, that they bear witness with one unvarying voice to the inspiration and authority of the sacred writings. 'While they had no definite theory of inspiration, they held in the most decided manner, the divine origin, authority, and perfection of the Holy Scriptures'.

Among the later Fathers Augustine was pre-eminent, the chief of all the Western theologians (died A.D. 430). In his view the apostles were comparable to hands which wrote down that which Christ, the head, dictated. He terms Scripture 'the style, to be regarded with reverence, of the Holy Spirit'. To the famous Jerome, his contemporary, he explained his belief in inspiration in the following words: 'I most firmly believe that none of the authors of the canonical books committed any error in writing. If I meet with anything in these writings that seems contrary to truth, I do not hesitate to affirm that the manuscript is faulty, or that the translator has not caught the sense, or that I do not understand it'.

It is but right to add that the one voice to the contrary, or at least a voice that does not fully concur with the unanimous remainder, is that of Theodore, Bishop of Mopsuestia (near Tarsus, Cilicia: he died in 428). He was a friend of the famous Chrysostom. He stated the view that there were degrees of inspiration. To Solomon he ascribed, not a gift of prophecy, but that of wisdom only, and judged of the Book of Job and the Song of Songs from the merely human angle. The Fifth Ecumenical Council, held at Constantinople in 553, expressed its disagreement with such views.

The exception proves the rule. It is virtually with one consent that the Early and Late Fathers, differing as they do on so many other matters, proclaim their common belief in the doctrine of inspiration. In his book entitled *An Introduction to the Study of the Gospels,* Bishop Westcott supplies an Appendix on 'The Primitive Doctrine of Inspiration', and concludes with the words, 'The unanimity of the early Fathers in their views on Holy Scripture is the more remarkable when it is taken in connection with the great differences of character and training and circumstances by which they were distinguished. In the midst of errors of judgment and errors of detail they maintain firmly with one consent the great principles which invest the Bible with an interest most special and most universal, with the characteristics of the most vivid individuality and of the most varied application. They teach us that Inspiration is an operation of the Holy Spirit acting *through* men, according to the laws of their constitution, which is not neutralized by His influence, but adopted as a vehicle for the full expression of the divine Message . . . They teach us that Christ—the Word of God—speaks from first to last; that all Scripture is permanently fitted for our instruction; that a true spiritual meaning, eternal and absolute, lies beneath historical and ceremonial and moral details. They teach us that this view was in their time no late invention, but a tradition which they received and transmitted, each according to his skill endeavouring to carry out the principles which he had learnt'.

The Middle Ages

The Middle Ages need not detain us in our inquiry. The church of this period maintained a belief similar to that of the Fathers. Extravagances occasionally appeared. An abbot of Tours claimed the infallibility not only of the received text but even of translations and commentaries. He was answered by an archbishop of Lyons who showed what great absurdity would follow from such a view. The noted Peter Abelard of France (1079-1142), who was renowned for bold speculations, departed from orthodoxy in averring that the Prophets sometimes had the gift of prophecy and sometimes spoke from their own minds. He was a lone voice. More dangerous was the Mysticism that sprang up in sundry places. To the mystic the devout soul is in a condition of constant inspiration and the rhapsodies of the specially favoured ones amount to much the same thing as biblical inspiration. They failed to distinguish between the work of the Holy Spirit in producing a measure of 'illumination' in the mind of every regenerated person, and His unique work in producing God-breathed Scriptures from the pens of 'holy men of God carried along by Him' (2 Pet. 1:21), just as in modern days many are prepared to equate the genius of a Milton or a Wordsworth with the inspiration of an Isaiah or a John.

The Doctrine of the Reformation

The 16th-century Reformation, following upon the Renaissance, gave a strong impetus to the doctrine of inspiration. The sufficiency of the Scriptures for salvation became a Reformation watchword. Whereas Rome sought refuge from reformation in emphasis upon tradition, the reformers took their stand upon the Word of God written. And they not only affirmed its 'sufficiency' in all matters pertaining to God and to godliness—a part of their protest all the more necessary on account of Rome's claims for tradition and the continuing voice of the church as heard from St. Peter's—but they gave equal stress to its 'perspicuity', that is to say, to the inherent capacity of Scripture to explain and interpret itself, and particularly so to the regenerated mind. In this way they opposed the claim of Rome that the Church of Rome was alone competent to instruct the individual Christian as to the meaning of the Word. The medieval church had monopolized the right of interpretation. This concept was projected into modern times by such Roman Catholic theologians as Cardinal Robert Bellarmine (d. 1621), Rome's foremost protagonist in the late 16th and early 17th century. 'It is plain', he wrote, 'that Scripture is not the judge of controversies, because it admits of various senses, nor can Scripture itself declare which is the true one. Besides, in every well-ordered state, the law and the judge are distinct. The law prescribes what is done and the judge interprets the law, and decides accordingly. The question is about the interpretation of Scripture, but it cannot interpret itself. We say that the Church (of Rome) is the judge of the true sense of Scripture and of all controversies, that is, the Pope with the Council in which all Catholics are assembled'.

It was to counter this claim that the reformers spoke much of the Bible's perspicuity and its easy-to-be-understood teaching on all matters essential to faith, to the saving of the soul, and to the living of a godly life. Erasmus, half-reformer though he was, was at least worthy to be followed on this point. His much-quoted words as to the value of Bible-reading for the 'common or garden' individual strike an eminently sound note (they occur in the preface to his Greek New Testament, 1516): 'I would that they (the words of Scripture) might be read and known not merely by the Scots and the Irish, but even by the Turks and the Saracens. I wish that the farm worker might sing parts of them at the plough, that the weaver might hum them at the shuttle, and that the traveller might beguile the weariness of the way by reciting them', words echoed unmistakably by William Tyndale in his equally famous reference to 'the boy that driveth the plough'. And again to quote Erasmus: 'These sacred books present us with a living image of His (Christ's) holy mind . . . I should prefer to hear young maidens talking about Christ than some who in the opinion of the vulgar are consummate rabbis'. And again: 'They (the Scriptures) will give Christ to you in an intimacy so close that He would be less visible to you if He stood before your eyes'.

But long before Erasmus and Tyndale and their fellows, Wycliffe had pointed the way to the true doctrine. He asserted that 'God has spoken through the prophets and apostles as through authentic notaries. Therefore Scripture grounds its authority and absolute truth above all the writings of men'. He roundly declares that the Bible 'is, as a matter of fact, the Word of God, the will and testament of God the Father, the charter written by God'.

Continental Reformers

It was said of Montesquieu's book, *The Spirit of Laws,* in the 18th century, that 'the human race had lost its title-deeds; Montesquieu found and restored them'. There is some truth in this, but much more is it true that the Reformers of the 16th century gave back to men the long-lost Scriptures, title-deeds, if believed, to 'a better country, that is, an heavenly'. Without exception, the Reformers are full-throated in their witness to the inspiration and perspicuity of the Scriptures. In Luther's case, however, we frankly admit that certain of his occasional sayings might appear to cast doubt upon a whole-hearted adherence to the doctrine propounded. Great theologian though he was, Luther was no systematic theologian. Neither his writings nor his 'obiter dicta' are all of a piece. Within the brief, though extensive, coverage of this article we cannot engage in a detailed study of the matter, though far be it from us to gloss over it or cast it to the limbo of silence. It is, however, not inexplicable. The primary fact is that the Lutheran trumpet in the main gave no uncertain sound in respect of the inspiration and authority of the Word. To Luther, Scripture, in its entirety, was the Word of God, the Book 'written by His finger', the final court of appeal, 'a spiritual light far brighter even than the sun, especially in what relates to salvation and all essential matters'. One of his two most renowned works, that on 'The Bondage of the Will', speaks strongly on these matters. He terms it 'shameless blasphemy' to say that the Scriptures are obscure (see particularly pages 123-136 in the modern translation by Packer and Johnston).

Set over against this, however, is the notorious fact that Luther could speak disparagingly of the Epistle of James, and could speak of the Book of Revelation as neither prophetic nor apostolic. In respect of James, he asserted that 'in comparison with them (*i.e.* Romans, Galatians and sundry other portions of the New Testament specially esteemed by Luther), James is a right straw epistle, for it has no evangelic manner about it. It has no syllable about Christ, not even naming Him except once at the beginning'.

It might seem, therefore, that the summoning of Luther into the witness-box augurs ill for our case. But it is not really so. In so far as he speaks with double voice—and he rarely does so in comparison with the number of his testimonies to the authenticity of the Word as a whole—he is guilty of a false judgment, but it is based upon the very intensity of his convictions concerning the doctrine which stands in the forefront of all Reformation teaching, that of Justification by Faith. Christian folk, when pressed into a tight corner by relentless logic, have sometimes made amazing and totally unwarranted admissions which, in their senses, they have repudiated; and it was virtually so with Luther when, faced by an apparent contradiction between the Pauline doctrine and that of James, he fell into a woeful imbalance. What he did was rather to challenge the agreed canon of Scripture than to deny the full inspiration and authority of all that he was convinced belonged to the true canon. Thus, in commenting on Hebrews, which he confessed to be canonical, he could say, 'One letter, yea a single tittle of the Scripture, is of more and greater consequence than heaven and earth . . . The Holy Ghost is neither foolish nor drunk to utter a tittle, much less a letter, in vain'. And again—we quote from his Commentary on Galatians—'Neither am I to be believed, nor the Church, nor the Fathers, nor the Apostles, nor an angel from heaven, if we teach anything against the Word of God'. The same conviction was in his mind as he answered King Henry VIII of England in 1522, 'Against all the acts and words of angels, men and devils, I set the Scriptures and the Gospel . . . Here I stand and here I defy them. The Word of God I count above all else, and the Divine Majesty supports me; hence I should not turn a hair were a thousand Augustines against me, and am certain that the true Church adheres with me to God's Word'.

If we run into difficulties in handling Luther we meet with no such embarrassment in assessing the testimony of other Reformers. The First Helvetic Confession (1536), which had been drawn up by Zwingli, states that 'Canonical Scripture, the Word of God, given by the Holy Spirit and set forth to the world by the prophets and apostles, the most perfect and ancient of all philosophies, alone contains perfectly all piety and the whole of life'.

Of all the Reformers, Calvin's witness is of superlative value. He was indisputably the greatest Protestant theologian of the Reformation period, and indeed of all subsequent periods, and his writings have had an influence second to none on his own and later centuries. He speaks invariably in the following strain:

'Holy men of God (2 Pet. 1:21) were *moved*—not that they were bereaved of mind as the Gentiles imagined their prophets to have been, but because they dared not to announce anything of their own, and obediently followed the Spirit as their guide, who ruled in their mouth as in His own sanctuary. Understand by *prophecy of Scripture* that which is contained in the holy Scriptures'.

'(Holy Scripture) is the eternal and inviolable truth of God . . . and since God has seen fit to give us in the Scripture an abiding record of His truth, it is needful for believers to know with certainty that the Scripture has come down from heaven'.

'The highest argument used in Scripture is always that the speaker is God: "Thus saith the Lord".

'Whoever wishes to profit in the Scriptures, let him first of all lay down as a settled point that the Law and the Prophets are not a doctrine delivered according to the will and pleasure of men, but dictated by the Holy Spirit'.

'By its own majesty the Word commands our reverence; nevertheless it does not really affect us until it is sealed on our hearts by the Spirit. Being enlightened by His power we no longer owe it to our own judgment or to that of others (*i.e.* the Church) that we believe the Scripture to be from God, but for reasons beyond human judgment we are perfectly certain, as if we beheld in it the glory of God Himself, that it came down to us by the instrumentality of men from the very mouth of God'.

'We subject our judgment and intellect to it (the Word) as something beyond all dispute'.

'We owe to the Scripture the same reverence that we owe to God because it has proceeded from Him alone and has nothing belonging to man mixed with it'.

Readers of Calvin's Institutes will find much else to the same effect.

English Reformers

English Reformers bear a similar testimony to God's Word written. Those who have acquaintance with the remarkable series of volumes published in the mid-19th century by the Parker Society cannot but assent to the fact of the unanimity of their witness on this matter. At whatever point they are sounded they give a clear ringing note. Thus Cranmer speaks:

'If thou be desirous to know whether thou be in the right faith or no, seek it not at man's mouth, for "all men be liars". Seek it not at a proud, glorious and wavering sort of bishops and priests, but at God's own mouth, which is His Holy Word written, which can neither lie, deceive, nor be deceived . . . Try every spirit, but allow none further than they agree with the written Scriptures. God's Word trieth all things, whether they be good or evil, true or false. That is the very touchstone'.

'Cleave ye fast to the sound and certain doctrine of God's infallible Word, written in the canonical books of the New and Old Testament, which is able sufficiently to instruct you to eternal salvation through Jesus Christ our Lord' (Remains: pp. 13, 14, 19).

Cranmer apart, no man spoke with greater acceptance for the Church of England in Tudor days than John Jewel, Bishop of Salisbury. We quote from his famous *Apologia Ecclesiae Anglicanae,* commonly known as Jewel's Apology:

'We receive and embrace all the canonical Scriptures, giving thanks to our God, who hath raised up unto us that light which we might ever have before our eyes, lest, either by the subtlety of man or by the snares of the devil, we should be carried away to errors and lies . . . They be the very sure and infallible rule whereby be tried whether the church doth stagger, or err, and whereunto all church doctrine ought to be called to account. Against these Scriptures neither law nor ordinance nor any custom ought to be heard, no, though Paul's own self, or an angel from heaven, should come and teach the contrary.'

To the same effect is the testimony of John Hooper, the martyred Bishop of Gloucester:

'I believe that the Word of God is of a far greater authority than the church, the which Word only doth sufficiently show and teach us all those things that in any wise concern our salvation, both what we ought to do and what to leave undone. The same Word of God is the true pattern and perfect rule, after the which all faithful people ought to govern and order their lives, without turning either to the right hand or to the left hand, without changing anything thereof, without putting to it or taking from it, knowing that all the works of God are perfect, but most chiefly His Word' (Later Writings, p. 43).

The testimony of John Whitgift, Archbishop of Canterbury during the last twenty years of Elizabeth's reign, is of interest because of the contrast that he sets up between the Book of Common Prayer and the Scriptures:

'You affirm that I say, "The Book of Common Prayer to be a perfect and absolute rule to govern this church, wherein nothing is wanting, or too little, nor nothing running over, or too much". If I have said any such thing, quote the place, that the reader may consider of it, and know that you speak the truth. But if I never spake or writ any such thing, then you are a false witness . . . I have learned with St. Augustine to give this reverence only to the writers of canonical Scriptures, that I think none of them to have erred in writing. And I do firmly believe that only the books of the canonical Scripture are of that absoluteness and perfection that nothing may be taken away from them, nothing added to them.'

The Voice of the Puritans

Among the Reformers there is no dissentient voice; English or Scottish, they present one unvarying body of witness. As for the Puritans, no one who knows anything of their outlook would for a moment deny that they bear the same unflinching testimony to the integrity of the Word. Their thoughts are set forth with the utmost precision and clarity in the *Westminster Confession* of 1647; indeed, its first Chapter is entitled 'Of the Holy Scripture'. It defines in ten paragraphs the belief of Puritan England and Scotland:

Para. IV. 'The authority of the Holy Scripture, for which it ought to be believed and obeyed, dependeth not upon the testimony of any man or church, but wholly upon God (who is truth itself), the author thereof; and, therefore it is to be received, because it is the Word of God.'

Para. VII. 'All things in Scripture are not alike plain in themselves, nor alike clear to all; yet those things which are necessary to be known, believed and observed for salvation, are so clearly propounded and opened in some place of Scripture or other, that not only the learned but the unlearned, in a due use of the ordinary means, may attain unto a sufficient understanding of them.'

Para. IX. 'The infallible rule of interpretation of Scripture is the Scripture itself; and therefore, when there is a question about the true and full sense of any scripture (which is not manifold, but one) it must be searched and known by other places that speak more clearly.'

Para. X. 'The supreme Judge, by which all controversies of religion are to be determined, and all decrees of councils, opinions of ancient writers, doctrines of men, and private spirits, are to be examined, and in whose sentence we are to rest, can be no other but the Holy Spirit speaking in the Scripture.'

To such findings let the whole Church of God say Amen!

What of Today?

And what shall be further said? The time would fail the writer to speak of Anglicans, Methodists, Nonconformists, Brethren and others of recent date who have strenuously affirmed in more or less the same terms the same unyielding convictions, and who have 'professed a good profession before many witnesses'. It is for us their successors in 'the long cloud of witnesses' to 'show the same path to heaven'. Across the centuries, crossed and inter-crossed as they are by the 'ringing grooves of change', it is for the Christian today to confess the same 'truth unchanged, unchanging', and to say, as Luther told the Emperor Charles V at the fateful Diet of Worms, 'I am bound by the texts of the Bible; my conscience is captive to the Word of God'.

The Inspiration and Authority of Scripture in the Modern World

By David G. Fountain

Previous articles have dealt with the inspiration and authority of Scripture as attested by Scripture itself, and as a doctrine of the Christian Church through the centuries. The question may be asked, 'Why is it necessary to have a third article relating to the postion as it stands today?' There are two main reasons. This doctrine has been assailed in a new way, and answers need therefore to be given that have not been given before. Furthermore, the doctrine has to be understood and applied in a contemporary situation.

Frequently in the past doctrines have been formulated as a result of the emergence of false teaching. Points that were always held but never clearly defined have been clarified as a consequence of being assailed. It is fitting, therefore, for us to consider the way in which the inspiration and authority of Scripture is being attacked today, so that a positive understanding of the position can be arrived at.

The Modern World

We live in an age that considers itself to be 'grown up', and that looks down on the past. This is no new thing. In the early eighteenth century, when rationalism was a powerful influence in this country, men felt that their society had arrived at its destination. In the present day men make the mistake of assuming that the scientific progress evident everywhere to a hitherto undreamed of extent is an indication that man himself is making moral progress. This analogy between science and morality is pressed further. It is assumed that, since it is evident that many of the scientific theories which held good for so long have been proved inadequate, it is now possible to debunk the spiritual and moral principles held by former generations. It is argued that it was not indeed wrong for them to work on outmoded ideas in the realm of science and morality, and we can advance on them both. They *had* to pass through such a period just as a child must have time to grow up. Men no longer need the restraints placed upon their forefathers, just as children, when grown up, no longer need parental discipline. It does not suit people, however, to press the analogy between science and morality into the realm of the absolutes. In an age when men are working on absolutes in the scientific realm, they disregard increasingly absolutes in the moral realm. There is no denial of the fact that there are unchanging scientific laws, but the idea of absolute moral standards is challenged. Furthermore, the application of this idea of moral progress and the consequent change in standards creates problems. If it was good for an unsophisticated community to practise stricter moral codes than advanced countries today, what about the areas of the world that are still 'adolescent'? Do they have a different standard from those that are more advanced?

What has been abundantly clear in recent years, according to Walter Lipman in America's *Newsweek,* is that while there is tremendous scientific advance, there is increasingly unrest and a challenge presented to all the basic institutions of society. Scientific progress is being achieved at the same time as a moral regress. The Word of God tells us that the heart of man is 'deceitful above all things and desperately wicked' (Jeremiah 17:9). The Christian is not at all surprised at what is happening in the world. Its course has been predicted in the Word of God. Furthermore, the Scripture has predicted the very assault made upon the Word of God itself. All men are basically the same, 'There is none righteous, no, not one . . . There is none that seeketh after God' (Romans 3:10, 11). This is human nature left to itself. The twentieth-century man is the same below the skin as all former generations.

The Doctrine of Inspiration Under Attack. Wrongly Defined

Along with the rejection of many doctrines held by the whole professing Christian Church, the doctrine of the verbal inspiration of the Scriptures was broadly jettisoned just under a century ago. It had been believed by almost the entire Christian world that the Scripture did not merely contain the Word of God, but that it was itself God's Word, the words themselves being inspired. Then the theory of Evolution gained favour, and men began to approach the Bible in a new way. They considered themselves capable of judging it and passing sentence upon it, rather than being subject to the judgment it made of men. Instead of letting its statements expose their prejudice and corruption, men approached it with a readiness to find fault. It was treated as if it were like any other ancient book, and theological considerations were carefully put on one side when its claims for itself were considered. It had to be proved to be true according to the method of textual criticism used when examining classical writings, before it was accepted as authentic. Men believed they should approach the Bible from a 'natural' point of view. Sir Frederic Kenyon (1903) expressed himself as follows: 'It is important to recognize from the first that the problem is essentially the same, whether we are dealing with sacred or secular literature, although the difficulty of solving it, and likewise the issues depending on it are very different. It is important, if for no other reason, because it is only in this way that we can meet the hostile critics of the New Testament with arguments, the force of which they admit. If we assume from the first the supernatural character of these books and maintain that this affects the manner in which their text has come down to us, we can never convince those who start with a denial of that supernatural character. We treat them at first like any other books, in order to show at last that they are above and beyond all other books.'

'Although Kenyon probably advised this oblique approach with the best of intentions, still the course which he advocated is wrong. Orthodox Christians must not stoop to conquer. We must not first adopt a neutral position toward the Bible in order that later we may persuade unbelievers to receive the Bible as God's Word. There are several reasons why we must not do this. In the first place, if we take this step, we are doing a sinful thing. We are not only allowing unbelievers to ignore the divine inspiration and providential preservation of the Bible, but we are even doing this ourselves. In other words, we are seeking to convert unbelievers by the strange method of participating in their unbelief. In the second place, when we approach unbelievers from the neutral position, we are endorsing their false method of textual criticism, a method which does not apply to the real, divinely inspired, providentially preserved Bible but to a false Bible of their own imagination, that is to say, an uninspired Bible whose history is basically the same as that of any other book. And in the third place, when we take up this neutral position, we are not doing anything to convert unbelievers to the orthodox Christian faith. On the contrary, we are confirming them in their confidence in the essential rightness of their unbelieving presuppositions.'*

Scientific investigation became the arbiter in matters that relate to Divine inspiration. Some who were anxious to hold to the older view of inspiration adopted the new approach to prove that it was entirely reliable, but in so doing they conceded the vital matter of approach. Spurgeon was among the few who saw where it would all lead. We take an example of what was happening in the 1890s from W. B. Glover's *Evangelical Nonconformists and Higher Criticism in the 19th Century.* Alfred Cave, a Congregational scholar, gave some lectures in which he made an attempt to give the traditional views of the Bible a firm foundation. The first three chapters after the Introduction deal with Genesis. Lecture II attempts a proof of the historical accuracy of Genesis by showing that the principal stories recounted there have their counterparts in the mythologies of other peoples widely scattered over the world. He deals in some detail with the flood and gives accounts of the legends of Babylon, Egypt, India, Persia, China, Japan, Siam, Tartary, Borneo, Phrygia, Greece, Rome, Scandinavia, and Wales. Then in considerably less detail he discusses the idea of chaos, the order of creation, creation

**Believing Bible Study,* by E. F. Hills, pp. 50, 51.

of man from earth, creation of woman from man's rib, Eden, the serpent as the source of evil, etc. For all these he shows counterparts in the myths of other peoples. This, he says, proves conclusively the historical accuracy of Genesis because there is no other way to account for the widely-scattered accounts.

Lecture III gives additional proofs. Cave affirms an agreement between science and Genesis on such matters as the single origin of the race, the essential unity of languages, etc. That these matters were controversial among scientists he does not recognise; he simply appeals to the authorities with which he is in agreement.

Cave had not attained to a *sound* critical position, but he had unconsciously surrendered the old traditional approach. The welcome he received among conservatives simply indicates how far conservatives had moved in the previous decade. Spurgeon, who had not budged an inch, is the exception that clarifies the rule. Spurgeon could see no purpose in any critical study of the Bible. Right-minded men needed no such prop for their faith in God's Word, and obviously the judgment of those perverted by unbelief was not to be trusted in so vital a matter.

Spurgeon was quite right in his contention that Cave had conceded so much as to compromise the whole traditional view of the Bible. The interesting thing is that this reaction was not more widespread. In fact, Spurgeon was so far behind the general movement of opinion that his own more logical judgment was scarcely understood. The 'Congregational Review' declared: 'The attack of Mr. Spurgeon upon it (Cave's Lectures) remains absolutely unintelligible to us. No stronger vindication of what may be regarded as the old orthodox view has appeared for many a day.'

This point is vital since there are those in these days who make the same mistake. The late Charles Breed in his *Lectures on Christian Doctrine,* published by the Strict and Particular Baptist Ministers' Fellowship, in his chapter on the inspiration of Scripture, makes this very point. 'Frequently the common approach to the question of inspiration, whilst well meaning, is unhappily a misguided one. It is a popular mistake to suppose that the inspiration of Scripture can be proved by logical argument. Many well-meaning attempts have been made to do this, but all have failed. Something more is necessary. It is not possible to prove the inspiration of Scripture by philosophical discourse, by logical arguments, or by intellectual exercise alone, but once the true foundation has been laid, then logical arguments can serve their turn . . . It is always possible from the logical point of view, that there should be some other explanation of those biblical characteristics which we do not know. These matters are confirmatory for those who believe in inspiration, but they are not proof.' He goes on to give the reasons and grounds for believing in inspiration: 'The man who knows God as Father, by spiritual instinct recognizes that this Book is his Father's word, and thereby he knows that this is the Word of God. I would remind you that the Scriptures themselves recognize this fact. John 7:17, 'If any man will do His will, he shall know of the doctrine, whether it be of God, or whether I speak of Myself.' John 8:43: Jesus is speaking to some Jews who had professed belief in Him, 'Why do ye not understand My speech? Even because ye cannot hear My word.' Of course they could hear His voice, the sound of what He was saying, but they could not hear Him, they could not understand. So in 1 Cor. 2:13, 14, 'Which things also we speak, not in the words which man's wisdom teacheth, but which the Holy Ghost teacheth; comparing spiritual things with spiritual. But the natural man receiveth not the things of the Spirit of God; for they are foolishness unto him: neither can he know them, because they are spiritually discerned.' A spiritual discernment is necessary. Once more, in 1 Thess. 2:13, 'For this cause also thank we God without ceasing, because, when ye received the word of God which ye heard of us, ye received it not as the word of men, but as it is in truth, the word of God, which effectually worketh also in you that believe.' These passages are sufficient to show the principle of which I have been speaking, that of recognizing the Word of God, in consequence of the inner work of God.' The Christian believes in the inspiration and authority of Scripture because of his faith in God Himself. His confidence in the Word of God does not lie in the conclusions of the labours of literary and historical critics.

An objection will be raised immediately based upon the difficulties that are encountered in a belief in verbal inspiration. Faith and confidence in Jesus Christ is based on a knowledge of Him, and such knowledge suffices to enable us to trust Him with that which cannot be understood. The Christian knows enough about Jesus Christ to trust Him implicitly with all the manifold difficulties he meets. The life of the Christian is a life of faith. He remembers that when he was a child he used to do puzzles, and if a piece did not fit, he did not assume immediately that the puzzle was worthless, but he patiently persevered. The Christian knows that there are answers to problems raised; many of them have been solved already. But at the same time he knows that God's method of revelation is not such as to satisfy an unbelieving mind. There were many who demanded proof from the Lord Jesus that He was all He claimed to be. There was quite enough proof, and those who objected were merely making excuses. When He was at Nazareth they were convinced of His remarkable power. What troubled them was the question, 'Whence hath this man this wisdom and these mighty works?' (Matt. 13:54). It was too humiliating to them that one brought up among them could be so favoured. They realized that the reports about Him were true as soon as He began to speak, but they could not bear the implications and they demanded proof. The Jewish leaders who demanded proof from the Lord Jesus said among themselves, 'This man doeth many miracles. If we let him thus alone all men will believe on Him: and the Romans shall come and take away both our place and nation' (John 11:48). They were convinced by the evidence, but it was the *implications* that worried them. There was sufficient evidence to believe that the Christ was all that He claimed to be. There were difficulties at the same time. How could the Son of God come in the *way* that He did? He seemed so unlike the Messiah they were expecting. Christ revealed Himself in such a way in order to make faith necessary. Faith finds the evidence that is given to be sufficient. It does not demand an exorbitant amount. To use a natural illustration, we trust certain people because we know them, not because we know everything there is to know about them, but because we know *sufficient* to have confidence in them. Apologetics do not establish faith, but confirm it. Scientific investigation and argument presented by godly scholars are very helpful in removing objections that the doctrine of verbal inspiration is unscientific, but it does not make faith unnecessary.

The first assault on the Scripture in the late 19th century led men to defend the traditional doctrine in the wrong way, and most professing Christians soon abandoned the older view of inspiration. This defence is still adopted by some, but it is clear that Spurgeon was right and that he recognized what would happen.

The Doctrine of Inspiration Wrongly Interpreted

The assault upon the integrity of the sacred text has been followed in more recent years by a much more subtle approach. Men say that God continues to speak today as in the days when the Scripture was being written down. The idea that we are shut up to a book written so long ago appears as an insult to modern man. The result is an appeal to the idea that God is still *revealing truth.* This is a serious assault upon the *uniqueness* of God's Word. The Papacy has always claimed for Church tradition equal authority with the Scriptures, while the cults all appeal to special revelations. This always leads to a rejection of the basic message of the Scriptures. In practice, tradition and the later 'revelations' are given undue prominence and overlie the Gospel message, rendering of none effect the Word of God. Modernistic scholars, while not believing in the specific 'revelations' of the cults, make the revelation of God subjective only in order to accommodate the older situation to the present. This is the only way they can deal with the problem of reconciling obvious contradictions that arise between the message as it has been believed formerly and as it is now taught. Sometimes men appeal to the familiar statement of John Robinson, the famous pastor of the Pilgrim Fathers: 'I am thoroughly persuaded, I am very confident, the Lord hath more truth yet to break forth out of His holy Word.' They forget that he was not speaking about 'inspiration', but 'illumination'. He believed that the vision was *sealed up,* the faith had been once delivered to the saints, the message *had* been preached by Christ and confirmed by them that heard Him. He did not believe that God still inspired men in such a way as to reveal new truth, but rather that He gave light and understanding that men might interpret the Scriptures more clearly. He went on, 'For my part, I cannot sufficiently bewail the condition of the Reformed churches who are come to a full stop in religion and will go at present no further than the instruments of their first reformation.' His conviction has been borne out by the fact that much light has been shed upon the Scriptures subsequently concerning the doctrine of the Church. Many would feel, furthermore, that in these present days further light has been given on the question of the Second Coming, so that as the end appears to draw near, light on different passages has shone forth. Calvin was noble enough not to comment on the Book of Revelation because he felt he had not sufficient light. Those who believe in the inspiration of the Scriptures are decided upon the point that Christ is God's *last* Word to man, and that the faith *has been* delivered once for all. Attempts in recent years, as referred to in the foregoing, to add to the revelation or to misrepresent the method of inspiration, far from helping us in these present days, have undermined confidence in the sacred record itself. God is well able to throw light upon the sacred page for the needs of our present day, but His Word is unique, it cannot be added to. To regard it in any other way is to destroy its authority.

It may be argued that we teach that the early Christians had a closer access to God in view of the fact that God was speaking to them His very Word, and that therefore they were in a more advantageous position than ourselves. It needs to be remembered that Christ, when He was upon earth, was rejected by men who could see Him with their own fleshly eyes. Furthermore, He told His disciples it was expedient that He should depart so that the Holy Spirit might enter into their hearts after He had gone. This is still the experience of the child of God, which is more intimate than that known by the disciples during our Lord's earthly ministry. Others object by saying, 'How can this be, since what can be more personal than to hear God actually speak?' They say that in order to meet the present situation God must deal in the same way in these days. The Christian, when he approaches the Scriptures, prays the same prayer as David when he said, 'O Lord, open Thou mine eyes that I may behold wondrous things out of Thy law'. When his eyes are opened, he sees wonderful things in the Word of God; the Word of God is itself alive, and quick and powerful. It does not need to *become* alive to him; *he* needs to become alive to *it,* and this is the work of the Spirit, which is the same today as ever it was. Our need in these days is to become alive to God. He is as *near* as ever He was. He speaks as directly through the written Word as through an audible voice in the days of the early church. God does speak to modern man, but it is through the same Word that He has ever chosen to speak to man down the ages. What modern man needs is the work of the Holy Spirit to open his eyes to understand the message of the Gospel. There is nothing wrong with the Scriptures. We should view them as perfectly sufficient and adequate for men's present need and not regard them as anything less than the very best that man can have today.

The Doctrine of Inspiration Wrongly Presented

Many who accept the view that the Scriptures are complete, and that men need the work of the Holy Spirit to open their eyes to an understanding of their contents can yet handle the Scriptures in such a way as to deny this teaching. The very approach they make to the subject of the presentation of the truth carries with it an implication that it is not absolutely necessary for men to be enlightened by the Spirit. The problem, they say, is concerned not with man's inability to receive the truth but with the natural difficulty he finds in *understanding* it. The barrier in the mind of man is considered to be natural rather than spiritual. The great problem appears to them to be one of communication. However, because the Scripture is the Word of God a man must know God Himself before he can understand the meaning of His Book. Yet much emphasis is placed upon the need to present the message to man in a way that will appeal to his understanding. It is put like this, 'If only we can present the truth in a way that will appeal to a man intellectually, we can win him. If only we can put the Word of God in a reasonable, easily understood form, we shall win men.'

According to this view the problem is one of communication and of convincing men intellectually. In these days men are more concerned about *reaching* men with the Gospel than making sure that it is the *Gospel* that reaches men! The great cry is that the need of our day is to find a method of getting the truth across. We are even told that men are seeking the truth today more than ever before' (quotation from Fact and Faith Film Advertising Strip). All the emphasis is on the presentation. The result is that the content of the message suffers. Men are prepared to sacrifice accuracy in the Scriptures for readability. Even such conservative groups as the I. V. F. have placed readability *before* accuracy in a guide to a selection of Bible translations. This principle has been applied to the translation of the Scriptures. The spate of modern translations exemplifies the modern approach. By and large, each succeeding translation becomes more popular and less accurate. The whole concept of verbal inspiration is threatened. We are given to understand that verses of Scripture can be interpreted in many different ways. The question is not what the writer meant, but what he *could* mean! What would we think if our letters were handled in a similar way? The idea is fostered that accuracy does not matter. This looseness in translation work goes back a long way (see article on the Greek text by Bishop D. A. Thompson, *Bible League Quarterly*, No. 272, January, 1968). Those who have held to verbal inspiration have been willing to use translations that they know full well are corrupt, because the language used is more up-to-date.

A clear example of the way in which concessions have been made by Evangelicals is the changed attitude in recent years towards the Revised Standard Version. When it first appeared over fifteen years ago it was disapproved of, in the main, by Evangelicals. They listened to men like Oswald T. Allis. In his criticism of the R.S.V. he answers the question, 'Is the R.S.V. a liberal version?' 'If by a "liberal" version is meant a version which represents a lax and "liberal" attitude to the question of the plenary, verbal inspiration and the divine authority of Scripture, then R.S.V. is clearly such a version. Sufficient evidence has been given to show that it is governed by a very different conception of what is meant by an 'accurate' version from that to be found in A.V. and R.V. This was to be expected. Thirty-five years ago Doctor Moffatt in the Preface to his *New Testament: A New Translation (1913)*, in discussing the difficulties which the translator faces in trying to make an accurate and idiomatic translation, made this significant statement: 'But once the translator of the New Testament is freed from the influence of the theory of verbal inspiration, these difficulties cease to be so formidable.' Moffatt's own translations give a clear indication of the amount of freedom which he felt a translator was entitled to exercise in this regard. And while R.S.V. does not go as far as he did, it shows the same determination not to be fettered by the ipsissima verba of Scripture. The R.S.V., as we have seen, supplies the gist of the passage but constitutes a paraphrase rather than a translation. While insisting that the translator must confine himself to translation, its authors have also insisted that it is the duty of the translator to assume the role of interpreter, and to regard it as his function not only to tell us what the writers said, but what they meant by what they said.' Allis compares it to the Authorized Version: 'We believe, and we think we have proved, that the Revised Standard Version represents a radical departure from the high standard of accuracy in translation which was set by the Authorized Version more than 300 years ago and which the English Revised Version and American Revised Version felt called upon to maintain. We cannot escape the conclusion that the standard of accuracy represented by R.S.V. is quite a different one. "New manuscripts," "papyri", "better understanding of vernacular Greek", "necessity of modern diction", and the like, may be responsible for many of the changes to be noted here. But most influential of all in determining the character of the version has been, we believe, the determination of the revisers to establish their right to exercise a freedom in the rendering of Holy Scripture, which might be tolerated in dealing with many books of merely human origin, but which is quite incompatible with the divine origin and authority of the Bible. Plenary inspiration, an inspiration which extends to the words of Scripture—this is the only inspiration which gives the Bible real authority as the very Word of God—has accuracy of translation as its necessary corollary. The freedom with which R.S.V. treats the text of Scripture indicates the low conception of its inspiration entertained by the revisers. It is this more than anything else which makes the R.S.V.

"important". It represents a type of translation which, certainly in the case of a "standard revision" of the A.V., would have aroused a storm of protest fifty years ago.' In *Christianity Today* Allis made a remarkable statement: 'Should R.S.V. attain to anything like the popularity which its publishers anticipate, this will be indeed an important event. It will be a signal triumph for Modern Liberalism.'

In recent years the R.S.V. has become the most widely used of the modern versions. This is not because it is a new and accurate translation. It is surely because of the change in the theological climate. Those who have been more opposed than any others to the circulation of the Scriptures, *i.e.* the Roman Catholics, have sufficient confidence in the text of the R.S.V. to use it themselves. The pragmatic approach predominates. The ultimate step in Bible translation will be the New Common Bible, which will include very likely, the Apocrypha, acceptable to both Roman Catholics and Protestants. We shall have within the same covers the Words of God and the words of men. The doctrine of inspiration and authority will in this manner be overthrown. Men have made the presentation of the Gospel more important than the Gospel itself!

Conclusion

The root cause of all these changes lies in a denial of the depravity of human nature and the need to be truly dependent upon God. The present situation can never be remedied by anything different from the Gospel. There have been periods in the history of the Church when the authority of the Scriptures has been very small, but a dramatic change has followed and the Word has assumed great power, leading to the salvation of multitudes. It could be the same today. In the past it did not come about as a result of the abandoning of doctrines previously held, or the discovery of novel methods of presentation, but by the power of the Holy Spirit working through the same message as was preached by the Apostle Paul: 'All Scripture is given by inspiration of God, and is profitable for doctrine, for reproof, for correction, for instruction in righteousness: that the man of God may be perfect, throughly furnished unto all good works' (2 Tim. 3:16, 17).

O Word of God incarnate,
O Wisdom from on high,
O Truth unchanged, unchanging,
O Light of our dark sky,
We praise Thee for the radiance
That from the hallowed page,
A lantern to our footsteps,
Shines on from age to age.

The church from her dear Master
Received the gift divine,
And still that light she lifteth
O'er all the earth to shine:
It is the golden casket
Where gems of truth are stored;
It is the heaven-drawn picture
Of Christ, the living Word.

It floateth like a banner
Before God's host unfurled;
It shineth like a beacon
Above the darkling world:
It is the chart and compass
That o'er life's surging sea,
'Mid mists and rocks and quicksands
Still guides, O Christ, to Thee.

O make Thy church, dear Saviour,
A lamp of burnished gold,
To bear before the nations
Thy true light as of old;
O teach Thy wandering pilgrims
By this their path to trace,
Till, clouds and darkness ended,
They see Thee face to face!
(*William Walsham How,* 1867)

The Authority of Scripture (2)

By Dr. D. Martyn Lloyd-Jones
(an extract from a sermon on Ephesians 6.14:
'Stand therefore having your loins girt about with truth')

There can be no doubt whatsoever that all the troubles in the Church to-day, and most of the troubles in the world, are due to a departure from the authority of the Bible. And, alas, it was the Church herself that led in the so-called Higher Criticism that came from Germany just over a hundred years ago. Human philosophy took the place of revelation, man's opinions were exalted and Church leaders talked about 'the advance of knowledge and science', and 'the assured results' of such knowledge. The Bible then became a book just like any other book, out-of-date in certain respects, wrong in other respects, and so on. It was no longer a book on which you could rely implicitly. There is no question at all that the falling away, even in Church attendance, in this country is the direct consequence of the Higher Criticism. The man in the street says, 'What do these Christians know? It is only their opinion, they are just perpetrating something that the real thinkers and scientists have long since seen through and have stopped considering'. Such is the attitude of the man in the street! He does not listen any longer, he has lost all interest. The whole situation is one of drift; and very largely, I say, it is the direct and immediate outcome of the doubt that has been cast by the Church herself upon her only real authority. Men's opinions have taken the place of God's truth, and the people in their need are turning to the cults, and are listening to any false authority that offers itself to them.

We all therefore have to face this ultimate and final question: Do we accept the Bible as the Word of God, as the sole authority in all matters of faith and practice, or do we not? Is the whole of my thinking governed by Scripture, or do I come with my reason and pick and choose out of Scripture and sit in judgment upon it, putting myself and modern knowledge forward as the ultimate standard and authority? The issue is crystal clear. Do I accept Scripture as a revelation from God, or do I trust to speculation, human knowledge, human learning, human understanding and human reason? Or, putting it still more simply, Do I pin my faith to, and subject all my thinking to, what I read in the Bible? Or do I defer to modern knowledge, to modern learning, to what people think today, to what we know at this present time which was not known in the past? It is inevitable that we occupy one or the other of those two positions.

The Protestant position, as was the position of the early Church in the first centuries, is that the Bible is the Word of God. Not that it 'contains' it, but that it is the Word of God, uniquely inspired and inerrant. The Protestant Reformers believed not only that the Bible contained the revelation of God's truth to men, but that God safeguarded the truth by controlling the men who wrote it by the Holy Spirit, and that He kept them from error and from blemishes and from anything that was wrong. That is the traditional Protestant position, and the moment we abandon it we have already started on the road that leads back to one of the false authorities, and probably ultimately to Rome itself. In the last analysis it is the only alternative.

People will have authority; and they are right in so thinking. They need authority because they are bewildered; and if they do not find it in the right way they will take it in the wrong way. They can be persuaded even though they do not know the source of the authority; in their utter bewilderment they are ready to be persuaded by any authoritative statement. So that it comes to this, that we are back exactly where Christians were 400 years ago. The world talks about its advance in knowledge, its science, and so on, but actually we are going round in cycles, and we are back exactly where Christians were 400 years ago. We are having to fight once more the whole battle of the Protestant Reformation. It is either this Book, or else it is ultimately the authority of the Church of Rome and her 'tradition'! That was the great issue at the Protestant Reformation. It was because of what they found in the Bible that those men stood up against, and queried and questioned and finally condemned the Church of Rome. It was that alone that enabled Luther to stand, just one man, defying all those twelve centuries of tradition. 'I can do no other' he says, because of what he had found in the Bible. He could see that

Rome was wrong. It did not matter that he was alone, and that all the big battalions were against him. He had the authority of the Word of God, and he judged the Church and her tradition and all else by this external authority.

We are back again in that exact position, and I am concerned about the matter, not only from the standpoint of the Church in general, but also from the standpoint of our own individual experiences. How can we fight the devil? How can we know how we are to live? How can we answer the things we hear, the things we read, and all the subtle suggestions of the devil? Where can I find this truth that I must gird on, as I put on all this armour of God? Where can I find it if I cannot find it in the Bible? Either my foundation is one of sand that gives way beneath my feet, and I do not know where I am, or else I stand on what W. E. Gladstone called 'The Impregnable Rock of Holy Scripture'.

Why should we return to the Bible?

Why should we return to the Bible, why should we believe it? Because we should not be as children, 'carried about by every wind of doctrine, by the sleight of men, and cunning craftiness, whereby they lie in wait to deceive'. The only way to avoid such a catastrophe is to have a compass, to have a chart, to have an authority, to have something solid on which we can base our whole life, and if necessary sacrifice our lives for it.

(i) because 'the world by wisdom knew not God'

But—to speak more in detail—the first answer is that the Bible itself claims that it is this authority. Sometimes it does so explicitly, and at all points it does so implicitly. No man in and of himself can ever arrive at a knowledge of God. That is the whole basis of the New Testament teaching, as it was the whole basis of the apostolic teaching. I cannot understand how anyone can hold any other view who has read the first two chapters of Paul's First Epistle to the Corinthians. The Apostle lays down the following as his fundamental position: 'For the preaching of the cross is to them that perish foolishness; but unto us which are saved it is the power of God'. Then he goes on: 'For it is written'—he is quoting from the Old Testament—'I will destroy the wisdom of the wise, and will bring to nothing the understanding of the prudent'. 'Where is the wise?—where is the scribe? where is the disputer of this world?' That is to say, where is the man who relies on modern knowledge and science and learning, and on his own ability and on what the philosophers are saying? Then Paul continues: 'Hath not God made foolish the wisdom of this world.' How? Paul answers, 'For after that in the wisdom of God the world by wisdom'—by philosophy, by learning, by knowledge and understanding and human reason—'the world by wisdom knew not God'. It had failed to find Him; but when the world had failed, then it 'pleased God by the foolishness of preaching'—by what the world regarded as the 'foolishness' of the thing preached, the 'foolishness' of the Gospel and the message of the Gospel—'to save them that believe.' The Apostle states there the whole position; and there is no answer to it. This is where we see the wisdom of God. People often ask the question: 'If God had proposed to send the Messiah, the deliverer, His own Son, into this world, as He had foretold throughout the centuries, why did He wait so long to do so? Why did He not do so much earlier?' The answer is that God sent His Son into the world with His message after He had given the world a full opportunity to deliver itself, and particularly through Greek philosophy. All the great Greek philosophers—Plato, Socrates, Aristotle, and the rest—had lived and died before the Lord Jesus Christ came. They represented man at his very acme. There is no question but that the flowering period of the human intellect in so many senses was reached in the great era of Greek philosophy which preceded the coming of the Lord Jesus Christ. There you have man's ability and thinking at its very best and highest; but it proved quite unable to rise to a knowledge of God. 'The world by wisdom knew not God,' and it never has known Him ever since, and it never will.

Yet, to-day, men continue to put their trust in human philosophy. The Church is doing so; she is quoting the philosophers, finding 'insights' in a variety of religions and in the philosophers' teachings, whether they are Christians or not. If they are able men, men of learning and deep thinkers, it is argued that they must have something to tell us! But that is a complete denial of the whole basis of apostolic preaching.

'The world by wisdom knew not God': and the reason for that is obvious. It is obvious because of the character of God. In 1 Corinthians, chapter 2, Paul says that 'the princes of this world did not know' and did not recognize our Lord. 'We speak wisdom,' says Paul, 'among them that are perfect; yet not the wisdom of this world, nor of the princes of this world, that come to nought' (v. 6). Human wisdom, even in its princes, its greatest men, is inadequate; it will never bring us to the truth. It is because God is what He is! God is infinite and absolute and eternal in every respect. God is! And the moment you realize that truth, you see how man can never possibly arrive at a knowledge of Him. How can the finite encompass the Infinite? How can mortal man arrive at a real knowledge of the immortal God, the God who says, 'I am that I am', the God who is from eternity to eternity, absolute in every respect, the God who is 'light and in Him is no darkness at all'.

Even if man were perfect he could not arrive at a knowledge of God the infinite, for in comparison with God he is nothing. If you can encompass any knowledge with your brain it means that your brain is greater than the thing that you encompass. So when man tries to understand God, and to find Him by his own searching and power and intellect and understanding, he is postulating that he is greater than God, and that God is someone open to examination. The very idea is monstrously ridiculous.

But when we realize that man is not only finite but also sinful, and fallen, and unclean, and twisted, and perverted, the position becomes still more ridiculously impossible. Take the Apostle's argument: 'What man knoweth the things of a man, save the spirit of man which is in him?' (1 Cor. 2:11). There must be a correspondence. If you want to appreciate music you must have some musical sense. There are people who have no appreciation of music at all. They may have great intellects, but they are tone deaf, they have no appreciation. There must be some correspondence before there can be understanding. And the same applies to the spiritual realm. God is not only infinite and absolute and eternal; 'God is light, and in Him is no darkness at all'. There is no communion between light and darkness, there is no correspondence between black and white. God is everlastingly holy, and every one of us is sinful and unworthy and vile. And the result is, as the Apostle says, that to every such 'natural' person the things of God's Spirit are 'foolishness' (1 Cor. 2:14). Man by nature not only cannot arrive at the knowledge; when he is given the knowledge he rejects it with scorn. It is nonsense to him, it is foolishness. 'The Greeks seek after wisdom,' but the Gospel is 'foolishness' to them. It is so utterly different from what they believe, and what they are, and what they have. And it will be so throughout eternity. The passing of the ages makes no difference. God does not change, man does not change, sin does not change, and therefore, whatever we to-day may know scientifically which our forefathers did not know, makes not the slightest difference. So we are back again in the old position, 'The world by wisdom knew not God'. It could not know. 'The natural man receiveth not the things of the Spirit of God . . . neither can he.' Man cannot, because of the greatness of God and his own weakness and ability and sinfulness.

(ii) because God alone can give man wisdom

We are all therefore in this position, that by all our efforts we can never arrive at this knowledge of God. Well, then, is knowledge possible? If I am to gird my loins about with truth, how can I find it? There is but one answer: if we are to have any knowledge of truth at all, then God must give it us. It has to be revealed to us. 'It is high, I cannot attain unto it,' says the Psalmist (Psalm 139:6). But God, if He so chooses, can give us the knowledge which we desire. And the whole message of the Bible from beginning to end is just this, that He has done so. 'In the wisdom of God when the world by wisdom knew not God, it pleased God by the foolishness of preaching'—by the message which He sent out through His servants—'to save them that believe'. That is another way of stating the fact of revelation.

Consider for a moment the way in which the Apostle Paul stated the matter when he was preaching at Athens, and addressing Stoics and Epicureans. It is, to me, not only the tragedy of tragedies, but most inexplicable that the Christian Church in the last century deliberately brought philosophy back into the Church and put it in a central position. It is a fundamental denial of the whole of the Gospel. And she is still doing so. We are to stand before the world and say what Paul said at Athens: 'Whom ye ignorantly worship . . .' (Acts 17:22ff). They were trying to find Him; they had not only erected temples to all their various gods, but there was this strange altar bearing the inscription, 'To the unknown God'. They had a feeling that He was there somewhere. The most primitive races have a belief in some supreme God. They do not know Him, they are trying to find Him—and so were the Greeks! 'The unknown God!' And Paul looks at them and says, 'whom ye ignorantly worship'—or try to worship—'Him *declare* I unto you'. He is making a declaration. Here are people fumbling and groping in the dark, and then a man with authority comes and says, 'Him declare I unto you'. Here is knowledge, here is the information. That is revelation! That is the whole biblical position. In our inability, in our finite condition, in our sinfulness, we cannot, and we never shall be able to arrive at a knowledge of God. And we are shut up to this position, that if God is not pleased to give us the knowledge, to give us revelation, we have nothing, we are undone, we are hopeless, 'we are without God, in the world'. But, says the Bible, God has done this very thing! That is the whole glory of the message, that is the good news of the Gospel of salvation; God has been pleased to give us this revelation. That is the message of the whole Bible; that is what it is proclaiming from beginning to end. 'In the beginning God . . .' It is an authoritative statement. How does Moses make the authoritative statement? It was given to him. So you find the author of the Epistle to the Hebrews saying that it is 'through faith we understand that the worlds were framed by the word of God'. We know it 'by faith'; it was given; it is a revelation.

(iii) because Old Testament and New Testament alike are 'God-breathed'

Such is the claim of the Old Testament; and the Old Testament in this matter is as important as the New Testament. The two go together, the one leads to the other. Moses wrote his five books, not by his own wisdom, not by his own philosophy. He does not give us his own ideas and understanding. The truth was revealed to him and he was enabled by the Spirit to write it. When you come to the prophets, you find exactly the same thing. Not a single prophet ever stood up and said, 'I am saying this because I have thought very much about this subject; I have meditated and read much about it, and I have come to this conclusion'. That is not what they say. Instead, they speak about 'the burden of the Lord'; 'the message of the Lord came unto me', or 'the Spirit of God came upon me'. Some of them did not want to give the message. Jeremiah says, 'I wish I had not got to speak, I only get into trouble when I do speak'. He decided more than once that he would never speak again, but he said 'The Word of God was like a fire burning within me and I could not refrain'. That is their position. The Psalmist says much the same thing.

The Bible is the result of God disturbing men by the Spirit, giving them the message, and then enabling them to deliver it in speech or in writing. And the Apostles, writing in the New Testament about these very things, fully confirm what the Old Testament claims. Take the famous statement of the Apostle Paul to Timothy in 2 Timothy 3:16: 'All Scripture is given by inspiration of God'. It is 'God-breathed'. It has come from God. He has 'breathed' it into men. It is not of men, it is not human literature, its source is divine. 'And it is profitable for doctrine, for reproof, for correction, for instruction in righteousness, that the man of God may be perfect, thoroughly furnished unto all good works.' The truth is the girdle which you have to put on around your loins. Peter confirms that in his own language in an important statement in his Second Epistle, chapter one, verse nineteen to the end: 'We have also a more sure word of prophecy; whereunto ye do well that ye take heed, as unto a light that shineth in a dark place, until the day dawn, and the day-star arise in your hearts: knowing this first, that no prophecy of the scripture is of any private interpretation'. Peter does not mean that you and I cannot interpret it as we read it, but that 'no prophecy of scripture' is the result of any private human excogitation; it is not the result of human reason and thinking and understanding. The prophetic writings do not give us a man's own private interpretation of contemporary events and his attempt to forecast the future—it is not that! Peter goes on to day, 'Prophecy came not in old time by the will of man but holy men of God spake as they were moved by the Holy Ghost'; they were 'carried along by', 'borne along by' the power of the Spirit. The claim is made first in the Old Testament; and we find it stated explicitly in the New Testament.

But over and above the testimony of the Apostles Paul and Peter to the Old Testament writings, we have our Lord's own attestation of them. Read the four Gospels and note how He quotes Scripture, and always as the final authority. Notice that He says on one occasion, 'The Scripture cannot be broken' (John 10:35). He quotes from Genesis as well as the other books. He talks about man at the beginning, obviously accepting the teaching about Adam and Eve and the first marriage and so on. There is never any question about the authority of the Old Testament anywhere in the whole of His teaching. He accepts the entire Book. And note how after His resurrection when He talks to the two on the road to Emmaus whose faith had been shaken, and who were dejected and disappointed, 'O fools,' He says, 'and slow of heart to believe all that the prophets have spoken'. And so He began to take them through the Scriptures—Moses and the prophets. He showed them in the Scriptures 'the things concerning himself'. He had already said to the Jews, 'The Scriptures testify of me' (John 5:39). And then, later, when these two from Emmaus had arrived back in Jerusalem, where the entire company had assembled, and some were still somewhat bewildered and unhappy and not able to understand exactly what was taking place, we read in Luke 24:44: 'And he said unto them, These are the words which I spake unto you, while I was yet with you, that all things must be fulfilled, which were written in the law of Moses, and in the prophets, and in the psalms concerning me'. He teaches plainly the authority of the Old Testament; He refers to prophecy as foretelling—and foretelling accurately! The knowledge could only have come from God, and it had been recorded by God's servants. 'Then opened he their understanding, that they might understand the Scriptures.'

(iv) because our Lord Jesus Christ Himself guarantees the authenticity of Scripture

The Old Testament Scriptures are authoritative because they are the Word of God. When you come to the New Testament the same holds good. There is the towering figure of our Lord Himself, with all that He says about Himself, and what He claims for His teaching. He does not hesitate to speak with authority; and the people recognized it. They said that 'he taught them as one having authority, and not as the scribes' (Matt. 7:29). 'I say unto you'—this carpenter, this man who had come out of Nazareth of all places, this man who had never been trained in the schools of the Pharisees, stands and speaks with authority. He claims to be the Son of God, not a human teacher. He has come from God. He is the Son of Man who comes down from heaven and who is still 'in heaven'. 'Before Abraham was, I am,' He says. That is His claim everywhere. He commands them to listen because of the unique authority that belongs to His Person, and therefore to His teaching. That anyone could read the Scriptures without noting these claims would indeed be inexplicable were it not that we know how sin blinds, and how sin fills us with such prejudice that we cannot see. The crime to-day is that people are sitting in judgment, not only on the Scriptures, but also on the Lord of the Scriptures! They say that He was wrong in His belief in the Old Testament and that 'He was a child of His age'. They do not hesitate to say that He was wrong in certain claims which He made for Himself. People who speak thus abandon all authoritative utterance, for there is no alternative. The supreme and only authority is the One who is the Son of God and who has come out of the eternal bosom. He was 'with' God. He has looked into the face of God. And He has come on earth and He has revealed God. 'No man hath seen God at any time; the only begotten Son, who is in the bosom of the Father, he hath declared him' (John 1:18). And what do we know apart from this revelation?

This is the beginning of the matter, the foundation, the bare minimum, the absolute. We either take everything from this, or we have no authority at all. You either submit completely to it, or else one man's opinion is as good as another's—and that means that you have no authority at all. Before you can ever succeed in girding your loins about with truth you have to come to God's Word as a little child, or, to use the stronger word that Paul uses, you have got to come to it as a 'fool'. 'If any man seemeth to be wise in this world' he says, 'let him become a fool that he may be wise' (1 Cor. 3:18); which means, 'Let him say he knows nothing, let him say that his philosophy is of no value to him, let him agree that "the world by wisdom knew not God" and cannot know God, and that therefore he knows nothing, and is prepared to bend his knees and to look up and receive the divine revelation'.

In other words, if we are to gird our loins about with truth, we have not only to admit that we know nothing, but that before the Holy Spirit works upon us and gives us enlightenment we cannot even receive God's revelation. The natural man cannot do so; 'but God hath revealed them unto us by his Spirit; for the Spirit searcheth all things, yea, the deep things of God' (1 Cor. 2:10). If you want to be girt about with truth you have to come as a little child, acknowledging not only your weakness and insufficiency and inability and complete impotence; you have got to realize that the Spirit of God must work upon you and enlighten you and cleanse your understanding and give you an anointing before you can receive the revelation that God has graciously been pleased to give us. Here is the authority—God's revelation, which we can receive and understand as the result of the working of the Holy Spirit of God within us and upon us.

Do you know where you stand? What are you fighting with? How do you face the future? How do you deal with temptation and the devil and all the uncertainty of life to-day? Here is the only answer. May God give us grace and strength to have our loins girt about with truth.

Hugh Latimer.—An old-time Bible book and teacher. From an old print.

The Infallibility of Scripture

By C. H. Spurgeon

(a message based upon 'The mouth of the Lord hath spoken it' Isaiah 1:20)

What Isaiah said was spoken by Jehovah. It was audibly the utterance of a man; but, really, it was the utterance of the Lord Himself. The lips which delivered the words were those of Isaiah, but yet it was the very truth that 'The mouth of the Lord hath spoken it.' All Scripture, being inspired of the Spirit, is spoken by the mouth of God. However this sacred Book may be treated nowadays, it was not treated contemptuously, nor negligently, nor questioningly by the Lord Jesus Christ, our Master and Lord. It is noteworthy how He reverenced the written Word. The Spirit of God rested upon Him personally, without measure, and He could speak out of His own mind the revelation of God, and yet He continually quoted the law and the prophets, and the Psalms; and always He treated the sacred writings with intense reverence, strongly in contrast with the irreverence of 'modern thought'. I am sure, brethren, we cannot be wrong in imitating the example of our divine Lord in our reverence for that Scripture, which cannot be broken. I say, if He, the anointed of the Spirit, and able to speak Himself as God's mouth, yet quoted the sacred writings, and used the holy Book in His teachings, how much more should we, who have no spirit of prophecy resting upon us, and are not able to speak new revelations, come back to the law and to the testimony, and value every single word which 'The mouth of the Lord hath spoken'!

The like valuation of the Word of the Lord is seen in our Lord's apostles; for they treated the ancient Scriptures as supreme in authority, and supported their statements with passages from Holy Writ. The utmost degree of deference and homage is paid to the Old Testament by the writers of the New. We never find an apostle raising a question about the degree of inspiration in this book or that. No disciple of Jesus questions the authority of the books of Moses, or of the prophets. If you want to cavil or suspect, you find no sympathy in the teaching of Jesus, or any one of His apostles. The New Testament writers sit reverently down before the Old Testament and receive God's words as such, without any question whatever. You and I belong to a school which will continue to do the same, let others adopt what behaviour they please. As for us and for our house, this priceless Book shall remain the standard of our faith and the ground of our hope so long as we live. Others may choose what gods they will, and follow what authorities they prefer; but, as for us, the glorious Jehovah is our God, and we believe concerning each doctrine of the entire Bible, that 'the mouth of the Lord hath spoken it.'

Our Warrant for Teaching Scriptural Truth

We preach because 'The mouth of the Lord hath spoken it.' It would not be worth our while to speak what Isaiah had spoken, if in it there was nothing more than Isaiah's thought; neither should we care to meditate hour after hour upon the writings of Paul, if there was nothing more than Paul in them. We feel no imperative call to expound and to enforce what has been spoken by men; but, since 'The mouth of the Lord hath spoken it,' it is woe unto us if we preach not the gospel! We come to you with, 'Thus saith the Lord,' and we should have no justifiable motive for preaching our lives away, if we have not this message.

The true preacher, the man whom God has commissioned, delivers his message *with awe and trembling,* because 'The mouth of the Lord hath spoken it.' He bears the burden of the Lord and bows under it. Ours is no trifling theme, but one which moves our whole soul. They called George Fox a Quaker, because when he spoke he would quake exceedingly through the force of the truth which he so thoroughly apprehended. Perhaps, if you and I had a clearer sight and a closer grip of God's Word, and felt more of its majesty, we should quake also. Martin Luther, who never feared the face of man, yet declared that when he stood up to preach he often felt his knees knock together under a sense of his great responsibility. Woe unto us if we dare to speak the Word of the Lord with less than our whole heart, and soul, and strength! Woe unto us if we handle the Word as if it were an occasion for display! If it were our own word, we might be studious of the graces of oratory; but if it be God's Word, we cannot afford to think of ourselves: we are bound to speak it, 'not with wisdom of words, lest the cross of Christ should be made of none effect'. If we reverence the Word, it will not occur to us that we can improve upon it by our own skill in language. Oh, it were far better to break stones on the road than to be a preacher, unless one had God's Holy Spirit to sustain him; for our charge is solemn and our burden is heavy. The heart and soul of the man who speaks for God will know no ease, for he hears in his ears that warning admonition: 'If the watchman warn them not they shall perish; but their blood will I require at the watchman's hands.' If we were commissioned to repeat the language of a king, we should be bound to do it decorously lest the king suffer damage; but if we rehearse the revelation of God, a profound awe should take hold upon us, and a godly fear lest we mar the message of God in the telling of it. No work is so important or honourable as the proclamation of the gospel of our Lord Jesus, and for that very reason it is weighted with a responsibility so solemn that none may venture upon it lightly, nor proceed in it without an overwhelming sense of his need of great grace to perform his office aright. We live under intense pressure who preach a gospel of which we can assuredly say, 'The mouth of the Lord hath spoken it.' We live rather in eternity than in time: we speak to you as though we saw the great white throne and the divine Judge before whom we must give in our account, not only for what we say, but for how we say it.

Dear brethren, because the mouth of the Lord hath spoken the truth of God, we therefore endeavour to preach it with *absolute fidelity.* We repeat the Word as a child repeats his lesson. It is not ours to correct the divine revelation, but simply to echo it. I do not take it to be my office to bring you new and original thoughts of my own; but rather to say, 'The word which ye hear is not mine, but the Father's which sent me.' Believing that 'The mouth of the Lord hath spoken it,' it is my duty to repeat it to you as correctly as I can after having heard it and felt it in my own soul. It is not mine to amend or adapt the gospel. What! Shall we attempt to improve upon what God has revealed? The Infinitely Wise—is he to be corrected by creatures of a day? Is the infallible revelation of the infallible Jehovah to be shaped, moderated, and toned down to the fashions and fancies of the hour? God forgive us if we have ever altered His Word unwittingly; wittingly we have not done so, nor will we. His children sit at His feet and receive of His words, and then they rise up in the power of His Spirit to publish far and near the Word which the Lord has given. 'He that hath My word, let him speak My word faithfully,' is the Lord's injunction to us. If we could abide with the Father, according to our measure, after the manner of the Lord Jesus, and then come forth from communion with Him to tell what He has taught us in His Word, we should be accepted of the Lord as preachers, and accepted also of His living people far more than if we were to dive into the profound depths of science, or rise to the loftiest flights of rhetoric. What is the chaff to the wheat! What are man's discoveries to the teachings of the Lord! 'The mouth of the Lord hath spoken it;' therefore, O man of God, add not to His words lest He add to thee the plagues which are written in His Book, and take not from them, lest He take thy name out of the Book of Life!

Again, dear friends, as 'The mouth of the Lord hath spoken it,' we speak the divine truth *with courage and full assurance.* Modesty is a virtue; but hesitancy when we are speaking for the Lord is a great fault. If an ambassador sent by a great king to represent his majesty at a foreign court, should forget his office and only think of himself, he might be so humble as to lower the dignity of his prince, so timid as to betray his country's honour. He is bound to remember not so much what he is in himself, but whom he represents; therefore, he must speak boldly and with the dignity which beseems his office and the court he represents. It was the custom with certain Oriental despots to require ambassadors of foreign powers to lie in the dust before them. Some Europeans, for the sake of trade interests, submitted to the degrading ceremony; but when it was demanded of the representative of England, he scorned thus to lower his country. God forbid that he who speaks for God should dishonour the King of kings by a pliant subservience. We preach not the gospel by your leave; we do not ask tolerance, nor court applause. We preach Christ crucified, and we speak boldly as we ought to speak, because it is God's Word, and not our own. We are accused of dogmatism; but we are bound to dogmatize when we repeat that which the mouth of the Lord hath spoken. We cannot use 'ifs' and 'buts', for we are dealing with God's 'shalls' and 'wills'. If he says it is so, it is so; and there is an end of it. Controversy ceases when Jehovah speaks.

Stewards of the Word of God

Those who fling aside our Master's authority may very well reject our testimony: we are content they should do so. But, if we speak that which the mouth of the Lord hath spoken, those who hear His word and refuse it, do so at their own peril. The wrong is done, not to the ambassador, but to the King; not to our mouth, but to the mouth of God, from whom the truth has proceeded.

We are urged to be charitable. We *are* charitable; but it is with our own money. We have no right to give away what is put into our trust and is not at our disposal. When we have to do with the truth of God we are stewards, and must deal with our Lord's exchequer, not on the lines of charity to human opinions, but by the rule of fidelity to the God of truth. We are bold to declare with full assurance that which the Lord reveals. That memorable word of the Lord to Jeremiah is needed by the servants of the Lord in these days: 'Thou therefore gird up thy loins, and arise, and speak unto them all that I command thee: be not dismayed at their faces, lest I confound thee before them. For, behold, I have made thee this day a defenced city, and an iron pillar, and brasen walls against the whole land, against the kings of Judah, against the princes thereof, against the priests thereof, and against the people of the land. And they shall fight against thee; but they shall not prevail against thee; for I am with thee, saith the Lord, to deliver thee.' When we speak for the Lord against error, we do not soften our tones; but we speak thunderbolts. When we come across false science, we do not lower our flag: we give place by subjection—no, not for an hour. One word of God is worth more than libraries of human lore. 'It is written' is the great gun which silences all the batteries of man's thought. They should speak courageously who speak in the name of Jehovah, the God of Israel.

I will also add that, because 'The mouth of the Lord hath spoken it,' therefore we feel bound to speak His Word *with diligence,* as often as ever we can, and *with perseverance,* as long as ever we live. Surely, it would be a blessed thing to die in the pulpit; spending one's last breath in acting as the Lord's mouth. Dumb Sabbaths are fierce trials to true preachers. Remember how John Newton, when he was quite unfit to preach, and even wandered a bit by reason of his infirmities and age, yet persisted in preaching; and when they dissuaded him, he answered with warmth, 'What! Shall the old African blasphemer leave off preaching Jesus Christ while there is breath in his body?' So they helped the old man into the pulpit again, that he might once more speak of free grace and dying love. If we had common themes to speak about, we might leave the pulpit as a weary pleader quits the forum; but as 'The mouth of the Lord hath spoken it,' we feel His Word to be as fire in our bones, and we grow more weary with refraining than with testifying. O my brethren, the Word of the Lord is so precious that we must in the morning sow this blessed seed, and in the evening we must not withhold our hands. It is a living seed and the seed of life, and therefore we must diligently scatter it.

How precious is the Book divine,
By inspiration given!
Bright as a lamp its doctrines shine,
To guide our souls to heaven.

Its light, descending from above,
Our gloomy world to cheer,
Displays a Saviour's boundless love,
And brings His glories near.

It shows to man his wandering ways,
And where his feet have trod;
And brings to view the matchless grace
Of a forgiving God.

When once it penetrates the mind,
It conquers every sin:
Th' enlightened soul begins to find
Two striving powers within.

It sweetly cheers our drooping hearts,
In this dark vale of tears:
Life, light, and joy it still imparts,
And quells our rising fears.

This lamp, through all the tedious night
Of life shall guide our way:
Till we behold the clearer light
Of an eternal day.

(*J. Fawcett*)

Section Three

The Bible: Addresses and Articles

Contents: Section Three

The Bible: Addresses and Articles

The Bible a Miracle

By Prebendary H. E. Fox

More than thirty years ago I was a young minister, without a grey hair in my head, away on the other side of the water in Westminster. It was about the time that Mr. Spurgeon was writing and speaking about what was called in those days the 'Down Grade,' and I, as a young minister, perhaps with the impertinence of the young, ventured to address him a letter on my own behalf, telling him how heartily I thanked God for his testimony and admired his courage. Among some of the treasures which I own in my library is the reply of that good man, written in the kindest, I would say most brotherly spirit, appreciating my sentiments, and showing that standing side by side as we were on the 'Impregnable Rock of Holy Scripture,' in whatever else we might differ, we were one there.

The Bible is a miracle, and I should like to give you an illustration of that, and a very remarkable one, which I observed in the public press only a few days ago. The Edward Seventh Professor of Literature, a very well-known writer, was lecturing in Cambridge upon Elizabethan Literature. He said some hard things about it; in fact, he went so far as to use the word 'detestable.' One merit, however, he discovered in it. 'It was struggling, fumbling, to say something that was to make something. It was not like modern jargon, trying to dodge something.' He adds, 'The Elizabethan writers were alive, and unconsciously for the most part, were striving to philosophise the vocabulary of English prose and find a rhythm for its periods.' That is not very high praise! Then he goes on to say that 'as happens sometimes, a miracle took place. It was a double miracle.' Speaking briefly of the influence which Shakespeare had upon the poetry of England, he referred to what was a greater miracle. He meant the Authorised Version of the Bible. 'Individual genius such as Shakespeare's we may allow to come in the course of nature. But how forty-seven men, not one known outside this performance for any superlative talent, could have brought that marvel to birth, and after no very long gestation—well, he had a somewhat sceptical mind, but he admitted that before such a wonder as that the most sceptical mind must stand humble and aghast.' 'When a nation had achieved the manner of diction they found in the wonderful language of the Authorised Version, those glorious rhythms,'—he is speaking, you see, only of its literary features,—'simple men, holy and humble men of heart, like Izaak Walton and Bunyan, had their lips touched and spoke to the homelier cadences. Proud men, scholars—Milton and Sir Thomas Browne—practised the rolling Latin sentences, but on the nobler cadences of our Bible they too fell back.' 'The Bible controls its enemy Gibbon as surely as it haunts the curious music of a light sentence of Thackeray. It is in everything we see, hear, feel, because it is in us, in our blood.'

Now I ask you, friends, if a literary man, not approaching it at all from the point of view of this meeting, if such a man can thus eulogise and describe as a miracle this Authorised Version of the Bible, what are we to say of the original? If you call the Authorised Version a miracle, infinitely greater is the miracle of that of which the Authorised Version is a translation. For here you have not a company of men meeting together and discussing and comparing notes, learning something from one and something from another; but you have a series of writers totally separated from each other by time and circumstances, not merely of one age, but living in many ages, men of totally different types of character, men of different professions, kings, poets, priests, fishermen, husbandmen, statesmen, composing a Book which is not merely, as sometimes it is called, a 'Library of Books,' but itself a complete Book; a Book with such a unity running through it from the beginning to the end, that you could not take out one part—hardly a chapter—without mutilating the whole. Was there ever such a miracle?

A friend of mine, I remember, some years ago wrote a little book, in which he compared the Bible to a great statue, put up to commemorate, say, our Sovereign. Suppose that every country in the Empire had each contributed a different part of that statue, one an arm, another the body, another a leg, and so forth. Suppose that every part of the body, coming from places far apart, as from Canada, from India, from the Cape of Good Hope, or elsewhere, fitted so absolutely accurately into each other that you could hardly see where they were joined, what would you call it? Would you say that it was an accident, or had there been some intelligent mind controlling the whole, some great artist conceiving the idea and communicating the plans to all those separate sources? And this is the fact that meets us in the Bible—that supernatural Power which has been controlling the universe controlled the minds of the writers of the Bible, so that it has come down to us—this Word of God.

Sir, I am proud of a phrase in our Anglican Prayer Book which calls the Scriptures 'God's Word written.' I know no finer definition of it, and I tell you why, because I believe that that was the attitude which my Blessed Lord took when He looked at the Scriptures of His day, which, remember, were just the Scriptures of our day, less the New Testament. There is not a Book in our Old Testament which was missing from the Old Testament of the Lord. Our Lord's appeal again and again was, 'What hath the Scripture said?' It is worth the study to try to trace out in the discourses and words of our Lord how His mind seems to have been saturated with the Scriptures, so saturated that in almost every case—I think I should say in every case—there seems either some direct or indirect allusion to the written Word of God.

And how does God communicate it to men? That is a mystery of which I have no knowledge. I shrink myself from any definition of Inspiration, just as I cannot express to you all that Incarnation is or how it is. But I believe from the bottom of my heart in the fact of a Divine origin, and if so, then Inspiration is Plenary; and it must have been verbal. How is thought communicated from one being to another? How are you taking in—imperfect as my expression may be—how are you taking in what I am saying to you, except as I express myself in words? How does the Almighty communicate Himself, except by those methods which He has given Himself to man, the power of speech and the mental faculty to comprehend what is said and then act upon it?

There are two words in the Greek language which we translate as 'word.' One is that which you find in the first chapter of John's Gospel, the word *'logos'*. Another very common expression on our Lord's lips is the Greek word *rhema,* which is literally, 'something spoken.' The word *'logos'* may be used in a larger sense, such as 'a discourse,' 'an argument,' as well as a particular word. But *'rhema'*—I think I am right in saying so—means actually the word spoken which is heard. Again and again our Lord has used this term. 'The words that I speak unto you, they are spirit, and they are life.' 'He whom God hath sent speaketh the words of God.' 'He that rejecteth Me, and receiveth not My words (*'rhemata'*) hath One that judgeth him.' In His great prayer recorded in John 17 He says, 'Thy Word (*logos*) is Truth'; and I believe by that He includes the whole sum of that which had been spoken both through Him and by the mouth of His Servants the prophets of old time.

The difficulty which a great many people find in accepting this view of the Old Testament lands them in a greater difficulty still. I have many friends, ministers, who I believe to be devout and earnest Christian men, but I know of some to whom I have put this question, 'Do you accept the teaching and example of our Blessed Lord, recorded in the Gospel, as the supreme standard of all Christian doctrine and practice?' Not seldom I have been met with a refusal, and why? Because they know perfectly well that if they accepted that test I should put to them another question, 'Then why do you not believe the Old Testament?' because the Rationalistic spirit of the day, which challenges the authority of the Old Testament, has no alternative but to refuse the authority of Christ also, or to surrender its false premise. What a position for a Christian man to find himself in! You would think that when faced with such a conclusion he would at once say, 'Well, then, my premise must be wrong.' But, unhappily, that is not the way the human mind works. Man clings dearly to his prejudices, however broadminded he may think he is; and the Higher Criticism would not have so large a following were it not for the pride of the human heart. 'The natural man receiveth not the things of the Spirit of God, for they are foolishness to him, neither can he know them, for they are spiritually discerned.' But to the man, whosoever he be, who has submitted his will to the Lord Jesus Christ, and who will say to Him, 'Lord, I believe everything Thou dost tell me,' the solution becomes easy; difficulties disappear.

The Bible League stands for this, the Holy Scriptures as given by God, and as witnessed unto by the Lord Jesus Himself, both before His death and after His resurrection.

There are two results which I think we may see from this attitude of mind towards the Scriptures. The Bible has one feature which distinguishes it from every other religious book in the world, just as Christianity differs from every other religion in the same respect. In all the other religions in this world religion is not necessarily connected with conduct; the Bible unites the two. As you believe in the Lord Jesus Christ, so will be your morality. The Hindu may be the most devout believer in his religion; yet it does not affect his ethical standards. So it is with the Buddhist; so it is with the Mohammedan; so it is with the Confucianist. Any of them may combine their religious creeds with lives utterly vicious and vile. With one who wholly believes the Bible and lives out his faith that is impossible. The Bible, from beginning to end, denounces sin in every shape and form. It alone produces the remedy—it alone effects the cure.

Then notice another thing: in every human religion, even if it preaches a true morality—and there is a true morality preached in some of the world's sacred books—there is no power that can lift a man out of a selfish or immoral life. It is the Bible only that not only shows a man how this can be done, but also enables him to do it. When the Lord Jesus Christ comes into a man's soul, it changes his character. He hates that which he before loved, and he loves that which he before hated. There comes what we call 'Conversion.' It is the Spirit of God entering into the man. I do not know, Sir, what your experience is of dealing with people in conversion, but I used to see a great deal more of it than, unhappily, I have the opportunity of seeing now; and I used to observe this, that in every case of conversion it was some Word of God that had brought about the result. Perhaps the individual was not always able clearly to trace it at first, but I have often asked the question, 'What was the Scripture that led you to the Lord?' Some said one and some said another. We are born again of the Word, as well as of the Spirit.

Then another blessed thing is this, that the Bible is the greatest unifying agency in the world. Our Lord, looking into the great vista of the future, and speaking of those who would come to believe on Him through the word of His servants, multitudes of millions yet unborn, spoke of them as the 'other sheep' whom He must bring. 'And they shall hear My voice,' He adds,—and what then? 'There shall be one flock, and one Shepherd.' And depend upon it, dear friends, the closer we come round the Bible and the Lord Jesus Christ, as revealed in the Bible, the closer we shall be to one another. I believe if true unity is to come, it will certainly not come by uniformity—it will come to us just in proportion as each believer hears the voice of the Lord Jesus Christ speaking to him. We stand apart from each other because we keep our ears closed, or we do not listen to the voice as we ought to listen to it, or we listen to a little part of it, or we put our own poor foolish interpretations upon it, instead of taking it just as it came from Him. Just in proportion, I repeat, as we hear and obey the Voice we shall be one.

Then mark another thing: wherever the Bible goes, in whatever translation, it has just the same power. It has been translated into many languages, and it produces the same effect everywhere. How can you explain that? 'Another miracle,' you say. Yes, far greater even than that of the Authorised Version. The translation may sometimes not be as perfect as it might be; still there is power in it, extraordinary power, even in a fragment. I could tell you of cases which I have known in the Mission Field again and again.

A man whom I knew well told me this story. He was an old man when he told me. As a lad he had learned a sentence from a Sanskrit book in his school: 'He is the great Teacher, who can teach men all things.' That fired his imagination. He spent years going through the country asking where that great Teacher was. He could not find him; no one could tell him where he was. There were many wise men who said they could teach him much, but they could not teach him everything. He came back. He met an English officer, Captain Haig, as he then was, engaged in engineering works. On the Lord's Day he would gather such of his labourers and clerks as would come, and read the Scripture to them. Only one Gospel had been translated at that time, the Gospel of Matthew. One day he was reading that passage in the Sermon on the Mount, where our Lord speaks of praying to our Father who is in secret, and He will reward us openly. The young man jumped up and said, 'Sahib, let me see that Book! for there is the Great Teacher who will teach me all things!' The Holy Spirit had gripped that man's soul, and he saw the great truth which some Christians do not see, that He who could penetrate the secret things and manifest them openly must know all things. Captain Haig had to go away soon afterwards, and that young man studied that single Gospel in a way in which I am afraid few of us read our Bibles. He read it on his knees. When the Captain came back he found that man was a thorough-going Christian, converted to God with no one to teach him but that single Gospel of Matthew. That young man afterwards became a catechist, then a teacher in a school, then a pastor, and then for many years he was a faithful minister to his own people; and there are hundreds of those poor Telugu people now rejoicing in the Lord Jesus Christ who were brought to God literally through that single text of the Word of God.

I could tell you of many other instances. Here is a power that Almighty God has put into the hands of His Church. What are we about that we are not using it? It does not require much courage to stand up for the Bible. It does not cost us great pains to speak for it wherever we go. If the Bible is to us the Book most precious of all books, if we know what the Bible is to our own souls, surely we should not be loyal to our Master if we did not defend it, and endeavour in every way, whether through the Bible League or in other ways, to get people to know and love this priceless Word of God.

Nehemiah's Wall. Bishops' Bible (1568).

Criticism and Evidence*

By Harrington C. Lees

Let us think of the cause for which the Bible League exists, and of the reasons why we are met together. I take it we are none of us here to defend the Bible, and I certainly would not join in carrying on a League that existed for that purpose. I would as soon think of putting a fence round the Matterhorn to keep the goats from butting into it, or of putting a tarpaulin over Vesuvius to keep the rain showers from extinguishing it, as of trying to defend God's Book by a man-organised League.

To those of us who look at the history of the books which make up the one Book, and see how they climbed into men's hearts and esteem, until these sixty-six books are known as 'The Book' throughout the whole of the civilised world, and in ever-increasing measure are asserting their position, and dominating every other form of published literature, there is no doubt whatever as to the hand of God being behind the Book and the voice of God being heard through the Book. And when we see, further, the results that inevitably follow its planting in the wildest and most degraded countries, and behold the elevation of the people who read it, in every case where it is given a fair trial, and its principles are imbibed and followed, again we say we know that God is in it.

We have seen from the study of history that, in the times of the fiercest attacks upon it, it has won its most marvellous victories. Take the most dangerous assault to which the Bible was ever subjected in the Christian era—I mean in the persecution by Diocletian. In the year 301 an edict was issued that the Christian books must go, because it was felt that it was no good killing Christians so long as you left the Book. It only made more Christians, and the thing to do was to kill the Book. That was a wise conclusion to come to, provided that the Emperor had power to carry it out. He did his best, and everywhere throughout the Empire Christians were bidden to give up the sacred writings. Some did, and it became a serious matter afterwards in ecclesiastical circles to adjudicate as to their fitness for Church-office. But what happened? Within twenty-five years of that time the Emperor Constantine was on the throne proclaiming that the Christian religion was to be the religion of the Empire, and he ordered that fifty magnificent copies of the Bible should be placed in the churches of Constantinople, the newly-made capital of his Empire. That was God's reply to the challenge of another Roman Emperor.

We are not here to defend the Bible, but we are here because we see that there is a real danger in the insistence on and the popularizing of certain theories in regard to the trustworthiness of the Bible. When the Dervishes made their raid on Abyssinia, in order that they might know their path back they bent the young saplings, and now you may trace their route by the warped and twisted trees which you can find along the road that they took. And we are here because we have seen—and we are afraid of seeing again—in the case sometimes of instructed souls, who ought to be able to look after themselves, and in the case of uninstructed souls, who cannot do so, we have seen the warp in the spiritual life as a result of the imbibing of views of the Bible which are widely promulgated to-day. We are here to endeavour to meet that challenge.

We must remember that when we step off the platform of unquestioning faith into the arena of discussion and argument, we must face the issues involved. That is to say, it is a perfectly tenable position to say, 'I believe because it is in the Bible, and the Bible is the Word of God.' That is unquestioning faith. But when a man says, 'I believe the Bible because—' (whatever the cause in mind may be), he steps down from the platform of unquestioning faith into the arena of argument, and he must be prepared to face the issues. You must meet argument by argument, theory by fact, and criticism by criticism. For it is not criticism in itself that is wrong; it is, as we conceive, many of the critics who are wrong. I think it is necessary to remember that this League exists to meet criticism with criticism.

*Address at Annual Meeting of Bible League in 1915.

It is an appalling thing that it has even been seriously argued that fraud may be pious. But we begin now to understand how some German critics could take that view. To them it was as harmless to make up a scrap of paper as to tear it up. Many of our English scholars swallowed the theory with a wry face. And many smelled the reek of hell in it and revolted, although they have often found other ways of coming to practically the same conclusion. But this is certain, the book which sternly denounces fraud has not sprung from impostors.

Now I do not want to underrate, or to appear to underrate, the question of 'sources,' which is often at the bottom of the critical question. If I may say so in his presence, Sir William Ramsay's suggestions as to the position of Philip and Philip's daughters and Rhoda in the compilation of the Acts are among the most illuminating things one has seen for some time. But when the issue is placed before us in this plain form, as a choice between fact, history and truth, or invention, jugglery and fraud, then we are not concerned to hesitate a moment: our reply is unquestioning and plain. And I think it is somewhat pitiful to note the chilly attitude of many critics towards the archaeologists, because after all the archaeologist is dealing with facts that in the majority of cases cannot be questioned.

I learned from Sir Robert Anderson the extraordinary value of indirect evidence with regard to the truth of a document or a witness. For instance, there is in the ancient records of Whitby the statement that a Pope sent a Bull to a Synod held there centuries ago, and the King, who was presiding, tore off the leaden seal in a rage and threw it out of the open window over the cliff. Well, the document says so, but who is to know if it is true? Not more than a score of years ago in some digging at the foot of the East Cliff, that leaden seal was dug up. If any man questioned the truth of the old chronicle, do you suppose he questioned it after the seal was found? It was the value of indirect testimony.

More than a thousand years ago a Saxon Christian King, Edmund, was murdered by Danish invaders in the village of Hoxne, in Suffolk. They fastened him to an oak tree, and shot him dead; and in that village long centuries after there was a great oak known as King Edmund's Oak. But who was to know that the story was true? In 1848 the old oak blew down, and they found embedded a foot deep in the ancient bole, at the height of a man's breast, the iron head of an arrow.Nobody had seen King Edmund killed there, but this was indirect evidence. The story was confirmed. And a very large amount of the work we now have in a number of the volumes of Sir William Ramsay, for instance, is just that kind of evidence which is most stimulating to the Bible student. Similar work has been done by Professor R. A. S. Macalister, who, in his book on Gezer, has shown how the Old Testament, when put to the same proof, holds the same reassuring evidence. For instance, the Chronicles speak of giants at Gezer. The books of the Chronicles are supposed to be discredited as history, but in 1 Chronicles 20 we are told David killed certain giants at Gezer. The word 'giants' does not mean monstrosities, of course, but it does mean men of extraordinary stature; and Professor Macalister, in his report, speaks of finding skeletons of unusual length at Gezer. About fifteen years ago my friend, Dr. H. Martyn Clarke, spent a holiday in the old land of the Philistines, and, alluding to the story of the men with six fingers and six toes, he said he found a family of men in those villages with just that malformation of the hand—a double thumb. I merely mention this to show that with regard to some of the unlikely things in the Bible you find extraordinary evidence even at the present day. Professor Macalister has given us another sketch in his book of the conformation of the great hall of the men of Gaza and the wooden pillars on stone bases, by dislodging which Samson was able to do the extraordinary feat that set the world wondering.

So I venture to say that the Bible records ring true wherever a man is really fair to them. And by that I mean, that he does not press them to mean what they have not said, or try to evade what they do say. I remember a man taking me to task because I said that if it were proved that the whole of the wall of Jericho did not fall it would not disprove the Bible. As a matter of fact the Bible says the whole of the wall did not fall down: Rahab's house had stood on the wall and Rahab's house was left standing. In this connection it is worth noting that Pére Vincent, the French archaeologist, is filled with wonder at the confirmations of the Jericho story which have been discovered. So also in the matter of interpretation. Adherence to the document more than to the commentator is desirable. What a man thinks is not necessarily the real interpretation. New light may lead to a different understanding of the unchanged text.

So we go on with confidence. This is the justification of our position. This is the task we have to address ourselves to. And we claim that in taking this position of confidence we are not obscurantists, hiding our heads and pretending things are not happening; we are not unscientific, refusing to accept fresh evidence; and we are not behind the times, holding to the threadbare arguments. We claim that those men are obscurantists who, in the face of new archaeological discoveries, refuse to reconsider their philological position; we claim that those men are unscientific who hold theories that new facts have proved to be unsound; we claim that a man is behind the times who goes on following up dicta emanating from Berlin in spite of the fact that a British archaeologist has placed on record discoveries that place the New Testament and, we believe, the Old as well, beyond many of the challenges and assertions that have been made in recent days. So we look up into the Face of God, and thank Him who has given us the means whereby with unshaken confidence we may go to those whose minds have been unsettled and confirm their faith and reinstate their souls.

Title-page to King James's, or The Authorised Version, 1611.

The Egyptian Watermark in the Pentateuch

By Dr. Melvin Grove Kyle

There are marks of early authorship in the diction of the Pentateuch which do not seem to admit of any other explanation than that of early production itself. A host of treasure-seekers in Egypt—Chabas, Brugsch, Naville, Lieblein, indeed every Egyptologist—in searching about its ruins have found now and then an empty matrix, so to speak, and some Old Testament writer has furnished a literary gem whose every peculiarity fitted exactly into it. Certain books of the Bible purport to have had Egyptian sources or associations, and there are certain literary correspondences which substantiate the claim, certain linguistic gems for which the exactly fitting matrix has been found in Egypt. Thus these correspondences become witnesses; witnesses which cannot lie, for their points of peculiarity are too many, and incapable of being suborned, as their testimony is incidental and lies outside the domain of human intention. They testify to two points, closely related and material, in the great controversy over the Pentateuch; (1) the *truth* of the patriarchal story, (2) the *time* of the Pentateuchal record. There is found in the Egyptian language a long list of Hebrew words of such meaning and use and at such a time as to indicate the presence and wide influence of Semitic people in Egypt, exerted by large numbers present for a long period. There is striking indication also of the slavery of this Semitic people. All which creates a presumption in favour of the early writing down of the patriarchal narrative. But we will confine ourselves to linguistic evidence bearing directly upon the question of the date of the composition of the Pentateuch.

We take this matter up to determine whether the critical indictment against Moses be a true bill, or whether it is possible to vindicate his authority, or at least render innocuous the insinuations made against it. The witnesses to be called are *Egyptian* words in the *Hebrew* Bible, accrediting the authorship of the records in the same age as the events recorded.

In Bible lands names are significant. Among the first questions asked concerning a new missionary is: "What does his name mean?" Alas for the missionary whose name either by translation or transliteration into Arabic conveys a disagreeable impression to the Egyptian mind! Now ancient Egypt had 'lords many and gods many.' Fond parents named their little one after the god most honoured at the time concerned. But one god was in favour at one epoch, and another god at another. Besides, the ascendancy of certain deities was localized in certain parts of Egypt at certain periods of Egyptian history. It thus comes about that papa and mamma in naming the baby in Old Egypt were constructing a kind of chronological index to Egyptian history—indeed, one of the best we possess. We may be sure that 'George Washingtons' did not become numerous in America until after 1776, nor 'Abraham Lincolns' until after 1861!

Thus it happens that Joseph's Egyptian name, *Zaphnath-Paaneah,* and the name of his wife, *Asenath,* have been important witnesses on the Pentateuchal question. Strange to say, they have been summoned to testify on both sides. Some years ago M. Kraal argued from the then known data that names of this meaning were unknown among the Egyptians until about the time of Ahab, thus shutting Moses completely out of the case. Now the critical analysers of the Pentateuch have persistently quoted this opinion of Kraal from that day to this, as may be seen in the Bible Dictionaries of the last quarter of a century, and in the works of Adam Smith and Driver. It is a very convenient way when you wish to find something and find just what you need, not to find anything more. Having found what suited their theory, these men have ignored every discovery on the subject since made. Yet Lieblein in his study of Egyptian names has pointed out among the names of Hyksos kings who lived and ruled in Egypt about the time of Apophis, the traditional Pharaoh of Joseph, three kings' names formed with the significant and troublesome part of Joseph's name. No one would ever learn from critical discussions of this subject that Lieblein's identification of Joseph's name is better etymologically, and far more phonetically exact, than any other identification suggested. Asenath also has been identified as a name in use from the 11th dynasty, long before the time of Joseph, until the 18th, near the time when that king arose 'which knew not Joseph.'

Thus these two names, instead of being fatal to the early authorship of the story, actually accredit the authorship at an age not much later than that of Moses. For are we to believe that some scribe of the days of Hezekiah or of the exile was an Egyptologist, who dug up the forgotten archives of the Hyksos period which later generations had done everything in their power to eradicate, and carefully selected names that would support his desire to have the people receive this story as genuinely Mosaic? Or did some happy chance direct his genius in inventing names for his heroes and heroines? Surely none will pretend that Providence took a special part in this plan to impose a new book on an unsuspecting people under the name of a very early author.

Another word from the same region and period bears testimony to the same effect, the Egyptian word 'Aat.' We have heard much in recent days about the 'Yellow Peril.' Old Egypt in the Hyksos days had also its 'yellow peril,' which became a reality. They called it the *pest.* They applied this term "aat" to the Hyksos tyranny, and to all things associated with those foreign kings. Indeed so spiteful was the national hatred against these people that it has never been possible to learn from the Egyptians the ethnic name of their oppressors. So Joseph said to his brethren, 'Every shepherd is an *abomination* to the Egyptians.' Being not a proper name but a mere epithet, the author of Genesis did not transliterate the word 'aat,' but translated it into Hebrew by the equivalent *toabah.* The Hyksos were driven from Egypt by Amasis, and that ogre of the eastern horizon disappeared from Egyptian imagination, history and language. National pride scorned to make mention of the time of humiliation. And yet we are asked to believe that some time before the epoch of Jeremiah, or even in the era of the Exile, some Jewish priest, complying with the desire of a designing priesthood to foist on the people a new book in the name of Moses, attained to such a philological nicety as the special use of this term long after that special use ceased to be current in Egypt.

In his *English Note-books,* Nathaniel Hawthorne relates how in the fifties Englishmen tried to palm themselves off on the American consul in Liverpool as Americans, and how he was always able to detect them, much to their amazement. Everyone betrayed himself by the word *been,* which true Americans invariably pronounced like "bin" and the English like "bean." The truth is that art can never perfectly supply the place of experience in the use of words. The possibilities of variation in the employment of words is so infinite that sooner or later art will stumble or fall. Where there is no stumbling we may be certain that we are dealing not with fiction, but experience.

The Pentateuchal documents manifest a proficiency in the choice of words that plainly shows that we are not in the presence of the art of the pious romancer or interested forger, but of experience only to be supplied by actual residence or extended intercourse. The Peruvians have a word *pampas* for dry, upland pasture which has found such acceptance with the Latin-Americans that its use has spread over much of the arid region of South America (and beyond it) as the most fitting name for this particular kind of pasture-land, and for no other. Egypt also has its peculiar pasturelands, those among the luxuriant grasses of the swamp lands along the Nile and its canals. The distinctive word for them was *akhu.* The Hebrews themselves had many expressions for the grass of the field, especially five words—*desheh, hatsir, yerek, eseb,* and *asab.* These are used throughout the Old Testament. They had no need at home for such a distinctive term as the Egyptians employed, for they had no *such* pasture-lands. Even when they 'sat by the rivers of Babylon,' had they needed such an expression, it would have been the Babylonian and not the Egyptian word they would have taken. Yet in Pharaoh's dream, a story born in Egypt, growing up in Egypt, and never quite losing sight of Egypt, the meadow in which the kine fed is called by the Egyptian word *akhu*; and in the Book of Job, where are other marks of Egyptian association, when it is said, "Can the *flag* grow up without water? (8.11)" this same Egyptian word is used; and nowhere else is it found in the whole Bible. Was this probably art, or was it more probably experience?

Linen was largely devoted to sacred uses in Egypt. The mummy-cloth has been found on the most critical examination to be every thread of it linen. Priests also were clad in linen. For this fine linen the Egyptians had a distinctive word, *shesh.* What figures more conspicuously in the description of the Hebrew priesthood, belonging (we are told) to a much later period, than its "fine white linen"? Now the Hebrew language had four words of its own for linen—*bad, pishteh, sadin,* and *aitun,* which are used throughout the Old Testament. In one instance (Prov. 7.16), in a book having no Egyptian associations, even when the linen of Egypt is mentioned, it is designated by a pure Semitic word, *aitun.* But in the Pentateuch the Egyptian word *shesh* is used thirty-four times for the fine linen of the priests, which they had brought with them from Egypt.

Bayou is an American provincialism, confined to the region of the lower Mississippi. In Louisiana it simply means a channel for water, and 'the bayou' means the particular channel at hand. The ancient Egyptians had a word of very similar meaning, belonging to the Nile valley. The term *yeor* was applied indiscriminately to the river, and to the numerous canals by which the water was conducted through the land. It was not a proper name for the Nile, which the Egyptians called *hapi,* but a common noun like *bayou,* which upon becoming definite meant the particular channel at hand. It is thus used both in Egyptian and Coptic. In this sense it was taken over by the Old Testament, and especially the Pentateuch. The word occurs in sixty-six passages in the Old Testament. In but one of these, Dan. 12. 5-7, where it occurs four times, is there any doubt about its reference to Egypt; and there in any case it follows on an extended prophecy relating to Egypt, and might be accounted for by the colouring of the context. In all the other sixty-five passages, it is unquestionably used of the streams of Egypt. The Biblical writers no more think of using *yeor* of streams elsewhere than American writers would talk of *bayous* in New England. The use of this word moreover is almost entirely confined to the Pentateuch, or to prophecies relating to Egypt. Such an extended use as this cannot be credibly accounted for except as the result of experience.

But a further peculiarity requires notice. Hebrew has two words, *nahar* and *nakhal,* for 'river' which supplant *yeor* in all those parts of the Bible not purporting to speak of Egypt. In the Pentateuch these words are of very frequent occurrence, but *not of the streams of Egypt.* So strictly is this distinction observed that when mention is made of the little desert stream, called the 'river of Egypt,' which marked the borderland, it is not called *yeor* at all, but *nakhal.* Such perfect accuracy as this throughout an extensive literature seems incredible in any writer not to the language born. And when the various portions of the Pentateuch are attributed to several different writers in different lands and distant ages the phenomena present a literary impossibility.

The author of the Pentateuch must have been familiar by actual use with the Egyptian tongue. That anyone should have imitated colloquial peculiarities so perfectly at so great a distance in days of so little intercourse is incredible, not to say inconceivable. 'Romancers,' 'historical novelists,' 'pious allegorists,' must have been skilful beyond the imagination of the heart of man to conceive, to have attended over so wide a field without a single mistake to such a little thing. This does not indeed prove that Moses wrote the Pentateuch, but it does point to the Mosaic age as the date of its composition, and it proves that the theory of its late authorship is not supported by archaeology in the matter of literary characteristics.

The theory of the late date of the authorship of the Pentateuch, however beautifully it may work out as a theory, is not established until corroborated by independent facts. The literary analysis itself is but the theory in the concrete; for having decided upon criteria of analysis suited to the theory of a late date, and then parcelled out the materials to the various documents according to the criteria, it is found that the results support the theory. Of course! As when a crippled man puts down his own crutch to support himself on it, he finds that it reaches to the ground. It was made exactly the right length to do so!

The Integrity of the Old Testament

By W. E. Vine

A fuller consideration of this subject than otherwise might have been the case has, happily, been forced upon us of late by the theories and methods of what is known as Higher Criticism. We say 'theories and methods' for this reason, that, a particular theory having first been formed, it became the basis for the application of methods of interpretation in conformity thereto. These have consisted in a process of elimination, inversion, recasting and disintegration of the Scriptures in a manner unparalleled in literary history.

Against the Critical hypotheses the very stones of archaeological discovery cry out. But the most cogent testimony is the self-witness of the Bible. To this latter side of the subject the present article will be confined. The Scriptures give evidence of being a revelation from God to man, a revelation exhibiting a designed development, an advancing plan, a continuously progressive unfolding of the Divine purposes relative to the establishment of the Kingdom of God upon earth and the whole scheme of the redemption of man. Each step in the progress, each action in the development itself, constitutes a partial revelation of the Divine character and attributes.

The self-discovery of God to man in the Scriptures is not something incidental or episodic, it is woven into the complete fabric of the Volume in such a manner that to recast the various parts deprives the Book at once of its greatest essential feature. The disclosure of God, His Person and His operations, grows with regularly increasing intensity as man, under the Divine discipline, is able to bear it. The records of the supernatural acts by which God revealed Himself, for instance, to Abraham and to Moses are not the unbridled imaginations of unknown redactors endeavouring to glorify remote traditions. Those acts respectively have a place in the unveiling process by a design of each which becomes self-evident as we review the whole. Each revelation of God, in whatever way it was given, while complete in itself for the immediate purposes for which it was bestowed, contributed its own share towards the completion of the entire design; and not only so, but each had also its own part in the Divine method with man in that era in which the particular revelation was given and thus in influencing the affairs of that era. To disintegrate the books of the Old Testament with a view to adapting them to an imagined necessity that Israelitic history should be found to conform to a progression observed in the case of other nations, is to miss the scope and purport of the Book and to mar its Divinely imparted beauty.

The place held by the Pentateuch, for instance, and the order of its component parts as they stand in our Bibles, is necessary to the consistency of plan, continuity of purpose and coherence of thought of which the Volume throughout gives evidence, and to which Christ and His Apostles bear witness. To take one instance illustrative of this—one out of a number the enumeration of which would carry this article beyond its due limits,—in the third chapter of the Epistle to the Galatians, verses 15 to 29, the historical position assigned by the Apostle Paul to God's covenant with Abraham is not only the position likewise assigned to it by the book of Genesis, but is also regarded by the Apostle as the pivot of the whole subsequent system of the progressive dealings of God with Israel and with the human race at large. From the standpoint of that covenant he traces the circumstances attendant upon both the Law and the Gospel, and all is in entire conformity to the consistency, continuity and coherence which we have noted above as characterising the Scriptures in the order allotted to them in our Bibles. The same is true of the corresponding passage in Romans Chapter 4.

The position of the Pentateuch in the Bible is in accord with the Divinely designed arrangement displayed throughout it, by which the gradual unfoldings of God Himself and of His providential dispositions are made known. The Divine method is to impart a revelation in a manner suited to human conditions at any given time. When that particular revelation has done its work, or has met with man's complete failure, through unbelief, to discharge his responsibilities regarding it, God discovers Himself in another way. Each discovery has its appropriate place in the entire plan until the whole is realised and disclosed in Christ, first as the Redeemer and Lord, and eventually as the recognised Sovereign over the Kingdom, the Kingdom of God in visible glory. The Divine wisdom and glory shine out in the succession of events which lead to, centre in, and issue from Sinai as well as in those which relate to Calvary. Recast the books of the Bible and you spoil the Volume. Redistribute the parts and you mar the whole. Change the order and you confuse the revelation.

The Pentateuch is the key to the whole position. We shall perhaps best illustrate the integrity of the Scriptures in this respect if we trace retrospectively the place occupied by the Pentateuch in the history of Israel from the post-exilic times of Ezra and Nehemiah back to the days of Uzziah. Our survey must perforce be brief. Three periods will suffice.

1. *The time of Ezra, after the return from the Captivity, i.e., the middle of the 5th century B.C.*

It is a matter of general consent that the Pentateuch was the ecclesiastical and municipal code of Israel at that period. Now the Higher Critical theory assumes that the Priests' code, a large part of Exodus, all Leviticus, and most of Numbers had been put together in the Exile. We go therefore to the books of Ezra and Nehemiah to see if the contents lend any support to the supposition. They show not a single vestige of anything indicative of such recent editings. They render incredible the assumption that the Pentateuch was the outcome of a recent redaction. Everything testifies against its being a brand new compilation. Notice, for example, the effects of the reading of the Law by Ezra. The first reading occupied half a day, 'from early morning until midday' (Neh. 8.3). The people were stirred to the depths of their souls: 'All the people wept when they heard the words of the Law.' Day by day they gathered 'to give attention' to it. Following upon this the seven days' feast of tabernacles was observed throughout the land according to the instructions of the book of Leviticus (ch. 23), a feast which, by the way, had been last observed 'in the days of Joshua the son of Nun' (verse 17). A few days later they assembled 'with fasting, and with sackcloth, and earth upon their heads, and . . . . separated themselves from all strangers, and stood and confessed their sins and the iniquities of their fathers.' A fourth part of the day they read the Law, and a fourth part they confessed and worshipped the Lord. In their following prayer they recounted their history from the call of Abraham onward in the order given in the Pentateuch and subsequently. As a result of these solemnities the nation made a written covenant with God 'entering into a curse, and into an oath, to walk in God's Law, which was given by Moses the servant of God' (9.38 and 10.29).

We are invited to believe that this devotion of the people was adherence to a compilation made by some unnamed writers during the exile, attempting by methods of imposture to glorify the national beginnings, working up an archaic tradition of Sinai, fabricating the tabernacle and its ritual, and putting words into the mouth of Jehovah. The idea is grotesque as well as incredible. The exile had been a time of heart-searching. Imposture was unlikely. Its reception still more so. Yet according to the Critical hypothesis these worthy exiles were the dupes of artifice and imposition, misled by unrestrained imaginations.

We are to imagine, forsooth, that the priests and Levites under Ezra put away their strange wives in obedience to instructions contained in a compilation of this character; that a production pieced together by fraudulent methods brought back the nation to such a realisation of its covenant relationship with God as to impress the heathen around and permanently to shape the ideas, lives and condition of the people; and that what has become an imperishable treasure of the human race, making its sanctifying influence felt among the nations, was a patchwork framed by questionable means, by persons whom the literary world is forced to call, J, E, D, Ph, Pg.

"And twenty more such names and men as these,
Which never were, and no man ever saw."

2. *The Reformation under Josiah.*

Our retrospect now takes us back almost two centuries. Let us see the evidence provided by 2 Kings 22, 23, as to the character and scope of the Law at that time. The book of the Law, lost and forgotten in the preceding period of degeneracy, is discovered amidst the debris of the dilapidated house of the Lord, brought to the king and read before him. Overwhelmed by the disclosure of its contents, he rends his clothes, and sends to enquire from the Lord concerning it. The awesome utterance of the prophetess leads the king to assemble the elders and people of Judah at the Temple, there to hear 'all the words of the book of the Covenant.' A solemn covenant is thereupon made by king and people to confirm the words of the book. The reformation begins, the land is purged from idolatry, and the Passover is kept 'as it is written in this book of the Covenant.' 'There was not kept such a Passover from the days of the Judges that judged Israel, nor in all the days of the kings of Israel, nor of the kings of Judah.'

According to the Critical view the book of the Law then existent consisted of Deuteronomy and Exodus 20-23, the rest of Exodus, all Leviticus and Numbers being put together at the time of the exile. Some have even ventured to suggest that the book discovered in the Temple was the production of Hilkiah the discoverer!

Now the instructions concerning the Passover in Deuteronomy are confined to eight verses of the sixteenth chapter, whereas the arrangements for the observance of this Passover are given fully in 2 Chron. 35.1-19. In the first place there are details which show that the feast was carried out according to the instructions given in Exodus 12 and 13. The brief reference in Deut. 16 does not, for instance, contain a mention of the prescribed day of the month, the fourteenth day, or of the sprinkling of the blood (*cf.* 2 Chron. 35.11 with Exodus 12.7 and 22). Then again, the whole circumstances related concerning Josiah's observance of the Passover make it extremely improbable that the solemnities were based upon the condensed passage in Deut. 16.1-8, rather than upon the complete narration of Israel's deliverance from Egypt and the complete instructions in Exodus. Furthermore, the narratives in 2 Kings and 2 Chronicles show how profoundly the people were impressed by the sense of their covenant relationship with the Lord, a relationship established by the Passover feast at its inauguration appointed as described in Exodus, and not incidentally as in Deuteronomy. A comparison of the character of the Divine decrees, ordinances and pledges, as given in Exodus 12 and 13, at the time of the nation's deliverance, with the character of the injunctions in Deut. 16.1-8, will surely convince any unbiassed mind which of the two records inspired the people to the extent described in 2 Kings.

3. *The period from Uzziah to Hezekiah as represented in the prophecies of Amos and Hosea.*

We again go back the length of about a century and a half. The Critical view regards Israel at this period as a nation gradually emerging from a state of original polytheism to monotheism, in accordance with the naturalistic theory of an evolutionary religion similar to those exhibited in the history of certain other nations. What then do we find from the self-witness of the Scriptures now before us? Israel is here also regarded as having been in covenant relationship with God from the inception of its national existence. These prophets speak of Jehovah as a Being who in promise and act has bound Himself up with the nation itself from the dawn of its history. 'When Israel was a child, then I loved Him, and called My son out of Egypt' (Hos. 11.1); 'I am the Lord thy God from the land of Egypt' (12.9; 13.4); 'Hear this word that the Lord hath spoken against you, O children of Israel, against the whole family which I brought up out of the land of Egypt, saying, You only have I known of all the families of the earth' (Amos 3. 1,2). Hosea goes further than this; he depicts the Divine relationship with Israel from the beginning as that of husband and wife (chap.2). The nation, however, has broken the covenant, treacherously departed from her Husband, and played the harlot: 'they have gone a whoring from under their God' (Hos. 4.12); 'they have transgressed My covenant and trespassed against My Law' (8.1); 'they have rejected the Law of the Lord, and have not kept His statutes' (Amos 2.4). They brought sacrifices and offerings to God forty years in the wilderness, and then turned to worship Siccuth and Chiun (5.15, 26).

Obviously the evidence of these prophets is directly opposed to the views of Higher Criticism. The writings of Amos and Hosea entirely discountenance the idea of a gradual transformation from polytheism to monotheism. Their prophecies, expressive of the national consciousness from its earliest days, breathe a sublime monotheism so pronounced that it forms the dominating feature of the prophets' testimony, the keynote of their remonstrances, and the basis of their hopes of national prosperity. He gives himself an impossible task who seeks to square the writings of the prophets with the theory of a slow development from beginnings on a par with the conditions of pagan tribes.

If the critical hypothesis is right the precepts referred to will be found to be limited to the portions of the Pentateuch mentioned above, namely, Exodus 20 to 23 and Deuteronomy. We find the contrary to be the case, however. The commandments mentioned by these prophets as having been broken by the people are given in various other parts of the Pentateuch. For instance, Amos refers to the breach of the prohibition against giving the Nazarite strong drink (2.11,12), a commandment enjoined in Numbers 6.3. Again the law which prohibited the compulsion of the poor to render bond-service, which likewise had been transgressed (Amos 2.6), is given in Lev. 23.29. Further, the daily sacrifices referred to in Amos 4.4 were enjoined not in Deuteronomy but in Numbers 28.3,4; and the sacrifice of thanksgiving with cakes of leavened bread (Amos 4.5) was enjoined in Lev. 7.13.

The conclusion which is forced upon us, therefore, is that the Critical theory is wrong, that the more the Scriptures are searched the greater will be the exposure of the fallacy of Critical assumptions, and that the Pentateuch in its entirety is in its right position at the beginning of our Bible. The Critics have never disproved the Mosaic origin of the Pentateuch, nor have they proved the existence of the imaginary compilers in the period of exile. Notwithstanding all that they have put forward, we believe that in the Bible as we have it God has revealed Himself in the order recorded therein, that the Mosaic arrangement of books is the Divine arrangement, and that unity coupled with progressive revelation characterises the whole.

The theory that because in Deuteronomy the Levites are predominant, while in Exodus, Leviticus and Numbers the priests predominate, therefore these three books are of later date than the first mentioned, is without a particle of evidence to substantiate it. The order in the Pentateuch as we have it is as follows: First, Jehovah claims the whole nation as His priests; then, through the failure of the nation, He claims the firstborn, on the ground of redemption, to represent the nation; then the tribe of Levi as representing the firstborn; and then Aaron's sons. This order is in keeping with the whole scheme of the Old Testament. In every case the progress of Divine revelation is not that of natural development, or the outcome of national progress, but is rather God's counterpart to a national decline. His dealings with the nation are at the same time consistent with the relationship of the nation to Himself, a relationship initially established by His own Covenant.

The priesthood, consequent on its failure in Eli, gives way in turn to the prophetic office in Samuel (Acts 3), for that was a day when Israel openly abandoned God as their King, thus consummating the sin they had conceived in the desert when they sought a Captain to return to Egypt. When all else fails God does not, and each development of His revelation is the witness to His sufficiency. The godly ones in the nation are sustained by the prospect of some better thing, which in His grace is superior to all the powers of evil, namely, the kingdom of God introduced at the coming of Christ.

The Bible throughout, in the order in which it has been arranged for us, exhibits one connected and orderly record of the dealings of God with the souls of men. There is found to be as distinct a relation of the books of the Old Testament to one another, the historical books to the devotional, and the devotional to the prophetical, as is seen in the case of the Gospels to the Acts, the Acts to the Epistles, the Epistles to the Apocalypse, in the New.

On reading through the Volume, the Creation, the Fall, the Divine operations in the Antediluvian, Patriarchial, Mosaic, Post-Mosaic, Regal and Post-Regal times, pass before us in a succession which displays a Divinely appointed progress of revelation. We see first in the book of Genesis the inability of fallen man to retain the knowledge of His Creator and restore his own righteousness, and then in the remaining books of the Pentateuch his inability to recover himself even by means of a Divinely given Law. The books of Joshua and Judges disclose in the record of Israel's degeneracy the lamentable depravity of man even under Theocratic institutions. The same feature is presented to us in a different phase in the historical books which follow. The devotional books next express the spiritual aspirations of those who, under the power of God's Law, sought with deep yearnings to feel after Him. Finally, the prophetic books, while denouncing the nation's apostasy, prepare the way for the New Testament by holding out the prospect of the spiritual power and triumphs of Messiah's kingdom.

What has been pointed out above is entirely confirmed by the teaching of our Lord as recorded in the Gospels, and by His method of handling the Old Testament Scriptures. When to the two disciples on the way to Emmaus 'He interpreted in all the Scriptures the things concerning Himself,' He began 'from Moses' (Luke 24.27).

Referring to the Divine injunctions to Israel in the matter of circumcision given in the book of Leviticus, He speaks of them as the Law of Moses (John 7.23), and states that Moses gave the nations the Law (5.19). Elsewhere He assigns to Moses passages from Exodus, Leviticus and Numbers, as well as Deuteronomy. For instance, He says, 'Now that the dead are raised, even Moses showed at the bush, when he calleth the Lord the God of Abraham, and the God of Isaac, and the God of Jacob' (Luke 20.37). The quotation is from Exodus 3 again. His reference to Moses in His conversation with Nicodemus (John 3.14) is from Numbers 21, and His reference to the manna as given from God under the leadership of Moses (6.32) is from Exodus 16. The legislation regarding divorce in Deut. 24 He also ascribes to Moses (Matt. 19.8).

Clearly, our Lord's view regarding the authorship and date of the Pentateuch was not that of Higher Criticism. We are compelled to choose one or the other, to decide between the credentials of Christ and those of Modernism, between the impregnable rock of His testimony and the shifting sands of Higher Critical theories. The choice is not difficult. The self-witness of Scripture decides the matter for us.

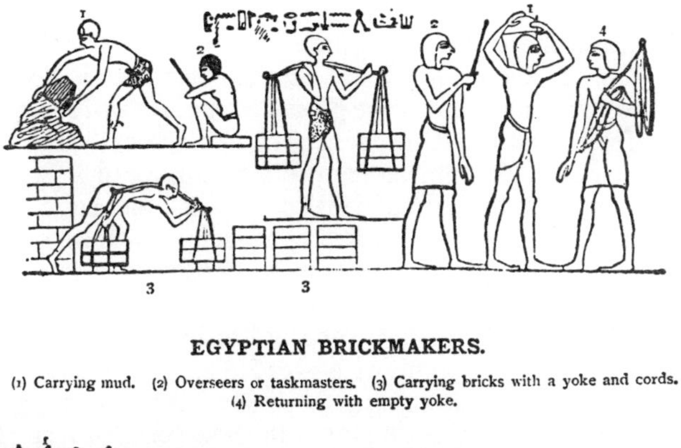

EGYPTIAN BRICKMAKERS.

(1) Carrying mud. (2) Overseers or taskmasters. (3) Carrying bricks with a yoke and cords. (4) Returning with empty yoke.

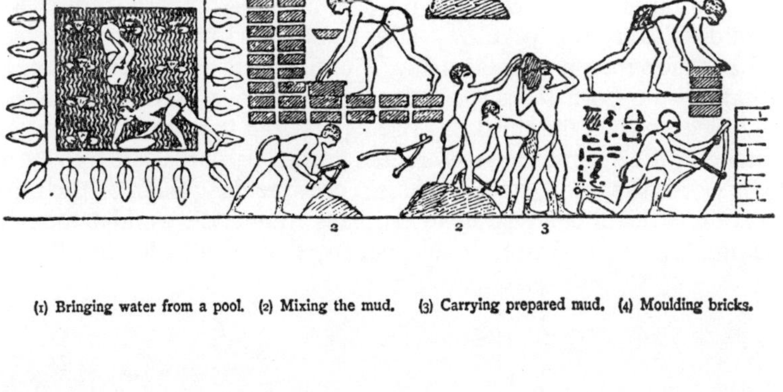

(1) Bringing water from a pool. (2) Mixing the mud. (3) Carrying prepared mud. (4) Moulding bricks.

"Raised on the Third Day, according to the Scriptures."

By W. S. Moule

The Apostle Paul speaks of the Scriptures as God-breathed, and the evidences for a Divine character attaching to Holy Scripture are varied and manifold. Some of the most convincing are those which may be drawn from hidden harmonies and latent connections between the books. These are constantly met with by the reverent student, and being so clearly undesigned by the writers, their cumulative effect on the mind is irresistible. They simply demonstrate the presence of a Divine Author in all Scripture, directing and correlating the works of His human agents. My contribution to this meeting of witness to the Bible will be to draw your attention to one such harmony.

It is suggested by some words of Paul in writing to the Corinthians. When we follow up the suggestion the harmony stands revealed.

Some Christians in Corinth were saying that there is no such thing as a resurrection of dead men. But, says Paul, all apostles preached and all Christians believed that Christ became a dead man, dead and buried, and that He has been raised. What then becomes of their theory that dead men do not rise? Christ, according to apostolic testimony and Christian faith, *has been raised,* and then, he adds, as a further element of the witness, that this resurrection took place *on the third day, according to the Scriptures.*

He means that not only did the apostles bear witness that Christ's resurrection took place on a definite day, the third day, but that the Scriptures had already marked the day. John corroborates this when he tells us in his Gospel that after the event His disciples remembered the words of Jesus about His Body being destroyed and restored in three days, and they believed the Scripture and the word that Jesus had spoken.

Following up this suggestion then, we look for some special prominence given to resurrection on the third day, first in the words of Jesus, next in the older Scriptures, and then, finally, we look for some *reason* for it in the scheme of the Divine revelation.

It may be necessary to say one word in passing on the exact time indicated. You know that it is variously stated that the resurrection was to take place *in a space of three days, within three days, after three days,* and even that Jesus was to be *three days and three nights* in the heart of the earth; but I think it can easily be shown that all these are equivalent in Scripture usage to the expression most commonly used—*the third day,*—meaning the first day of death and burial, the second day of lying in the grave, and on the third day resurrection. I may say that the difficulty which *we* feel, with our more precise ways of speaking, is not at all present to Eastern minds, which to this day think and speak in similar language.

To return then to the rising on the third day. The Lord Jesus, we find, laid special emphasis on the time. When the Jews pressed Him for a sign, twice over He gave this as a sign—'Destroy this temple, and in three days I will raise it up'. 'As Jonah was three days and three nights in the whale's belly, so shall the Son of Man be three days and three nights in the heart of the earth.' The words made a deep impression on the Jews. When they had destroyed His body, when it was actually committed to the ground, the words haunted them still. Shall we not say, haunted them the more? 'Sir, we remember that that deceiver said, while he was yet alive, After three days I will rise again; command therefore that the sepulchre be made sure until the third day.' But precisely on that third day He rose as He had spoken. To His disciples the Lord Jesus spoke repeatedly in open terms, The Son of Man must be crucified, must be killed, and on the third day rise again from the dead. And they forgot, until the women were reminded by the angels; then they remembered His words, and told the vision to the rest. As they recalled His words they were struck by this report reaching them on the third day—it was at least a coincidence; but, as the disciples going to Emmaus argued, the women, though they had seen a vision of angels saying that He had risen, could not say that they had seen *Him.*

Jesus Christ then took them to the Scriptures. To the Scriptures now let us go, not merely for a death and resurrection, but for a resurrection from the dead *on the third day*. Some have said that there are no such Scriptures. It seems to me, however, that there are *exactly seven*. This in itself is a significant fact, if it is a fact, for seven is the number of the Divine covenant, and we are face to face here with one of the mysteries of the covenant.

We notice again that these seven Scriptures are made up of three typical histories, three typical ordinances, and one prophecy. Three is the number of Deity, and the subject here is 'the working of the strength of God's might which He wrought in Christ when He raised Him from the dead.' The thing is doubled to us by three histories and three ordinances, because, like Pharaoh's dreams, it speaks of something established by God, which God will surely bring to pass. And then, finally, a single prophecy is added, which not only throws a strong light backwards and forwards, but brings the total number of the Scriptures bearing on this important truth to seven, and so stamps it with the mark of the covenant of salvation.

Let us take the three histories. There is the story of Isaac, the child of promise, the child long expected, the child miraculously born, by the expulsion of Ishmael exhibited in his father's home as an only child, whom Abraham loved. And then the Divine command comes to Abraham, 'Take now thy son, thy only son whom thou lovest, and offer him up for a burnt offering on one of the mountains which I will tell thee,' and so that son willingly offers himself in obedience to his father's will. Like our Lord Jesus, who offered Himself a sacrifice to God for a sweet-smelling savour. But there is more in that offering than mere obedience and devotion; a real death took place, and a substitutionary death. God provides a ram which dies on the altar instead of Isaac, and so this picture of Christ's offering is made complete and true to its type. Now we must all have noticed the significant note that 'on the third day' Abraham reached Moriah, so that 'on the third day' he received Isaac back from death in a figure. The story would be complete without this note of time, yet there it lies on the surface of the story, and according to this Scripture Christ was raised on the third day.

There is the story of Joseph, the son of his father's love, predestined for high honour, separate from his brethren, envied and rejected, sold to foreigners, falsely accused, imprisoned for another's sins, exalted to the right hand of power, saviour of the nations, and, last of all, of his own house,—is not this a picture of the Christ, and is not Joseph's imprisonment a picture of His death, not for His own sins, but for that of others? Here again there comes the note of time, 'after two full years.' That is, *in the third year* Pharaoh has his dreams, and Joseph is exalted to the kingly throne. There is no doubt a reason why the special phrase, 'in the third year,' is avoided here, perhaps, for one thing, because the measure of time is in years not days; but we meet with the exact period later in the history. When Joseph was about to be reconciled to his brethren, as the first step towards securing their penitence, he puts them all together in ward three days, and on the third day he brings them out with the words, 'This do, and live.' We can scarcely doubt that this period was determined by his own term of imprisonment, a day for a year; it may also have its own typical significance as regards the future restoration of Israel; but at all events we find here once more in a typical history a sign that the Christ will be raised on the third day.

There is the story of Jonah. Here is a prophet sent first to Israel, then to a foreign nation, with a message which leads to repentance and remission of sins. Now between these two missions Jonah is three days and three nights in the whale's belly, and in his miraculous restoration is a sign to the Ninevites and to Israel. According to this history also the Christ must be raised on the third day.

We have looked at these as three detached histories. Now let us look at them in combination. They are connected by the occurrence in each of the three-year or three-day period, due in each case to direct Divine action, for God stopped Abraham's journey at Moriah on the third day, God sent Pharaoh's dreams in the third year, God spake to Jonah's fish on the third day. They are evidently thus intended to be viewed in combination, and at once we see *how the typical histories more and more approximate to the actual experience of Christ. Isaac* is three days under sentence to die, but he still lives and moves in the world with Abraham and his young men. *Joseph* goes deeper, for he is shut off for three years from the life of the world, yet he is still active in prison. *Jonah* goes deeper still, when he is enclosed in a dark cavern, and plunged beneath the waters, cut off from the life of men, for three days, yet he still lives in the whale's belly. None actually reach, though they steadily approximate to, the experience of our Saviour, who in full reality went down to the grave and to Hades till the third day.

Once again we see how the histories combine to present a perfect picture of our Christ. *Isaac* shows our Lord in His office as Priest, offering Himself for our acceptance and blessing. *Joseph* shows Him exalted to be a Prince and a Saviour, our great and glorious King and Benefactor. *Jonah* shows Him as God's Prophet to the nations, Himself the great credential of His mission.

How comes it, do you think, that there is this gradation in the three detached experiences, and this completeness in their combination? Is not the Christian explanation also the rational explanation, that these Scriptures are God-breathed? The typical foreshadowing of a resurrection on the third day might, we think, have rested there, so definite and complete are these three histories in their witness; but yet it could scarcely have been absent altogether from that whole series of Divine ordinances which prefigured that first declaration of apostolic testimony and Christian faith, that Christ died for our sins. And so, in connection with the Law of Offerings, we find a second three-fold indication that He who died for our sins would rise on the third day.

Take the four great offerings which foreshadowed the dying of Jesus Christ—the burnt offering, the peace offerings, the sin and trespass offerings. There is only one of these the ritual of which is capable of illustrating a resurrection after three days, for the burnt offering was totally consumed on the altar, while in the sin and trespass offerings all the fat ascended on the altar, certain other portions of the animal were consumed by the priests as part of the ritual, and the remainder was at once removed by fire in a clean place; but the flesh of the peace offerings was reserved to form the basis of a feast of communion. Here then was an opening for the illustration of the truth of resurrection on the third day, and here, sure enough, we find it. There are two rules which govern the treatment of the flesh of the peace offerings (Lev. 7); one is that it must be kept free from all contact with corruption; the other is that whatever remains on the third day must not be eaten, but removed at once by fire. *The no-corruption rule* enacts that unleavened bread only must be used at the sacrificial meal, and if the flesh accidentally touches an unclean thing, it is at once disqualified for use, and must be removed by fire; nor must a ceremonially unclean person eat of it under penalty of being cast off from God's people. *The third day rule* is even more strongly emphasised—the flesh may be eaten on the day of sacrifice, or on the morrow, but *not* on the third day—'That which remaineth of the flesh of the sacrifice on the third day shall be burnt with fire. And if any of the flesh of the sacrifice of a man's peace offerings be eaten on the third day it shall not be accepted, neither shall it be imputed to him that offereth it, it shall be an abomination, and the soul that eateth of it shall bear his iniquity.' The energy of language marks the importance in God's eyes of this point of ritual; the impossibility of the victim remaining in a state of death on the third day, is essential to the picture of the reconciling Saviour. So Paul declares to those who denied the apostolic witness of Christ's third day resurrection—'Christ may have died, but if He remained dead and did not rise on the third day, as we preached, our preaching is vain, your trust is vain, you are yet in your sins.'

It is intensely interesting to note here a minor regulation which tended still more to lay stress on the point we are considering. Peace offerings might be offered either in fulfilment of vows, or as freewill offerings, or as thanksgiving offerings. In he first two cases the rules were as I have stated; but for the last a curious exception is admitted. Three kinds of cakes formed the sacrificial meal, all of which must be unleavened, *except* in the case of thanksgiving offerings, when *one* kind was leavened so far relaxing the no-corruption rule; but this led to a tightening up of the closely connected rule, the sacrifice for thanksgivings could not be reserved at all but must be eaten on the day of offering, and the remainder at once removed by fire; the exception in one rule, admitted no doubt for special reasons, leading at once to greater stringency in the other rule, drew attention to both as of primary importance, and according to this Scripture the crucified Lord must after death be preserved from all corruption, and not continue in the state of death on the third day. This is the first of the ritual laws to foreshadow Christ's resurrection on the third day.

Take next the Law of the Passover. I need scarcely say that the Passover ritual signified our redemption by the death of Jesus Christ. It also was of the nature of a peace offering, for it provided for a sacrificial meal. Here then we find the rule of no-corruption enforced, for no leaven was admitted to the paschal meal, and it was followed by seven days of eating unleavened bread. But, as originally instituted, we search in vain in the Passover ritual for the third day rule. Turn, however, to where the Passover is put into its place in the whole scheme of the set-feasts (Lev. 23), and the omission is rectified in the most remarkable manner. On the third day after the Passover, the day following the first day of unleavened bread, a sheaf of barley, the firstfruits of the year's harvest, must be waved in the tabernacle. Once more this point of ritual is emphasised—'You shall eat nothing of your harvest until this self-same day, until you have brought this oblation: it is a perpetual statute for ever.' Christ, slain as our Passover, must rise like the harvest from the buried seed, Christ must be raised on the third day from His crucifixion, Christ must be raised as the firstfruits of all the buried seed in God's acres—there it all lies in the ordinance of the Passover.

We have seen two ritual laws; where is the third which will complete the series? It will be found in *the ritual of the red heifer* (Num. 19). Major ceremonial uncleannesses lasted seven days, and on the eighth day, after ablutions, the defiled person was clean. Certain uncleannesses, including defilement by contact with dead bodies, excluded the defiled person from the camp for seven days. The ordinance of the red heifer was given to enable persons defiled by contact with the dead to remain in the camp till the period of defilement was over. For this purpose a substitute was permanently provided. A special sin offering was sacrificed, and its ashes laid up permanently outside the camp in preparation for symbolic use. When a man became liable to exclusion from the camp these dead ashes, as it were, at once took his place, and he himself was exempt; but if nothing further had happened until the seven days were over, it would have been fatally unlike the great reality. What then is the Divine regulation? *On the third day living water shall be put to the ashes,* and the unclean person shall be sprinkled with it, and again there comes the unfailing note of emphasis—'He shall purify himself with the water on the third day, and on the seventh day he shall be clean; but if he purify not himself on the third day, then the seventh day he shall not be clean.' So once more we come back to the truth that He through whom we are restored to fellowship with God died for our sins indeed, but rises on the third day. If it were not so, we should not be clean, could have no rightful place in the camp of God. So three ritual laws re-enforce three typical histories, and according to these Scriptures Christ has been raised on the third day.

To all this one striking prophecy is added. It is found in the Book of Hosea (ch. 6), in connection with predictions concerning the future of Israel. The whole book predicts the rejection of Israel for a long period, and then a final restoration, and at last we come to these words of God—'I will go and return to My place, till they acknowledge their offences, and seek My face: in their affliction they will seek Me earnestly.' Then follow what appear to be the words of Israel at last returning to God—'Come, and let us return unto the Lord; for He hath torn and He will heal us; He hath smitten and He will bind us up. After two days will He revive us; on the third day He will raise us up, and we shall live before Him.' Instinctively our minds go back to the history of Joseph's reconciliation with his brethren, and their three days' incarceration which preceded it, and we think that some special experience of the kind awaits Israel in the last days. But, if so, we know that it is based on a similar previous experience of their Joseph, and this seems present to the mind of the Holy Spirit in Hosea, for He continues—'And let us know, let us follow on to know Jehovah. His going forth (does He not mean His death and resurrection on the third day?) is sure as the morning. And He will come (also in due time) unto us as the rain, as the latter rain that watereth the earth.' I cannot now elaborate this shining prophecy, which throws its light backwards and forwards over all these Scriptures of Christ being raised on the third day.

But there—in briefest outline—are the seven Scriptures of which I spoke, given significantly at each great epoch of the history of the chosen people—*one* at the very commencement, in the history of Abraham's son; *one* at the going down into Egypt, in connection with Joseph; then the whole group of ritual laws in connection with the Exodus, and for perpetual memory in Canaan; *one* again in connection with the first proclamation of the Gospel to the Gentiles; and *one* in reference to a still future restoration of Israel. I ask you, is this chance, or is it God?

It remains only to seek a reason in the scheme of Divine revelation for the importance so evidently attached to a resurrection of Christ on the third day. Why was there such definiteness in marking the day, and why was the resurrection fixed for the third day, and not the second, or fourth, or fifth? And here we may mark—

1. The Divine wisdom which secured that the Scripture should foretell and the Apostles proclaim and Christians confess not merely that Christ has been raised, but that He rose on a definite day. We find in the Acts Peter so preaching to Cornelius and his friends, and St. Paul says here that all the Apostles did the same, and all Christians believed the same, a statement which is borne out by the presence of the words, 'On the third day He rose again from the dead' in Christian creeds. It is precisely this element in the Apostles' witness to the resurrection which puts it beyond doubt that the resurrection of Christ which they preached is something which happened to His dead and buried body at a definite time in the past.

2. And so St. Paul uses the fact as a starting point for his teaching, that something will happen to *all* dead bodies at a definite time in the future. When we look for the resurrection of the dead and the life of the world to come we mean nothing less than this, that as Christ had His day, so every man will have his resurrection day. Christ, the firstfruits, then, at His coming, those that are Christ's, in a moment, in the twinkling of an eye, when He comes—a definite thing on a definite day—the dead bodies shall be raised incorruptible.

3. But all this might just as well have been shown by a resurrection on the second or fourth or fifth days. All that was needed was a definite date, why then must the resurrection take place on the *third* day? I think we may find a reason by considering those three days in the history of Jesus. On the first day we see Him under condemnation, bearing our sins in His own Body on the tree. On the second day we see Him freed from condemnation indeed, for the sin-bearing was finished, and His Spirit was in Paradise, yet his Body of humiliation still remained, only its natural tendency to corruption was by Divine power restrained, and the desecration from without was by providential arrangement averted—so was our Lord on the second day. But on the third day, in a moment, in the twinkling of an eye, all is changed,—the grave is empty, the body of His humiliation is risen and becomes the body of His glory, alive for evermore.

Have we been reading the Lord's history or our own? Why, *both*. We too have been under condemnation, but now that is all past, there is no condemnation to them who are in Christ Jesus.

We now, like Him, are dead to this world, but alive to God. We too have our no-corruption, and no-desecration rule and power. We, like Him in His second day, are waiting for our resurrection day. And, dear friends, be sure, be confident, our third day is coming. Look at Jesus, the Author and Finisher of our Faith. He has run the race from start to finish, we still are in our second day, waiting for the redemption of our body when Jesus comes.

There are *only* three stages for all of us, for we shall not all sleep, but we shall all be changed, and so only three days for our Lord Jesus from His death to His resurrection.

Why I Believe the Old Testament to be True

By Dr. R. Dick Wilson, of Princeton, U.S.A.

Time would fail me to give all the reasons why I believe the Old Testament to be true. I have been giving reasons for thirty years or more, and I cannot sum up the results of forty-five years of investigation in forty-five minutes. Of course, I have the ordinary reasons for believing the Bible to be true. I still think that it gives the best philosophical explanation of the universe. It tells how God, the Cause of all things visible and invisible, fore-ordained all things for His glory, and that He is surely bringing His purposes to pass. The Bible, when looked upon comparatively, stands out as the one great Book of God known in the world to-day. We sometimes forget that the Bible itself is a fact in evidence. It is a work that we have in our hands. Howsoever it may have come, we have it, and we can compare it with all the great philosophical works of the past and present, and all the great religious works produced in all countries, and I believe it to be better than any of the rest; it justifies itself as God's Book. In fact, it is the only Book that pretends to be the Book of God, the only Book that from beginning to end has 'Thus saith the Lord.'

I am not going into subjective matters, though I love subjective matters. The philosophers, of whom, according to the last History of Philosophy I acquired, there were just about a thousand in Germany alone, think that they have in their little heads produced an explanation of the universe which is better than that in God's Word.

The Lord did not call me to be a philosopher. I never thought that I knew more than Jesus Christ. Talking to one of our philosophical theological professors some time ago, I asked him this little question—this is one of the greatest writers in America, and one of the wisest men, at least in his own conceit, that we have in the whole States—I said, 'Suppose we had a statement in the New Testament which purported to have been made by Jesus Christ, and there was absolutely no doubt about the text; you knew that He said it, and you are certain that you understood exactly what the Lord meant, would you believe it because the Lord said it?' And his answer was, 'Certainly not'! 'Well,' I said, 'that looks as if you were the Lord, not He.' And he did not dispute that.

I have never doubted that Jesus Christ knew more even about the Old Testament than I do. Furthermore, I might expand that a little—for I have a little bit of egotism in me. Indeed, I have so much egotism that I am not going to give the conduct of my soul into the hands of any man, though he be a professor or even the Archbishop of Canterbury or the Pope. My soul is too big for any mere man to direct. But I will take God, and if Jesus Christ is God, as I believe, I am willing to submit my soul for time and eternity into His keeping. Let me give up the Bible and I will make my own philosophy. I will say, like the old Epicurean, 'Let us eat and drink and be merry, for to-morrow we die.' That is the matter with the world to-day which has given up its Christ. I do not believe any man to-day without revelation knows anything more about God than Plato did. I have some conceit, but I have never had enough to buck up against Plato. I always thought Plato was better at philosophy than anything I could possibly be. An old professor at Berlin used to tell us boys there in the University that all the philosophers since have not produced anything equal to Plato. So that if I wanted philosophy I suppose I might go to Plato. But while he said that he believed in God, he added that, if we were to know anything about Him, He Himself must send a messenger to teach us. I do not believe we have any right to call these man-made systems 'theology'—they are anthropology. And I do not want their anthropology, I will make my anthropology for myself. There is only one theology, and it is God-made and God-given.

Now, I might give an account of the many investigations I have made. The reason I became a specialist was because I was not satisfied with the old defences, especially of the Book of Daniel, and I thought that it would be a worthy labour if somebody could devote his life to the preparation necessary for the defence of the Old Testament, philologically, and palaeographically, and historically, against all comers. And according to the principle of law which requires that a man who is called upon as an expert should first show his right to speak as an expert, I would say to this audience that, at any rate I have made a good and strenuous attempt to prepare myself to speak. After I had become able to read about a dozen languages, and had taught about eight of them, and had been instructor in a theological school for a year, I started across the water to prepare myself to give my life to the defence of the Old Testament. I came over to Oxford and saw Professor Sayce, who was then a young man. He advised me to go to Germany, and I went, and instead of just hearing lectures from the professors giving the results of their labours I made a plan like this: I was then twenty-five, and I laid out a plan of forty-five years' work. The first fifteen years of the time I determined to give to the acquisition of the languages necessary to enable me to read the ancient documents which alone give first-hand information with regard to Old Testament history. Those languages are Hebrew and all the cognate languages; secondly, all languages into which the Old Testament was translated up to the year 600 after Christ; and, thirdly, such languages as Egyptian and Persian which would throw light upon Old Testament history. The second fifteen years of my plan were to be devoted to the study of the text of the Old Testament, and the third fifteen years I was going to give up to the Higher Criticism. One of your professors from England, who was in America some years ago, said that every man ought to be asphyxiated when he was forty-five years of age. I just change that a little, and say that any man who attempts to write anything upon the Higher Criticism of the Old Testament before he is forty-five years of age ought to be asphyxiated. Why? Because he does not know enough to write upon such a subject.

I studied at the University of Berlin, and then went back to America to be a professor. The Lord has given me a chance to carry out that plan from that day onwards, and I am now in my forty-fifth year of the fulfilment of that plan. During the first fifteen years I devoted myself to the languages—in that time a man can get a working knowledge of the languages if he keeps at it. In the second period I studied the Old Testament text, studying every letter in the Old Testament in Hebrew, comparing it with all the ancient versions, and making notes. I knew nothing, and know nothing yet, about Old Testament texts or Babylonian or Egyptian or any other ancient documents except what I get by hard work and the first-hand investigation of the documents themselves. A short time ago a young professor brought out a book about the Old Testament. He said in the introduction, 'I have not an idea of my own in this book'—which was true! The only idea was the way in which he had made this book. It consisted in the gathering together of all the opinions of all the men who thought like himself. At the end he had fifteen pages of what he called 'authorities,' and everyone of those authorities was a radical critic, except one, and that one was his predecessor in the Chair he then occupied, and for politeness' sake he had to put him in. That professor never cited the Old Testament text as an authority. He cited nothing but other writers, and often you will have to go through eight or ten of those writers before you get to any original statement made by anybody. I count none of these men an authority for me. The Old Testament itself is the only authority, and we can trace it back step by step through the present Hebrew MSS. in existence—one very good one over here in the British Museum, more than one, but one very fine—we can trace these manuscripts to where they first begin, about 916 A.D., and from that we can get back by Massoretic notes and translations until we come to the time of Christ. There is absolutely no doubt scientifically that we have the same Hebrew Bible to-day substantially that was used by Christ and His Apostles, and to which they gave their approbation.

Why do I say that? I know it. I have been teaching that subject for thirty or forty years. I have been teaching textual criticism of the Old Testament for forty years, and, mind you, not to dull fellows. The dull fellows never take my classes. The men preparing for their Master's degree and for their degrees in philosophy in Berlin and Leipsic, and Columbia and Pennsylvania, the brightest men going, are the men who have been taking my teaching. At the end of my teaching they are more conservative than I am—that is because they have not gone through my difficulties. If there is any difficulty I have my boys go straight to the Hebrew manuscript, straight to the Massoretic notes, and straight to the Greek version, so that they can testify at first hand that the Old Testament is to-day substantially what it was in the time of Christ.

I remember when I was first asked that question I used to stop at the Septuagint version in the third century B.C., and so satisfied myself that I had the Bible of Christ and His Apostles, and that was good enough for me. And if there is anybody here who has not a chance to go back further, I would advise him to say that that is good enough for him too. That is the Bible we have got. There has never been a version made in good faith, translated into any language—and they all were made in good faith until the last few years—which has not contained the plan of salvation, the Old Testament history, the life of Christ, the witness of the Apostles, and the great doctrines of the Church sufficient unto salvation for everyone that believeth. There are people who are throwing dust in the eyes of the Church as though you could not depend on the English text. There are professors in your English universities who give out the impression that you cannot depend upon the English version or upon the Hebrew original of the Old Testament. Either they mean to deceive or they do not know what they are talking about.

All the books on the Old Testament written twenty-five years or so ago are out of date because we have discovered so many original documents in the last thirty years. All these theories—the Wellhausen theory, for instance, still taught in many of our theological schools—are out of date. Just a few months ago I received the prospectus of a great German magazine. The magazine was started when I was in Berlin as a student in 1882. It was a great protagonist of the Wellhausen theory, and it flourished more or less until about a year ago. Wellhausen himself died a couple of years ago. Now comes this prospectus announcing a new series of this Magazine of Old Testament Science, and here is what the Editor says: 'What we forty years ago thought to be a science of Old Testament criticism we have now found not to have been science at all, and it will be the endeavour of this review to reconstruct, if possible, a new science of Old Testament criticism.' That puts me in mind of the story told about Abraham. He walked out and saw the sun and bowed down and worshipped the sun, but by and by the sun set. He said, 'I worship not that which sets.' The moon came up, and he began to worship that, but the moon also set, and then there came the stars, and he said, 'I will worship the stars,' but by and by their light went out, and he said, 'I worship not that which goes out.' Then it was that the father of the faithful said, 'I worship Him who made the sun and the moon and the stars.' I worship not these sciences that set. But why call them science at all? Rather call them theories that come and go.

Let me tell you further, the Bible is all right, but there is a great deal of trouble in its interpretation. They used to hit the Bible because of certain troubles in translation. I get many letters on that subject to-day. The Bible was in Hebrew, and the translation is merely an interpretation. Any faults you find in your version are not the faults, necessarily, of the Hebrew. I do not pretend to understand everything in the Old Testament. But what I want to show you is why I believe we have got the original Bible to interpret. You say, 'What is the use of that?' Well, here is a new translation of the Bible put out within the last year. It is a new translation of the Old Testament in which the translator claims the right to change the Hebrew text whenever it suits him. I am not exaggerating one bit. He even puts a part of the second chapter of Genesis at the head of the first. A man can have his view about such matters, but when he is translating the Old Testament Scriptures he ought to translate the Scriptures as they stand. These great professors claim the right to change the text whenever it suits them.

Some years ago I was talking at Berlin University about a professor who brought out commentaries on Samuel and Kings, and I asked the other professor to whom I was speaking what he thought of this man's commentary. His reply was, 'It is very fine, providing you accept his text.' Here was the manner of this craftsman. He would go on commenting on Samuel and Kings, and whenever he got stuck and came across something he could not understand or translate he would say, 'There is something the matter with the text here, and would proceed to change the text to something which he could understand!' Imagine a school where the examination is on Julius Caesar's Commentaries on the Gallic War, and the boys are told to translate a page, and whenever they came to a word they do not understand, just to put in a word they do understand. Well, every boy would take a hundred.

But I was hunting for years for some way of showing that we could get back of the Greek translation of the third century in our scientific confirmation of the Old Testament Hebrew text, and finally I struck on the proper names, especially the proper names of the kings, more particularly those that are mentioned, not merely in the Old Testament text, but in their own monuments, or in monuments contemporaneous with the kings mentioned. I found there were forty-one names of kings which are mentioned either on their own monuments or on monuments contemporaneous with themselves. These forty-one names contain 191 consonants—you know that the original Hebrew text has no vowels. Everybody wants to see how the wheels go round. I found that out of those 191 consonants found in our present Hebrew text which are employed in the writing of those names of the forty-one kings, there are only two or three about which there could be any controversy as to their being proper renditions of the original name.

I am going to make a preliminary statement here. Let us take the life of Alexander the Great. I want to show that it is not a thing to be expected that proper names should be handed down correctly for two or three or four thousand years, and that it is a remarkable phenomenon that these proper names of Kings should have been handed down correctly. In the case of the Life of Alexander the Great we find three Greek manuscripts that have been collected and also a Syriac translation. You will remember that there was a contest, and the names of the contestants are given in Greek and also in Syriac. President Woolsey, of Yale University, brought out a long article in which he contrasted the Greek with the Syriac. When it came to the names of these contestants, he could hardly recognise one of them in the Syriac translation. If you take the names of the Kings of Babylon as given in Ptolemy, where you would have expected them to be given very accurately inasmuch as Ptolemy's Canon does give the years of the reigns of these kings with almost absolute accuracy, you find that among the proper names of the kings out of a list of twenty there are just two which agree with the Babylonian original. I could go on multiplying instances of this kind, for I have been gathering them up for a good many years, but I want you to understand that to transmit properly proper names for thousands of years is one of the most wonderful phenomena in connection with historical documents.

Let me show you how I did this. (Here you have the British Museum which will give you all the stuff you want with which to test what I say.) In the first place, we have a number of Egyptian kings mentioned in the Old Testament—Shishak, Neco, and others. You go to the Museum and take your Hebrew Bible with you, and you look at the way in which the names of those kings are spelt in the Bible, and then at the way in which they spell themselves in the old cartouches. You will find that those names have been handed on letter by letter in the manuscripts. The Assyrian kings, such as Sargon and Shalmaneser and Sennacherib, you will find again have their names spelt in the Bible text in Hebrew with absolute accuracy in every case. Out of the 191 consonants in only two or three cases could there be any dispute. But the most marvellous perhaps of all the names is that of Xerxes. Xerxes is found in Herodotus, who was a contemporary. Yet you could never transliterate Xerxes into the form you find in the Old Testament Hebrew, namely, Ahasuerus. That would be impossible. They did not do it that way. But take Xerxes. As spelled in the Bible, Xerxes is nearer to the original form on the Persian monuments as spelled by Xerxes himself than you will find anywhere else. In considering the Book of Daniel, you see the importance of this fact. How would some Hebrew writer, writing in Palestine in the second century B.C., get Ahasuerus out of Xerxes? Yet it is said by the critics that the writer of Daniel got his ideas from the Greek literature! I was telling the above facts to a certain professor, and he said that the name of Xerxes alone was enough to confound all the critics. In the Bible it has been handed down all these centuries or millenniums absolutely correctly. These names prove first that the writers of the Hebrew Bible somehow or other were able to spell the proper names of all the kings of Egypt, Babylonia, Assyria, and Persia correctly. The Hebrew writers spell the names of the Egyptian kings just as the Egyptian kings themselves spell them. They spell the names of the Assyrian kings with the same accuracy. And they have handed down *mirabile dicta.* They have handed it down *verbum dicta.*

And, let me tell you, proper names are more easily changed than any other words. You will find more mistakes of transmission in proper names than anywhere else.

Now a second point. The Bible gives the names of these kings in their proper chronological order, from all these various countries, nine or ten of them. We have got the Egyptian list from the Egyptian monuments. Synchronously the Bible gives every king his right and proper place in the scheme of Old Testament history. How could such documents have been produced in the year 300 B.C.? Where were the sources of their information? They would have to read Egyptian and Assyrian and Babylonian and Persian. We have to imagine somewhere an unknown writer who knows all these languages and has access to all the original documents sitting down and writing this history. What I have been telling you about Assyria was not known from 612 B.C., when Nineveh was destroyed, till less than a century ago. Nobody on earth knew how to spell the names of these Assyrian kings. No Greek document gives us the names of these Assyrian kings. Yet when these documents that have been buried for 2,500 years are unearthed and brought to light and read we find our old friends Tiglath-Pileser, and Shalmaneser, and Sargon, and Sennacherib, and Esarhaddon. Is not that a wonderful thing? I thank God who has given us so much stuff that a man may work all his life, and then not learn more than a little.

But I want to speak on this one point. The text, as far as we know, is all right. There is no man to-day that knows enough to attack successfully that Old Testament Hebrew text. You have got to take your Bible straight. If it is true, then take it on. Because that is what it says of itself. It is the will of God for our salvation, and we have to take its 'don't' as well as its 'do.' I am a very happy Christian, especially have I been so these last five years. I spend my time on these studies. I read dictionaries just as you read novels. I am losing my faith in man. 'Put not your trust in princes.' I change the text, and say, 'Put not your trust in professors.' Believe me, a professor does not know anything more about an ancient document without having studied it than you do yourself. A professor can only know about an ancient document by learning the script of it, by learning the language in which that doctrine is written, and by studying dictionaries and grammars and translations and all that. If a professor has not studied those ancient documents and languages he is no better able to testify than you are—that is all. And that means that he is not able to testify at all.

I lectured over in China. There are some very polite ladies in China, and after I had lectured some thirty times they surprised me by getting up a little farewell testimonial, and a young lady, who was of a Confucian family, said—and I was never so pleased in my life—'Hereafter when anyone comes to us and says anything against the Bible we will simply say, "How do you know so much, and where did you get your evidence?" ' The Church has been listening too long to men who claim to know more than is revealed in the Word of God.

Some years ago I was lecturing in one of our big university cities, and up came four brilliant students of the university. What these students of the university did not know about ancient history was not worth knowing! They began to quiz me on the Pentateuch. I was a little astonished at their questions, so I said, 'See here, when did you read this book last? Have you ever read it?' And they all with one accord began to make excuse! There was not one of them that had ever read the five books of Moses. There are people who, because they have made a great reputation along the line of chemistry or physics or biology, are thought worthy of all deference in these other matters.

My time has gone. I have taken full measure of it, though my lecture this morning is not as long as some that I have given. I have talked for three hours and twenty minutes, though I ought to add that that was with an interpreter, and the interpreter took two-thirds of the time. But I put this final sentence. Whenever you hear me advertising a lecture on biology or chemistry or physics, or even German, why then I will remove all this objection to these professors getting up to lecture on Old Testament history and the doctrines of the Church. There are scientists and scientists, and although my science is of a different sort, I claim to be every bit as much of a scientist as any of the others.

Historical Accuracy of the Old Testament

The External Testimony

By Dr. Robert Dick Wilson, of Princeton, U.S.A.

It has been charged against my method of defence of the Old Testament *that it is harmonistic.* I take the term as a word of honour; a word of common-sense; a word of commendation for our rationality. When a man goes to treat a book like the Bible, he should have a purpose in his mind. He must come to it with some theory of God and the universe and man, and no man ever, as a matter of fact, does write about the Bible but that he has come to it with some theory in his mind about it. It is not a matter of harmony, *it is a matter of theory that causes the harmony.*

Now the *Christian goes to the Bible with a theory of the universe.* He believes that God is the cause of all things; that there is a purpose and end in the universe; and that this end is the glory of God. And with this theory in mind, a man who thus believes comes to the Bible, and necessarily in his treatment of it tries to make all that it contains to harmonise with God and the universe and men, with the cause and purpose of all things.

I claim also that those very men that made that charge, as if it were a reproach, come to the Bible also with a theory of the universe. Take Buckle in his History of the Intellectual Development of Europe. Buckle has a theory, and he tries to harmonise the history of the human race with that theory. His theory is the evolutionary theory of history, and he has three great forces—physical, moral, and intellectual,—and he claims that the intellectual is the greatest of the three: that it controls the physical advancement of men, and that it shapes and moulds his moral status.

Or take that greater leader of modern Socialism, Karl Marx. He holds that the motive force behind man in history is the necessity of economic conditions; that the physical environment of men in the struggle for existence in this world, as it has been in the past, has shaped and moulded the history of the human race.

H. G. Wells, in his history which has been so much talked about lately, also has a theory of evolution, and he attempts to harmonise with that theory the whole history of man. It is very hard to tell what Mr. Wells does believe, for he belongs to that great school of thinkers who are fond of calling themselves rationalists; people that reason things out and are casting reproach upon us old-time traditionalists who believe that there were great thinkers of old, some who had revelations given to them, like Isaiah, Moses, and Paul; the Son of God Himself, who came down from the Father to reveal His will to man; great philosophers like Plato, Aristotle, Augustine, who investigated the human mind in the history of man, and who left us their thoughts for us to study.

I say H. G. Wells belongs to that vast human throng of thinkers (they are very fond of calling themselves thinkers) who go to bed at night and write as if, after ten hours' rest, they might waken up the next morning with a grand new system of the universe, ready-made, to be written about and exposed for general acceptance to all the rest of the human race, but with the great reservation that they themselves have the right to change their system overnight again and broach an entirely new theory of the universe along with the development of man. A brand new system of religion over night! Puts you in mind of going down the street and you see a little notice above a cobbler's shop, 'Shoes repaired while you wait.'

We can read ordinary philosophers like Plato or Augustine and find out what they mean, but these modern philosophers of the School of Wells; you read ten pages like the conclusion of his history, and you will pardon me for not being more exact. It is very difficult to quote Mr. Wells and say he believes this and thus and so, for he varies like the weather-cock. You look up and it is pointing north—no, it is pointing quite south, and you never exactly know where to find it. He is like that little animal which I call the evanescent imp—you think you've got him, but he is not there. Just read that last chapter of his history and see if you don't agree with me. It is hard to find out what he means, but he is an evolutionist all right, and he claims that education is everything; only educate the human race in science—that is the principal thing. Only get them to believe that they came out of something or another, it is not very clear what or how. Somehow, they came through somehow. Granting all that, however, when he comes down to the present he is going to get us out of all our troubles simply by education—à la Wells. But how that's going to get us out of our moral difficulties is not quite clear.

You know, I studied in Berlin for two years. I know the German method. I lived in the midst of it. Their principle of cult is the development by each man of his own soul, his intellect, his aesthetics, his morals. But those men never seem to have any motive. Not one of these evolutionary thinkers has any cause back of the universe, nor back of man. What made these things evolve; what started the whole creation and life on this line of evolution? What kept it going? What is the force, the energy? There is something back of it all that made it go, and Wells and the rest of them, Marx and Buckle, and all of them, have no place to go to. They have no heaven; they have no hell; they have no future for you or the human race. It is a movement from nowhere to nowhither.

Now that may satisfy the minds of some, but I think the Christian system of history is more rational than any evolutionary system that has ever been thus far propounded. Because whatever else you may say of this system revealed in the Bible, you must admit that it has power sufficient to have produced all the effects that are visible or have been visible in the history of the human race. *Here is a God in whom all things consist.* Ah, that satisfies my mind, and if you embrace it, it will satisfy yours. Just make the God big enough—a God that fills space and time, and made the stars and sun and angels and principalities and powers, and man, with all his genius and all his capacity; a God that has a purpose in the creation of all these things—THE GLORY OF GOD. Get that thought into your mind. Carry it with you all through your life, that *the Glory of God is the purpose of all things visible,* the manifestation of His wisdom and power and grace and mercy in the salvation of men. That satisfies.

Around this central thought it is the duty of every Christian to harmonise and centralise all his own life and the life of the whole world now and in the past; and therein we can rest content.

I have dwelt upon this because I want you all to understand I have a method in my madness. I have thought of what I am talking about here. I want you to understand that the method is largely the trouble with all our modern thinking people in the discussion of the Bible. If you go to the Bible with a theory that there is no God, or that He has never revealed Himself, or that He takes no interest in human affairs, of course you will throw the Bible away, for it is full of God as the sparks fly upward. But if you go there with the belief *that there is a God, and that He has revealed Himself,* then the Bible is an easy Book. Its miracles and its predictive prophets are just the thoughts of God expressing themselves a little ahead of time in His prediction, manifesting themselves by the manipulation of forces unknown to us in its miracles, all conspiring together to manifest the one true God to His ignorant sons of men.

Now, these critics of the Bible that go to the Bible in order to find fault have a most singular way of *claiming to themselves all knowledge and all virtue and all love of truth.* One of their favourite phrases which you will find in every book they have written in the last 25 years in this country is, '*All scholars believe or agree.*'

Methods of Study

But sometimes one professor knows more than all scholars, whatever they may agree on. They will admit that when it is a matter of Hebrew. I claim one man may know more Hebrew than fifty or perhaps a thousand, or maybe than a million, or perhaps all the world. Do you catch the trend of that remark? When a man writes a book and gains a point by saying, 'All scholars agree,' *I wish to know who the scholars are and why they agree.* What's back of that? *Where do they get their evidence from to start with?*

I remember some years ago I was investigating that word, *Baca,* which you have seen in your English Bible—'Going through the valley of Baca, make there a well.' So I looked and found in the Hebrew dictionary that there was a traveller named Burkhart, who said the word 'Baca' meant Mulberry Trees. That wasn't very enlightening. I couldn't see how mulberries had anything to do with water. I looked up all the authority of the scholars in Germany and England since Burkhart's time, and found they had quoted Burkhart. *Just one scholar back of it.* When I was travelling in the Orient, I found we had delicious water here and there. The water sprang up apparently out of the ground in the midst of the desert. I asked my brother, who was a missionary, where this water came from. He said, 'They bring this water from the mountains. It is an underground aqueduct. They cover it over to keep it from evaporating.' Now *the name of that underground aqueduct was Baca.*

My point is that you ought to be able to trace back this agreement of the scholars to the original scholar that propounded the statement, and then *find out whether what that scholar said is true.* What was the foundation of his statement?

Next, we come to the *second charge* that is made against the defence of the Bible. *First, they say we use the harmonistic method, and, secondly, we don't use the historical method.* I enjoy Higher Criticism. When I want to have a little fun—if you will pardon me for taking amusement out of so serious a matter—I get a work by one of those higher critics, and I can hardly read a page or two without enjoying one of the heartiest laughs you could ever imagine an Irishman having. They charge we don't use the historical method, and if you will pardon me for saying it in this language, I throw it in the teeth of the man who says it.

What is the historical method? (1) The first principle of the historical method is that as far as possible every document must be judged first of all *by contemporary evidence;* (2) a second principle is that the contemporary evidence must, if possible, *be from the locality in which the events transpired;* (3) a third principle would be that the man that gave this corroboratory evidence should have had *knowledge of the languages spoken* at that place, at that time, so as to enable him to get first-hand information; (4) and lastly, he must have had *honesty enough,* been unbiased enough, when he gave us this information, *to have given us the true information.*

You lawyers, or those that have studied the law of evidence, will see that I am just giving the law of evidence. A first-class witness must have lived at the time that the thing occurred, and have been there, and must have had eyes to see if he says he saw, and ears to hear if he says he heard. And he must have had intelligence enough to judge of what he saw and heard and to repeat it—a good memory, if possible—and then honesty not to perjure himself.

Now this method, you see, is merely an application to historic documents of what could apply to an ordinary witness in a court of law. *Now, then, that's a method that I pursue in all my works.*

What is an Expert?

If a man is called as an expert the first thing that has to be done is to establish the fact that he is an expert. *One expert may be worth more than a million other witnesses that are not experts.*

Suppose I study and can read Babylonian to some extent. I might know more Babylonian than this whole audience; at any rate, if I could read any and you could read none, I would be more expert than you. Now listen to this: Before a man has a right to speak about the Old Testament history and language and paleography *I think it is about time for the Christian Church to demand that such a man shall establish his right to speak as an expert upon this question.*

I say here that, in my opinion, no man under 50 has any right to discuss the great questions concerning the origin and the transmission of the Old Testament books, and if you will look into the history of the Church in the last 130 years you will find that *most of these assaults on the Bible have been made by young men of 30 and 40 years of age.* This is true to-day. Eloquent preachers, rhetoricians, fine appeals, exaltation of alleged scholarship, you mark my word. There is no man or woman living that can know enough by 40 to write much worth reading about the Old Testament. *Worthwhile writing on such a subject cannot be done by neophytes.* It can't be done. One of the first things I tried to impress upon my students at Princeton was that there are many things that are not to be determined by native brilliancy. Facts in evidence don't depend on brilliancy. *A brilliant man who wasn't there can't serve as a witness;* whereas a clodhopper who saw the deed would make a first-class witness. And I had just to keep repeating that until I got it into them eventually.

For 45 years continuously, since I left college, I have devoted myself to the one great study of the Old Testament in all its languages, and in all its archaeology, in all its translations, and as far as possible everything bearing upon its text and history. I tell you this, so that you may see why I can speak and do speak as an expert.

Courage for Ministers

I am tired of those ministers of the Gospel that are always apologising for the remnants of the faith that they now possess. Why should a man who professes to believe in Jesus Christ always be going about searching, as it were, for further evidence against that book? Why shouldn't he be determined to stand by his colours and defend the faith until it shall be absolutely certain that there is absolutely no possibility of standing longer? The result of my 45 years of study of the Bible has led me all the time to a firmer faith that *in the Old Testament we have a true historical account* of the history of the Israelite people, and I have a right to commend this to some of those bright men and women that think they can laugh and smile at the old-time Christian and believer in the Word of God. The most critical, radical Review in Germany had an article by a professor twelve years ago, in which he said over his own signature that no man to-day has a right to deny the possibility of Israelite history as recorded in the Old Testament. I just want you to know I do not stand alone! That's the position of a radical. The trend of things to-day is to a belief in the veracity of the history of the Old Testament.

The Law of Evidence

It is the custom nowadays to distinguish between the law of evidence as used in courts and in science and in history. There is a distinction here that many fail to observe. And yet it is necessary for all real, clear discussion of matters of history. It is not fair for anybody to demand a scientific demonstration of a historical fact. Strictly speaking, we know nothing except what we can investigate and test for ourselves. You who have studied chemistry and heard lectures know how the professor can demonstrate a fact by an experiment before your eyes. You see that and you know it, and this is said to have been demonstrated by evidence that enables you to say, 'I know.' When it comes to a case of law, and in court a decision is to be taken, certain rules are laid down and only certain kinds of evidence are admitted. Hearsay evidence and second-hand evidence are excluded. A decision when made is made on the grounds of probability. You cannot get to a scientific demonstration. If a man has been killed once, you cannot have him killed over again to see how it was done. A jury must come to a decision on the merits of the case.

When we come to historical questions, however, it is not necessary to come to a decision. Matters are to be decided on the ground of probability. Probability in one man's mind may be different from the probability in another man's mind. It is not necessary to come to any decision. It may not be important enough. But whenever you do come to a decision, you come to a decision on the ground of belief that there is preponderate evidence in favour of a certain decision. Now all historic questions are decided on that ground. Strictly speaking, you can never know how the world was made. You can believe what the Word of God says about it. You may know by reading that the Word of God says a certain thing, and on the ground of that knowledge you have the belief that what it says is true. No scientist to-day has the right to speak scientifically of the creation of the world, for he was not there, and he cannot test creation. He can believe. You may believe. He may believe that the world was made in a certain way, but he cannot prove it, and he cannot test it, and he cannot say, 'I know.'

Law of Historical Evidence

Now the law of evidence in historic matters has lately been discussed by two different schools. (1) One contends that nothing in any historic record is to be believed in a single sentence unless you can produce corroborative evidence in proof of it. You may be able to prove every other sentence or statement in a document, but according to this school you could not believe the intervening statements unless you were able to bring corroborative evidence for them. If you take that position, there is scarcely anything recorded in the history of the world that can be believed. (2) There is a saner view very well put forward by Mr. George, of Oxford University, England, in *Historical Evidence*, a book I strongly recommend. He maintains what I think is the correct view, that if you take any historic document and *can test it at certain points* as to the statements made in it, and you find it stands the test that can be made, *you are safe in presuming that when the documents cannot be tested they are true also.* That is the only way in which we can treat the history of the past. It is coming to be the prevalent view, and it is the view upon which I proceed.

Evidence of Historic Documents

Now the law of evidence in general is the same in courts of law as with reference *to historic documents.* You will find that in a case at law, when there is something beyond the range of ordinary comprehension and knowledge, the court will summon experts. Sir James Stephens' great work on the *Digest of the Law of Evidence,* the highest authority about it in England, says:

'Testimony of experts as to what the evidence really is, is especially necessary as to all subjects requiring special study or experience, such as all matters of science and art. It is a general rule of evidence that witnesses must give evidence of *facts,* not opinions.'

When you read a book like Dr. Driver's on the *Introduction to the Literature of the Old Testament,* you will find that *these critics are always citing their own opinions or the opinions of those they call authority.* I want you to observe I call no man authority in my studies, whether a German professor, an English professor, or an American professor. *The only authorities I recognise are the original texts, which I cite in testimony.*

The Making of an Expert

Now then, have I a right to be called an expert? I am before the jury in the court. I am going to give a little account of my life. When I was in the Seminary, *I used to read my New Testament in nine different languages,* one after the other, in fifteen weeks, a different language every fifteen weeks. And I learned my Hebrew by heart, so I could recite it without the intermission of a single syllable, and the same of David and Isaiah and other parts. This is a very good way of learning a language.

As soon as I graduated from the Seminary, I became a teacher of Hebrew for a year, and then I went to Germany. When I got to Heidelberg I made a decision. I decided—and I did it with prayer—to consecrate my life to a study of the Old Testament. I was 25 then, and I judged from the life of my ancestors that I would live to be 70, so I would have 45 years to work. I divided the period in three parts. The first 15 I would devote myself to a study of the languages necessary. For the second 15 I was going to devote myself to the study of the text of the Old Testament, and I reserved the last 15 years for the work of writing out the results of my previous studies and investigations so as to give these results to the world. And the Lord has enabled me to carry out that plan almost absolutely to a year.

I went to Berlin and pursued a different method from what most of our young men do when they go abroad. Most of our students from Princeton, Union, Harvard, used to go to Berlin, and they went into the lecture room, and they heard the professors give lectures which were the results of their own labours. They got everything second-hand. *They took everything because the professor said it.* That wasn't what I went to Germany for. I could get plenty of that in America. You can get all kinds of opinions in our universities and theological seminaries. I went there to study so that there would be *no professor on earth that could lay down the law for me or say anything without my being able to investigate the evidence on the ground of which he said it.*

Now I considered then, and I consider now, that what was necessary in order to investigate the evidence was, first of all, to know the languages in which the evidence is given. And so I went to Berlin and studied under Dillman, Schrador, Lachou, Burgsch, Straek, and others as teachers, and devoted myself almost entirely to the study of the languages bearing upon the Bible, and determined that I would learn all the languages which throw light upon the Hebrew, all the cognate languages, and also all the languages into which the Bible had been translated down to 600 A.D., so that I could investigate the text of the Old Testament for myself. I determined that no man on earth should ever make a charge against the Old Testament based upon any items of evidence that I should not be able to investigate for myself. *Don't imagine for a moment that you are going to be an Old Testament critic by reading other people's books* on it, or that you have a right to speak upon it because you have read a lot of books in English, and perhaps even in German, or maybe gone through Berlin.

Follow the Critics to their Lair

What we need in the Church to-day are more men that are able to *follow the critics up to their lair, and slaughter them in their den.* It makes me sad to hear these old ministers of the Gospel and Christians lament all the time about the attacks being made here and there upon the Bible, and *they never do one thing to train the men to fight their battles for them,* and you know perfectly well that you cannot defend the Old Testament Scriptures unless you have made the preparation.

I never bothered myself about getting a place when I got back from Germany. I studied ten hours a day. I never could study twelve. That was too much for me. But, excepting Sundays, and for the past forty years, about ten hours a day has been my regulation. I devoted three hundred and twenty days a year to this one subject.

The Work of the Expert

I claim to be an expert. I defy any man to make an attack upon the Old Testament on the ground of evidence that I cannot investigate. I can get at the facts if it is linguistic. If you know any language that I don't know I will learn it. Now I am going to show you some of the results.

After I had learned the languages I got to work on investigation of every consonant in the Old Testament in Hebrew. There are about one million and a quarter consonants, and it took me many years to read the Old Testament through and look at every consonant in it and gather the variations found in the Old Testament text as far as found in manuscripts or in the notes of the Massorites, or in the versions or in the parallel passages or in the conjectural emendations of critics, and classify them and put them in form for use. I prize this textual criticism very highly.

If you ask me a question, as the boys do, 'Professor, has this change taken place? Does this change take place?' etc., I don't answer questions from memory. My plan, as you see, has been to reduce the Old Testament criticism to *an absolutely objective basis,* on the ground of evidence and not opinion. I scarcely ever express an opinion based on my own subjective belief. I try to drive everything from subjectivity to objectivity, from my own personal view or opinion to the real facts and evidence in the documents. And so if you ask me, 'Does this letter ever change?' I take my little concordance and say, 'This letter changes here and there and elsewhere.' Purely objective.

In order to carry out textual criticism, anybody that goes into it will have to be a master of the science of paleography (the science of ancient languages) and of philology; he will have *to be the master of a dozen languages at least,* so that every word may be thoroughly investigated.

The text of the Old Testament is the basis of your history, theology, and faith in the document. In any document brought before any court of law, the fundamental thing of all is to *first get your text,* just as you catch your hare before you cook it. So don't depreciate what I am saying about the text. *The text is fundamental to everything about history and about the Bible.* If you can't get the text and a good enough text to believe that it gives substantially what the original writers wrote, then you can't be sure of what the original writer says.

So this is the fundamental thing I am talking about to-day. The result of those 30 years which I have been putting on the text has been this: there is not a page of the Old Testament (there were about 1,390 in the Old Hebrew Bible), there is not a single page of that but what you can read and be sure that you can depend upon the contents of the page. *You can be absolutely certain that we have the text substantially of the Old Testament that Christ and the Apostles had and that was in existence from the beginning.*

Results the Critics Tested

I remember when it was considered very unprofitable to read over those long genealogies in the first chapters of First Chronicles—nine chapters of proper names, and we wondered why they were in the Bible. Let me tell you this. To-day in scientific criticism of the Old Testament the proper names are the most necessary factor to consider. The way in which they are written and all that is connected with the proper names—they have come to be the very foundation of scientific criticism of the Old Testament.

Now, there are 29 kings whose names are mentioned not merely in the Old Testament, *but on documents written in their own time,* and many of them under the supervision of the kings themselves; written in Egyptian, Assyrian, Persian, and on monuments and other documents which come from the time of the kings themselves. There are 195 consonants in these 29 proper names. We find that in the documents of the Bible, the Hebrew Bible, of these 195 consonants *there are only two or three* about which there would be any question of their being written in exactly the same way that they were written on their own monuments by the men themselves or under their direction some 4,000 years ago—some about 2,400 years ago. Think of names being handed down for 2,400 to 4,000 years, *so that every letter is clear and correct—that is a wonder!*

Let me give you some comparisons. One man blamed me for not referring to the classical writings more in discussing certain questions in my first book on Daniel. Now, here is a list made by a great scholar—the greatest scholar of his age; he was the librarian at Alexandria in 200 B.C., and he made a list of the kings of Egypt, 38 of them. *Only three or four of them are recognisable at all.* Here is a great librarian who wrote in Greek; he made a list of 41 kings of Assyria; *in only one of them can you tell what is meant, and that one is not spelled right.* Here is Ptolemy. Well, Ptolemy has a list of the kings of Babylon and Persia. He has 18 kings of Babylon. *Not one of them is spelled right.* You could not make them out if you did not know from other sources what he means.

I want you to know that there is no book in the world that has been handed down as has the Bible. And we to-day study every consonant of the Bible.

If anyone talks against the Bible, ask him about the names of those kings. Here is another thing. There are 29 kings of Egypt, Israel, Judah, Moab, Damascus, Tyre, Babylon, Assyria, Persia; 10 different countries mentioned among these 59, both in the Bible and on the monuments, some can trace them. *Every one of these is mentioned in the Bible as king of the right country. Every one of the 59 is mentioned in the correct chronological and synchronous order.*

I wish I had hold of one of those bright mathematicians—about 14 years old. I would give him a little problem in arithmetic. If you had *ten lines of kings* extending for sixteen hundred years, and you were set the problem of picking out twenty-nine kings out of these ten lines (i.e., dynasties) and putting them in a record or story of any kind, what would be the probability of any person being able to get the twenty-nine kings *in the right place, in the right time, and synchronise them properly?* The chance of getting them right *would be one to infinity*—no chance at all. It would be absolutely impossible for you to get them right. *But the Bible has them right.* The Bible of the Old Testament shows its historicity by the fact that those names of twenty-nine kings are in their right places. Remember, some of these kings reigned, like Rameses II., for 52 years; some for two months. Why, if you were going to write the history of this century and had to get these little things in the Balkans and Germany and Austria and Italy down right in their synchronism and in their relativity, you would find it a big problem. *But the Bible has its kings right.* That is a lesson in paleography, all right, in historical chirography.

The Critics' Language Test False

As to the contention of the critics that Aramaic is evidence of the date of documents, I got the conviction that these critics said things about Aramaism they could not substantiate. I took a Hebrew dictionary and went through it from the first word to the last, and gathered up results. Then I went to the Arabic and gathered results. I gathered up the whole number of the relevant words and compared them with the Babylonian language. Then I gathered up my results and could speak with some facts back of me. It makes four volumes of stuff.

I carried this investigation on according to the scientific method, and found there is little in the claim to Aramaism in the Old Testament. There are only five or six of these words in the whole Old Testament that could be even considered doubtful, and the whole argument dropped to the ground.

The brainiest man on earth can know no more about a subject like that than you do, by birth. Some of these men demand of us more belief in their inspiration or revelation or secret internal means of information than has ever been claimed by us for any prophet in the Old Testament, or apostle in the New Testament. I tell you the day is at hand when the Church, instead of covering, and seeming, as many so-called Christians do, to rejoice in the supposed victories over the Bible truth, will demand that any one who attacks the Bible will produce his evidence. Believe no man who makes a statement against the Bible without bringing evidence, and if he brings evidence and you cannot investigate it, call in an expert that can; and try out your expert, too.

Sixty years ago there was no Babylonian known. People read the Old Testament, and when they found a form of a noun or verb that did not suit the Hebrew, they said it was Aramaic, and that everywhere it appeared it marked the books as late. So the critics in Germany and some of them in this country had just to open their mouths and say anything at all, and everybody believed it, because it came from a professor.

God and the Monuments against the Critics

You know the principles of the English language—the parts of speech. Now in Hebrew there is a noun ending in '*ooth,*' rhyming with 'booth.' The Lord has given us Babylonian. *God kept those monuments for this time.* The Babylonian documents take us back before the time of Abraham, and we have more literature from the time of the kings in Gen. 14, than from the time of Tiberius Caesar, the time of our Lord.

In these documents from the time of this old king we find nouns ending in '*ooth,*' and down from that until the end of the Kingdom of Babylon, and the destruction of the city, you find them. It is found not in Aramaic alone, but in Hebrew and Babylonian languages as well. The whole foundation falls from under the old argument.

Daniel in the Critics' Den

The claim of the critics to destroy the historicity of *Daniel* by making the book late owing to the character of its language, and the usage as to the names of the kings is equally groundless.

I stand for what I say here. I have worked for three years on a great thesaurus of the titles of the kings, and everybody who writes either for or against me used my own works to get his information.

They used this particular testimony to prove that Daniel is not like the other books of the sixth century B.C. (when Daniel was written). But critics have not produced a single example to prove that the form "X the King" was used subsequent to Nehemiah. None of the recent documents, nor any of the late portions of the Old Testament, nor the Psalms, Proverbs or Job use the order which they claim is late. Their theory breaks down.

The critics are very fond of the phrase, 'All scholars are agreed,' but if the greatest of their scholars will make such a blunder, what dependence will you place upon him when he steps beyond the bound of knowledge into the limitless regions of imagination? *The charges of the critics are false;* and upon what ground or law of evidence are we to be convinced that these documents are false, when charges absolutely unsupported by evidence are made against them?

I never believe any man who says something against the Bible out of his own imagination. I would not believe any man on earth, even if he brought up evidence, until I had investigated every item of the evidence. I commend this to you, and if you have not the knowledge to investigate the charge made, *have faith enough to believe the Bible until the charge is corroborated.*

Dr. Driver in the Lions' Den

One illustration more. Dr. Driver, in the best book the critics have, says, in speaking of the phrase 'King of Persia,' used in the very end of the author of Ezra-Nehemiah, that there were no kings of Persia when the book Ezra-Nehemiah was written.

I would like to repeat this: that the writer of the Book of Ezra-Nehemiah would not have needed to use this title while *Kings of Persia* were still *Kings of Persia,* nor was it usual thus to do.

I don't know what you think of that. It affects not only Ezra—Nehemiah, but Chronicles and Daniel. If that statement is true, it knocks the historicity of all four. It is the greatest statement the critics have made. It appeals to history and to fact.

If you want to find out anything about this subject, there is not one of you who has any right at all to contradict anything I say, unless you can read Egyptian and Babylonian and all the rest, going to the original documents to see what is there. I will not take a translation.

Dr. Driver says he read *forty titles in a translation,* and when I was answering that, I said that I had found *two thousand six hundred and fifty-six in the originals,* where the titles are, with all particulars concerning them.

The critics say it was not usual to give the title 'King of Persia' while there were Kings in Persia; consequently the books must have been written after they ceased to exist. [The Persian Empire fell under Alexander the Great (Greece), B.C. 331; the Old Testament history closes B.C. 488.] If this were true, it would bring these books down to Greek times. It is sufficient answer to this assertion to say that eighteen different authors in nineteen different documents from Persian times use this title altogether thirty-eight different times; at least six different times it is used of Cyrus [B.C. 536-530], and is used also of Artaxerxes III. [B.C.358-338]. The title occurs in the Persian, Greek, Babylonian, Aramaic, and Hebrew; it was used in the countries of Media, Babylon, Assyria, Greece, and Palestine, and, according to Herodotus, in Ethiopia.

The Witness of Comparative Religions

I must close. But before closing this review of the lines of defence of the Old Testament Scriptures, I must emphasise the strongest of them all—their great religious ideas.

A study of the religious systems of these ancient peoples has revealed to us a groping after God, but nowhere among all the nations is it recorded that a clear apprehension was attained of one living and true God, the Creator and Preserver, the Guide, the Judge, the Saviour, and the Sanctifier of His people.

Other religions are outward; concerned with words and deeds. Their sins are offences; their substitutions are material equivalents; their atonements are physical; their resurrection is a crownless expectation; their judgment is without mercy, and a future life with joy is for the few and great.

The Internal Witness of the Old Testament to Divine Origin

The Old Testament religion is essentially inward of the mind and heart; love, joy, faith, hope, and salvation through the grace of God alone. How account for this religion? The prophets say it came from God. No other theory of its origin will account for its results, its superiority, its influence. We add to the prophets' statement *evidence which all the quibbling of the critics cannot impugn.* The prophets say they had their ideas from God. If not, from whence? If so, the greatest of all miracles has happened, involving all the rest, for *if God spoke through the prophets, the revelations of His will could not be bound by the shackles of time and circumstance.*

The prophets who spoke for Him, *spoke not as men of their own time, but as men of all time;* as men who spoke of Him who knows the end from the beginning and has all power in heaven and on earth. The modern critical school is antagonistic to the fundamental conception of the prophets' mission as it was spoken by the prophets themselves. They say that *God spoke to them,* and *they spoke for God.* The critics say that *they gave utterance to the ideas of their times; that they were limited by the time and place of their prophecy.*

But if this were all the source of their information, how then does it come that not from the oracles of Thebes and Memphis, nor from the temples of Babylon, nor from Delphi and Rome, nor from the deserts of Media, but from the sheepfolds and dungeons, from the lowly cots of captives on the banks of the river came forth these great words of hope and salvation and glory for a sin-cursed world! Words that have made the desert heart rejoice and blossom like the rose in the sunlight of God's favour, in the revivifying atmosphere of His presence.

'God with us.' This is the. key to unlock the mysterious chambers of the Old Testament.

The Springs of Scripture are in God

By A. E. Hughes

For a moment I fancy myself travelling in some Eastern land beneath the blaze of the burning sun. Being thirsty, I come across two wells. One is shallow. The water it contains is mere surface water from the rain that has fallen round about and percolated through the ground into the well. It is what we call in the East a cistern, which sometimes runs dry, as did the pit in which Joseph was placed. But the other well is different. It is a deep well. Here is a well which has touched some hidden spring. It has an abundant supply of what the woman of Samaria would have called 'living water,' water clear and cold; it is a well that never runs dry, and the water of which is practically unaffected by the sides of the well through which it rises. I drink of each well. The first may be welcome in hot weather, but the other is more welcome. Without being told, I think I can tell the difference between those two wells.

We are like thirsty souls travelling through a world that will never satisfy the needs of any of us. Our soul-thirst needs quenching. And so we turn to this Book, the Bible. It is a well. But of what kind? I indeed have turned to it under great conviction of sin and it has met my need. I have turned to it in the bitter sorrows of life and it has met my need. I have turned to it, I have recently done so, in the most heart-breaking bereavement, and again it has met my need.

There are some who tell us that here we have hardly more than the thoughts and words of men, and that, being human, they were liable to mistakes in regard to the history they record, the facts they state, and the doctrines they teach. Paul, the Apostle, they say, for instance, was quite wrong when he talked about the fall of man. If only Paul had lived in these enlightened days, if only he had had the knowledge of evolution which people now have, he would have seen his mistake. But, if so, the well that these people offer me to drink from is a very shallow one. The Bible, as they regard it, is a well which contains only surface water, spoiled by very much human imperfection. If that be so, I cannot fully trust it. Therefore it would fail to meet my need. How contrary that is to the experience of multitudes, and to my own!

As I drink of the Bible well I have water so clear, so pure and so fresh—though, indeed, it is an old well—that I can almost tell without any other information that it is no surface well, that its source is deep, that it comes from some hidden spring, and that the water has not been appreciably affected by the human channels of translators and copyists all down the centuries.

This Book makes the claim for itself that all Scripture is given by inspiration of God. That is its own claim, and Inspiration means God breathing out, and minds being breathed into, men writing under the breath of God. That is the claim that it makes for itself. At times those men wrote just as simply and personally as you or I would write, unconscious of any power behind them. At times they did not understand the full meaning of what they did write, but whichever it was, if that text be true, the Spirit of God was breathing upon and into their minds, keeping them from error, and guiding and controlling their words. They were moved by the Holy Ghost. The figure is that of being borne along, like a sailing ship with the wind behind it, right across the ocean.

Now the question comes to us, Is that claim of the Bible as being the inspired Word of God one upon which we can depend? Is it justified or is it not? First of all, I would speak of the most wonderful unity of this Book. For there are about 40 writers who were employed to write the 66 books in the Bible. Those writers divide themselves into two groups, so that we have two volumes, the Old Testament and the New Testament. Attempts are made to differentiate between the two. We are often told that the God of the Old Testament is not the God of the New; at least we are told that the Old Testament writers had a very poor and imperfect view of God, and that we to-day know much better than they knew what God is. Of course, to those who speak and think like this, the Bible is not and cannot be a well of real living water, but is rather surface water, a Book which has been marred by the imperfections of the writers. But let us suppose the same thing in regard to another book. Take '*Pickwick Papers,*' for instance, and let me suppose that I knew nothing about its authorship. This book is in two volumes, and one of them falls into my hands. I do not know at the time that there is another volume. When I have finished reading the first volume, I feel that there must be a sequel; or if it is the second volume which has come into my hands, I feel that there must have been something earlier. It needs a preface to help me understand it. Then suppose that instead of having only the one volume, I find the other, the first or second, whichever it may be, and it just answers my question, and meets my need for something else, so that as I read the two I am convinced that there cannot be a separate author for each because there is such a unity between them.

In just the same way, if I had only the New Testament or only the Old, I should find it incomplete. I cannot understand Leviticus unless I have Hebrews, nor Hebrews unless I have Leviticus. I feel that the Ten Commandments want some further explanation, and that the Sermon on the Mount needs a basis. I need an explanation of the Gospel in Isaiah, and I find the four stories of Jesus Christ in the New Testament give just the explanation that I need. I see the connection between the Passover Feast and the Lord's Supper, between Daniel and Revelation, and, as with the two volumes of Dickens, so, when I see the wonderful completion of the one volume by the other in the Book, I feel and realise that the two volumes are volumes of the same Book, that they must have had the same author.

If you go from book to book through the Old Testament teaching in regard to the Messiah that was to come, you find a wonderful variety of teaching. But when you come to the New Testament, while the writers simply tell their story as truthful men—never altering one word, as if trying to bring it into harmony with the old prophecy,—yet in a marvellous way you find that all these old foretellings harmonise in the Gospel story, so much so that the Risen Lord Himself was able to give a Bible reading on the day of His resurrection, when 'Beginning at Moses and the prophets, He expounded to them in all the Scriptures the things concerning Himself.' He Himself was fulfilling all those marvellous prophecies.

Now if 40 parts of a great house were all designed by 40 different architects, I fancy there would be some discrepancies, and you would observe a lack of harmony and symmetry in the house or building. In looking at most houses you can see at once that the house must have had one plan, one designer, and one architect. Thus in this wonderful Book, with its two volumes by 40 writers, one can tell on looking at it that it must have had one architect and one designer, and that architect and designer was God.

Another thing to confirm our faith in this Bible answering its own claim is its completeness. Did you notice that word we read just now with regard to the man of God being perfect—or as we may read that word, complete—thoroughly furnished unto all good works? The Bible gives us a complete knowledge. We need the whole of the Bible and nothing more is needed as a revelation from God than we have in the Bible. In the case of other books, have you noticed this difference, that everybody is out for the latest edition? But, when it comes to the Bible, we do not talk about an up-to-date edition. What we really want above everything else is the oldest edition, and, if some older manuscript of Hebrew or Greek in regard to one Testament or the other were to be found, that MS. would be worth more than its weight in gold. We go back to the old in this case; we believe that the old is God's revelation; and yet the old is always up-to-date.

There are some people who tell us that we are putting a dead hand on progress by claiming for the Bible what we do, and that what we need is continually new light. Yes, we do need new light, and new light is constantly bursting forth from these very pages. It comes, not independently of, but through the old Book. When we think about new light in science, new knowledge of things, new uses of things, we must remember that the things already exist. There was the same force years ago in the River Shannon as there is to-day, but it was not used for the purposes of electricity as it is now. There was the same force in Niagara a hundred years ago, but it was not applied as it is to-day. So the Christian has all that he needs for knowledge and use in Christian living here in this Book; but oftentimes the same Spirit which inspired men of old to write the sacred pages casts new light upon His own Word and gives new blessing, and men are led to use what they had before but did not know how to use. I would say, beware of any new light, if light it be, that contradicts the sacred Scriptures and is out of keeping with the Bible.

Finally, just a word about the testimony to the Bible given by our Lord and His Apostles. They always looked upon these Scriptures as infallible. Our Lord set His seal upon them. In that remarkable story of Abraham and Dives, you remember how Abraham said, 'If they hear not Moses and the prophets, neither will they be persuaded though one rose from the dead.' Moses and the prophets were enough for those Old Testament believers, and that was proved to be true because, not long afterwards, One did rise from the dead; there was indisputable evidence that the Lord Jesus was risen, and yet the majority of the Jews rejected the One Who had so risen.

The question really before us comes to this, What think ye of Christ? If you and I cannot trust the Old Testament, if we cannot trust what He taught and believed about the Old Testament, how can we trust what He revealed and taught in regard to the way of salvation and other things?

The real danger at the moment is not from attacks from the outside. You remember how in the old city of Troy there was little danger from attacks from without, but, when the men foolishly brought into the city that wonderful horse, then a new danger, unknown before, was created within. The danger to-day is not from the attacks of the open infidel, but it is from the attacks which come from within the citadel, from those who profess and call themselves Christians, inside the camp of Christ. Yet as we see these dangers, we look above them, above the fallible teachers to the great Teacher Himself, and we believe Him to be true.

Some 150 years ago the celebrated Lord Chesterfield, who was an unbeliever, and whose life did not commend his faithless faith, was in Paris, and was addressed by a celebrated lady there. 'My lord,' she said, 'how is it, if the Bible and your Christianity are so full of fables and so obsolete, that you have 500 or 600 brilliant and able men in your Parliament who still keep the Bible and Christianity as the basis of your country's law and order?' 'Madam,' he replied, 'this is only a temporary makeshift. We are casting about for something better, and as soon as we have found something better the Bible and Christianity will remain no longer.' That is more than 150 years ago, and the world has been casting about for something better and has failed to find it. By the grace of God we mean to continue in the things that we have learned and of which we have been assured, and we are thankful that we have in the Holy Scripture words inspired by God's Holy Spirit, which, though written so many years ago, are a living message to our hearts and our souls to-day.

PSALM 87

1 *The nature and glory of the church.*

4 *The increase, honour, and comfort of the members thereof.*

A Psalm or Song for the sons of Korah.

1 His foundation *is* in the holy mountains.

2 The LORD loveth the gates of Zion more than all the dwellings of Jacob.

3 Glorious things are spoken of thee, O city of God. Selah.

4 I will make mention of Rahab and Babylon to them that know me: behold Philistia, and Tyre, with Ethiopia; this *man* was born there.

5 And of Zion it shall be said, This and that man was born in her: and the highest himself shall establish her.

6 The LORD shall count, when he writeth up the people, *that* this *man* was born there. Selah.

7 As well the singers as the players on instruments *shall be there:* all my springs *are* in thee.

The Miraculous Unity of the Bible

By Dr. Basil F. C. Atkinson

We are so much accustomed to speak of the great Book as the Bible and to think of it as a unity, that we are inclined to forget the diversity of time and authorship that characterises its various parts. All the writers of the Bible, with the probable exception of a single New Testament author, belonged to the same race. This fact, however, may be said to be the only tie that bound them together. Their social positions, their occupations, their standards of education, the circumstances of the times at which they lived, differed greatly. Even more striking is the fact that from the days of Moses to those of the Apostle John, who was the latest New Testament writer, there extends a period of fifteen hundred years. How can any set of writings produced at intervals over such a period of time exhibit any sort of unity, even allowing for the fact that the later writers were familiar with the work of the earlier, which we may say to have been generally but not necessarily invariably the case? In the history of our own nation such a period would run from the first landing of the English, from the last days of Roman occupation, to the present day. It is inconceivable that any set of writings could show any consistency or possess a thread of narrative or teaching that could be traced from beginning to end. If it can be shown that the Bible as a whole possesses consistency and unity, if it can be shown that it may rightly be regarded as a single book, then a miracle has been proved, and the Divine origin of the Bible may be said almost to have been demonstrated by that fact alone.

Such unity and consistency can be shown to exist, and shown without much difficulty to an unbiassed and attentive mind. The efforts of rationalistic criticism during the last two or three generations to disparage that unity have served only to bring it into fuller relief, and for some time there have appeared signs that those efforts are approaching exhaustion.

The unity of the Bible can be seen from at least three separate angles. First we can distinguish a literary unity. We can see that the various parts dovetail together like a single composition. Secondly, we find from beginning to end an undeviating consistency in the presentation of certain great doctrines or principles. These doctrines concern spiritual or eternal things, which cannot be known by man apart from revelation. They have been, however, during the whole known course of the history of the human race the subject of speculation, and if the doctrines taught in the Bible had not been derived from revelation, the speculations of the various authors, covering such a wide range of time, must have been widely different from each other, and the confusion that might have been expected to exist in such a collection of writings would have resulted. Thirdly, there is a dominant theme that runs throughout the whole having a continual unifying effect. There is a key that brings relevance to any apparent irrelevancies. There is a commanding Personality who passes majestically across the scene from one end of the Bible to the other, as the sun passes daily across the heavens. There is no need for us to remind ourselves that this Person is Jesus Christ our Lord.

Let us look at each of the three aspects of unity in greater detail. The Bible in its original form consists of seven great divisions, three in the Old Testament and four in the New. In the Old Testament there are the Law, the Prophets and the Psalms (see Luke 24.44), in the New first the four Gospels, secondly the Acts and Catholic Epistles, thirdly the Pauline Epistles including Hebrews, lastly the Apocalypse. The Law consists of the five books, Genesis to Deuteronomy; the Prophets of the historical books, Joshua to Kings, followed by Isaiah, Jeremiah, Ezekiel, and the twelve minor prophets; the Psalms of the following nine books, Psalms, Proverbs, Job, Song of Solomon, Ecclesiastes, Esther, Daniel, Ezra, and Nehemiah and Chronicles.

The five books of the Law form an obvious unity of narrative and teaching. It is irrelevant to our theme whether that unity is the work of a single author, or of an editor manipulating and combining past material, which latter conception however is a theory that we may be permitted to say we entirely reject. However it came about the unity is there. Now notice how smooth is the link by which we pass over into the Prophets. 'Now after the death of Moses the servant of the Lord . . .' The transition is effected without lurch or jolt. The story is taken up where it was laid down. We may pass from the last chapter of Deuteronomy to the first chapter of Joshua without noticing any break in the narrative. The history passes on through the four books and ends at a point only too suitable for its conclusion, the disruption of the Kingdom of Judah, the taking of Jerusalem, the burning of the Temple and the captivity of the people. We turn over the page to the first chapter of Isaiah. The visions of the great prophets are dated in a way which presupposes our knowledge of the books of Kings, while the message of the prophets not only presupposes our knowledge of the historical books but arises directly out of the conditions which they describe. The historical facts are enlarged and illuminated as we read the pleadings and denunciations of the great prophets, and the inner reasons for the climax of tragedy are laid bare to a much greater extent than they were in the historical account.

The connection of the prophets with what goes before is also clearly seen in the theme which forms the second part of the message of the prophets. The prophets' message is two-fold. Denunciation of sin, prediction of certain judgment to come upon the city and people are followed by and interwoven with prophecy of a glorious future, when a King would reign in righteousness, an everlasting covenant would be made with God's people, they would all have one Shepherd, their sins would be forgiven, and the Lord Himself would dwell in their midst for evermore. This theme is definitely supplementary to, and intentionally explanatory of, the tragedy of which we have read in the historical books. Joshua, it is true, is a triumphant book, but through Judges, Samuel and Kings we pass further and further downwards to the depths in an ever-gathering darkness, broken only temporarily here and there by the glories of the reigns of David and Solomon, the faithful witness of Elijah and Elisha, the reformations effected by Hezekiah or Josiah. We start to read Isaiah and the prophets that follow him in and from these depths, as it were, and we are not spared a continuation, even intensification, of the darkness. But through it shines a glorious light. In Isaiah it is most brilliant, in Jeremiah it is least strong, in Ezekiel it blazes out and covers the second part of the book. From the lowest point of disaster we begin to rise with our eyes looking forward to the future. The purpose of God is not utterly broken by the sin and failure of Israel and Judah. His mercy is not clean gone for evermore. He has a purpose of glory and blessing which He intends to carry out in His own time in the future. We might add that this theme again is only an intensification of the isolated promises that flit through the Book of Moses, with which it establishes again a definite connection of thought.

On finishing the Prophets we take up the Psalms, a series of nine books which deal more with the spiritual life of the individual and its problems than with that of the nation, which also lift the veil to disclose the action of spiritual forces in the affairs of men to a greater extent than the previous books. Is there a violent break between the last chapter of Malachi and the first Psalm? It is quite true that we must not expect the Psalms to continue a thread of narrative or of teaching that we might have previously noticed, seeing that they consist of a series of hymns written on various occasions and intended for the use of God's people under both the Old and New Covenants. Yet the obvious contrast between the last sentence of the Prophets and the first sentence of the Psalms is more likely to be designed than fortuitous. '. . . Lest I come and smite the earth with a *curse.*' '*Blessed* is the man.' . . And at the end of the last of the three Old Testament divisions we find the books of Chronicles, which summarise all that has gone before, beginning with Adam and ending with the restoration from the Babylonian captivity. 'The Lord his God be with him, and let him go up.' If this sentence breaks off at a comma, it does so designedly, the design being easily visible to those who have studied the theme of the Bible as a whole. We have already read the book of Ezra—Nehemiah: 'his God be with him, and let him go up to Jerusalem, which is in Judah, and build the house of the Lord God of Israel.' But at the end of the Old Testament the sentence is broken off. We have reached the conclusion of the Old Testament, but not the end of the Bible. We are in the middle of a sentence. God has more to say. At sundry times and in divers manners God has spoken to us by the prophets. 'The Lord his God be with him, and let him go up . . .' Go up where? The New Testament completes the sentence. To Jerusalem, yes, but not to Jerusalem which is in Judah. To Jerusalem which is above, which is the mother of us all.

We take up the opening chapter of the Apostle Matthew's Gospel, and find that we have made a transition less abrupt than that between Malachi and the Psalms. The first section is unintelligible without a knowledge of the Old Testament, indeed without a considerably close knowledge of its history. Not only must we know epoch-making facts such as the key promises to Abraham and David, but we must know the stories of the four women mentioned in the genealogy if we would catch the beauty and pathos that lie behind the fact of their being mentioned.

The Book of Acts takes up the story of the Gospels where it left off, the Epistles follow naturally from the Acts. The Epistles of Paul, closely linked and arranged in definite order, follow without difficulty the catholic epistles. They end with the delightful affectionate personal epistle to Philemon, bringing the affairs of the Kingdom of God into the matters of everyday life, or rather illustrating the fact that the circumstances of everyday life only constitute a means of contact between the Saviour and the needy world.

Then follows the epilogue, the marvellous book of Revelation, almost every verse of which contains an allusion to something in the Bible that has gone before. The closing five verses are the closing verses not of revelation only but of all the Scriptures. The thrice-repeated 'Come,' the solemn admonition not to add to or take from the Word of God, the forward look to the appearance of the Lord, the grace as if the pierced hand were raised in blessing. Who can say that in reading the Scriptures he has not been reading a book which hangs together throughout and proceeds in an intentional order by a designed route to an appointed end?

We now turn to the second set of facts which reveal the unity of the Scriptures. We will examine the teaching of the Bible on three fundamental themes, first the existence of one eternal God who created the world, life, the heavens, all we see about us, and all else that is in being; secondly the fact that the relationship between this God and man is fundamentally in the moral sphere, in other words, that the supreme and only essential question for man is the difference between right and wrong; thirdly the fact that all men fall short of the moral standard required by God.

The opening verses of the Bible lay the foundation of the revelation of the Person of God. 'In the beginning God . . .' 'In the beginning God created the heaven and the earth.' What is the first of the commandments of the moral law? 'I am the Lord thy God. Thou shalt have none other gods but Me.' What does Moses tell us? 'Hear, O Israel. The Lord thy God is one Lord.'

We pass to the prophets. Is there any deviation from this teaching. 'Hereby ye shall know that the living God is among you,' says Joshua to the people. What an emphatic exposition of this revelation of the being and nature of God lies in the very expression, 'the living God.' It occurs again in the first Book of Samuel on the lips of the young David as he prepared for the contest with Goliath. Listen to Solomon as he dedicates the temple: 'there is no God like Thee,' 'will God indeed dwell on the earth? behold, the heaven and the heaven of heavens cannot contain thee'; or to Hezekiah: 'Thou art the God, even Thou alone, of all the Kingdoms of the earth; Thou hast made heaven and earth . . . Of a truth, Lord, the Kings of Assyria have destroyed the nations and their lands, and have cast their gods into the fire: for they were no gods, but the work of men's hands, wood and stone.'

Again we need only remind ourselves of the great section of Isaiah's prophecy beginning with chapter 40 in which the true God deliberately sets Himself in contrast with the idols of the nations, of the word of revelation to Jeremiah, 'I fill heaven and earth,' of the Psalmist's statements, 'The gods of the nations are but wood and stone, but Thou art He that made the heavens.' 'The sea is His and He made it, and His hands formed the dry land.' The same teaching of the relationship between God and nature is set forth in detail in the concluding chapters of the Book of Job. What is the great Nebuchadnezzar obliged to confess? 'The most High ruleth in the Kingdom of men, and giveth it to whomsoever He will.' What did Nehemiah believe? 'I prayed unto the God of heaven.' This revelation of the one true eternal God is made throughout the Old Testament against a background of continual unfaithfulness to Him and of sinful devotion to idols.

When we reach the New Testament, assertions of the existence of the one true living God are less numerous. The days of idolatry had been long over for the Jews. But the truth is no less emphasised. It is assumed behind the whole New Testament scene, which crumbles to pieces meaningless without it. And here and there definite assertions are made. Our Lord repeats the words of Deuteronomy, 'the Lord thy God is one Lord.' The early church resorts to prayer and addresses the One who made heaven and earth, the sea and all that is in them' (Acts 4.24). The Apostle Peter speaks of 'a faithful Creator.' The Apostle Paul is emphatic: 'One God and Father of all, who is over all and through all and in all.' At the end of the Bible we find just the same thing: 'I am A and Z, the beginning and the end, saith the Lord,' 'He that is and that was and that is to come.'

We challenge anyone to find any teaching about the being and nature of the Creator different from this from one end of the Bible to the other. If it be objected that other gods are mentioned, the answer is simple enough. The Bible always speaks the warmhearted language of everyday life. It speaks of other gods because the idols of the nations were commonly spoken of as such. The Old Testament writers who mention other gods no more believed in their objective existence, than does a teacher of Greek history and literature to-day believe in the existence of Zeus, Athene and the rest, though he may frequently speak of 'the gods.' In Old Testament days the issue between faithfulness to the true God and going after other gods was a live issue. The heathen and the apostate Israelites believed in the reality of other gods. It may have been some who so believed whom David thinks of when he tells Saul that there were those attempting to drive him out to serve other gods (1 Sam. 26.19). It is no safe conclusion from this remark of David's that he himself believed in the reality of other gods. Nor should any such conclusion be drawn from the ironical remark of Jephthah to the Ammonites, 'Wilt not thou possess that which Chemosh thy god giveth thee to possess?' If the Bible mentions other gods, it says frequently that they 'are but wood and stone.' The writers no more believed in them than the Apostle Paul when he says, 'though there be that are called gods, whether in heaven or in earth (as there be gods many, and lords many)' (1. Cor. 8.5). Again we may remind ourselves that there is a mystery of evil behind heathen idolatry. If the Lord's words to Moses, 'Against all the gods of Egypt will I execute judgment,' seem to imply some objective existence in the objects of Egyptian worship, the words of the Apostle in 1 Cor. 10.20 supply an explanation, 'the things which the Gentiles sacrifice, they sacrifice to devils.'

We must pass on to the next fundamental principle of Biblical revelation, which is that God is essentially a moral Being, concerned always with right and wrong of which He himself is the sole and perfect and personal arbiter, and that He has created human beings as moral beings and responsible as such. This principle is so firmly embedded in every chapter of the Bible, so patent to the eye, that it needs little ilustration. In heathen religions and in degraded forms of Christianity we sometimes find religion divorced from morality. There is not so much as a hint that the two are not vitally interrelated in any page of the Scriptures. The God whom we serve is a holy God. The first book of the Bible contains almost at its threshold the story of the fall of man, the second gives us the ten commandments of the moral law. The historical books are concerned all the time with burning moral issues which in every case affect the course of history. How familiar is the expression of the moral principle, 'God will render to every man according to his works!' 'The Lord is our judge,' says the prophet Isaiah. 'God the judge of all,' exclaims the writer of the Epistle to the Hebrews. The prophets continually predicting a blessed future describe it as a time when God will write His law on men's hearts. The Christian, though justified by faith (itself a fact implying God's judgment and His requirement of moral perfection) is not allowed, if he would be true to the Scriptures, to fall into anti-nomianism. And the Bible shows the conclusion of this world's history to be a day of judgment when 'the dead were judged . . . according to their works.' If it be suggested that the ceremonial law, to which so much detailed attention is given in the book of Leviticus for example, is not concerned with moral issues, we deny the suggestion, and reply that its whole purpose is to illustrate the incompatibility between the holiness of God and sin.

The third great doctrine which appears consistently throughout the Bible is that of the fallen and corrupt nature of man. Certain clear declarations are made on this point. The book of Genesis asserts, 'every imagination of the thoughts of his heart was only evil continually' (Gen. 6.5), 'the imagination of man's heart is evil from his youth' (Gen. 8.21). The prophet Jeremiah affirms, 'The heart is deceitful above all things, and desperately wicked,' and David in the fifty-first Psalm (verse 5), 'Behold, I was shapen in iniquity; and in sin did my mother conceive me.' The Apostle Paul says plainly, 'All have sinned, and come short of the glory of God' (Rom. 3.23), 'In Adam all die' (1 Cor 15.22).

Is this doctrine of the corruption of human nature taught consistently throughout the Bible? Let us look at Scriptural history and biography. From Exodus to Kings the Old Testament tells the story of the increasingly deep corruption of a nation that had had every spiritual privilege and the light of revelation continually burning in its midst. That fact has a significance greater perhaps than is ordinarily realised. Even more significant are the facts revealed in the biographies not of wicked men, but of those who fall in the class that the Bible refers to as 'the righteous,' or 'saints.' There is not a man whose life-story is given us, about whom some imperfection is not made apparent. The most upright Old Testament character is that of Joseph, but even he as a youth incurred his father's displeasure by a boastful attitude. Noah fell under the influence of drink, Abraham lied through cowardice, Isaac did the same, Jacob bargained with his brother and deceived his father. Judah ancestor of our Lord, takes part in a sordid story of immorality, Moses loses his temper and disobeys an express command of God, Aaron (actually described as 'the saint of the Lord') makes an idol, Joshua gives way to despair, Samson fails all his life to restrain his passions, David commits adultery and murder, Solomon allows the practice of idolatry beneath his eyes, Elijah shows cowardice and weakness, Elisha hesitates to leave all for the Lord's service, Hezekiah gives way to pride and boasting, Josiah shortens his life by rashness, Jeremiah cries out, 'Cursed be the day on which I was born,' and attempts to resign his ministry, Daniel is found confessing his sins. The New Testament tells the same story. Peters denies his Lord, all the disciples forsake Him and flee, Mary the mother of Jesus misunderstands His purpose and ministry, Paul quarrels with a fellow-missionary. One character, one life alone stands out in Scripture in a blaze of sinless glory, in whose radiance the purity of Joseph or the devotion of Paul appear as stained and feeble. Now all these facts not only provide a consistent picture of the corruption of human nature, but constitute a proof of Divine inspiration, for the imperfections of the heroes of human composition are veiled in silence. Only the Holy Spirit provides true biography.

We now turn to the supreme theme of the Bible. There is a pervading unity in the fact of a single Person passing across its pages from beginning to end. There is the Figure who walks in the garden with Adam, seen no longer after the fall. But immediately comes the first of Bible prophecies: '. . . It shall bruise thy head, and thou shalt bruise His heel.' Thus early this victorious scion of the human race steps upon the scene. If we were to stop to find Christ in all the Scriptures, this paper would, I think literally, never end, for I believe this may be one of our occupations for eternity. We must, however, follow Him through each book as He most prominently appears. We cannot at once leave Genesis. There is the Visitor who with two angels sought the hospitality of Abraham, there is a ram caught in a thicket by his horns, there is one who was separate from his brethren.

Exodus tells us of One who spoke to Moses from the burning bush; also of a Passover lamb without blemish, of a throned One who was seen by Moses and Aaron, Nadab and Abihu and seventy of the elders of Israel. In Leviticus we find animal after animal portraying the victim of sacrifice, Numbers shows us a serpent on a pole lifted up to heal the dying. In Deuteronomy the outline is clear. 'The Lord your God will raise up unto you a Prophet like unto me.' Thus the Law tells us of a human being, a Prophet, yet of One throned in majesty, One whom Abraham worshipped, a Lamb whose blood is shed.

We pass on to the books of the prophets. The conquest of Canaan is not carried out by the Israelites alone. There is a great Person who leads them, before whom Joshua falls in worship, the Captain of the Host of the Lord. In the book of Judges, where the critical or superficial mind might be least inclined to look for it, there is a blaze of glory from the rays of the Scriptures' Sun. Twice appears the Angel of the Lord, twice He demands sacrifice, and the second time—let us note this detailed, marvellous type—He himself ascends up to heaven in the flame from the altar. Is this some vulgar piece of mediaeval-like wonder-working, invented by an ingenious mind to make a sensational story? No, indeed! What a sacrifice! What a picture! What a way into heaven! 'Who through the eternal Spirit' (here we have the fire) 'offered Himself without spot to God.' Just as in the book of Genesis Christ was seen mirrored through the life of Joseph, so now in the books of Samuel we see His form through the life and career of David, though the glass is more deeply stained here, making its beauty in part indistinct. But here is one who is the Lord's Anointed, a victorious one, highly-favoured, full of grace and virtue, destined for a Kingdom in which at first another rules, rejected and driven to and fro, but in the end coming in to his glory and subduing all things unto himself. The Song of Hannah at the opening of the book speaks of God's King and God's Anointed. If in the books of Kings we can detect no rift in the clouds through which the radiance from this supreme Person shines, we see a line of Kings preserved in a small Kingdom while dynasty after dynasty of Israel is swept away, and our eyes are directed forward to the fulfilment of the promise made to David's house.

As we reach the great prophets, the sun begins to send forth a clear, brilliant light, brighter than any before. It has climbed higher in the heavens now. Isaiah gives us eight definite predictions of Christ, beginning with His miraculous birth, and covering His infancy, ministry, death and burial, and the continuation of His work by the preaching of the Gospel in the world. Jeremiah tells us of the Branch raised up unto David to execute judgment and justice in the earth, whose very Name is to be 'the Lord our Righteousness.' Ezekiel has much to say of the Prince who will enter the House of God by the east gate and go out by the way by which He came. 'One Shepherd,' he calls Him, 'My servant David.' Micah tells us of One coming out of Bethlehem, whose goings forth have been from everlasting, Zechariah of the smitten Shepherd and of the meek King of Zion riding on an ass' colt, Malachi says that the Lord whom we seek shall suddenly come to His Temple. So the picture grows more definite. Our thoughts are turned to a coming One, everlasting, yet born at Bethlehem, a prophet performing works of mercy, despised, suffering, rejected, dying for His people's sins, becoming His people's righteousness.

The Psalms fill in more detail for us. 'Yet have I set My King,' Jehovah exclaims, 'upon My holy hill of Zion.' 'Kiss the Son, lest He be angry.' Then there is the crucified One of Psalm 22, the triumphant answer to the repeated question of Psalm 24, 'Who is this King of Glory?' the Good Shepherd of Psalm 23, the King of Psalm 45, David's Lord, the eternal High Priest of Psalm 110, to say nothing of the One from whose heart come the mysterious prayers of Psalms 38, 40, and 41, and many another. Can we find this great Person in the book of Proverbs, a collection of moral maxims, among which there might well be no room for Him? Who is it that we hear speaking under the name of Wisdom throughout the eighth chapter? What is the answer to the mysterious question of chap. 30, verse 4, 'Who hath ascended up into heaven, or descended? Who hath gathered the wind in His fists? Who hath bound the waters in a garment? Who hath established all the ends of the earth? what is His Name, *and what is His Son's Name,* if thou canst tell?' Job in his extremity cries, 'I know that my Redeemer liveth, and that He shall stand at the latter day upon the earth,' and speaks of a Daysman between God and man. The Song of Solomon is the love-song of a heavenly Lover. Has the Preacher anything to tell us of the Coming One? Is not his book an exception, breaking the unity in this matter? If it did, we could hardly complain, or admit the defeat of our contention. The book is short, and the writer leads us among the thick clouds of the vanities of this world. But all at once and for a moment these clouds part. Here is a heartening ray from the Scripture's Sun, whom we are beginning now to know so well. 'One Man among a thousand have I found,' says the Voice of God through the Preacher. Our hearts joyfully echo the words, and later in thunderous tones that same Voice cries openly from heaven, 'This is My beloved Son, in whom I am well-pleased.' Even the little book of Esther, in which Jehovah's Name is not openly mentioned, speaks of one whom the King delighteth to honour, carrying on in this connection quite closely the thought of Ecclesiastes. The prophet Daniel knows of Messiah the Prince, who was to be cut off and have nothing, knows the very epoch of His appearance on earth, and in his own experience knew of a Hand that touched him and set him upon his knees and the palms of his hands. In Ezra-Nehemiah we read of Zerubbabel and Jeshua, pictures of the Governor and High Priest to come, and as we open the last of Old Testament books we find a long genealogy, whose collateral lives are dealt with shortly and quickly, but which passes itself onward and onward through time to a point in the future to be reached in the beginning verses of Matthew's Gospel.

At length we open our New Testaments, and all clouds disperse. We are in a blaze of noon-day glory. Henceforward Jesus Christ, revealed, incarnate, holds the field. Prophecy is unsealed. 'The book of the generation of Jesus Christ.' How well the first evangelist in his opening verses lays the rock foundations of the Gospel! 'Thou shalt call His Name Jesus, for He shall save His people from their sins.' 'His Name shall be called Emmanuel.' We pass four times through the life of Jesus Christ, three times along ways that lie parallel, the fourth by one where all the time we see the Divine Majesty flashing through His human life. Every section, every verse describes and is centred upon Jesus Christ, Emmanuel, the King, the Servant of God, the Son of man, the Everlasting Father. And the purpose of His coming into the world is as plain as may be. 'The Son of man is come to seek and to save that which was lost.' Thus the death of the One, so eagerly foreseen by the Old Testament prophets, the description of which occupies the central place in Scripture, is found to be the solution of the problem raised by the three great doctrines we considered in the second section of this paper, the holiness of God, the responsibility of man, and the sinfulness of man's nature.

There is not a New Testament book among those left which does not centre round Christ. The Acts describes how the Apostles Peter and Paul went out to preach Him, a Prince and a Saviour, the one to the House of Israel, the other to the ends of the earth. 'Who art Thou, Lord?' '*I am Jesus.*' That is the central scene and conversation of the book. 'Be patient therefore, brethren,' says the Apostle James, 'until the coming of the Lord.' Jesus Christ is to the Apostle Peter a Lamb without spot, whose precious blood redeems where gold and silver are of no avail. 'We beheld His power and coming,' he says, as he looks back to select the most striking of the sacred memories of his life. The Apostle John writes that those to whom he writes might join in a fellowship which is with God and with His Son Jesus Christ. For him the supreme error is to deny that Jesus Christ has come in the flesh. Again his heart is warmed with tenderness towards those who went for His Name's sake, the beloved and glorious Name, which it is not even necessary for him as he speaks of it to mention. There are those against whom the Apostle Jude would warn his hearers. Who are they but those who by teaching and conduct deny our only Master and Lord Jesus Christ?

What shall we say of the writings of the Apostle of the Gentiles? His first great foundation epistle expounds the Gospel of God concerning His Son, and centres round the One whom God set forth a propitiation through faith in His blood. He knows that as in Adam all die, so in Christ shall all be made alive. The love of Christ constrains him. The life that he lives in the flesh he lives by faith of the Son of God who loved him and gave Himself for him. In Him, he tells us, we have the redemption, the forgiveness of sins. To the Apostle, to live is Christ. God has highly exalted Him and given Him a Name that is above every name, that in the Name of Jesus every knee should bow. 'Let this mind be in you,' he says, 'as was in Christ Jesus.' Again Christ is the First Cause, the Firstborn of every creature (that is to say, 'begotten of His Father before all worlds')'. 'The Lord Himself,' the Apostle tells us in radiant expectation, 'shall descend from heaven with a shout.' 'The Lord Jesus shall be revealed from heaven in flames of fire.' Then the Apostle, or one well taught by him, shows us how God has spoken His last word, having 'in these last days spoken unto us by His Son, Who being the brightness of His glory and the express image of His Person, by whom also He made the worlds, when He had by Himself purged our sins, sat down on the right hand of the Majesty on high.' 'There is one Mediator,' says the Apostle, 'between God and man, the Man Christ Jesus.' 'Remember,' he says, 'Jesus Christ raised from the dead, of the seed of David, according to my gospel.' He tells us to wait for the blessed hope and appearance of the glory of our great God and Saviour Christ Jesus. He rejoices in being the prisoner of Christ Jesus.

Finally, once more we reach the great epilogue. What do we find? The great High Priest in His glorious majesty going about trimming His lamps, His face as when the sun shines in its strength. 'I am He that liveth and was dead, and behold, I am alive for evermore, and have the keys of death and of the grave.' We see also the Lamb in the midst of the throne, and One riding to victory upon a white horse.

Here after all in the Christ of God lies the miracle of the unity of the Bible, which is not a literary miracle only, great as that aspect of it may be, but a miracle of the grace and love shown by the Supreme Holiness to a fallen, needy and miserable world.

אִגֶּרֶת אֶל־הָעִבְרִים

1 הָאֱלֹהִים אֲשֶׁר־דִּבֶּר מִקֶּדֶם פְּעָמִים רַבּוֹת וּבִדְרָכִים א
שׁוֹנִים אֶל־הָאָבוֹת בְּיַד הַנְּבִיאִים דִּבֶּר אֵלֵינוּ בְּאַחֲרִית
2 הַיָּמִים הָאֵלֶּה בְּיַד בְּנוֹ׃ אֲשֶׁר־נְתָנוֹ לְיוֹרֵשׁ כֹּל וְגַם־
3 עָשָׂה בְיָדוֹ אֶת־הָעוֹלָמוֹת׃ וְהוּא זֹהַר כְּבוֹדוֹ וְצֶלֶם
עַצְמוּתוֹ וְנֹשֵׂא כֹל בִּדְבַר גְּבוּרָתוֹ וְאַחֲרֵי עֲשׂתוֹ בְנַפְשׁוֹ
4 טָהֳרַת חַטֹּאתֵינוּ יָשַׁב לִימִין הַגְּדֻלָּה בַּמְּרוֹמִים׃ וַיִּגְדַּל
מְאֹד מִן־הַמַּלְאָכִים כְּפִי אֲשֶׁר הַשֵּׁם אֲשֶׁר נָחַל יָקָר
5 הוּא מִשֶּׁלָּהֶם׃ כִּי אֶל־מִי מִן־הַמַּלְאָכִים אָמַר מֵעוֹלָם
בְּנִי אַתָּה אֲנִי הַיּוֹם יְלִדְתִּיךָ וְעוֹד אֲנִי אֶהְיֶה־לּוֹ לְאָב
6 וְהוּא יִהְיֶה־לִּי לְבֵן׃ וּבַהֲבִיאוֹ אֶת־הַבְּכוֹר שֵׁנִית
7 לָעוֹלָם אֹמֵר וְהִשְׁתַּחֲווּ־לוֹ כָּל־אֱלֹהִים׃ הֵן עַל־
הַמַּלְאָכִים הוּא אֹמֵר עֹשֶׂה מַלְאָכָיו רוּחוֹת מְשָׁרְתָיו
8 אֵשׁ לֹהֵט׃ אַךְ עַל־הַבֵּן אֹמֵר כִּסְאֲךָ אֱלֹהִים עוֹלָם וָעֶד
9 שֵׁבֶט מִישֹׁר שֵׁבֶט מַלְכוּתֶךָ׃ אָהַבְתָּ צֶּדֶק וַתִּשְׂנָא רֶשַׁע
עַל־כֵּן מְשָׁחֲךָ אֱלֹהִים אֱלֹהֶיךָ שֶׁמֶן שָׂשׂוֹן מֵחֲבֵרֶיךָ׃
10 וְעוֹד אַתָּה אֲדֹנָי לְפָנִים הָאָרֶץ יָסַדְתָּ וּמַעֲשֵׂה יָדֶיךָ
11 שָׁמָיִם׃ הֵמָּה יֹאבֵדוּ וְאַתָּה תַעֲמֹד וְכֻלָּם כַּבֶּגֶד יִבְלוּ׃
12 כַּלְּבוּשׁ תַּחֲלִיפֵם וְיַחֲלֹפוּ וְאַתָּה הוּא וּשְׁנוֹתֶיךָ לֹא
13 יִתָּמּוּ׃ וְאֶל־מִי מִן־הַמַּלְאָכִים אָמַר מֵעוֹלָם שֵׁב לִימִינִי
14 עַד־אָשִׁית אֹיְבֶיךָ הֲדֹם לְרַגְלֶיךָ׃ הֲלֹא־הֵם כֻּלָּם רוּחוֹת
הַשָּׁרֵת הַשְּׁלוּחִים לְשִׁמּוּשׁ בַּעֲבוּר הָעֲתִידִים לָרֶשֶׁת
אֶת־הַיְשׁוּעָה׃

THE EPISTLE OF PAUL THE APOSTLE
TO THE

HEBREWS.

CHAPTER I.

1 *Christ in these last times coming to us from the Father,* 4 *is preferred above the angels, both in person and office.*

GOD, who at sundry times and [a] in divers manners spake in time past unto the fathers by the prophets,

2 Hath [b] in these last days [c] spoken unto us by *his* Son, [d] whom he hath appointed heir of all things, [e] by whom also he made the worlds;

3 [f] Who being the brightness of *his* glory, and the express image of his person, and [g] upholding all things by the word of his power, [h] when he had by himself purged our sins, [i] sat down on the right hand of the Majesty on high;

4 Being made so much better than the angels, as [k] he hath by inheritance obtained a more excellent name than they.

5 For unto which of the angels said he at any time, [l] Thou art my Son, this day have I begotten thee? And again, [m] I will be to him a Father, and he shall be to me a Son?

6 [2] And again, when he bringeth in [n] the firstbegotten into the world, he saith, [o] And let all the angels of God worship him.

7 And [2] of the angels he saith, [p] Who maketh his angels spirits, and his ministers a flame of fire.

8 But unto the Son *he saith,* [q] Thy throne, O God, *is* for ever and ever: a sceptre of [3] righteousness *is* the sceptre of thy kingdom.

9 Thou hast loved righteousness, and hated iniquity; therefore God, *even* thy God, [r] hath anointed thee with the oil of gladness above thy fellows.

10 And, [s] Thou, Lord, in the beginning hast laid the foundation of the earth; and the heavens are the works of thine hands:

11 [t] They shall perish; but thou remainest; and they all shall wax old as doth a garment;

12 And as a vesture shalt thou fold them up, and they shall be changed: but thou art the same, and thy years shall not fail.

13 But to which of the angels said he at any time, [u] Sit on my right hand, until I make thine enemies thy footstool?

14 [x] Are they not all ministering spirits, sent forth to minister for them who shall be [y] heirs of salvation?

The Bible and Comparative Religion

By W. W. Lucas

There is an idea abroad in the theological colleges and missionary societies that Christian preachers and teachers should study the other religions of the world. The Word of God has something to say upon this subject, which should be carefully borne in mind. Deut. 13 is a chapter of terrible judgments in which the children of Israel are commanded to put to death (1) any prophet or dreamer (verses 1-5), (2) any relation (verse 6), and (3) to destroy any city (verses 12-15) which should seek to entice Israel away from Jehovah their God and Saviour.

In order to obviate this great sin, the Lord gave to Israel His laws, and He commanded them to root out all the heathen religions from the Promised Land. Deuteronomy 12.3 gives us an idea of the extent to which those heathen religions were to be shunned. They were to be utterly cast out. The Lord commanded that Israel should destroy the very *names* of the false gods, and to banish them from the Promised Land. How could those names be allowed to exist side by side with the Memorial Name of Jehovah (verse 5). This destruction of the names of the false gods obviously would not leave the children of Israel much opportunity to study the false religions which supported their claims.

In the same chapter (verse 30) Israel is told to beware that they *enquire not* after those heathen gods saying, 'How did these nations serve their gods?' This would prevent their displaying any interest in the tenets or practices of false religions.

God not only warned Israel against practising the 'doings' and *walking in* the ordinances of the heathen (Lev. 18.1-3), but forbade them even to *learn* their ways; for in Jer. 10. 1, 2 we read, 'Hear ye the word which the Lord speaketh unto you, O house of Israel: thus saith the Lord, learn not the ways of the heathen . . . for the customs (Heb., statutes) of the heathen are vain.' In the second Commandment the three snares which produce ungodliness and lead to final rejection of God are met. First, man is forbidden to *make* an image; next, he is forbidden to *bow down* (i.e., show respect) to it; and, third, he is told not to *serve* it. When this is done the offence of ungodliness is complete (Ex. 20.4, 5), and God leaves the offender to an appropriate judgment (Deut. 4. 23-28) until he repents and returns to the living God.

This warning applies to the Christian Church which is brought out of the world into a better promised land than Palestine, the Kingdom of God. The Christian is a son of Abraham by faith, and as a citizen of heaven (Phil. 3.20) he is warned to beware lest any man spoil him through philosophy or vain deceit after the tradition of men, after the rudiments of the world, and not after Christ (Col. 2.8).

The law of the Lord is perfect, and its function is to convert the soul: the judgments of the Lord are true and righteous altogether (Psa. 19.7-9). He could not bestow any recognition upon false teaching, for He is of purer eyes than to behold evil, and cannot look upon iniquity (Hab. 1.13). Our Lord, when preaching the Kingdom of God, neither taught nor directed His disciples to teach other religions. He early sought His Father's Word (Luke 2.49). 'My doctrine is not Mine,' He said, 'but His that sent Me' (John 7.16). Just before His death He said to the Father, 'I have given them Thy Word' (John 17.14), and, 'I have given unto them the *words* which Thou gavest Me' (John 17.8).

Not only was the Law thus set apart and sanctified by God in Israel, but the historical portions of His Word were proclaimed to contain the only true account of the 'former things' (Isa. 43.9, 12). The Gentile nations are described as people with eyes, but blind, and people with ears, but deaf (verse 8). Having seen and heard nothing, they are exhorted to read the history of the former things recorded by God's witnesses, Israel (verses 8-10). The heathen religions have plenty of material with which to spin mental and moral theories, but such discussions lead to nothing. O that all Christians could recover a childlike faith in the *facts* recorded in Scripture! Not until then can preaching and teaching be wholly acceptable to God and receive His fullest blessing. An Indian barrister recently wrote from Bengal asking a Christian in this country to suggest portions of Scripture suitable for an opera descriptive of the Christian religion. Similar operas, he said, had already been written and rendered by the circle to which he belonged on other religions. The opera was to be written so as not to hurt the religious susceptibilities of the Hindoos, and to show the essential oneness of the two religions—Christian and Hindoo. The reply referred to the *facts* of the Christian faith, and stated that they precluded any possibility of reconciliation between the two religions or any mere discussion of moral principles (see Deut. 33.8-10).

The Law was given in order that the days of Israel in the Promised Land might be 'as the days of heaven upon the earth' (Deut. 11.21). In the same way the Bible is given to the Christian as the hand-book of the 'kingdom of heaven.' Hence the necessity of keeping it pure and undefiled by man-made teachings.

The purpose Jehovah had in view in entrusting to Israel His Law was made known to them just before the Law was given. It was that they might be unto Him a kingdom of priests and an holy nation (Ex. 19.6), and so become supreme teachers and leaders. The blessings which were promised for obeying the Law without adding to or diminishing ought from it (Deut. 4.2) are set forth in Deut. 4.5-8, and include a recognition for the nations around. 'Behold, I have taught you statutes and judgments, even as the Lord my God commanded me, that ye should do so in the land whither ye go to possess it. Keep therefore and do them; for this is your wisdom and your understanding in the sight of the nations, which shall hear all these statutes, and say, Surely this great nation is a wise and understanding people. For what nation is there so great, who hath God so nigh unto them, as the Lord our God is in all things that we call upon Him for? And what nation is there so great, that hath statutes and judgments so righteous as all this law, which I set before you this day?'

Having seen what were the commands of God concerning the 'other religions of the world,' let us see how sadly Israel neglected the warnings given to them, and the manner in which they erred. We shall find the account of this in 2 Kings 17. They first *feared other gods* (verse 7), like many people to-day who consider that they should pay deference to every man's religious views. This deference begets in time a superstitious 'fear' of their gods. Next Israel *walked in the statutes* of the heathen (verse 8). This alienated their minds from Jehovah, for we read that when He told them to turn from their evil ways and keep His commandments and His statutes, according to *all* the law which He commanded their fathers, they would not hear. Indeed we read that by this time they *preferred* the statutes of the heathen, and did not *believe in* the Lord their God (verses 13, 14). It is bad to prefer false teaching to the Word of God, but we now observe that this preference led to a want of faith in Jehovah Himself, for we are told that they would not hear, and they *did not believe in* the Lord their God (verse 14). As a consequence they then actively *rejected* His statutes and His covenant, and followed after vanity. If a man rejects the Word of God there is nothing else for him to follow after. Believing no longer in God, and having rejected His statutes, they develop a partiality for the *heathen themselves.* When they followed after vanity, 'They went after the heathen that were round about them, concerning whom the Lord had charged them that they should not do like them.'

Matters continued to go from bad to worse in a natural sequence. In verse 16 we learn that they then left *all* the commandments of the Lord. Their career in the Promised Land is finally consummated in verse 17, where we read that they 'sold themselves to do evil in the sight of the Lord.' Having commenced to err by learning the ways of the heathen, Israel in due course ended in moral as well as in doctrinal ruin. The Lord then cast out from His sight the whole seed of Israel (2 Kings 17.20), and brought upon them 'the fruit of their thoughts, because they have not hearkened to My own words, nor to My law, but rejected it' (Jer. 6.19). Finally, Israel having been cast out of the Land which is the glory of all lands, those very heathen nations whose ways they had learned came and occupied their beloved Land, and set up and worshipped their heathen gods there (2 Kings 17.24-41).

It is a grave error for young Christians who are Sunday School teachers, and those who are preparing to become preachers of the gospel at home, or in the mission fields, to read books which teach that heathen religions have a 'comparative value.' Those who study the Bible deeply, and with a heart full of faith, find that it meets every need and solves every problem in human life and experience (2 Tim. 3.15, 17). The Bible, therefore, should be the dominating study for Christians on all questions of faith and morals. It is not necessary for missionaries to learn the errors of the false religions in order to combat them successfully. They have simply to 'bear witness to the truth,' as Christ did, and to defeat error by truth. The heathen will bring forward their own difficulties and opinions, and a man who knows his Bible can meet them from God's Word. God invites all the nations to do this (Isa. 43.9), and He calls Israel (verse 10) and the Church (1 Tim. 3.15; John 17.17) to be His witnesses—witnesses who were saved by Him, and became qualified to witness for Him when there was no false god among them (Isa. 43.12). When there is no false god, God can say, 'I have declared and saved, and I have showed.' The Christian should not go to the nations with natural religions in his head. He has to witness for God only, and therefore he needs only the Word of God. Let not the Christian sow tares. Many others will do it. Offences will come, but woe unto those by whom they do come. Christians must sow only the 'good seed.' The good seed is the Word of God. False teaching reaches our notice readily enough from many sources. It is not necessary to acquire it by study.

A knowledge of God's Word and its application under the guidance and power of the Holy Spirit provide light which the heathen require. Let them expound their views, and the Scriptures and the power of God will condemn those views without any previous study of false teachings on the part of the missionary. The Word of God is a sword, which, when used by the Holy Spirit, is capable of effecting all the Divine purposes connected with mankind, and it is not rendered more effective by an admixture of base metal with the pure steel. How earnestly Christians should contend for the faith and for that alone!

The Greeks were the most intellectual of the Gentile nations, but the Apostle Paul told them that they were ignorant of Divine things. Their ideals were mere 'idols of the heart' (Ezek. 14.3-5), and gave them no entrance into the Kingdom of God. Did the Greek religion awaken the Apostle's curiosity or interest? No, we read that his spirit was stirred within him (Acts 17.16), and his one and only concern was to preach Christ to them. Their 'superstition' and their 'devotions' failed to arouse his admiration. In reminding them that their poets affirmed God to be the Creator of all, Paul was merely affirming a truth that was universally known. It was not part of a creed. A poet, ordinarily, is a secular person who echoes the sentiments of the human heart, and not a teacher of revealed truth. This is further shown from the fact that Paul called the poets, 'your own' poets. Had they been divinely inspired they would have been God's poets and writers, as are the writers of the Scriptures. The Athenians, we read, spent their time to 'hear or tell' some new *thing* (Acts 17.21). Paul preached a Person—God, who made the world and all things therein, seeing that He is Lord of heaven and earth—and who made of one blood all nations of men—that they should seek the Lord (Acts 17.24-27). Man was therefore made *that he might seek after the Lord.*

A Christian's duty is not to hear or tell some new thing, nor should he study heathen religions and philosophies with that end in view. He is commissioned to proclaim to men the fact that God now commandeth all men everywhere to repent; because He hath appointed a day in the which He will judge the world in righteousness by that Man whom He hath ordained; whereof He hath given assurance unto all men in that He hath raised Him from the dead (Acts 17.30, 31).

A 2,000 Years Old Manuscript of Isaiah Discovered

By P. J. Wiseman

Early this year (1948) some Arabs unexpectedly discovered a number of earthenware jars in a cave near the Dead Sea. These jars were obviously very ancient, they were covered with linen and the linen covered with a black wax in order to protect the contents from damage. When the jars were opened they were found to contain ancient manuscripts.

By the end of February of this year some of the manuscripts had reached the Syrian monastery of St. Mark, in Jerusalem. Two members of the fraternity asked the experts in the American School of Oriental Research to examine four of them; two were of parchment and two of leather.

On examination one of these rolls was found to be the complete text of the Book of Isaiah. Students will be aware that the oldest manuscript of Isaiah hitherto in our possession is a copy made in the ninth century A.D. We know, however, that it is a faithful copy of copies written at a much earlier date and that it does not materially differ from the roll of the prophet Isaiah from which our Lord read in the synagogue at Nazareth.

One very ancient manuscript of the Old Testament was found some years ago, but it is only a tiny fragment containing a part of the sixth chapter of the Book of Deuteronomy and including the Ten Commandments. This is known as the 'Nash Papyrus' and is very ancient; from the type of Hebrew script and other characteristics scholars have determined that it must have been written in the first century B.C.

Fortunately one of the experts who examined the newly found roll of the Book of Isaiah was acquainted with the script used in this fragment called the 'Nash Papyrus,' and the similarity of the writing impressed him. It became apparent that the long manuscript of Isaiah which he was investigating must be as old as the tiny fragment of the Book of Deuteronomy and therefore a thousand years older than any other manuscript of Isaiah hitherto discovered.

Photographs of the ancient type of script used in writing this newly discovered manuscript of Isaiah have now reached America and Professor Albright, of John Hopkins University, who some years ago identified the date of the 'Nash Papyrus,' has stated that the manuscript must have been written at an even earlier date, not later than the second century before Christ.

Students will be glad to learn one fact of considerable importance. This newly discovered manuscript is complete up to and including the sixty-sixth chapter. Readers of the *Bible League Quarterly* will be aware of the many critical conjectures about the composition of Isaiah. The book has been divided into two main sections—chapters 1 to 39 and chapters 40 to 66,—but not even the whole of the first section has been allotted to Isaiah the son of Amoz, while chapters 40 to the end have generally been attributed to a so-called Second, or Deutero-Isaiah. Many of the critics were not content with these two main divisions and asserted that many of the later chapters were merely appendices and had been written at an even later date than that of the so-called Second Isaiah. They said that some of the later chapters of the second section were written at a late date by some person or persons unknown who attached them to the end of the Second Isaiah. Other critics produced the idea that at some date later still, an unknown editor or editors had inserted editorial additions to these added chapters.

Further attempts were then made by such writers as Kayser (*Die Theologie des Alt Testament in iher geschichtlichen Entwickelung dargestellt,* page 191). Others declared that the later chapters exhibited 'an advanced apocalyptic' and it was argued that consequently this must bring these portions down to a very late date. Some said that the date of these appendices must be placed in the time of the Ptolemy and Seleucid empires, that is between 312-64 B.C. Stade, for instance, maintained that some of the events recorded in these chapters were written after the persecution of Antiochus Epiphanes in 169 B.C.

This new discovery now puts us in possession of a manuscript complete to the last chapter, written in the second century before Christ, and completed by the scribe before the dates on which many of the critics asserted portions of it were written. This newly found roll is no doubt a copy of a manuscript which must have been written some time earlier. Although we await further detailed information, that which we already have makes it clear that the conjectures of the critics are obviously absurd

CHINESE BIBLE

'Thy word is a lamp unto my feet,
and a light unto my path.'—Ps. 119.105.

Supposed Contradictions in the Scriptures

By J. Willoughby

Some have supposed that in the Scriptures there are contradictions by which the doctrine of their Divine Verbal Inspiration is shown to be false. There is, however, a vast difference between merely *seeming* contradictions and *real* contradictions.

I was once listening to a trial in the Rolls-Court in Dublin. There had been a dispute in connection with some place of worship, and on one occasion a number of persons prevented a certain minister from preaching therein. At the trial the minister, in reference to this occasion, was asked the question, 'Were you able to preach?' His answer in effect was, 'No.' The caretaker of the building, when giving evidence regarding the same minister and the same occasion, was asked the question, 'Was he able to preach?' His answer in effect was 'Yes.' The two answers seemed flatly contradictory. There was, however, only a *seeming* contradiction. The minister meant that on the occasion in question he was prevented from preaching. The caretaker meant that the minister possessed preaching ability.

Suppose the following: Some person tells me that in a certain town there is a general who has a brother, an admiral. Some other person tells me that the admiral has no brother. These may seem to me to be contradictory statements, until I discover that the general is a lady in the Salvation Army. If in the Bible what looked as like real contradictions as the foregoing at first did, sensible people would say that some explanations might show the statements to be consistent, while foolish people would say that the statements exploded the doctrine of Verbal Inspiration.

According to Ezekiel the Lord said that Zedekiah would be brought to Babylon. According to the same prophet the Lord said that Zedekiah would not see Babylon. These statements might seem to us to be contradictory, if we had not read in Jeremiah 52.11, or in 2 Kings 25.7, that before Zedekiah was brought to Babylon his eyes were put out.

According to Luke the men who journeyed with Paul to Damascus heard the voice speaking to him from heaven. According to Paul himself they did not hear the voice of Him that spoke from heaven (Acts 9.7; 22.9). These statements might seem flatly contradictory, if we were not aware that the Greek verb rendered by 'hear,' like the English verb 'hear,' sometimes means 'understand.' Luke meant that those journeying with Paul heard the sound of the voice; Paul meant that they did not understand its meaning. Possibly the Lord then spoke not in Aramaic or Greek, but in Old Testament Hebrew which perhaps only Paul there and then understood. In the original of our Lord's utterance the word for 'Saul' is not the Greek form, but is a transliteration of the O.T. form.

In Mark 10.46 we read, *"As He went out of Jericho* . . . blind Bartimeus, the son of Timeus, sat by the highway-side begging," and according to Mark, Bartimeus cried to the Lord, and received his sight. In Luke 18.35 we read, '*As He was come nigh unto Jericho* a certain blind man sat by the way-side begging,' and according to Luke the blind man cried to the Lord and received his sight. The contexts appear to show clearly that both passages refer to the same event, but according to the former the Lord performed the miracle '*as He went out of Jericho*' or shortly after, and according to the latter, '*as He was come nigh unto Jericho.*' Must there not certainly be a contradiction here? Not at all! It is said that in apostolic days there were in Palestine two places, each called Jericho, with the same road running through both, and manifestly if the miracle had been performed after the Lord had gone out of the one, and before He had entered the other, both statements would be perfectly true. It would not be at all remarkable, if a new city were built near an old city, and called by the same name. It is said that after apostolic days there were three places in Palestine each called Jericho.

According to Matt. 20.29 on one occasion when the Lord had passed through Jericho two blind men cried to Him and received their sight, but, manifestly, if Bartimeus and another blind man thus cried and received their sight, it would be still true that Bartimeus had cried and received his sight. There would be no contradiction.

I think some people suppose the accounts of what was written on the cross to be contradictory, but look at the following diagram:

'This is	Jesus	of Nazareth,	the King of the Jews.'
'This is	Jesus,	....	the King of the Jews' (Matt. 27.37).
....			the King of the Jews' (Mark 15.26).
This is	....		the King of the Jews' (Luke 23.38).
....	Jesus	of Nazareth,	the King of the Jews' (John 19.19).

Let us suppose the following: Four persons meet a man who says, 'I am going to London to see a friend who is unwell.' According to one of the four, the man said, 'I am going to London.' According to another he said, 'I am going to see a friend.' According to another he said, 'I am going to see a friend who is unwell.' The four statements are different, nevertheless each statement is correct. No one of the four persons says he is giving the man's statement in full.

Now consider the diagram. Putting the four accounts of the evangelists together, we see that written on the cross was the sentence, 'This is Jesus of Nazareth, the King of the Jews.' According to Matthew there was written thereon, 'This is Jesus, the King of the Jews,' and this is correct. According to Mark there was written, 'The King of the Jews,' and this is correct. According to Luke there was written, 'This is the King of the Jews,' and this is correct. According to John there was written, 'Jesus of Nazareth, the King of the Jews,' and this is correct. Each statement is verbally accurate both in the English and in the original. No one of the Evangelists says he is giving the writing in full. There is no contradiction whatever.

Some think the following statements to be contradictory: 'So David bought the threshing-floor and the oxen for fifty shekels of silver' (2 Sam. 24.24). 'So David gave to Ornan for the place six hundred shekels of gold' (1 Chron. 21.25). The 'place' referred to in the latter was the 'place of this threshing-floor' (v. 22). The floor was, of course, only a very small part of the area on which the temple was afterwards built on Mount Moriah, and it may be that the 'place of this threshing-floor' was the rest of that area. In the two passages two purchasing transactions which may have taken place on the same day are referred to—the giving of the 50 shekels of silver for the floor and the oxen, and the giving of the six hundred shekels of gold for the 'place of this threshing-floor.' There is no contradiction.

Although there may *appear* to be contradictions in the Bible we may be quite certain that there are no *real* contradictions in view of the very strong reasons which we have for believing that the Scriptures were all written or dictated by prophets of God, including apostles, and that the words thus written or dictated were all supernaturally given by the Spirit of God.

Witnesses to Isaiah's Authorship of the Prophecy of Isaiah

By W. E. Dalling

While we have the new evidence of the true antiquity of the prophecy of Isaiah before us in the two-thousand-year-old manuscript, confirming the view that it was truly the work of one man whose name it bears, it is helpful to remember the witness of many ancient writers, who knew nothing of the jig-saw book the critics play with.

From the original simple theory of two authors of Isaiah, Ewald has postulated seven; but this is not complex enough for Cheyne who hints that there might well be more. Most critics agree in suggesting three main parts, the work of different authors: Chaps. 1 to 39; 40 to 55; and 56 to the end. They attribute the second part, 40 to 55, to an unknown writer, Deutero-Isaiah , and the third part to Trito-Isaiah.

In the New Testament Isaiah is referred to by name as the writer of the book no less than twenty-one times, and quotations and allusions to the book number nearly ninety. In bringing forward the witness of the New Testament writers we will confine ourselves to the direct mentions of Isaiah as the writer of the parts erroneously rejected by the critics, only stating the other references where Isaiah is named from Isaiah 1 to 39, without comment. Nor do we lack confidence when we set the witness of the inspired writers of the Old and New Testaments over against the confused and conflicting conjectures of the critics, and declare that the former speak with divine authority no God-fearing believer dares to deny.

The authority of the statements of the critics of this prophecy is destroyed by their mutually destructive views. There are but two things on which all are agreed:

(a) That no prophecy can be accepted.

(b) That the authors of chapters 40 to 66 are unknown.

But when we examine their reasons for these bold statements, we find:

(a) That their 'evidence' is subjective.

(b) That they disagree as to what *is* evidence.

Some base their divisive findings on alleged differences in style, while others declare that no argument from style is valid! Thus it is clear that their castle of criticism built on the clouds of imaginative hypotheses, has neither substance nor foundation, but is blown about with every wind of changeful minds. Evidently it was as impossible for the modernist's god to have named Cyrus two centuries before he was born, as it was to predict the virgin birth of our Lord, and the deliverance of Israel from captivity! Such revelations present no difficulty to an Almighty God—the God of John the Baptist, Matthew, Paul, and of all true believers.

But what of our witnesses?

The Witness of Ezra.

This valuable evidence from the sixth century B.C. shows Cyrus's knowledge of Isaiah 44.28: 'Thus saith Cyrus king of Persia, The Lord God of heaven hath . . . charged me to build him an house at Jerusalem, which is in Judah' (Ezra 1.2).

Isaiah's prophecy concerning Cyrus has been incontinently rejected as ever having been written by him on no other ground than that of human unbelief; for the critics have roundly declared that Cyrus could not have been named nearly two hundred years before he was born. Nor could he have been by an uninspired writer—but is God limited in His knowledge and His revelation? Cyrus accepted the command, and declared that it was because of Isaiah's prophecy that he ordered the Temple to be rebuilt and handed back the vessels of the house of the Lord to Sheshbazzar the prince of Judah. Evidently Ezra and Cyrus knew nothing of the critic's puppet Deutero-Isaiah.

The Witness of Ben Sira.

Jesus the son of Sirach, also called Ben Sira, was the author of Ecclesiasticus in the very early part of the second century B.C. He gives valuable evidence to Isaiah's authorship of the parts assigned by the critics to Deutero-Isaiah and to Trito-Isaiah. For in Ecclesiasticus 48.24, 25 he makes reference to Isaiah: 'He saw by an excellent spirit what should come to pass at the last, and he comforted them that mourned in Sion. He showed what should come to pass for ever, and secret things or ever they came.' This is an unmistakable reference to Isaiah 40 and the subsequent chapters. Evidently Ben Sira, who lived over twenty-one centuries nearer to the time of Isaiah than do the critics of to-day, knew nothing of the creatures of unsanctified imagination. No Deutero- or Trito-Isaiah existed for him.

The Witness of Josephus.

' "Thus saith Cyrus the King: Since God Almighty hath appointed me to be king of the habitable earth, I believe that he is that God which the nation of the Israelites worship; for indeed he foretold my name by the prophets, and that I should build him a house at Jerusalem, in the country of Judea." This was known to Cyrus by his reading the book which Isaiah left behind him of his prophecies . . .' This testimony was given by Josephus in the first century A.D., in Antiquities 11.1, para. 1, 2; and clearly confirms the witness of Ezra, showing that this educated Jewish historian had no doubts of Isaiah's authorship.

The Witness of John the Baptist.

The voice of no authorized prophet of Jehovah had been heard since that of Malachi, till John the Baptist burst forth from the desert with his searing message from God. Great was the wonder, and various the conjectures of his hearers. His identity and authority were of the utmost importance. He was pressed to declare himself. What was the reply that he gave to the priests and Levites who had been sent by the Jews of Jerusalem? John boldly claimed that Isaiah had prophesied his coming: 'I am the voice of one crying in the wilderness, Make straight the way of the Lord, as said the prophet Esaias' (John 1.23 and Isa. 40.3).

This appeal to Isaiah's prophecy is the earliest recorded in the New Testament. Further, it is from the section of Isaiah unanimously rejected by the critics and assigned by them to some unknown writer. John the Baptist lived comparatively near the time assigned by the critics for the writing of this part of the book. That John was 'filled with the Holy Ghost, even from his mother's womb' (Luke 1.15) is a matter of indifference to the destroyers of God's Word. While it is true that John was neither sinless nor infallible, it is easier to believe the testimony of this Spirit-filled prophet as to the author of Isaiah 40.3, than it is to believe the guesses of those who avowedly deny prophetic utterances.

The Witness of Matthew.

John the Baptist made his appeal to Isaiah 40.3, so does Matthew (Matt. 3.3). Matthew was one of the twelve. During his companying with his Lord it is evident he was not taught to reject this part of Isaiah as not being his work. The Lord warned against false teaching, tradition, and wrong exegesis, but it is clear that no doubt of Isaiah's prophecy mars Matthew's mind. It was to Isaiah God gave the prophecy concerning John the Baptist, and Matthew's faith was confirmed as he saw the inspired record fulfilled before his wondering eyes.

While Matthew appeals to the critics' Deutero-Isaiah to prove that John the Baptist is the forerunner of the Messiah, he turns to the same section to show that Isaiah prophesied of the Messiah Himself. There he finds that the healing ministry of our Lord was declared in Isaiah 53.4, 'When the even was come, they brought unto him many that were possessed with devils' (demons) 'and he cast out the spirits with his word, and healed all that were sick: That it might be fulfilled which was spoken by Esaias the prophet, saying, Himself took our infirmities, and bare our sicknesses' (Matt. 8.16, 17). Matthew saw this prophecy fulfilled in rich and glowing detail. No unknown writer happened by chance to foretell the future, but Isaiah the Spirit-filled prophet was the bearer of the glad news of healing and life to come.

Matthew's other reference is in Matt. 12.17-21, where he quotes Isa. 42.1-4, as showing Isaiah's true prophecy concerning the ministry and methods of our Lord. Isaiah's prophecy, knowing no bounds of time, because his words were from the timeless God, sees through the centuries the outflow of divine grace to the Gentiles through the Messiah who had the Spirit without measure. Matthew trained by none other than the Lord Himself, recognises both the writer and Subject of the prophecy. This disciple is unaware of the 'assured' findings of the critics. He quotes from Isa. 9.1, 2, as well as from 42, and mentions but *one* writer, Isaiah, for all his quotations from this prophecy.

The Witness of Luke.

Luke, a Gentile physician, well trained in the best Greek culture of his day, is a more independent witness than Matthew or Paul. His medical training would have made his powers of observation and analysis acute, while his Gentile origin would free him from Hebrew traditions. His attitude to the Old Testament, and to the prophecy of Isaiah will be important.

What do we find? Surely his clear mind will penetrate the subterfuge of any imposter who might have tampered with Holy Writ! Any Deutero- or Trito-Isaiah will be unmasked, for Luke wrote his gospel and history only some three centuries after the date assigned by the critics to some of their unknown writers, who, they allege, have added to the book.

But no! Luke quotes from Isa. 40.3-5 and Isa. 53.7, 8. Here is his witness when referring to the ministry of John the Baptist: 'As it is written in the book of the words of Esaias the prophet, saying, The voice of one crying in the wilderness, Prepare ye the way of the Lord, make his paths straight' (see Luke 3.4-6).

In Acts 8.28-33 we have a twofold witness, that of Luke and of Philip. The evangelist had joined the Ethiopian who 'read the prophet Esaias,' the portion being Isa. 53. Luke records that this was Isaiah's prophecy, and Philip recognises the Lord Jesus as the suffering Servant of Isaiah 53.

Luke still held the view of the authorship of Isaiah that he held when he wrote his gospel. Evidently no one had convinced him that Isaiah had not written it all—even if any had tried! There is power yet in his writings because he had no doubts about his God's ability to forecast the future. He so gloried in God's power and knowledge that we find no attempts made to reduce the sacred oracles to the dull level of mere human history.

The Witness of Paul.

Paul refers to six passages in Isaiah in his quotations where he mentions the name of the prophet; four are Rom. 9.29 from Isa. 1.9; Acts 28.25-27 from Isa. 6.9, 10; Rom. 9.27,28 from Isa. 10.22, 23; and Rom. 15.12 from Isa. 11.10. The other two passages are from the critics' Deutero-Isaiah: Rom. 10.16 from Isa. 53.1 and Rom. 10.20, 21 from Isa. 65.1, 2.

Let us remember that Paul cannot be dismissed as unworthy of a hearing, for he was a scholar, and had been taught by Gamaliel, the greatest Hebrew teacher of his day. It is clear that Paul has not been convinced by Gamaliel that Isaiah was not the author of his prophecy. There is no evidence that Gamaliel ever held such a view. When Paul finds many in Israel rejecting the Messiah he quotes from the rejected section a prophecy of this disbelief: 'Lord, who hath believed our report?' (Rom. 10.16). For him this is no unauthoritative word of some unknown writer, who audaciously palms off his work on Israel as the work of the God-inspired prophet Isaiah. But he appeals to it as a divine prophecy then being fulfilled before his eyes.

Nor is this the only occasion that Paul appeals to this section of the prophecy. He sees the mighty sweep of inspired thought that not only declares Israel's disobedience, but embraces the knowledge of the Gentiles' reactions. 'But Esaias is very bold, and saith, I was found of them that sought me not; I was made manifest unto them that asked not after me' (Rom. 10.20, 21).

Again Paul's appeal is one confidently made to an accepted prophecy. No poisonous breath of doubt blows across the sacred page. Paul's God was greater far than the god of the modernist. His God's power and knowledge were not exhausted by the interpretation of past and current history, they embraced the remote future. Jehovah's eye pierces the centuries. The god acclaimed by the critic is one whose sight is limited as man's, whose sphere of knowledge is bounded by the horizon of the Present, and whose revelation can cast no ray of light into the dim recesses of the future. Paul sought to turn the thoughts of the Athenians from the Unknown god to Him whom he knew; from the god of man's speculation to the true God of revelation. That God could reveal the future was no stumbling-block to Paul, nor should it be to any true man of faith trusting in a living God.

The Witness of John.

John quotes Isaiah and mentions him by name twice. John 12.39-41 refers to Isaiah 6,9, 10; and John 12.38 refers to Isaiah 53.1, this latter passage being in a disputed section of the prophecy. John wrote of our Lord: 'But though he had done so many miracles before them, yet they believed not on him: that the saying of Esaias the prophet might be fulfilled, which he spake, Lord, who hath believed our report, and to whom hath the arm of the Lord been revealed?'

The apostle John was one who had been the most intimate with our Lord. It is incredible that the great Expositor of the Old Testament could teach John for over three years and not warn him against forgeries in the Holy Scriptures, had they existed. Nor can we believe that the critics know more about the Old Testament than did our Lord—the Incarnate Word.

The oceans of divine truth imparted to the apostle are unruffled by the winds of false doctrines. No clouds of doubt cast their dark shadows there. The Isaiah of Isa. 6 is the Isaiah of Isa. 53; no destructive critic's disfiguring scalpel dismembers the prophecy for John, it is a God-breathed unity.

The Witness of our Lord.

Twice does our Lord mention Isaiah and his prophecy. Isa. 6.9, 10 is quoted in Matt. 13.14, 15; Isa. 29.13 in Matt. 15.7, 8. Once He reads from Isa. 61.1, 2 (Luke 4.17-19).

This last quotation is from the critics' Trito-Isaiah. If the validity and authority of this were in question, if some writer had dared to palm off his writings as those of God's inspired prophet Isaiah, is it conceivable that He who is the Truth would both accept them and read them publicly, declaring their fulfilment and so perpetuating the 'pious' fraud?

Our own personal contacts with a modernist principal of a theological college, have shown that denial of the authority and inspiration of the Old Testament always reflects upon the knowledge and teaching of our Lord. It would be beyond the scope of our subject if we dealt at length with this question, but it is necessary that we should again declare that He who is Truth could never teach or perpetuate anything false.

Our minds will be neither darkened nor confused by His teaching. He gives confidence and not doubt. He speaks with authority, not with empty words of confused thinking. He gives objective facts and not subjective theories. The foundation of His teaching is the rock of inspired truth, and not the sand of shifting speculation.

Against the literary butchery of the critics we have heard the witness of Ezra, Ben Sira and Josephus, all of whom tell nothing of the dismemberment of Isaiah's prophecy. To their witness we have added more from the New Testament: John the Baptist, Matthew, Luke, Paul and John all testify to the unity of the book. The New Testament writers have quoted from the various parts of the prophecy, naming *one* writer only—Isaiah.

Lastly, the greatest of all is the testimony of our infallible Lord. With confidence and in public He reads the ancient prophecy, declaring its fulfilment in His own appearance and work.

Let us not heed modern critical statements born of pride and unbelief! No presumptuous rejector of divine truth must rob us of this priceless treasure. But as humbly we read the inspired Word, and ponder the glorious revelation of Isaiah, God will speak truth and life to our souls. We shall know the truth, and the truth will set us free.

The New Testament Use of the Old Testament Scriptures

By Fred Mitchell

It is quite patent to any reader of New Testament Scripture that it is shot through with Old Testament quotation and allusion, so much so that the New Testament will be little understood, and certainly not fully appreciated, apart from the background provided by the Old Testament.

A story was told some time ago of a missionary handing an epistle to a native. This native read through the portion in his own language and came back saying, 'Please, sir, this does not begin at the beginning. It refers me back to something which was written before.' The missionary then gave him a copy of Matthew's Gospel. Imagine the feelings of the missionary when a few days later the native appeared a second time, pointing out that this referred him further back still. The Old Testament is indeed the background of the New or, to quote Augustine's well-known couplet:—

'In the Old the New lies hid,
In the New the Old lies open.'

Otherwise, how can we begin to understand the full New Testament teaching of atonement, redemption and the forgiveness of sins unless we are acquainted with—

the Exodus from Egypt,
the Offerings in Leviticus, and
the Day of Atonement?

For lack of such acquaintance, one of our modern preachers, dealing with our beloved and basic doctrine of Atonement by Blood, said recently, 'When I forgive my son, I don't require that there shall be any atonement or shedding of blood. I forgive him because I love him.' But we do well to remember, and this the Old Testament serves to do, that God thinks differently from this minister on the basic subject of sin.

Number of Quotations.

The number of Old Testament quotations in the New Testament has been variously estimated by different scholars. One well-known Bible student finds 160 direct quotations. A well-known Handbook of the Bible gives 263 direct quotations and 376 indirect quotations, but two such scholars as Westcott and Hort say there are 1,279 quotations from the Old Testament in the New Testament. Again, if you take Westcott and Hort's figures, out of those 1,279 they give 61 quotations from Isaiah, while there is another very devout student of Scripture who says the New Testament contains 122 quotations from Isaiah. The numbers vary greatly but they all go to emphasize the very large portion of the New Testament which is taken up by Old Testament quotations direct and indirect and by allusion to its history and teaching.

The Purpose of the Old Testament Quotations in the N.T.

These may be said to fall into three main classes.

The Old Testament is quoted for Argument, for Comment and for Comparison. Let us examine these three classes.

For Argument—and that in a number of ways.

First, *History in the Old Testament is recalled, Mark* 2.25.

You will remember that when the disciples were plucking the ears of corn Jesus said, 'Have ye never read what David did, when he had need and was an hungered.' History is recalled in argument.

Secondly, *Prediction is fulfilled,* John 19:24.

When they were casting lots for Christ's robe they said, 'Let us not rend it, but cast lots for it, whose it shall be, that the Scripture might be fulfilled, which saith, They parted my raiment amongst them and for my vesture they did cast lots.' And on the day of Pentecost, Acts 2:16, Peter said in answer to the question, 'What meaneth this?','This is that which was spoken by the prophet Joel.'

Thirdly, *Commandment is renewed.*

Of this use of the Old Testament, Mark 12:29 is one of many examples. 'And Jesus answered him, The first of all the commandments is . . . And thou shalt love the Lord thy God with all thine heart . . . And the second is like, namely this, Thou shalt love thy neighbour as thyself.' The old commandment is repeated in the New as an argument for spiritual as against formal religion.

Fourthly, *Principle is taught by quoting the Old in the New.*

Matthew 9:13. Jesus said: 'But go ye and learn what that meaneth, I will have mercy and not sacrifice . . .'

Quotations which are made for Comment.

These are sometimes for Correction and sometimes for Confirmation.

First, *for correction or completion,* that is to say, where the New Covenant completes or supersedes the Old. For example, Matthew 5:21, 22 quotes Exodus 20:17 with a comment. 'Ye have heard that it was said by them of old time, Thou shalt not kill; and whosoever shall kill shall be in danger of the judgment: But I say unto you, That whosoever is angry with his brother without a cause shall be in danger of the Judgment.'

But some *Quotations are for Confirmation only.* Romans 4:8, 9—'Blessed is the man to whom the Lord will not impute sin.' Psalm 32:2—'Cometh this blessedness upon the circumcision only?'

Then there are *Quotations for Comparison,* usually connecting an Old Testament event or prophecy with a New Testament subject and I quote one example only although many can be supplied. Matthew 12:40—'For as Jonah was three days and three nights in the whale's belly, so shall the Son of man be three days and three nights in the heart of the earth.' A quotation for comparison!

Differences in Quotations.

Now let me try to deal with some of the difficulties arising mainly out of differences of quotation. It may be well at this point to remind you that the quotations of Old Testament Scriptures in the New Testament are *sometimes direct from the Hebrew Old Testament and sometimes from the first translation of the Old Testament into Greek,* that is, from the Septuagint, the first complete translation made about 250 years B.C. Some quotations are abbreviated, whereas others give only the sense of the text. There are very few quotations in the New Testament direct from the Hebrew and they are mainly found in the Gospel according to Matthew where perhaps one would most expect them. We have by far the greatest number of quotations in the New Testament from the Septuagint, that Greek translation of the Hebrew Old Testament. Strangely enough all the quotations in the Epistle to the Hebrews are made from this Greek translation, the Septuagint, and not from the Hebrew, which at least may suggest that it was the popular version in the days of our Lord and certainly used among the common people who knew Greek better than Hebrew. As an example of this, note the quotation of Isaiah 53:8 in Acts 8:33 where you will remember Philip interpreted the text as the Ethiopian was reading that portion in the desert. The Hebrew as in the Revised Version is, 'By oppression and judgment He was taken away.' The Septuagint translation is, 'In His humiliation His judgement was taken away.' It is the latter translation which was used by Philip and read by the eunuch, and which appears in our New Testament.

Some Old Testament texts are abbreviated. There is a classic example which we have noted in Luke 4:18, 19. When Jesus went back to Nazareth where He had been brought up and went into the synagogue, He said: 'The Spirit of the Lord is upon me, because he hath anointed me to preach the gospel to the poor . . . to preach the acceptable year of the Lord.' He had made this very interesting omission from the prophecy—'and the day of vengeance of our God.' The obvious reason is that the day of vengeance was postponed that the period of Gospel preaching may have its full course.

There are some texts which are used not so much as direct quotation as for giving the sense of them. I could quote a number here. Isaiah 29:16 reads: 'For shall the work say of Him that made it, He made me not? or shall the thing framed say of Him that framed it, He hath no understanding?'; but Romans 9:20 takes the sense of that and says: 'Shall the thing formed say to Him that formed it, Why hast Thou made me thus?'

Difficulties with Quotations.

There are difficulties which arise in the believing mind when considering these New Testament usages of Old Testament Scripture. A number of serious problems have arisen in my own mind, such as these:—

When the New Testament differs from the Old Testament, which is inspired?

When the Old Testament text or the meaning is changed, is this permissible?

When the purpose of the Old Testament text is not as originally intended, is this justified?

And our love of Scripture forbids us to ignore any difficulties, rather, we should seek a solution of them.

Where the Text is Different.

May I remind you first how some of these problems arose. First of all let us think *how the New Testament quotations differ from the Old,* for this is exceedingly common. It must be noted first of all, and as already mentioned, that the quotations of Old Testament in the New Testament are made from various sources.

In the Gospels we have a Greek record of speech which was often in Aramaic. The Aramaic speech in turn would be a translation and quotation either from the original Hebrew or from a Greek translation of the original Hebrew. That will show a little of the intricacy, and I hope the marvel of inspiration. When we turn over the pages of the New Testament and read an Old Testament quotation there, it comes to us first through the original Hebrew, then translated into Greek, then spoken in Aramaic, then written down in Greek and finally translated into English, and wonder of wonders, the truth is preserved through all the processes.

In the epistles, the Septuagint, the Greek translation of the Old Testament, and sometimes perhaps other and clearer translations, are quoted, so we have in the Old Testament passages quoted in the New Testament a passage which has already passed through two or three languages before it is finally translated into the English of our Bibles.

Where the Text is Changed.

I reminded you that the Old Testament text or meaning may be changed in the New Testament. Here is an instance. Psalm 68.18, speaking about the Messiah who was to come, reads,'Thou hast received gifts for men' in the Hebrew and in the Greek translation. However, Paul quoting in Ephesians 4:8 says, 'He gave gifts unto men.' Which is inspired? I would answer "Both," for taken together the two sides of that transaction are both related for us, one in the Old Testament and the other in the New Testament. The combined teaching is that Christ exalted, opened His hands to receive gifts from His Father and then opened His hands to give the same gifts to His people.

Sometimes the meaning is deliberately changed, Let me give you that interesting illustration from Psalm 24:1—'The earth is the Lord's and the fulness thereof.' Paul uses this in an interesting way in I Cor.10, verses 26 and 28. First, to support the principle of eating whatever is set before us—'For the earth is the Lord's and the fulness thereof.' 'If any of them that believe not bid you to a feast, and ye be disposed to go; whatsoever is set before you, eat, asking no question for conscience sake.' Secondly, if the food be known to have been offered to idols, then, for the sake of him who provided it as well as conscience sake, we should do without it. In other words, if you are invited to a feast, eat whatever is set before you because it is part of the fulness of the earth, but if you find out it is sacrificed to idols, then for his sake who showed it and for conscience sake it is better not to eat it; there is much more, 'for the earth is the Lord's and the fulness thereof.'

Where the Purpose is Changed.

An Old Testament text with a two-fold meaning has its original meaning used and then its meaning changed. This may be used to declare the mind of God on the conduct of believers in certain circumstances—here again the original text is deliberately changed as to its purpose or meaning. Isaiah 59:20, 21, 'And the Redeemer shall come to Zion and unto them that turn from transgressions in Jacob, saith the Lord.' Romans 11:26, 27, 'There shall come out of Zion the Deliverer and shall turn away ungodliness from Jacob.' In the original 'the Redeemer shall come *to* Zion.' In the quotation, 'There shall come *out of* Zion the Redeemer'—the first, to them that turn from transgression, and in the quotation to turn them from their transgression.

I have made some suggestions of the use which is made and the problems which arise and have given some indication of how those problems arise. Now I want to draw to a conclusion by stating

Some Principles and Explanations.

These have already helped my own heart and helped to clarify my own mind.

First, Christianity is based on the divine religion of Israel; the New Testament is based on the Old. The one was preparatory, the other fulfilment; thus the Old Testament and the New Testament are inseparable. There is a tendency these days to applaud the New and to discredit the Old. They are bound together as the one revelation of God, as well as in the covers of our one Bible. Christ and His apostles bring to light the hidden moral and spiritual truths which are wrapped up in the Old Testament passages, so that the Old Testament Adam anticipates the New Testament Second Adam. The Exodus of the Old Testament anticipates the Redemption and Deliverance of the New Testament and this helps us to see that there is often both a partial and complete fulfilment of the same prophecy. Here is a classic example. Matthew 2:15 quotes Hosea 11:1. The first quotation in Hosea refers historically to the calling out of the people of God from Egypt, the first Exodus or Redemption. The second refers to the calling out of the Son of God from Egypt for the fulfilment of the second Redemption. The first reminds us of God's unchanging love to his rebellious people in bondage to Pharaoh although they afterwards turned to Baalim. The second instance refers to God's concern and love in the ordering of the ways and works of His Son, our Lord Jesus Christ. Here let me quote from Dean Alford:—

> 'This citation shews the almost universal application in the New Testament of the prophetic writings to the expected Messiah, as the general antitype of all the events in the typical dispensation. It seems to have been a received axiom of interpretation (which by its adoption in the New Testament received the sanction of the Spirit Himself, and now stands for our guidance) that the subject of all the allusions, the one represented in all dark sayings, *was HE who was to come* or the circumstances attending His advent and reign.'

That is to say, the main purpose of the Old Testament was to portray Christ to men; 'The testimony of Jesus is the spirit of prophecy.' Of the Old Testament Scriptures Christ said, 'These are they which testify of Me,' and whatever may have been the local or temporary meaning to either Israel or an individual, the final and full fulfilment is in Christ, and therefore their ultimate design is unaffected. Returning to Hosea 11:1 and its quotation in Matthew 2:15, the *local* meaning concerns God's people from exile, the *ultimate* meaning concerns God's Son from His exile. Thus we have the principle of Consecutive Fulfilment which is fundamental in the understanding of God's revelation. We find a text like this in Isaiah 6:9, 10. 'Hear ye indeed but understand not' is stated as being fulfilled in Matthew 13:14 and again three years later in John 12:38, 39 and yet again 37 years later in Acts 28:25. If men harden their hearts then the same prophecy is fulfilled at any time, for God changes not.

What of the various versions—Which is true? The answer is that both the Old Testament original and the New Testament quotations are true for the same Spirit has inspired both Testaments. Both are used to convey the message of God to men, and when God used a Greek translation or His apostles gave a New Testament interpretation, Divine authority is stamped on the translation or the comment.

Is it justifiable to change, abbreviate, and use for other than its original purpose an Old Testament passage? Yes, the Holy Spirit who inspired the Old has the right to handle His own Word as He wills. Only we are to remember that it is His prerogative and not ours. In other words, He may take a text out of its context but we must hesitate to do so.

I close with a practical lesson. In the use of Scripture in learning God's will for our lives, the Lord in His mercy may use a text of Scripture in other than its plain meaning in the context in guiding us to a decision. He has a right to take out a text to illuminate the path of His servant, but we must beware of isolating Scriptures and using them thus. We have no right to close our eyes and open our Bible expecting to find God's direction for life and action. If however we are in deep perplexity of soul and spirit and are looking to God for light, His Spirit who wrote the Book and dwells in our hearts can take anything He has written and apply it to our need at the time of crisis.

The Old Testament is used in various ways in the New Testament. However the Holy Spirit may use it, He stamps its use with the same Divine authority. I close by declaring unqualified and growing confidence in the Word of God as written, thanking God that He has preserved me in that strong confidence these past years.

PSEAVME CL.

Soit ioint auec la voix
Le plaiſant ſon de haut-bois,
Pſalterions à leur tour,
Et la harpe, & le tabour
Haut ſa louange reſonnent,
Phifres eſclattent leur ton,
Orgues, muſette & bourdon
D'vn accord ſon los entonnent.

Part of Psalm 150 (from Calvin's Psalter, 1562)

Chapters and Verses

By Dr. Henry S. Curr

The average Bible reader and student takes for granted the arrangements of its contents in chapters and verses. Indeed this method of producing and printing Holy Scripture had gained such a hold on the hearts and heads of the Christian public that a great deal of comment, which was not invariably favourable, was aroused when the Revised Version was first issued from the press in 1881. Chapters and verses were not omitted, but they appeared in a new position on the page so that they ceased to occupy the prominent place which they had held since the publication of the Authorised Version in 1611. Editions of Holy Scripture, in which chapters and verses are relegated to even less conspicuous situations, have now become fairly common, but editions which depart from the traditional method do not seem to enjoy such a large vogue as might well be expected in these days when so many radical changes are accepted as a matter of course.

The abiding popularity of chapters and verses is all the more striking because the practice cannot claim any very great antiquity. The first division into chapters was the work of Stephen Langton, Archbishop of Canterbury (1150-1228). He was dealing, of course, with the Vulgate, the great Latin translation of the Bible, made by Jerome in Bethlehem at the close of the fourth century. The modern division into chapters was the work of Cardinal Hugo de Sarieto, who died in 1263. As for the verses, these have been largely the work of Jewish scholars in the ninth century. Another arrangement as to verses is probably the work of Athias, a Jewish scholar, who completed the task in 1661. The division of the New Testament into verses was the work of Robert Stephen in 1551. It is related of him that the task was undertaken as he rode to the South of France, probably to occupy the weary miles and hours to the best advantage. They have remained unchanged.

Division Ordained by God.

That is, humanly speaking, the account of the origin of this eminently distinctive feature of the Bible, but it cannot be considered to do complete justice to the facts. Dr. H. C. G. Moule, a former Bishop of Durham, once wrote of the Bible that it is the book with which God always had His way, that way which is perfect. There can be no doubt whatever that the division of the contents of the Bible into chapters and verses was ordained by God for the simple reason that Old and New Testaments could never have wielded the unique influence which they have done on human history if it had not been for the introduction of chapters and verses. Is it too much to suggest that the Bible, deprived of chapters and verses, would have been like Samson shorn of his locks, and consequently weak as other men? It is not disputed that the absence of chapters and verses made no difference to the immeasurable influence of the Bible on Jew and Gentile prior to their introduction, but it may be argued that, since the Reformation, the impact of Holy Scripture on man's affairs might never have attained to its actual dimensions without these features. It seems, therefore, justifiable to contend that the use of chapters and verses can be traced, in the last analysis, to the mind and will of God.

It has been said that God does His perfect work with imperfect instruments. That is true of chapters and verses. They are open to a good deal of criticism regarding which more will be said. But it can safely be argued that their advantages far outweigh their drawbacks, numerous and serious although these may be thought to be. The full force of that observation will be apprehended and appreciated better, if we pause to enquire as to the purpose which the Bible has been designed to serve. That question is not so easy to answer as might be supposed since the appeal of the Bible is universal, knowing no distinction of race, culture, or language. It has been felicitously, if quaintly likened, to a river in which a child can paddle, and an elephant can swim. Nevertheless, it must be contended that the Bible is primarily designed for the man in the street. One of the greatest claims ever made for the Living Word can be transferred with the necessary modification to the Written Word. Of the Son of God it is stated that the common people heard Him gladly. Of the Word of God it may be said with equal force that the common people read it gladly. That is quite compatible with what has been said regarding the infinite profundity of Holy Scripture. Dr. Benjamin Jowett, the great Master of Balliol College, Oxford, is credited with the characteristically caustic observation that it is no sign of superior intelligence to alienate the ordinary run of people.

The Value of the Division.

The introduction of chapters and verses has been responsible in no small measure for the widespread appeal and influence of the Bible. The wayfaring man, though a fool or otherwise, does not read very much of anything. The Bible would be left unread, if it were not for the fact that the chapters and verses make the perusal of small portions possible, while the contents make them profitable. At the present moment, the Scripture Lesson in a service can hardly be too brief. It is doubtful if there ever was a period when the Bible was read on a large scale by a large majority of such as profess and call themselves Christians. Without offering any opinion on the merits or demerits of such practices, the fact remains that the form of the average Bible lends itself to a type of reading which no other book receives. Who can content himself with a single scene from one of Shakespeare's plays?

Again, one must turn to the immense results which have been produced by verses or parts of verses, when used in preaching, or in conversation, or in meditation. It is related of Principal James Denney, the great New Testament scholar, that in criticizing a student's sermon he began by remarking that there was nothing wrong with the text. The seed is ever and always the Word of God. But, since it is so obvious, the subject need hardly be pursued along these lines. Attention had rather be drawn to the fact that no book is so widely quoted as the Bible both consciously and unconsciously, since many words and phrases in daily speech are derived from its pages. The Scriptures lend themselves to quotation like no other book. Would it be feasible to argue that that could never have happened if it had not been for the use of chapters and verses? A loaf will not be eaten until it be sliced.

Some Negative Drawbacks.

Chapters and verses cannot, however, be regarded as an unmixed blessing, and reference must now be made to some of their drawbacks. It may be said at once that these are negative in character rather than positive. Neither chapters nor verses do any mischief or if they do it is negligible. Their defects rather lie in the direction of obstruction and obscuration. Thus the division into chapters is far from ideal. That statement can be tested by the simple device of turning to the lectionary prefixed to the Prayer Book. If the long list of lessons, intended for use in public worship, be carefully scanned it will be found that in a much larger number of passages than might be expected, the verses, averaging about twenty or twenty-four, include parts of two chapters. In a few cases the lesson begins towards the end of a chapter. The classic instance is the closing verse of 1 Corinthians 12—'But covet earnestly the best gifts; and yet shew I unto you a more excellent way.' Then follows the prose poem which has few rivals, even in the Bible, forming a different and distinct chapter. A less well-known example is furnished by John 2:24, 25 and 3:1, 2—'But Jesus did not commit himself unto them, because he knew all men, and needed not that any should testify of man; for he knew what was in man. There was a man of the Pharisees named Nicodemus, a ruler of the Jews; the same came to Jesus by night, and said unto him, Rabbi, we know that thou art a teacher come from God: for no man can do these miracles that thou doest, except God be with him.' The connection of the three verses is as subtle as it is close, but that is concealed by the chapter division.

A more serious defect is also illustrated in these verses. That is concerned with sentences. The difficulty does not assume the same proportions in the Old Testament as in the New, since the sentences of the former tend to be more concise and crisp in accordance with the genius of the Hebrew idiom. In the Pauline Epistles, for instance, the misleading effect of the division into verses is more manifest. An excellent example is provided by a superb passage in the first chapter of the Epistle to the Ephesians. It will be found that a single sentence covers verses 3-12. Schoolboys might find it very helpful to parse it as a test of their mastery over the rules of English syntax. Such cases are more numerous than might be thought since few people pay attention to the elaborate punctuation of the sacred page, a wonderful guide for intelligent reading aloud.

The drawbacks just mentioned are far outweighed by the signal service which has been rendered by chapters and verses. It is remarkable that the contents of the Bible lend themselves to such treatment, although their authors were unaware of their very existence. Other books would suffer irreparably if they were printed like Holy Scripture. It would be rash and foolish to claim that it is the only collection which benefits by such treatment. There may well be others, but there cannot be another which owes so much of its unique appeal and power to the fact that it has been handled in this fashion

Laudate nomen. Psal. CXXXV. N.

He exhorteth all the faithfull to praise God for his maruailous workes, & graces wherewith he hath declared his maiestie, to the confusion of all Idolaters.

Praise the Lord, praise him, praise him, praise him with one accord: O praise him still all ye that be the seruants of the Lord, O praise him ye that stand and be in the house of the Lord: Ye of his Court and of his house praise him with one accord.

3 Praise ye the Lord, for he is good,
sing praises to his name:
It is a comely and good thing,
alwayes to do the same.
4 For why? the Lord hath chose Jacob,
his very owne you see:
So hath he chosen Israell,
his treasure for to be.

5 For this I know, and am right sure
the Lord is very great:
He is indeed, aboue all gods,
most easie to entreat.
6 For whatsoeuer pleased him,
all that full well he wrought:
In heauen, in earth, and in the sea,
which he hath framd of nought.
7 He lifts vp clouds euen from the earth,
he makes lightnings and raine:
He bringeth forth the winds also.
he made nothing in vaine.
8 He smote the first borne of each thing,
in Egypt that tooke rest:
He spared there no liuing thing,
the man nor yet the beast.

9 He hath in thee shewed wonders great,
O Egypt voyd of vaunts:
On Pharao thy cursed King,
and his seuere seruants.
10 He smote then many nations,
and did great acts and things:
He slew the great and mightiest,
and chiefest of their Kings.

11 Sehon King of the Ammorites,
and Og, King of Basan:
He slew also the Kingdomes all,
that were of Canaan.
12 And gaue their land to Israell,
an heritage we see:
To Israell his owne people,
an heritage to be.

Psalm 135 (after Sternhold and Hopkins)

'The Battle of the Scrolls'

(The above is the title of an article in the current *Calvin Forum* from the pen of the Rev. Simon J. De Vries, pastor of the Northside Christian Reformed Church of Passiac, New Jersey. It has reference to the Hebrew manuscripts, commonly known as the *Dead Sea Scrolls*—sometimes designated by a later title, the *Qumran Scrolls*—which were discovered in a cave near the Dead Sea in the year 1947. The finding of these manuscripts—which included a complete copy of Isaiah—wrought such havoc amongst many of the higher critical theories concerning the Old Testament that energetic, not to say violent, efforts have been made by some to prove that they belong to Christian, and not pre-Christian, times; hence the allusion to 'the battle' in the title of Mr. De Vries' article. We have hereunder made extensive quotations from it, accompanied by a few footnotes concerning certain technical terms employed by the author which may not be familiar to some of our readers· and the matter is so important that we desire all believers to be acquainted with it.—Editor.)

Eight years have passed since the scholarly world came into possession of one of the greatest manuscript discoveries of modern times. It was in the spring of 1947 that Bedouins of the Ta'amireh tribe entered a long-forgotten cave near a place called Ain Feshka, high on a bluff overlooking the Dead Sea, where they discovered a cache of ancient Hebrew scrolls stowed away in tall clay jars. Originally there had been a great number of these jars in the cave, but long ago in early Christian times the cave was plundered and only a few intact manuscripts besides a great quantity of fragments were left behind. The Bedouins gathered up the scrolls that were left, recognizing their commercial value, and brought them to Jerusalem to be sold.

Eventually four of these scrolls came into the hands of the bishop of a Syrian monastery, Mar Athanasios Y. Samuel by name, who allowed them to be studied by various scholars and to be transported to America, where they have been published by the American Schools of Oriental Research. These four scrolls include a complete copy of the book of Isaiah, a 'commentary' on Habakkuk, a sectarian scroll of discipline, and an—up until the present—unopenable scroll of a Lamech apocalypse. Recently Mar Samuel has sold these four scrolls for a tidy sum to the Hebrew University in Jerusalem.

Other scrolls have already been in the hands of the Hebrew University, where Prof. E. Sukenik has carefully prepared them for publication under the title, *Otzar Ha'Megillot Ha'Genuzot,* meaning 'Treasury of Hidden Scrolls.' This volume includes the extant portions of another Isaiah scroll, a sectarian apocalypse titled 'The Battle of the Sons of Light against the Sons of Darkness,' and a collection of 'Hymns.'

In addition to these intact scrolls, numerous fragments of various manuscripts have been collected by scholars who visited the cave during February and March of 1949. These too are of great scholarly interest. Fragments of almost every Old Testament book have been identified among them. Of particular interest are those of Leviticus and Daniel. Of the book of Isaiah, fragments of ten different manuscripts have been found—these in addition to the two intact scrolls already mentioned.

Since the discovery of the first cave in 1947 several other caves have been entered in the same vicinity and scrolls of lesser antiquity have been found.

Scholastic Excitement

In the eight years which have passed since these scrolls first came to light, members of our circles have learned something of them from newspaper notices and from an occasional article disclosing their general importance appearing in our own periodicals. But otherwise they have gone virtually unregarded among us. This is in stark contrast to the general feverish excitement of the scholarly world. This is a great thing in biblical studies! Hebrew and Semitic scholars everywhere have been studying the scrolls with avid interest. In various countries a disproportionate number of pages in the scholarly journals have been devoted to them. Book after book concerning them has come from the press. Thus in 1952 a Dutch scholar was able to compile a bibliography on the Dead Sea Scrolls of over three hundred titles. By this time the number probably approaches a thousand.

Apparently biblical scholars have recognized how enormously significant the Dead Sea Scrolls are. If we ask why, the answer is simple to give: they are concerned about them because (1) they appear to be older than Christianity itself, dating by the best estimates from the second or first century B.C. and (2) objective study of them is forcing drastic changes in many of the most vital theories of Bible critics, much to the discomfort of some. A discovery so significant could not but provoke a veritable flood of discussion. Perhaps it should surprise no one to see certain normally sedate scholars losing their equilibrium and at times even their tempers as they enter what may well be called 'the Battle of the Scrolls.'

Development of Archaeology

Literary criticism has long been able to go to the greatest lengths in questioning the integrity of the Old Testament because it reasoned in the abstract, largely apart from faith and with little objective data to challenge its claim. The development of archaeology as an exact science has forced a change in this situation. Increasingly, archaeology has learned to speak with authority. The millions of dollars spent on expeditions to the Near East have produced an ever-increasing harvest of concrete data. Mound after mound has been excavated; temples and palaces have yielded their secrets; inscriptions almost beyond number have been found and studied; works of art, coins, and household utensils have been forced to reveal their story; and the humble potsherd, found in great numbers in every ancient site, has told the clearest tale of all, because by its evidence the chronology of Bible times has been fixed with amazing exactness. By careful study of this information the Palestinian archaeologist has forged for himself a sharp and accurate tool, so that he can now speak with authority where previously every whim of interpretation prevailed.

Conservative Christians, who have often winced before the sharp attack of criticism, ought to be grateful for the fact that these archaeological investigations have tended to corroborate the traditional view of Old Testament origins. Point by point, concrete discoveries have verified the witness of the Old Testament, and because it has been their aim to be honest with facts, many of those scholars who have actually done extensive work in Palestine have moved toward a more conservative position. A notable example is the renowned William F. Albright, who accepts many of the views of higher criticism but nevertheless believes firmly in the basic integrity of the Old Testament writings. This man, Prof. Albright, has probably done more than any other to put Palestinian archaeology on a truly scientific basis. And as we might expect, it is also he who has been in the forefront in making clear to the world the importance of the Dead Sea Scrolls for the understanding of the sacred Scriptures.

These newly-discovered manuscripts promise to do much to fill a serious gap in our knowledge of biblical times—the gap between the finish of the Old Testament Canon and the beginning of the New. No Bible book enlightens us, except by inference, as to conditions in this period. The apocrypha and pseudepigrapha do not provide sufficient light for full understanding. Josephus and the secular historians are not always reliable. Archaeological remains from this period have been relatively scanty. Thus, because positive evidence to the contrary has been so often lacking, scholars were able boldly to assert their opinions. The trustworthiness of the Masoretic Text[1] was denied, to use an example. Or, to use another, high dates were assigned for the composition of certain New Testament books because of what were considered to be advanced theological ideas appearing in them. But now we have the Dead Sea Scrolls! They have come as a light in the darkness to show us that after all the Masoretic textual tradition does date from before Christ and that many of the theological ideas in question were already common among the Israelites long before the New Testament began to be written.

[1] The *Massorah* (variously spelt) is, broadly speaking, the authorised Jewish text of the Hebrew Old Testament.

Critics must think Again

Thus the study of the Dead Sea Scrolls threatens a revolution in many points formerly believed to be firmly established by higher criticism. First, the study of the Old Testament will be profoundly affected. As already stated, the new scrolls make clear the general trustworthiness of the Masoretic Text, so that light-hearted textual emendations are now definitely a thing of the past for any scholar who values his reputation. On the other hand, the scrolls have provided new evidence of a parallel Hebrew recension[2] underlying parts of the Greek Septuagintal version, demonstrating that its witness will likewise have to be taken more seriously than it has been in certain circles.

The Dead Sea Scrolls also give welcome light on the status of the Canon in pre-Christian times because whenever they quote the canonical Scriptures they clearly regard them as fully established and authoritative. This is of greatest importance in regard to those books which critics have dated very late. Duhm, for instance, made almost all the Psalms and parts of Isaiah post-Maccabean, i.e., from the late second century or even from the first century B.C. But the Dead Sea Scrolls quote these very writings as scripture! Prof. Albright emphasizes the importance of this point in one of his many articles on the subject . . .

And thus new questions are being raised all along the line. Jewish history and theology of the inter-testamentary period must come in for fresh study. Formerly, the Pharisees and the Sadducees monopolized the interests of scholars, but now greater attention will be given to a third sect of the period . . . that of the Essenes, since the community which possessed the Dead Sea Scrolls was very likely an Essene group. Moreover, new consideration will have to be given to the old theory that Aramaic was the only spoken language of the common people in pre-Christian and early-Christian Palestine. Now a community has been discovered from that period which actually spoke Hebrew, as appears from a study of the documents they left behind! It would certainly appear that at least a part of the Jewish people retained Hebrew as a living language for a much longer period than was formerly supposed.

The Scrolls and the New Testament

But this is not all. The Dead Sea Scrolls (or Qumran Scrolls, as they have been called more recently) are perhaps equally important for the New Testament. First, they promise a sizeable contribution to a greater understanding of the influence of legalism, apocalypticism,[3] and monastic asceticism upon the religious atmosphere of New Testament Judaism.

Second, they reveal that a certain tradition in Judaism expected the Messiah, not from David, but out of Levi and Aaron. Third, it is possible that they will help explain something of the spiritual climate which prepared the way for John the Baptist's preaching, for in them, too, we find a strong expectation of the coming of the Kingdom of God combined with an urgent call to conversion. Again, they show that the great antithesis between Light and Darkness, between Christ and Belial, expressed so forcefully in John's Gospel and in Ephesians, can no longer be taken by anyone as evidence of the dependence of these books upon such late documents as the Epistle of Barnabas or the Didache.[4] This antithesis is already the leading theme of our pre-Christian Qumran scrolls. And thus we might continue, but these examples must suffice. Only the future will tell how extensive the influence of the Dead Sea Scrolls will be.

The Date of the Scrolls

But this influence depends entirely upon the evidence for a pre-Christian date for the origin of the Dead Sea Scrolls. Most of those who have studied the evidence have conceded a pre-Christian date.

[2] A revision, or re-examination, of the Hebrew text.

[3] Here probably meaning the expectation of the first coming of Christ.

[4] Early sub-apostolic Christian writings, variously dated, of value in many ways, but not accepted as part of the canon of the New Testament.

The writer of this article personally accepts that evidence and welcomes the consequences. But there is no unanimity among scholars in dating the scrolls. On the contrary, there has arisen a very vigorous opposition to a pre-Christian date from many quarters. While Prof. Albright and many others have staunchly defended the early date from the time of their discovery, various scholars have arrayed themselves against them, claiming a post-Christian origin for the scrolls. Most colourful, and probably most notorious, is Prof. Zeitlin, writing in the *Jewish Quarterly Review.* He has been extreme unto absurdity in his heated opposition, affirming vehemently that the scrolls are medieval, and hinting darkly that they were deliberately 'salted' in the Qumran cave in order to give the false impression of great antiquity. Another Jewish scholar, T. Wechsler, has dared to accuse Bishop Samuel of disposing of a synagogal Haftaroth-roll (which would be post-Christian) which was originally with the other four scrolls in his possession, in order deliberately to destroy evidence of lateness for the find . . .

Flimsy Arguments

The fact is, most of the arguments of the opposition are too flimsy to bear their own weight. It is not too harsh to say that pure bias has led some of these scholars to their denial of the antiquity of the scrolls. Often conservatives have been charged with obscuring facts for the sake of theory—and probably justly so in some instances—but here we observe scholars who pride themselves on their scientific objectivity deliberately ignoring objective facts in order to save their theories! One of them is reported to have exclaimed, 'I don't care how much evidence you claim to have for an early date! I *know* that these scrolls are medieval, and I'll never believe otherwise.'

Prof. Albright expresses his exasperation at this cavalier attitude in words worth quoting. Recalling that formerly various scholars of reputation similarly refused to accept the spectacular discoveries of archaeology, such as the ruins of Pompeii and Herculaneum, the decipherment of cuneiform, and the Elephantine papyri, all of which they called fakes and forgeries, Prof. Albright writes the following:— 'In none of the similar episodes of the past two centuries . . . has there been such wide refusal on the part of scholars to accept clear-cut evidence . . . Individual leaders of the movement are naturally swayed by different motives, often complex and frequently more or less unconscious. Certain of these leaders are moved by the very elementary instinct for preserving personal theories. Others seem to react violently against innovations likely to threaten the critical schools to which they belong. It is quite true that the discovery of the Scrolls menaces the insecure foundations of many speculative hypotheses of both Old and New Testament scholars, not to mention students of rabbinics.'

All who are content to let the evidence speak for itself will be convinced that these scrolls do indeed date from the centuries before Christ, that they belonged to a semi-monastic Essene brotherhood living in the lonely Judean desert in expectation of the triumph of righteousness, and that they were probably deposited in the cave by members of the brotherhood for safe-keeping against the ravaging Romans at the time of the Temple's destruction.

First there is the archaeological evidence . . . The scrolls were stored in tall clay jars with lids, all of Hellenistic or early Roman origin. The linen used to wrap the scrolls has been subjected to a radio-carbon test and has yielded a medial date of 35 A.D. Nothing whatever younger than 70 A.D. was found in the cave, except for a few late Roman lamps left by the original plunderers, and a quantity of cigarette butts left by the recent Bedouin intruders.

Internal evidence likewise speaks for a pre-Christian date. After studying carefully the historical references in the sectarian scrolls of Qumran, the English scholar, H. H. Rowley, has assigned their composition to the early Hasmonean age before 100 B.C., and he concludes that our scrolls, copied from the originals, could not have been deposited in the cave later than 70 A.D. Similarly, the forms of the letters, the spelling of the words, and the vocabulary fit properly only in pre-Christian times. The theological ideas likewise are those of pre-Christian Judaism . . .

Authority of Scripture Confirmed

The 'Battle of the Scrolls' will probably continue for a long time. We would like to believe that in the end the facts will prevail against prejudice and that all logical deductions will be drawn. Those who hold to traditional Christianity may well rejoice in the discovery of these scrolls, for if they do anything they tend to confirm the authenticity and authority of the Holy Scriptures. It is of course true that the Scriptures do not depend for confirmation upon anything outside themselves. They are God-breathed and bear their own unique authority. And the only force that can persuade a man to accept this authority is the *testimonium Spiritu Sancti,* the voice of the Author of these words Himself. Nevertheless let us who accept the authority be grateful for every vindication of God's Word. Let us thank God for this clearer light upon the distant origins of our holy faith . . .

QUMRAN

The Whole Counsel of God

By C. H. Spurgeon

(*Editor's Introductory Note.* Amongst the evangelical reprints recently issued by the Banner of Truth Trust is a relatively small volume entitled *Revival Year Sermons*; the sermons being those preached by C. H. Spurgeon in the Surrey Gardens Music Hall during the year 1859. In a specially interesting and informative foreword by the publishers reference is made to the phenomenal spiritual power resting upon the young preacher, then no more than twenty-four years of age, and of the almost incalculable influence which he exercised, even at that early period, both by tongue and pen. So great was the desire to hear him that buildings of ever-increasing capacity had to be sought to accommodate even part of the crowds that thronged to listen. During 1857 and the two following years the evening services on Sunday were held in the Exeter Hall, capable of holding some 3,000 persons, while the morning meetings were held in the Surrey Gardens Music Hall, which seated more than three times that number. On special occasions Spurgeon preached in the open air, and when he did so it was no unusual event for ten thousand people to assemble, and for his voice to reach the utmost fringe of the crowd.

The spiritual results were no less remarkable, the conversion of the unsaved, from all ranks of society, and the quickening of believers, keeping pace with the growth of the listening multitudes.

It is our personal judgment that Spurgeon, not only at that period, but throughout the remaining thirty-three years of his ministry, maintained a truer and more Scriptural balance between the doctrines of Divine sovereignty and human responsibility than did many both before and after him. He was a firm believer in what are known as 'the five points of Calvinism'; he preached them without apology or diminution; he regarded them, indeed, as central to the gospel. 'The doctrine' he said 'which looks at first as though it would hush every exertion with indolence, and make men sit down with listlessness and despair, is really the trump of God to awaken the dead.' Yet he saw that it was a doctrine that could be sorely abused; and throughout his life he fought against such over-statement of it as brought it into disrepute. He saw, too, that there were other doctrines taught in Scripture, complementary to the 'five points,' no less Divinely inspired, and no less assuredly to be taken into account; nor did he forget that when the utmost has been said there remains much that is too vast for human comprehension. 'Who can find out the Almighty to perfection?' It is by way of illustration of this that we have selected the following extract from Spurgeon's sermon on closing the services in the Surrey Gardens. We may add that the volumes will well repay the study of those who in particular are earnestly desiring to witness another visitation of grace such as that which blessed the British Isles in the years of Spurgeon's prime. E. J. Poole-Connor.)

Taking as his text Acts 20:26, 27, after introduction, the preacher said:—

Now I must bring down the apostle's saying to these modern times; and I take it, if any one of us would clear our conscience by delivering the whole counsel of God, we must take care that we preach in the first place the *doctrines of the gospel.* We ought to declare that grand doctrine of the Father's love towards his people from before all worlds. His sovereign choice of them, his covenant purposes concerning them, and his immutable promises to them, must all be uttered with trumpet tongue. Coupled with this the true evangelist must never fail to set forth the beauties of the person of Christ, the glory of his offices, the completeness of his work, and above all, the efficacy of his blood. Whatever we omit, this must be in the most forcible manner proclaimed again and again. That is no gospel which has not Christ in it, and the modern idea of preaching THE TRUTH instead of Christ, is a wicked device of Satan. Nor is this all, for as there are Three Persons in the Godhead, we must be careful that they all have due honour in our ministry. The Holy Spirit's work in regeneration, in sanctification and in perseverance, must be always magnified from our pulpit. Without his power our ministry is a dead letter, and we cannot expect his arm to be made bare unless we honour him day by day.

Upon all these matters we are agreed, and I therefore turn to points upon which there is more dispute, and consequently more need of honest avowal, because more temptation to concealment. To proceed then: I question whether we have preached the whole counsel of God, unless predestination with all its solemnity and sureness be continually declared—unless election be boldly and nakedly taught as being one of the truths revealed of God. It is the minister's duty, beginning from this fountain head, to trace all the other streams; dwelling on effectual calling, maintaining justification by faith, insisting upon the certain perseverance of the believer, and delighting to proclaim that gracious covenant in which all these things are contained, and which is sure to all the chosen, blood-bought seed. There is a tendency in this age to throw doctrinal truth into the shade. Too many preachers are offended with that stern truth which the Covenanters held, and to which the Puritans testified in the midst of a licentious age. We are told that the times have changed: that we are to modify these old (so-called) Calvinistic doctrines, and bring them down to the tone of the times; that, in fact, they need dilution, that men have become so intelligent that we must pare off the angles of our religion, and make the square into a circle by rounding off the most prominent edges. Any man who doth this, so far as my judgment goes, does not declare the whole counsel of God. The faithful minister must be plain, simple, pointed, with regard to these doctrines. There must be no dispute about whether he believes them or not. He must so preach them that his hearers will know whether he preaches a scheme of freewill, or a covenant of grace—whether he teaches salvation by works, or salvation by the power and grace of God.

But, beloved, a man might preach all these doctrines to the full, and yet not declare the whole counsel of God. For here comes the labour and the battle; here it is that he who is faithful in these modern days will have to bear the full brunt of war. It is not enough to preach doctrine; we must preach *duty*, we must faithfully and firmly insist upon practice. So long as you will preach nothing but bare doctrine, there is a certain class of men of perverted intellect who will admire you, but once begin to preach responsibility—say outright, once for all, that if the sinner perish it is his own fault, that if any man sinks to hell, his damnation will lie at his own door, and at once there is a cry of 'Inconsistency! How can these two things stand together?' Even good Christian men are found who cannot endure the whole truth, and who will oppose the servant of the Lord who will not be content with a fragment, but will honestly present the whole gospel of Christ. This is one of the troubles that the faithful minister has to endure. But he is not faithful to God—I say it solemnly, I do not believe that any man is even faithful to his own conscience, who can preach simply the doctrine of sovereignty, and neglect to insist upon the doctrine of responsibility. I do assuredly believe that every man who sinks into hell shall have himself alone to curse for it. It shall be said of them as they pass the fiery portal: 'Ye would not.' 'Ye would have none of my rebukes. Ye were bidden to the supper and ye would not come. I called, and ye refused; I stretched out my hands, and no man regarded. And now, behold, I will mock at your calamities. I will laugh when your fear cometh.' The apostle Paul knew how to dare public opinion, and on one hand to preach the duty of man, and on the other the sovereignty of God.

I would borrow the wings of an eagle and fly to the utmost height of high doctrine when I am preaching divine sovereignty. God hath absolute and unlimited power over men to do with them as he pleases, even as the potter doeth with the clay. Let not the creature question the Creator, for he giveth no account of his matters. But when I preach concerning man, and look at the other aspect of truth, I dive to the utmost depth. I am, if you will so call me, a low-doctrine man in that, for as an honest messenger of Christ I must use his own language, and cry: 'He that believeth not is condemned already, because he believeth not on the Son of God.' I do not see that the whole counsel of God is declared, unless those two apparently contradictory points are brought out and plainly taught.

To preach the whole counsel of God it is necessary to declare the promise in all its freeness, sureness and richness. When the promise makes the subject of the text the minister should never be afraid of it. If it is an unconditional promise, he should make its unconditionality one of the most prominent features of his discourse; he should go the whole way with whatever God has promised to his people.

Should the command be the subject, the minister must not flinch; he must utter the precept as fully and confidently as he would the promise. He must exhort, rebuke, command with all long-suffering. He must ever maintain the fact that the preceptive part of the gospel is as valuable—nay, as invaluable—as the promissory part. He must stand to it, that 'By their fruits ye shall know them'; that 'Unless the tree bring forth good fruit it is hewn down and cast into the fire.' Holy living must be preached, as well as happy living. Holiness of life must be constantly insisted on, as well as that simple faith which depends for all on Christ.

To declare the whole counsel of God—to gather up ten thousand things into one—I think it is needful that when a minister gets his text, he should say what that text means honestly and uprightly. Too many preachers get a text and kill it. They wring its neck, then stuff it with some empty notions and present it upon the table for an unthinking people to feed upon. That man does not preach the whole counsel of God who does not let God's Word speak for itself in its own pure, simple language. If he finds one day a text like this: 'It is not of him that willeth, nor of him that runneth, but of God that sheweth mercy,' the faithful minister will go all the lengths of that text. And if on the morrow the Spirit of God lays home to his conscience this: 'Ye will not come unto me that ye might have life,' or this other: 'Whosoever will, let him come,' he will be just as honest with his text on that side as he was on the other. He will not shirk the truth. He will dare to look at it straight in the face himself and then he will bring it up into the pulpit, and there say to it: 'O Word, speak for thyself, and be thou heard alone. Suffer me not, O Lord, to pervert or misinterpret thine own heaven-sent truth.' Simple honesty to the pure Word of God is I think requisite to the man who would not shun to declare the whole counsel of God . . .

The question, however, is suggested, is there any temptation which arises to the man who endeavours to do this? Is there anything which would tempt him from the straight path and induce him not to preach the whole counsel of God? Ah, my brother, little do you understand the minister's position, if you have not sometimes trembled for him. Espouse but one phase of the truth, and you shall be cried up to the very heavens. Become such a Calvinist that you shut your eyes to one half the Bible, and cannot see the responsibility of the sinner, and men will clap their hands, and cry Hallelujah! and on the backs of many you shall be hoisted to a throne, and become a very prince in their Israel. On the other hand, begin to preach mere morality, practice without doctrine, and you shall be elevated on other men's shoulders; you shall, if I may use such a figure, ride upon these asses into Jerusalem; and you shall hear them cry, Hosanna! and see them wave their palm branches before you . . . Yes, all these things cast their little weight into the scale; and they have a tendency, if a man be not kept right by God the Holy Spirit, to make him diverge a little from that narrow path, in which alone he can stand if he would declare the whole counsel of God. Ah, friends, there are honours to be had by the man who will espouse the opinion of a clique; but while there are honours, there are far more dishonours to be gained by him who will stand firm to the unstained banner of truth, singly and alone, and do battle against mischief of every shape, as well in the church as in the world. Therefore, it was no mean testimony that the apostle asked for himself, that he had not shunned to declare the whole counsel of God.

But, then, let me remark further, while there is this temptation not to declare all the counsel of God, the true minister of Christ feels impelled to preach the whole truth, because it and it alone can meet the wants of man. What evils has this world seen through a distorted, mangled, man-moulded gospel. What mischiefs have been done to the souls of men by men who have preached only one part and not all the counsel of God! My heart bleeds for many a family where Antinomian doctrine has gained the sway. I could tell many a sad story of families dead in sin, whose consciences are seared as with a hot iron, by the fatal preaching to which they listen. I have known convictions stifled and desires quenched by the soul-destroying system which takes manhood from man and makes him no more responsible than an ox. I cannot imagine a more ready instrument in the hands of Satan for the ruin of souls than a minister who tells sinners that it is not their duty to repent of their sins or to believe in Christ, and who has the arrogance to call himself a gospel minister, while he teaches that God hates some men infinitely and unchangeably for no reason whatever but simply because he chooses to do so. O my brethren! may the Lord save you from the voice of the charmer, and keep you ever deaf to the voice of error.

Even in Christian families, what evil will a distorted gospel produce! I have seen the young believer, just saved from sin, happy in his early Christian career, and walking humbly with his God. But evil has crept in, disguised in the mantle of truth. The finger of partial blindness was laid upon their eyes, and but one doctrine could be seen. Sovereignty was seen, but not responsibility. The minister once beloved was hated; he who had been honest to preach God's Word, was accounted as the off-scouring of all things. And what became the effect? The very reverse of good and gracious. Bigotry usurped the place of love; bitterness lived where once there had been a loveliness of character. I could point you to innumerable instances where harping upon any one peculiar doctrine has driven men to excess of bigotry and bitterness. And when a man has once come there, he is ready enough for sin of any kind to which the devil may please to tempt him.

There is a necessity that the whole gospel should be preached, or else the spirits, even of Christians, will become marred and maimed. I have known men diligent for Christ, labouring to win souls with both hands; and on a sudden they have espoused one particular doctrine and not the whole truth, and they have subsided into lethargy. On the other hand, where men have only taken the practical side of truth, and left out the doctrinal, too many professors have run over into legality; have talked as if they were to be saved by works, and have almost forgotten that grace by which they were called. They are like the Galatians; they have been bewitched by what they have heard. The believer in Christ, if he is to be kept pure, simple, holy, charitable, Christ-like, is only to be kept so by a preaching of the whole truth as it is in Jesus. And as for the salvation of sinners, ah, my hearers, we can never expect God to bless our ministry for the conversion of sinners unless we preach the gospel as a whole. Let me get but one part of the truth, and always dwell upon it, to the exclusion of every other, and I cannot expect my Master's blessing. If I preach as he would have me preach, he will certainly own the word; he will never leave it without his own living witness. But let me imagine that I can improve the gospel, that I can make it consistent, that I can dress it up and make it look finer, I shall find that my Master is departed, and Ichabod is written on the walls of the sanctuary.

How many there are kept in bondage through neglect of gospel invitations! They are longing to be saved. They go up to the house of God, crying to be saved, and there is nothing but predestination for them. On the other hand, what multitudes are kept in darkness through practical preaching. It is do! do! do! and nothing but do! and the poor souls come away and say: 'Of what use is that to me? I can do nothing. Oh, that I had had a way shown to me available for salvation.' Of the apostle Paul we think it may be truly said, that no sinner missed a comfort from his keeping back Christ's cross; that no saint was bewildered in spirit from his denying the bread of heaven and withholding precious truth; that no practical Christian became so practical as to become legal, and no doctrinal Christian became so doctrinal as to become unpractical. His preaching was of so savoury and consistent a kind, that they who heard him, being blessed of the Spirit, became Christians indeed, both in life and spirit, reflecting the image of their Master.

The Holy Scriptures: The Task of the Translators and the Story of the Early Versions (Part I)

By Bishop D. A. Thompson

There can be few nobler or more fruitful tasks than that of translating the Word of God from the languages in which it was originally written into that of another spoken on the earth today. It is a work in which there are many and great difficulties and not a few perplexing problems. An idiom or word in the Hebrew or Greek may have no precise equivalent in that other tongue. Indeed there are backward and pagan tribes having no words at all for some of the greatest in Holy Writ such as 'God' (with the attributes ascribed to Him therein), 'grace', 'sin' and 'forgiveness'. In these cases a word has to be coined or a phrase composed to express the fact to those to whom the sentiment is altogether new. The translator requires, therefore, the highest linguistic ability and the utmost clarity of thought as well as extensive theological knowledge, all wedded to deep spiritual understanding.

The believer owes, under God, more than he can ever repay to the first writers of Holy Scripture, and to the many transcribers and translators whose labours have issued in the Bible he uses. The least he can do in discharge of only a portion of his indebtedness is to remember fervently in prayer those now engaged in this great work of translation, that they may be vouchsafed those mental gifts and that help from above vital for the production of a worthy version.

The Translator and the Translation

The translation can rarely be considered apart from the translator. The version is his child. As he is in linguistic stature, spiritual discernment and soundness in the faith, so will be his translation. Ideally, he needs to be a genius in languages and a master of the rules of grammar, while even more essential he must be born of the Spirit (John 3, 5 and 6), filled with the Spirit (Eph. 5:18), enlightened of the Spirit, guided by the Spirit and prompted by the Spirit. The highest academic distinctions, invaluable as they are, will yet, without the spiritual qualifications, be wholly insufficient for this sacred task and may lead to serious blemishes in the version. The translator, however, divinely gifted not only with the intellectual but also with this spiritual equipment, will then be a 'man of the Book', loving it, believing it wholly without reservation, living in it, and dominated by Him of whom it testifies from beginning to end; all of which are essential links in the chain of the production of a faithful translation. But with any one or more of these elements missing, there is every likelihood of grievous defects in the work.

Laws Governing Accurate Translation

Certain other great principles underlying accurate renderings of Holy Scripture must be appreciated if various versions are to be examined and criticized.

Perhaps the first to be borne in mind is, that the translation of each and every section, however small, must be consistent with the volume as a whole.

The Divine Library has but one Author, the Holy Spirit, who used many writers (2 Peter 1:21). He never contradicts Himself. Thus Holy Writ, considered merely as literature, displays marvellous variety and miraculous unity. One portion may be the complement of, but is never contradictory to, another. Scripture is the best exponent of Scripture. Hence, if in a passage considered in isolation, there may be more than one rendering, that one is to be given in the translation which is in harmony with the immediate and the remote context, and indeed with all else that is in the sacred volume.

This has special pertinence to that great Figure who overshadows everyone else and everything else in the Holy Bible—our Lord and Saviour Jesus Christ. He is the touchstone both of our faith and of the quality of a version. He not only stands out above all others and all else but should be seen to do so. The Book as a whole, from beginning to end, reveals Him as perfect God and real but sinless man, the Son of God in a unique sense (the equivalent of saying that He is God the Son, the Second Person of the Holy Trinity), virgin-born, omniscient, whose death on Calvary's tree was the atonement for penitent believing souls, who rose bodily from the grave, ascended into heaven, and will return to this earth in power and great glory. It cannot be stressed too strongly or appreciated too highly that not one of these statements concerning Emmanuel is dependent upon only one text but upon many, and in some cases literally hundreds. They are of such supreme importance and so inter-related that they stand or fall together; if one is questioned or denied, sooner or later the others will be too. They are the very warp and woof of divine revelation.

Thus as surely as the answer to the question, 'What think ye of Christ?' (Matt. 22:42) reveals the soundness or otherwise of the faith of that person who vouchsafes a reply, so the rendering of the words and phrases which have to do with the stupendous facts concerning the Person and the Work of our Lord is a gauge by which to estimate the quality and worth of a version.

This is a point of cardinal importance and must not be overlooked in appraising modern translations. The older English versions in accurate renderings of the Hebrew and of the Greek and in conformity with the testimony of Scripture as a whole present the Saviour as the Son of God in that unique sense already indicated. But in many passages in some of the present-day translations some of these facts concerning the Redeemer are toned down, obscured, evaded and, in an indirect way, denied.

The Rise and Development of 18th Century Scepticism

The explanation is extremely sad but simple, and very briefly, without entering into detail, the history of this apostasy must be sketched. In the latter half of the 18th century the Protestant Churches were almost dead and rapidly losing even the little influence they still retained over the people. Some of the leading ecclesiastics—especially those on the continent of Europe—distressed by the increasing godlessness of their generation thought that they saw the reason and the remedy for this declension. They considered that it was due to the fact that it was held that the essential elements of the Christian Faith were supernatural in character; and that if the Bible were expounded in a different way, eliminating the miraculous in Christianity, the drift from the Churches would not only be arrested but reversed. So these misguided and grievously erring theological professors and pastors declared that much of the Old Testament must be regarded in the same way as many a passage of the classics of Greece and of Rome, i.e., as mythical, legendary, unhistorical in character, and definitely not inerrant.

The rejoinder of the conservatives was logical and convincing. They pointed out that this novel view was inconsistent with the attitude of our Lord and His apostles to those Holy Oracles. They showed that the Son of God believed implicitly in the sacred writings, regarded the earlier books as historical and wholly reliable, and the prophetic portions as already, or else sure to be, fulfilled; and that the same was true of the apostles. They concluded that this new approach to the Old Testament, being diametrically opposed to that of our Lord and His closest followers, and which had never been held by any school of thought within the Universal Church before, must therefore be rejected.

The Sceptics' attack on the New Testament and the Person of Christ

Then the innovators, instead of recognizing the force of this argument and in penitence abandoning their false conception, propounded another theory to evade the supreme, final and infallible authority of Jesus Christ our Lord. They declared that the books of the New Testament and especially the gospels were not to be taken at their face value, because, so they affirmed (although wholly contrary to facts), these precious documents were not written at the early dates usually assigned them but at least a century or more after the death of Christ. And thus, these critics contended, the gospels did not record the true facts concerning the birth, Person, and works of the Saviour and an accurate recapitulation of His discourses, but their distortion after they had passed from one person to another, and from the first to the second and then from the second to the third generation, in the process of which they were added to, exaggerated and idealized. In other words, according to these critics, the four testimonies of the earthly life and teaching of the Saviour express the delusions of the Christian

Church of the second century, which had grown up in the popular mind spontaneously and without conscious or deliberate fabrication on the part of anyone, as the real outlines of the form and teaching of Jesus became blurred in the memory of mankind. They attest, not the facts of the early first century, but the beliefs of the middle of the second century.

The rest of the New Testament suffered similarly at the hands of those who must be described as deluded teachers. According to them many of the epistles had been written not by the apostles but long after their decease, and so were marked by many aberrations if not falsifications.

It is neither possible nor necessary here and now to trace the course and development of this scepticism through its various phases of religious Rationalism, Higher Criticism, Liberalism, Modernism, Barthianism and Neo-Orthodoxy. It is true that later critics in dating the books of the New Testament have receded, in some cases considerably, from the figures of their predecessors, but broadly speaking their contentions and the results are the same. It must suffice to point out to the reader that it produced a thorny problem for these neologians—that of removing from the Christ as He is set forth in the Holy Oracles those attributes ascribed to Him, those facts concerning His works, and those statements found in His discourses, which according to their ideas should have had no place in the pages of the New Testament. In due course, instead of the Christ of God these deceived and deceiving authorities presented various Christs of their own imaginations.

Amongst these critics there was to be found every degree of unbelief, from the moderate to the extreme, and according to their grade of scepticism, so was their Christ.

Christ robbed of the recognition of His uniqueness

There was first questioned, and then denied, one, more, or all of those great doctrines which Evangelicals hold are vital to the Gospel—the virgin-birth, the sinlessness, the omniscience, infallibility, atoning-death, bodily resurrection, ascension and coming again of the Saviour. Some of these liberals conceded Divinity to the Lord Jesus but on the express understanding that it differed from humans in degrees only, not in kind. So, by these men in this way[1], the Jesus Christ of Holy Scripture and of History was shorn of His essential Deity and of the supernatural. There was the evasion and the denial that He was the Son of God in that unique sense which means that He is God the Son, the Second Person of the Blessed Trinity. There was thus presented a Jesus Christ who was the most godlike man who ever walked this earth without being God manifest in the flesh with all the attributes of Deity.

All this has a most important bearing upon some recent versions of Holy Scripture. These anti-Christian views—for on reflection they cannot be less than that—have, alas, leavened the professing Protestant world. Very large numbers of the theological professors, and of the lecturers in the colleges, and as a consequence most of the preachers, are infected, more or less, with these apostate ideas, and this to a far greater extent than the usual occupant of the pew realizes. Some of

---

[1] Scholars of the highest eminence, such as for example the late Professor Sir William Ramsay, who spent many years in archaeological work along the routes of the journeys of Paul, both testing and confirming up to the hilt the historical accuracy of the apostolic writings, have pointed out a fact which is of the most damaging nature to these negative theories. It is that these critics did not begin to suspect a late origin for the Gospels and other New Testament books on account of the indications which they had detected in them. On the contrary; having formed for other reasons, mainly sceptical, the belief that the books must be incorrect and unhistorical, they framed the theory of their late origin, and then set to work to find in them the required indications of lateness. The real ultimate case of their eagerness to discover grounds for the support of their theory lay in their preconceived idea that the Word, who was with God and was God, could not have become flesh. Their theory of the New Testament was a subterfuge to undermine and invalidate the infallible authority of Christ and His endorsement of the Old Testament. See *The Historical Jesus,* ch. VII in *The Education of Christ* by Sir William Ramsay, one-time Professor of Humanity in Aberdeen University.

those who have been or are engaged in translating Holy Writ are earnest men, not sparing themselves to excel in their task, but are to be pitied for they have never really been instructed in the truth. From their childhood they have heard, not evangelical exposition of the Word of God and of the gospel (such as is found in the writings of the late Bishops J. C. Ryle and H. C. G. Moule and the sermons of C. H. Spurgeon), but their caricature. They have had instilled into their minds at Sunday and day schools, in their place of worship and at college, the subtle errors of modern theology (rather neology). Hence they have approached their sacred work ignorant of the truth and with a distinct bent towards the liberals' conception of Jesus. Thus their renderings in some passages concerning the Son of God not only fail to do justice to His pre-eminent uniqueness but actually, indirectly and directly, deny it and prepare the ground for the reception by the undiscerning reader of some of those sceptical doctrines of the critics. This will be apparent in the examination of the two most widely circulating versions of this last generation.

The Verbal Inspiration of Scripture

Another essential factor in the production of worthy versions of the Word of God is the honouring of the doctrine of Verbal Inspiration. The right faith is, as is evident from the attitude and teaching of our Lord and His apostles, that every word that Moses and the other writers of Holy Scripture penned was exactly what God Himself willed to be written. It is not possible to deal with this fundamental doctrine of apostolic Christianity in this article[2]. It must suffice to quote the weighty pronouncement of the late Rev. R. Wright Hay, the one-time secretary of the Bible League: 'How the Spirit caused men to produce writings, the very words of which He could authenticate as His own, we do not pretend to say: but that He did cause this to happen we affirm. And we believe that the pass which we are seeking to defend is the Thermopylae of the Christian faith; and that if once it is surrendered among the churches of Christ, there is nothing for the Holy Spirit to use to prevent the enemy coming in like a flood'. These words are even more apposite to this generation than they were to his readers of thirty or forty years ago. For today an ever increasing number of commentators and translators repudiate this doctrine, and have no compunction in what virtually amounts to tampering with the traditional text of Holy Writ. Those who have thus abandoned the faith of the apostles, when dealing with a sentence or a passage which (largely owing to the antiquity and consonantal nature of the Hebrew) presents a difficulty or problem, instead of confessing their own limitations and waiting patiently and prayerfully for fuller light, hesitate not to pronounce the text 'corrupt', even 'desperately corrupt'. Then one will substitute for it what in his judgment he considers it should read, while another introduces a different re-construction and others still more variants. As a general rule there is no unanimity amongst them as to what the text should be. Thus they make the slight difficulty 'confusion worse confounded'. They are frank enough to call their alteration 'conjectural emendations' and 'corrections' (usually denoted by the letters Cn). *Chambers' Dictionary* defines 'conjecture' as 'a forecast; an opinion formed on slight or defective evidence; an opinion without proof; a guess'. The critics therefore confess that their dealing with the time-honoured text of Scripture is on the basis, not of facts, but of opinions which lack proof and are guesses. It has already been shewn that these opinions are biassed, being definitely antagonistic to the only logical approach to the Bible and to Christianity, which are founded on the substantiated claim that God has intervened in the affairs of the world ruined by the Fall, and that intervention is supernatural in character. It might be added that the whole ministry of these Modernists, by pen through commentaries, and in lecturing and speaking, is, broadly speaking, of a similar character. Their employment of the word 'conjectural' shows that their service, rather dis-service, is an airing of opinions which are without proof and merely guesses. In the final analysis, moreover, they are antichristianism presented in a most subtle manner. Their view-point is not only illogical, full of uncertainties and inconsistencies, but raises far larger difficulties and problems than taking God's Word just as it is.

[2] Dr. J. C. Ryle, first Bishop of Liverpool, treats of this in his tractate, *The Inspiration of Scripture.*

Further, some of these critics declare that the abandonment of the doctrine of the Verbal Inspiration of Scripture gives them a freer hand in translation work[3]. In the light of this confession, it is therefore not surprising that many of their renderings reflect their extreme liberal views.

These preliminary observations should emphasize the fact that the Bible is the unique book of the world's literary productions, witnessing throughout its pages to that unique Person, even our Lord and Saviour Jesus Christ, who alone of all who have walked this earth, was and is perfect God and real yet sinless man, thus necessitating a unique approach for the study of the Holy Oracles and their translation. Any other approach will be defective. Hence those who have abandoned the apostolic faith cannot but be unreliable expositors and translators; they will steer the soul toward shipwreck instead of building it up on its most holy faith (1 Tim. 1:19 and Jude 20).

A brief reference to the Samaritan Scriptures and other early sacred literary activities is essential, if that chain of events which led to the production of the Authorized Version, and in the last hundred years of further revisions and new translations of the Bible, is intelligently to be followed.

The Samaritans and their Religion

Certain matters relating to the origin of the Samaritan people and religion, and to their holy books are the subject of controversy amongst the learned and it is not possible to be dogmatic on some points. It is certain, however, that the Lord delivered the northern Kingdom of Israel for its apostasy into the hand of the King of Assyria, who deported its inhabitants to the far corners of his empire, and substituted for them a new body of settlers from the region of the Tigris and the Euphrates (2 Kings 17:1-24).

Probably there was a remnant of Israelites who escaped this deportation and remained in the land and intermarriage took place between them and the newcomers. Consequently a new race arose, later to be known after their capital as the Samaritans, amongst whom there lingered something of the religious tradition of the dispossessed Israelites. At the beginning of this new chapter in the history of this part of Palestine, ravages of lions were attributed by the people to the anger of 'the God of the land', and on their appeal to the Assyrian king an Israelitish priest (apparently with assistants, 2 Kings 17.27) was sent to instruct them. At first their religion was of a motley kind, 'they feared the Lord and served their own gods' (2 Kings 17:33). But the reformation and revival of true religion, which took place in Judah in the reign of King Josiah, penetrated this northern region (2 Kings 23:1-20, 2 Chron. 34:1-7), and these Samaritans seem to have submitted to the destruction of their idols and nominally to have adopted the pure revelation of God.

Shortly after this Judah for its apostasy was delivered into the hands of Nebuchadnezzar and the majority of its people was taken captive to Babylon. Seventy years later many of the exiles returned and re-established the southern state. The relations between the Jews and the Samaritans were not good, and there was constant friction and hostility between them (see books of Ezra, Nehemiah and John 4:9).

Scripture makes it clear that Nehemiah had occasion to deal sternly with one of the grandsons of the high priest for defiling his priesthood by transgressing the marriage law (Neh. 13:28). Josephus declares that this expelled priest was Manasseh, and that when Nehemiah drove him away he went to his father-in-law Sanballat, who then built a temple on Mount Gerizim and made his son-in-law the high priest. In this way the Samaritans built up a rival system of worship to that at Jerusalem (John 4:20).

The Samaritan Pentateuch

Manasseh had sufficient regard for the Law of the Lord to make the five books of Moses (Genesis, Exodus, Leviticus, Numbers and Deuteronomy), slightly amended, without any other books of the

---

[3] See for example Dr. Moffatt's preface to his translation of the New Testament—'Once the translation of the New Testament is freed from the influence of the theory of verbal inspiration, these difficulties cease to be so formidable'.

Old Testament, the basis of the life and worship of the Samaritans. Their Pentateuch is written in the old Hebrew characters that were extant before the beginning of the use of the square letters adopted by Ezra. It has been maintained independently, with its own transmission by copyists, and translated into a few other languages since the fifth century B.C. Hence its origin goes back further than any version, and this makes it of special interest to Biblical scholars even if its value for textual criticism is small.

Some authorities have thought that this recension was made from a copy of the Law carried into the northern kingdom at the time of the secession of the ten tribes. There can be little doubt that there were copies in Israel during the days of its kings, although neglected and largely forgotten, and maybe one or two were left behind when the Assyrians deported the people. It is more than likely that a copy or copies were introduced by Josiah when he suppressed the idolatry of the northern state (2 Kings 23:15-20); or it may be that the priest whom the Assyrian king despatched to instruct the people took a copy of the Law back with him. Or Manasseh himself could have taken a copy of these books when he left Jerusalem for Samaria. Whether one, some or all of these likelihoods is the historical fact, is immaterial. What is certain, is that Manasseh had a copy of the Pentateuch as it was written before Ezra's inspired editing and transcribing into the new alphabetical characters, and that this Samaritan high priest and other leaders altered it slightly so as to conform to the ecclesiastical course the people were to pursue.

The Variations of the Samaritan Pentateuch

One of the most striking deliberate changes in the Samaritan text is the substitution, in Deut. 27:4, of 'Gerizim' for 'Ebal' to point to the pre-eminence of the former, the site of their temple, over the latter, and to reflect adversely on Jerusalem and its holy shrine. Other differences introduced are (a) alterations in the ages given in the genealogical tables found in Genesis chapters 5 and 11· (b) the weaving of apparently rabbinical tradition into the text as, e.g., in Gen. 4:8 where to 'And Cain said to Abel his brother' is added 'Let us go into the field', and likewise in Gen. 7:3 to the reading 'of fowls also of the air' is added 'which are clean'. These additions are probably correct as matters of fact but uninspired. Further, anthropomorphic expressions are modified to comply with Samaritan theology and idiom, and sentences here and there are recast under the idea of clarifying the sense, or avoiding some difficulty or conforming to some parallel passage.

The Samaritan Pentateuch was known to the early church, and renewed interest was evoked when copies were secured for the libraries of Western Europe in the 17th century. It was critically studied by such scholars as Archbishop Ussher (1581-1656), Dr. Kennicott (1718-1783), and others nearer this time. Their opinions differ as to its textual value but all are agreed that it does furnish evidence as to the general accuracy of the work of the Massoretes.

The Targums

No account of the transmission and translation of the Word of God would be complete without a reference to the Targums or Aramaic paraphrases and expositions of the Old Testament. It has already been noted that when the Jews were taken captive to Babylon, Hebrew soon became a language known and spoken only in the select circles of the learned. The vast majority of the rising and succeeding generations did not trouble to learn it. They spoke solely the language of those amongst whom their lot was cast. This was Aramaic[4] (but at a later date must be added Greek and other tongues). Thus it came to pass that when large numbers returned to the land of their forefathers to repopulate it, the tongue of the reconstituted state was not what it had previously been, Hebrew, but Aramaic. As a consequence whenever the Hebrew Scriptures were read at the public services in the rebuilt Temple in Jerusalem, or in the synagogues of the homeland or of the dispersion, there was of necessity begotten the custom for a scholarly official to translate the Hebrew text of the lessons into the language (Aramaic) which the people understood and spoke. This was obviously what took place when Ezra returned to the sacred city, and the people assembled for instruction in the things of God.

'The book of the law of Moses' was brought before them and it is recorded that Ezra and his colleagues 'read in the book of the law of God distinctly, and gave the sense, and caused them to understand the reading' (Neh. 8:8). The first extemporaneous translations developed in process of time into paraphrases and even expositions, became stereotyped, and were eventually committed to writing as the Targums (i.e., the Translation, Paraphrase, or Interpretation). Amongst the best Targums are those of the Pentateuch by Onkelos, a literal translation, and on the Prophets by Jonathan ben Uzziel which is a paraphrase. There were other Targums covering almost the entire Old Testament. These Targums are a valuable aid in determining the text as read at Jewish services, and in discovering the meaning the Jews attached to it, especially any difficult passages.

It is of interest to note that the awe-ful words of our Lord on the Cross, 'Eli, Eli, (or 'Eloi, Eloi'), lama sabachthani?' (Matt. 27:46; Mark 15:34) meaning 'My God, my God, why hast Thou forsaken me?' were partly from the Hebrew and partly from the Aramaic paraphrase of Psalm 22, verse 1. In the light of the facts cited it is not surprising that many other Aramaic words and expressions have inevitably passed into the Greek of the New Testament such as: 'Abba' meaning 'father' (Mark 14:36; Rom. 8:15; Gal 4:6); 'Aceldama' that is to say, 'The field of blood' (Acts 1:19); 'Ephphatha', that is, 'Be opened' (Mark 7:34); 'Mammon' denoting 'riches' (Matt. 6:24); 'Maran-atha', the prayer, 'Our Lord, Come' (1 Cor. 16:22); 'Talitha cumi' which is 'Damsel, arise' (Mark 5:41).

---

[4] Noah's son Shem begat Elam (from whom were descended the Elamites), Assur (the progenitor of the Assyrians), Arphaxad (ancestor of Abraham and so of the Jews) also Aram (see Gen. 10:21-31; 11:10-29). Arams's descendants, the Aramaeans, occupied that part of what is now called the Middle East to which his name was given, and which stretched from the Lebanon mountains to the Euphrates (Num. 23:7). Greek writers applied to the people of this region the term Syrians, perhaps a corruption of Assyrians: hence the name Syria, the usual rendering of the Authorized and Revised Versions. To the various parts of Aram were given different names: Aram—Naharaim, i.e., Aram between the two rivers, more familiarly known under the Greek word 'Mesopotamia' (Ps. 60 title; Gen. 24:10; Deut. 23:4; Judges 3:8-10; 1 Chron. 19:6; Acts 2:9 and 7:2) wherein lay Padan—Aram (Gen. 25:20; 28:2, 5, 6, 7; 31:18; 33:18; 35:9 and 26; 46:15); Aram—Zobah (ps. 60, title); Aram—Damascus or Syrians of Damascus (2 Sam. 8:5; Isa. 7:8; Amos 1:5); Aram—Bethrehob (2 Sam. 10:6); Aram—Maachah (1 Chron. 19:6 and 7); Aram—Geshur (2 Sam. 15:8). All these people and their languages were related even if distantly. Of the Aramaic tongue there were two branches, the Eastern or Chaldee and the Western (Mesopotamian or Palestinian). The latter was known also as Syriac. The Palestinian was of three kinds: Jerusalem, Samaritan and Galilean.

(continued on page 277)

The Holy Scriptures: The Task of the Translators and the Story of the Early Versions (Part II)

By Bishop D. A. Thompson

The Spread of the Greek Culture and Language

Another great change affecting the speech not only of the Jews but also of the inhabitants of all the lands of the Eastern Mediterranean seaboard was in store. In less than three hundred years the Babylonian Empire (whose most illustrious ruler was Nebuchadnezzar, see Daniel, chapters 1 to 4) was absorbed by the Medo-Persian (under the Cyrus whose edict permitted the Jews to return to Jerusalem—2 Chron. 36:22 and 23, Daniel 6:28), which in turn was overthrown by the armies of Greece under the astounding generalship of Alexander the Great. This ambitious ruler and brilliant administrator died (B.C. 323) at the early age of thirty-three in Babylon, which he had intended to make the capital of his new empire. This extended from Greece in the west to the frontier of India in the east, and from Persia in the north to Egypt in the south. Wherever the Greek armies marched and Greek officials directed the life of the people, there too, Greek culture spread and the Greek language became the medium of communication. (Even the ruling and learned circles of Rome fell under the spell of Hellas, so that when this city became the mistress of the world, her officials were perhaps even more at home in her Greek-speaking eastern possessions than in the lands to the west of the capital where Latin had become the common tongue).

Through Alexander's conquests many lands hitherto backward were opened up to trade, industry and a higher standard of living. He founded new cities and gave special privileges to enterprising and trustworthy merchants who would settle in them and the older commercial centres, and develop the trade of his empire. Amongst those who responded to these opportunities for advancement and wealth were the Hebrews of the dispersion—the descendants of those who had been deported from the northern kingdom to Assyria and from the southern to Babylonia. Thus representatives of the twelve tribes became scattered abroad (James 1:1), finding homes in all the leading cities of the Greek dominions, preparatory to penetrating the chief centres of population in the west also, including Rome itself. It was not long before these Jews no longer spoke and understood the Aramaic of their immediate forbears and could only converse in Greek. Wherever they settled they established synagogues, but as few could follow the reading of the Hebrew Scriptures or the Aramaic paraphrases which followed, they realized their need for a Greek translation of their holy books. At the same time the earnest and thoughtful heathen neighbours of these Jews, who wanted to know about their religion, displayed an interest in having their sacred writings rendered into the language which half of the known world of that time could understand. In the wonderful Providence of God this felt need from these two sources was marvellously met.

The Septuagint

Alexander's policy for Egypt led to something approaching a revival of its ancient glories. He founded a new city by the delta of the Nile and named it after himself. Alexandria soon became the leading sea-port, naval base and capital of the land. To it Jews of the dispersion flocked in such large numbers that it was not long before they were about one-third of the population. When Alexander died, one of his generals, Ptolemy, made himself the ruler of the country and founded that dynasty of Macedonian kings which extended from B.C. 323 to B.C. 30. The first two of these monarchs, Ptolemy I (B.C. 323-B.C. 285) and his son Ptolemy II (B.C. 285-B.C. 246) were patrons of the arts and promoters of scientific research. They established in their capital the biggest library of the ancient world, boasting a collection of over one-fifth of a million books. It would appear that the librarian Demetrius Phalereus felt that a copy of the Scriptures translated, however, into the Greek, as they were unintelligible in the Hebrew, ought to have a place on the shelves. As the suggestion was favoured by the local Jews and met with the approval of the highest authorities in Jerusalem, the work of producing the first, the most famous and in some respects the most important version of the Old Testament went forward. The details concerning this epoch-making undertaking are uncertain. One tradition asserts that Eleazar the high priest sent seventy-two aged and skilful interpreters, six from each tribe, to Alexandria; that they were hospitably received and translated the Law, i.e., the Pentateuch, in seventy-two days. This belief of roughly seventy men completing their task in approximately seventy days led, it is thought, to the version being called the Septuagint, from the Latin word 'septuaginta' for seventy, and hence usually written LXX. Another theory is that the name is derived from the fact that the seventy members of the Egyptian Jewish Sanhedrin sanctioned the translation.

These matters on which there can be no dogmatism are immaterial. What is beyond dispute is, that the first five books of the Bible appeared in Greek about the beginning of the third century B.C.; that the translation of the other books of the Old Testament followed; and that they were welcomed by the world-Jewry of those days. It is evident that the version is the work of many translators as differences in the quality, style and method of the various parts show. In some books the translation is excellent, in others very poor, being either too slavish or too free. In spite of its linguistic blemishes, the Lord of the Word used it marvellously for the extension of His Kingdom. It circulated all over the world of that day wherever Jews were to be found. It introduced the Revelation of the true God to inquiring Pagans. It thus, in no small way, helped to prepare Jewry and the world for the coming of the Son of God, and for the rise and rapid spread of Christianity. It was known to and used by our Lord and His apostles, for some of the New Testament quotations from the Old Testament are according to this version (others being direct translations from the Hebrew, doubtless to ensure a better rendering and greater accuracy). It was the Old Testament of the early Christian Church to which was added the New Testament written in the common Greek of that time, with which Bible as the Sword of the Spirit the first Christian generation waged such mighty warfare, overthrowing the strongholds of Satan, that in less than three hundred years the civilized world acknowledged, at least outwardly, the Lordship of Christ. In these ways God used this Greek Version for the working out of His purposes.

The Apocrypha

It is at this period that some other Jewish writings, uninspired and known collectively as the Apocrypha, make their appearance. This literature, consisting of fourteen books with a total of one hundred and seventy-two chapters, varies greatly in character and value, from accurate history and lofty thoughts to unreliable records, worthless legends and doctrinal errors such as the merit-earning power of alms (Tobit 4:7-11) and prayers for the dead (2 Mac. 12:44-46, especially Douay Version).

'Apocrypha' is the Greek for hidden or secret things. The word itself has an interesting and illuminating history in the course of which it changed its meaning and came to denote that which is unauthorized and spurious. This arose from its use in connection with the mystery religions of those times. The public, reading the books of these religions, understood them in the natural sense. But those who aspired to the inner circle, the 'initiates' were told by the priests that the stories of the gods and goddesses, and all the particulars and details of the rites and ceremonies connected with them, had a hidden meaning. The leading priests, known as hierophants, who prepared the probationers for full membership by instructing them in these hidden meanings, required them to keep this information, usually designated as knowledge and wisdom, to themselves, as a secret not to be imparted to those outside their privileged company. This stood in marked contrast to Christianity and the Bible, whose 'mysteries' were set forth plainly in the Word of God for all to read, mark, learn and inwardly digest, and where wisdom and knowledge, while hid in Christ, were for all who repaired to Him in faith (Matt. 13:11; Rom. 11:25 and 16:25; 1 Cor. 2:7 and 8; Eph. 1:9; 3:3-12; 6:19; Col. 1:25-29 and 2:3). As the influence of Christianity and its impact upon the heathen increased, the latter began to feel that the 'hidden meanings' were unauthorized by the deities and spurious. So the connotation of 'apocrypha' changed and when Jerome applied the word to these Jewish and to some subsequent writings it implied that they lacked the authority of God since they were without the inspiration of God, and, as Scriptures, were not holy but spurious. Never once does any one of its writers declare 'The Word of the Lord came unto me, saying', or any equivalent formula.

Summary of the Apocrypha

The First Book of Esdras is an uninspired history of the Jews from the time of Josiah to that of Ezra; the second book is a religious treatise, largely apocalyptic in character resembling somewhat the visions granted to Daniel and to John under the symbolism of beasts. *Tobit and Judith* are romantic, but fictitious, narratives of a Jewish hero and heroine. The addition to *Esther* amplifies parts of the Scripture narrative, without furnishing a new fact of value and often contradicting it. *Wisdom* is an imitation of the book of Proverbs. *Ecclesiasticus* is an ethical treatise reflecting parts of Proverbs, Ecclesiastes and Job; and the section towards its close in praise of famous men (44:1—50:21), part of which is often read at memorial services, is finely written. *Baruch* is a feeble imitation of Old Testament prophecy. *The Song of the Three Children,* the *Benedicite* of the Anglican Prayer Book, is on the whole a most noble hymn with its refrain, 'Praise Him and magnify Him for ever'. It was designed to follow Daniel 3:23; as *The History of Susanna* was intended to precede that book, and *Bel and the Dragon,* in which the wisdom of the prophet Daniel is praised, to conclude it. *The Prayer of Manasses* is a compilation of Old Testament passages. *The First Book of the Maccabees* is valuable as a history of the Jewish war of independence, under the Maccabee family of Levites in the second century B.C. The second book deals with a portion of the same period but is much less valuable and reliable.

The Apocrypha not Inspired but merely Human

It is necessary to reiterate, because of the misconception which abounds on this subject, that this particular literature was not inspired and so is not part of the Word of God, although occasionally found bound up with it. The Apocrypha was never given a place in the Jewish canon of the Old Testament. It is not quoted in the New Testament. It was not recognized as a section of the Divine Oracles by the Primitive Church. It ought to have been kept as a volume of uninspired Jewish writings distinct from the Old Testament or the Holy Bible. But while it was not included at first in the LXX, its various books unfortunately found their way into later copies, inserted in places that seem appropriate. So certain portions came to be read in churches as setting forth instruction in manners and providing examples of noble living, but never with the intention that they were to be regarded as part of the Holy Scriptures. In the fourth century, Jerome, one of the then outstanding leaders of the Church, made it clear that these apocryphal books were not of the Divine Library (as he styled the Canonical Books of the Bible) and must only be valued as throwing light upon the times when no prophetic voice was heard—those four hundred years following the death of Malachi and terminating with the commencement of the Gospel story. In spite of this, however, the good man, under pressure from Rome and against his better judgment, translated and included most of these uninspired books in his Latin version of the Bible, the Vulgate, as it became known. This regrettable concession paved the way to one of the great errors of the Church of Rome. Its Council of Trent in 1543 declared the Apocrypha (with the exception of I and II Esdras and The Prayer of Manasses) to be of equal authority and value with the sixty-six books of Holy Writ, and pronounced an anathema against anyone who rejected the dogma. The Reformed Churches, faithful custodians of the truth of God, made suitable reply. The Church of England in the sixth of her thirty-nine Articles published in 1562 calls the Apocrypha books which 'the Church doth read for example of life and instruction of manners; but yet doth it not apply them to establish any doctrine'. The Westminster Confession of Faith (1646) declares that 'The books, commonly called Apocrypha, not being of divine inspiration, are no part of the canon of the Scripture; and therefore are of no authority in the Church of God, nor to be any otherwise approved, or made use of, than other human writings' (chapter 1, section 3).

The Apocrypha was included in some of the early English versions of the Bible but began to be omitted in the Puritan era. When inserted it was placed between the Old and New Testaments. In 1826 the British and Foreign Bible Society decided (and rightly) against its inclusion in any volumes issuing from its press.

The Unprecedented Sacred Literary Activity of the Early Christian Church

With the incarnation of the Son of God followed by His atoning death, bodily resurrection and ascension, and also the outpouring of the Holy Ghost, a new era in the world's history commenced. As the Lord had raised up a succession of holy men to write the books now known as the Old Testament, and then in His Providence had brought about their translation from Hebrew into Greek and their diffusion throughout the leading cities of the civilized world, so He worked in a similar way at the very threshold of the new dispensation that the written record of Divine revelation might be complete. The God of Truth moved certain of the apostles (Matthew, John, Paul, James, Peter and Jude) and two apostolic men (Mark and Luke) by the Holy Spirit, to pen those gospels and epistles which came to be called the New Testament, and that in Greek, the language in which they could penetrate the highest circles as well as influence the largest possible number of ordinary folk. This new collection of books was the perfect complement of the earlier compilation. It was not long before the holy Church throughout all the world acknowledged these sixty-six books, constituting the Holy Bible, as distinct from all other literature, as having the authority of God, because having the inspiration of God, and therefore being inerrant and the sole rule of faith and practice.

The missionary zeal of the apostles and of the first generation of converts led to a world-wide expansion of the Church. By the end of the first century of this new age there was no part of the Roman Empire where believers in the Lord Jesus were not to be found, and before the close of the fourth, Christianity had triumphed over Paganism. This issued in an unprecedented demand for copies of the Holy Oracles for use in places of worship and by individuals who could both afford to purchase and were able to read the same. Moreover the large numbers who became obedient to the faith from amongst those people who did not know or were not sufficiently familiar with Greek as to be able to follow clearly the reading of the Scriptures in that tongue, emphasized the need for translations, which were undertaken with surprising speed. This is the more remarkable when it is remembered that during the three hundred years which followed the birthday of the Christian Church there were frequent outbursts of savage persecutions against the followers of Christ, when to confess His Name and to possess and to reverence copies of the Word of God entailed the most serious consequences, often involving the faithful in being thrown to wild beasts in the arena or being burned alive.

Early Versions

One of the first translations was that from the Hebrew Old and the Greek New Testaments into the tongue of the mass of the people of the Roman Province of Syria, the Aram of previous times. It is known as the *Peshitta* or *Peshito,* a word inferring that it is the correct and simple rendering. It was circulating in the second century. By reason of its elegance it has often been called the 'Queen of Versions'. About the same time the Septuagint and New Testament were rendered into the Latin spoken in North Africa, where it was well received. But its provincialisms grated on the ears of those speaking the same tongue in and nearer Rome; a revision was called for, and from its being made in Italy it was known as the *Itala.* Towards the close of the second century the Bible was rendered into the two leading Coptic dialects of Egypt, the *Memphitic* (spoken in the north) and the *Thebaic* (for the south). The turning of Ethiopia to Christianity in the early fourth century was followed by the translating of the Holy Scriptures into *Giz* or *Ethiopic.* About a hundred years later the *Armenian* and *Gregorian* versions appeared. A little earlier Ulphilas, Bishop of the West Goths, produced a translation for his people. In the ninth century the brothers Cyril and Methodius of Thessalonica, missionaries to Bulgaria and Moravia, first reduced the Slavonic language to writing and then rendered the Word of God into that tongue. Those who spake Arabic were not overlooked: divinely-raised-up labourers entered this field too, that the former might, like those already mentioned, hear and read in their mother tongue, the wonderful works of God.

Revisions of the Septuagint

It has already been pointed out that this version was not a uniformly good translation, nevertheless this rendering of the Hebrew text into Greek, by Jews for Jews, was well-received by Jewry and used in the synagogues for some eight or nine generations. But about the beginning of the second century of this era satisfaction gave place to heart-searching, suspicion and prejudice, accompanied by a general desire that there should be a revision. There was a cause for this revulsion towards the Septuagint. Earnest Christians used it to show that Jesus of Nazareth in His Person, earthly life, atoning death, resurrection and ascension fulfilled those Scriptures which the Jews themselves admitted were prophetic of the Messiah. The inference was obvious: Jesus was the Messiah, Christianity was Judaism come to its full flowering: and the Saviour was the Second Person of the Holy Trinity. Some Hebrews saw the truth of this, yielded to it and confessed the faith of Christ. Most Jews, however, while they could not deny the logic of this reasoning were unwilling to assent to its conclusions. These justified their attitude by contending that the Septuagint was an unworthy translation of the Hebrew, and that this applied particularly to the Messianic portions. From that time to this the leaders of Israel have urged that the Hebrew of certain of these passages should be rendered in a different way. They give it a sense which does not, directly or indirectly, point to the Messiah as being the Second Person of the Godhead. Their renderings, dictated by their doctrinal viewpoint, have been largely adopted by the Modernists, and are reflected in the English language revisions of the Bible which have emanated this last generation from liberal translators. That these Jews and Modernists, are mistaken—that they have failed to give the proper sense of the Hebrew—will be shewn from the pages of the infallible New Testament, as this study proceeds.

There can only be one explanation of the fact that men of such undoubted scholarship and learning should so grievously err. It is that they are spiritually in the dark and without a personal experience of the saving grace of God; that they approach their work of translation and exposition of the Word of God biassed against the fact that God the Son became real but sinless man without ceasing to be God, and are prejudiced against everything of a supernatural character which is recorded in the Gospels concerning the Lord Jesus Christ.

Jewish Revision of the Septuagint

This impulsion for a new translation of the Old Testament into Greek first found expression in the work of Aquila. It appears that he was a native of Pontus and a nephew of the Emperor Hadrian (76-138), who employed him in the rebuilding of Jerusalem, which was to be called Aelia Capitolina. It is believed that Aquila turned from Paganism and made a profession of Christianity, but on being reproved for practising astrology he became a proselyte to Judaism. He seems to have come under the influence of Rabbi Aquiba and through him undertook to make a fresh translation of the Hebrew Scriptures to counteract the use of the Septuagint made by the Christians in advancing their doctrine.

His translation was very literal and accurate except in key Messianic passages where his determination to checkmate the Christian appeal gets the better of his intention to be correct in his renderings. He definitely and deliberately mistranslates in Isaiah 7:14 so as to undermine the doctrine of the virgin birth of the Saviour, a falsification which Modernists have welcomed and adopted, and as will be seen later, is retailed in liberal versions like Dr. Moffatt's and the American Revised Standard.

Other work on the Septuagint

Aquila's work was followed by another revision undertaken by Theodotion, said to have been a Jewish proselyte of Ephesus, and who probably joined the Ebionites, believing in the Messiahship but not the Deity of Christ. A third translation, elegant but sometimes lapsing into paraphrasing, came from the labours of Symmachus, a Samaritan Ebionite.

The work of these three men in this particular field of endeavour was consummated by that of Origen (185-254). This distinguished Church philosopher (from whose expositions of Scripture and of doctrine, evangelicals would often have to dissent) was concerned for the preservation of the purity of the text of Holy Writ. With this end in view, he devoted many years to the study, along lines of his own devising, of the text of the Old Testament. Origen is thus the pioneer of that worthy science, Textual Criticism.

Origen arranged the Hebrew text and four different versions in six parallel columns for purposes of comparison. In the first column he wrote the Hebrew text, in the second he transliterated the Hebrew into Greek letters, in the third he placed the version of Aquila, in the fourth that of Symmachus, in the fifth the Septuagint, and in the sixth the revision of Theodotion. From these six columns his work takes its name of Hexapla. Later he prepared a smaller edition containing the last four columns only, hence called the Tetrapla. He had his own system of marking and of making notes.

These valuable volumes were deposited in the library founded by his disciple Pamphilius at Caesarea in Palestine. They seem to have been destroyed when the city was sacked by the Saracens in the seventh century.

Jerome and the Vulgate

It is impossible to follow the story of how the Bible has been passed on from one generation to another, and translated into the mother tongues of the leading nations of the earth, without a brief sketch of the life, work and character of Eusebius Sophronius Hieronymus more familiarly known as St. Jerome (c. 340-420). He was borne at Stridon, a town on the border of Dalmatia, of Christian parents of wealth and standing. After instruction at home he was sent to Rome where he received the best education possible in those days. Impressed by the stories of the martyrs told by eye-witnesses of their sufferings, Jerome confessed the faith of Christ. He returned home with the scholar's tastes and cravings for knowledge. The next years (360-379) were devoted to travels in the west, further studies, and then a tour along the route of the missionary journeys of the apostle Paul. At Antioch one of his closest friends and companions died of a fever and he himself became dangerously ill. These things made a deep impression on him spiritually, and as he was recovering he resolved to devote himself more fully to the Scriptures. He sought to perfect his knowledge of Greek and began studying Hebrew. After being ordained presbyter he visited Constantinople and then returned to Rome (382). Here the Pope Damascus whose life and policies seem a strange mixture of good and evil, recognizing Jerome's great gifts, directed him into the channel of translating the Word of God. For various reasons, including the changes in language which come with the years, the old Latin versions, already mentioned, called for revision. So Jerome began what was to be his great life work, and which was to bear fruit in every succeeding generation. His first efforts were concentrated on the Psalter. He produced a new translation for Rome and Italy, and another for use in Gaul.

Protestants who will admit that they owe not a little to this Latin father deeply regret that he was deficient in his knowledge of evangelical truth, and was an enthusiast for monastic life.

During his sojourn in Rome (382-5) he ministered to a number of widows and maidens, and extolled the supposed virtues of celibacy. When he left for the East many of them, including two of considerable wealth, Paula, a widow, and Eustochium, her daughter, accompanied him, all vowed to live according to this erroneous idea, which is without the warrant of Holy Writ and in due course was fruitful of many evils. Eventually they settled in Bethlehem, where Paula built four monasteries, three for nuns and one for monks. She was at the head of the nunneries until her death in 404, when Eustochium succeeded her; Jerome presided over the fourth monastery.

The Bethlehem Days

Here, Jerome with his outstanding abilities settled down to his great literary works. He wrote a number of commentaries, and historical sketches, and translated many of the sermons and theological treatises of preachers and writers of earlier days. But he is chiefly remembered as the translator of the

Hebrew Old Testament and Greek New Testament into the Latin which was the *lingua franca* of the western division of the Roman Empire at that time. Hence it is known as the Vulgate, a word derived from the Latin intimating that it is the translation into the tongue of ordinary people (of that part of the world), as indeed it was when it first appeared, although it ceased to be with the passing of a few generations, as will be outlined later.

(continued on page 284)

The Holy Scriptures: The Task of the Translators and the Story of the Early Versions (Part III)

By Bishop D. A. Thompson

In this great undertaking the dispositions of Providence and the wisdom displayed by Jerome are clearly discerned. Bethlehem was not far from Caesarea with its famous library housing Origen's Hexapla, and other manuscripts and books indispensable to the textual critic and scholar. To this lovely seaport and cultural centre Jerome was able, with comparative ease, to journey to consult those authorities which would enable him to ascertain as far as was humanly possible the original text of Holy Scripture, which he then translated to the best of his great abilities. For this painstaking care to eschew all corruptions of the text many of his contemporaries gave him abuse rather than gratitude· and the eminent scholar, 'whose temper was none of the best, retorted by expressing the contempt which knowledge feels for blatant and aggressive ignorance'.

Further, in Palestine and centred particularly in Tiberias, only a little further from Bethlehem than Caesarea, there was found the very cream of the Jewish learning of those times. And Jerome was great enough and wise enough to tap this fund of sacred knowledge in pursuit of his determination to translate the Old Testament direct from the Hebrew. He mentions the help he received from a rabbi from Lydda and from Rabbi Ben Anina, who came to him by night secretly for fear of the Jews! But perhaps still greater was his debt to a rabbi from Tiberias. The significance of this, arising from the educational and religious activities pursued within this town must not be overlooked. When the Romans destroyed Jerusalem in A.D. 70 they spared Tiberias becasue its citizens favoured rather than opposed the victors' arms. So this place was one of the few that emerged from that desolating conflict unharmed, and to prosper, while all around felt the impoverishing effects of that cruel strife. In the light of this fact it is not surprising that the Sanhedrim, dispossessed of the capital, fixed its seat here early in the second century. Tiberias then, like a magnet, drew to within its walls, those pious Jews who were devoted to the study of their sacred Scriptures. Academies sprang up and soon became famous as halls of learning, giving to Jewry the Misnah (about 220 A.D.) and the Talmud (420 A.D., the year Jerome died). In this town, too, the guild of the Massorites—whose profound knowledge of the Hebrew text was priceless—made its home. So Jerome through his contact with the helpful rabbi from Tiberias was really drinking of the Massoretic stream which flowed from the work of Ezra. And in this way the Lord completed his equipment and qualifications for the translating of the Word of God. Thus, too, Bethlehem, Caesarea and Tiberias, all famous in the annals of the Bible, made each its own special contribution to that great work.

The Vulgate

It took Jerome almost twenty years to render the Holy Scriptures into the Latin of his day. Under pressure from Rome and against his better judgment, he included most of the Apocrypha in his work, but made it clear and left it on record that the latter is not part of the Word of God. On account of its intrinsic worth his version soon drove its predecessors from the field. In process of time its text underwent corruption but there were recensions to restore its purity by Alcuin, at the instance of Charlemagne at the beginning of the ninth century; by Lanfranc; and later, through the expressed wish of the Council of Trent (1546) by Pope Sixtus V (1590) and his successor Clement VIII (1592). The Vulgate has the distinction of being the first book ever to be printed, being issued from the newly invented printing press, 1455.

It has been said that Jerome 'is one of the few Fathers to whom the title of Saint appears to have been given in recognition of services rendered to the Church rather than for eminent sanctity. He is the great Christian scholar of his age, rather than the profound theologian or the wise guide of souls'. These remarks are very true provided the endorsement does not cover the Roman Catholic doctrine of sainthood reflected therein. Jerome was not an attractive character. He could be very bitter and his pen vitriolic. In controversy he too often mingled personal abuse with legitimate argument. This weakness mars his letters, which are valuable for their history of the man and his time.

Diocletian reorganized the Roman Empire, and that reorganization rapidly led, territorially, administratively and also ecclesiastically into the permanent division of East and West. Jerome's lot was cast in those days of change. The East, as has been seen, was, if the expression may be used, well catered for in respect to versions of Holy Scripture. Each of its groups of peoples early had the Word of God in its mother tongue. Jerome's work was, that the whole of the West might have a good and dependable version in the language that all of its several countries or provinces could follow. And it was so, but only for a very short time. Another confusion of tongues, a second Babel, through the irruption of the Barbarians, was to overwhelm the West, and render the Vulgate, so soon after its completion, useless to the people. The Church of Rome did little, if anything at all, to remedy this disaster. But in the mysterious Providence of God, catastrophe in the East together with the invention of printing brought about revival in the West. This, however, was not till the fifteenth century. Then Jerome's and the Greek versions of the East became the well-spring of new translations and of undreamed of circulations of the Holy Scriptures, first in Europe and then throughout the whole world.

A Lesson from the Primitive Church

One of the great truths which emerges from the study of Church history is, that the primitive churches felt it imperative to give the Word of God to every soul in its mother-tongue, whereas when the Church of Rome became corrupt it vehemently opposed this principle.

This monument of Jerome's scholarship and industry is a landmark in the story of the versions. It became the Bible of the whole western church in the Middle Ages and remains the Bible of the Roman Catholic Church still. It is the father of other versions like that of Wycliffe, and has made direct and valuable contributions to other translations, although it is not without blemishes. It gave terms to, and helped to mould, the technical language used in theology.

The God of Abraham praise,
Who reigns enthroned above,
Ancient of everlasting days,
And God of love.
Jehovah, great I AM!
By earth and heaven confessed;
We bow and bless the sacred Name,
For ever blest.

The God of Abraham praise,
At whose supreme command
From earth we rise, and seek the joys
At His right hand;
We all on earth forsake,
Its wisdom, fame, and power;
And Him our only Portion make,
Our Shield and Tower.

The God of Abraham praise,
Whose all-sufficient grace
Shall guide us all our happy days,
In all our ways:
He is our faithful Friend;
He is our gracious God;
And He will save us to the end,
Through Jesus' blood.

He by Himself hath sworn—
We on His oath depend—
We shall, on eagles' wings upborne,
To heaven ascend:
We shall behold His face,
We shall His power adore,
And sing the wonders of His grace
For evermore.

The whole triumphant host
Give thanks to God on high:
'Hail, Father, Son, and Holy
Ghost!'
They ever cry.
Hail, Abraham's God and ours!
We join the heavenly lays;
And celebrate with all our powers
His endless praise.

(*Thomas Olivers,* 1770)

Why I prefer the Authorised Version of the English Bible

By E. J. Poole-Connor

I have recently been studying afresh the parables that are found in the thirteenth chapter of Matthew, and have been again struck by the fact that the Lord impresses upon His disciples that the supreme power by which the kingdom of heaven would be set up would be by the sowing of the seed of the Word of God. This surely includes the circulation of copies of Holy Scripture, and the blessing of the Holy Spirit upon its reading to the knowledge of the way of salvation. The apostle Peter tells us that we are 'born again, not of corruptible seed, but of incorruptible, by the word of God, which liveth and abideth for ever'.

One of the reasons why I have such a strong preference for the Authorised Version is the fact that it was translated by men who clearly recognized that Holy Scripture is the inspired Word of God. In the earlier editions of this Version there was a very long preface which is found in very few editions of the Scriptures today. In it the translators bear testimony to their belief that the sacred volume was not of man but of God, that it was not human but divine, and much more to that effect. In those days people wrote very voluminously and the preface would cover several pages of close print· but the greater part of it was a recognition of the fact that they were entrusted with a very solemn responsibility in translating what they knew to be the Word of God. This sense of responsibility is manifest on almost every page of their work. I do not think that in any subsequent version in the English language there has ever been so clear a recognition of the divine inspiration of Holy Scripture as was then expressed. In the New English Bible there is a somewhat perfunctory prayer that God may bless the translators' labours; but I might almost say that as much is said about Dr. Dodd (who was the Chairman or Director of the panel of translators) as about God Himself. Other versions, such as Moffatt's and Phillips' translations, have no such clear recognition of Holy Scripture as being the veritable Word of God as that of the Authorised. This is one reason why I have so great a preference for the King James's version.

II

Another reason why I honour and respect the A.V. is that the men who translated it thoroughly understood and valued the great truths that were embodied in the Reformation of that period. It was not very long before its publication that there had been a breakaway from the Church of Rome, and the men who met together to give us the Authorised Version were fully acquainted with all the distinctions of doctrine between the teachings of the Church of Rome and those of the Protestant Reformers. They were very careful to put into exact language the particular truths for which Protestantism stands. If you will look through the New Testament in particular with that thought in mind you will see how clearly it is to be noted. This cannot be said of the N.E.B. It has, in the interests of the ecumenical movement, corrupted the Word of God (2 Cor. 2:17). It has given an interpretation of certain texts according to Roman Catholic errors instead of translating them. It has rendered John 1:42 'You shall be called Cephas (that is, Peter, the Rock)' instead of 'Cephas, which is by interpretation, a stone'. There is a big difference between an immovable rock and a small stone, a pebble. So, too, the N.E.B. in Matthew 16:18 reads, 'You are Peter, the Rock; and on this rock I will build my church' whereas the A.V. has, 'Thou art Peter, and upon this rock I will build my church'. Holy Writ gives the title 'The Rock' to the Lord Himself—2 Sam. 22:2; Ps. 18, vv. 2,31 and 46; 31:3; 42:9; 1 Cor. 10:4; the apostle was a stone and no more than a stone. Further, nowhere in the Greek text does our Lord, during His years of public ministry, address Mary as 'Mother'. There is reason for this. Without entering into detail, it may be said that it was to indicate His unique Sonship and absolute independence of her, and as if to warn in advance against the use of the expression 'Mary, the

Mother of God'. The A.V. correctly translates the original of John 2:4 'Jesus saith unto her, Woman, what have I to do with thee? mine hour is not yet come'; the N.E.B. deliberately falsifies the verse to, 'He answered, "Your concern, mother, is not mine. My hour has not yet come".' Likewise the A.V. accurate rendering of John 19:26 is, 'Woman, behold thy son': the inaccurate N.E.B. wording is, 'Mother, there is your Son'. In these flagrant mis-translations the N.E.B., as has been truly said, 'outpopes the Pope and outRomes Rome'. In contrast we have in the Authorised a truly Protestant Version without the least unfaithfulness to the original Scriptures.

III

Further, in common with multitudes of others, I have a very great respect and admiration for the Authorised Version because of the majestic English into which it has been rendered by the translators. This came about very largely in the over-ruling providence of God. Some little time before the Reformation, Europe had been awakened by what was called the Renaissance, or Revival of Learning. The human mind, after many years of bondage, began to regain its freedom; a number of Greek manuscripts were discovered which helped to enlarge the thought and enlighten the understanding of mankind in many ways; and amongst other results of this Renaissance, or rebirth of learning and intellect which, as I have said, preceded the Reformation by some few years, was that the English language attained a power and purity such as it had never before known. Some of us at school had to read the plays of Shakespeare, chiefly because of the wonderful English in which they were written; and that same beauty and majesty of language is found in our Authorised Version. Yet it reads quite simply. There are very few passages that the ordinary person cannot understand. What are commonly called 'archaic' passages are very few; but its dignity and its rhythm are alike most impressive. How important a part of public worship is the careful and measured reading of Holy Scripture! There is a music in it which attracts the mind by its richness and beauty.

When we turn to some other versions, and in particular to the New English Bible, it is like coming down from a heavenly region to a very earthly region indeed. There are phrases in the New English Bible which are really very little removed from slang, and there are expressions that very much grate upon us, however sincerely we try to be fair in our estimate of it. For instance, it says concerning certain things that Stephen said to the Jewish Council that it 'touched them on the raw'. Imagine that being read from the pulpit! In Matthew 25, where we have the Parable of the Talents, when the faithless steward presents his excuses for not using the money entrusted to him, the New English Bible makes the master say, 'You lazy rascal!' instead of 'Thou wicked and slothful servant'. The latter is a dignified phrase; moreover, we have to remember that the words are an intimation of what our Lord Himself will say to an unfaithful servant in the day of reckoning. Can we imagine that in the solemnity of our Lord taking account of our stewardship He would say, 'You lazy rascal'? It is almost an insult to put such a saying into His mouth. I must confess that I am constantly irritated as I read the New English Bible; there are so many things in it that do not ring true, that lower the dignity of the Word of God. Another instance of this is that it makes our Lord say after His resurrection to His disciples when they were fishing, 'Shoot the net to starboard'. Now as a matter of fact the term 'starboard' was never known until centuries after, and then only at first amongst the Vikings, because of the way by which they steered their vessels. Our Lord would not have used such a word. He said exactly what the Greek text says He did—'cast the net on the right side of the ship' (John 21:6). The New English Bible translation seems to show a kind of smartness, a parading of knowledge of nautical terms. The whole version has come down to a much lower level, merely regarded from the standpoint of the English into which it has been rendered. This is something which greatly influences me in regard to the matter of preference.

IV

Then there is an aspect of the question which touches on a somewhat intimate and experimental side of Christian life. To very many of us, when the Lord has spoken to us personally through His

Word, it has been through the Authorised Version. I remember my dear father, who was a very saintly man, saying to me when I was a boy that one object which God had in giving us Holy Scripture was that He would have a channel of communication with His people, and I am sure that every one of you now present can remember occasions when the Holy Spirit has laid a particular passage of Scripture upon the mind as God's personal word to you. My father was once deeply in prayer concerning his family, and after he had been pleading with the Lord for some time God gave him the word, 'All thy children shall be taught of the Lord'; a promise which has come true, as I can here testify. May I venture to add that the Lord has never spoken in my own experience in anything other than in the language of the Authorized Version? It is very dear to many of us on that very ground. We do not claim that it is inspired as was the original, but we do believe the Lord greatly helped those who gave it to us.

I close by relating an instance which occurred during my pastorate of the Talbot Tabernacle, in that part of London which then included not only very aristocratic quarters but also districts where men of very low character had their dwelling. In one of these was a young man who took up boxing and made some success of it, and that led him into bad company. He got into the circle of a gang of thieves, and fell into much evil. After a time he was taken by the police and put in prison. One day while there he began to rail on God and on Scripture for permitting this to happen; but in his cell there was a Bible which he opened at random at the 50th Psalm. These are the words that he read—'But unto the wicked God saith, What hast thou to do to declare my statutes, or that thou shouldest take my covenant in thy mouth?' It was as if God spoke to him audibly, saying, 'What right have you to quote Scripture and cavil at my dealings?' He read on: 'Seeing thou hatest instruction and castest my words behind thee. When thou sawest a thief, then thou consentedst with him, and hast been partaker with adulterers. Thou gavest thy mouth to evil, and thy tongue frameth deceit . . . These things hast thou done and I kept silence; but I will reprove thee'. He knew that every word of the Psalm was true, and he realized that it was God speaking to him through it. When he reached the verse 'Now consider this, ye that forget God, lest I tear you in pieces and there be none to deliver', he flung himself on his knees, and cried, 'O God, don't go on any further, I cannot bear it'. But he picked up the Bible again and read, 'Whoso offereth praise glorifieth me; and to him that ordereth his conversation aright will I show the salvation of God'. He took that word 'conversation' to mean 'speech' and he went on his knees again and spoke to God now very differently. He cried for salvation and received it. He later became a member of my church, and a very godly man.

CHAPTER 3.

1 *He advertiseth him of the times to come,*
6 *describeth the enemies of the truth,* 10
propoundeth unto him his own example,
16 *and commendeth the holy scriptures.*

THIS know also, that [a]in the last
days perilous times shall come.
2 For men shall be [b]lovers of their
own selves, [c]covetous, [d]boasters,
[e]proud, [f]blasphemers, [g]disobedient
to parents, unthankful, unholy,
3 [h]Without natural affection,
[i]trucebreakers, [5]false accusers, [k]in-
continent, fierce, despisers of those
that are good,
4 [l]Traitors, heady, highminded,
[m]lovers of pleasures more than
lovers of God;
5 Having a form of godliness, but
[n]denying the power thereof: [o]from
such turn away.
6 For [p]of this sort are they which
creep into houses, and lead captive
silly women laden with sins, led away
with divers lusts,
7 Ever learning, and never able [q]to
come to the knowledge of the truth.
8 [r]Now as Jannes and Jambres
withstood Moses, so do these also
resist the truth: [s]men of corrupt
minds, [t6]reprobate concerning the
faith.
9 But they shall proceed no further:
for their folly shall be manifest un-
to all *men*, [u]as their's also was.

a 1 Tim. 4. 1. ch. 4. 3. 2 Pet. 3. 3. 1 John 2. 18. Jude 18.
b Phil. 2. 21.
c 2 Pet. 2. 3.
d Jude 16.
e 1 Tim. 6. 4.
f 1 Tim. 1. 20. 2 Pet. 2. 12. Jude 10.
g Rom. 1. 30.
h Rom. 1. 31.
i Rom. 1. 31.
5 Or, *makebates*, Tit. 2. 3.
k 2 Pet. 3. 3.
l 2 Pet. 2. 10.
m Phil. 3. 19. 2 Pet. 2. 13, &c. Jude 4, 19.
n 1 Tim. 5. 8. Tit. 1. 16.
o 2 Thess. 3. 6. 1 Tim. 6. 5.
p Matt. 23. 14. Tit. 1. 11.
q 1 Tim. 2. 4.
r Ex. 7. 11.
s 1 Tim. 6. 5.
t Rom. 1. 28. 2 Cor. 13. 5. Tit. 1. 16.
6 Or, *of no judgment.*

10 [x]But [7]thou hast fully known
my doctrine, manner of life, pur-
pose, faith, longsuffering, charity,
patience,
11 Persecutions, afflictions, which
came unto me [y]at Antioch, [z]at Ico-
nium, [a]at Lystra; what persecutions
I endured: but [b]out of *them* all the
Lord delivered me.
12 Yea, and [c]all that will live
godly in Christ Jesus shall suffer
persecution.
13 [d]But evil men and seducers shall
wax worse and worse, deceiving, and
being deceived.
14 But [e]continue thou in the things
which thou hast learned and hast
been assured of, knowing of whom
thou hast learned *them*;
15 And that from a child thou
hast known [f]the holy scriptures,
which are able to make thee wise
unto salvation through faith which
is in Christ Jesus.
16 [g]All scripture *is* given by inspira-
tion of God, [h]and *is* profitable for
doctrine, for reproof, for correction,
for instruction in righteousness:
17 [i]That the man of God may be
perfect, [2k]throughly furnished unto
all good works.

u Ex. 7. 12. & 8. 18. & 9. 11.
x Phil. 2. 22. 1 Tim. 4. 6.
7 Or, *thou hast been a diligent follower of.*
y Acts 13. 45, 50.
z Acts 14. 2, 5.
a Acts 14. 19, &c.
b Ps. 34. 19. 2 Cor. 1. 10. ch. 4. 17.
c Ps. 34. 19. Matt. 16. 24. John 17. 14. Acts 14. 22. 1 Cor. 15. 19. 1 Thess. 3. 3.
d 2 Thess. 2. 11. 1 Tim. 4. 1. ch. 2. 16.
e ch. 1. 13. & 2. 2.
f John 5. 39.
g 2 Pet. 1. 20, 21.
h Rom. 15. 4.
i 1 Tim. 6. 11.
2 Or, *perfected.*
k ch. 2. 21.

The Testimony of Chemistry to the Accuracy of Scripture

By Dr. Arthur C. Custance

It is a curious thing that, while we often hear it said that the Bible is completely unscientific, it is constantly being confirmed by Science. And while many are also saying that its proposals for dealing with human problems are hopelessly outdated, its precise analysis of the root of these human problems is constantly being validated. The idea that the real trouble in society stems from the fundamental wickedness of the human heart has consistently been repudiated by 'moderns' who, at the same time, constantly refer back with confidence to the views of Freud who affirmed precisely the same thing—that human nature is essentially bad. This odd double vision which denies the truth in the Bible and acknowledges it everywhere else is one of the evidences of the noetic effects of sin, and demonstrates clearly how great a need there is for a man not only to have his spirit re-born (John 3:3) but his mind renewed (Rom. 12:2).

Recently, while searching for something else in scientific literature, I came across three items which illustrate how faithfully Scripture deals with facts. And part of this remarkable quality is that statements are often made which, superficially viewed, appear to be absurd and yet are set forth without apology or explanation, as being unquestionable. It is as though the author knew He was speaking the truth, and knew also that in due time the truth of His words would be established.

The first of these little items has to do with the use of straw in bricks. The early chapters of Exodus tell how the Israelites in their servitude were required to make a quota of bricks, using straw, supposedly as a binder, and that these bricks were used for the building of what we might call 'grain elevators' in our modern world, which were situated in places called Pithom and Raamses. Some years ago, Edouard Naville discovered the supposed site of one of these places in which the lower courses of brick contained free straw, the middle courses stubble, and the higher courses little or no straw at all. This circumstance was believed to confirm the story of Exodus 5:6-19, where it is recorded that the hardships of the Israelites were increased by taskmasters who forced them to gather the straw themselves whereas formerly they had been supplied with it.

After reading in Naville's account how a visitor to the site had expressed interest in the absence of straw in the upper courses of brick, Professor Eric Peet of Liverpool University pointed out with a show of superior wisdom that it was no surprise to him at all.[1] For, he said, 'It is almost inconceivable that any traveller in Egypt should make this statement with regard to the use of straw in bricks, for though straw has been used both in ancient and modern times, its use is somewhat rare, more particularly in ancient times'. He proceeded to point out that the Nile mud makes perfectly good brick without any binder, making the assumption (as most of us have done) that straw served *this* purpose only.

The Professor's assumption cannot be justified. Edward G. Archeson, in a Paper printed in the Transactions of the American Ceramic Society in 1904, described certain experiments he made as the result of a chance discovery, which led to a technique for greatly improving the strength and impact resistance of bricks.[2] He was surprised to discover on one occasion that certain German clays were far superior to local American clays for the making of pottery, both with respect to plasticity and tensile strength. His surprise sprang from the fact that the clays did not feel or look different nor did chemical analysis reveal any essential differences. However, being a novice and unaware of previous research work done in this field, he came to the subject with an entirely fresh mind and soon found that

[1] Peet, T. E., "Egypt and the Old Testament", University of Liverpool Press, 1922, p. 99.
[2] Acheson, Edward G., "Egyptianized Clay", *Transactions of American Ceramic Society,* N.Y., 6th Annual meeting, February, 1904, pp. 34 and 39.

'residual' clay differed from water-laid or sedimentary clays, the latter being superior even though their compositions appeared to be identical. He hazarded a happy guess that the process of water-laying had introduced some component which had hitherto escaped recognition. To make a long story short, he discovered that gallo-tannic, when introduced into clay, not only improved the tensile strength of the finished brick, but considerably shortened the time required for drying it since less water was required to make it readily mouldable. His conclusion was that gallo-tannic acid was being introduced into water-laid clays by water which had itself percolated through vegetation and in doing so had picked up the modifying chemicals. Thus Acheson concludes:

> 'It was therefore possible perhaps for the Egyptians to produce a *sun*-dried brick of greater strength from the straw-treated clay than from the same clay untreated *and burned.*
>
> The addition of either tannin or straw emulsion to the clay diminished the amount of water that was necessary to produce a sufficiently plastic mass for moulding.'

In other words, less water was required (important in a dry country), less shrinkage occurred, there was less cracking, less time to 'temper', and there were fewer lumps: by contrast there was increased plasticity, greater density, greater tensile strength and increased hardness. And, incidentally, Acheson's discovery accounts for the fact that even stubble served a useful purpose—which seemed much less likely to have been the case if it was to constitute a binder only. Thus it appears that the ancient Egyptian technicians were wiser as technicians than was Professor Peet as a Professor!

I came across the second confirmation while studying the literature dealing with ion exchange surfaces. The book I was studying opened with a very brief historical review of the development of ion exchange resins. On the very first page I came across this statement:[3]

> 'The treatment of waters by solid absorbents such as sand is probably as ancient as civilization itself . . .
>
> A recent interpretation of the miracle supposedly performed by Moses as he led the Israelites safely through the wilderness suggests the possibility of ion exchange. In order to make the "bitter" water of Marah potable (fit to drink) during their journey through the wilderness, Moses found a tree "which when he had cast it into the waters, the waters were made sweet".
>
> It has been suggested that the oxidized cellulose of the tree had entered into an exchange reaction with the bitter electrolytes of the water, rendering the water drinkable.'

There are some readers who may be disturbed to discover that what they had always thought of as a miracle now turns out to have been a straightforward chemical process, and to them such findings may even appear sacriligeous. We shall return to this question in a moment, but there is one more 'unexpected' testimony that I should like to put on record first.

I suppose it does not occur to one, normally, to ask how salt can lose its saltiness. It is difficult to see how it could. After all, salt is salt. And yet Jesus said that this could happen.

Recently in *The New Scientist* under the caption, Trends and Discoveries,[4] the editors report that the question was asked of chemists, 'Why did biblical salt lose its savour?' Apparently quite a few answers were received. And here I quote their report:

> 'One biblical passage must have puzzled many chemists. In a letter to *Chemistry and Industry,* D. F. Perriman asked for an explanation of that part of the Sermon on the Mount (Matt. 5:13) in which Jesus refers to salt losing its savour as if this were a common experience to his audience.
>
> 'In a subsequent issue of the same journal, a number of correspondents rose to the challenge, and a general consensus of opinion was apparent. The suggestion is that salt in biblical times was a very impure product, obtained by natural or artificial evaporation of Dead Sea Water, and was further contaminated by insoluble solids, like sand and calcium sulphate . . .
>
> 'The high concentration of magnesium chloride in Dead Sea salt renders it deliquescent (easily washed out by absorption of water from the atmosphere), and it might easily absorb so much water

[3] Kunin, Robert, and Robert J. Myers, "Ion Exchange Resins", John Wiley, N.Y., 1950, p.1.

[4] *The New Scientist,* July 15, 1965, p. 155.

on being stored that the soluble salts would gradually be leached out, leaving only an insoluble and tasteless residue.

'R. Child (in a letter) quoted a passage from the 17th-century traveller, Henry Maundrell, who described a natural deposit of salt bearing out this explanation: "I broke a piece of it, of which that part that was exposed to the sun, rain, and air, though it had the sparks and particles of salt, yet it had perfectly lost its savour; the inner part, which was connected to the rock, retained its savour as I found by proof (i.e., taste)".'

I am sure that if any one had ever said to me, How in the world can salt lose its salty taste? I should have been completely at a loss as to how to answer the question. But there it is: now we have the answer. I'm quite sure, as someone once said, that no man living knows enough to be able to challenge the truth of the Bible with success. But the question is whether we might not suffer a great loss if in the course of time we were to find the natural explanation to every event recorded, even those which we have always assured ourselves were miraculous. It is worth asking whether this could ever occur, or, to put the question in a slightly different way, whether there is some element about miraculous events which is entirely beyond investigation in this sense. Augustine said that miracles were not contrary to nature, but contrary to what is *known* of nature. This is a profound statement, but I think it carries an implication which is not true: namely, that the more we know of nature, the less room for miracle there will be. I believe that there are areas which will prove beyond investigation. Moreover, I believe that one of the most important elements in miracle is in the timing of the event. As an illustration, it now appears that when the waters of Jordan were held back for the Israelites to cross, a natural dam may have occurred some distance upstream as the result of the swollen waters undercutting a cliff (Josh. 3:16). The miracle here is not so much in stopping the waters but in the fact that the waters stopped at the very moment the feet of the priests stepped into it. And I believe that in the every-day experience of the child of God, there are to be observed recurrent miracles of this kind in which God's provision is precisely timed to fit the need.

Nevertheless, in the meantime, there are events for which we have no explanation, which are indeed contrary to what we know of nature and yet which we know to be a fact. In his Harveian Oration for 1965 before the Royal College of Physicians in London, Sir Theodore Fox made this observation:[5]

'To contemplate the Universe is to stand even more abashed. For somehow, at some time, all that we see and touch and hear must have emerged from Nothing. To us this transformation of nothing into something is contrary to reason; and the creation of the universe is a mystery that man may never be able to understand. Yet the universe seems to exist; and we must beware of making excessive claims for any system of thought that finds the origin of the universe impossible'.

Even the most scientific mind is, therefore, faced with the necessity, in this one instance at least, of accepting as fact what cannot reasonably be so. Nor would it answer the question to argue that the universe has always existed, for this is no more readily conceivable. In either case we are forced to believe what is inconceivable. The Christian certainly has no need to be ashamed of his confidence in the Word of God even though there may be things written there which appear to the world to be both irrational and inconceivable.

[5] Fox, Sir Theodore, "The Purposes of Medicine", *The Lancet,* London, October 23rd, 1965, p. 804.

Bible Distribution

an address by C. H. Spurgeon

Scatter the Bible without stint, strew the sacred pages 'thick as leaves in Vallambrosa'. Put it into the hand of prince and peasant, leave it in the waiting-room and the car, give it to the sceptical philosopher and the unsophisticated child. 'In the morning sow thy seed, and in the evening withhold not thine hand.' Spread the Scriptures till they are as universal as the light, as all-pervading as the air, as all-refreshing as the dew.

What is the Bible to us that we should wish to spread it throughout the habitable earth? The answer is a large one. First, it is to us

The Umpire of Truth

Let the umpire be where he can be heard. The Scripture is our court of appeal; let it be open to all comers. Every man must have an anchorage for his faith; even for his unbelief he needs some form of holdfast. The disputer of this world believes in himself, and so he ends the matter. The Roman Catholic finds his anchorage in the infallibility of the Pope, and submits his reason to the traditions of his Church. You and I find our anchorage in the infallibility of Scripture. The Holy Ghost moved holy men of old to write this Book, and we believe that every word of it is inspired, and that if we could get absolutely the exact words in which it was written at the first, we should have a book as perfect, certain and immutable as God Himself. We know that in any one version of it there may be minor errors of copyists, which could not have been avoided unless a miracle had been wrought every day for thousands of years; but allowing for that, we hold that the volume containing the Old and New Testaments is God's revelation of Himself to us in words—a revelation to read it. We desire to see the truth triumphant, and error defeated; and therefore we scatter the Bible. We would see the divided church once more purged of heresies, and united in one Lord, one faith, and one baptism; and therefore we scatter the Bible. If this Book be the test of truth, those who are the children of truth are the most deeply concerned to see it brought to the front.

'This is the judge that ends all strife,
Where wit and reason fail.'

Let us proclaim the judgments of this judge in all places. To me one text of Scripture is worth seven years of argument. Fathers, schoolmen, reformers, Puritans, bishops, and even ecclesiastical courts are nothing in comparison with this oracle of God.

The text-book should be accessible to every man. No one should be allowed to go abroad into an atmosphere loaded with superstition and scepticism without bearing the antidote with him. We should not merely provide it for him when he seeks it, but we should suggest his use of it by furnishing an abundant supply. Every man should be able to judge of the truth and value of the teaching of the pulpit and the press by having in his hand the law and the testimony by which all must be judged.

Brethren, the Bible is to us, next,

The Storehouse of Truth

It not only helps us to judge what is truth, but it tells us what truth is. Shall we not wish that all our neighbours should possess such a treasure? Will we allow one poor wandering gipsy or street-beggar to be without the book which makes wise the simple? The marvellous fulness of Holy Scripture reminds me of certain of our coal-mines. Coal is found upon the surface, and it gladdens the cottager's hearth without costing him labour in coming at it. Even thus there are truths in the Bible which are conspicuous to every reader, and are learned without study or research. When the surface-coal is gone, the miners dig down till they come to another seam, and the same thing is done many times: they go further into the bowels of the earth, and they find still more treasure. In such mines there is no exhaustion; so long as the expense of the descent can be borne, the enterprising digger may go far down under the bottom of the mighty sea, and still find full veins to reward him. Men exhaust a coal-mine, but they will never work out the Biblical mine, nor come to the end of the truth that is in God's Word. I do not know what truth is not in the Bible. A band of eminent men once taught that all science is to be found in the Bible: they conceived it to be a thesaurus of philosophical and physical truth, as well as of theological truth, and they said that all discoveries which are made externally by science might have been made within the inspired volume if we had looked for them. They asked if the circulation of the blood was not taught by Solomon long before Harvey's day, and if the rotundity of the earth and its position in space were not clearly indicated? All things were and are known to that great Author who inspired the writers of this Book, and it is small wonder if His omniscience betrays itself. When our very wise men have discovered all they can, it may be that their wisdom will become sufficiently prudent to look up to the foolishness of God; but as yet the foolishness of God is wiser than men—the Book in which God conceals the secrets of nature is yet too bright for mortal eye.

What a storehouse it is, since a man may continue to preach from it for five-and-twenty years, and still find that there is more to preach from than when he began to discourse upon it! What pyramids of books have been written upon the Bible, and yet we who are students find no portion over-expounded, but large parts which are scarcely touched. If you take Darling's Cyclopaedia, and look at a text which one divine has preached upon, you will see that dozens have done the same: but there are hundreds of texts which remain like virgin summits, whereon the foot of preacher has never stood. I might almost say that the major part of the Word of God is in that condition; it is still an Eldorado unexplored, a land whose dust is gold. This is a tempting subject. The Word of God is the great Popular Educator, the treasurehouse of wisdom and knowledge, and surely, we who desire to see around us a holy, happy, instructed people, must most anxiously desire that all men should read and believe, and understand the message of the Lord.

Next, far and wide disperse the Holy Word, because it is—

The Great Exemplar of Morals

To whom shall we go for help in this matter if we forget this thrice-holy Book? The common novels of the day are sorry teachers of morality; they teach a great deal more of immorality. The religious fiction of the day is little better: it is either goody-goody, teaching men and women how to be babies, or else it is suggestive of doubts which minister weakness to the soul. And what are all the essays and the theories of reviewers? What are all the tomes of the sages, and the gatherings up of centuries? London would become a field of blood if its only force for the maintenance of law, order, and right were found in the current literature of the period apart from the Bible and religion. The Scriptures give us a perfect law, and fix its commands upon the firm foundation of God's claim to man's obedience. It reveals to us the perfect example of our Lord Jesus Christ, and gives us the most powerful motives for copying that example, by attracting our love to Him on account of His life and death on our behalf. It supplies virtue with courage, and gives zeal to justice. If we would create a thoroughly moral people, it can only be done in connection with the diffusion, belief, and practice of the Scriptures. The spread of sound morals is an absolute necessity of good government, especially in our great cities. Sin is a political danger. But the people's morals cannot be cared for except upon the basis of religion, and there is no religion but that of the cross. Banish religion and you destroy virtue. We will not say that no infidels have been moral, but we do say this, that unknown to themselves they were under influences which sprang out of religion and its outgrowths, and so they were not fair specimens of what atheism alone would produce. Go to France in 1797, and see what happens to a nation when the sacred volume is removed and its teachings are derided: there the gospel of Pandemonium brought forth its Millennium, and anarchy created upon earth the express likeness of hell. If you would settle the pillars of order upon the basis of liberty, let the Word of God be in the hands of all your citizens: and if you would go on to build an enduring empire, which shall be a temple of blessings to all mankind, let the sacred page be every day more studied, better understood, and more heartily practised.

Holy Scripture is not only the teacher of morals, but it is—

The Great Enforcer of Truth

Other books tell us the truth, but this puts us in love with it; they instruct us, but this converts us. That is a fine example which is told of Junius, who had been for years an infidel. His father persuaded him to come home, and being grieved at his opinions, begged him, for the love of his father, to read the New Testament. He said he would read it once; and here is his testimony concerning it: 'When I opened the New Testament I first fixed my eyes on that august chapter with which St. John begins his Gospel: "In the beginning was the Word, and the Word was with God, and the Word was God". I read part of the chapter, and was soon convinced that the divinity of the argument, and the majesty and authority of the style, did far excel all the eloquence and art of human writings: my whole body trembled, my mind was astonished, and I was so affected all that day that I knew not where or what I was. O my God, Thou wast mindful of me, according to the multitude of Thy mercies; and in pity broughtest home Thy lost sheep into Thy fold'.

The Word not only contains the truth, but it distils a certain secret unction by which that truth penetrates the heart. The Spirit of God is usually pleased to bless the Word of God to the conversion of men. It is a self-evidencing Book, proving its own inspiration by its effects on the soul. I find when I question people about their conversion that it is almost always a text of Scripture that God has blessed to that end. I may have expatiated on the text in my sermon, but the main instrument which the Lord has employed has been the passage itself. It is God's Word, and not our comments upon it, which He usually blesses to the conversion of men. Have you not all felt, who know the Lord, that a wondrous charm is in the Word of God, by which men are gently led to the Saviour? Was it not by one touch of Scripture that the scales were made to fall from your eyes, and you saw the light? *Lex lux:* the law is light. The Bible itself is a preacher, yea, an army of preachers in one: its silent tongue has more eloquence in it than all the tongues of all God's ministers; and often those who have not been led to faith by human voices have heard in the Bible the 'still small voice' of God Himself, and bowed before the throne of the Most High. If you want sinners converted and souls saved, spread the sacred Scriptures. You cannot tell where God will bless them; sow them beside all waters.

Let us spread the Holy Scriptures also, and perhaps chiefly, because they are—

The Very Throne of Christ

I hate to hear Scripture and Scriptural doctrine made into a great stone to roll at the door of the sepulchre of a dead Christ. This may be done by teaching a creed, and forgetting the living personality of our Lord. I have heard of Christians whose principal talk is about 'the church'. God bless the church! But it is not the chief object of our affection. Christ—Christ crucified—must ever stand first. I have joined the society of 'know-nothings'; not the American 'know-nothings', but the old Pauline know-nothings; for I determined to know nothing among you save Jesus Christ and Him crucified. Those who are of that persuasion will be sure to love the Word of God, for it is full of Jesus. 'The Scriptures are the swaddling-bands of the child Christ Jesus'; so St. Augustine used to say. The Scriptures are those beds of choicest flowers where He is ever present—'He feedeth among the lilies'. This is the garden where He delighteth to walk. In the Scriptures, as in the Temple, everyone speaks of His glory. All the prophets and apostles point to Him and with one voice cry, 'Behold the Lamb of God which taketh away the sin of the world'. The ivory palaces of inspiration are fragrant with cassia and myrrh, and all that myrrh and holy perfume come from the presence of Christ in the midst of them. Oh! you who love the Incarnate Word, spread the inspired Word which does Him honour. Oh! you that feel that He loved you and gave Himself for you, if you desire to bring Him an acceptable sacrifice, spread the Word of God all over the world, till every creature shall read the glowing page.

Last of all, let us spread the Bible, for we have no idea how greatly it is—

(After a painting by Thomas Sadler: the only portrait painted during Bunyan's lifetime (1628-88): now in the National Portrait Gallery)

The Consolation of the Afflicted

and the comforter of the poor and troubled. It nourishes the souls of the famished ones. I know many persons who cannot get out to a place of worship, for they have been bedridden for many years; but the Psalms of David, and the blessed words of the Saviour, such as, 'Let not your heart be troubled: ye believe in God, believe also in Me', have been their daily food.

I have heard it whispered by some of God's people sometimes, 'We know not where to get the gospel. We have a preacher, but he is a dry bone; there is no marrow in him, for there is no Christ in his preaching'. When you hear a sermon that has no Christ in it, you are to be pitied: if you hear that man again it is your own fault, and you will deserve to be blamed. I would not give a man a second chance to preach me a Christless sermon. 'That is hard', say you. If a man were to advertise that he could make bread without flour, he might add, 'But I will never do it'. It may be so, but let us judge by an analogy. When I get the idea that a gentleman believes in a gospel in which Christ is not first and last I leave him alone in his glory. Christ must be all in all, or the gospel is not preached. When people live in a region where an adulterated gospel is served out, what a blessing it is that they can go and get the bread of life at first hand from their Bibles! If you live in a region where the milk is watered down, the best thing is to keep a cow of your own: to have your own Bible is like keeping your own cow; from it you get 'the sincere milk of the Word'. And what a blessing it is to be able to have God's Word at so small a cost! Time was when your forefathers would have given all they were worth if they could have had such a treasure. You have it in all your homes; therefore take care that you have it in your hearts.

When we think of the many, many poor people in this great city of ours that suffer very much, and yet are happy because they live on the Word of God as their daily manna; when we think of the many who are full of diseases, whose very bones decay, and yet are joyful and sing all day long because the holy promises are their comforters; when we think of the many that are almost homeless, scarcely knowing where to lay their heads, and are, nevertheless, supremely blessed through the grace of God, we cannot but adore the sacred Scripture, which is the meat and drink of their souls. Take the Bible away! You might as well strike the sun from the firmament, or dry up all the rivers and springs.

I was sitting under a beech tree in the New Forest some time ago, thinking and meditating on that tree. The beech is a very wonderful tree, exhibiting many curious habits and growths. If any tree has intellect it is the beech tree. I was meditating upon my friend the beech, and looking up through the interlaced branches and enjoying the shade, when I saw a squirrel up in the tree, and I said to myself, 'Ah, I do not value this tree as the squirrel does. He knows the trunk avenue, and calls it his High Street, and then he knows all the branch streets, all the little thoroughfares, and the nooks where he can hide himself away. This tree is his town, and he almost counts the leaves as he runs about it. Moreover he has a little store of nuts somewhere in his own private bank, and this tree is a sort of mother and father and general provider for him. He can tell me what sounds it makes at midnight, and what creaking of the branches he hears when the storm is out; for this tree is his world, it is everything to him'.

Now, we ministers go to the Bible for our texts, and value it for that purpose; and ordinary readers go there, and see much of poetry, and much that is interesting and instructive in it; but the poor sinner, heavy-laden with his sins, how precious it is to him when first it reveals his Saviour; and afterwards, when he is worn and weary with the cares of life, how precious is the Word to the believer when it assures him that his bread shall be given him and his waters shall be sure. We do not know the value that one line of Scripture has in the eye of one of God's saints whom that Scripure has sustained. Whenever you give a Bible, you bestow a priceless treasure upon the man who receives it; therefore, do all that you can to spread the Word of God. The Bible is not Christ, but it points to Him. You may not rest in your Bibles as though they could save you, but you must go to Christ Himself for salvation. But still, when you have once believed in the Lord Jesus, set about leading others to Him, and how can you do this more surely than by seeing to it that the Scriptures are scattered everywhere? Farewell.

"One that Findeth Great Spoil."

(Psalm 119.162)

By Dr. W. L. Wilson (of Kansas City, U.S.A.).

I have been thinking that infidelity and atheism and evolutionism, and so forth, have no trophies of grace. Once when Dr. Ironside was preaching a very noted atheist elbowed his way through the crowd and challenged him to a debate. Dr. Ironside said he would be very glad to accept the challenge, with one provision, that this infidel would have on the platform two people whose lives had been transformed through his message, and he himself would have on the platform one hundred people whose lives had been transformed through his message. The atheist disappeared through the crowd. Beloved, the only message that transforms lives is the message of this precious Book.

My text is found in Psalm 119. I think Ezra wrote this Psalm. He 'prepared his heart to seek the law of the Lord, and to do it,' and that is what we have in this Psalm, is it not? 'I rejoice at Thy word, as one that findeth great spoil' (verse 162). That is his personal testimony. I love that verse, I have underscored it in my Bible. It is wonderful really to love the Word of the Lord.

I remember a man who used to work for me as a janitor telling me one day that his wife's birthday came in the following week and he wanted my wife to go and help him purchase a present for her. I said to him: 'How would you like to give her a Bible?' 'Oh, that would be fine;' he said, 'if hers is worn out she would like to have a new one, I am sure.' I got a lovely Bible for him to give to her. During the night he took a ribbon and tied it round the Bible and then he tied the ribbon round her wrist. When she woke up in the morning she tried to lift her hand and could not lift it because of the weight of the Bible; she looked down and found that she had a beautiful new Bible. She took it up and pressed it to her breast, and then she lifted it and kissed it and said: 'Lord, thank You.' She loved her Bible.

'One that findeth great spoil.' Let us think together a little what that means. As you know, finding great spoil means going into the enemy's camp after the enemy has deserted it and getting jewels and silver and gold, as the lepers did from the camp of the Syrians; then they hid the spoils and went and told the king about them. That is what we should do. We find precious things in the Word, and we should hide them in our souls and then go and tell our neighbours and friends about them.

I want to think with you of some of the things that we find in the Word of God. First, let us think of the perfection of the words that we find there, how the Spirit of God has chosen words to convey to us God's mind. My father-in-law said to me once: 'If you want to convey God's thoughts to the people, use God's words.' Here is an example. 'He was delivered for our offences.' Why did not He say, 'delivered for our sins,' or 'delivered for our transgressions,' or 'delivered for our iniquities.' All those statements are true, but He chose a word that covers every possible thing that could be wrong in our lives, in order to show us how completely the Lord Jesus paid the penalty for our sins, for everything wrong—our offences. Our Lord wanted us to know that everything in our lives that could possibly hurt the heart of God was covered by the precious Blood. Then think of these lovely words: 'He bore our griefs and carried our sorrows.' Why did He say the two things—griefs and sorrows? I suppose that most of us in this room belong to the Lord Jesus and are saved; if any of you are not saved I hope that you will be before you leave this room and that you will make Christ your own. We who are saved are quite happy in the knowledge that He bore our sins in His own Body on the tree, and we rest in that and in the knowledge that He bore our griefs and carried our sorrows. See how completely the Lord has supplied this resting place for our hearts. Griefs are things that happen and that we can repair. You lose your purse and you can get another, your house is burned down and you can build another, but if you lose an arm you cannot get another. Griefs are things that are temporary: sorrows are things that are permanent. You lay some precious one in the tomb—that is permanent and that is a sorrow. You have a slight accident with your car—that can be repaired and that is a grief. Our blessed Lord carried both our sorrows and our griefs. How do we carry our own griefs? We go about with a heavy heart when we ought to be singing, grieving when we should be praising. Do we who are in this room really believe that the Lord Jesus bore our griefs and carried our sorrows, so that we can go singing to carry the sorrows of others? You remember Gal. 6. 2: 'Bear ye one another's burdens, and so fulfil the law of Christ.' How can we bear one another's burdens if we are weighed down with our own? We cannot. Our blessed Lord assures us that He took ours, so that we may go and bear the griefs and share the sorrows of others.

Then think of the certainty of the words. Think of the words in the Old Testament; 'He was wounded for our transgressions.' He had not been then; those words were written seven hundred years before He died for us. 'He was bruised for our iniquities'—He had not been when those words were written. Why are they in the past tense? All these precious truths in the Old Testament are in the past tense because whenever our Lord decided upon a thing it was done, so far as He was concerned. I might say with reference to my will: 'I have left all my property to my wife'; I have not yet, but I have made out the will and it is signed and witnessed, and it is all done so far as I am concerned. Similarly, when our blessed Lord says something it is in the past tense; as far as He is concerned it is done; it is only waiting until the time when it should be accomplished. Think of our certainty and then think of the fulness of the revelation of God. I take the Book of Genesis and it tells me something. Evolution does not tell me anything. Think of the seven beginnings in Genesis. There is the beginning of the natural creation; that is the first revelation, because that is the sphere of God's grace. Then there is the beginning of man, who is the subject of God's grace; there is the beginning of sin, which is the reason why there is God's grace; there is the beginning of sacrifice, which is the means of God's grace; there is the beginning of Israel, the channel of God's grace; there is the beginning of the nations at the Tower of Babel, which are the scope of God's grace; and there is the beginning of the life of faith, which is the result of God's grace. Those seven precious beginnings of grace run all through the Word for the blessing of our hearts.

I like to talk to so-called scientists about the origin of things. As you know, there are 92 chemical elements and everything that you see is made of some of those 92 chemical elements.* The human body has 16 of them in it and we know what they are. Every year I get from our Bureau of Chemistry in Washington a qualitative analysis and a quantitative analysis of the human body. The chemical elements are always the same in quality but not in quantity. I can take those 16 elements to my chemical laboratory, but I cannot put them together and make a baby boy out of them. My Lord can do it, but I cannot. I say to my Professor of Chemistry: 'Tell me, where did gold come from? Gold, silver, platinum, radium, sodium, chlorine, bromine—what started these things?' and he has to say: 'I do not know.' I was talking with an atheist the other day, one of our collegers. He said to me: 'Wilson, do you believe that Lazarus came out of the grave?' 'Yes, indeed I do; I know he did.' He said: 'You look like an intelligent man,' and I said: 'Thank you for the compliment. I am intelligent on that subject. I believe God's Word. That man came out of the tomb just as surely as you are standing in that pair of shoes.' He said: 'How did he come out?' I said: 'That is the second question. I say that he heard the voice of Jesus Christ and he came out. But when you ask me how, I say I do not know. Is the reason why you do not believe the story because you do not understand how he got out?' 'Certainly,' he said. I said: 'Well, tell me: how does a butterfly get out of a cocoon?' 'I suppose it bites its way out.' 'Is that so? How many teeth has a butterfly got?' 'I do not know; I do not think it has any teeth.' 'No, it has not even a mouth, let alone teeth. That is one thing you do not know.' 'Well, I suppose it must burn a hole through the cocoon with acid.' 'Would not it be a strange thing if a butterfly had in its body an acid so strong that it would make a hole in a cocoon but would not hurt the butterfly?' 'I never thought about that.' 'That is two things you do not know. Now how does the butterfly get out?' 'I suppose it must swell up and burst its way out.' I looked at his hands, which were great big hands, like a blacksmith's, and I said: 'Did you ever try to tear a cocoon open with your hands?' 'Yes, I have many a time.' 'Did you ever do it?' 'No, I never could.' 'But you are so simple that you think a soft tender butterfly could swell up and burst its way out, when you cannot tear the cocoon with your big strong hands?' 'That is

*Since 1938, when this Address was delivered in London, other elements have been discovered, bringing the present total (1984) to 103.

quite right. I did not think about it.' 'That is three things you do not know I am still waiting for you to tell me how a butterfly gets out of its cocoon.' He turned two or three colours and said: 'Brother, I don't know.' I said: 'And I do not know how Lazarus got out, but he came out.' Again, how does a bean come out of the ground? We see the ground breaking; large clods are broken and pushed up, and we go out and lift up a heavy clod, weighing two or three pounds, and underneath are two soft velvety leaves. They have broken the hard ground and pushed up that clod, and yet if we pull them up and place them on a table and put a piece of blotting paper on them it will smash them down flat. How does that happen? How is it that beans always grow up a pole from left to right and hops always grow up a pole from right to left? If we unwind them and wind them up in the opposite direction they will die. Why? I do not know. Why is it that God has made life to come in series of seven? The eggs of the potato beetle hatch in one week, hen's eggs in three weeks, ostrich's eggs in six weeks, snake's eggs in seven weeks. It is always in weeks. The period of gestation of a cat is eight weeks, a dog nine weeks, a guinea-pig ten weeks, a whale forty-three weeks, a human being forty weeks, a bear twenty-six weeks. Why is it always in series of seven? Beloved, everything our blessed Lord does is absolutely right.

I want you to think of a strange thing about the Bible that you may not have noticed before, that all the thirteenth chapters, except the 'love chapter,' have sorrow and trouble in them. The thirteenth chapter of Genesis tells us about a family quarrel between Abraham and Lot; the thirteenth verse of the thirteenth chapter of Exodus is: 'And every firstling of an ass thou shalt redeem with a lamb; and if thou wilt not redeem it, then thou shalt break his neck'; the thirteenth chapter of Leviticus tells us about the leper having to dwell outside the camp, away from his home; the thirteenth chapter of Numbers describes the report of the twelve spies, ten of whom brought an evil report; the thirteenth chapter of Matthew refers to the burning of the tares in the fire, and the thirteenth chapter of Revelation describes the beast, the anti-Christ. Every chapter in the Bible numbered 5 has something in it about human weakness. In the fifth chapter of Genesis we find the words, 'and he died,' eight times; in the fifth chapter of the Gospel according to St. Mark we read about the man dwelling among the tombs, whom no man could tame; in the fifth chapter of the Gospel according to St. John we read about the infirm man at the Pool of Bethesda who had no man to put him into the water, and in the fifth chapter of Revelation we read about the book that no man could open.

Is not the accuracy of this Book wonderful? Have you ever noticed how scientifically accurate it is? 'All the rivers run into the sea, yet the sea is not full; unto the place from whence the rivers come, thither they return again.' There is evaporation, gravitation, precipitation, and gravitation again and evaporation, and then the clouds going back over the hills, and precipitation. An atheist said to me once: 'Wilson, I do not believe that Book. There is not a word of truth in it.' I read that verse to him, and he said: 'Any fool knows that verse is true.' I said: 'Thank God. Shake hands with a fool.' Another friend said to me: 'Wilson, do you believe the Old Testament is true?' I said: 'Not only true, but accurately true.' He said: 'There is not a word of truth in it. It is a lot of old stories.' I said: 'If there is a verse there that is true, will you let me prove it?' 'Certainly.' I turned to the last verse of chapter 30 of the Book of Proverbs: 'Surely the churning of milk bringeth forth butter, and the wringing of the nose bringeth forth blood,' and I said: 'I am ready to do it right now to prove that it is so.' The Word is absolutely accurate. When I was studying these things in school my professor did not like it because I carried my Bible with me, and he used to sneer at me. One day he said: 'Wilson, there is a verse in your Bible that is so absurd that I do not see how you can believe it. It says that God weigheth the mountains in His scales. What kind of scales did God have to weigh Mount Everest?' I could not tell him, and I said: 'I do not know, Professor. I know it is so if God says it is so. Some day I will find out.' Next year I studied chemistry, and I found out something that I did not know before—that all chemicals are put together by weight and not by measure. I went into the office of my physics professor, and I said: 'Professor, I have found the meaning of that verse. Every stone, every ounce of soil in Mount Everest or any other peak is put together by weight. God weighed the mountain, exactly as the Word says.' That professor committed suicide; he did not really possess anything; he knew physics but he did not know the Maker of heaven and earth.

Then think of the lovely peculiarities. I have been practising medicine for 34 years. I have brought many a baby into the world and married them off when they got old enough, led them to Christ and brought their babies into the world and buried them when they died. I sit on the platform in my Gospel Hall and look down on my congregation, and I know everything about them. I was there when they were born; I have seen them get saved and be baptised; I know their stories. Dr. Luke, as you know, wrote the longest book in the New Testament; it has 24 chapters—not so many as Matthew, but the chapters are longer. Luke shows the peculiarities of the physician in his writings. For instance, when he writes about those who were eyewitnesses of these things from the beginning, he uses the word from which we derive 'autopsy'; he looked at the inside of them to see if they were true; he performed an autopsy on these stories to see if they were facts, and then he gave us the facts. Dr. Luke tells us about a woman who came and touched the hem of the Lord's garment; Matthew and Mark tells us about that too, but they say that she had suffered many things from the physicians, and Dr. Luke omits that when he tells the story. Matthew and Mark tell us about Malthus' ear being cut off; Dr. Luke says it was the right ear. Matthew and Mark leave him with his head bleeding and his ear on the ground, but Dr. Luke, like a good physician, records the surgical operation and tells us that the Saviour put the ear on again. Matthew and Mark tell us about the man possessed with a devil that threw him to the ground, and Luke adds that it did not hurt him.

Have you ever thought, beloved, that in this Book we find how to live a happy life, how to die a happy death, and how to have a happy eternity? It is the only book in the world that tells us how to be happy when we are miserable. My father-in-law was a great man of God. He said to me once: 'Walter, it is a lovely thing to live by faith and show it.' I did not know just what he meant; I was very young then. He had a big tent factory, at which he made tents and awnings and all kinds of canvas things, and he did not believe in insurance of any kind; he had no insurance on his life or his property or his business, or anything else. One night the factory caught fire through spontaneous combustion, on the fourth floor. I heard on the telephone that it was on fire and I hurried down; my father-in-law came down from his house, and we stood together watching the fire. The heat was intense; we could not get near the place. The firemen poured water on it, but it was burning like a volcano, and as it burned the flames shot out like a geyser of fire. The noise was deafening; all the sirens were blowing and the heat and steam were dreadful. It was a terrible sight. The factory burned right through to the sub-basement and it was a complete wreck; nothing was left. I put my arm through his and said: 'There goes the last thing you have got on earth. What are you going to do now?' He put one arm round me to hold me close to him and he said: 'Walter, you are quite mistaken. You see, that was not my business. That belonged to my Father, and I was just running it for Him. I will go home now and see what job He wants me to do next.' The next day, which was Friday, he was up at 7 o'clock for breakfast. On Saturday night we had street meetings in the town, and on this Saturday he was there as usual, singing the hymn that we have sung this afternoon, 'The gospel of Thy grace.' That was his favourite hymn, and there he was, singing it at the top of voice, penniless; all he had was a pile of ashes.

Most of us pray 'Our Father, who art in heaven,' and then we live like a lot of orphans who have not any father at all. That is just the truth, is it not? But think of the beauties of the Word—great spoil—something that meets one's need. A boy went to his pastor and sneered at his words, and said: 'I do not believe what you are preaching; it is not inspired at all.' The pastor very wisely said to him: 'Go home and write out the 23rd Psalm, and bring it to me and then repeat what you have said.' Is not that Psalm inspired? Has it not sung its way through prison bars and into the homes of sickness and sorrow and into death chambers? Has not many a weary soul laid its head on that precious Psalm and gone home to be with the Lord, and has not many a fine strong man read it and been braced for the battle? What is there like it in all the world? 'The Lord is my Shepherd.' This precious Book brings to you and me a personal God whom we can have. 'O God, Thou art *my* God.' I wonder whether each of us here has a God that is our own God, or do we just know that there is a God?

Some years ago I started a new system with the Lord. It has been a great blessing to my heart. I started keeping a prayer book. On the left-hand side of the page I write the date and the thing I ask my

Lord for; I leave the right-hand side of the page blank, and when He answers my prayer I put the answer down and until He answers it I keep on reminding Him of it. That is the way with children; they ask their father for something and then they wait about near him until he answers them. Have we learned, beloved, to lay hold of God? 'O God, Thou art *my* God.' David said that when he was hiding in a cave, with nothing in the world but trouble, with thorns and briers and thistles to sleep on, hunted like a deer by Saul and his men, and without one earthly comfort. That did not turn him against God, but it brought him to God, and he said: 'Because Thy loving kindness is better than life, my lips shall praise Thee.' I wonder whether we have a God like that! This precious Book brings us to a personal God, that we may know and have Him and be rich in His presence. And what rich people we ought to be! Each one of us ought to be a fountain—'There shall be in you a fountain springing up.'

I was at a Bible Conference two years ago, and they put me in a cottage where I had to pump the water. When I pumped no water came, so I went out to complain about it. I did not know anything about pumps. I saw a boy about 12 years old and he asked me what was the matter. I said: 'They have put me here with a broken pump.' He said: 'Cannot you get any water?' and I said: 'No.' He smiled and he picked up a tomato can that was behind the pump and went down to the lake and filled the can with water; then he came back and poured it into the pump and worked the handle, and soon I had the whole lake at my disposal. The boy said to me: 'You see, Mister, if you don't put none in you don't get none out.' A great many people are like that, waiting for some interesting speaker to come and pour a little in, and then they get along all right. I heard the pump make a strange noise afterwards, and it was as dry as ever; I could not get a drop out. Are not Christians sometimes like that? The Lord does not expect us to be like dry pumps but wells of water springing up, so that everyone who comes near us gets the water of life brought to hand.

I want you to think of the gender used in certain passages of the Bible. 'Go to the ant, thou sluggard. Consider her ways and be wise.' It says '*her* ways,' because we never see a male ant; the male ants stay down in the ground and take care of the babies and the ladies come up and do the work. Solomon knew that very well; he was a zoologist; he had studied all kinds of animals and plants. 'The spider taketh hold with her hands, and is in kings' palaces.' Why '*her* hands'? Because we do not see male spiders unless we look carefully for them. They are tiny as compared with the female spiders, and they never spin webs. The Scriptures are absolutely accurate. If the Bible says the Lord has blotted out all your sins, THEN HE HAS DONE SO. I love that little touch about the flies in Exodus 8.31. I will read it to you: 'And the Lord did according to the word of Moses; and He removed the swarms of flies from Pharaoh, from his servants, and from his people; there remained not one.' Think of that—not one fly was left! See how accurate the record, see how complete His work. Everything He does He does to a finish.

Let us learn to love our Bibles, read them and pore over them, saturate our souls with the Word and be ready to give it out to others. It is God's fountain of blessing for our own souls and for the souls of others.

Lamp of our feet, whereby we trace
Our path when wont to stray;
Stream from the fount of heavenly grace,
Brook by the traveller's way·

Bread of our souls, whereon we feed;
True manna from on high;
Our guide and chart, wherein we read
Of realms beyond the sky:

Pillar of fire through watches dark,
And radiant cloud by day;
When waves would whelm our tossing bark,
Our anchor and our stay·

Word of the ever-living God,
Will of His glorious Son;
Without Thee how could earth be trod?
Or heaven itself be won?

Lord, grant us all aright to learn
The wisdom it imparts;
And to its heavenly teaching turn
With simple, childlike hearts.
(*Bernard Barton*, 1826)

Section Four

The Bible and Archaeological Discoveries

Contents Section Four

The Bible and Archaeological Discoveries

Archaeological Discoveries at Megiddo*

By G. Ernest Wright

Megiddo was one of the towns smitten by Israel under Joshua and given to Manasseh (Josh. 12:21 and 17:11, 12); but Manasseh failed to drive out the inhabitants. It stood in an important position on the southern edge of the plain of Esdraelon and commanded one of the passes, from the north into the hill-country, which were critically important on many occasions in Judah's history. Solomon placed one of his twelve commissariat officers, Baana, over it (1 Kings 4:12), and raised a levy for building there (1 Kings 9:15). Ahaziah died there (2 Kings 9:27), and there Josiah received his mortal wound (2 Kings 23:29, 30 and 2 Chron. 35:22).

Megiddo in the Time of David and Solomon

The great problem at Megiddo is the question as to what ruins belong to the time of David and Solomon in the tenth century. In *Megiddo 1: Seasons of* 1925-34 (1939) the excavators published a remarkable series of constructions in Stratum IV which they attributed to the time of Solomon. A new stone city-wall was erected around the perimeter of the mound, slightly over one-half mile in circumference. Its average width was about 12 feet. In certain areas it was made of roughly coursed rubble, but in others, perhaps where extra strength was needed, blocks of hewn stone were carefully fitted together along the faces of the wall. At the east were the remains of what was once an excellent palace, presumably for the local governor, set in a walled courtyard of its own.

Most interesting of all, however, were the remains of four large buildings which were once stables for horses. Careful measurements indicate that the capacity of these stables was 480 horses. In addition, there was a small stable unit adjoining the palace which could have housed about a dozen more. The typical unit was about 80 feet long; it contained a central passage about 10 feet wide, paved with crushed, unslaked lime. This passage was flanked by two rows of stone pillars which served as tie-posts (the tie-posts were preserved) and as supports for the roof. Between the posts were mangers, each hollowed out of a solid block of limestone. Behind them on each side was an aisle, parallel to the central passage and of equal width, in which the horses stood. These aisles were paved with cobblestones to keep the animals from slipping. Five of these units were put together to make each of the three larger stables; the fourth stable employed but two units. Each unit held about 30 horses, except in one of the large buildings where the aisles were slightly smaller and would have held only about 24 horses.

A Solomonic Gateway

There was also discovered the finest fortified gateway yet found in Palestine. The excavators believe it to be Solomonic, which it certainly is. The gate with the four doorways is unique, though double and triple doorways have been found a number of times at other sites. The masonry was massive and the workmanship excellent. The stones were cut and fitted together in a regular bonding pattern on the wall faces, while the interiors were filled with mud and rubble. The masonry was laid dry without mortar, but the joint between any two stones is said to have been so perfect that not even a thin knife blade could be inserted between them. The width of the main doorway between the tower piers was about 14 feet; this may have been the only one provided with wooden doors. There were probably two of them, one on each side; when open they could be swung back into the side chambers. A stone socket on which one of the doors turned was found in place. Outside the gate was a strongly fortified courtyard with a small outer gate; from the side of the latter a series of steps led down the steep slope of the mound for the use of pedestrians. As Dr. Albright was the first to observe, the main gate with the four doorways is remarkably similar in plan to the east gate in the enclosure to the

*Abridged from an article in 'The Biblical Archaeologist', vol. xiii, No. 2 (1951).

Solomonic temple in Jerusalem, as described in Ezekiel 40:5-16—a further witness to the importance of Ezekiel 40-42 for the reconstruction of the Jerusalem temple.

In the light of our present evidence we can reconstruct the events which occurred in tenth century Megiddo with some probability as follows: As the Israelite King David in the early part of the tenth century sought to extend his control over all Palestine, he was forced to attack certain strong cities in the north in order to secure his dominion over Esdraelon and the northern Jordan Valley. In so doing, he destroyed Beth-shan which guarded the eastern opening of the Esdraelon into the Jordan Valley. At the same time he probably destroyed Megiddo V. Various bits of evidence for reoccupation in Stratum V A—IV B have been found; but the largest construction thus far discovered is that of the palace. It was provided with its own walled enclosure and covered gateway, thus suggesting that the mound's fortifications at the time were by no means strong. Whether the V city-gate was still in use or completely in ruins we have no means of knowing. It is likely that David was responsible for the building of the palace as the residence of the official in charge of the Esdraelon district.

In the reign of Solomon Megiddo was made the capital of his fifth administrative district (cf. Westminster Hist. Atlas, p. 48 and Pl. VII A), which included the Esdraelon and extended to the Jordan Valley. Its governor was Baana, son of Ahilud (1 Kings 4:12). An elaborate plan for the rebuilding of the city was evolved and carried out by extremely able architects. The new fortification wall and gate were built. It is also highly probable that the various stables for horses were erected (cf. 1 Kings 9:15-19), since the city gives evidence of having been planned and built as a whole.

When Pharaoh Shishak conquered Megiddo toward the end of the tenth century (in the fifth year of the reign of Rehoboam)[1], he seems to have destroyed the Solomonic city-gate so that a new one of three entry-ways was erected. Otherwise the main Solomonic constructions continued in use throughout the ninth century in Stratum IV proper. They were finally destroyed toward the end of that century (probably in the wars with the Syrians alluded to in 2 Kings 13:3-17), so that the eighth century city of Stratum III was rebuilt on an entirely new plan.

We are greatly indebted to the Oriental Institute of the University of Chicago for providing us with such a feast of interesting material.

[1]925 B.C.

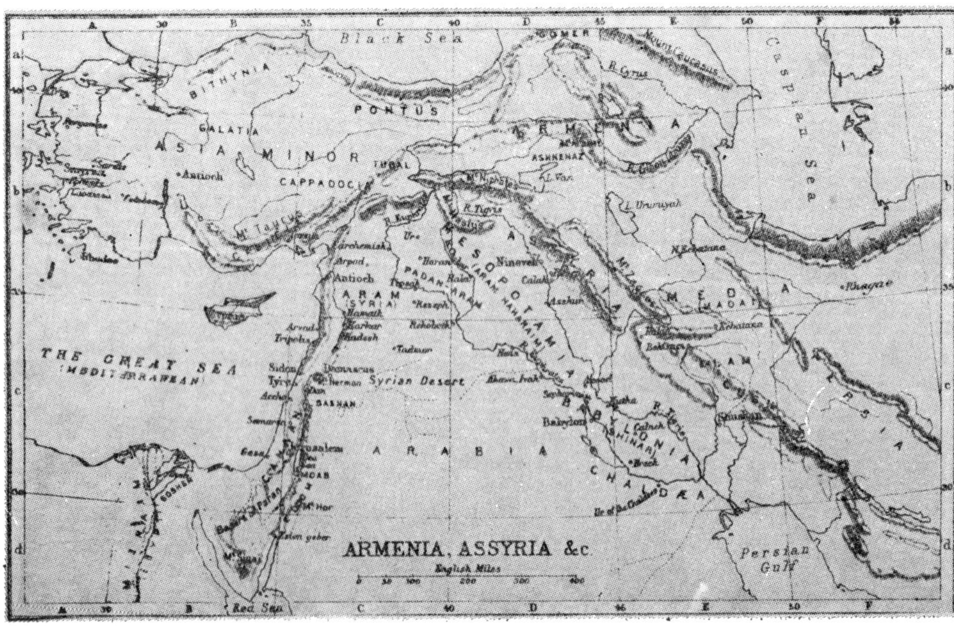

The Problem of the Teraphim (*Genesis 31:34-35*)

By Dr. Allan A. MacRae

All through the ages interpreters of the Book of Genesis have puzzled over the great importance attached by Laban and Rachel to the household gods which she stole. Why should Laban have been so excited about the loss of these 'teraphim' that he should think it worth while to gather an expedition and pursue Jacob many days in order to attempt to get them back? It could not be because they were of gold, as the amount that could be hidden (Gen. 31:34, 35) would not suffice to pay the cost of Laban's expedition.

The documentary hypothesis maintains that this portion was not written by Moses, but by someone who lived many centuries later.

Very recently the solution to this mystery has come to light. A great many clay tablets have been excavated at the town of Nuzi, in northern Mesopotamia, in the region in which Laban lived and from approximately the same period. From them we learn that at that time the possession of a man's household gods by a son-in-law was acceptable in court in that region as evidence that he had designated that son-in-law as heir to all his possessions. This explains why Rachel was anxious to keep the teraphim, and why Laban was so determined, if possible, to get them back, and thus to prevent Jacob from securing what was left of his property after his death.

We are glad indeed to note that Jacob made no use of the household gods. He never sank so low as to take advantage of Rachel's theft. Instead, we find that later on he buried the household gods at Shechem.

Thus these clay tablets discovered at Nuzi throw a wonderfully interesting and informing light upon this narrative in Genesis, and at the same time give strong evidence that the account was written near the time of the event, when it would have been clear to everyone, rather than long after, when the meaning of this important feature would have been forgotten.

The Assyrian Account of the Deluge,
inscribed in cuneiform characters on a terra-cotta tablet, from the Library of Assur-bani-pal, king of Assyria (B.C. 668-626), at Nineveh.

The Bible and Modern Archaeological Discovery

An address given at the Bible League Annual Meeting, 1951.

By D. J. Wiseman, O.B.E.

I feel very honoured to be asked to address you this evening on such an important subject as that chosen in the title—"Modern Discovery and the Bible." I would, however, commence by taking the liberty of changing the subject and emphasis to "The Bible and Modern Archaeological Discovery." I do this for an important reason. In the Bible we are dealing with a unique book and a unique type of knowledge—revelation by the Source of all true wisdom. It will be seen that on the main purpose of the Bible as God's revelation of Himself to men, archaeology can have nothing to say. Much that the Bible tells us cannot be put to an archaeological test. The revelation that God is One, the Creator, that Christ is the Incarnate Word of God and through Him alone is eternal life, is beyond the question of archaeology or of any human science. Yet being a revelation set in a time and in a geographical background which we can know from other sources there is much that we can learn from the honest and industrious research of many scholars as they reconstruct the story of the past from countless though often fragmentary finds. It is to my father, who was himself a member of your Council, that I owe, under God, my interest in Near Eastern antiquities and more especially my reverence for and interest in the whole Word of God. While still young I developed an eager desire to be able to read the tablets of Abraham's time and the brick of Nebuchadressar which lay in his study. Now I have come to try to tell you about some of the recent discoveries and their bearing on the Bible.

The Essential Truth of God's Word.

We commence with the words of Psalm 119:160, 'Thy Word is true from the beginning: and every one of thy righteous judgments endureth for ever.' One attempt to translate this is 'The beginning of Thy word is true.' Of course this is quite correct in that the *source* or commencement of God's Word, being God Himself, is Truth; but I believe this verse can mean more than that. The Hebrew word here translated 'beginning' (*rosh*) means literally 'head' and can be used for 'summing up.' The capital asset of Thy words is truth, and it is from this so-called bias that I am not ashamed to say that I commence my investigations. Men will argue that it does not matter if the Bible is true or accurate in its historical presentation so long as we accept the ideas. It does, for you cannot divide the Biblical truth or ideas from the written word or the historical setting. It is in the latter that we can legitimately test the Biblical *facts* by other external *facts*.

A Great Increase in Literary Evidence.

During the last fifteen years[1] which, with the lacuna caused by the war, can be considered modern, more than fifty thousand documents written in the cuneiform script have been recovered from ancient Iraq alone. From this one country which figures so largely in the early pages of the Scriptures about half a million such records have been unearthed in the last 120 years. Yet despite the great increase in our knowledge which must result from such additions to our source material it must be realised that these come from only 30 different ancient cities, and at least 3,000 ruin mounds (Arabic *talls*) remain undug. But when you realise that the Bible covers God's actions with His people not only in the land of the Tigris and Euphrates but also in Syria, Palestine, Egypt, and even Turkey you can see what a vast field there is to cover and what must necessarily be as yet grave limitations in our knowledge of these countries as recovered through the science of archaeology. The fact that as yet nothing has been found of a people, city, custom, or word mentioned in the Bible cannot of itself be used as an argument against the truth of the Biblical record. For example, during the last few years the Horites or Hurrians are becoming increasingly knowable and Genesis 10 is now a genealogical and geographical list of

[1] 1936-51.

which only a few names still await more evidence for us to be able to place them. While there is much still unknown, the increase in literary evidence has widened and deepened our understanding of many Hebrew and Greek words to the extent that a new translation of the Bible has been demanded and is now being made.

Old Testament Records Independent of Babylonian Records.

Another result of this modern evidence is a new examination of old theories. It has become a habit for many to assume that the Old Testament draws perhaps directly upon Babylonian sources for its earlier accounts. Dr. Alexander Heidel, of Chicago, a Christian scholar and leading Assyriologist, has devoted much time to comparing the six main Sumerian and Babylonian Legends of Creation with the Hebrew account. In his *Babylonian Genesis* he clearly shows that there is no confirmed relationship between the Biblical and c.2000 B. C. epics. He shows that there is no interdependence verbally, but that the Babylonian accounts have preserved amid their confused record a germ of the truth which is so clearly expressed in the Divine record. These elements, such as the creation of man by God (the Babylonians say gods) from dust in order to serve his Maker, show that the clearer and more spiritually stated facts in the Old Testament record this first historical event faithfully. The same can be said of the Biblical account of the Flood.*

New Facts about Abraham.

Excavations at Nuzi, in Central Iraq, have brought to light 20,000 clay tablets dated in the sixteenth century B.C. From these we get a clear account of the daily life of these people and of the customs which must have prevailed from the time of Abraham. It was customary for childless folk at Nuzi to adopt a son to serve them during life and to provide for them at death. Such was the case with Abraham's first heir Eliezer (Gen. 15:2-3). If there was a child born after the adoption the adoptee had to yield up his right of inheritance. This helps us to understand the legal implication of Genesis 15:4. When Sarah provided the slave Hagar to bear children to Abraham she would seem to be conforming to the practice of her day. A Nuzi contract says that 'if Gilimninu (the bride) fails to bear children, she shall take a woman of Lullu-land (a slave) as wife for Shennima (the bridegroom) . . . Gilimninu shall not send the handmaid's offspring away.' Abraham needed special assurance from God before he broke the contemporary custom (Gen. 21:12). Many a Nuzi son would spend his days working as a slave for his future father-in-law in order to earn the right to his bride. Laban tried to avoid his side of the bargain. In a similar way many comparisons can now be made between the Hurrian (Biblical 'Horite') customs and the records of Genesis 12-36. Archaeology has painted in the background to our Biblical knowledge of the Patriarchal days.

The discoveries at Abraham's home town—Ur of the Chaldees—have been long well known. Yet the thousands of cuneiform tablets from that flourishing seaport are as yet not fully published. Recent translations of some of these make us astonished at the high state of culture in Abraham's time. History books, works on botany, medicine, law, and legends form but a few of those available to the thoughtful man of that time. I think this will help us to realise how great was the faith of Abraham to leave such a highly civilized place to go out into the northern desert.

A month ago I was working with the Anglo-Turkish expedition in the Haran area, Abraham's first stopping-place. Further work on this place, which abounds with legends of Abraham's sojourn—such as the Well outside the city named after him—will not merely give us more information about the worship of the moon-god Sin, who had such a power in Ur's religious life, but also help our knowledge of the Aramaeans.

We may also find yet more evidence concerning the Hurrians—the Biblical 'Horites' and 'Hivites'—whom I have already mentioned. These people can be traced as far south as Egypt and individuals bearing Hurrian-type names, such as Alian (and several names in Gen. 36), Shamgar (Jud.

*A. Heidel. *The Gilgamesh Epic and O.T. Parallels.*

3:31) and Eli-hipa (A. V. Eliahba) (2 Sam. 23:32), occur in the Old Testament at the same dates as they are attested in extra-Biblical documents. It is interesting to see yet another people, unknown a generation ago apart from the Biblical record, become known to us in detail.

The Limitations of Archaeology.

A word of warning may be necessary here. We are not defending the Bible for the Bible speaks clearly for itself. We must realise the limitations of archaeology as of any branch of science, for only a small part of the available territory has been explored, and to present a whole picture the few facts must often be supplemented by reasonable conjecture based upon them. For example, if I excavate a house I may seek to reconstruct the life of the people who lived there. Should the walls show traces of burning I would like to know why and when this occurred. The latter, apart from any surviving trustworthy records, would be hypothesis, and we must never talk of derivatives from the facts as if they were the facts themselves. For long it has been customary to treat the events of Genesis 14 as if the five named kings who opposed Abraham were known to us beyond doubt. One Tidal *may* be Tudhaliash, the Hittite. The name of Chedorlaomer has never been found on a cuneiform tablet as is often claimed, nor has a form Amraphel (Ammu-rapi-ilu?) been attested for the Babylonian Hammurabi. The latter's date is now c. 1750 B.C., so that if he is to be identified with the raider of this chapter the date of Abraham would need to be reduced. You will thus see the difficulties which are raised by a number of hypotheses! It is more truthful, scientific, and above all honourable to God's Word, to say that as yet we do not know the answer to this and many other problems. Beware of rushing into any interpretation of Scripture on the basis of conjectures.

Archaeological Light on Biblical History.

Modern discoveries have helped us in the understanding of various passages. No longer are the laws promulgated by Hammurabi the oldest code known to us from any source. My friend, Dr. Francis Steele, of Philadelphia, has published part of the Code of Lipit-Ishtar, written at least two hundred years earlier, from which Hammurabi borrowed. A study of all the Old Testament legislation shows that only in a very few 'statutes' is there even similarity of wording (but not penalty) with other contemporary laws. These are introduced by the common case-law formula, 'If a man . . . then . . .' There is no evidence for this having been borrowed from other nations rather than 'common law.' Never has there been found such a high and religious standard of law worded in the direct way (i.e., 'Thou shalt . . .') so characteristic of the Old Testament. These laws are given in the name and authority of God.

The Names of Biblical Kings.

Let me refer to another interesting aspect in which archaeology strengthens our trust in the details of Biblical History. Among the Assyrian cuneiform records we now have a reference to every major King of Israel and Judah who had direct contact with the Assyrian Empire. These occur in the same chronological order and with their names spelt as recorded in our Hebrew Old Testament.

Ration Books.

Among the administrative documents of Nebuchadrezzar II of Babylon have been found a number of 'ration books' showing the food allowances granted to prisoners of war held in the city between 595-569 B.C. The lists are headed with the name of Jehoiachin of Judah and followed by details of his family, the craftsmen and others recorded in 2 Kings 25 and Jeremiah 52. What is even more important is that kings and men of other countries, whose overthrow by the Babylonians was foretold by the prophet Jeremiah, figure in these prison lists. Here is proof—were such needed—of prophecy fulfilled and of the downfall of Tyre and Sidon, Moab, Egypt, and other territories.

The Population of Nineveh.

For the last two seasons' excavations at Calah (Genesis 10:11) I have been privileged to work with Professor Mallowan and have had the responsibility of reading the inscriptions as they have come to light. Among many interesting finds have been a number relating directly to the Bible. One inscription tells us in detail how Tiglath-pileser III invaded Phoenicia and Philistia in 734 B.C. and, having captured Gaza and the 'city of the River of Egypt,' returned via Judah as recorded in 2 Kings 15. A large royal stele ends with the details of the city's population in 879 B.C.—a grand total of 69,574 persons. When you realise that the size of Calah which is about one-third the size of ancient Nineveh (taking the known city walls as the boundary) is known to us, it is clear that the many arguments brought against the final verse of the Book of Jonah must fail. Nineveh could easily house 'more than six score thousand persons that cannot discern between their right hand and their left hand' (Jonah 4:11). At Calah too we found at the lowest level of occupation primitive walls which are characteristic of the earliest civilisation in S. Babylonia. It may well be that further work may give more evidence that the city was founded by immigrants from the south as indicated in Genesis 10.

The Dead Sea Manuscripts.

Before I close you will expect me to make some reference to the recently publicised find of Hebrew Manuscripts found in a cave west of the Dead Sea. Among these are two copies of Isaiah, the older of which is well worn and contains all 66 chapters. The majority of scholars date this copy in the middle of the second century B.C. Although there is much controversy over the dating there is unanimity in that all state this to be the oldest MS. of an Old Testament book yet available to us. Moreover, the evidence from the cave where the scrolls had been hidden shows that they must have been stored in the Hellenistic-type jars before 63 B.C. So great is the interest in these finds that the modern resources of nuclear physics have been brought to bear on the question. "Carbon 14 tests" made on the linen covers which sealed the scrolls in jars indicate a date of plus or minus 200 years from 33 B.C. The final conclusions of scholars on this archaeological—even if accidental—find will be awaited with interest. Meanwhile it is said that this old text remarkably confirms the Massoretic Hebrew text of the ninth century A.D. on which our modern English versions are based.

The Earliest Archæological Record of Christianity.

There is one other very recent discovery which merits our attention. Professor Sukenik of the Hebrew University cleared a number of rock-hewn tombs outside Jerusalem. He concludes that they belong to the first half of the first century and must be dated before the fall of Jerusalem. The contents—mainly inscribed sarcophagi—are 'the earliest record of Christianity' and bear the personal names of Miriam, Simon, Jesus and Simon Barsabas, probably the very man named in Acts 1:23 and 15:22. This Jewish scholar, who certainly has no wish to promote belief in the New Testament, says this is the most remarkable discovery showing the accuracy of the account of the early Church.

After this rather sketchy review of some of the recent archaeological finds, perhaps you will allow me one final word from Proverbs 21:28, ' A witness to lies shall perish, but the man who hears speaketh constantly.' This applies both to the Bible and to our individual lives. A false witness shall perish—fade away—and if God's Word is in any way or part a witness to lies, nothing we can say or do and no external evidence that we can bring can keep it alive. But if, as I believe, it is the very voice of God to man speaking constantly, eternally, consistently, then it is going to endure. 'My word,' says the Lord, 'shall never perish.' Further, we believe that this Book has come down to us through godly men who have heard and recorded the voice of God. Thus their written words are consistent and not contradictory even though the writers be widely spaced in time and circumstance. There is a special application of this verse to our daily lives and to our attitude to God's Word. Great is our responsibility as we interpret His words, for many of our difficulties which we encounter arise not merely from a misinterpretation of archaeological evidence or hypotheses but from a failure to understand God's Word aright, that is, to hear His voice. We must be men who hear God's word constantly and learn and live by it that we may never be a witness to lies which must surely perish.

The Bible and Scholarship

An Address delivered at the Annual Meeting of the Bible League, 1954,

by D. J. Wiseman, O.B.E.

When I was privileged to address the Annual Meeting of the Bible League three years ago, I was given as my subject *The Bible and Modern Archaeological Discovery*. I then sought to show how the discoveries made by that branch of science were continuing to illustrate Biblical times, customs, places and words, and in many instances to provide direct corroboration of historical facts recorded in the Bible. While this is by no means the aim or bias of Near Eastern archaeology it is not surprising that since 1951 there should be a number of finds or research works which had a direct application to the Scriptures.

OLD TESTAMENT MANUSCRIPTS

The discovery and importance of the complete scroll of Isaiah, called after its find-spot the Dead Sea Scroll of Isaiah, is well known as being the oldest complete manuscript of any Old Testament book known to us. The worldwide interest which it caused had its repercussions even among the Arabs inhabiting the barren Judaean hills, and led them to search for other caves or likely hiding places. Soon a steady flow of inscribed fragments came into the hands of a Bethlehem dealer and this led to authorised and expertly-led expeditions to seek out the sources from which the literary treasures came. Excavations at the original cave helped to confirm that the Isaiah scroll, generally dated c. 160 B.C., was one of a cache stored away before the fall of Jerusalem in 70 A.D., when the neighbouring Essene settlement was abandoned. A search of twenty-eight nearby caves resulted in the finding of fragments of Leviticus, written in a Phoenician script (and therefore earlier than the 5th century B.C. and probably than Ezra), also parts of Exodus, Jeremiah, Psalms and Ruth.

Further south, at Wady Murabba'at, on the west bank of the Dead Sea, excavators cleared two caves early in 1952. Coins and dated Hebrew letters showed that these had been occupied during the second Jewish Revolt in 124 A.D., though the fragments of the Pentateuch, Isaiah, and other books both canonical and apocryphal, found there may well be earlier. With other cave explorations and finds made by Arabs many thousands of fragments are now in the hands of the Transjordan Antiquities Service. Although the great jig-saw puzzle being pieced together by an international team of scholars is still incomplete we already know that all the books of the Old Testament are represented with, at present, the one exception of Esther. The texts, which are at least as old as the days of our Lord, in general confirm the Massoretic Text on which our English translations are based. Since a number of the manuscripts are in scripts which antedate the square Hebrew characters, and are written on parchment, leather or papyrus, while others are written in Greek and conform rather to the Septuagint translation of 245 B.C., the advance in our appreciation of the transmission of the Biblical text is very great. There can be no doubt that the Old Testament consonantal text has been most diligently passed down to us through the centuries.

At the same time these finds will increase the understanding of Jewish sects in the time of our Lord. If the quantity of finds are a safe measure it is not without significance that the largest number of scrolls or fragments are of the books of Deuteronomy, Psalms and Isaiah, which are so often quoted by Him. Already the finds, which include a page of extracts being "the testimony of the prophets concerning the Messiah," have given a much needed new breath of air to Old Testament textual research, and have enabled many of the hypotheses of the Higher Critical studies to be replaced by factual evidence. Old Testament studies may soon place us in the same virtually undisputed positions as marks the New Testament text.

NEW TESTAMENT FRAGMENTS

In the face of such a wealth of new Hebrew manuscripts recent discoveries of fifth and eighth century A.D. New Testament fragments have almost been overlooked by Bible students. From a grotto near the brook Kedron, outside Jerusalem, came fragments of Greek codices in uncial characters of the Gospels by Mark, John and the Acts, and palimpsests of Luke, John, Acts and Colossians. These will add to our knowledge of the texts used by the early Church at Jerusalem.

While such welcome light shines on the Old Testament text it must be stated that recent researches have continued to illuminate the Old Testament in other ways. The last ten years has seen a virtual reinstatement in scholarly circles of the historicity of the Patriarchal narratives. The following example can be added to those given in my previous address.

ABRAHAM AND THE CAVE OF MACHPELAH

In a recent study of Genesis 23 Professor M. R. Lehmann has shown how applicable are the Hittite Laws (c. 1800-1200 B.C.) to this account of Abraham's negotiations for the purchase of the cave of Machpelah. It has been customary to suppose that the central point of the negotiations was the price only, and that the first courteous rejection in which Ephron, a Hittite, offered the use of part of the property, was countered by Abraham's request for the outright purchase of the cave. Ephron, with oriental politeness, then offered it as a free gift; to this Abraham shows his desire to make a money payment (v. 13). The negotiations are concluded by Ephron mentioning his price of 400 shekels, which Abraham immediately pays. Now, the current Hittite laws required any purchaser or inheritor of a *whole* estate to perform certain feudal services to the king. It would appear that Abraham's second request was only for the cave 'at the edge of his field' (v. 9). Lehmann therefore concludes that while Abraham wished to avoid unnecessary obligations Ephron seized the opportunity to sell the whole property (the Hebrew *nathan* is used in its technical sense of 'sell' throughout this chapter). This interpretation shows that the negotiations revolved round the question of full title and consequent responsibilities—the exact nature of which are not stated in the Biblical account as they are not in contemporary legal documents—rather than the matter of the price.

The Biblical account of this transaction remarkably preserves the correct legal terminology of the day, with which we are now familiar from the many Old Babylonian real-estate contracts which have been discovered. The purchase price was paid, or rather 'weighed,' since these were pre-coinage days, and designated as 'silver of the merchants.' The transfer of ownership was made by the transfer of the silver before witnesses. The contract correctly designated the boundaries of the field and includes the trees within the property transferred—the latter is a characteristic feature of Hittite business documents. As Dr. Lehmann has rightly emphasised, "We have thus found that Genesis 23 is permeated with intimate knowledge of intricate subtleties of Hittite laws and customs, correctly corresponding to the time of Abraham and fitting in with the Hittite features of the Biblical account. With the final destruction of the Hittite capital of Hattusas about 1,200 B.C. these laws must have fallen into utter oblivion. This is another instance in which a late dating must be firmly rejected. Our study again confirms the authenticity of the 'background material' of the Old Testament, which makes it such an invaluable source for the study of all aspects of social, economic and legal aspects of the period of history it depicts."

THE DESOLATION OF BABYLON

Another example of the way in which scholarship illustrates the text of Scripture comes from an Assyrian inscription of Sargon II, King of Assyria (722-705 B.C.), found during our season's excavation at Nimrud (the Biblical Calah*) last year.

This is a unique text in that it is written with an unusual disregard of chronology, the events of the king's reign being woven into a literary composition of high merit, rare in early Semitic literature

*Genesis 10:10-11.

outside the Hebrew Scriptures. It gives a new account of the siege of Samaria, whose fall Sargon accomplished in 721 B.C., when taking over the operation from his predecessor Shalmaneser V, just as is so carefully stated in 2 Kings 17:3-6. He took away from the city "the gods in whom they trusted"—a striking testimony to the polytheism of Israel at this time. But I wish to draw your attention to Sargon's description of Babylon, written soon after its capture in his operations against Merodach-Baladan in 710-709 B.C., that is, towards the end of Isaiah's ministry in Judah. The king describes the desolation in the area of Babylon as follows: "At that time the track which leads from . . . to approach Babylon, the cult-centre of the gods Enlil and Ninlil, was not open, the road was impassable. The country had become a desert from days long past, and any passage through the centre of it was impracticable and the way most difficult; there was no prepared path. In the inaccessible tracts thorn, thistle and jungle prevailed over all. Dogs and jackals assembled in their recesses, and bunched together in herds like sheep. In this desert country Aramaeans and Suti, tent-dwellers, treacherous fugitives and plundering folk, had pitched their dwellings, and put a stop to any passage across the area. There were settlements among them which for many days past had lapsed into ruin. There were no channels or furrows over the cultivated ground which was criss-crossed (with dried-up irrigation works) like a spider's web. Their rich meadows had become like a wilderness, their cultivated grounds were bereft of the sweet harvest song, and grain was quite cut off . . ." You will have noticed the expression "thorn and thistle over all" which uses identical Semitic words to the Divine curse upon the ground as a result of sin, following the Fall of Man (Gen. 3:18, cf. Hosea 10:8). How striking this is when we read the almost contemporary prophecy of Isaiah concerning the fall of Babylon, a prophecy all the more remarkable since it was written at a time when Babylon was, as we now know, an insignificant part of the great Assyrian Empire.—The few changes from the Authorised Version found in the following quotation result from recent linguistic discoveries.

"And Babylon, the choicest of kingdoms, the most splendid of the Babylonian Chaldeans' beauty-spots shall be as when God overthrew Sodom and Gomorrah. It shall never be inhabited nor be dwelt in from one generation to another; neither shall the Arab pitch his tent there; neither shall the shepherds make their fold there. But wild beasts shall lie in groups there and their houses be full of jackals; and ostriches shall dwell there, and goats stretch themselves out there. Moles shall be in their desolated (widowed) places, and lizards in their (princely) luxurious palaces. Her appointed time is near to come and her days will not be prolonged" (Isaiah 13:19-22).

Such examples, taken from the great mass of recent material resulting from research work in subjects which have a direct bearing on Bible studies, will be multiplied so long as the kindred disciplines of history and philology are pursued. It is hoped, for example, that in this next year some of the correspondence written in Palestine in the days of Tiglath-pileser III (the Pul of 2 Kings 15), will be published, and thus throw new light on the conditions. As with the publication of the Tell-el-Amarna, Ras Shamra, Mari, Nuzi, and other groups of cuneiform tablets, these documents will stir us to a better understanding of the Old Testament.

By taking such examples of the results of one branch of science I am aware that I do insufficient justice to the help brought by other branches of science to Biblical exegesis. Nor have I forgotten that the scope of my subject requires me to think of scholarship as a whole. Many Evangelicals have come to view scholarship as something anti-Biblical, even sinful, and contrary to faith and, generally, to the Faith. This is unfortunately true when men make their scholarly pursuits—even their own natural and therefore sinful and biassed thought—an end in themselves. Moreover for a long time Bible 'scholarship' has been dominated and deadened by an unquestioning acceptance of Higher Critical theories, which undermine the authority of the Bible. In the last 150 years this has not only permeated the ranks of scholars, but influenced the popular view of the Bible. For many men 'scholarship' has made the Bible a dead and dull book. But that is not true scholarship which, seeking to find but a segment of truth, will not accept the revelation of the Truth Himself. In the same way that I have just used a special methodology* and branch of scholarly research (which we may call—for want of a

*i.e., a scientific method of approach.

better comprehensive term—Biblical Archaeology) by taking *facts* from it and seeking to compare it with *facts* presented in the Bible, even so we must both acknowledge the help which scholarship can give and, with due care for the truth, use its findings for our greater understanding of the Christian faith, and of the text on which the great and fundamental doctrines of our Evangelical Faith are based. Our faith cannot of itself avoid an intellectual element. Knowledge, however slender it may be, is necessary to 'saving faith,' for no man can trust God without knowing something about Him.

I am reminded of some of the remarks of Dr. Gresham Machen in his addresses to the Bible League on *The Importance of Christian Scholarship.* "True (i.e. Christian) scholarship is of importance *for Evangelism* both because of its relations to faith and for a right presentation of the faith. Gospel preaching, according to the New Testament, was the setting forth of facts about Jesus Christ, His life, His miracles, His substitutionary death, and His resurrection. This was the method of the scholar Paul, as of all the Apostles. The simplicity of the Gospel lies not a little in our ability to understand it and proclaim it. A true knowledge, usually the result of much study and drawing even unconsciously on the great resources of Christian learning, leads to ability to proclaim and make plain the Truth which alone can make men free."

THE BIBLE AND THE SOURCE OF TRUE SCHOLARSHIP

Not only does the Bible exhort men to use (not blindly trust) their minds, but it is itself the source or vehicle of true scholarship—the knowledge of God. Indirectly, since the time when the Renaissance of learning fathered and preceded the Reformation, the Bible has been a stimulus for men to think deeply, not only about God, but also about the world He has created. For many centuries all English scholarship was closely tied with Biblical studies and depended for its sustenance and encouragement—or the lack of it—upon the theological climate of the day. Moving away from Biblical principles some scholars have run into moral difficulties, such as those which face nuclear physicists today. The implications, methods and results of scholarly research demand, as Professor C. A. Coulson has on more than one occasion reminded us, the Divine domination and control of men's thoughts and desires, and therefore of their work. The Christian Faith alone provides this power to co-ordinate the very scholarship it would stimulate. If it is absent one of the many secular and materialistic philosophies will be adduced in its place, with anti-christian results; that is, results which err from the truth.

I would therefore make a plea that the Bible League should actively encourage Christian scholarship. This is vital if the object of *promoting* the reverent study of the Holy Scriptures is to be forwarded. The *Quarterly* will then increasingly have within its pages articles, as in the past, which will carry weight, through both evangelical circles and beyond, because of their sound learning and constructive nature. True Biblical scholarship is necessary, too, if that other part of our one aim is to be obtained—'to resist the varied attacks made upon their Inspiration, Infallibility and Sole Sufficiency as the Word of God.'

SCHOLARSHIP IN DEFENCE OF THE BIBLE

We are always quick to call to our aid those results of scholarship which directly confirm the Scriptures, and rightly so. Yet it often requires a trained mind both to analyse and explain the attacks made upon the Bible—our first speaker tonight is a good example of this. Evangelicals must encourage those of their number with any special gifts, especially of the mind, not to hide them, but to develop them for the benefit of the Church.This will require both prayer by the many, and patient hard work by the few, to ensure that we have men able to help in defence against attacks which, in our day, are principally aimed at our Faith via our minds. Today one is not popular, even among Evangelical Christians, if one enters into argument or controversy, in the finer sense of these words. Yet the New Testament is full of argument in defence of the one Faith. Error comes in and takes root through ignorance (the lack of true scholarship). 'Ye do err,' said the Lord Jesus Christ, 'not knowing the Scriptures and the power of God.' While argument or apologetic cannot, of course, make a man a

Christian it may be used by the Holy Spirit, in so far as it is true in itself, both to turn men to God and keep them in the Faith. Such a work, requiring an unswerving faith in, and deep knowledge of, the Scriptures, and a mind illumined by that same Holy Spirit who alone can enable the gift of scholarship to be rightly applied, is still the task of the Bible League.

NAMES of ASSYRIAN, BABYLONIAN, and PERSIAN KINGS mentioned in the Bible.

1. D.P.[1] **Tukulti - pal - ishar - ra** — *Tiglath - pileser.*

2. D.P. **Pu - lu'** — *Pul.*

3. D.P. D.P. **Shulma - nu - asharid** — *Shalmaneser.*

4. D.P. **Shar - gi - na** — *Sargon.*

5. D.P. D.P. **Sin - akhi - ir - ba** — *Sennacherib.*

6. D.P. **Ashur - akh - iddin - na** — *Esar-haddon.*

7. D.P. D.P. **Ashur - bani - pal** — *Asnapper* (Ezra iv. 10).

8. D.P. D.P. **Marduk - pal - iddin** — *Merodach-baladan.*

9. D.P. **Bel - shar - uṣur** — *Belshazzar.*

10. D.P. **Nabu - ku - dur - ri - u - ṣu - ur** — *Nebuchadnezzar II.*

11. D.P. **A - me - lu - D.P. Marduk** — *Evil - Merodach.*

12. D.P. D.P. **Nirgal - shar - uṣur** — *Nergal-sharezer.*

13. D.P. **Kur - ra - ash** — *Cyrus.* (in Persian **K - u - r - u**) — *Cyrus.*

14. D.P. **Da - ri - ya - mush** — *Darius.*

15. D.P. **Ar - tak - shat su** — *Artaxerxes.*

[1] D.P. = Determinative Prefix

The Dead Sea Scrolls, Why Important?

By Dr. Oswald T. Allis

[We again bring before our readers some further information concerning the Dead Sea Scrolls. The following article is taken, by permission, from *The Sunday School World,* of America. It will help to explain what the *Scrolls* are, and why they are important to the lovers of God's Word. We are grateful to be allowed to use it.—The captions are our own.—EDITOR.]

PART I

It is a truism to say that the past century has been pre-eminently the age of discovery and recovery. The physicist has been discovering the mysteries of the atom and introducing the nuclear age; the archaeologist has been recovering the forgotten past of mankind. The results in the one field have been almost as startling and revolutionary as those in the other. In both fields the great advances have sometimes been the result of careful planning and research; sometimes they have been quite accidental. This has been especially true of archaeology. Some discoveries have been the result of laborious digging for ten, twenty, fifty, or even more feet into ancient mounds. Others have been come upon by chance.

But the exploiting of these chance discoveries has given scholars abundant work to decipher, evaluate, and correlate the materials that have been discovered. The El Amarna Letters discovered in the year 1887 are still a mine of information. The Ras Shamra tablets, first discovered in the year 1930, opened up many vistas which are still to be fully explored. Within a decade the Dead Sea Scrolls have aroused an interest and enthusiasm which equals if it does not surpass the excitement which was caused a century ago when the palaces of Sargon and Sennacherib and the library of Ashurbanipal began to yield up their treasures.

A New Field of Research

The Dead Sea Scrolls are especially interesting and valuable for a number of reasons. The first of these is that they have opened up an entirely new field in Palestinian exploration and research. Until the year 1947 when this epoch-making discovery was made, exploration in the Holy Land had been, as compared with that in Egypt and Babylonia, sadly unrewarding. Aside from the Siloam inscription, the Moabite Stone, and the more recently discovered Samaria Ostraca and Lachish Letters, very little documentary material had been discovered. And thus the archaeologist was largely dependent on 'sequence dating,' derived from the different patterns of pottery found in the various strata of the excavated sites, for the relative age of occupancies which had left no written history behind them. The fact that Palestine was so unproductive of literary remains was variously explained. One explanation was that the Hebrews might have used perishable materials, leather or papyrus, to write on and that owing to the widely different climate there, such perishable documents as have been found in Egypt, had perished centuries ago. This suggested explanation has been remarkably confirmed by the discoveries made since the year 1947 near the Dead Sea.

So much has been written about these discoveries that a detailed account is hardly necessary. Some seven miles south of Jericho in the lofty cliffs which skirt the western shore of the Dead Sea, Arab boys discovered a cave in which there were at least eleven scrolls which apparently owed their preservation to the fact that they had been placed in jars, many fragments of which were lying in the cave. When first offered for sale their value was not recognized and it was only by happy accident that they finally got into trustworthy hands and that most of them have since been published. This initial discovery led to extensive search, both of the cave itself and of the neighbouring country.

Why the Scrolls were Hidden

Since the cave where the scrolls were discovered was about two miles from a spring known as Ain Feshka, they at first went by that name. But much nearer to the cave there was an ancient ruin known as Khirbet Qumran. Excavation of this ruin proved it to be the remains, not, as had been supposed, of a Roman fort, but of what appeared to be a monastery or community centre with large rooms and many cisterns. Connected with it also was a large cemetery. Coins which were discovered in the course of the excavations indicated that the site had been occupied in Maccabean and in Roman periods up to the time of the siege of Jerusalem by Titus. A number of caves were discovered in the vicinity, several within a stone's throw. It was concluded that most of the persons who were connected with the community lived in near-by caves and that when they fled from the Roman advance they hastily secreted these and many other scrolls in the caves. In one of these caves which is now called 4 Q (that is, fourth Qumran cave [the first or Ain Feshka cave is now called 1 Q]), great quantities of manuscript fragments were also discovered, some of them as a result of digging three or more feet below the present floor of the cave. In 3 Q two badly corroded bronze rolls were discovered. Quite recently the discovery has been announced of a complete Pentateuch, whether in one or five scrolls is not clear. If true, this reported discovery will be of very great interest.

An Epoch-making Discovery

The first question raised regarding the scrolls was naturally as to their date. The chief determining factor was at first the style of writing (palaeography) and the patterns of the jars which were found in the cave. Some scholars, notably Professor W. F. Albright, dated them at once as early as the latter part of the second century B.C. Some other scholars placed them much later, even as late as the Middle Ages. Later discoveries, notably the coins found in the Khirbet, a carbon 14 test, and the internal evidence of some of the documents themselves, have convinced many, perhaps most, scholars that the early date is approximately correct and that all the manuscripts were placed in the caves before 70 A.D., it being recognized, of course, that the date of the production of the manuscripts might have been very considerably earlier.

The early date of the manuscripts makes their contents a matter of great importance. They are practically all religious, either Biblical or extra-Biblical. The strictly Biblical material consists either of manuscripts of the Biblical books or of commentaries upon them. The most extensive of all the scrolls is the so-called St. Mark Isaiah (now known as ɪQɪs ^{a}). There is another Isaiah scroll which is incomplete (ɪQɪs ^{b}). Besides these there are almost innumerable fragments, mostly small, many of which have been already identified as belonging to all of the books of the Old Testament with the possible exception of Esther. Scholars who have been working with these fragments and trying to piece them together believe that they have identified fragments of approximately ninety different Biblical manuscripts, including ten or more different scrolls of Genesis and an equally large or larger number of scrolls of Deuteronomy, Isaiah, and the Psalms. Considerable fragments of Daniel have been identified; and it is interesting to find that in this early manuscript the change from Hebrew to Aramaic takes place in 2:4 just as in the Massoretic Text (abbreviated as M.T.). It is claimed that fragments of forty-seven out of fifty-seven columns of a manuscript of the Books of Samuel have been identified. In the case of some of the fragments of the Pentateuch and of Job, the script that is used is not the so-called 'Square Letter' which has been in use for centuries but the earlier Phoenician or 'Coin Letter,' which is so called because although it was the older script it was still used on Maccabean coins. Whether this means that these fragments in the Phoenician Script are considerably older than, for example, the two Isaiah scrolls is an interesting question, which it may prove difficult or impossible to answer.

When we consider the fact that up to a decade ago the oldest scroll of any book or books of the Old Testament dated from about the tenth century A.D., the discovery of this extensive material may be regarded as epoch-making! It carries us back by the means of manuscript evidence a thousand years nearer to the original documents of the Old Testament than we were a decade ago. Consequently these discoveries are of very great significance. They are important in themselves. But they are also important because of the promise which they hold out for the future.

Possibly More to be Found

If there lay hidden in caves in the Wilderness of Juḍea such a wealth of Biblical material, dating from a period regarding which we had relatively little information, it would seem to be quite obvious that there must have been many others living at about that time and even much earlier who studied, copied, and treasured the Oracles of God, and who might have left behind them similar stores of documents. These discoveries, breath-taking as they are, may be but the harbingers of greater discoveries which may be made at any moment. At least we now know what we may hunt for and hope to discover.

But a word of caution is in order as we proceed to examine these newly discovered Biblical texts. It is to be remembered that the fact that they are, relatively speaking, quite old does not necessarily prove that they are good. A quite recent copy of an old document, if it has been carefully made, may be better and more dependable than a poorly made copy which is many years, even many centuries older, especially if the older copy is in bad condition, fragmentary, or illegible in spots. New Testament scholars are well aware that the value of a manuscript is not determined solely by its age. Readings which are quite probably false appear in some manuscripts which are quite ancient. It is important to bear this in mind as we examine this new material for Old Testament study.

The Massoretic Text (M.T.) of the Hebrew Bible has been regarded as the standard text for many centuries. It was prepared by Jewish scholars who were responsible for the safeguarding of the sacred text and for vocalizing and punctuating it. This work was both important and necessary because Hebrew was originally written without vowels. This characteristic was due to the fact that in it as in other Semitic languages the root which determines the basic meaning of a word is consonantal, usually tri-consonantal. For example, the root *KTB* has the basic meaning 'write.' The supply of vowels or adding of formative consonants modifies the meaning. *KaTaB* (using small letters to indicate the vowels) means 'he wrote,' *KoTeB* means 'writing' or a 'writer,' *KaTaBTa,* 'thou hast written,' *MiKTaB,* 'a writing.' All are simply modifications of the root *KTB.* Only under certain circumstances were weak consonants, for example, *w or y* used to indicate long vowels, as in the Hebrew word *KaTaBTiY,* 'I have written.'

When Hebrew was a spoken language, the consonantal text was sufficient for the average reader, who would only occasionally be in doubt as to the correct pronunciation and exact meaning of an unusual word or of a difficult passage. The scribes and doctors of the Law were expected to know the meaning. And even today in Jewish synagogues the rolls which contain the sacred Scriptures are unvowelled. The Massoretes who vocalized, or as we often say, 'pointed' the Hebrew text, did their work with great care. In order to safeguard the text they counted not merely the verses, but the words and even the letters of each book. If in copying two mistakes were made on a single page they might be corrected, if more than two it must be recopied. Most scholars have been ready to admit that the Hebrew text in use today is practically the same as the one which was accepted as authoritative as early as the second century A.D. It is very significant that while our Lord reproved the Jews for setting at naught the Word of God by their traditions, He never accused them of falsifying the *text* of Scripture. Jesus and His opponents both appealed to the Scriptures as a body of writings mutually accepted as of divine authority. This implies that at that time the text of the Old Testament was fully established and generally accepted.

The Scrolls and the Massoretic Text

Such being the case, the question at once arises whether the newly discovered Dead Sea manuscripts agree with the Massoretic Text. The answer cannot be an unqualified 'yes.' There are variations which must be carefully studied. But on the whole these ancient texts support the Massoretic Text. No very important variations have been reported. Much has been made by some scholars of the fact that in some places the scrolls or the fragments appear to follow the Greek Septuagint version instead of the Hebrew. Professor Millar Burrows of Yale, who has probably studied the scrolls as carefully as any other scholar, was a member of the Committee which prepared the Revised Standard Version Old Testament. He has pointed out that that version adopted thirteen readings in the 1QIs [a] scroll which differed from the Massoretic Text. But he has recently expressed the opinion that a mistake was made in accepting some of them.

One of these cases where the writer believes the new reading is clearly wrong is Isaiah 3:24, 'instead of beauty shame,' where the Authorized Version renders 'burning instead of beauty.' The word rendered 'burning' in that version is *KiY*. This word is usually a conjunction meaning 'that,' 'for,' 'because.' It is of very frequent occurrence. But there is another root in Hebrew which occurs several times, both as noun and verb, and means to 'burn' from which *KiY* can quite well be derived. So 'burning' or 'branding' is a perfectly proper rendering here. It is highly probable that the scribe who copied this passage in the new scroll misunderstood the word *KiY*, thought a word was left out, and supplied the word 'shame' to fill out the sense. But this spoils the phrase. 'Beauty' is *YoPiY* and there is clearly a wordplay between *KiY* (branding) and *YoPiY* (beauty) which the Authorized Version tried to bring out by using slightly similar sounding words. Compare, for example, Isaiah 5:7 where there is a wordplay on the words 'judgment; (*mishpat*) and 'oppression' (*mispach*) and on 'righteousness' (*tsedaqah*) and 'cry' (*tse'aqah*).

Need for Careful Study

We have already referred in a former article to the scroll reading in Isaiah 52:14, where *MaSaHTiY*, 'I have anointed,' is apparently to be read instead of *MiSHaT** 'a marring.' The final "y" which appears in the first Isaiah scroll (1QIs [a]) indicates that the word is to be read as first person singular of the perfect of a verb *MSH*, 'to anoint', instead of a noun with formative element 'm' from the root *SHT* '*to destroy.' But the second Isaiah scroll* (1QIs [b]) although fragmentary is well preserved at this point and it plainly reads *MSHT*, agreeing with the Massoretic Text. Scholars who have studied this scroll report that it follows that text more closely than does the first scroll, which is characterized by a very full writing of the vowels by means of the semi-vowels or vowel-letters. It seems quite probable that the final 'y' which is added to this word is due to a misunderstanding on the part of the scribe. He thought *MSHT* had the meaning 'I have anointed' and consequently added the 'y' of the usual spelling of this word. These examples illustrate the arduous yet important task which awaits scholars in studying and evaluating the new materials which have been so recently and so suddenly placed before them. They should be studied carefully. Some of them may supply readings which will help us to correct passages in the Old Testament which are obscure and where errors may have occurred in copying the text. For example, in Isaiah 21:8 the 1QIs [a] scroll reading 'he who saw' (*HR'H*) may seem better than the reading of the Massoretic Text 'a lion' (*RYH*). But 'like a lion' makes good sense (see Revelation 10:3). The reading given in the scroll was one suggested by Lowth nearly two centuries ago, but was not generally accepted by critics. And in the scroll it may represent an attempt to clear up a difficult reading. It is certainly a cause of gratitude for all Bible lovers, that the new discoveries in the main, support the accuracy of the Massoretic Text and illustrate the care with which it has been transmitted.

Commentaries also Discovered

In this respect the commentaries which have been discovered are of especial interest. The longest and most important of them covers most of Habakkuk 1-2. But fragments of commentaries on Micah, Nahum, and Psalm 37, have also been published. They follow a uniform pattern. A verse or portion of a verse is quoted and then an interpretation follows. The most important thing is that the Hebrew text is quoted accurately, even when the interpretation is decidedly free, fanciful, and even fantastic. The Biblical text as quoted may differ somewhat from the Massoretic Text. But these variations seem to represent merely a different reading of the original and do not indicate any desire to twist the Scripture itself in the interest of some special interpretation.

*The *S* in these words is to be pronounced as *SH* and the *H* like the *CH* in 'loch.'

This feature is significant because it reminds us of a fact which is illustrated by the extra-canonical books (Apocrypha, etc.) and which has been known to us for centuries. This fact is that along with the scrupulous, almost superstitious care with which the Jews guarded the text of the Scriptures, they allowed themselves great liberties, in the Apocryphal and other extra-canonical books, in expanding and embellishing the incidents which they found described or suggested in the sacred text. The additions to Esther and to Daniel which are found in the Greek Septuagint, are an illustration of this trait, as are also the Song of the Three Children, Bel and the Dragon, Susanna and the Elders. They are fanciful, unhistorical, even fantastic, and breathe a spirit which is quite different from that of the Old Testament itself.

One of the scrolls which were found in the first cave was a tantalizing mystery for a long time because of the extreme difficulty of unrolling it. It was called the Book of Lamech, because his name was read in a readable portion of it. It has recently been successfully unrolled; and it has proved to be a midrash or fanciful expansion of narratives contained in the Book of Genesis. The legible portion deals with Genesis 12-15. Thus, while the Biblical account simply tells us that Sarai was very beautiful, this midrash goes into a more or less elaborate description of her charms. We have another example of the same romantic interpretation of Biblical history in Josephus' stories about Moses' exploits as the general of Pharaoh in a campaign against the Ethiopians. The Jews and also the Arabs invented the most marvellous stories about the Old Testament characters. Those about Solomon and the queen of Sheba are perhaps the most familiar to us. Consequently it is not at all remarkable that among the manuscripts discovered in these caves there should be a midrash containing fanciful stories regarding Abraham and his wife. But it is not at all probable that this midrash will be found to contain any new stories which equal, not to say surpass in absurdity those which are already known to us.

There is, we repeat, an amazing difference between the scrupulous care with which the Jews safeguarded the very letter of Scripture and the extreme liberties which they permitted themselves in expanding and embellishing it in their commentaries and other writings. It is from these latter that modern writers of 'historical' novels dealing with Biblical times have taken many of the fantastic stories which they use to give realistic and novel appearance to their presentation of ancient times.

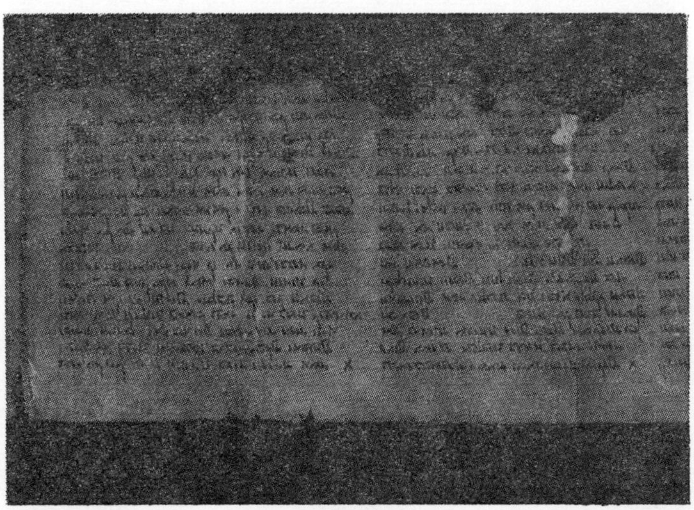

Part of Commentary on Habakkuk (from Dead Sea Scrolls)

Modern Discovery and The Bible

By Dr. Allan A. MacRae
(an address delivered in 1952)

We live in a time of vast discoveries. Within the past few centuries the size of the world has far more than doubled, not only geographically, but in many other respects. In his latter days Sir Isaac Newton made extensive studies of Biblical prophecy. In discussing a verse in Daniel, he ventured the prediction that at some time in the future people might travel as fast as sixty miles an hour. Voltaire pointed to this as evidence that a great scientist could become so confused by religious superstition as to be led into utterly fantastic ideas. Yet within two hundred years Newton's prediction was fully realized, and the speed of today's airplanes make sixty miles an hour seem slow.

In every department of life discoveries have rapidly followed one another. A book of science written even a few years ago is now hopelessly out of date. Has the spiritual realm been affected in the same manner? Has the Bible been replaced by later and better studies in the same field? Surely this would be the case, if the Bible were merely a record of human ideas and observations. But it claims to be something far different from that. It claims to be a revelation from the Creator of the Universe of facts and principles which mankind could never have discovered in any other way.

Revelation not Unscientific

This idea of 'revelation' seems fantastic to many. They assert that we who live in an age of science ought to be scientific and to abandon what they consider to be medieval nonsense. Let us examine this attack, and see whether it is unscientific to believe in revelation. In doing so we shall discover that revelation, instead of being out-of-date, is actually so vital a part of scientific method that without it little progress in any science would be possible. Revelation is simply communication from one personality to another. Without such communication knowledge would die with its discoverer, and the process of gathering facts through the co-operation of many observers, and of interpreting these facts by the combined work of many thinkers, would be impossible. If revelation ceased to be a factor, science would quickly go back to the dark ages. No man living has the ability or the time to gather all the facts and reach all the conclusions involved in any one branch of thought. He must receive many communications from others.

I fear that many philosophers today are like an untravelled man who stands on the western shore of Ireland and looks at the ocean. He has never gone farther west; has neither talked with anyone who has visited America, nor read a book on the subject. But he is possessed of rare mental gifts, and he desires to apply his powerful mentality to the problem of western exploration. He looks westward at the waves and the sky, and undertakes to determine what sort of a land lies beyond the sea. How big is it? What kind of soil does it have? Do its rivers run from south to north like the Nile, or from west to east like the Danube, or from east to west like the Clyde? Is it inhabited? Are its people civilized or savage? What language do its people speak? Upon these and many other questions he might ponder at great length. His intellectual ability might be far above the average, but his conclusions would be utterly worthless. No one could possibly learn the answers to these questions unless he could either travel westward himself, or could receive a communication by word of mouth or in writing from someone who had done so. When facts are accessible to us it is our duty to examine them carefully and critically and to reach our own conclusions about them. When they are not accessible to us we should seek to learn them by revelation from one who knows them, for there is then no other way.

Revelation a Necessity

When it comes to the facts concerning the meaning of the universe, its beginning and its coming fate, the reality and nature of eternal life, and the being and attributes of God, the facts are utterly inaccessible to the natural man. No matter how capacious his intellect may be, he can learn them only by revelation from one who knows about them. And the only one who can possibly know about them is God Himself, the Creator of the universe. In studying theology or learning facts in the spiritual realm it is not unscientific to desire a revelation from God; on the contrary, it is unscientific to seek information regarding this realm in any other way, since the facts are completely inaccessible to us apart from such a revelation.

The vital question therefore is this: Is the Bible such a revelation? If it is, it can never become out-of-date. New light may break from its pages. Students may discover teachings in it which had previously not been grasped. But always it will remain formative. It will be the infallible source of all our knowledge in the spiritual realm—the sole authority by which the truth or falsity of human ideas may be judged. Human writings in this sphere, as in all others, will be replaced by better ones; but this Book, if it is God's Revelation, can never become out-of-date or be proven to contain error.

In no field of thought has modern discovery opened wider horizons than in that of ancient history. Through the work of archaeology whole civilizations, previously unknown, have come to view. As a result of its advances ancient history now extends back twice as far as was the case a century ago. This provides a crucial test for the claims of the Bible. If it is the work of man, we can expect its statements about ancient history to become outmoded and to be proved false at many points. If, however, it is a revelation from God, we can expect it to meet every fair test to which it may be put.

A century ago the Bible stood practically alone in its accounts of events prior to 500 B.C. Other ancient writings that had come down to us gave practically no dependable information about events before that time. A few myths and legends from Greek tradition seemed to be our only non-Biblical source. The Old Testament alone claimed to describe events extending many centuries back of 500 B.C. It mentioned great nations, otherwise absolutely unknown to us. Mighty conquerors crossed its pages, whose very names were otherwise forgotten. Great cities were described which otherwise had left no trace. Under these circumstances it was easy for men who opposed the doctrines of the Bible to say that its history was largely fictitious, and to develop theories which assumed the Old Testament to be a compilation of discordant material, most of it written long after the time of the events with which it claimed to deal. These theories, generally known as the Higher Criticism, came to be widely accepted, and by 1900 many were ready to assert that the views of the Graf-Kuenen-Wellhausen school were accepted by nearly all scholars.

Higher-Critical Theories Discredited

Even before that time, however, a new movement was well under way—the movement of archaeology. During the past century, archaeology has so increased our knowledge of ancient history that it now extends just as far back beyond 500 B.C. as the whole period since that time. Under the excavator's spade great cities have emerged from the dust in many parts of the world, but particularly in Egypt, Mesopotamia, and Palestine. Remains of houses, temples, and palaces have been dug up. Beautiful works of art have been discovered. A new world has emerged from below the surface of the earth and many a fact mentioned in the Old Testament now finds specific and exact corroboration in these new discoveries. The Old Testament history no longer stands alone. It takes its place in that larger world history which gradually comes to light as new factors are discovered. The Bible becomes clearer as we come to understand it, not as an artificial production, but as a Book which gives us an accurate picture of the way in which God revealed Himself in the midst of striking historical events.

A world of life and movement, glory and tragedy, effort and achievement, long ago disappeared from sight. Only an occasional reference in the Bible kept alive the memory of its greatness. Then the excavator's spade unearthed its remains. What a striking illustration of the statement in 1 Peter 1:24-25: 'For all flesh is as grass, and all the glory of man as the flower of grass. The grass withereth, and the flower thereof falleth away: but the word of the Lord endureth for ever.'

Nineveh was for a time the capital of most of the civilized world. Nation after nation fell before the onslaught of her armies. A few verses in the Old Testament tell of her greatness. The most impressive are in the Book of Jonah, with its reference to Nineveh as a city so large that it would take three days to walk around it. One hundred and twenty years ago, no trace of Nineveh remained above the ground. Sceptics derided the Biblical statements about it. 'Surely,' they said, 'if there had actually existed in ancient times a city as great as modern Paris or Berlin, some trace of it would remain, so that we would at least know where it was.' Then in 1842 the French vice-consul, Emil Botta, crossed the upper Tigris River opposite modern Mosul and began to excavate a series of deserted mounds. There, under the sand of the ages, he found evidence of a city just as large and just as great as it was pictured in the Bible. The ancient glory of Nineveh had crumbled into dust, while the Bible remained and kept alive the memory of its long-forgotten greatness.

Isaiah 20:1 refers to an Assyrian king named Sargon. Early in the past century many doubted the very existence of this monarch. The name was not found in any of the Greek writers, and occurs only once in the Old Testament; they therefore considered that it must be used in error for some other person. Then an English excavator went to Khorsabad, a mound in the desert a few miles from Nineveh, and found that it contained the palace of a mighty ruler. Remarkable pictures, bas-reliefs, and statues, proclaimed the greatness of the conqueror who lived there, and the inscriptions gave his name as Sargon. Thus one of the mighty conquerors of world-history disappeared from sight for more than two thousand years, his name forgotten, save for its use to date the giving of a portion of God's Word—another striking illustration of Peter's words: 'For all flesh is as grass, and all the glory of man as the flower of grass. The grass withereth, and the flower thereof falleth away: but the word of the Lord endureth for ever.'

Discoveries in Palestine

Some have been privileged to pay a visit to Palestine and there to see the remains of ancient Jericho. The city which Joshua destroyed was partially excavated over forty years ago, and the work was carried to completion twenty years later. It was very impressive to see the strong walls of this powerful fortress, lying on their sides, just as they fell. The excavators reported that the remains were different from those of other cities. The wall had not been broken through with a battering ram, nor were the people starved into submission and the walls left standing. The condition of the walls showed that they had fallen outward suddenly, in a great cataclysm. There the stones lie today, mute evidence of the great divine intervention described in the Book of Joshua. How could discoveries go further, to show the accuracy and dependability of the Word of God?

Recently excavation has commenced on another mound, about a mile from Old Testament Jericho, containing the remains of the city of Jericho of the time of Christ. Although results are still necessarily somewhat tentative, it is fairly certain that a portion of King Herod's winter palace has been uncovered. There is evidence of the sophistication and luxury of this outpost of Roman life in Palestine. Herod had spent a number of years of his early life in Rome. Perhaps he brought Roman architects all the way to Palestine to build his luxurious palace overseeing the Jordan Valley. As its features come to life we see again an illustration of the way the human glory disappears, while God's Word abides.

Extremely interesting is the new light shed on the times of Solomon by the excavations between 1925 and 1939. A few years ago no evidence remained, aside from Biblical statements, of the greatness of this son of David. Naturally unbelievers scoffed at it, declaring that the Biblical statements were grossly exaggerated. Now evidence has come to light, at Megiddo (New Testament Armageddon) and elsewhere in Palestine, and also further south at the shores of the eastern branch of the Red Sea, of the great building activities of Solomon. It proves him to have been far more powerful than any other ancient Palestinian ruler, and also to have utilized scientific knowledge unparalleled in ancient times. Modern engineering principles, rediscovered within the past century, were employed by Solomon a thousand years before the time of Christ. Proof is now available that he was a great mercantile expert, a scientific leader, a man whose empire was of tremendous importance. Aside from the Biblical statement all contemporary evidence of Solomon's greatness completely disappeared. Now the Biblical statements about him are proved to be true, and not in the least exaggerated. Again we think of 1 Peter. Human greatness disappears and is forgotten; only God's Word abides for ever.

The Case of Sennacherib

Naturally we do not expect always to find material verbally reproducing the statements of the Bible. Most of our written material comes from Mesopotamia or Egypt, rather than from Palestine. Its political and geographic viewpoint is quite opposed to that of the Hebrews. This makes the essential agreement all the more striking. The Bible tells how another great Ninevite conqueror, Sennacherib, the son of Sargon, overran Palestine and threatened to seize Jerusalem. Isaiah told Hezekiah not to fear: God would protect Jerusalem and would deliver it from the boastful Assyrian. In three books of the Old Testament the deliverance is portrayed. The angel of the Lord attacked the host of Sennacherib in the night, and when Sennacherib awoke in the morning, he found that thousands of his men were dead, and he had no choice but to return across the desert to Nineveh without conquering Jerusalem. We should hardly expect archaeological evidence from Nineveh to present these facts in quite the same way; kings do not boast of their defeats, and least of all such a one as Sennacherib. But Sennacherib's annals have come to light, and in them we read of his great campaigns and victories. City after city was conquered by him, many of them far stronger than Jerusalem. In the account of this third campaign he tells of the Jewish opposition. He mentions Hezekiah, a king of Judah, as one who was especially obnoxious to him. After seeing what he did to his other enemies, we are ready to read about a great victory over Hezekiah. Instead, we find these words: "Hezekiah, king of Judah, I shut up like a bird in a cage in his capital city of Jerusalem." It sounds like a strange anticlimax, after he has described his victories elsewhere. It was all he could find to boast of! It testifies to the fact that he failed to conquer Hezekiah or to take Jerusalem.

Another interesting feature emerges in this connection. Sennacherib set up in his palace a great bas-relief portraying his conquest of a certain city. In a series of incidents the pictures show him attacking the city, breaking through its walls, leading out its people as prisoners and seizing their property as booty. One expects to find that this is one of the great foreign capitals that Sennacherib captured, but the inscription with it shows that the city involved is Lachish, the second of the cities of Judah, and inferior to Jerusalem in importance. Having failed to take Jerusalem, he put up a monument to his lesser conquest in Judah. Shall we call the picture "Sennacherib's consolation prize"?

A Strange Situation

It is fascinating to study archaeological evidence, and to see, at point after point, evidence of the accuracy of the background of the Biblical accounts. In these days when unbelief has become more widespread than ever before, God has caused the buried past to give up many of its treasures, making clear the accuracy and dependability of the Bible. A fog of unbelief covers much of the world, but never was unbelief less reasonable than today, when so many new evidences of the truth have become available. Nevertheless a strange situation still exists. On the one hand scholarship, which fifty years ago had to so large an extent accepted the Higher Criticism, is being led further and further away from the critical views, as a result of the new light from archaeology. Among scholars there is an increasing retreat from the theories of Wellhausen. Trained scholars are giving up many of its most fundamental positions, because the new material from archaeology is showing them to be untenable. On the other hand the ecclesiastical world, which until recently stood largely in opposition to the Higher Criticism, has now capitulated to it, at least as far as many of the leading denominations in America and in Europe are concerned. But solid fact and evidence is on the side of the Bible-believer. Most of the apparent difficulties in the material and historical statements of Scripture, as seen by critics of a half-century ago, are now easily solved. In all other spheres of thought, new discovery causes books to become out-of-date, and leads to the preparation of better ones. In this case alone, a book is shown, as new discoveries are made, to be more dependable and true. There is only one explanation. The Bible is not a product of human observation or of human wisdom, but is a revelation from God. 'Holy men of God spoke as they were moved by the Holy Ghost.' It, and it alone, is God's Word. It is our only guide to eternal life. It shows us our lost condition. It X-rays our hearts and demonstrates that they are altogether wicked and corrupt. It shows our condition to be humanly incurable. Only eternal suffering can lie ahead of sinful men. But the Bible message does not stop there. It shows that God has made provision for the salvation of all who will put their trust in the Lord Jesus Christ, who purchased redemption for us by His death at Calvary. Let us rejoice in this salvation, and let us declare it to others, that they also may be saved.

EXTRACT FROM A CUNEIFORM TEXT recording the siege of Jerusalem, inscribed on a clay cylinder of the Annals of Sennacherib (B.C. 705–681), now in the British Museum.

The substance of Sennacherib's account is as follows:—"Six and forty of the fenced cities, and the fortresses, and the villages round about them, belonging to Hezekiah the Jew, who had not submitted to my rule, I besieged and stormed and captured. I carried away from them two hundred thousand and one hundred and fifty souls, great and small, male and female, and horses, mules, asses, camels, oxen, and sheep without number. In his house in Jerusalem I shut up Hezekiah like a bird in a cage. I threw up mounds round about the city from which to attack it, and I blockaded his gates. The cities which I had captured from him I took away from his kingdom and I gave them to Mitinti, king of Ashdod.' . . . .

New Light on Some Old Testament Problems

An address at the Annual Meeting of the Bible League, 1957.

By D. J. Wiseman, O.B.E.

My subject tonight has to be limited because of many factors, not the least of which is that there seems to have entered into the Bible League an unwitting tradition that I should address its Annual Meeting every three years. In 1951 I sought to cover the archaeological discoveries made in the preceding ten years. The fact that three years later in an address on 'The Bible and Scholarship' four new archaeological discoveries bearing on the Bible could be described, is some indication of the rapid progress being made in the accumulation of evidence in this branch of science. It is sufficient here to note that discoveries continue which, when fully evaluated, will further our understanding of the Scriptures. The excavations at Hasor which have laid bare an Israelite royal store-city, produced inscribed sherds with the name of Pekah, and contain evidence which fits best the later date (Thirteenth Century B.C.) for the entry of the Children of Israel into the Promised Land. The clever decipherment of an inscribed stone lintel from Siloam, near Jerusalem, provided us with one of the oldest Hebrew monuments. This was part of the impressive tomb of Shebna, the Steward of King Hezekiah, for the construction of which he was rebuked by the prophet Isaiah (22:15-19). Interesting though these points are, my purpose is to deal at greater length with recent discoveries which throw light on two historical matters concerning which there has been a considerable divergence of opinion for many years.

The Capture of Jerusalem

Last year I published four new texts belonging to the famous Babylonian Chronicle, a contemporary native historical record of which parts previously furnished the outline of historical events from 747-648, 616-609 B.C., that is, down to the fall of Nineveh and the end of the Assyrian Empire.[1] This means that our knowledge of subsequent events had to rely on the history of Josephus as the only extra-Biblical source. As a result diverse interpretations have been presented. The date of the Battle of Carchemish, when Nebuchadnezzar defeated Necho of Egypt, has never been conclusively fixed. Now the Chronicle tells of the heavy defeat they suffered when, after the battle at Carchemish, the Babylonians chased the Egyptians as far as Hamath and defeated them so utterly that 'not a man escaped to his own country. At that time Nebuchadnezzar conquered the whole of the Hatti-land' (i.e. Syria and Palestine). In the following year, 604 B.C., 'all the kings of Hatti came before him and he received their tribute.' Among these must have been Jehoiakim of Judah, so that it is no wonder that Jeremiah could write 'Nebuchadnezzar king of Babylon came up, and Jehoiakim became his servant three years: then he turned and rebelled against him . . . And the king of Egypt came not again any more out of his land; for the king of Babylon had taken from the river of Egypt (the *Nahalmusur* or *Wady el-Arish*) unto the River Euphrates all that pertained to the king of Egypt.' (2 Kings 24:1, 7).

The Babylonian Chronicle also tells us how one city, Askelon, resisted Nebuchadnezzar's advance in this same year (604 B.C.). The city was sacked and its king captured. There can be no doubt that this severe act so near to Jerusalem caused a deep impression and underlined Jeremiah's message of warning of the dangers which would follow opposition to Babylon. The same month as Askelon fell, a solemn fast was proclaimed in Jerusalem (Jer. 36:9). Nevertheless, we know that the prophet's numerous opponents favoured Egypt, and it has not always been possible to see why, for Egypt was thought to have been weak and powerless at this time. We can now see that this was not the case, for we learn that in 601 B.C. Nebuchadnezzar marched to battle with Egypt. On hearing of his approach Necho II called out his army and both forces met in open battle. With characteristic frankness the

[1] D. J. Wiseman, *Chronicles of Chaldaean Kings (626-594 B.C.) in the British Museum, 1956.*

Babylonian chronicler states that both sides suffered heavy losses. Since Nebuchadnezzar's army remained at home for eighteen months re-equipping it seems that the outcome of the battle was a severe set-back for them. The Egyptians were sufficiently strong to deter Nebuchadnezzar from attacking them during the next thirty years.

We can see then why Jehoiakim revolted from Babylon in this year, probably after the battle, and put his trust in Egypt. Nevertheless, Jeremiah still perceived which was the stronger nation and continued to warn his neighbours of impending reprisals. His oracles against the Arab tribes of Kedar and Hasor (49:28-33) once thought by many critics to be a late reflexion of attacks on these tribes by Ashurbanipal in 648 B.C., or a confusion with Nebuchadnezzar's later raids into Arabia in 681 B.C., can now be seen in a new light. In December, 599 B.C., the Babylonian armies, according to the Chronicle, plundered these very tribes, taking from them their possessions, animals and gods. (cf. Jer. 49:29).

But most striking of all this new contemporary evidence is the Chronicle's entry for the next year, Nebuchadnezzar's seventh regal year. It reads: 'In the month Kislev of this seventh year, the king of Babylonia mustered his troops and, marching to Hatti-land (Palestine) besieged the city of Judah (Jerusalem). On the second day of the month Addar he seized the city and captured the king. He set up there a king after his own heart. He received a heavy tribute and sent it back to Babylon.'

I submit that no more direct contemporary historical allusion, so comprehensive or clear, to any Biblical statement has hitherto been found. The capture of Jehoiachin, the placing of the Babylonian nominee Mattaniah on the throne, the taking of the temple vessels and the despatch of the prisoners (included in the tribute) to Babylon are included. The very date for the commencement of the crucial Jewish Exile is now known for the first time (16th March, 597 B.C.).

An end is thus put at last to those criticisms which found disparities in the three Biblical accounts of this one cardinal event. The city's fall 'at the turn of the year' (2 Chron. 36:10) can be readily understood, for at the end of this month, two weeks later, the New Year began. This was Nebuchadnezzar's eighth year when, according to 2 Kings 24:12, the prisoners began their long desert march into exile. A small Babylonian tablet has once again provided evidence which, as it were in a single stroke, rendered invalid years of hypothetical discussion and disputation.

Darius the Mede

One of the major historical problems of the book of Daniel has been the references to Darius the Mede. It recounts how after the death of Belshazzar, Darius the Mede received the kingdom (v.31). He was aged sixty-two at the time (v.31) and was the son of Ahasuerus (9:1). One of his major acts of government was to organise the kingdom into one-hundred-and-twenty satrapies (6:1). One statement—'so Daniel prospered in the reign of Darius, and in the reign of Cyrus the Persian' (6:29 A.V.)—would seem to imply that he was succeeded by Cyrus the Persian. The Septuagint shows that the translators took this to be the meaning. If this is so then it implies that Darius followed Nabonidus, and his co-regent son Belshazzar, who were both killed at the fall of Babylon in 539 B.C., and was himself succeeded by the conqueror of the ancient city, Cyrus. The fall of Babylon to Cyrus is clearly outlined in the contemporary Babylonian Chronicle. This and other Persian and Babylonian records make no reference to any intervening ruler but clearly state that Cyrus himself took over the Neo-Babylonian empire from Nabonidus after a brief period of fifteen days in which Babylon itself was under a military governor named Gubaru (Gobryas).

There have been numerous attempts to identify this Darius. The most common are to associate him with Gobryas, with Cambyses or with a fictitious Cyaxares II. Among anti-critical orthodox writers within the last fifty years, Wright and R. D. Wilson have argued for the identification with Gobryas and Boutflower with Cyaxares II. Other candidates include Astyages. Despite much ingenious reasoning, some of it in the pages of the *Bible League Quarterly,* the growing contemporary evidence does not point to any such predecessor of Cyrus as ruler in Babylon. As a result it is still generally agreed within the critical school that 'he (Darius the Mede) has no place in history, and that he is a fictitious creation out of confused traditions.'[2] This strong assertion is strengthened by Rowley's sound historical arguments to show how that this Darius cannot be Cambyses, Gobryas, Astyages or Cyaxares if the details in Daniel are to be accepted. One of the main arguments against the historicity of this ruler has been the well-known fact that the kingdom of Media was incorporated in the greater realm of Persia when Cyrus overthrew Astyages in 550 B.C. It has been generally assumed that the kingdom of Media ceased to exist, and that the later style 'king of the Medes,' if this is to be read into the simple ethnic description 'the Mede' applied to the Biblical Darius, is incongruous in 539 B.C.

In the light of these statements a discovery made last autumn at Haran, formerly Abraham's sojourning place, is of special interest. Three paving stones of the Great Mosque there were discovered to be re-used older Babylonian inscribed monuments. When these were read they proved to be new records of the reign of Nabonidus, the last native king of Babylon (556-539 B.C.), and of his aged mother the high-priestess of the Moon-god, Sin. While these are of wide historical interest there is one point in the texts, which are as yet unpublished, of special importance for our problem. Two texts tell how the people rebelled against Nabonidus' religious innovations, directed to secure the worship of Sin. When plague followed, the king withdrew to Arabia where he set up a kingdom centred on Tema, and seems to have been supported by Jewish exiles. He remained in exile for ten years by which time he says the attitude of the Babylonians had changed, as had the economic position, and he was able to return. The text says of this time, his tenth regnal year, i.e., 546 B.C., or later, that 'the kings of Egypt, of the Medes and of the Arabs, who had been hostile, sent messages to me to make an alliance.' This royal inscription will, of course, silence the criticisms that no one was called 'king of the Medes' after the annexation by Cyrus of that province in 550 B.C. While a few Greek authors imply that Astyages had a son, Herodotus (1:109) and other evidence shows that Astyages was the last Median king. The most likely person who might have borne the title was Cyrus himself who had incorporated Media while he was 'King of Anzan' a province of Persia. This later title, with that of 'King of Persia, king of the lands,' is attested as his in many Babylonian documents. It would now seem that even before Cyrus took the title 'King of Babylonia' on conquering that country in 539 B.C. he was known there as 'King of the Medes.'

If this new evidence is to help us it remains to see if Cyrus himself could be the 'Darius the Mede' of Daniel. I have elsewhere stated that the phrase 'and Daniel prospered in the reign of Darius, and in the reign of Cyrus the Persian' could equally well be translated 'and Daniel prospered in the reign of Darius, *even* in the reign of Cyrus the Persian.' There is a striking parallel in 1 Chronicles 5.26 which is now translated 'and the God of Israel stirred up the spirit of Pul, king of Assyria even (not 'and' A.V.) the spirit of Tiglath-pileser, King of Assyria and he carried them away.' Years before the Bible League was founded scholars used to argue against the historicity of Pul but all such criticisms died away when contemporary Assyrian and Babylonian tablets revealed that Pul(u) was the native name of Tiglath-pileser himself, and used by him as his royal title in Babylonia. In 1 Chronicles 5.26 as in Daniel 6:29 the writer's aim would be to acquaint the reader with the two names in use by the one person. This would accord with Josephus' claim that Cyrus had another name among the Greeks (Antiq. 10, 11:4).

An examination of the Biblical references to Darius shows that these may equally well fit the evidence of Cyrus' life as we now know it. The Babylonian Chronicle clearly describes how Cyrus took over the government of Babylonia, entering the city a fortnight after its fall and being received by the inhabitants who spread palm-branches before him. Governors were appointed for all the Babylonian provinces, though the number of 120 as in Daniel 6:1 cannot be checked. An unpublished tablet in the British Museum may well be part of the orders given to these men. Cyrus' act in placing his generals and others as governors of important parts of his realm was an innovation, since the Medes previously had sub-vassal kings ruling over any conquered territories. For this reason the introduction

[2] H. H. Rowley, *Darius the Mede,* p. 5.

of 'satraps' may well have been worthy of special mention. It is certain that satrapies existed before the days of Darius II.[3]

As to the exact age of Cyrus when he took over Babylon there is some doubt, but most authorities have noted that he may have been about 62 years old.[4] Indeed this has been used as a prime argument against the other 'identifications' of Darius. Cyrus had been a general in the service of his uncle Cyaxares, according to Xenophon, and had been king of Persia for some years before annexing Media in 550 B.C. He died in 529 B.C., according to Babylonian records, after only nine years' reign over his new dominion. Cyrus was certainly over 46 years old when he came to the throne,[5] and if the exact figure given by Herodotus is correct must have come to the throne in 558 B.C. This advanced age is made all the more likely when we know that his grandfather was already ruling Persia (*Parsumas*) in 640 B.C.

There remain two difficulties for which I do not profess to know the answer if the equation of Cyrus as Darius the Mede is to be maintained. Was Cyrus a 'Mede'? It might be argued that 'the Mede' is an abbreviation for the title 'King of the Medes,' and does not denote his origin and was thus omitted in Dan. 6:29. In the light of the recently discovered Babylonian inscription there seems little point in arguing that Cyrus was a Mede by his marriage to a daughter of Cyaxares,[6] for there can be no question of the close connection of the ruling families of Persia and Media. The other difficulty is closely linked, for Cyrus, if the same person as Darius, was the son of Ahasuerus (Xerxes),[7] though the origin and predecessors of Cyrus are by no means clear. Cyrus is usually recorded as the son of Cambyses I. It would have to be assumed that Cambyses had another name, whether personal or dynastic, of Xerxes. Only further evidence can prove or disprove such a bold assumption.

The implications of this argument based on new evidence may well be far reaching. If it is right, then the historical character of Darius the Mede, being none other than the well known ruler Cyrus, could no longer be questioned. Such statements as 'the claim of the book of Daniel to be a work of history written by a well-informed contemporary, is shattered beyond repair by this fiction of Darius the Mede'[8] would be indefensible. It would give a new light to the predictions of the overthrow of Babylon by the *Medes* (Jer. 60:9-41; 51, 11:20; Isaiah 13:17) and to the linking of Elam (the state of Anshan) and Media in the same action (Isaiah 21).

These two examples will perhaps serve to show how many passages of Scripture, though seemingly difficult to understand in themselves, may in time find some solution as our knowledge increases. Such new light has often been the result of archaeological discovery. Whether we find the answer soon or have to wait until the day when we shall know 'even as we are known' can never be foretold. One thing is sure—problems, and indeed theories to solve them, may come and go, but 'The Word of the Lord endureth for ever.'

[3] *Revue Biblique*, 48.
[4] Rowley, *op. cit.* p. 55.
[5] Sidney Smith, *Isaiah XL-LV*, p. 32.
[6] Xenophon, *Cyrop.* VIII v. 19.
[7] Dan. 9:1.
[8] Rowley, *op cit.*, pp. 59-60.

The Topography of Jerusalem in Old Testament Times

By S. M. Houghton

It is unthinkable that the city of Jerusalem should ever cease to be a subject of outstanding interest to Christians. Much of the 'wealth of sacred story' gathers around it. Here many of the Old Testament narratives are centred. From the days of Abraham and his mysterious encounter with Melchisedek, priest of the most high God, to the days of Zacharias son of Barachias who was slain between the temple and the altar, Jerusalem is of surpassing importance in Jewish, and indeed in world, history. Here, too, much of New Testament history was wrought out. Kings and priests and prophets, whose names are still household words, trod its streets and played their part for good or ill in the tangled drama of national life. Above all, the Saviour Himself here ministered, suffered, died, and rose again. From a near-by hill He ascended into the heavens: and when He comes again, the King of glory, 'the flaming of His advent feet' will be witnessed on the self-same Mount. Dull must the Christian be of soul if he is not stirred by the age-old story of the city over which his Saviour wept. All national histories, graphic and thrilling though they be, are eclipsed by the story of the earthly city of God.

It is not proposed in this article to give even a bird's-eye view of Jerusalem's history. Its setting in the national history of Israel is much the same as the setting of the history of London in the history of England. It would almost be true to say that the history of Jerusalem *is* the history of Israel. The capital city is the heart of the body politic, and in the case of Israel it is also the religious centre. The Saviour gave expression to this when He said, 'It cannot be that a prophet perish out of Jerusalem' (Luke 13:33). Upon Jerusalem's high stage, in the full view of Israel, and portrayed for all the world in Hebrew literature, the 'long cloud of witnesses' showed the same path to heaven, the path from earth to the Jerusalem which is above. So much is this the case that the witnesses yet to come remain identified with the city 'where also our Lord was crucified' (Rev. 11;8).

The Importance of Topography

For an understanding of Jerusalem's fascinating story the reader must acquaint himself with the main features of the city's topography. He must acquire a working knowledge of the situation of its surrounding valleys and of its principal gates. He must get fixed in his mind the position of its temple and its 'high palaces'. He must grasp the significance of the Bible's use of certain prepositions as indicative of height and depth: thus a person leaving the city of David for another site in the neighbourhood (as Pharaoh's daughter going to the house built for her by Solomon) not merely went out of the city but went 'up out of it' (1 Kings 9:24). When attention is given to these matters, the story of the capital city of Jewry can be followed with a more intelligent interest. Just as many British people who do not live in London would feel somewhat ashamed if they remained in ignorance of the locations within the capital of Westminster Abbey, the Tower of London, Buckingham Palace, St. Paul's Cathedral, and suchlike places, so the reader of Scripture should aim at a topographical knowledge of the main sites of the Holy Land, and of the main features of the city around which so much of sacred history revolves.

Considerable difficulties have existed for those who have endeavoured in the past hundred years to solve the topographical problems which Jerusalem presents. Probably more frequently than any other city, Jerusalem has been captured and destroyed. It has been termed 'the twenty-seven-times-sacked city'. Yet upon the ruins of the old city a new city has invariably arisen. Jerusalem has proved indestructible. 'In many places', wrote H. V. Hilprecht in his *Explorations in Bible lands,* 'the debris that conceals the old city from our sight is over 100 feet deep. Laborious and expensive excavations are therefore everywhere necessary in order to arrive at any degree of certitude regarding the form of the ancient city. In many places these are impossible, inasmuch as upon the debris the new houses of the modern city have been built, underneath which digging cannot be done'. Jerusalem's very indestructibility has been in itself the greatest of hindrances to the archaeologist. Whereas Babylon and Nineveh, for example, are desolate ruins where 'diggers up of the past' have had free scope, Jerusalem has risen phoenix-like from its ashes and the excavator is correspondingly handicapped. And outside the bounds of the modern city, as in the valley of the Kidron and the Valley of Hinnom, the presence of thousands of graves, both Jewish and Moslem, renders the task of the archaeologist one of great difficulty. In the temple area, again, investigation is all but forbidden upon religious grounds. Yet, in spite of such difficulties, in recent years a considerable fund of knowledge has accumulated, and agreement has virtually been reached by experts on certain matters which have been long in dispute.

The Geographical Setting

Apart from the significant fact that Jerusalem is situated near the point where three continents meet, its vast importance in human history owes little, if anything, to its geographical situation. It is not on the sea-coast, nor is it easy of access from the sea, for the roads from the Mediterranean wind through steep and rugged mountain passes. Unlike many great capitals, ancient and modern, it is not situated on a river. Nor has it been a mart of nations, situated where trade-routes converge. It lies on no great highway. The surrounding country is not remarkable for any special degree of fertility: on the contrary it is somewhat more arid and less productive than other parts of the Holy Land. Notwithstanding these seeming disadvantages, Jerusalem, as the 'city which God chose to place His Name there', has established itself in the affections of the Jewish people and in the interest of Christians as has no other city on the face of the earth.

The traveller goes up to Jerusalem. If he journeys there from the shores of earth's central sea, he climbs 2,500 feet above sea level: if he makes the ascent from Jericho at the northern end of the Dead Sea, he rises 3,800 feet. Palestine has a backbone of mountains which form the watershed between the Mediterranean Sea and the Jordan Valley, and on the summit of this watershed Jerusalem is situated. It is surrounded, however, by hills of slightly greater height, so that no extensive prospect is to be met with, except to the south-east where there is a gap in the outer ring, and the mountains of Moab, at the western edge of the great Arabian desert, are to be seen 25 or 30 miles away. But it must not be supposed that Jerusalem is actually shut in by mountains. The words of Psalm 125:2 must not be interpreted as indicating the presence of towering peaks and mountain battlements; it is rather an allusion to the 'protection afforded the city by the wild hills cut up by a thousand ravines which guard it on every side, and render any approach difficult, especially to a large armed force'.

'Beautiful for elevation, the joy of the whole earth
Is Mount Zion, on the sides of the north;
The city of the great king.
  For lo, the kings were assembled,
They marched on together.
  They beheld and so they marvelled,
They were troubled, they hasted away;
Trembling took hold upon them there,
Pain, as of a woman in travail'. (Psalm 48).

The Geology of Jerusalem

Geologically considered, Jerusalem rests on the chalky limestone of the Judean hills. Beds of limestone having a gentle south-easterly slope are found immediately below the city. The lower strata reach ground level on the western ridge of the city and consist of a hard stone suitable for building and for paving stones. Above these are beds of softer fine white limestone, known as Melekeh or royal stone. This has been used extensively for building purposes: underneath the city ancient quarries exist which probably supplied all the stones needed for the construction of Solomon's temple. On this

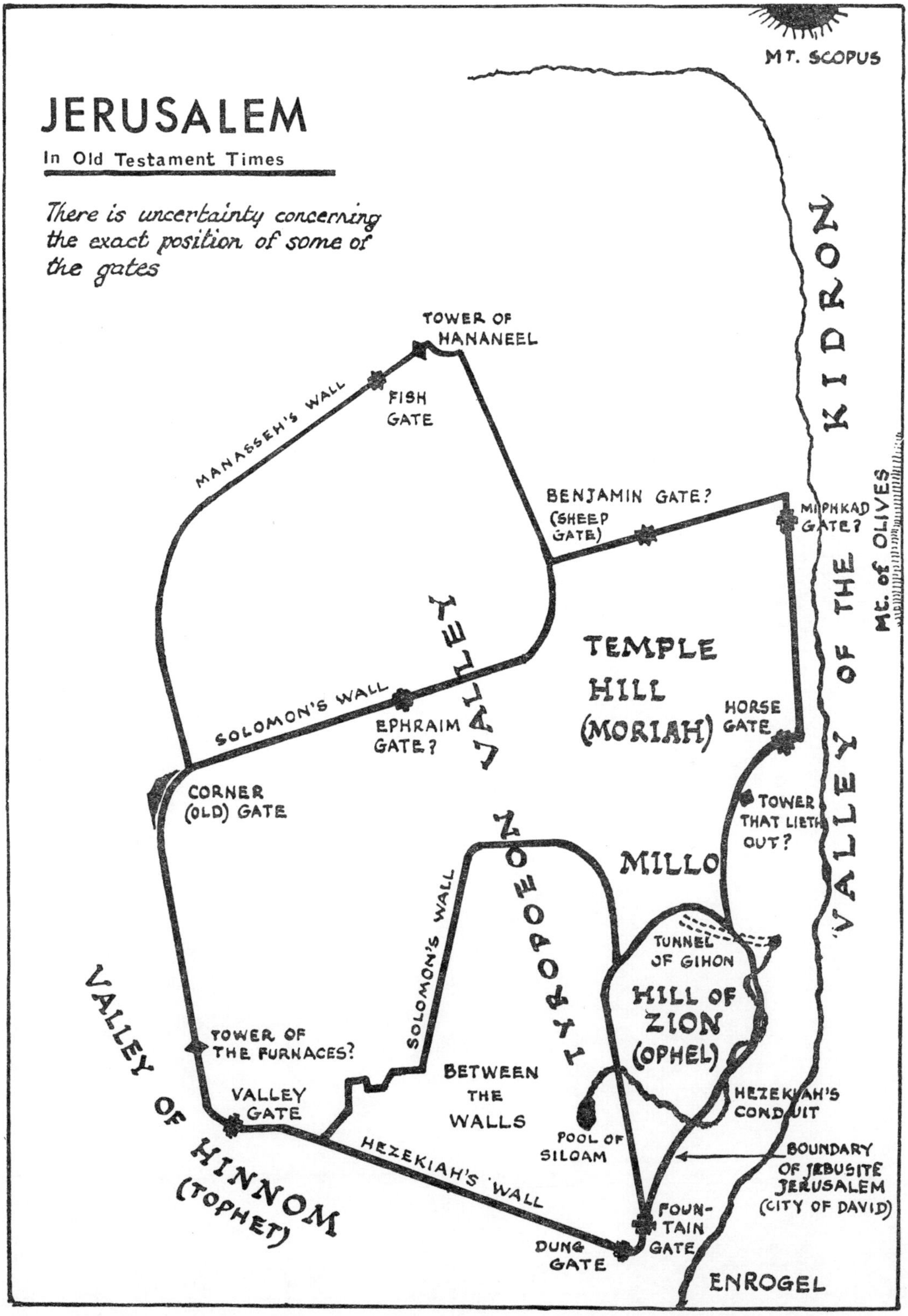
JERUSALEM
In Old Testament Times
There is uncertainty concerning the exact position of some of the gates
MT. SCOPUS
KIDRON
TOWER OF HANANEEL
FISH GATE
MANASSEH'S WALL
BENJAMIN GATE? (SHEEP GATE)
MIPHKAD GATE?
MT. of OLIVES
VALLEY OF THE KIDRON
VALLEY
TEMPLE HILL (MORIAH)
SOLOMON'S WALL
EPHRAIM GATE?
HORSE GATE
CORNER (OLD) GATE
TOWER THAT LIETH OUT?
TYROPOEON
MILLO
SOLOMON'S WALL
TUNNEL OF GIHON
HILL OF ZION (OPHEL)
VALLEY OF HINNOM (TOPHET)
TOWER OF THE FURNACES?
BETWEEN THE WALLS
VALLEY GATE
HEZEKIAH'S CONDUIT
POOL OF SILOAM
HEZEKIAH'S WALL
BOUNDARY OF JEBUSITE JERUSALEM (CITY OF DAVID)
FOUNTAIN GATE
DUNG GATE
ENROGEL

softer rock rest more beds of hard grey limestone, which appear on the slopes of the Mount of Olives to the east of Jerusalem. The rocks of the district contain no metals and such clay as occurs is of rather poor quality. Much of Jerusalem's limestone is porous. The rain sinks through it to considerable depths and is deflected by harder underlying rocks towards the south-east of the city where are found the only well and spring in the neighbourhood.

Ravines around Jerusalem

On three sides Jerusalem is surrounded by deep-cut ravines. In ancient times they were much deeper than they are today. Great accumulations of debris, much of it the result of the oft-repeated deliberate and systematic destruction of the city, have reduced the depth by 50 or 60 feet in some places, with the consequence that modern visitors often fail to appreciate the military advantages of the site as estimated by its defenders and attackers in the centuries before Christ; and those who study the site from photographs are likewise easily deceived. Modern science has completely altered conceptions of military strategy, but in ancient days Jerusalem was regarded as occupying a well-nigh impregnable position, the Gibraltar of the Palestine highlands. Lamentations 4:12 shows the sense of surprise which affected the kings and peoples of the earth 'who would not have believed that the adversary and the enemy should have entered into the gates of Jerusalem'. Joshua failed to capture the city (then called Jebus), and David, ere he took it, had to meet the taunts and jeers of its Jebusite inhabitants who mocked him with the news that the citadel could be well defended by the blind and the lame.

To the east of the city is the famous Kidron Valley, which separates it from the Mount of Olives. Further north it separates the city from the mountain now known as Scopus. It deepens rapidly towards its southern end and becomes a narrow ravine 'with tolerably precipitous sides'. When it leaves the neighbourhood of Jerusalem it runs on towards the Dead Sea and becomes increasingly rugged. A brook used to flow down the valley but now it is dry, except after heavy rains. This is probably accounted for, in part, by the masses of debris which have raised the level of the valley. David, fleeing from his son Absalom, crossed the Kidron valley as he went 'toward the way of the wilderness' (2 Samuel 15:23), and the Lord also did so as He went to Gethsemane on the night of His betrayal (John 18:1).

To the west of Jerusalem runs the Valley now called Wadi-el-Annabeh, which turns abruptly eastward as soon as it has passed the city's western ridge, deepens rapidly, and joins the Kidron at the so-called Well of Job (Bir Eyyub) at the city's south-east corner. It was anciently called the Valley of the Sons of Hinnom, or the Valley of Hinnom. The point of juncture is about 350 feet below the site of the temple. It was in the Valley of Hinnom that Manasseh introduced the worship of Moloch and 'caused his children to pass through the fire', for which reason the godly Josiah, his grandson, defiled the valley, making it a receptacle for the bodies of criminals. A fire was kept perpetually burning there and worms were continually gendering in the putrifying flesh. The valley thus became a vivid image of hell, as the fit place for all unfit for the city of God. The term Gehenna, as used in the New Testament and translated 'hell', is really a Greek form of the name Ge-Hinnom (valley of Hinnom). Tophet was a spot in the Valley of Hinnom (2 Kings 23:10). It is referred to several times by Jeremiah and was apparently the centre of idolatrous worship, on which account it came to be regarded as a fit symbol of the place 'ordained of old' for the punishment of the ungodly. It is of interest, too, to note that Aceldama, 'the field of blood' (Matt. 27:6-8) was situated in the same locality. It was in this area that a bed of clay, suitable for the use of potters, was located. Probably the clay was so far exhausted by the time of Christ's betrayal that the field where it had been worked was of no further value to potters. It could, therefore, be applied to a different use, while it retained its ancient name of 'the potter's field'. Furthermore, the Valley of Hinnom was the boundary fixed in the days of Joshua between the tribes of Judah and Benjamin (Josh. 15:8 and 18:16). The temple hill, therefore, was actually situated within the territory of Benjamin, which lay to the north of the valley.

Between the Kidron and Hinnom valleys occurs a third valley, probably as deeply cut in the rock as the others, but so completely filled with the debris of centuries that it has lost much of its ancient character and is now a comparatively slight trough dividing the hills which form its flanks. It runs from north to south, thus dividing ancient Jerusalem into eastern and western portions, the western portion being the more extensive of the two. It is not mentioned in the Old Testament, but Josephus, the Jewish historian of the first century A.D., calls it the Tyropoeon, or the Valley of the Cheesemongers. It has been calculated that in early times this central valley was from twenty to ninety feet deeper than it is today.

Thus Jerusalem is situated on a chalky plateau, an infertile tongue of land of about 900 acres in extent, divided by the Tyropoeon into two parts. The northern side is the only side not cut off by ravines from the surrounding country. Andrew Bonar, in his pleasant book called *Palestine for the young,* compares the valleys to 'fosses scooped out by the Creator, to make Jerusalem secure as a fortress: while on its north side the ground was in a great measure level, that the city might be approached as by a natural drawbridge'. It remains to be noted that the east and west ridges of the plateau were again split by cross valleys into separate spurs (some like to find seven hills within the city's bounds). A small side valley opening out from the Tyropoeon divides the western ridge into a northerly half, which is linked with the highland to the north (Mt. Scopus) and into a southerly isolated half. The parallel east ridge is broken into three spurs, the central spur being that occupied by the temple. But these matters can best be learned from maps.

Water Supply

The small southern spur to the east is of particular interest because it is undoubtedly the site of the Jebusite city captured by David, which henceforth was called the City of David (Prof. Geo. Adam Smith suggests 'Davidsburgh'). Before proceeding further, however, with the problem of identification of localities, we must give attention to the all-important matter of Jerusalem's water-supply, for the location of springs of water helped to determine the history of the city, particularly in its early stages.

Modern Jerusalem obtains most of its water from rock-cisterns, with which the city is well-supplied, and from aqueducts. It possesses only two natural sources of water-supply in its own neighbourhood, and these, strikingly enough, are the only two mentioned in the Scriptures. They are both situated in the place where the geological factors outlined above would lead us to expect them—near the confluence of the three principal valleys, and at their lowest point. Here the waters which have percolated through the limestone of the plateau find a vent. There is no doubt that the spring and well of today, which are known respectively as the Virgin's Fountain (or the Staircase well; so called because of the flight of steps which leads down to it) and Job's well, correspond with the sources of water supply which the Old Testament calls Gihon and Enrogel. It was at Enrogel that Adonijah proclaimed himself king, in David, his father's, old age, and at Gihon that Solomon was proclaimed king on the instruction of David (1 Kings 1:9, 33). Joshua 18:16 makes it clear that Enrogel was to be found in or near the valley of Hinnom, and this is a sufficient and sound reason for identifying it with the present Job's well. Gihon is stated in 2 Chronicles 33:14 to have been in the valley of the Kidron ('the valley'=*nahal*=the brook, i.e., the Kidron), and it could not have any other location than the Virgin's Fountain.

Zion, the City of David

It is important to note that these two sources of water are in the immediate neighbourhood of the eastern ridge. The western ridge is without a natural water supply. It follows, therefore, that for use as a fortress in ancient times, the eastern ridge would probably be chosen in preference to the western ridge. That such was actually the case is the view of most modern archaeologists, who have forsaken the older belief, dating from the days of Josephus, that the south-west ridge was Zion, the city of David. Certain considerations still cause a few scholars to adhere to this identification, and a few also hold that both eastern and western hills were included within Jebusite Jerusalem. The south-west hill is about 100 feet higher than the south-east hill, and to that extent it overlooks it. It is much broader than the hill to the east, and affords much more room for settlement. Using modern weapons, a force occupying the higher hill would have a considerable advantage over a force occupying the lower hill. In ancient warfare, however, this would not be the case. Nor does the smallness of the eastern hill provide an argument in favour of the traditional view. Ancient fortresses in Palestine were notoriously small. Gezer, Jericho, and Samaria afford illustrations of this. It was customary to mass the houses together within the natural limits of a fortress and to accept a great congestion of population as a necessary evil, if evil it was held to be. Economy of space was all-important and all other considerations, including sanitation, were regarded as of comparatively small moment.

It will be taken as proved, in the remainder of this article, that the south-eastern hill was Zion, David's city. It was usually known as Ophel.* The identification seems fully to correlate with Old Testament information. It is indeed the problem of the water supply which gives finality to the identification. A completely sterile hill could not endure a siege, and the western hill would not be chosen as a fortress-site for this reason. R. A. Stewart Macalister, in Volume III of the Cambridge Ancient History, writes with great assurance on this matter: 'The argument from proximity of water, together with the great strength of the Eastern Ridge (within the limitations of ancient warfare), has gradually convinced all but a few, who still cling to the former identification; and it has been powerfully, one might almost venture to say overwhelmingly, reinforced by the most recent excavations'.

The Jebusites and their Tunnel

These recent excavations are of outstanding interest, and they throw valuable light on several Old Testament situations. They show how the inhabitants of the city of David solved the problem of water-supply. Naturally it was only the upper part of the hill which constituted the ancient city. It was, as with many other sites in Palestine, a case of 'a city set on a hill'. Its crags were natural walls of defence ('the munitions of rocks') and these were made still more formidable and unscaleable by a wall, which made it a virtual impossibility for the city to be taken by direct assault. Yet Enrogel and Gihon were in the valley, outside the walls, and it was essential for the inhabitants to have a supply of water which could not be cut off by an enemy. In addition, it was a toilsome matter for the women of the city to descend the very steep slope of the hill into the Kidron valley in time of peace, and even more so to make the ascent back again with their heavy water jars. The Jebusites found a very ingenious solution of their difficulty. Macalister, in the work already quoted, describes it thus: 'A tunnel was constructed which may be likened, very roughly, to the letter Z, except that the central member should be vertical and not oblique. The upper horizontal stroke represents a passage that starts from an opening inside the city: the lower, another passage running inwards from the end of the cave in which the water rises. The water-drawers made their way along the upper tunnel, lowered their buckets down the vertical shaft, and so drew up water that flowed into the lower tunnel. We may suppose that the outer entrance of the spring was concealed temporarily or permanently, with masonry, thus preventing the access of enemies who would find no water in the neighbourhood except perhaps at Bir Eyyub, some distance down the valley'.

David Captures the City

It is clear from 2 Samuel 5 that David experienced unusual difficulty in capturing the hill fort on Ophel. Finally he offered the position of 'chief and captain' of his army to the man who by valour and skill effected the capture. The task involved 'getting up to the gutter' in order that the Jebusites might

* Later the name 'Zion' was extended to a wider area, and became a synonym for the whole city of Jerusalem whose inhabitants are referred to as 'the daughters of Zion' (Song of Sol. 3:11; Isa. 3:16, 17; 4:4).

be smitten. The term used for 'gutter (*zinnor*) has presented much difficulty to translators.* It appears to mean a watercourse of some kind. In older times it was supposed to mean a gully on the hill of Ophel, but more recently it has been thought that it refers to the rock-hewn passage leading through the hill from Gihon into the heart of the fortress. The work of climbing the vertical portion of the shaft (44 feet high) must have been supremely difficult, if one may judge from the condition of the shaft when re-discovered in 1867 by Sir Charles Warren, and named after him. The walls of the shaft were very smooth (this is supposed to show that the women of the city used buckets of skins, which polished the rocky sides) and provided no hand-grip or foothold. At one point the passage is so small that a man of more than normal girth would have difficulty in worming his way through. But the task was accomplished successfully by Joab, who thereby proved his courage and resourcefulness. Macalister writes of his feat thus: 'I myself followed Joab's example when I explored the tunnel—I passed through at dead of night . . . Wading through the water in the cave, carrying their weapons and probably a rope, they entered the tunnel that opens at the back of the cave. They would follow it west for 32 feet, after which it turns abruptly north and runs for 23 feet by a branch passage impassable except at low water. Here in Joab's time the tunnel ended in a chamber, at the side of which rose a vertical shaft about 50 feet high. Some expert climber in the party clambered up . . . With the help of a rope another and then another drew himself up until they were all landed safely in the little chamber at the top of the shaft. From this they passed along the upper passage, which gradually rises by a gentle slope to the flight of steps at the end. Mounting these, they stood within the city'.† It has been conjectured that the Jebusite women left a rope always dangling down the shaft and that this proved the solution to Joab's problem. We do not know, but it is all but certain that it was by this perilous enterprise that the Jebusite stronghold fell to David and became his capital city. It has been further supposed that a Jebusite within the city must have assisted David to capture it. Another expert in archaeology writes: 'Unless we suppose that Joab had a confederate inside the city, or that the rope was habitually left dangling in the shaft, I do not think that it was possible for any man to climb this shaft' (J. Garrow Duncan). It has even been supposed that Araunah, the owner of the threshing floor on Mount Moriah which David bought for the temple-site, was the Jebusite who became confederate with the Hebrews, but there is no proof of this. It is curious, however, that he should be spared after the capture of the city, and that he should be allowed what was obviously a privileged position as a landed proprietor.

---

*W. F. Albright (leading Palestinian archaeologist of recent years) has stated that in his view the word 'gutter' probably means 'hook'. He compares it with a similar word used by the Assyrians for apparatus for scaling walls. Yigael Yadin, Professor of Archaeology at the Hebrew University of Jerusalem, in his recent book, *The art of warfare in Biblical Lands in the light of archaeological discovery (1963),* supports a supposition of the late Professor Sukenik that the Hebrew word '*Zinnor*' should not be translated as 'gutter' but as a weapon rather like a three-pronged pitchfork or a trident. 'The Hebrew letter for "and" is "w", and "w" is also the Hebrew suffix for "his". By moving the letter "w" back one space in the text and reading it as the suffix of "*Zinnor*" rather than a prefix for the succeeding word, we would get the following phrase which would make the action clear: "Whosoever . . . smiteth . . . the lame and the blind with his trident . . ." '. If this solution is to be adopted, obviously the supposition that '*Zinnor*' refers to the underground water-tunnel is no longer tenable. Prof. Yadin also offers his own solution to the problem of the 'blind and the lame' (2 Sam. 5:6). Following the suggestion of Josephus, most writers have supposed that the phrase is used by the Jebusites contemptuously. Yadin, however, sees in it a resemblance to a Hittite oath-taking ceremony in which a curse involving blindness and deafness is pronounced upon enemies. In other words, the Jebusites felt that David's determination to capture their city could only be countered by means of magic. Hence David offered a substantial reward to the man who would defy the curse and become leader of the desperate attack: 'So Joab the son of Zeruiah went first up, and was chief'. (Pages 268-270).

† Quoted from *Bible and Spade* (S. L. Caiger).

Hezekiah's Tunnel

At a later date other devices were arranged for conducting the waters of Gihon into Jerusalem. At a time unknown, but probably in the days of the early monarchy, a simple aqueduct was cut into the side of the hill, and covered over with masonry, to conduct the overflow of the Gihon spring to a spot at the south end of Ophel called the old Pool of Siloam, known nowadays as the Red Pool. It is to this channel in the hillside that Isaiah appears to refer (8:6) when he speaks of "the waters of Shiloah which flow gently" (that is to say, they lack the rush and tumult of an ordinary stream). The term 'Shiloah' means 'Sent' or 'Conducted' (compare John 9:7). Hezekiah was not satisfied with these arrangements. He gave careful, and doubtless prayerful, thought to the question of the water-supply of Jerusalem, now threatened by the kings of Assyria, and in a skilful way he both denied water to the Assyrians and conserved it for his own use. (See 2 Chron. 32:2-5: 'Why should the kings of Assyria come, and find much water?'). His method was the construction of another tunnel, from Gihon to the southern end of Ophel, to replace the former surface channel. Its value lay in the fact that it was completely hidden from the enemy. The work also included the building-over and concealing of the spring of Gihon. About the same time, apparently, Warren's Shaft was deliberately closed and rendered useless. The water was not conducted through the new tunnel to the old pool, but a new pool was made, not far from the first but on somewhat higher ground, inside Ophel. Both pools can still be seen: the Upper Pool is known as the Pool of Siloam, and the Lower is considered to be the same as the King's Pool referred to in Nehemiah 2:14. J. Garrow Duncan, in *The accuracy of the Old Testament,* reports that the women of Jerusalem still draw water and wash in Hezekiah's pool, which continues to receive the entire overflow of the Gihon spring. The overflow from the pool ran down to water 'the king's garden' (Neh. 3:15).

Hezekiah's engineers commenced to excavate their tunnel from Gihon and Siloam simultaneously, and accomplished successfully the difficult feat of making both ends meet. We can admire their skill the more when we realise that the tunnel is by no means the shortest distance between the two points. For a reason unknown, but possibly to avoid disturbing the tombs of the kings of Judah, the Siloam end of the tunnel makes a considerable detour. In its middle course it appears to wind about because the engineers found it impossible to keep to one direction. More than once they left a part of the tunnel to form a small cul-de-sac, which indicates that they were not always sure of their way. But the tunnel (about a third of a mile in length) was completed successfully. Its height varies from 11 feet at the Siloam end to 6 feet at Gihon. At most intermediate points it is very much less.

The Siloam Inscription

To celebrate the completion of the work the famous Siloam inscription was engraved by Hezekiah's workmen. It was discovered about 6 yards from the Siloam end of the tunnel, and consists of six lines of Hebrew. Professor A. H. Sayce, in *The Higher Criticism and the verdict of the monuments,* writes thus about it: 'In the summer (of 1880) some native pupils of Mr. Schick, a German architect long settled in Jerusalem, were wading in the Pool of Siloam and the part of the tunnel which opens into it, when one of them slipped and fell into the water. On rising to the surface he noticed what appeared to be letters cut in the rock . . . Mr. Schick visited the spot and at once saw that an ancient inscription had been found . . . In the winter after the discovery I arrived at Jerusalem, and one of my first visits was to the newly-found inscription . . . Not only was it difficult to determine the forms of the letters . . . it was necessary to sit for hours in the mud and water of the channel deciphering them as best one could by the dim light of a candle. It was not until three afternoons had been spent in this fashion that I had the satisfaction of obtaining a text . . . which proved to be a record of the construction of the conduit written in pure Biblical Hebrew. The inscription consists of six lines but a few letters have been destroyed by the wearing away of the stone. The translation of it runs thus:

"(Behold) the excavation! Now this is the history of the excavation. While the excavators were lifting up the pick, each towards his neighbour, and while there were yet three cubits (to excavate, there was heard) the voice of one man calling to his neighbour, for there was an excess in the rock on the right hand (and on the left). And after that on the day of excavating the excavators had struck pick against pick, one against the other, the waters flowed from the Spring to the Pool for a distance of 1,200 cubits. And a hundred cubits was the height of the rock over the head of the excavators". The inscription . . . is full of linguistic interest, as it proves the identity of the Hebrew spoken in Jerusalem before the Exile with that of our present Old Testament books. At the time when the inscription of Siloam was written the Hebrew language was already that which is embodied in the Biblical text'. (For those interested, a facsimile copy of the lettering is given in *The city of Jerusalem* by C. R. Conder, page 67).

The Millo

We must return from Hezekiah, however, to the work of earlier Hebrew kings. Scripture tells us very little about Jebusite Jerusalem or Jebus (Judges 19:10). Its area was comparatively small, as already noted. Probably it did not exceed twelve acres. Its greatest length was about 410 yards and its greatest width about 135 yards. 1 Kings 11:27 appears to mean that David had breached the walls of the city in his attempt to capture it, and that this breach remained unrepaired until Solomon's reign. It is in connection with David that we first read of Millo, or The Millo (2 Samuel 5:9 and 1 Chron. 11:8). The name appears to mean 'The Filling', and may conceivably apply to the filling of a breach in the wall. Much more probably, however, it meant the tower or citadel (it is translated 'citadel' in the Septuagint Version) which filled up or completed the defences of the city of David on the north side where its defences were most easily assailable. It was from the north side that the city was almost invariably taken. This explanation receives support from the use of the word Millo in 2 Chron. 32:5, where we are told that Hezekiah strengthened 'the Millo' in the city of David. Here a citadel or tower of defence seems the only appropriate meaning of the word.

Ophel

J. Garrow Duncan, in the work already mentioned, has interesting comments on the word 'Ophel', a common name for the south-east hill overlooking the Kidron and Hinnom valleys. He points out that the word in Hebrew means a hill or a swelling, and is twice used in the Old Testament as a medical term meaning a boil or tumour (Deut. 28:27 and 1 Sam. 5:6). In 2 Kings 5:24 it is translated 'tower'. Micah 4:8, literally translated, reads, 'O tower (or stronghold) of the flock, Ophel, daughter of Zion, etc.' Here the suggestion is that Ophel is an important adjunct of Zion, the temple hill, and that it is merely a part of a larger Jerusalem. Doubtless the expansion of the city outside the narrow limits of the Jebusite stronghold commenced as early as David's reign, when its choice as a capital would give it outstanding importance and necessitate an expansionist policy. Whether it reached across the Tyropoeon to the western hill before Solomon's reign is uncertain, but probably it did not. David's personal attention seems to have been given to the fortification of the portion of the wall upon the Kidron heights immediately to the north of Gihon. Here the wall terminated at that time in 'the tower that lieth out' (Neh. 3:26). This has been fairly recently identified. Its discoverer describes it as one of the finest pieces of city fortification of the Canaanite and Hebrew periods yet discovered. Near it was David's own house, of which no trace has been found. That it stood as high as possible in Ophel is clear from Neh. 3:25, and from the fact that David, resting on the roof of his house, could overlook other houses of the city (2 Sam. 11:2). (Note the expression used of Uriah—'down to his house'—in verses 8, 9, 10, of 2 Sam. 11).

The Temple Hill

In Solomon's reign interest is naturally concentrated on the development of the temple hill which lay due north of Ophel, and reached to a greater height. 2 Chronicles 3:1, which calls this hill 'Moriah', is undoubtedly intended to imply that it is the hill on which Abraham offered up his son Isaac, as narrated in Genesis 22. The name occurs only in these two passages. In other words, Genesis 22 is divinely intended to be, not only a fore-view of the sacrifice of the Son of God Himself, that 'miracle of time', but also an indication of the locality where the Messiah should in the fulness of time offer Himself without spot to God. It is in keeping with this that we are told that Abraham took a three days' journey from Beersheba before reaching the mountain chosen by God for the sacrificial act. The circumstance that a certain Jebusite named Araunah used the temple rock as a threshing floor in the later days of David indicates the eminence of the site. Possibly, too, it indicates that Araunah had become a worshipper of the God of Israel. Why Araunah and his sons (four are mentioned in 1 Chron. 21:20) were spared when Ophel was captured we can only conjecture. The statement of 2 Sam. 24:23 is of particular interest. Many scholars have been loth to believe that Araunah (or Ornan) had been king of Jebus and have preferred to translate, with the Revised Version, 'All this, O king, doth Araunah give unto the king'. But this involves a change both of order and tense, for the Hebrew clearly reads, 'The whole gave Araunah the king to the king'. Rather than tamper thus with the text, it is simpler and better to take the statement as it stands and to accept it as one of the unexplained mysteries of the Scripture.

Solomon levelled the hill of Moriah to provide a suitable platform for the temple: its natural slope towards the south-east was only corrected by much labour. The site is now occupied by the Mohammedan mosque of Omar. The dome of the mosque (*Es-Sakhra*) is exactly over the top of the mount, and encloses a portion of the hill left in its native ruggedness. It rises five feet above the pavement of the mosque and is approximately sixty feet long by fifty broad. It was probably used as an altar from primeval times. H. V. Morton, in his book, *In the steps of the Master,* writes, 'Lying behind an intricate screen of metal-work is a huge, unsmoothed slab of the living rock. It is black in colour and polished in surface . . . It is as if the sharp top of a mountain were pushing its way through the floor of a house'. The top of the mountain it undoubtedly is, and one may suppose that it was deliberately left in its natural state by Solomon when his workmen levelled the rest of the summit.

Solomon's Temple

Of Solomon's temple, and house which stood south of the temple, no trace remains, but we have good reason to know the source from which he obtained his building stone. Last century, near the Damascus Gate on the north of the city, there was discovered a narrow entrance into subterranean caverns. These were the rock whence the temple was hewn and the hole of the pit whence it was digged. Used as quarries for building stone, they are very extensive, and contain a labyrinth of passages. Immense pillars of rock are left standing in the more commodious areas to support the roof. Here undoubtedly the immense stones for the temple were chiselled and dressed before being built into the fabric on the rock above.

> 'No workman steel, no ponderous axes rung,
> Like some tall palm the noiseless fabric sprung'.
> (R. Heber).

Some stones are left in the quarries, half-cut out and then abandoned. Niches in the rocks indicate where lamps were placed to give light to the masons. Masons' marks abound. It is evident that the dressing of the stones took place in the quarries, for large quantities of stone chippings remain as proof of this. About 1870, shafts sunk by Sir Charles Warren through the debris which has accumulated to a depth in one place of as much as 125 feet below ground level in the temple area, have reached the actual foundations of the original temple and have furnished proof that the stones had been lowered into their places ready dressed. Had this not been so, stone chips would have been found near the foundation stones, but in the mould close up to the wall, the only remains discovered were pieces of broken pottery and fragments of ancient lamps for burning fat or oil. The absence of chippings furnishes a remarkable confirmation of the truth of the Old Testament story. Sir Charles Warren's workmen also discovered letters and marks in red paint on certain of the stones. In one case the paint had run to the other side of the stone, which made it clear that the mark had been made before the stone had been laid in position. These marks were undoubtedly made by Phoenician masons and were instructions to the actual builders where to lay each stone. Similar marks have been found in ruins in the city of Tyre. The original entrance to the quarries was probably near the present Damascus Gate, a position which would make the process of moving the stones down to the temple area a comparatively easy one. It is probable that they were run along the side of the Tyropoeon on rollers and brought to their exact position in the wall, so that there would be no occasion to lift them, a matter of considerable difficulty with such 'great stones' as were prepared for the lower courses of the building (1 Kings 5:17-18). One of the stones which has been discovered and measured weighs over 100 tons. It is a gigantic block of hard limestone, 26 feet long, over 6 feet high, and 7 feet wide.

The Walls of Jerusalem

The actual area enclosed by the walls of Jerusalem at different periods is a matter of considerable uncertainty. It is highly probable that the Jerusalem of today excludes almost completely the site of Jebusite Jerusalem which became the city of David. Incidentally, this fact has facilitated excavations and made important discoveries possible. The Old Testament narrative seems to imply that David's city had one gate only, for we are told that when Absalom set about the task of fomenting rebellion "he stood beside the way of THE gate" (2 Sam. 15:2). On the other hand, the fact that it was possible for him at one time to dwell two years in Jerusalem without seeing the king's face (2 Sam. 14:28) implies that the city had extended its boundaries considerably, and this is what might have been expected after it became Israel's capital city. It was probably in the reign of Solomon that the west ridge began to be occupied. More than one historian has supposed that the west hill would be a suitable site for the dwellings of the heathen wives of Solomon, who must not defile the temple of the Lord by their too-near presence. Certain it is that, whereas David only built or repaired the wall of the city of David (2 Sam. 5:9), Solomon 'built the wall of Jerusalem round about' (1 Kings 3:1). Solomon's wall apparently did not include the Tyropoeon within the limits of the city. It ran along the heights of Ophel bordering the Kidron, and on towards the north so as to embrace the temple hill. Turning sharply westwards, it crossed the Tyropoeon and reached the Valley of Hinnom near the present Jaffa Gate: then, turning south, it followed the line of the Hinnom Valley until the Valley turned eastwards. Encircling the western hill, the wall then turned north again, recrossed the Tyropoeon near the south-west corner of the temple area, and ran along the western slopes of Ophel until the circuit of the citadel was complete.

The Gates of the City

The situation of the various gates of the extended city cannot be stated with exactness in all cases. On the north side—the weak side of Jerusalem from the military standpoint—were the Benjamin Gate, also called the 'higher gate of the house of the Lord' (2 Kings 15:35, Jer. 20:2, Ezek. 9:2), the Ephraim Gate (2 Kings 14:13), and the Corner Gate, (stated to be 400 cubits from the Ephraim Gate, and therefore probably the modern Jaffa Gate). On the side of the valley of Hinnom was the Valley Gate (2 Chron. 26:9). Overlooking the Kidron valley was the Horse Gate ('the way by which the horses came into the king's house': 2 Kings 11:16, Jer. 31:40). Probably all these gates existed in the days of Solomon. At a later date Manasseh extended the boundaries of the city northwards, the only suitable area for extension. It is probably he who constructed the so-called Second Wall. It ran as far north as the Fish Gate (2 Chron. 33:14), used by Tyrian fishmongers who naturally entered Jerusalem from the north. It probably corresponded with the modern Damascus Gate, though it may have been situated a little distance down the Tyropoeon from this gate.

Nehemiah's Jerusalem

The Book of Nehemiah gives a very full account of Jerusalem's gates and towers, and should be carefully studied by all who wish to get an intimate acquaintance with the topography of the city. The account of the rebuilding of the wall by Nehemiah commences on the north side with the Sheep Gate, which is generally considered to be identical with the Gate of Benjamin. Westwards from this was the

Tower of Meah (the Hundred) the Tower of Hananeel, and the Fish Gate built by Manasseh (Neh. 3:1-2). The Old Gate next mentioned (6) was probably at the spot where the Second Wall joined the old wall of Solomon, and seems to have been identical with the Corner Gate already mentioned. The Broad Wall (8) was probably that which ran along the slopes of the Valley of Hinnom in its southerly stretch. Towards the southern end of this wall was the Tower of the Furnaces (11), followed by the Valley Gate (13) which seems to have been situated near the spot where the Valley of Hinnom begins to take an easterly course. The Dung Gate and the Gate of the Fountain (14, 15) were located between the Pool of Siloam and Enrogel. Next mentioned are the 'Turning of the Wall' (20) and 'the tower which lieth out from the king's high house' (25). These were situated on the slopes of Ophel overlooking the Kidron valley. Finally the Horse Gate near the temple area (hence repaired by the priests) and the East Gate are mentioned (28, 29). The Gate Miphkad (31) seems to refer to the gate at the north-east corner of the city where the wall turned towards the Sheep Gate at which Nehemiah's orderly survey commenced.

'The City of the Great King'
(Ps. 48:2; Matt. 5:35)

Probably no city has had such a varied and chequered history as Jerusalem. Its story is the story of the Jewish people. It has been the stage where a large part of the drama of world history has been enacted. Of the events it has witnessed we might well say, 'These things have not been done in a corner'. Its age-long tribulations have been endured before the eyes of the world. To the archaeologist it has been a site of surpassing interest, hampered though he has been by the present occupation of the city, and by the religious fanaticism of large elements of its modern population. 'You begin digging in the streets of Jerusalem', writes a historian of 1887, 'and you come upon house-tops at all varieties of level underground! It is probable that we have there traces and remains of older and more numerous generations than in any other city under the sun' (quoted by C. H. Irwin in *The Bible, the scholar and the spade*). To Jew and to Gentile alike it remains the key-stone of the great arch of prophecy which spans the ages, one day to be glorified in the advent of the King-Messiah when He shall return to Zion and turn away ungodliness from Jacob.

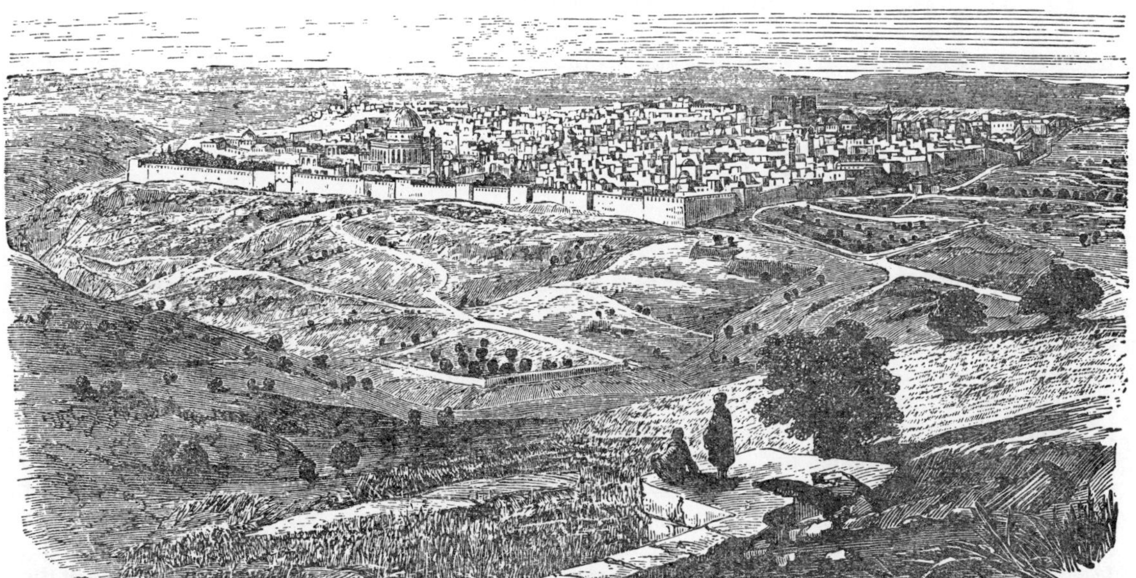

Jerusalem from the Mount of Olives.

Masada

(a chapter in Palestinian history and archaeology)

By S. M. Houghton

The establishment of an independent Jewish State once again in Palestine after the lapse of many hundreds of years will rank in Christian eyes as one of the most interesting and significant events of modern history. That Britain played a leading part in bringing it about is plain matter of fact. From the time of the Balfour Declaration of 8th November, 1917, which recognised Palestine as a 'national home' for the Jews, to the 14th May, 1948, when the new Jewish State was created, Britain was intimately involved in all that happened in the Holy Land, and not a few of her nationals were following events with much more than political and economic interest. In so far as the Christian faith has a geographical centre, Palestine is that centre; there the Son of God took up His earthly residence; there He died, there He was buried (a fact which is a basic part of the Gospel: 1 Cor. 15:4), and from its sacred soil in resurrection life and body He returned to the heaven of heavens from which He came. Who that bears the Christian name could not but be interested in such a land?

Yigael Yadin

As a direct result of Israel's re-occupation of its ancient God-allotted territory, or at least of a part of it, the work of the archaeologist has received tremendous stimulus. Hitherto, in Palestine, the recovery of the past by archaeological 'digs' has been largely in Gentile hands, but since 1948 the Jew himself, not surprisingly, has 'taken pleasure in' Israel's 'stones, and favoured the dust thereof'. The resulting discoveries have thrown further light on biblical history and on its significance for the sons and daughters of Abraham.

The Jewish Archaeologist-in-Chief is Yigael Yadin, now Professor of Archaeology in the Hebrew University of Jerusalem, and formerly Chief-of-Staff of the Israeli military forces at the time of their War of Independence. In the nineteen-fifties he directed the excavation of Hazor, twelve miles north of the Sea of Galilee, where a coalition of Canaanitish kings was broken and overwhelmed by the Hebrews as narrated in the Book of Joshua. In an expensive quarto volume, lavishly illustrated in colour and published in 1963, Yadin deals with the entire subject of warfare in Bible Lands throughout the whole of the Old Testament period. Then, too, he has been responsible for much research work on the Dead Sea scrolls and for the full exploration of caves difficult of access in the Judean desert where other ancient historical documents have been discovered. Yadin's latest written work is a fascinating account of the excavation and exploration of Masada, Herod the Great's fortress, where Jewish Zealots made their last stand against the Romans in the years 73-75 A.D. In addition to a text of great clarity, it supplies 96 illustrations in full colour and many in black and white, as well as excellent maps and plans.

A Palestinian Gibraltar

Masada, 'a place of gaunt and majestic beauty' is situated close to the Dead Sea at a spot where, in the first century A.D., the frontiers of Judaea and Idumaea were contiguous. It is a kind of Palestinian Gibraltar, an elevated rock eminently suited to be a defensive post, and of such a character that an attacker required the utmost military skill and tenacity if he was to achieve success. The capture of Jerusalem in 70 A.D. was no easy task even for the most determined and experienced of enemies; for Masada to fall to its foes required an even greater call upon military prowess and endeavour. Hitherto, Flavius Josephus the Jewish historian of the first century A.D., has been the chief, and indeed the only authority, for happenings at Masada, even as it is upon him also that we depend for our detailed knowledge of the siege and fall of Jerusalem. But Yadin now puts our knowledge of events at Masada upon a new and firmer basis. He points out from time to time in his book that Josephus had a very accurate knowledge of Herod's great fortress, but here and there the spade of the archaeologist is able to correct Josephus, a surprising thing after well-nigh two thousand years of change and decay.

Herod the Great

The story really begins with the fortification of Masada by Herod the Great. Actually, according to Josephus, 'Jonathan the High Priest'—scholars are not absolutely certain which of two Jonathans is meant—made the first attempt to fortify Masada, but it was Herod the Great who, about thirty years before the birth of Christ, commenced building work there on a vast scale. It was obviously in his mind to construct a fortress-residence to which he might retreat or retire whenever the mood seized him, or whenever the political horizon became black with clouds. Josephus hints at two kinds of danger; first, that arising from the Jews themselves who, one may judge, must have felt Herod's rule to be harshly oppressive; second, it appears that the famous Cleopatra, Queen of Egypt, was anxious to obtain possession of Judaea, and to this end urged her lover, Mark Anthony, the friend of Julius Caesar, to destroy Herod; but apparently the opportunity did not present itself. Herod, however, scented ever-present danger, and Masada was his rock of refuge. God, said the Psalmist, is 'the rock of my refuge'(Ps. 94:22). Herod had no such defence. Maybe he hoped that, if things came to the worst, he could escape from Masada into his native Idumaea, despite the curse which Isaiah had pronounced upon that land (Isa. 34:5). Perhaps we do not give too much play to imagination if we suppose that Herod, ensconced in his all but impregnable palace-residence, gave his own interpretation to further words of Isaiah (33:16): 'He shall dwell on high (literally so); his place of defence shall be the munitions of rocks; bread shall be given him (he built storechambers where he built up abundant stocks of food); his waters shall be sure' (with enormous labour, rock-hewn cisterns were constructed, to contain the occasional deluge which visited this parched wilderness country).

Masada was not merely one of a series of Herodian fortresses which included Herodion (a little to the south of Bethlehem) and Machaerus (where at a later date John the Baptist was imprisoned and beheaded) which occupied a site in Peraea, on the opposite side of the Dead Sea from Masada. From the first, Herod intended it to be a royal residence, sumptuously equipped, where his subjects might contemplate him as 'a king in his beauty', dwelling in 'the land that is very far off' (Isa. 33:17). With immense labour (not his own) he reared a complex of buildings on the top of the rock. They included a casemate wall of dressed stone which made the complete circuit of the summit and was not much less than a mile in length. It was covered with white plaster, which causes Josephus erroneously to state that it was of white stone. Thirty-eight towers were built on the wall and within them and the wall itself were over a hundred rooms, some of them of considerable size. In the west-centre of the lozenge-shaped summit a palace was erected. It contained a throne room and was clearly intended to serve as the official residence of the king from which the business of the Kingdom could be conveniently (or, as far as subjects were concerned, inconveniently) transacted. Three smaller palaces stood near-by, complete with swimming pool.

Herod's Private Residence

At the northern end of the rock was built, with incredible labour, a three-tiered palace-villa, Herod's private residence, upon which he bestowed his utmost care and thought. Josephus described it thus:

> 'The wall of this palace was very strong and high, and it had at its four corners towers sixty cubits high. The furniture also of the edifices and of the cloisters and of the baths was of great variety, and very costly; and these buildings were supported by pillars of single stones on every side; the walls also and the floors of the edifices were paved with stones of several colours. He also had cut many and great pits, as reservoirs for water, out of the rocks . . . as if there had been fountains there. Here was also a road digged from the palace, and leading to the very top of the mountain, which yet could not be seen by such as were without (the walls)'.

Yadin's excavations substantially confirm all that Josephus says, and add very considerably to our knowledge. The residence was built literally on the edge of an abyss, and to render building possible, large supporting walls up to eighty feet high were constructed. This enabled the king to build at three levels, the lowest being a hundred feet below the summit, and the middle tier sixty feet. Magnificent frescoes supplied ornamentation, and no effort was spared to render the building 'exceeding magnifical'. A bath house contained a *frigidarium* (cold room), a *tepidarium* (tepid room), a *caldarium* (hot room), and an *apoditerium* (disrobing room). Heat was supplied by the use of a hypocaust after the approved Roman fashion. Storerooms—about fourteen in number—stood side by side in rectangular pattern. Each such room contained one commodity—oil, wine, flour, and so on. Certainly Herod's garrison could have sustained a long siege if it had been beleagured in Masada. Some of the sherds of broken wine jars found by the archaeologists bore the name of the Roman consul for the year 19 B.C. (C. Sentius Saturninus) and supplied the added words, 'To King Herod of Judaea'. This particular vintage had been sent to the King from Italy. Yadin comments that this was the first time archaeology had yielded an inscription with the name of Herod.

We cannot doubt that Herod had chosen the northern face of the rock from purely personal motives. Heat with wind came from the south, even as Christ reminded certain hypocrites (Luke 12:55). To the north of Masada's summit was shade and shelter, and Herod was consulting his own comfort by requiring his engineers to construct his private residence in an almost impossible, and certainly for them a highly dangerous, spot. But the views were wonderful.

Bible Scrolls Found

One of the most interesting of the finds on Masada was that of a synagogue, the original Herodian building having been later modified by the Zealots who took possession and defied the Romans. Without doubt this is the earliest synagogue discovered in Israel. It was oriented towards Jerusalem as required by 'the tradition of the elders'. Embedded in its floor was found an ostracon (potsherd) inscribed 'Priestly tithe', together with many vessels, including a wash-basin. But the most interesting aspect of this discovery was that of a piece of rolled scroll. It was found in what the Jews termed a 'geniza', a pit especially dug to receive copies of sacred writings which were no longer usable, either through age or tattered condition or because use had revealed copyists' mistakes. The Jews could not bring themselves to destroy such scrolls any more than Bible-loving Christians today can find it in their hearts to do away with Bibles which have become defaced and soiled.

The scroll discovered at Masada contained a part of the prophecy of Ezekiel, and included (*mirabile dictu*) chapter 37 with its vision of the dry bones. It was a find which seemed strangely remindful of the miracle which constitutes Israel's sad but wonderful story. Spiritually, Israel has been for long centuries a dry-bone nation which recently, by a significant national re-awakening, has returned to its own land after a 'captivity' lasting wellnigh two millenniums. Alas that it still remains blind (though only in part: Romans 11:25) to the true cause of the divine wrath which rendered its land and its people desolate! Yet if Israel has not yet risen spiritually from its ancient grave, the day has dawned when the 'stone shall cry out of the wall, and the beam out of the timber shall answer it'.

A further exciting discovery was made in one of the rooms of the casemate wall. Under much debris a collection of miscellaneous articles was found, including vessels, mats, baskets and leatherware, together with 17 silver shekels in excellent condition, all dated from the period immediately before the fall of Jerusalem, and inscribed 'Jerusalem the holy'. Nearby was a piece of creased and blackened parchment which contained Psalms 81 to 85. By the use of infra-red rays they could be deciphered with comparative ease, and, says Yadin, 'like the other biblical scrolls which we found later, this section from the Book of Psalms is almost exactly identical (except for a few very minor changes here and there) to the text of the biblical books which we use today. Even the division into chapters and psalms is identical with the traditional division'.

In the same locality the diggers discovered two fragments of the Book of Leviticus, and elsewhere a copy of Psalm 150: 'Praise ye the Lord . . . Praise Him with the sound of the trumpet'. 'The writing was so faded', runs the record, 'and the colour of the parchment so light that it almost escaped our notice, and indeed when it was being cleaned one of the volunteers thought what she was holding in her hand was a piece of newspaper'. Actually it was a scrap of white leather.

Another discovery was that of a part of a scroll which contained the Apocryphal Book of Ecclesiasticus, dated in the first half of the first century B.C. Still another, described by Yadin for certain reasons as an 'archaeological miracle', was a copy of chapters 8 to 12 of Leviticus. This scroll, he adds, was 'absolutely identical with the traditional text of Leviticus. Moreover, there was the same division into sections, the traditional division into 'open' and 'closed' ones, that is, sections which begin after an empty line-space at the end of the previous one, and those which begin after a small space in the same line'. The discovery of this fragment seemed to be simplicity itself. It happened on the first day of the second season of excavation. A young lad from a *kibbutz* in Galilee (communal settlement), pottering about among surface debris, discovered the Leviticus fragments scattered around, apparently on or very near the surface, and to the amazement of workers they could be immediately identified and read. It was surmised that they had been blown to the spot of their discovery by the wind or thrown there by an uninterested Roman soldier after the capture of Masada.

The Fall of Masada (73 A.D.)

The story of the capture of the palace-fortress is gruesome in the extreme. It took place shortly after the siege and fall of Jerusalem and its temple as prophesied by the Lord (Luke 19:41-45; 21:6. Four years before the Holy City was captured by Titus in 70 A.D., a group of Jewish Zealots had captured Masada from the Roman garrison which held it. After the fall of their capital, they were joined by a few desperate men who had some-how evaded the Roman patrols and had survived the hazardous thirty-mile journey south-wards to the Judaea-Idumaea border. It did not consist with Rome's pride of arms to permit this last picket of resistance to continue, and in 72 A.D. the Roman Governor, Flavius Silva, laid siege to 'the rock'. The Tenth Legion was served by thousands of Jewish prisoners who had no option but to labour without respite for the overthrow of their brethren. Supply lines had to be maintained, no less than eight camps had to be built, and—most hated task of all, perhaps—Masada had to be completely surrounded by a wall over two miles long to prevent the escape of the beleaguered. But the Roman general was not content merely to watch and wait until at long last the Zealots were starved into surrender. He contrived a means to break into the fortress. A huge ramp was constructed up the western side of the rock. It can still be seen, little changed from the time of its construction. It enabled the Romans to use battering rams and other military machines against the Jewish wall of defence.

It is to Josephus that we again have to turn for a detailed account of the awful horrors that ensued. His narrative seems highly dependable and includes an account of the last desperate measures taken by the besieged to rob the Romans of some of the joys of victory. The Jewish commander was Eleazar ben Yair. When the Romans had completed their ramp and reached the walls of the fortress, it was soon realised by the defenders that, within days or even hours, the final break-through by the Romans would take place. Eleazar thereupon decided that it was preferable for the Jews to die by their own hand rather than die at Roman hands or live to grace a Roman triumph. Josephus supplies us with the speech by which he persuaded his fellow-soldiers and their wives to accept such a fate and to die bravely. Presumably he learned its content from two Jewish women who (together with five children) escaped by hiding. There were 960 people in Masada at the time of its fall. The final act of desperation Josephus describes thus:

> They then chose ten men by lot out of them to slay all the rest; everyone of whom laid himself down by his wife and children on the ground, and threw his arms about them, and they offered their necks to the stroke of those who by lot executed that melancholy office. And when these ten men had, without fear, slain them all, they made the same rule for casting lots for themselves, that he whose lot it was to first kill the other nine, after all, should kill himself'.

It seems likely that the archaeologists have discovered the very ostraca which were used in the casting of lots. Eleven have come to light, different from all other such finds in Masada. One of them is inscribed, 'Ben Ya' ir' and it is highly probable that this is the lot of Eleazar himself, the commander who survived to the bitter end. The mortal remains of the dead have been found, in part, and include one of the most pitiable finds of all, the plaited hair still attached to the scalp of a young woman whose skeleton was found near that of a warrior and child. Her leather sandals were not far away.

Already, before the capture of Masada, to commemorate the triumph over Jewry, Rome had issued a special coin inscribed 'Judaea capta'. It depicted a captive Jewish woman in the garments and posture of extreme grief. Behind her (doubtless to assist in identification) is a palm tree, and behind the palm tree a Roman soldier in an attitude of triumph.

'Is it nothing to you, all ye that pass by? Behold and see if there be any sorrow like unto my sorrow, which is done unto me, wherewith the Lord hath afflicted me in the day of His fierce anger . . . The Lord hath trodden under foot all my mighty men in the midst of me; He hath called an assembly against me to crush my young men; the Lord hath trodden the virgin, the daughter of Judah, as in a winepress. For these things I weep; mine eye, mine eye runneth down with water, because the comforter that should relieve my soul is far from me; my children are desolate, because the enemy prevailed . . . the Lord hath commanded concerning Jacob that his adversaries should be round about him'. (Lamentations of Jeremiah 1:12-17).

'Pray for Jerusalem, Christians, Pray'

Masada comes within the scope of the Lord's own prophecies as previously mentioned. Its capture by the Roman legions serves as an appendix to the story of the fall of Jerusalem. The exploration of its ruins by Yigael Yadin and his team of helpers recruited from all parts of the world is one of the outstanding triumphs of modern archaeology. Although, strictly speaking, as history it is extra-biblical, it cannot but interest the Bible student. It serves to illustrate certain aspects of sacred story, and once again to call attention, if not to the spiritual condition of Israel today, at least to its amazing vitality as a nation. Yet we cannot but pray that the Lord will arise and have mercy upon His earthly Zion, and that the time to favour her, even the set time, may in His mercy soon come.

'There shall come out of Zion the Deliverer, and shall turn away ungodliness from Jacob: for this is my covenant unto them, when I shall take away their sins . . . for the gifts and calling of God are without repentance.'

MASADA

An aerial view of the zealots' stronghold at Masada in Israel, where some 960 Jews committed suicide in AD 72, sooner than surrender to the Romans – the Roman siege ramp is still clearly visible on the lower right.

Section Five

Scripture Versus The Theory of Evolution

Contents: Section Five

Scripture Versus The Theory of Evolution

The Origin and Fixity of Species

By John Leslie

'We do not know,' says Sir Oliver Lodge, 'how the different species originated; and as to the origin of variations, we are still largely in the dark, in spite of a great accumulation of knowledge and admirable work.' (*Evolution and Creation*, page 108.) What the evolutionist needs is not so much an accumulation of knowledge as a sense of relative values—a sense which would enable him to distinguish between the true and the false, or between the scientic and the unscientific.

I wonder if Sir Oliver has studied the origin of species as recorded in Genesis, and studied it with scientific acumen and spiritual perspicacity?—'And God said, Let the waters bring forth abundantly the moving creature that hath life, and fowl that may fly above the earth in the open expanse of heaven. And God created great whales, and every living creature that moveth, which the waters brought forth abundantly, after their kind, and every winged fowl after his kind. And, again, God said, Let the earth bring forth the living creature after his kind, cattle, and creeping thing and beast of the earth after his kind: and it was so' (Gen. 1:20-25).

The Word of God not only gives the three main divisions of the universe—the super-organic, organic, and inorganic; it also teaches the law of biogenesis in conjunction with the origin and fixity of species; and yet Sir Oliver Lodge confesses that 'he does not know how the different species originated'; and that, 'as to the origin of variations, he is still largely in the dark'!

'Although there are,' says Darwin, 'two or three million of species on the earth, it must be said to-day—in spite of all the efforts of trained observers—that not one change of species with another is on record.' While, over half a century later, Sir Arthur Keith emphasizes this confession by likewise admitting that 'no one has succeeded in producing a new species.'

And why? Because Genesis tells us that all types of creation had a direct and separate basis in the inorganic, and have stamped and indelibly impressed on their respective nuclei the great and wondrous words, '*after his kind*'—words which indicate the specificity and immutable fixity of the different species,—an immutability which the evolutionist (on his own admission) is powerless either to gainsay or reverse.

Now, if it has been found impossible—a question which I have put from time to time, but which still waits an answer,—if it has been found impossible to change one species of bird into another species of bird, or one kind of animal into another kind of animal, how much more impossible would it have been to have changed an animal into a man? Or if, in other words, the blood or life of one species of animal is so radically different from the blood or life of another kind of animal, how much greater must the difference be between the blood of an animal and that of a man?

THE ORIGIN OF MAN

'If man was naturally evolved,' writes Professor J. A. Thomson, 'the factors in the process require elucidation, but in regard to these we can only speculate.' (*Outlines of Zoology*, p. 793.) But why does the professor speculate when he may have ascertained factors and unchallengeable certainties?

The main and indispensable originating factors—according to the law of biogenesis—consist of the Great First Cause, the protoplasm, the organism, and the environment. Well, if the evolutionist condescends to look, he shall find these factors in Genesis 2:7: The Lord God (or Great First Cause) formed man of the dust of the ground—the protoplasm or basis of life; and breathed into his nostrils the breath—or physical and spiritual nuclei—of life; and man became a living soul—or an organism in correspondence with an environment whose centre and circumference is God.

Man is thus connected—vitally and uniquely connected—both with the physical and the spiritual, for he is endowed with two distinct—yet closely related—nuclei. He has a nucleus within a nucleus: a nucleus for corresponding with the physical environment and a nucleus for communing with the spiritual; while the action and interaction of these two nuclei so influence and modify the human organism as to distinguish it from all other types of creation.

"But," asks the quasi-creationist, "is there not a suggestion of evolution in the Scripture which reads, 'My substance was not hid from God, when I was made in secret and curiously wrought in the lowest parts of the earth?' " (Psa. 139:15).

This Scripture is quoted by certain men who, not fully grasping or comprehending the fundamentals of creation, are of the opinion that, after all, there is a suggestion of a modified form of evolution in the origin of man. But what are the facts?

The term *substance,* as used by David, refers to the protoplasm or basis of life; while the phrase, 'In the lowest parts of the earth,' signifies both the original place from which the *dust* was derived (inorganic) and eventually the womb in which the protoplasm and bioplasm—body and spirit—were united (organic).

Strictly speaking, however, the word '*substance*' refers to the dust of which the body is composed, and to the dust alone. When body and spirit are separated at death, 'the dust returns to the earth as it was, and the spirit unto God who gave it' (Eccles. 12:7).

The 'dust of the ground,' generally speaking, is the raw material which is found, more or less—and in some shape or form—throughout the physical universe. It consists mainly of hydrogen, nitrogen, oxygen, carbon, phosphorus, sulphur, etc., and is the material which God used as the protoplasm or physical basis of life (Gen. 2:7). In this Scripture, the Supreme Potter reaches down to the inorganic, and by applying the law of biogenesis to the dust thereof, raises it to organized life and organized existence.

'God said, Let us make man in our own Image, after our Likeness, and let mankind have dominion over the fish of the sea, and over the fowl of the air, and over every creeping thing that creepeth upon the earth. So God created man in His own Image, in the Image of God created He him; male and female created He them' (Gen. 1:26, 27). Will the evolutionist or the *pseudo-creationist* point to any other Scripture which speaks of an animal or a bird or a fish as having been created in the Image of God?

'What is man?—how is his origin more divine than the origin of any other organism?' demands the Higher Critic! The Bible answers the question by telling us that 'God has made man a little lower than the angels and has crowned him with glory and honour . . . God has put all things under his feet: all sheep and oxen, yea, and the beasts of the field; the fowl of the air and the fish of the sea' (Psa. 8).

Now, if the beasts of the field and animals in general had the same specific origin and divine birthright as man, why should the latter have dominion over them? And if they are of the same blood-relationship as man, why does the evolutionist break the sixth commandment by killing and eating his *brother* organisms? My humble opinion is that the Higher Critics and Evolutionists would be well advised if they *religiously* avoided all reference to the physiological and psychological aspects of the respective species, and confined themselves exclusively to the culinary.

'My substance,' says the Psalmist, 'was not hid from God, when I was made in secret, and curiously wrought in the lowest parts of the earth' (Psa. 139:15)—a Scripture which should be read in the light of another Scripture, namely, 'The dust [the body or physical substance] shall return to the earth as it was, and the spirit shall return unto God who gave it' (Eccles. 12:7).

The evolutionist teaches that the word *substance* represents David himself physically and spiritually, but if this is true, how can he be *dead* and buried in the earth, and at the same time *alive* with God in heaven?

'Thou, O Lord, art our Father,' says the Prophet, 'we are the clay, and Thou art our Potter; and we all are the work of Thy Hand.' (Isa. 64:8). God is just as much our Potter to-day as He was in the days of David, or in the days of Adam and Eve, for He enables us to assimilate the dust, clay, or physical basis of life from different sources—from various kinds of food, and direct from the atmosphere, which receives its main supply—by volcanic action—*from the lowest parts of the earth;* and He so fashions this clay as to ensure not merely immutable fixity for the species, but even unchangeable identity for the individual.

SOUL AND SPIRIT

Soul signifies self-consciousness, and spirit God-consciousness; while the union of these respective elements of consciousness results in what the Bible calls 'a living soul.' In other words, soul might be likened to psychic protoplasm, and spirit to psychic bioplasm, whose union and inter-communion would generate spiritual life and spiritual correspondence, and would thus enable the soul to enjoy the consciousness both of nature and super-nature.

But this type of life—*soul* is the more scientific term—this kind of life is characteristic of man and of man alone. It is therefore both unscriptural and unscientific to say—as some critics do—that the phrase 'living soul' is applicable to the animal as well as to man. In Gen. 1:20-25, the terms applied to fish, fowl, and animals in general are discreetly introduced and scientifically qualified, for they not only indicate the origin, but also the specificity of the organism—as, for example, 'Let the waters bring forth abundantly the moving creature that hath life, and fowl that may fly above the earth in the open expanse of heaven; and God created great whales, and every living creature that moveth . . . *after their kind,* and every winged fowl *after his kind* . . . and, again, God said, Let the earth bring forth the living creature *after his kind,* cattle and creeping thing and beast of the earth *after his kind.'* But in the case of man, 'God breathed into his nostrils the breath of life, and man became a 'living soul' (Gen. 2:7).

In differentiating thus between the origin of the animals and the origin of man, the Authorised and Revised Versions of the Bible are genetically and specifically sound, because the term 'life' and the phrase *after his kind* signify the blood or animating principle of the organism with special reference to classification; whereas the word *soul* includes not merely the physiological, but also the spiritual characteristics of man: 'God breathed into man the breath of life'—He imparted to man His own breath and His own likeness; for man was created in the Image of God (Gen. 1:26, 27). And this will account for the uniqueness of man; for his uniform substance; his uniform structure, and his uniform likeness; or, as the Darwinist would phrase it, for the uniform nature of his species.

Man must therefore be considered as in a class by himself, because in complexity of correspondence, he is superior—immeasurably superior—to all other forms of creation, for he has capacities and correspondences with which, in all the brute creation, there is nothing to compare, and which link him to a kingdom which man alone is capable of corresponding with both intellectually and spiritually.

THE ORIGIN OF WOMAN

'The Lord God caused a deep sleep to fall upon Adam, and he slept: and God took one of his ribs, and closed up the flesh instead thereof; and the rib, which the Lord God had taken from man made He a woman, and brought her unto the man' (Gen. 2:21, 22).

'I reject this record,' exclaims the Evolutionist, 'because it outrages the rules of propagation, and is therefore unscientific.' But in what particular respect is it unscientific?

In the creation of Adam, as previously expounded, the Creator reached down to the inorganic, and by applying the law of biogenesis to the dust thereof raised it to organized life and organized existence. He now subjects the organism to a far-reaching operation, and to prevent the subject from suffering pain, He causes a deep sleep to fall upon him. As the result of the operation, a rib, or *vitalized* cutting, is taken from Adam's side, on the basis of which the Creator fashions the woman.

Now, if mere man can propagate plant-life by means of a cutting from the living plant in the vegetable kingdom, and considers the process scientific, why should it be deemed *unscientific* on the part of the Creator to propagate human life by means of a rib or cutting from the living *plant* in the kingdom of man?

In the hands of the Creator, this rib or cutting—which represented the inorganic in vital union with the organic—was no doubt fashioned in such a way as to ensure completeness in the womanhood of Eve. She was part of Adam, and yet so differentiated, in the process of transplantation, as to be fitted in every way to partner him in matrimony.

THE UNBRIDGEABLE GULF

By way of emphasizing what has already been expounded, I desire to repeat—with all the clearness and force I can command—that each type of creation had a direct and independent basis in the inorganic—that every species of animal was created and fashioned after its kind; and that man, although also having a direct and independent basis in the inorganic or 'dust of the ground,' is nevertheless absolutely and irreconcilably distinct from the animal, not merely physiologically, but also as regards his moral and spiritual relationships with God.

To the animal, God is simply the Creator, but to man He is both Creator and, in Christ, Father. In the Lord's Prayer, we are taught to say, 'Our Father, who art in heaven,' but throughout all the realms of organic creation, man alone has this prerogative—and why? Because men and women are the offspring of God, and not the offspring of animals.

Genesis teaches the separate origin and immutable fixity of species, and the Darwinist acknowledges—indirectly acknowledges—the truth of that teaching. If, therefore, the gulf which separates one species of animal from another is unbridgeable, how much more so is the gulf which separates the animal from man? And what right—moral or scientific—has the Evolutionist to persist in preaching a doctrine which runs counter not only to the facts—the irrefutable facts—of creation, but also to the dictates—the accusing dictates—of his conscience?

Ere God had built the mountains,
Or raised the fruitful hills;
Before He filled the fountains
That feed the running rills;
In Me, from everlasting,
The wonderful I AM
Found pleasures never wasting,
And Wisdom is My Name.

When, like a tent to dwell in,
He spread the skies abroad,
And swathed about the swelling
Of ocean's mighty flood,
He wrought by weight and measure,
And I was with Him then;
Myself the Father's pleasure,
And Mine, the sons of men.

Thus Wisdom's words discover
Thy glory and Thy grace,
Thou everlasting lover
Of our unworthy race:
Thy gracious eye surveyed us
Ere stars were seen above;
In wisdom Thou hast made us,
And died for us in love.

And couldst Thou be delighted
With creatures such as we,
Who, when we saw Thee, slighted
And nailed Thee to a tree?
Unfathomable wonder,
And mystery Divine!
The voice that speaks in thunder
Says, Sinner, I am thine!

(William Cowper)

The Creation Story True

By 'Quartus'

In touching upon the Creation, as portrayed in Genesis, it is impossible for us to trip lightly over ground which has been a battlefield for at least two generations. The battle is not yet over; but there has been advance upon one side, and retreat upon the other, and it already seems evident enough that those who have had to fight *pro aris et focis,* for altar and home, will not only preserve them, but be enriched with spoils besides. They will understand better, and value still more highly, the book for which they have striven. We cannot, therefore, ignore the conflict, and we must indicate in a word or two how it has fared and is now faring with the claims of Scripture, and with the theories which have been set up in opposition to its teachings.

How much depends for us upon the absolute truth of these first chapters of Genesis would call for some larger mind than ours to fitly say. The roots are there of sentiments which bind man to man, and men to God. These chapters contain, for one thing, the charter of our liberties. If we all have descended from a common ancestry, and have all alike been born with the likeness of him who was made in the likeness of God, then every human life is sacred, and all men are equal. The Creator may have offspring who have wandered 'into a far country,' but there are no essentially inferior races. For another thing, these chapters are the assurance of present dignity and future destiny beyond earth's highest dream. If these first words of Scripture are neither legend, nor myth, nor dream, nor guess, but literal and absolute truth, then they are not man's words, but His to whom alone His works were known; and if God has not only created us, but has Himself told us this story so simply, and yet so fully, do we need anything more to prove that God loves the world?

There is power, accordingly, as well as preservation for us, bound up with the early chapters of Genesis. We have some interest, therefore, in the question as to whether they are a product of fiction, or a record of fact; and, fortunately, this is a question which we are able to settle in the most effective way. The Scripture has committed itself to the most definite and precise statements. For example, its first words inform us that

The Universe has had a Beginning

This, though one of faith's commonplaces throughout all ages, has not been universally believed. The opposite view has been entertained by those who professed to be exponents of philosophy and science. Ocellus Lucanus, who was earlier than Plato, held that the universe was incapable of either beginning or end. Aristotle and many of his followers maintained the same opinion, and held that every species of animals, mankind included, had existed from eternity. But science has spelled out, letter by letter, the truth which has been from the first the heritage of belief. Geology has traced the earth's story from the time of the primal fire. The earth has not always been as it is now. Animal life has had a beginning; plant life has had a beginning. There was a time when neither existed, and when they could not have existed even in germ. There was a time when even the soil, which now covers the earth's surface, was not. Going still further back, we come to a point when the quaternary strata that underlie the soil began to be. Descending further still, we come to the beginning of the tertiary, and then of the secondary, and last of all, of the primary formations. Where geology stops, chemistry and astronomy take up the tale. The globe on which we dwell was once, like the sun, a mass of flame. To the flaming hydrogen, oxygen seems to have been added, with the result that water was formed, in which the strata were laid that eventually belted and bound in the burning mass. Whence the gaseous matter came science cannot tell us, though, 'by faith, we understand that the worlds were framed by the word of God, so that the things which are seen were not made of things which do appear.' But science testifies to this, that the book, which stated that the universe had a beginning, has stated a fact. In that matter Scripture has been right; every opposing philosophy and so-called science have been wrong; and those who have scorned or slighted these words of the Bible, have done it to their own hurt. Turning from its teachings, they have erred from the truth.

That is one test; here is another. The Scriptures declare that all vegetable and animal

Life has been Created

It is true that the account in the first chapter of Genesis leaves this somewhat indefinite. The earth receives God's command to bring forth vegetable life, and the waters to bring forth animal life. There might be room there, accordingly, for evolution to find a place. But there is a feature of the Pentateuch, and specially of Genesis, which marks the unity of the books, and which had a good deal to do with the point before us. Genesis is really a series of genealogies. We find the beginning of one of these sections, for example, in chap. 6, verse 9: 'These are the generations of Noah: Noah was a just man and perfect in his generations, and Noah walked with God.' Now, Noah was mentioned before; for, just as he is the first link in this new part of the chain, so he was the last link of that which preceded The new reference to Noah is not, however, a mere repetition. Fresh details are given; the story becomes fuller, and then flows on. In the first verse of the fifth chapter we find the beginning of another section, and mark again the same features. Adam has not only been mentioned in the three preceding chapters, but much of his history, including even the birth of Seth, has been told. Here, however, we now read: 'This is the book of the generations of Adam,' and we find once more fresh details, among them the age of Adam when Seth was born. The reader will now see why we have pointed out this feature of the book. In the fourth verse of the second chapter we read: 'These are the generations of the heavens and of the earth,' etc. It is the beginning of a new section, and not, as some have imagined, a new and independent account. The heavens and the earth have had the beginning of their story told already; but it is briefly recounted anew with fresh details. Among these are the following: 'The Lord God made . . . every plant of the field before it was in the earth, and every herb of the field before it grew' (verse 5); 'and out of the ground the Lord God formed every beast of the field, and every fowl of the air' (verse 19). It might be urged that these last words refer merely to the beasts of the field, and the birds which were created for man's special use. But, if this be so, the inference is that the Creator was repeating a process which He had previously followed. The teaching of Genesis plainly is, that the varied life which fills the earth is the product of distinct and separate creations, and not of evolution of higher from lower forms, or of any one species from another.

Now, many may have passed over these words in Genesis without pausing to think of what they mean; and some may have been positively troubled by them, as if too loud a challenge were given here to science, and as if the issue might not be quite favourable to the claims of Scripture. But it must be admitted that the statement is in wonderful harmony with all we know of God. It is eloquent of His love. The Lord delights in His works. His hands have fashioned them each one, and each has come forth with the glory of the Divine touch still clinging to it. And it is eloquent of God's wisdom. Each living thing was made perfect, was brought up fully to the Divine ideal, and, then, at the very height of its capability, was set free to send forth the broadening stream of life, and use, and beauty, with which it was to gladden the ages. Is this a statement, however, which is in accord with facts as ascertained by science? Is it true that life has entered the world through creative acts, and that each species of animals and of plants is the result of distinct and separate creations?

The first of these two questions is answered by a unanimous affirmative. At this point Darwin arrested his theory in its majestic sweep. It could account for much; it explained well-nigh everything; but it could not account for the beginning of life. There was a time, he knew, when no life existed in the earth, and he knew, also, that there was a gulf between the living and non-living which no law and no force in nature can bridge. Life, then, must have been produced by a power outside nature; in other words, it was produced by creation. Everyone will remember Darwin's 'primordial forms,' rude but mighty potential germs of the life which was to be. With these evolution could begin and fill the earth; but, as out of nothing nothing comes, without these evolution itself never could have existed.

This acknowledgment, let it be remembered, has been extracted in the face of the strongest determination to exclude the supernatural from the explanation of the universe. Darwin did not make it because he loved to believe that there is a God who created, and who still rules over all; and Huxley and Haeckel are but representatives of many who would gladly deny this miracle if they could. These have made the attempt, and have signally failed, their attempt and failure only lending mightier emphasis to the truth from which they tried to escape. Certain words still float about, the ghosts of the effort. They are 'protoplasm' and 'Bathybius.' A preserved specimen of a gelatinous mud, dredged from the sea, at a depth of some miles, was sent to Huxley. He placed it under the microscope, when, lo! that which had been the quest of his life was found. He saw before him a shapeless network, which was undergoing a continual change. The gelatinous clod was alive! Here was the true Eve, the mother of all living! Huxley proceeded at once to label his discovery, and to introduce it to the world. He called it not only *Bathybius* (that which lives at great depths), but *Bathybius Haeckelii,* in honour of Haeckel, the German scientist and atheist. The discovery was made in 1868. The public were, of course, electrified, and many concluded that belief in creative acts had received its death-blow. Bathybius, however, was to die first. Whatever else may be said of science, this must be confessed, that it is marked by uncompromising honesty. At a congress of German Naturalists, held at Hamburg in 1876, Professor Moebius, of Kiel, startled the assembly by demonstrating that Bathybius owed its existence to a mistake. Many specimens of the gelatinous mud had been dredged up from great depths in the course of the *Challenger* expedition. They had been placed under the microscope, and had been long and diligently examined, with the uniform result that no life or movement was discerned. It was plain that Huxley had been the victim of a mistake, and the origin of the blunder which had led to the supposed discovery of the origin of life was soon detected. It had been due to the alcohol which had been added to the sea-water in order to preserve the specimen; and Professor Moebius proceeded to electrify the Hamburg assembly by manufacturing, with the aid of a little alcohol, the far-famed *Bathybius* before their eyes. We have only to add, that Huxley manfully acknowledged his error.

So far, then, Genesis taught truth when it said that life has been the result, not of spontaneous generation, but of creation. While men of science erred, or hesitated, believers held the truth, and are now fully justified. And let it be noted and remembered, that the men who alone were able to answer this question rightly, were the men who loyally accepted the statements of Scripture. What, then, of the further assertion that the various species of plants and animals are results of distinct creative acts? Can this be sustained? And has the faith, which has received it unquestioningly, been rejoicing in the light of truth? Everyone is aware that one of the most imposing assaults which this belief has ever had to encounter has been made in recent times. Development has never had another exponent like Darwin, and has never numbered such an array of supporters as it has done in recent years. If the distinct declarations of Scripture could be overthrown, then here, surely, we might expect to see its pretensions lie in hopeless ruin. What, then, up to the present hour, is the net gain of Darwinism, and the exact loss at this point of Scriptural authority? What judgment has scientific research passed upon the theory of development? Has it upheld or overthrown the doctrine that

Species are Distinct Creations?

One of the most thorough criticisms of Darwinism that has ever appeared was published in the *North British Review* for June, 1867, and will now be found in the first volume of the *Papers,* etc., of H. C. Fleeming Jenkin. The review is so able that Darwin himself was impressed by it, and, though it did not induce him to throw away his theory, it led him to modify it in one important point. The late Edinburgh Professor of Engineering did not approach the subject with any theological bias. Darwinism was questioned by one of the keenest and most scientific intellects of the time as to its pretensions to be regarded as an explanation of the present existence of life. The examination resulted in the verdict that Darwinism is a bundle of impossibilities. That we are not exaggerating that judgment the following quotations will show:—

'We are asked to believe all these may-be's, happening on an enormous scale, in order that we may believe the final Darwinian "may-be" as to the origin of species. The general form of his argument is as follows: All these things may have been, therefore my theory is possible, and since my theory is a possible one, all those hypotheses which it requires are rendered probable. There is little direct evidence that any of these may-be's actually *have been.*'

'In this essay an attempt has been made to show that many of these assumed possibilities are actual impossibilities, or, at the best, have not occurred in this world.'

He declares that Darwin's theory will be looked back upon with the kind of admiration with which we regard the exploded theories of antiquity, and will be held to mark at once the ignorance of the age, and the ability of the philosopher. He concludes with the words:

'A plausible theory should not be accepted while unproven; and if the arguments of this essay be admitted, Darwin's theory of the origin of species is not only without sufficient support from evidence, but is proved false by accumulative proof.'

Scientific men are marked by an unbending honesty, which is worthy of all admiration. Whatever theories they may favour, they will not misrepresent facts. There can be no doubt that the belief that the various species and genera of the animal and vegetable kingdom were gradually evolved from rude primordial forms is largely entertained; but scientists are constantly reporting results, the meaning of which is that they find no trace of evolution as a law of nature. No intermediate forms are being produced to-day. Species are not invading each other, and obliterating distinctions, or producing a new species by the intermingling of the old. Now, if evolution were a law of nature, and not a pure imagination, can anyone explain how it has been suddenly arrested? If it has done such mighty things in the past, why has it ceased its operations now? If it is the father and mother of us all, why has it so suddenly disappeared and left us orphans that must search earth and heaven in vain for the cause of our existence! We are told that it worked on till it produced man. It produced a being able to understand it, and then, overwhelmed by sudden modesty or fear, it rushed from the throne of the universe and buried itself in unfathomable nonentity! But, whatever the explanation may be, its guiding touch, if it was ever felt, is felt no longer. There are variations, it is true. But it is equally true that these variations have narrow and impassable limits. Man, with all his knowledge and all his care, cannot produce a single new species, or even a single permanent variation. Nature, instead of aiding him, obliterates his handiwork. The laws which rule over life to-day preserve, and do not destroy the distinction of species. Pasteur and Tyndall have proved, by exact experiments, that even microbes and germs keep the appointed limits, and produce, and are produced, after their kind.

It might be said, however, that, though we cannot discover development as an actual force to-day, it nevertheless operated in the past. But science does not treat this theory with any more complaisance than the other. The whole story of terrestrial life is contained in the strata that lie beneath our feet, and that tower above us in the mountain masses. They form a vast museum, in which we can still see the remains of all that the earth ever had to show; and the men who have searched this museum through and through say there are no intermediate forms there. Species are as distinct there as they are now. Like comes from like, not from unlike. But, say the Darwinians, the intermediate links have perished. What! all perished, and not one solitary result to be met with of one of the mightiest laws of the universe?

A theory which will save itself by so huge a supposition as that is invincible! It refuses to be disproved, and it is impervious to ridicule. It must, therefore, be allowed to die as all such fancies do die—of sheer exhaustion and neglect. It cannot long withstand constantly recurring disappointment and defeat. It demanded an almost infinite duration of life upon the earth to give evolution time to do its work. It is now scientifically proved that the entire existence of our earth, and of the planetary system, must be comprised within limits which will not allow the required interval. That was a cruel blow, and another, still more terrible, has most unwillingly been inflicted by one of the adherents of the theory. Dr. Dallinger has put the theory to the proof. He has carefully watched certain species of animalcules, entire generations of which come into being and pass away while the eye of the observer gazes on them through the microscope. He watched them for months. He subjected them to a temperature gradually raised till it reached the highest point compatible with the continuance of life. Under these changed conditions many millions of generations came and went, *but the species never altered.* It was at the end what it had been at the beginning.

In regard to

THE CREATION OF MAN,

Evolutionists and the Bible have been hopelessly opposed. The Scripture assures us that the first man derived neither body nor spirit from any pre-existing terrestrial life, but that God 'formed man out of the dust of the ground, and breathed into his nostrils the breath of life, and man became a living soul.' Darwin refuses to admit this as a scientific account of the origin of the human race. Man has clearly descended, we are told, from the ape, and Darwin has endeavoured to account for our mental and spiritual endowments by serving us heirs to whatever resembles them in the brute creation. We have derived our fidelity and reverence, for example, from the dog, etc. But here, also, the results of scientific research not only fail to support Darwin's theory, but really demonstrate its impossibility. There is a difficulty which will occur to everyone, and which may be said to stare the theory in the face. If apes have produced men in the past, how is it that they do not produce men now? Or, as one has put it, 'If monkeys ever became men, when did they leave off, and why?' Darwin's reply to this has been that we must not expect to mark a process which goes on through almost inconceivably slow and imperceptible modifications, and which has taken hundreds of thousands of years. It must be confessed that Lyell's geological calculations gave Darwin room and depth enough to float his theory; but Lyell himself saw reason to modify his conclusions. Calculating from the rate at which deposits are now made at the mouth of the Mississippi, he reckoned the age of a human skeleton, found at a certain depth, to be more than 100,000 years old. He confessed afterwards, however, that he had been mistaken as to his data, and cut down his calculation by one-half. Since his time, research has shown that the foundation for those vast numbers is an illusion; and Sir John Lubbock has reduced Lyell's 50,000 to 3,000, while Schmidt, the anthropologist, places it at 1,700 years!

The truth is that science has been romancing as to the age of man and of the earth. It has been blind to the facts of the rapidity of change. A thousand years seemed nothing to Lyell and Carl Vogt, and they threw in their ciphers with the most liberal hand. But, measured by changes, a thousand years is a vast period. The England of to-day is not the England of the beginning of the century. During that comparatively brief interval we have peopled New Zealand and Australia. And physical changes seem to hasten on with as rapid a foot. 'The estuaries around our south-eastern coast, which have been filled up in historical times, some within the last 700 years, to a height of thirty feet from their sea-level, by the gradual accumulation of soil, now look like solid earth, in no way differing from the far older land adjoining. The harbours out of which our Plantagenet Kings sailed, are now firm well-timbered land. The sea-channel through which the Romans sailed on their course to the Thames, at Thanet, is now a puny fresh-water ditch, with banks apparently as old as the hills. In Bede's days, in the ninth century, it was a sea-channel, three furlongs wide.'

Such facts as these have entirely revolutionised geological chronology, and the old talk of hundreds of thousands of years is no longer heard. A considerable number of scientists are now agreed that about 8,000 years covers the entire period of man's history as an inhabitant of the earth. The time required, therefore, for the slow developments of the Darwinian theory cannot be had, and, were the theory in every other respect an explanation of the origin of species, it would be set aside by this one fact as an explanation of the origin of man. But the theory is, besides, triumphantly disproved. Man can be traced along his entire history, from his earliest remains to the present hour. He appears suddenly, without any forerunners bridging the gulf between him and the ape, and he appears, in every respect, the same as he is to-day. Whence did he come? There is but one explanation that has professed to stand between us and belief in a miraculous creative act, and that explanation breaks down utterly. There are structural differences which separate man from the ape. For example, the biting muscles in man are attached to the temples. In the ape, with the evident intention of giving greater biting power, they are attached to a ridge which runs along the top of the skull—a ridge which has nothing like it in the human species. The difference in brain, also, is fatal to any theory of man's development from the brute creation. The greatest of all apes, the gorilla, has a brain of thirty-and-a-half cubic inches, while the medium size of the brain of the most degraded branch of the human family, the Australian aborigines, is ninety-nine-and-one-third, or more than three times as great. The brain, indeed, of a full-grown ape, is not half the size of that of a new-born child.

It might be suggested that, as there are differences between the brains of men, some being larger and some smaller, and similar differences between the brains of apes, a small-brained man and a large-brained ape may not show so wide a difference after all. But there is no more foothold here for the development-hypothesis than elsewhere. The difference in brain size between the highest and lowest human races is only a little over twelve-and-a-half inches, while that between the lowest man and the highest ape is over sixty-eight-and-a-half inches. That is, the difference which separates the lowest man from the highest ape is nearly six times greater than that which separates the lowest from the highest man. And this difference continues all through man's history. The skulls of the earliest men are larger, on an average, than those of men now existing. 'Nowhere,' says Dr. Frederick Pfaff—'nowhere in the older deposits is an ape to be found that approximates more closely to man, or a man that approximates more closely to an ape, or perhaps a man at all. The same gulf which is found to-day between man and the ape, goes back with undiminished breadth and depth to the tertiary period.' We therefore repeat our question—Whence did man, the crown and king of creation,—

Such splendid purpose in his eyes,
Who roll'd the psalm to wintry skies—

whence did he come? Science tells us that he was not produced by pre-existing life; that he came suddenly; and came perfect and complete, as he now is. Whence then, if not from the same hand that produced life at the first? Science, by removing every other explanation, has triumphantly proved the truth of the statement of Scripture, that man's life is due to a distinct and separate creative act.

It may seem, at first sight, that science can have little or nothing to say regarding

The Creation of Woman

But the family relationship is a fact, and a fact so unique, that science ought to have something to say regarding it. Wherever man is found, that relationship which we call the family, and which is endeared to us by the name of home, exists and distinguishes human life from every other upon the face of the globe. It must have its roots somewhere. We follow to-day the customs of our fathers, and, could we interrogate them, they would reply they followed, in this matter, the customs of their fathers. Custom, therefore, is in itself no explanation. It merely refers us back to the point at which the family relationship began. But seeing that from every portion of our widely scattered race we receive the same reply, it is plain that these lines of reference all meet in one centre, and that the origin of our race. There must have been something there which planted this institution so deep in the life of humanity that no vicissitude or change has ever been able to overthrow it. It must also have been something which appealed to man's mind and heart, as there is nothing in man's physical constitution which can account for it. What was it, then, that built this holy resting place for man? The Scripture story gives us the only answer. God's lowliness is as marked, both in nature and in grace, as His power. He dealt wisely, patiently, lovingly, with the man He had made. He was permitted first to realise the need of fit companionship, so that when the gift was bestowed by which the need was afterwards supplied, it might be rightly understood and valued. The creatures which God had made were brought to him, and he named them. It is a striking fact that these ancient names of the lower animals, as Max Müller has shown, are marked by clear penetrating intelligence. The distinctive qualities were grasped and formed into an epithet. The word for horse, for example, which the various races carried away from their central home, was 'the swift runner.' Man found a kind of companionship there; but the yearning for a full companionship, a communion of mind with mind, and heart with heart, on the same level of intelligence, sundered neither by height nor depth, a union of common purpose, desire and pursuit, a fellowship of joy and love—that yearning was not satisfied. It was only awakened and made to feel its strength. He looked around him and realised that, amid all the wonders of creation, and all the subjection, and reverence, and trust of lower life, there was no helpmeet for, or rather, as the word literally means, no help 'answering to' him, that is, of a like kind with himself. And then God gave him a help of like kind with himself. Taking from man's side a rib, which shielded the seat of life, He fashioned woman to be a still better protectress of man's heart and life. And man with quick intelligence read the Divine parable. He hailed her as part of himself, the completing of his being, and the queen of his home.

Here again, therefore, the explanation which science wants, but cannot of itself find, is supplied by Scripture.

There is one other feature of the creation-story which demands a glance before we close. The Scripture has all along taught

The Unity of Nature

This is taught not formally, but in effect. The unity of nature is the conclusion to which the simple-minded believer in these first chapters of Genesis has always been led. The world is the work of one Maker, and of one only. All has come into existence at His word. *He* spake, and it was done; *He* commanded, and it stood fast. Step by step the great creative work was advanced till the desired end was reached, the design was completed, 'and God saw everything that He had made, and behold it was very good.' With that belief men knew that the universe was a harmony and a unity, for it was the work of one Divine mind, and it still obeyed the behest of one Divine will. Now, starting from the other side, science has proved, and is demonstrating more fully every day, that nature is a unity. It has discovered, one after another, the great laws which bind the universe together. It has disclosed an adjustment here, and another there, all working and blending together to produce one result. Looked at from this point of view, the world is a scene of endless glory; wisdom triumphs everywhere; thought, that never lacks a fitting plan, surmounts every difficulty; all things become plastic at the touch of one hand; rude matter, the dust ground by icebergs from the rock, is transformed into beauty of herb, and tree, and flower, into luscious fruits and sweet odours, into soft, warm sentient frames that rejoice in nature's fulness. That is the daily testimony of science; but Scripture has placed him who received its teaching with simplicity of heart, in possession of all that from the beginning! The unity of nature has never found a grander or less faltering expression than in the Bible, and nowhere will an explanation of that unity be found but in these opening chapters of Genesis.

Whence comes this book? There is no other which can be named its equal to-day. There never has been another worthy to be called its peer. We are told that it has been 'evolved,' for if men have been lacking in explanations, they have been liberal in hypotheses. We are informed that Genesis was compiled from earlier documents. Where are they? Genesis has never claimed to be older than the time of Moses. We possess now the more ancient literatures of Egypt and of Babylonia, recalled, apparently, from the dead, for the exigencies of these last times, and now the evolutionists of Scripture, like the evolutionists of nature, must suffer their theories to be tested by facts. Where are the missing links between the heathen and the Biblical books? These are even more distinct and more widely sundered than man and the ape, and the ape might far sooner account for the origin of man than these literatures for the origin of Genesis. Whence, then, has Scripture come, if not from Him who created man at the first, and who, caring for man's every want has supplied also the light which has made him the possessor of a knowledge and a fellowship that are alike Divine?

The Theory of Evolution

By Dr. John R. Howitt (of Ontario, Canada).

The theory of evolution is a materialistic philosophy of life based upon suppositions which have not been verified by science. It is not a modern discovery. The late Sir William Dawson of McGill University, one of Canada's most distinguished scientists, has pointed out that the theory of evolution existed in the oldest philosophy 'in connection with the crudest and most uncritical attempts of the human mind to grasp the system of nature.' With the spread of Christianity, however, this crude concept rapidly disappeared but it was revived again in the year 1859 largely as a result of the publication of Charles Darwin's *Origin of Species.* Seventeen years before the publication of Darwin's famous book, however, Barnum, the great showman, exhibited the first department of missing links. His motto was 'the people like to be fooled.' In the revival of evolution the world has turned again to the age of mythology. Dr. C. S. Lewis of Oxford University has said, 'We may be living nearer than we suppose to the end of the Scientific Age.'

Evolution is the foundation stone of communism, based upon the false theory of automatic and inevitable progress. It is the foundation stone of militarism based upon the concept of the survival of the fittest. Two world wars were the logical outcome of evolutionary teaching and we are now preparing for the next world war. Evolution is also the foundation stone of atheism based upon a materialistic concept of life.

Evolution is not scientifically possible, however, because:—

(1) Acquired characteristics are not transmitted to the offspring. The habit of foot binding common among Chinese women for centuries has not led to any inherited deformity of the foot. Our domestic chicken is a descendant of the Roman fowl and no essential change has taken place in 2,000 generations of breeding. Mendel's law of heredity is still held as substantially true. Variations in animal and plant life are due simply to re-combinations of characteristics already present in the germ cells. Mutations are hereditary changes produced in the species. But mutations are always inferior and they would never survive for long in nature. Prof. H. J. Muller of Indiana University, who won the Nobel Prize in 1946, has stated that 'Most mutations are bad. In fact, good ones are so rare that we can consider them all as bad.' If mutations were the basis of new species it would be the survival of the unfit. Only in Russia where biology is based by compulsion on Soviet philosophy is it taught that acquired characteristics are inherited. If evolution were true the Russian school would be right but the science of genetics contradicts this false teaching. In a desperate attempt to overcome this insurmountable difficulty some geneticists are now trying to prove that acquired characteristics may sometimes be inherited which would be advantageous in a totally different environment, but such investigations simply demonstrate to what lengths scientists are forced to retreat in order to substantiate a theory which is obviously false.

(2) No indubitable or undisputed fossils have ever been found in the pre-Cambrian rocks. And moreover there are no transitional forms to be found in the geological record of species shading off into one another like the colours in the spectrum, as one would certainly expect to find in the geological record if evolution were an historical fact. There are no fossils with half-formed eyes and legs and wings or other organs.

(3) Similarly, if evolution were true we should find about us many half-formed structures in various species which in another 100 million years would be fully developed and useful organs. But these we do not find in nature. Text books on biology never even mention the subject, although they nearly all teach evolution. Why then, has evolution stopped just when man has supposedly discovered that it has been taking place for millions of years in the past?

Some animals have complicated organs which would have been quite useless until fully developed, as for example the web-spinning organs of the spider. How would it have been possible for these spinnerets to evolve gradually?

Similarly, there are many creatures which have instincts or habits that could not possibly have developed gradually, such as the habit of the water spider of constructing its diving bell, or the habit of the house martin of constructing its cup-shaped mud nest, attached to a wall or other vertical surface.

Dr. Julian Huxley, formerly Director of the United Nations Educational and Scientific Organization, has stated that, 'in conclusion we have the glorious paradox that this purposeless mechanism, after a thousand million years of its blind and automatic operations, has finally created purpose as one of the attributes of our own species.' Would it be unscientific to say that Julian Huxley's glorious paradox is far more incredible than the concept of special creation by God Almighty?

It is sometimes stated that all scientists agree that evolution is a fact, but this is not true. Many able scientists realize the fallacy of this theory and its devastating results in human experience. Many theories which have been almost universally accepted by scientists in the past have later been abandoned entirely and almost every science has undergone a great transformation in the past few years, especially physics and chemistry which are among the most exact of them all. If such revolutionary changes in theory and concept have taken place in recent years in what are supposed to have been the exact sciences we may reasonably anticipate similar revolutionary changes in the field of biology before long. In the meantime it may be stated that the theory of evolution will require much greater proof than is now available before it could rightly be accepted even as a theoretical basis for the study of biology. It is well to remember that science is not infallible.

The heavens declare Thy glory, Lord;
In every star Thy wisdom shines;
But when our eyes behold Thy Word
We read Thy Name in fairer lines.

The rolling sun, the changing light,
And night and day Thy power confess;
But the blest volume Thou hast writ
Reveals Thy justice and Thy grace.

Sun, moon and stars convey Thy praise
Round the whole earth, and never stand;
So, when Thy truth began its race
It touched and glanced on every land.

Nor shall Thy spreading gospel rest
Till through the world Thy truth has run;
Till Christ has all the nations blest
That see the light or feel the sun.

Great Sun of Righteousness, arise!
Bless the dark world with heavenly light;
Thy gospel makes the simple wise,
Thy laws are pure, Thy judgments right.

(*Isaac Watts*)

The Kingdom of Heaven and The Theory of Evolution

By Dr. Uuras Saarnivaara, (of Kauniainen, Finland.)

Scripture speaks of the kingdom of heaven in three main senses. First, that of God's kingdom of power, which is the entire physical universe with its innumerable galaxies, suns, and planetary systems. God is the Creator of all this, and He continues to uphold, guide and control it (Isa. 40:26). Second, that of God's spiritual kingdom of grace, whose members are saved and born-again children of God who live on earth and which, according to Paul, is 'righteousness, peace and joy in the Holy Spirit' (Rom. 14:17). It is of this kingdom that Jesus speaks in most of His parables, and which is sometimes called the 'kingdom of heaven' (so particularly in Matthew), and at other times the 'kingdom of God' (so particularly in Luke). Third, there is the kingdom of glory in the unseen world of God, and which will come in its fulness at the second coming of Christ.

The theory of evolution belongs primarily to the sphere of God's kingdom of power, or His visible creation. It has, however, serious repercussions both on one's understanding of the kingdom of grace and of the kingdom of glory. For example, Sir Julian Huxley, a noted British biologist and grandson of Thomas Huxley, the great Victorian protagonist of Charles Darwin's evolutionary hypothesis, said on the 26th of November, 1959, at the Darwin Centennial Celebration at the University of Chicago: 'In the evolutionary pattern of thought there is no longer need or room for the supernatural. The earth was not created; it evolved. So did all the animals and plants that inhabit it, including our human selves, mind and soul, as well as brain and body. So did religion'. 'Evolutionary man', Sir Julian continued, 'can no longer take refuge . . . in the arms of a divinized father-figure, whom he has himself created'.

At an earlier date (1954) Dr. Joseph Harountunian, professor of systematic theology at McCormick Theological Seminary in Chicago, in an article in *Theology Today,* the theological journal published by Princeton Theological Seminary, set forth the position of the Modernist and the so-called Neo-Orthodox in regard to these matters. The Evangelical believes that he is living in a world which had a beginning in the Creation and which is drawing toward its glorious consummation in the return of Christ. But, as Harountunian's exposition reveals, the Modernists and the Neo-orthodox cannot take the Bible literally at these points because they accept the evolutionary philosophy. They cannot say with assurance that God initiated the process of history with the creation of Adam and Eve. They declare that no one knows when or how the human race began. They cannot believe that this world will have a sudden end, and that God will create a new heaven and a new earth wherein dwells righteousness. The *Modernists* replace this biblical faith with a trust in a gradual development of earth and mankind into the kingdom of heaven, created by human, religious, moral and social efforts, and the *Neo-Orthodox* replace it with their view that what the Bible states of Christ's second coming and the kingdom of glory is symbolical of the coming of Christ into the life of a believer in the crisis of faith, which occurs at the moment of decision (see *The Reformation Review,* Oct., 1954, pp. 47 ff).

Thus the acceptance of the theory of evolution leads consistent scientists to the rejection of the faith in God and in His kingdom, in all its three meanings. The theologians who try to amalgamate the theory of evolution with the teachings of the Bible are led to change the scriptural teaching of the kingdom of grace and the kingdom of glory into something widely different, and so to adulterate the Christian faith in its foundations.

The basic and central conflict between the theory of evolution and the Christian faith in the kingdom of heaven pertains to the origin of the visible universe and particularly the world of life. According to the evolutionary theory, man was not originally created in the image of God, and his primeval state was not that of righteousness and holiness; rather, he has gradually evolved from a bestial stage to the cultural and moral level. Neither could he fall into sin and become a corrupt being, to be later redeemed by the blood of Jesus and be born again by the Spirit of God. If the theory of evolution is true, sin is not a fall from the original state, rebellion against God, slavery under the powers of evil, and the subsequent subjection to the wrath of God; it is simply the remainder of man's earlier animal inclinations and tendencies. Conversion and regeneration are consequently not the way to reform him; this must be done by improving the circumstances in which he lives, by education and further gradual development.

In short, if the theory of evolution concerning the origin of the world of life and of man is true, the biblical revelation of the establishment of God's kingdom, its history, nature and consummation is pure antiquated fancy. It must be substituted by a new religion. This, in fact, is the very thing that the Modernists and Neo-Orthodox have done.

Efforts to Reconcile the Evolutionary Theory with Christian Doctrine

Those who endeavour to reconcile the theory of Evolution with Christian teaching usually explain the Bible as being a book of religion and not a textbook of natural science. Only those parts of it are to be taken as divine revelation which speak of our salvation and our relationship to God; while the Scriptures which deal with things that belong to the sphere of nature and history are to be treated in the same way as other ancient literature; to be regarded as merely the views and opinions of the ancient Israelites, not as divine revelation. These Christians believe that the dilemma between Scripture and science can be overcome by drawing a line between revelation in the Bible on the one hand and human opinions on the other. Usually they do not draw this line mechanically, as between various parts or verses of the Scriptures; they rather explain that the same statements of the Bible may contain erroneous opinions, when looked at from the scientific and historical point of view, and divine revelation, when looked at from the religious point of view. But may we not ask: Who decides what in the Bible is Divine revelation and what erroneous human opinions? Will not the Bible in this case lose its authority, and the real authority rest with the interpreters of it, in other words, with men? Will not this view lead to rationalism? May we not also ask: Is it possible to think that statements which in certain respects contain erroneous human opinions can in other respects contain religious truths? Who will distinguish between the two in a reliable way? What becomes, in that case, of the authority of the Bible? Would not human reason become the final arbiter of what is true and what is false?

Some Christians use a different method. They take the Bible as it is, but modify the theory of evolution so as to fit into the framework of the Christian faith. Those who take this course explain that evolution has been God's method of creating the various forms of life. God "created" man of the dust of the earth by causing him to evolve gradually from some simple form of life through the stages of invertebrates, fishes, amphibians, reptiles and mammals, until he reached the human stage, both as to his body and mind. God Himself guided this process, and when the stage of humans had been attained, He took a couple of these human-like mammals and put an undying spirit into them, thus making them into His own image and taking them into fellowship with Himself. This was, according to their view, the 'creation' of Adam and Eve.

It may, however, be replied that this is very far from what the Bible tells of the creation of man, and consequently this interpretation leaves the authority of the Bible quite questionable. It may also be objected that if man was produced in this manner, there must have been a considerable population of man-like animals, from among whom God took the individuals of whom he made true humans. What happened to the rest of this population? It can hardly be assumed that God miraculously annihilated them, for science does not believe in miracles. If they continued to live on earth, there existed on it side by side two forms of life which were physically and mentally alike: true men with immortal souls and man-like animals without souls. Could inter-marriage be avoided between them? The entire thought is impossible and senseless, and shows the difficulties of this so-called 'theistic evolution' theory, accepted by so many Christians. Many other methods have been adopted in an effort to harmonize the Bible with the theory of evolution, but those just mentioned seem to be the most common.

The Actual Testimony of the Facts of Nature

Many Christians who feel unsatisfied with the endeavours to bring the Bible and science into harmony by changing either one of them or both, have attempted a different method. They take the Bible as it is and the results of science as they are, and seek to find whether there is any real conflict between the two. The first thing they set out to do is to determine the nature and areas of the alleged conflict between Scripture and science.

In this investigation they discover that the disagreement between the two does not pertain to what is called *microevolution*, or variation within the existing groups, but only to *macroevolution* (that is, the theory that all the various forms of life have evolved from a simple one-celled creature). The Bible admits microevolution but denies macroevolution. (An example of microevolution is the development of the various races of man, white, black, yellow, and the like, from the original pair).

The second observation is that the so-called *proofs of evolution,* such as similarities in the structures and physiological processes in the various groups of vertebrates, are no real proofs. They can be explained either by the theory of evolution or by the doctrine of creation. An American Christian biologist, Professor William Tinkle, of Tylor University, writes: 'Some say that species of animals that are somewhat alike must have a common ancestor. It rather proves that they were created by the same God' (*Look Again before You Doubt,* 1943, p. 5).

Neither can the results of modern *genetics,* or study of heredity, be used as proofs for macroevolution, and this for two reasons. First, genetics merely studies the manner and methods of heredity in plants and animals; it cannot show that evolution has actually taken place. Second, all the genetic study of the past decades has merely shown microevolution or variation within existing groups. Theodosius Dobzhansky, one of the foremost authorities in this field, writes: '... the fact (is) that systematic mutations have never been observed' (*Genetics and the Origin of Species,* 1941, p. 80). ('Systematic mutations' are hereditary changes which produce new forms that can be classified as new species). Since such mutations have never been observed, genetics proves only microevolution, and its findings are opposed to the theory of macroevolution; that is, development from a one-celled being.

The only field of natural science that might be able to produce proofs for macroevolution is *paleontology,* or the study of ancient forms of life with the help of fossils. If the various forms of plants and animals that now live on earth are descendants of lower and simpler forms, there should exist in the fossil-bearing rocks continuous series of forms from the earliest ones to the present ones; at least there should be considerable numbers of transitional forms between the various groups of life. No such gradient series, however, exist. Dr. Austin H. Clark of the United States National Museum writes: 'No matter how far back we go in the fossil record of previous animal life upon the earth we find no trace of any animal forms which are intermediate between the various major groups...' On this basis Dr. Clark draws the conclusion: 'There is not the slightest evidence that any of the major groups of animals arose from each other. Each is a special animal complex ... and appearing, therefore, as a special distinct creation'. (*New Evolution,* 1925, p. 189).

Thus, the real facts of natural science offer no proof for evolution, as the word is commonly understood. They rather point in the direction of special creation. The theory of evolution is maintained only by forcing these facts into its preconceived mould. Such a misuse of the facts is no science but unscientific natural philosophy.

The Origin of Man

What is true of the fossil history of plants and animals is also true of the fossil history of man. It was formerly thought that ancient men with sloping foreheads and prominent browridges such as the Trinil Man of Java (called *Pithecanthropus erectus* or *Homo erectus*), the Peking Man of China (called *Sinanthropus pekinensis*) and the Neanderthal Man of Central Europe (called *Homo neanderthalensis*) were earlier evolutionary stages of man, or connecting links between the humans and their animal ancestors. More recent discoveries of human fossils however, have antiquated this theory. There are particularly two discoveries of early human skeletal remains that have been decisive in disparaging the evolutionary theory of the origin of man: the one made in Swanscombe, England, and the other in Fontechevade, France. Both of them are remains of men who lived long before the so-called Neanderthal age and about the same time with or before the Trinil Man, and both of them are of the so-called modern type, with relatively erect foreheads and smooth brows.

Professor Rendle Short, a noted British surgeon of Bristol University, wrote as early as 1935: 'The most unexpected part of the paleontological evidence . . . remains to be mentioned: the further back we look for early man, the more like ourselves he appears to be'. (*Some Recent Literature Concerning the Origin of Man,* The Victoria Institute, 1935, p. 10). Later discoveries have confirmed this statement. J. O. Buswell, an American anthropologist, wrote in 1956: 'Those who hold the theory of evolution no longer believe that the older the fossil remains are the more ape-like they become . . . The famous missing link is now an antiquated concept'. Buswell quotes M. F. Ashley Montagy, a renowned British anthropologist. It is an erroneous assumption, he says, to equate 'primitiveness with morphologically brutal traits. The facts, as we know them, do not lend support to the notion of a beast-like early man' (*Introduction to Physical Anthropology,* 2nd ed. 1952). Buswell sums up the results of recent anthropological study in the words 'All men can be regarded as the same species, *Homo sapiens;* but they have been divided into races, both living and extinct, whose properties cannot be proven to be of different quality' (*The Creation of Man in Christian Life,* May 1956, p. 17).

Thus, science can merely state that man appeared upon the earth suddenly, in his final form. There are no intermediate forms that would indicate that he has evolved from an animal stage. How he came into existence is a riddle to the scientists. To the Christian this is no riddle, for he knows from the divine revelation in the Bible that man came into existence by the creative act of God. There is no real conflict between the actual facts of science and the biblical revelation. They merely supplement each other. The existing conflict is between the unscientific philosophical theory of evolution and the divine revelation in the Bible.

The Kingdom of Heaven and the Theory of Evolution

The kingdom of God is primarily concerned with the conversion and regeneration of men, with their coming to Christ and their salvation through repentance and faith in Him; not with their views on the origin of the universe and the various forms of life. There is, however, as we have seen, a very close connection between these primary concerns of the kingdom of heaven and the theory of evolution. A person who takes the theory of evolution as a well substantiated explanation of things cannot take seriously what the Bible says concerning sin and its consequences. What Christianity calls sin is to him mere remainders from an animal stage, and, according to his view, it can be overcome by further evolution, enlightenment, education, and other influences. The theory destroys one's sense of responsibility before God, makes any sense of guilt before God impossible, dulls the conscience and relegates the Christian doctrine of conversion and regeneration into the museum of antiquated ideas. It is useless to speak of Christ, of blood-redemption, of remission of sins and salvation, to a person who does not believe that he is a creation of God and responsible before Him. These blessed truths have sense only to those who believe that they are guilty before their Creator and going to hell unless they find pardon and grace with Him.

A person indoctrinated with the theory of evolution seldom attends evangelistic preaching. If he happens to come, it sounds foolishness to him, as failing to fit into the framework of his world view. It is true that the word of the cross is foolishness to the wise of this world even when they do not know the theory of evolution or do not think it. But this theory renders them much more immune to the biblical Gospel than they otherwise would be, since it strongly tends to make the biblical teaching concerning salvation impossible and ridiculous in their eyes. The First Article of the Creed, or faith in God as the Creator, is the foundation of the Second and Third articles which speak of Christ and redemption in

His blood, of the Holy Spirit and His work in the Church, and the last things. When the foundation is destroyed by the evolutionary theory, practically everything else that is genuinely Christian goes with it.

It is largely the theory of evolution that has led historians and sociologists, and even the students of the history of religion, to apply to their work the axiom that no supernatural factors can be accepted as explanations of the phenomena that are observed and studied. This axiom, which is the starting point of modern science, is in reality entirely unprovable, and therefore unscientific. Real science does not beforehand discard the possibility of certain factors. It takes the phenomena as they are and interprets them without preconceived ideas. If they plainly point to Divine activity and cannot be explained without it, science should not deny this possibility. When theologians have sought to attain the rank of scientists they have adopted the mentioned axiom and applied it to their work as much as possible. The consequence has been that not only pagan religions, but Christianity as well, have been viewed as products of human religious evolution. Julius Wellhausen, the actual father of modern Old Testament criticism, constructed his history of Israelitic religion after the pattern of the history of Arabic paganism. Since that time it has been common to present the history of biblical religion according to the idea that the religions of mankind have gradually evolved through the stages of animism, polytheism and henotheism to monotheism, or something like it. The belief that biblical history is the history of progressing divine revelation, and of God's dealings with men, is wholly discarded.

Evolution and Modern Ecumenism

The Ecumenism of the World Council of Churches is another natural outgrowth of the theological liberalism which is a cross-breed of Christianity and the theory of evolution. When all the members of Christian denominations are looked upon as members of the body of Christ and fellow travellers on the way of religious evolution, it is only consistent to think that their inner religious unity should be expressed also in an outward ecclesiastical unity. This goal of the Ecumenical Movement is thus a natural expression of the Liberal-evolutionistic theology that has become dominant in most great denominations. The matter is entirely different when only those born anew of the Holy Spirit are acknowledged as members of the Body of Christ, the true Church. In their case an outward union of church organizations has little or nothing to do with the true union of the children of God. Neither has it any significance for the building of the kingdom of heaven, for this kingdom is built only by seeking to lead people to true repentance and faith. This work of winning souls to Christ is not done by great ecclesiastical organizations and their resources of money and personnel. The kingdom of heaven on earth is the little flock of Christ's own. It is this flock, and this only, that God uses in building His kingdom. Neither liturgical pomp, nor skilful technique in canvassing and gathering church members, can accomplish this end. It may result in a great united World-Church, with large resources of money and personnel, and worldly honour; but it will be one which has given up faithfulness to Christ and to Divine Truth, and has thus become a representative rather of apostasy than of Scriptural Christianity.

All things bright and beautiful,
All creatures great and small,
All things wise and wonderful,
The Lord God made them all.

Each little flower that opens,
Each little bird that sings,
He made their glowing colours,
He made their tiny wings.

The purple-headed mountain,
The river running by,
The sunset, and the morning
That brightens up the sky;

The cold wind in the winter,
The pleasant summer sun,
The ripe fruits in the garden,
He made them every one.

The tall trees in the greenwood,
The meadows where we play,
The rushes by the water
We gather every day,

He gave us eyes to see them,
And lips that we might tell
How great is God Almighty,
Who has made all things well.
(*Mrs. Cecil Frances Alexander,* 1848)

A Surgeon Looks at Evolution

By Sir Cecil Wakeley, Bt.,
K.B.E., C.B., M.CH., D.SC., F.R.C.S., F.R.S.E.*

(President of the Bible League, 1952-79)

When I was a medical student, I was taught the theory of Evolution, but I never believed in it, because it was the exact opposite of what is written in the Holy Bible. As soon as I qualified I tried to find out if any of the evolution statements were true. I soon discovered that the human foetus does not go through the stages of evolution during development. The more I see of human embryology, the more I have to confess that we are 'fearfully and wonderfully made'. We are seeing today a sad state of affairs when men and women try to influence the course of nature. And what terrible deformities are produced in untold numbers of children!

It seems such a pity in a scientific age where precision and detail are so important that the vast majority of modern scientists believe in evolution, and yet all the basic facts are against such a theory.

I was told as a student over fifty years ago that the so called 'missing links' in the animal kingdom would be discovered in a few years. But none of these have materialized and scientists search for them in vain. We have seen the humbug and fakes of these so-called missing links in the Java man and Piltdown skull, and yet volumes have been written about these; they were nothing but the work of the Devil himself.

There is a great tendency today to disbelieve the Bible as a whole or in part, and yet many modern discoveries wonderfully corroborate the Old Testament history. We are told that the Gospel record of miracles performed by the Lord Jesus are fables and that indeed miracles never take place, but I suppose every doctor of experience has seen miracles occur, when the impossible takes place and a patient recovers from an incurable disease.

As long as man takes all the credit for his boasted progress and gives no thanks to God for the benefits that come on earth, so long shall we have trouble in the world.

I well remember the time when certain scientists asserted that there was no proof that a universal flood took place, but today geology supplies ample proof that the earth was covered with water after man and animals were created.

We must not be surprised that so many people believe in evolution, because if we read our Bibles, we can see clearly that these so called changes in belief are predicted. We are told that in the last days perilous times shall come. Men will be seeking their own ways and will acknowledge no God at all. Is not this what is taking place today?

The theory of evolution is the thin edge of the wedge towards atheism because if the Creation is a myth then why believe other parts of the Bible? This is a very insidious and crafty way of suggesting that the whole of the Bible is false.

St. Paul predicted that we should have to face such times as have now come upon us, when the great majority of the people in the world do not believe in the living God or in the Lord Jesus Christ.

St. Paul preached Christ crucified, which was a stumbling-block to the Jews and to the Greeks foolishness. The Greeks represented the scientific group of people, and do not the scientific people today consider the resurrection of Jesus Christ from the dead to be foolishness? St. Paul was not ashamed of the Gospel of the Lord Jesus Christ, and thank God there is a remnant in the world today who also are not ashamed of that Gospel.

If we are true Christians we shall have to stand up for our faith, but it is worth fighting for. In my opinion the Bible is the inspired Word of God and every chapter in it is true. The theory of evolution is the Gospel of the atheist and paves the way to the complete rejection of the Bible.

* *This testimony against the theory of evolution is the more valuable as it comes from one of the leading surgeons of this kingdom—for Sir Cecil is the former President of the Royal College of Surgeons.*

We are living in an age when there is interference with nature on every side, not only in the case of human beings, but also in animals and agriculture; and these are bringing about severe repercussions and unforeseen problems.

In my fifty years of surgical practice I have seen many changes—the disappearance of consumption in England because of new drugs, and the prevention of, or protection against, tetanus and infantile paralysis, to mention only a few. It may well be that in the not too distant future we may obtain a cure for cancer, but it is probable that other diseases will take its place.

What is wanted today in the world is a return to the Scriptures and a renewal of trust in the Lord Jesus Christ. May God grant us these blessings!

'Twas God that made the ocean,
And laid its sandy bed;
He gave the stars their motion,
And built the mountain's head;
He made the rolling thunder,
The lightning's forked flame;
His works are full of wonder,
All glorious is His Name.

And must it not surprise us
That One so high and great
Should see and not despise us,
Poor sinners, at His feet?
Yet day by day He gives us
Our raiment and our food;
In sickness He relieves us,
And is in all things good.

But things that are far greater
His mighty hand hath done,
And sent us blessings sweeter
Through Christ, His only Son,
Who, when He saw us dying
In sin and sorrow's night,
On wings of mercy flying,
Came down with life and light.

He gives His Word to teach us
Our danger and our wants,
And kindly doth beseech us
To take the life He grants;
His Holy Spirit frees us
From Satan's deadly powers,
Leads us by faith to Jesus,
And makes His glory ours.
(*George Burden Bubier,* 1855)

A Major Challenge to Evolution

(Darwin's Theories Severely Criticised)

By Bishop D. A. Thompson

Towards the close of the 18th century and during the first half of the 19th the various branches of science made prodigious advances. Some of the leading men of these expanding fields of knowledge began, alas, to question the biblical account of the creation, and with it much of the history recorded in the Old Testament. Worse still, ecclesiastical leaders began to conform to these novel scientific ideas, and to the extent to which they did so, they abandoned belief in the plenary inspiration and inerrancy of Holy Writ, and as a consequence in the trustworthiness and final authority of Christ's utterances, particularly when He referred to the Old Testament Scriptures. These churchmen, in an attempt to justify themselves and their illogical, compromising and unbelieving attitude, declared that much of the Old Testament was marred by inaccuracy, was unhistorical and legendary, and even mere folklore and myth. There were not wanting faithful and scholarly divines who maintained that the Bible was the infallible Word of God, that more knowledge and fuller light would vindicate its correctness in every detail and that scientists, sooner or later, would be brought to confess that every assumption or theory contrary to Divine Revelation had been a mistake and that such would be constrained to adopt other view-points which would be in harmony with the Scripture of truth.

Into this confused world of scientific and religious thought various ideas of evolution (instead of direct creation) began to be put forward. These ideas received definite shape and impetus through the researches and writings of Charles Robert Darwin (1809-1882). This naturalist had studied at both Edinburgh and Cambridge Universities. His *magnum opus, The Origin of Species* (published in 1859) did more than anything else to popularise the theory of evolution. Other eminent men developed it, and it spread with lightning rapidity; so much so that today these ideas of the origin of the universe and of all that therein is, are received as an oracle and taught in most schools, colleges and universities. The man who dares to question the assumptions which lie behind this theory is in danger of being regarded as unscientific, 'behind the times', out of step with his wise contemporaries, and indeed as 'a bit of a crank'. It must, however, be remembered that the theory is contrary to the sublime record of direct creation by Almighty God as recorded in the first two chapters of Genesis and endorsed by our Lord Jesus Christ (Matt. 19.4-6; Mark 10.6-8). Moreover it is built upon numberless assumptions and suppositions which, with pathetic disregard for the laws of logic, are frequently represented as proven facts. Frauds perpetrated by some of the theory's exponents—the best known relates to the Piltdown skull—have successfully hoodwinked for long periods most, if not all, of the leading advocates of Darwinism, and demonstrated the utter unreliability of conclusions to which, despite the exposure of the deception, they have stubbornly clung. Further, the theory has done immeasurable harm to the visible Church of God, undermining the confidence of many in the Word of God and the whole scheme of salvation. It has destroyed the faith of large numbers and led to the conception of creation without the Creator, that is, to Atheism. The strength of the resulting apostate movement in the professing Church can be gauged from the fact that Darwin was given the honour of burial in Westminster Abbey.

Until quite recently Darwin has been accorded a paean of praise. One of his devoted followers, Sir Arthur Keith, regarded him as amongst 'that small select group of great Englishmen', which included Shakespeare. But this estimate of the man and his work is now beginning to be revised if not reversed. It was only natural that early in the last decade certain scientists and humanists should consider how they could most appropriately celebrate the approaching centenary of the publication of *The Origin of Species* which would fall on 24th November, 1959. Several eminent scholars engaged in research work on the life, diaries, letters, character and achievements of Darwin so as to make a worthy literary contribution to the great occasion. Amongst them was Dr. Gertrude Himmelfarb who, in the centenary year, produced a work entitled *Darwin and the Darwinian Revolution.* In it she records that, in her opinion, Darwin was lacking alike in originality and integrity. Dr. A. C. Crombie of Oxford, writing in the *Listener* (3rd December, 1959), referred to the 'deception' of Darwin, and of his 'two faces'.

But perhaps the most striking criticism of Darwin and his theory of evolution is found in Everyman's Library, Number 811 (1956). Messrs. J. M. Dent & Sons, Ltd., the publishing firm, had brought out an edition of *The Origin of Species,* with an introduction by Sir Arthur Keith, in 1928. They decided that their contribution to the centenary celebrations should take the form of a fresh edition of this work, with a new introduction by a leading contemporary scientist so that the assessment should be fully up-to-date. They invited Professor W. R. Thompson, F.R.S., the distinguished director of the Commonwealth Institute of Biological Control at Ottawa, to undertake the writing of this preface. The sequence is best told in the Professor's own words forming the first two paragraphs of his introduction:

> 'When I was asked by the publishers of this new edition of *The Origin of Species* to write an introduction replacing the one prepared a quarter of a century ago by the distinguished Darwinian, Sir Arthur Keith, I felt extremely hesitant to accept the invitation. I admire, as all biologists must, the immense scientific labours of Charles Darwin and his lifelong, single-hearted devotion to his theory of evolution. I agree that although, as he himself readily admitted, he did not invent the doctrine of organic evolution, or even the idea of natural selection, his arguments, and especially the arguments in *The Origin of Species,* convinced the world that he had discovered the true explanation of biological diversity, and had shown how the intricate adaptations of living things develop by a simple, inevitable process which even the most simple minded and unlearned can understand. But I am not satisfied that Darwin proved his point or that his influence in scientific and public thinking has been beneficial.
>
> 'I therefore felt obliged to explain to the editors of the Everyman's Library, that my introduction would be very different from that of Sir Arthur Keith, and that I could not content myself with mere variations on the hymn to Darwin and Darwinism that introduces so many text-books on biology and evolution, and might well be expected to precede a reprinting of the *Origin.* They raised no objection, so my main difficulty was removed. I am, of course, well aware that my views will be regarded by many biologists as heretical and reactionary. However, I happen to believe that in science heresy is a virtue and reaction often a necessity, and that in no field of science are heresy and reaction more desirable than in evolutionary theory. I have written what I think should be written; but the responsibility of the editors of the Library is not involved' (page 7).

Here then is a biologist of the front rank who is neither satisfied that the theory of evolution has been proved, nor that its influence has been beneficial.

Amongst Professor Thompson's criticisms of Darwin's work are the following:

> 'Personal convictions, simple possibilities, are presented as if they were proofs, or at least valid arguments in favour of the theory' (page 11).
>
> 'Since no one has explained to my satisfaction how evolution could happen I do not feel impelled to say that it has happened. I prefer to say that on this matter our information is inadequate' (page 15).
>
> 'It does appear to me, in the first place, that Darwin in the *Origin* was not able to produce palaeontological* evidence sufficient to prove his views, but that the evidence he did produce was adverse to them; and I may note that the position is not notably different today. The modern Darwinian palaeontologists are obliged, just like their predecessors and like Darwin, to water down the facts with subsidiary hypotheses which, however plausible, are in the nature of things unverifiable' (page 19).

*Palaeontology—the study of fossils (like the Piltdown skull, etc.).

The following extracts from the Professor's Introduction would bear out the contention that Darwinism has been associated with fallacies, frauds and forgeries and is inimical to the Christian Faith:

'Haeckel† altered the illustrations . . . to fit his theory' (page 15).

'A long-enduring and regrettable effect of the success of the *Origin* was the addiction of biologists to unverifiable speculation. "Explanations" of the origin of structures, instincts, and mental aptitudes of all kinds, in terms of Darwinian principles, marked with the Darwinian plausibility but hopelessly unverifiable, poured out from every research centre' (page 21).

'The success of Darwinism was accompanied by a decline in scientific integrity. This is already evident in the reckless statements of Haeckel and in the shifting, devious, and histrionic argumentation of T. H. Huxley. A striking example, which has only recently come to light, is the alteration of the Piltdown skull so that it could be used as evidence for the descent of man from the apes; but even before this a similar instance of tinkering with evidence was finally revealed by the discoverer of Pithecanthropus, who admitted, many years after his sensational report, that he had found in the same deposits bones that are definitely human. Though these facts are now well known, a work published in 1943 still accepts the diagnosis of Pithecanthropus given by Dubois, as a creature with a femur of human form permitting an erect posture. Not long ago (1947), an exhibit in London, designed for public instruction, presented human development in such a way as to insinuate the truth of the 'biogenetic law', and in the same exhibit were problematic reconstructions indicating the descent of man and including the Piltdown type' (pages 21 and 22).

'Sir Arthur Keith said that Darwin himself had done more than anyone to lift 'the pall of superstition' from mankind and, in another place, that Darwinism is a 'basal doctrine in the rationalist liturgy'. These remarks suggest that in his opinion the decline of belief in the supernatural, and probably the decline of Christianity, is largely due to the influence of Darwin. I think there is much to be said for this view . . . Although the *Origin* contains no direct attack on the Christian concept of the universe, it is, on a number of crucial points, opposed to this concept . . . Darwin himself, though he once held some rather vaguely Christian views, abandoned them quite rapidly and soon ceased to believe in the Christian revelation' (pages 22 and 23).

'This doctrine of evolution by natural selection as Darwin formulated, and as his followers still explain it, has a strong anti-religious flavour. This is due to the fact that the intricate adaptations and co-ordinations we see in living things, naturally evoking the idea of finality and design and, therefore, of an intelligent providence, are explained, with what seems to be a rigorous argument, as the result of chance. It may be said, and the most orthodox theologians indeed hold, that God controls and guides even the events due to chance; but this proposition the Darwinians emphatically reject, and it is clear that in the *Origin* evolution is presented as an essentially undirected process. For the majority of its readers, therefore, the *Origin* effectively dissipated the evidence of providential control' (page 23).

'This general tendency to eliminate, by means of unverifiable speculations, the limits of the categories Nature presents to us, is the inheritance of biology from *The Origin of Species.* To establish the continuity required by theory, historical arguments are invoked, even though historical evidence is lacking. Thus are engendered those fragile towers of hypotheses based on hypotheses, where fact and fiction intermingle in an inextricable confusion' (page 24).

So at long last a highly-qualified biologist has rejected the theory of evolution associated with such names as Darwin, Huxley and Haeckel!

† E. H. Haeckel (1834-1919) was the arrogant and pugnacious German evolutionist who renounced Christianity, and denied the immortality of the soul and the existence of a personal God. Professor of Zoology at Jena University (1862-1909), he was the first to draw up (an imaginary) genealogical tree tracing the evolution of the human race, from protoplasm, through animals, chimpanzees, the *Pithecanthropus erectus* (ape-like man), to primitive and finally modern man.

Conservative Evangelicals should be deeply grateful to Messrs. J. M. Dent & Sons for giving publicity to the late Professor Thompson's criticisms. Their action stands in marked contrast to the policy of the British Broadcasting Corporation which propagates this unbiblical theory of evolution and refuses to allow those who share Professor Thompson's views to present their convictions over the air.

IN* the beginning
God created the
Heauen, and the
Earth.
2 And the
earth was with-
out forme, and
voyd, and darke-
neſſe was vpon
the face of the deepe: and the Spirit
of God mooued vpon the face of the
waters.
3 And God ſaid,* Let there be light:
and there was light.
4 And God ſaw the light, that it was
good: and God diuided † the light from
the darkeneſſe.
5 And God called the light, Day,
and the darkneſſe he called Night: † and
the euening and the morning were the
firſt day.

From the first edition of the 'Authorized Version' of the English Bible. Printed at London, 1611

Seven Sound Reasons for Protesting against the Theory of Evolution

By Dr. C. E. A. Turner

1.—The Theory is contrary to the discovered and tested Laws of Physics, Chemistry, Physiology, Genetics. The universe operates a process of action and reaction, producing stable states. There is no upbuilding of giant molecules needed for life, without human intervention or using life-processes. All creatures reproduce only their own kind, from their own gene pools.

2.—The Theory is absurdly illogical in alleging that inanimate matter produces life, that simple creatures transform into more complex, that the Creation arose by chance. All this is also contrary to experience.

3.—The Theory is called by its advocates an historical process—yet this depends upon historical evidence, itself dependent upon human testimony. This is both absurd and impossible over the hundreds of millions of years supposedly involved. Incessant search throughout the century since Darwin restated the ancient Greek Theory, has found none of the promised 'intermediates' between the species.

4.—Its devotees adopt highly questionable methods, avoiding debate. They fabricate genealogical 'trees', purporting to show the descent of man, and suggest that these are factual. They engage artists to produce pictures of imaginary prehistoric scenes that no eye ever saw, and based upon the scantiest material. They 'reconstruct' whole men and animals from a few fragments of bone.

5.—The Theory is criticised by many eminent modern scientists, unconvinced by its claims, and opposed to its trends. They include Prof. J. Doyle of Dublin University; Dr. Malcolm Dixon, F.R.S., Reader in Enzyme Biology at Cambridge; Prof. Ronald Good of Hull; Prof. W. R. Thompson, F.R.S., former Director of the Commonwealth Institute of Biological Control, Ottawa; Sir Cecil G. Wakeley, Bart., F.R.S.E., Past President of the Royal College of Surgeons, London.

6.—The Theory excludes the Creator, the existence of whom, as the Almighty, wise and beneficent Organizer, alone can give sense and purpose to His Creation. On the other hand, the Theory is embraced by atheists, communists and others, with intent to encourage or conform to the permissive fashions of a godless and degenerating society.

7.—The Theory is not in any form in accord with the Word of God, straightforwardly read and fairly interpreted.

And who but He that arched the skies,
  And pours the dayspring's living flood,
Wondrous alike in all He tries,
  Could raise the daisy's purple bud?

Mould its green cup, its wiry stem,
  Its fringed border nicely spun,
And cut the gold-embossed gem
  That set in silver, gleams within?

Then fling it, unrestrained and free,
  O'er hill and dale and desert sod,
That man where'er he walks may see
  In every step the stamp of God?

Teleology: Purpose Everywhere

By Dr. C. E. A. Turner

The word 'Teleology' is derived from the Greek 'telos' meaning 'end', or 'teleios' meaning 'complete', and 'logos' or 'word', 'body of thought'. The study is one of final causes, of purpose in nature. C. Wolf used the term in his book 'Logic', 1728.

While Aristotle taught purpose in nature, it was during the 17th century in this country that this subject developed. Together with the revival of interest in the Holy Scriptures at the Reformation went the expansion of the study of the natural world. So there occurred an increase in knowledge of both the spiritual and the physical.

The great Sir Francis Bacon saw the pursuit of natural science as being 'to the glory of God and the relief of man's estate'. The work of the leading Puritans was important here. John Wilkins, 1614-1672, Bishop of Chester, wrote 'A Discourse concerning the Beauty of Providence in all the Rugged Passages of it', 1649, and then his noted work 'On the Principles and Duties of Natural Religion', published posthumously in 1678. John Ray, an ejected minister at the Restoration of Charles II, devoted himself to natural science and produced a monumental and influential book in 1691. This is 'The Wisdom of God manifested in the Works of Creation'. Three times enlarged by him, it passed through some eight further editions up to 1827.

George Berkeley, 1685-1753, Bishop of Cloyne, an 18th-century philosopher, following this view, saw God's attributes in 'the works of nature, which discover so much harmony and contrivance in their make' as he wrote in his 'Treatise concerning the Principles of Human Knowledge', 1710.

Later William Paley's 'Natural Theology or Evidence of the Existence and Attributes of the Deity, Collected from the appearance of Nature', similarly exerted great influence, being required reading in the universities. It was in its 20th edition by 1820.

Today Dr. R. E. D. Clark's 'The Universe and God', 1939, and 'The Universe: Plan or Accident', 1949, cite plenty of evidence from modern discovery for the existence of the great Planner.

There seems to be purpose everywhere and in everything. Formerly this was recognized by many, but in modern times the subject has been disregarded and relegated to a mere half-column in the most recent edition of the Encyclopaedia Britannica. E. H. Haeckel, 1834-1919, the German zoologist, notorious for his faked diagrams to foster the theory of evolution, picked out exceptions to purpose, mocking the idea by using the term 'Dysteleology'. However, the advances of science have told against him. For example the idea of the uselessness of vestigial organs has been exploded as their purposes have come to light. Further, the intricate structure and inter-working of organs, cells and secretions all make the idea of chance less and less acceptable. The increased interest during recent years in the study of Ecology, or the relationship of plants to one another and to their environment, shows a greater recognition of purpose in the natural world.

It would be foolish to think that the purpose for everything is known. Much needs to be discovered about the value of disease, pests and weeds on the physical plane. But on the moral, an explanation is available in the doctrine of man's fall and punishment, following the intrusion of Satan, the Destroyer. Because all is not known, we do not reject the whole study, any more than the physician ceases his treatment or the researcher his pursuit of knowledge owing to lack of complete success.

John Ray stated that the works of God in creation show His wisdom in: I. Their Formation; II. Their Order or Harmony; III. Their End or Use. So we may think of how the complexities and varieties of structures and of the methods of functioning show the extent of the Creator's skill.

For a brief review of a sample of these wonders, the following five groups may be considered:

I. The Earth as a Planet

This sphere is unique within the limitations of our knowledge. Its range of temperatures and pressures, the composition of its atmosphere, the existence and amount of water and of numerous other compounds, make it eminently suited for the continuance of life as it was in the beginning. This is in complete contrast to the conditions obtaining on other planets and recently confirmed by the space probes. The now familiar lunar exploration has shown how inhospitable is that sphere to terrestial life. Neither can scientists conceive of any form of life that would be possible in the conditions found elsewhere than on the Earth.

II. The Properties of Matter

The law of gravity makes for stability and order, enabling work to be done and goods to be stored. The weightlessness of the lunar-nauts produced amusing results, but made many normal activities nigh impossible. The phenomena of magnetism and electricity have proved valuable in former times for giving direction and assisting detection by means of the ancient lodestone; while today much of the activity of modern man with his machines is due to the use of the forces and principles involved in these phenomena.

Much might be said of the general properties of the gases, liquids and solids found in the Earth. The melting points, boiling points, densities, solubilities, conductivities and the like suggest a Guiding Hand has adjusted them so that the materials are of use to man. Here, for example, the higher specific gravities of many ores is of assistance in their separation. Water, almost a universal solvent with its suitable temperature range from melting to boiling point, is a remarkable case of purpose. Its peculiar properties of having its maximum density at 4 degrees Centigrade, and its crystals floating, thus preventing complete freezing up and assisting unfreezing, adds to its unique value in the Earth.

III. Chemistry

In this sphere there are the remarkable cycles involving the elements oxygen, hydrogen, carbon and nitrogen. The simplest of these, for example, may be that in which oxygen is removed from the air and used by animals, and restored by plants, which will have absorbed it in the form of carbon dioxide produced from it by the animals. Thus a balance is effected to enable life to continue.

The element calcium, by means of a soluble chloride in milk and in the blood stream, supplies what is necessary to form the insoluble phosphate needed for the formation of bones and teeth. Yet this absorption is dependent on the presence of vitamin D in the food. The elements of the group, namely strontium and barium, have many similar properties, but cannot be so used, and are moreover lethal, as we think of the strontium fall-out from nuclear fission and the use of barium in poisons.

Carbon is another element with markedly unique properties. Its high valency and ability to combine both with the electro-positive element hydrogen and with the electro-negative oxygen make it the constituent of very many compounds in the natural world, so that Organic Chemistry is defined as that of the carbon compounds. Here again the most similar element to it, silicon, is very different, and could not conceivably be used as a substitute. In fact silicon itself is an element of first importance, being the next most abundant to oxygen in the Earth's crust, and forming the silicates, which are the basic substances of most rocks.

Single atoms of certain elements are vital parts of biologically important compounds. The familiar green colour of plants is due to chlorophyll. This is a very large molecule composed of many atoms, but within it is a single atom of magnesium. This compound is essential to life, being the catalyst enabling photosynthesis to build up compounds in plants.

Iron also occurs as four single atoms in the complex twin molecule of thousands of atoms and a molecular weight of about 68,000, known as haemoglobin. Here, owing to its special properties, it is able to combine ('rust') with oxygen to transport it to tissues where it is released and carbon dioxide removed. One author stated that iron rusting is an 'unfortunate' property, but here it is essential to life. Incidentally the rusting or oxidation of a number of metals helps to remove the remains of man's discarded and disfiguring machines!

Thyroxine, an essential hormone, is a complex compound secreted by the thyroid gland. It has been synthesized, and as such has proved a blessing in treating diseases of that organ. The presence of four atoms of the comparatively rare element iodine in the molecule produces its peculiar and important properties.

A certain sickness in some Australian sheep was shown to be due to the absence of cobalt from the soil. Subsequently it was found that a single atom of this element was an integral part of the complex compound known as Vitamin B 12. This is essential for the manufacture of red corpuscles in the bone marrow.

The assertion is therefore made that these elements situated in these vital components show the wise work of the Designer, rather than the blind chance processes of supposed evolution.

IV. The Biological Field

The fluids of the animal bodies all carry the signs of design. Blood, the carrier of the body, containing all the substances needed for its upbuilding and activities, as well as those to be eliminated, is wonderfully contrived. So too is the four-valve pump which controls its flow.

The miracle of the egg, with its peculiarly strong shell, is the story of two liquids and two cells which, without more than a steady application of gentle heat, can produce the new life of the creature which lays it. In all species the reproductive process is a miracle, beyond the conception of man's mind or remote chance.

Milk too is a marvel, eminently suitable for its purpose of feeding the young. Wonderfully secreted and containing all the substances necessary for the proper development of the off-spring, it also provides a valuable food in many cases for other creatures including man.

The alimentary canal with its attached glands and blood vessels is much more complicated, intricate and remarkable than the most sophisticated industrial plant. Essentially just one main tube, it is more than a factory producing a variety of products. Through a wise Designer, it, without apparent conscious direction, absorbs food, sorts, processes and allocates it, eliminating waste and keeping itself in constant repair. It uses and produces most complex chemicals in its digestive actions, which may be described in part, but which are neither understood nor reproduced in the laboratories of the most advanced scientists.

Even the air with its precise worldwide balance of suitable gases, small variations from which prove lethal, shows evidence of design to suit the various forms of life dependent on it. This view is rather to be preferred to that of its being accidental, or the result of some fantastic processes of evolution.

Numerous well-known structures of familiar creatures all point to design, rather than chance or some gradual development. The intricate organisation of the ant hill is one example. Similar are the wasps' nest and the beehive with the regular hexagonal cells. The queens, drones, workers and their particular functions suggest a Super-Organiser in at the beginning. The spiders with webs produced perfectly from the first, indicate something built-in, and that needs a Builder. Birds' nests of the many species are similar structures. Who too gave the birds their light strong feathers for flight and bones of minimal weight? Man's most intelligent efforts in this form of transport are extremely clumsy in comparison.

The fine formation and beauty of diatoms; of insects, especially butterflies and moths; of plants, particularly in their flowers and seeds, are indicative of the quality of the Designing Hand behind all. The Lord reminded men that Solomon in all his glory was not arrayed like one of these (Matt. 6.28-29).

V. The Inanimate Features of the Earth's Crust

These appear as designed for specific purposes. Thus in the rocks are to be found building materials, minerals, metals, fuel and the basis of soil. The mountains serve as watersheds, stores, shelters, boundaries and objects of beauty and recreation. The lakes are reservoirs, the rivers means of transport, communication and purification, while the seas are great food factories. Man is the centre of all this purpose. Sir Julian Huxley, as reckless and illogical as his ancestor T. H. Huxley, stated his 'glorious paradox' that blind chance gave rise to purposeful man. The truth is that the

Almighty Designer put purpose in creation which was provided for man and to be controlled by man (Gen. 2.8-9; Psa. 8.6). This control is seen increasingly through modern technology, although it often works blindly without a goal or Divine direction.

Evolutionists may declare, 'What was needed, came!' or 'What was present, was adapted by life!' But how did it come, how would the need be known, or how can adaptation occur without an Agent? Man for all his intelligence does not know where he is going, or what to adapt, neither can he, as the Lord said, add a cubit to his stature (Matt. 6.27). The creationist states, 'God foresaw and provided all'. Just as man is advised by a textbook or maker's handbook how to deal with a mechanism, so he needs to heed the Creator's Book, the Bible, in order to learn the right use of the Creation.

Give to our God immortal praise;
Mercy and truth are all His ways;
Wonders of grace to God belong,
Repeat His mercies in your song.

Give to the Lord of lords renown,
The King of kings with glory crown:
His mercies ever shall endure,
When lords and kings are known no more.

He built the earth, He spread the sky,
And fixed the starry lights on high:
Wonders of grace to God belong,
Repeat His mercies in your song.

He fills the sun with morning light,
He bids the moon direct the night:
His mercies ever shall endure,
When suns and moons shall shine no more.

He sent His Son with power to save
From guilt, and darkness, and the grave:
Wonders of grace to God belong,
Repeat His mercies in your song.

Through this vain world He guides our feet,
And leads us to His heavenly seat:
His mercies ever shall endure,
When this vain world shall be no more.

(Isaac Watts)

Creation versus Evolution

By Malcolm H. Watts

(The substance of a talk given to young persons to counter the teaching of evolution which is so widespread in schools.)

1. The very concept of 'creation' militates against the theory of evolution, for creation is an act and not a process of nature. The Bible insists that in the beginning everything sprang into being at the instant of a command: 'God said' and 'there was' (Gen. 1; Psalm 33.6, 9; Heb. 11.3). If things suddenly appeared out of nothing as God spoke and at the instant of command, then all process must be excluded. There is no necessity for God to work through process of gradual development. This even the devil conceded when tempting our Lord: 'If thou be the Son of God, *command* that these stones be made bread' (Matt. 4.3).

However, it may be objected that there is evidence of process in the things made. That must be granted, but it serves as no valid objection to the biblical doctrine of Creation. The serpent brought into being in a moment by means of Moses' rod doubtless looked as if it had gone through the stages of growth and natural change: indeed, a scientific contemporary of Moses would have so concluded, but it would have been a wrong conclusion. All statements concerning the origin and development of that serpent would really have been ridiculous. Science would have been confounded before the living God (Exod. 4.3 cf. the manna Exod. 16.14-35; the meal and oil 1 Kgs. 17.14-16, 2 Kgs. 4.1-7; the wine John 2.1-11; the bread and fish Matt. 14.19). 'One day' the Scripture says, 'is with the Lord as a thousand years' (2 Pet. 3.8) and, as the context speaks of Creation, it evidently means that God is able to do in one day what appears to have taken a thousand years to perform and perfect.

2. One of the concessions all too rashly made by certain modern Christians is that the Bible is an infallible guide only in matters of theology. It is said that the Bible nowhere claims to be a scientific text book. The matter is often set forth in this way: the Word of God may teach us 'who' created, but it is outside the province of the Word of God to teach us 'how' things were created. Now, scientific terminology is indeed absent from the Scriptures, but when in the sacred volume there are pronouncements upon matters of science, there is an almost incredible accuracy. Let me illustrate. Certain thinkers in earlier times fancifully conjectured that the world stood on the back of an elephant. Later minds cherished the notion that the world was in the shape of a table with legs resting upon some unseen foundation. Pindar expressed the view that the earth rested upon pillars. The inspired Word of God, as far back as the time of the patriarchs, revealed that 'He hangeth the earth upon nothing' (Job 26.7). The planet home of man for centuries was popularly believed to be flat (I believe there still is 'The Flat Earth Society'!) but scriptures written by Solomon teach the spherical form of our globe: 'He set a compass (lit. "a circle") upon the face of the depth' (Prov. 8.27). The ancients believed rather crudely that the stars of heaven were lamps in the great dome made by God. It was not until the appearance of the telescope that man really enjoyed a realistic conception of the immensity of space; yet, in the seventh century B.C., the thought was expressed and used as an argument for God's great faithfulness to His people: 'If heaven above can be measured . . . I will also cast off all the seed of Israel' (Jer. 31.37). The Bible does not err even with respect to science, and upon the subject now under consideration it emphatically states that each species is fixed and can only produce 'after his (its) kind' (Gen. 1.11, 21, 24). Such statements may be fully trusted.

3. If the early chapters of Genesis are interpreted in a way which denies their historicity, then the great principles of Biblical interpretation are destroyed. These chapters are written, not as fable or parable, but as sober matter-of-fact history and they have a place among the historical narratives of the Old Testament. Besides, the very law of God bears witness to its historicity and exact truthfulness (Exod. 20.11); the Saviour appealed to the early record (Mark 10.6-8); and the Apostles confirmed the traditional view of the Creation account (2 Cor. 4.6; 2 Pet. 3.3-6). Once the testimony of Genesis is rejected, the foundations of the whole Bible are shaken (see: Luke 3.38; Acts 17. 24-26; Rom. 5.12, 14; 1 Cor. 15.21; 1 Tim. 2.13, 14, etc.).

4. Evolution attacks the chief doctrines of the Christian Creed. 'In the beginning, God' is one of our most basic affirmations, but this is now challenged and Julian Huxley boldly asserts that 'God is unnecessary', believing that 'the Divine Father' is a conception man had in a primitive state, which conception is to be abandoned by ascending man. Again the Bible describes man at the first as made 'in the image of God', which means that he originally possessed righteousness, holiness and knowledge (Eph. 4.24; Col. 3.10). Man is not, therefore, a victim of nature and earth rising gradually to greatness. He is a fallen creature bearing full responsibility for his present state, and, furthermore, he alone is responsible for the presence of death in this world (1 Cor. 15.14).

Does the theory also affect the doctrine of the Mediator between God and man? Undoubtedly, for if men arrived by natural stages at the knowledge of the One True God, it is conceivable that men will one day outgrow the conception of God in Christ. Let the thought perish!

'Should all the forms that men devise
Assault my faith with treacherous art,
I'd call them vanity and lies,
And bind the Gospel to my heart.'
(Isaac Watts, 1709.)

5. Interestingly enough, in a letter to Huxley on August 8th, 1860, Darwin referred to Evolution as 'the devil's Gospel'. Evolutionary humanism desperately seeks to usurp the place which Christianity enjoys. It is man's poor and beggarly substitute for the gospel of grace. The treacherous thrust of this theory is to the heart of the Faith. 'We can,' wrote H. J. Muller, 'in securing and advancing our position, increasingly avoid the mis-steps of blind nature, circumvent its cruelties, reform our own natures, and enhance our own values.' That is a philosophy in which man is at the centre; it is a philosophy in which man is able to save himself; it is a philosophy in which man ascending has all the glory. The evolutionary system is the product of a world which knows not God and loves not Christ.

6. There is a God-made parallel between the natural 'creation' of the world and the spiritual 'creation' of the Christian (2 Cor. 5.17; Gal. 6.15); for the ways of God in nature correspond to the ways of God in grace. The Christian became a new creature, NOT by a process of gradual improvement, but the moment the life-giving voice of God penetrated into the regions of the soul; and it was precisely so when God made the world (see 2 Cor. 4.6). God acted in the old creation as He acts now in the new creation, and man tries to rob God of the glory in both of these: in the first by postulating an age-long improvement with the theory of evolution and in the second by inculcating a life-long endeavour with the teaching wholly concerned with morality and 'good works'. Even the Christian's experience, therefore, testifies against the unbelieving speculations of evolutionary thinking.

7. In a scientific work published some years ago the author wrote: 'It is an interesting thought to remember that the earth existed for thousands of millions of years before man came and that it will probably exist for thousands of millions of years after man has vanished.' Evolution leads us to that conclusion, but revelation leads us in another direction altogether. As the heavens and the earth were made for man, they made their appearance at the same time that man made his appearance (Isa. 45.18. Notice that it was not God's intention that the earth should lie waste and desolate). The same heavens and earth shall pass away when man passes away from this scene (2 Pet. 3.7). This means that the history of this world and the history of man began together and will conclude together; 'science falsely so-called' makes no allowance for such a supernatural opening and closing to history.

The prophetic scriptures warn us that the biblical doctrine of creation will be denied in the latter times for, according to Peter, scoffers shall arise, willingly ignorant of the fact that 'by the word of God the heavens were of old and the earth . . .' (2 Pet. 3.5). Through the revelation of God we understand that the worlds were framed by the word of God 'so that things which are seen were not made of things which do appear' (Heb. 11.3). Whatever the strange assertions of science may be, the Lord contends, saying: 'Where wast thou when I laid the foundations of the earth?' (Job. 38.4). God is the only infallible Scientist. Let God be true and let all the earth keep silence before Him!

Man and Animals: some of the Differences

1. An Animal is Not Religious

Man is incurably religious, but an animal is not. Man has an experience of spiritual order which is not accounted for on natural premises. Man cannot help but be religious. It is part of his nature; therefore, we find religions everywhere in the world. Man is God-directed. Even in his denial of God man struggles with the God question. Dr. J. H. Bavinck perceptively comments that 'in his religion man is aware that he is not alone because he knows that he is living in the immediate presence of someone who is infinitely greater than he'. Only in man—heaven and earth meet each other.

2. Animals Have No Sense of Time

Only man has a sense of the past, present and future. He has the ability to plan for the future and to build on past experience. Man can recall with fear or joy the past and knows that he has to meet the common enemy—death. An animal has no concept of time. It only knows the present and acts and reacts according to instinct.

3. An Animal Has No Aesthetic Experiences

No animal has artistic feeling or ability. Newspapers have told stories of monkeys dipping their paws into a paint pot, daubing on canvas and receiving a great art prize. This is the height of absurdity and the depth of bankruptcy of modern thought. Dr. Ramm remarks that a dog may hear better than any human being, but it can hardly enjoy a concert as a trained musician does.

4. No Animal Has a Conscience

Man has a conscience that witnesses against him when he does wrong (Rom. 2.15). When a man commits a crime, his conscience pricks his heart. An animal has no conscience. No dog has ever brought back to the butcher the meat it had stolen.

5. No Animal Has Moral Experiences

Man is a moral being. He is confronted with moral choices. He has the law of God before him which tells him what is right and what is wrong. The very law of God is even written in his heart (Rom. 2.15). The moral structure is fundamental to all normal people.

6. Animals Have No Language

The origin of language does not lie within a specific need of man, but in man's reasoning abilities. In language man has the key to communicate concerning the past, the present, and the future. Man has intellect, will, emotion and general ideas about space and time, and abstract concepts. An animal cannot communicate in language. The parrot utters cries, but 'no parrot ever yet spoke a true word'.

7. Animals Do Not Have a Concept of Violence

If human society, as well as man's conscience, are products of animal ancestry, why do we have violence? Only man kills at random and tortures members of his own species. The concentration camps of Nazi Germany were called 'bestial', yet no animal has ever, with such cold predetermination, killed such large numbers of its own kind.

8. No Animal is the Subduer of the Earth

Man is a worker and developer. He is the steward of the world and has become called by God to responsibly enfold creation through his work. Animals and plants are to be under his dominion. He is the scientist at work in God's laboratory—earth.

What is man? He is unique! He was created in God's very image and is precious in His sight. Man has a very special place in God's creation. He is neither junk nor animal to be cast aside at will. Scripture says of man: 'What is man, that thou art mindful of him? and the son of man, that thou visitest him? For thou hast made him a little lower than the angels, and hast crowned him with glory and honour. Thou madest him to have dominion over the works of thy hands; for thou hast put all things under his feet.'

(From *Bible-Science Newsletter,* June 1976.)

I sing the almighty power of God,
That made the mountains rise,
That spread the flowing seas abroad,
And built the lofty skies.

I sing the wisdom that ordained
The sun to rule the day;
The moon shines full at His command,
And all the stars obey.

I sing the goodness of the Lord,
That filled the earth with food;
He formed the creatures with His word,
And then pronounced them good.

There's not a plant or flower below
But makes His glories known;
And clouds arise, and tempests blow,
By order from His throne.

Creatures, as numerous as they be,
Are subject to His care;
There's not a place where we can flee
But God is present there.

In heaven He shines with beams of love,
With wrath in hell beneath:
'Tis on His earth I stand or move,
And 'tis His air I breathe.

His hand is my perpetual guard,
He guides me with His eye;
Why should I then forget the Lord,
Who is for ever nigh?

Coelacanth—'living fossil'

By S. M. Houghton

(The word is pronounced se—la—kanth; it is derived from two Greek words meaning 'hollow-spined'.) A problem for which evolutionists can supply no solution is mentioned from time to time in the secular as well as in the religious press. An article by D. Birch which appeared in the *Pretoria News* on the 3rd February last reminds its readers that 'it was in February, 1939—40 years ago—that the news of the amazing discovery of the Coelacanth was given to the world. And the world has not heard the last of this famous living fossil, for international co-operation may one day accomplish the feat of keeping one alive in captivity'. Mr. Birch supplies us with the following information:

'Late in the year 1938 the vessel, *Nerine,* was trawling over a bank 40 fathoms deep off the mouth of the Chalumna River, south-west of East London (Cape Province). Captain Goosen, master of the vessel, looked expectantly at the contents of the nets as they were brought in. First of all, there were two metric tons of sharks, and about one and a half metric tons of edible fish. At the bottom of the pile was a lizard-like blue fish, 1.52 metres long, the like of which no one had ever seen before. As Captain Goosen bent forward for a closer examination, the fish swivelled round and tried to bite him. Little did he know that very soon he would become the centre of the scientific world. The blue fish was left on deck where it lived for three hours.

'Captain Goosen had an arrangement with Miss Courtenay Latimer, curator of the East London Museum, whereby sharks and inedible fish were handed over to her. In due course the mysterious blue fish ended up along with all the others on the wharf where Miss Latimer was immediately fascinated once she had caught sight of it. She tried to identify it but without success. Even the Museum reference books gave her no clues. So she quickly sketched the fish, wrote down a description and posted a letter to Professor J. L. B. Smith of Rhodes University. She desperately wanted to preserve the fish. The cold storage people refused to help and even the mortuary declined. So she and her African helper, Enoch, trundled the fish on a two-wheeled handcart to an elderly taxidermist.

'Meanwhile, Professor Smith received Miss Latimer's letter and gazed at her sketch, remarking to his wife as he did so, "You'll think I'm crazy, but they've found a fish at East London of a type generally thought to be extinct for millions of years". It was even so. He had identified the fish as a Coelacanth which evolutionists regarded as having been extinct for more than 50 million years.' Mr. Birch continues:

'A rushed car trip to East London and Professor Smith's enthusiam knew no bounds. He ran his hands over the fish's limb-like fins, the cosmoid scales, the extra tail and the heavy head bones, and concluded that the fish was "a stray" and that its home was probably the islands and reefs off East Africa.

'Fourteen years passed before the next dramatic chapter in the story of the Coelacanth could be written. A leaflet printed in English, Portuguese and French, and distributed to ships and fishermen, offered a reward for Coelacanth. A black fisherman of Anjouan Island [one of the Comoro Islands in the Mozambique Channel between the African mainland and Madagascar], caught a Coelacanth. Bringing it ashore he was about to cut it up at the market place when a Black teacher recognized it and handed it to Captain Eric Hunt, the owner of a schooner, who then salted it and injected it with formalin. He also cabled Professor Smith. Amid much excitement the Prime Minister put his private Dakota aircraft at the Professor's disposal, enabling him to get to East Africa quickly and take possession of the Coelacanth. He then wrote a book on the fish called *Old Fourlegs* which was translated into nine different languages and even penetrated the Iron Curtain.

'When the Professor died, his wife took over much of his research work. She is still waiting for the most thrilling sight of all—an "extinct fish" swimming around in captivity. But there are difficulties, for the Coelacanth normally lives 300 metres below the surface and is subjected to 30 atmospheres of pressure. If caught it must needs be transferred to a special refrigerated pressurized tank—an expensive operation. In Mrs. Smith's view "it would be like taking a time-machine back to 300-million years ago".'

* * * * *

Let two further remarks suffice.

The Elder Pliny in his *Natural History* passed the observation, *Ex Africa semper aliquid novi* (Out of Africa something new always emerges). An incontestable fact deriving from Africa may serve to invalidate a theory produced in Europe or America.

The doctrine of evolution derives from theories which, however plausible and attractive to the natural man, are not supported by clear and indisputable factual evidence. They are based upon suppositions which are incapable of historic or scientific proof, and pertain to 'the wisdom of this world' which God in His wisdom renders foolish. The true knowledge of origins and beginnings depends upon revelation. The necessity of revelation drives us to Holy Scripture and to the unique Person of Him who was none other than 'God manifest in the flesh'. His is 'the last word' upon creation, for 'All things were made by Him and without Him was not anything made that was made'. 'Let God be true and every man a liar.' If it be asked, Does Scripture allow a belief in evolution, theistic or otherwise, we give an emphatic 'No' to the query. 'God's Word shall stand, His truth prevail, and not one jot or tittle fail'.

Coelacanth

I beg y continuance of your prayers for me, and rest
Sir, your most cordial and affectionate Friend and Servan-

Mat: Henry.

MATTHEW HENRY
(1662-1714)
(perhaps the most famous of Bible Commentators)

Section Six

Israel in Scripture

Contents: Section Six

Israel in Scripture

Israel's Unique History and Testimony

By David Baron

'To me the wonder of all wonders, and the most unmistakable proof of a Divine providence and rule—a miracle greater than Noah's ark, or Lot's wife, or the Burning Bush—is the Jew.' So spake the philosopher Hamann of Königsberg, who died in 1788, and who in his lifetime was called *Der Magus des Nordens*—'The Sage,' or 'The Wise Man of the North.' To this I would add a saying of our beloved and lamented friend, Dr. Adolph Saphir—viz., that 'The history of Israel is the history of miracle, even as it is the miracle of history.'

These sayings are true; and if men fail to see in the history of Israel, and in the present state of the Jewish people, most striking and manifest proof of Divine interposition and of the truth of Scripture, it can only be attributed to deplorable ignorance of both prophecy and history; or to the more solemn fact that this generation, so wise in its own eyes, is, by a process of self-hardening, becoming more and more dead to all sense of the supernatural.

Surely, even the least informed and the most superficial observer of things cannot but be struck with the peculiarities and uniqueness of the Jewish people; while philosophers and metaphysicians like Hegel have had to confess, that, judged by the principles of philosophy, and by known natural laws, the Jews and their history must remain an enigma—a problem which cannot be solved. But perhaps the most wonderful thing in connection with this unique people—that which distinguishes Israel from all other nations—is that their whole history, already covering a period of more than three thousand four hundred years since the Exodus, was all written in advance.

The passage I have chosen for our consideration serves to illustrate this:

Deuteronomy 4.25-21.

It is one of those germinal passages in the writings of Moses which form the basis of a great deal which is more fully unfolded in later Scriptures. It formed part of the farewell address of Moses to the children of Israel in the plains of Moab before ever they entered Canaan. This is what the Book itself tells us; and so far I see personally no reason, in the guesses and conjectures of a certain school of criticism, to oblige me to give up faith in the Mosaic origin and historic character of the Book of Deuteronomy.

Certainly the conclusions forced upon us in the study of the Book itself are that it is both historic and authentic. Historic *proof* or fact to the contrary there is none; and guesses and conjectures, however confidently made, are not sufficient to oblige us to regard the writer of this sublime Scripture as a forger and deceiver. Much, however, of what I am about to say in this exposition is not affected by the questions of the date and authorship of this Book. To return to our passage in Deuteronomy chapter 4, it is not too much to say that in these few verses we have a forecast of the whole history of Israel. From the top of Mount Pisgah Moses had a wonderful view. He saw the whole land spread before him. But from the top of the prophetic Pisgah, to which he was lifted by the Spirit of God, his view was still more wonderful.

His vision ranged through the centuries; he saw, not only the whole land, but *the whole history of the people,* spread before him, from the very beginning to the very end. By revelation he saw it, and by God's command he wrote in a book (Ex. 34.1-7; Deut. 31.24), in order that in ages to come, men, by comparing this Divine forecast with the actual condition of things, might learn to know that there is an omniscient God, who sees the end from the beginning—One who first makes His counsels known, and then causes all things to work together for the accomplishment of that which He declared beforehand should come to pass. That the prospective record which is given in this and other Scriptures, in relation to the history of Israel, has so far proved true, the peculiar people which already existed as a separate nation when Moses spoke three thousand four hundred years ago, still lives to testify.

In reading so-called higher critical literature on the Old Testament, I feel thankful to God for the continued existence of the Jewish people; for however easy some may find it to reduce the early *records* of Israel's history into myths and legends, it is not so easy to reduce into shadows and phantoms *a whole nation* whose past history is embodied in their present, and who by their very existence and solemn rites and observances bear witness, in a thousand ways, to the historic truth of those early records, which in the providence of God they have preserved for us.

But let us compare this forecast with the unquestionable facts of history. The forecast, in brief, is this: After sojourning for an indefinite period in the land, Israel would corrupt themselves and turn away from God, and become idolaters; and in consequence, they would soon perish from off the land of which they were about to take possession. Yet their destiny and experience would be unlike other people's, who, driven from their land, also perished from off the face of the earth by being either absorbed or exterminated. Something strange, something unique, something which, up to the time that this forecast was written, was altogether outside the experience of mankind, should befall them. Jehovah would scatter them among the nations, 'from one end of the earth,' as we are told in the twenty-eighth chapter, 'even unto the other.' Among these nations they would find no ease, nor would the sole of their foot have rest. For a long time they would be persecuted and oppressed.

Their plagues and their sorrows would be unlike those which any other nation on the face of the earth had experienced. Yet they would be preserved, and in the end a spirit of repentance would be given them. In the latter days there would be a restoration of the covenant relationship between Jehovah and His people. They would be blessed and be made a blessing. This is a meagre outline of the prophetic forecast, filled in by many striking prophetic details upon which I cannot touch.

And remember that there are other parallel but distinct lines of prediction in relation to this people, and to the land, and to the city, and especially in relation to Him who is both the climax and the solution of the mystery of Israel. But did it not seem to you as I summarised the Divine forecast as if I had been reminding you of well-known and universally acknowledged facts of history? This only shows how striking and manifest the fulfilment has been of the things which have been foretold.

And the purpose for which they are miraculously preserved is that they might bear witness among the nations. It is true that the testimony which they bear while in a condition of unbelief is, for the most part, though not wholly, passive; but still it is most valuable. How thankful, for instance, we should be that in these days, when even theological professors coolly assert that it is doubtful whether Abraham was an actual personality—that there is a whole nation who, whenever they name Abraham, say, 'Abraham abinu'—'Abraham, *our father*'; and when a Canon of the Church of England has the temerity to write that to him the actual existence of the personality of Moses is 'unproved and unprovable'; and when others who condescend to admit the existence of Moses as an historical personality confidently declare that he certainly had very little or nothing to do with the giving of the Law—that to this day there is a whole people scattered through the earth who, whenever they name the name of Moses, say, 'Moshe rabbinu'—'Moses, our teacher; Moses, our law-giver,' as if in solemn protest against those wild, unreasonable, and unjustifiable theories which are palmed off in the name of criticism.

And in this materialistic age, when men are denying God, not only as Redeemer, but as the Creator, it is something to have a nation who throughout their history have kept the seventh day as a reminder and testimony that in six days the Lord created the heavens and the earth, but rested on the seventh day.

How significant also are the various festivals which Israel continues to observe! For instance, there is the Passover, which celebrates the great historical event of the Exodus, and the wonders which God wrought for them in bringing them out of Egypt; there are the feasts of Weeks and of Tabernacles, which commemorate the experiences in the wilderness, and their entrance into the promised land; and the many other rites and observances which could only have originated in actual facts in their history, of which they are mementos.

'And as they observe the festivals, so they observe the law of Moses; and it is owing to that law of Moses that they are still in existence, for Israel is not like any of the other nations. Other nations, when they have reached, as it were, their highest point, and when they have been living in great civilisation and luxury, become effete, on account of their immorality, and on account of their wickedness; but Israel has never become effete.

'The sanctities of family life endure in Israel up to this day, owing to the law of Moses, owing to the ten commandments, owing to the ordinances which God gave to His people, and to God Himself watching over them. They are physically, as they ever were, distinguished by their longevity, distinguished by their tenacity and vigour of purpose, distinguished by their mental freshness, so that they are able to enter into any branch of study or into any occupation of life.'

'God's judgment of Israel is the most terrible thing in history—yet they have been preserved to this very day through the power of that very God who punished them so terribly. Here they are, a monument of the truth of God's Word—a monument also of God's faithfulness. None of the persecutions which they have endured have availed to destroy them, neither have they broken their energy, or subdued their indomitable will, or crushed their power of mind; and no sooner was the great pressure which the nations—so-called Christian nations—put upon them removed, than we see them prosper in every country, and take leading positions in every sphere of life, in commerce and politics, as well as in literature and art: showing that the Lord God has made them to be a peculiar people, a nation to be perpetuated; and that it was He who gave them nerve to endure, in order that in the future, when His grace shall melt their hearts, they may be a mighty instrument to show forth His praise. There is still visible among scattered Israel something of blessing and influence, the effect of God's training through so many centuries. Their history since the rejection of Christ is unspeakably sad; yet we cannot help noticing that in the midst of Christless Israel some traces of the grandeur and beauty of their fathers' house still linger.

'Behold their zeal for God, their zeal for the Scriptures, their zeal for the Sabbath day; behold the sacrifices which they make in order to carry out the injunctions of the law. Yes, there are many features in the Jewish character which we cannot explain in any other way than this—that there is still a blessing resting on them; that the voice of God which was heard upon Sinai has still its echo in their hearts and consciences; and that the prayers which have been offered up on their behalf, by patriarchs, kings, prophets, and saints, are still held in remembrance before the throne of God.'

(A. Saphir)

God of the covenant, Triune Jehovah,
Marvels of mercy adoring we see;
Seeker of souls, in the counsels eternal
Binding Thy lost ones for ever to Thee.

Not now by words bringing death to transgressors,
Grace unto life the new covenant brings,
Jesus our Surety, our Kinsman-Redeemer,
Round us the robe of His righteousness flings.

Blessings on blessings through ages unending,
Covenant fulness in glorious flood;
Ours is a hope which no mortal can measure,
Brought in by Jesus and sealed in His blood.

God of the covenant—changeless, eternal,
Father, Son, Spirit in blessing agree;
Thine be the glory, our weakness confessing,
Triune Jehovah, we rest upon Thee.

(Jessie F. Webb)

The Witness of the Jews to the Old Testament

By James Gosset-Tanner

In these days of doubt and unbelief, when all the foundations, on which we have hitherto relied, are shaken, and when those things which have been most surely believed for above 2,000 years are confidently denied, it is well for us to consider the reasons why we maintain the absolute genuineness and entire inspiration of the Old Testament.

It is evident to the unprejudiced Bible student that the various portions of the Bible, as they were successively written, were handed over to the heads of the Jewish Church, and accepted by them as inspired. We are told that 'Moses wrote the law, and delivered it unto the priests, the sons of Levi, and unto all the elders of Israel.' And he solemnly commanded them to read the law before all Israel every seven years, at the Feast of Tabernacles. He also ordered that the book should be kept in the side of the ark (Deut. 31.9-13, 25, 26). As soon as Moses died, the Lord's injunction to Joshua was, 'This book of the law shall not depart out of thy mouth; but thou shalt meditate therein day and night' (Josh. 1.8). There is copious reference to it in the subsequent books of the Old Testament, and very especially in the Book of Psalms. Joshua evidently wrote his own book (24.26), and, according to Jerome, the last eight verses of Deuteronomy. Other writings by Samuel, Nathan and Gad are alluded to from time to time. Bishop Westcott thought that the first step in the formation of a Canon at once familiar and authoritative was found when Isaiah spoke of 'the book of the Lord' as a general collection of sacred teaching (34.16). But he did not think that the Canon was finally settled until the days of Ezra and Nehemiah. In Daniel's allusion to 'the books' (9.2) he seems to mark the prophetic writings as already collected into a whole. And soon after, Zechariah speaks of 'the law' and 'the former prophets' as in some measure co-ordinate. By the year 131 B.C., when the Greek translation of the Wisdom of Sirach is believed to have been written, the threefold division of the Old Testament had been fully recognized, as 'the law, the prophecies, and the remainder of the books.' It is to this that our Lord set His seal when He said, 'These are the words which I spake unto you, while I was yet with you, that all things must be fulfilled, which were written in the law of Moses, and in the prophets, and in the psalms, concerning Me' (Luke 24.44). So He had often dwelt on this topic in former days, but then the understanding of the disciples was not opened to understand the Scriptures.

The testimony of Josephus is of great value. He writes: 'We have not an innumerable multitude of books among us, disagreeing from and contradicting one another, but only twenty-two books, which contain the records of all the past times; which are justly believed to be Divine; and of them, five belong to Moses. The prophets, which were after Moses, wrote down what was done in their times in thirteen books. The remaining four books contains hymns to God, and precepts for the conduct of human life. How firmly we have given credit to those books of our own nation is evident by what we do; for during so many ages as have already passed, no one has been so bold as either to add anything to them, or to make any change in them; but it becomes natural to all Jews, immediately and from their very birth, to esteem those books to contain Divine doctrines, and to persist in them, and, if occasion, willingly to die for them.'[1]

The translation of the Old Testament into Greek, commonly called the Septuagint, which was made, it is generally believed, about 285 B.C. is a strong proof that the Canon, as we now have it, was accepted by the Jews of Egypt and Palestine at that period. And the existence of the Samaritan Pentateuch, probably dating from the first Captivity of Israel, proves that though the Jews and Samaritans had no dealings with each other, they were united in believing the Five Books to have been written by Moses.

But by far the strongest argument is the seal our Lord set upon the Old Testament. What can be plainer than His words in John 5.46, 47: 'For had ye believed Moses, ye would have believed Me, for

[1] *Against Apion,* 633.

he wrote of Me. But if ye believe not his writings, how shall ye believe My words?' Other passages occur of equal value. Moreover, nearly all the books of the Old Testament are quoted in the New Testament by way of illustration, or proof. And the value of the preserving care exercised by unconverted Hebrews is fully recognized. Stephen alludes to it; and the Apostle Paul writes: "What advantage then hath the Jew? Much every way: chiefly, because that unto them were committed the oracles of God" (Rom. 3.1, 2). We know that lessons from the law and the prophets were regularly read in the Synagogues every Sabbath day after the return from captivity in Babylon, and it is a well-known fact that copies of the Old Testament were made by the Jews with scrupulous, if not superstitious, care.

On this Adolph Saphir well remarks: 'There is no other nation on the face of the earth that could have been induced to preserve books which so pictured their unthankfulness, their constant apostasies, comparing them with the other nations of the world, and saying in effect, "You are worse than any other nation—less loyal to Me than the other nations are to their false gods." Where is the nation which would have preserved for centuries such a record testifying against themselves?'[2] Again he says: 'This remains certain that, according to the commandment of God, all the books that we possess were gradually added and afterwards collected, and, 300 years before our era, existed among the Jews as the only authoritative sacred collection of books, and it is a very remarkable thing that the Jews never had any doubt about these books, although they possessed literature of every kind.' And he adds, with reference to the books of the Apocrypha, that 'the Jews never for a single moment acknowledged them as belonging to the Canon.' And he makes another important observation, that 'even the traditions, which were not committed to paper for eight centuries, were intended only to reverence the Bible, and the reason why, from the time of the Great Synagogue, it was forbidden to write any other tradition, was lest the commentary and the tradition should be confused with the written Word of God, the oracles that were committed to them. So even in their sin and in their tradition, which was contrary to the mind of God, God kept them faithful and loyal as conservators of His Word.' Again, 'because the Scriptures which contain the picture of Jesus remain in the hands of the Jews who have rejected Jesus, none can gainsay their witness.' He further remarks, that during all the period of their dispersion, Israel has been a witness for God. 'Monuments of marble are nothing compared with the nation of millions for eighteen centuries, under the greatest persecutions, and in the most diverse circumstances, commemorating continually the great facts that had been wrought out for them in days of old. There is the Sabbath day. Israel, up to this very hour, every seventh day, keeps the day which God commanded their fathers to keep. Look at all the festivals they keep. Look at the Passover, kept in every Jewish family. They read those chapters of Exodus. They sing hymns of praise. They break the unleavened bread, and all the members of the family partake of it. Shall I remind you of the Day of Atonement, when the Jews fast and humble themselves before God? or the festivals of Weeks and of the New Year? What wonderful mementoes all these are of the facts which took place? What else could have made them observe them, year after year, and century after century? And as they observe the festivals so they observe the law of Moses.'

In fact, we cannot help recognizing that the very existence of the Jews as a nation, and all their ritual, is a continual witness to the absolute truth of the Old Testament.

With regard to the preservation of the fifty-third chapter of Isaiah, Mr. Binney remarks: 'It was unquestionably in being—it was written and read—seven centuries before the events which are supposed to have fulfilled it. It is found in a Jewish, as distinguished from a Christian writing—in a writing admitted, preserved, believed, by those who have every reason for wishing this passage altered or expunged. After the appearing of Jesus Christ, a passage like this could not be introduced into the writings of Isaiah by Christians; the jealousy of the Jews would prevent that. It would not be introduced by the Jews; that would be inconsistent with their unbelief. To be here at all, it must have formed an original part of the prophetical Scriptures. Such it is admitted to be, and admitted by the

[2] *The Divine Unity of Scripture,* pp. 89, 93, 94.

Jew. The book was in the hands of both parties, and the passage in the custody of both; the Jew could not have expunged it, for the Church would have detected and denounced the fraud; the Christian would not, for he exulted in its existence and import.'

Moreover, is not the very existence of the nation of Israel, apart from any belief of theirs, a mighty testimony to the truth of the Old Testament Scriptures? Those writings abound with predictions of the sorrows, wars, and persecutions, which should come upon them. They also predict that they will not be annihilated by their enemies, but that they will emerge at length as a glorious nation, pre-eminent among the empires of the world. What has been their history during the last 2,000 years? Every effort has been made to exterminate them, by appalling cruelty and by banishment. Psalm 83.3, 4 has been fulfilled. At the present moment, the Anti-Semite passion is very prevalent in many professing Christian countries. Still, the nation exists; it amasses riches; it maintains its old ritual. And while other tribes, such as Briton, Saxon, Norman, Dane, have been fused together, and have lost their special characteristics, the Jews, though dispersed into every corner of the world, have continued distinct and separate. They have a marvellous vitality. And, as so many prophecies regarding them have come to pass, can we doubt that the remainder will be exactly and minutely fulfilled? All Israel will be saved when they see that Messiah whom they have rejected, in all His glory. Then will the nation not only be exalted in righteousness, but it will be dominant among the peoples.

In these days, when the so-called Higher Critics declare, 'We are the men, and wisdom will die with us,' the testimony of the Orthodox Jews to the truth of the Old Testament is most valuable, remembering as we do that they must be better acquainted with Hebrew than any among Gentiles.

And I should like to add that we are largely indebted to the special knowledge and grasp of the Scriptures, both of the Old and New Testaments, possessed by many Hebrew Christians. We think of the philosophic Neander, the accurate and spiritual Edersheim, the multi-form and genial Hellmuth, and, above all, the singular skill of Adolph Saphir, who united a wide acquaintance with general literature with a peculiar insight into the meaning of the Word of God, whose work on the Divine Unity of Scripture is a complete answer to the vain fancies of the present day. I would add the name of David Baron, whose mind is cast in the same mould. May we not believe that when Israel as a nation is converted fresh light will be thrown on many a passage of the Old Testament, and that the beauty, symmetry, and completeness of the Word of God will be more forcibly illustrated than before.

Behold, the mountain of the Lord
In latter days shall rise
On mountain tops above the hills,
And draw the wondering eyes.

The beam that shines from Zion's hill
Shall lighten every land;
The King who reigns in Salem's towers
Shall all the world command.

No strife shall rage, nor hostile feuds
Disturb those peaceful years;
To ploughshares men shall beat their swords,
To pruning-hooks their spears.

To this the joyful nations round,
All tribes and tongues shall flow;
Up to the hill of God, they'll say,
And to His house we'll go.

Among the nations He shall judge;
His judgments truth shall guide;
His sceptre shall protect the just,
And quell the sinner's pride.

Come then, O house of Jacob, come
To worship at His shrine;
And, walking in the light of God,
With holy beauties shine.

(Michael Bruce)

Robert Haldane on the Restoration of Israel (Part I)

[Robert Haldane was a Scot, born in London in 1764, but educated in Scotland. At the age of sixteen he entered upon service at sea under his uncle Viscount Duncan, and was present at the relief of Gibraltar. He left the navy shortly after to settle on his estate near Stirling. Though still unconverted he was concerned for the welfare of humanity, and, like Wordsworth, was stirred with new hopes for the regeneration of mankind by the French Revolution; but his whole outlook was profoundly changed by his personal experience of the saving power of Christ. From thence onward he spent time and talent and wealth in spreading the evangelical gospel. He built so many 'tabernacles' and supported so many preachers that in twelve years he had expended seventy thousand pounds. In 1816 he went to Switzerland and Geneva, and coming into contact with students for the ministry he took them through the Epistle to the Romans. This led not only to many individual conversions, but to a revival of religion, in both Switzerland and France. Amongst those converted were Merle D'Aubigné, Frédéric Monod, Louis Gaussen, and César Malan.

His exposition of the Epistle to the Romans was his *magnum opus,* although he wrote on many subjects; it is a truly magnificent piece of work. The late Dr. Reuben Saillens, with whom it was our privilege to co-operate in earlier years, said of him that he was 'an orthodox of the first water, but his orthodoxy was blended with love and life.'

While the Bible League stands firmly by the fundamental doctrines of the evangelical faith, and in particular affirms its unreserved belief in the verbal inspiration of the original Scriptures, it does not identify itself with any sectional interpretation of Bible teaching. If without controversy it can present both views upon any given theme, it believes it helpful to do so. Hence the present extract from Haldane's *Romans.* So many books and pamphlets have recently appeared in which it is sought to be proved that 'there is no future for the Jew' that a presentation of the opposite view from so orthodox a writer as Robert Haldane is thought by the Editor to be due.

(E. J. Poole-Connor)]

Rom. XI ver. 16.—*For if the first-fruit be holy, the lump is also holy; and if the root be holy, so are the branches.*

The whole of the Apostle's argument goes to establish the restoration of Israel. He shows that they were not cast off,—first, by his own example; and, secondly, by referring to the remnant among them according to the election of grace, which proved that they were not devoted to destruction like Sodom and Gomorrah, ch. 9.29. It was true that the predictions of which he had spoken were fulfilled; but although, consistently with these, they had stumbled, it was not that they should irrevocably fall; but this was the way in which God had appointed salvation to come to the Gentiles. Even in this, however, God had their restoration in view; for the kindness shown to the Gentiles would be the means of provoking their jealousy, and great as were the benefits which accrued to the world from their fall, those of their restoration would be still greater. The verse before us contains a third argument to prove the future conversion of the Jewish nation.

The Apostle here employs two similitudes, one taken from the law, respecting the first-fruits, by which the whole of the harvest was sanctified; and the other from nature, by which, under the figure of a tree, he evidences the truth he is exhibiting respecting the final restoration of the whole nation of Israel. By the first-fruit some understand the first Jewish converts; but it rather appears that both the first-fruit and the root refer to Abraham, as the first-fruit to God, and the root of the Jewish nation. As Abraham was separated to the service of God, so, in the sense of a relative holiness, all his descendants in the line of Isaac were holy, standing in an external relation to God in which no other nation ever stood. But Abraham was also personally holy; and so, in every age, had been many of his descendants through the heir of promise; and so, also, shall be an innumerable multitude of them hereafter. For, according to the figure here employed, they shall as branches be graffed in again, and so all Israel shall be saved.

It is therefore here shown that the future conversion of Israel is guaranteed by the peculiar covenant relation in which they stand to Abraham. Although the whole nation had never been internally holy, they had all along been in a peculiar manner separated or consecrated to God, in the same way as, according to the law, the first-fruits of the harvest were consecrated; for when the corn was kneaded, a cake of the first of the dough was to be given to the Lord, Num. 15.19-21; and thus the whole of the harvest was set apart or sanctified, 1 Tim. 4: 5. On this ground, Moses, even when reminding the Israelites of their unhallowed rebellion against God in the wilderness, declared, 'Thou art a holy people unto the Lord thy God: the Lord thy God hath chosen thee to be a special people unto Himself,' Deut. 7.6. And a little after, when rehearsing to them their several rebellions, and informing them that the Lord had pronounced them to be 'a stiff-necked people,' and when he claims the heavens and the earth, and all that they contain, as the property of Jehovah, he says to Israel, 'The Lord had a delight in thy fathers to love them, and He chose their seed after them, even you, above all people,' Deut. 10.15, and Deut. 4.37, 14.2, 26.19, and 32.8, 9. 'God,' it is also said, 'heard their groanings, and God remembered His covenant with Abraham, with Isaac, and with Jacob. And God looked upon the children of Israel, and God had respect unto them,' Exod. 2.24. Moses assured the people, the Lord 'will not forsake thee, neither destroy thee, nor forget the covenant of thy fathers which He sware unto them,' Deut. 4.31. And it is said by the Prophet Isaiah, 43.21, 'This people have I formed for Myself.' In like manner, when Samuel was in the strongest terms reproaching Israel for their rebellion, in forsaking the Lord and choosing a king, he still exhorts them to serve the Lord, notwithstanding their past wickedness. 'For,' he adds, 'the Lord will not forsake His people for His great name's sake; because it hath pleased the Lord to make you His people,' 1 Sam. 12.22. Innumerable declarations to the same effect are interspersed throughout the Old Testament. The Apostle's argument then is, that as the lump is holy through the offering of the first-fruit, and as the tree derives its character from the root, so the descendants of Abraham, Isaac, and Jacob, whom the Lord chose, were set apart by solemn covenant for His service and glory.

In consequence of God's love to the fathers, He delivered them from Egypt, and separated them by the Sinai covenant from all other nations as His peculiar people. But while that transaction announced the most important purposes, it was not faultless, Heb. 8.7. It pointed out their duty, but did not communicate those dispositions which are essential to obedience. It was therefore only a figure for the time then present, imposed on them for a season, Heb. 9.9, 10, and intended to be introductory to a better covenant, established upon better promises, by which the law was to be put in their inward parts, and God was to be a God to them in a higher sense than He was by that first covenant. This was taught them in the land of Moab, where God promised to circumcise their heart and the heart of their seed, and is repeated by Isaiah, 59.21, Jeremiah 31.31, and referred to by the Apostle in the 26th and 27th verses of the chapter before us. Thus Israel has been set apart as a holy people, devoted to the service of God, since the call of Abraham. Their unbelief has not made the faithfulness of God of none effect. Their rebellions have all been subservient to His eternal purpose. The tree was of the Lord's right-hand planting, a noble vine; many of the branches have been broken off, but still the root remains, bound round, as it were, 'with a band of iron and brass;' and the branches shall be graffed in again, by their partaking of the faith of Abraham. And as they were God's witnesses when enjoying His blessing in the land of Canaan, Isa. 43.10, 12, 44.8, and are His witnesses in their rejection, and in being 'left as a beacon upon the top of a mountain, and as an ensign on a hill,' Isa. 30.17, so shall they be His witnesses in their restoration. In God's treatment of them we see His abhorrence of sin. In them we behold a memorial of the severity of God, Rom. 11.22; but in them shall also be witnessed a nobler monument of His goodness.

The Apostle's argument, then, amounts to this—that as the lump is holy, through the offering of the first-fruits, so this is a pledge that the lump, or body of the nation, will yet be made holy. The restoration of Israel is not only plainly asserted by the Apostle here, but it is essential to the fulfilment of the parable exhibited in God's dealings with the nation of Israel. That nation was a type of the true Israel, and in God's dealings with them all the great doctrines of the Gospel are exhibited. It was therefore necessary that Israel should be restored, otherwise the parable which shadows forth the final preservation of the people of God, declared in Rom. 8.35, would have been incomplete. We see the sovereignty of God in choosing Israel, in bestowing on them so many great advantages, in punishing them so severely, and making the whole to redound to His own glory and the salvation of all who are ordained to eternal life. They have been the chosen instruments employed for the salvation of the world; and their last end, after all their wanderings, and all their rebellions, and all their unbelief, shall exhibit them as the true circumcision who rejoice in Christ Jesus. When, therefore, the calling of the Gentiles and the rebellion of Israel are announced in the strongest terms, it is immediately added, 'Thus saith the Lord, As the new wine is found in the cluster, and one saith, Destroy it not, for a blessing is in it; so will I do for My servants' sakes, that I may not destroy them all. And I will bring forth a seed out of Jacob, and out of Judah an inheritor of My mountains; and Mine elect shall inherit it, and My servants shall dwell there,' Isa. 65.8. 'As a teil tree, and as an oak, whose substance is in them when they cast their leaves, so the holy seed shall be the substance thereof,' Isa. 6.13. All this accords with those repeated declarations of Scripture already referred to, in which it is said that the Lord will never forsake His people, for His great name's sake. It likewise accords with the numerous and peculiar privileges conferred on Israel as a nation, as enumerated in the ninth chapter of this Epistle, and summed up in these words, 'Whose are the fathers, and of whom, as concerning the flesh, Christ came.' And consistently with the whole, it is declared in the sequel of the chapter before us, that the time is coming when all Israel shall be saved, and the natural branches, or descendants of Abraham, shall be graffed in again into their own olive tree. On these grounds it is evident that, while those whom the Apostle calls the 'rest' of Israel, had in the meantime fallen, and although successive generations should behold Jerusalem forsaken, and Israel wandering without a home through the world, yet the restoration of the nation shall hereafter testify the unchangeable faithfulness of that God who, in dividing to the nations their inheritance, 'set the bounds of the people, according to the number of the children of Israel.'

Zion's King shall reign victorious;
  All the earth shall own His sway;
He will make His kingdom glorious;
  He will reign through endless day.

Nations, now from God estrangèd,
  Then shall see a glorious light;
Night to day shall then be changèd,
  Heaven shall triumph in the sight.

Then shall Israel, long dispersèd,
  Mourning seek the Lord their God,
Look on Him whom once they piercèd,
  Own and kiss the chastening rod.

Mighty King, Thine arm revealing,
  Now Thy glorious cause maintain;
Bring the nations help and fhealing,
  Make them subject to Thy reign.

(Thomas Kelly)

Robert Haldane on the Restoration of Israel (Part II)

Robert Haldane's concluding comments on verse 16 are as follows:

Such is the method by which the Apostle in this verse continues to substantiate his declaration that God had not cast away His people. He had shown that their destruction could not have been intended, since a remnant was preserved; and he is now proving that, as a body, they shall finally be restored to God's favour. In declaring the peculiar privileges of Israel, derived from their first progenitors, the Apostle, by exhibiting their distinguished superiority over all other nations, lays a foundation for the forcible warnings which, down to the 23rd verse, he proceeds to deliver to the Gentiles who had been received into the covenant of God. Mr. Stuart remarks of this 16th verse, that it is *illustration* rather than argument; but it is an illustration which has been adopted by the Spirit of God as a pledge of the event. If it be not argument, it is evidence and is recorded as a revelation of the Divine purpose, that the lump, or body of the nation of Israel, shall yet be holy.

Ver. 17.—*And if some of the branches be broken off, and thou, being a wild olive tree, were graffed in among them, and with them partakest of the root and fatness of the olive tree;*

Before alleging anything further to prove the future conversion of the Jews, Paul here, and onwards to the 25th verse, continues to employ the figure of a tree and its branches. In doing so, he takes occasion to administer a salutary caution to the Gentile believers. In this and the following verses, down to the 25th, he warns them to beware of self-preference, or of being puffed up against the Jews, on account of the blessings with which they themselves were now favoured. The Jewish nation was God's olive tree. They were all the people of God in a typical sense, and the greater part of God's true people had been chosen out of them; but now, by their unbelief, some of the branches were broken off from the tree. By the term 'some,' as has been observed, verse 14, is meant not all, Heb. 3.16; for it implies that others, as the Apostle had shown, verses 2-5, remained. And among, or rather instead of, those that were broken off, the Gentiles, who were a wild olive, having had no place in the good olive tree, are now made the children of Abraham by faith in Christ Jesus, Gal. 3.26-29. They were graffed into the good olive tree, whose root Abraham was, and were made partakers of his distinguished privileges. It has sometimes been remarked that there is no graffing in the olive tree. But this makes no difference. The illustration from the process of graffing is the same, whether the operation be performed in the particular tree mentioned or not. Mr. Stuart says that the wild olive 'was often graffed into the fruitful one when it began to decay, and thus not only brought fruit, but caused the decaying olive to revive and flourish.' This, however, whether it be fact or not, is not to the purpose of the Apostle, for he is beating down the arrogance of the Gentile believers, and not pointing out the advantages they occasioned to Jews. Nor is the stock of the olive here supposed to be decayed, but to be full of sap and fatness, to partake of which, and not to benefit the fruitful olive, is the wild olive graffed into the tree.

Ver. 18.—*Boast not against the branches: but if thou boast, thou bearest not the root, but the root thee.*

It is probable, from what is here said, that even in the Apostle's time the Gentile believers were beginning to exhibit an overbearing disposition towards the Jews, and a complacent feeling of self-preference. At all events, the sin against which they are thus warned well describes the spirit that has long prevailed among the Gentiles who profess Christianity. What marvellous ignorance, folly, and vanity, are often displayed even in God's people! Nothing but the constant lessons of the Spirit of God will teach them that all spiritual difference among men is by God's grace.

But if thou boast.—Whenever Gentile Christians feel a disposition to boast with respect to the Jews, let them remember not only that the Jews were first the people of God, but that the first Christians were also Jews. The Jews received no advantage from the Gentiles; but, on the contrary, the Gentiles have received much from the Jews, from whom the Gospel sounded out—its first preachers being Jews, and of whom even Christ Himself, as concerning the flesh, came. The Gentile believers become the children of Abraham, and all the blessings they enjoy are in virtue of that relation. Hence the covenant, Jer. 31.31, includes all believers; yet it is said only to be made with the house of Israel and Judah.

Ver. 19.—*Thou wilt say then, The branches were broken off, that I might be graffed in.*

Ver. 20.—*Well; because of unbelief they were broken off, and thou standest by faith. Be not high-minded, but fear.*

The Gentile believers might reply, that the branches were broken off to give place to them, and in a certain sense this is admitted by the Apostle. But unbelief was the cause of the fall of the Jews, while it is by faith only that the Gentiles stand. It was not, then, on account of their superior merits that they were graffed into the good olive tree, since faith is the gift of God, bestowed on whom He will, and therefore leaves no room for boasting or self-preference. Among the Gentiles who professed the faith, there was soon a great falling away, and 'the man of sin,' though he boasts of being exclusively the good olive tree—the only true church—is broken off altogether, and doomed to inevitable destruction. It becomes all Christians to be humble, and to fear lest they also fall by error of the same kind. It is very usual, when they perceive the errors of other Christians, to glory over them. This is highly unbecoming. If a Christian understands any part of the will of God of which his brethren are still ignorant, it is God that has made the difference. A haughty spirit goeth before a fall; and if arrogance be indulged by any one, it is likely that God will give him up to some error as pernicious as that into which others whom he despises have fallen.

Ver. 21.—*For if God spared not the natural branches, take heed lest He also spare not thee.*

This verse contains another argument by which the Apostle urges the Gentile believers to humility and watchfulness. If the natural branches were not spared, this was an additional reason why those whom He addressed should be on their guard lest they also should fall through unbelief. It appears also to be a prophetical intimation of the apostasy of the great body of the professors of Christianity under the mystery of iniquity.

Ver. 22.—*Behold therefore the goodness and severity of God: on them which fell, severity; but towards thee, goodness, if thou continue in His goodness; otherwise thou also shalt be cut off.*

The Apostle lastly enforces his warning to the Gentile believers by four concluding arguments: First, he calls on them to behold the severity of God's strict justice in cutting off and casting out the unbelieving Jews. Second, to consider His goodness in conferring unmerited favour on the Gentiles, who had attained that righteousness after which they were not following. Third, to remark the necessity of continuing in that goodness, by abiding in the faith of the Gospel; and, Fourth, to observe the assurance that if they abide not in the faith, they should be themselves cut off.

Men generally form in their imagination the character of God according to their own inclination. It is the duty of the Christian to take God's character as it is given by Himself. His goodness is no evidence that He will not punish the guilty; and the most dreadful punishment of the guilty is consistent with the existence of supreme goodness in the Divine character. That God will yet lay righteousness to the line, and judgment to the plummet, is now seen in His treatment of Israel, whom He had so long spared after they had sinned against Him. Let none imagine, then, that He will spare them if guilty, because they have the name of being His people. Rather let them dread the more terrible vengeance on that account. The evidence that we are the true objects of the goodness of God here mentioned, is, that we continue in it, by continuing in the faith of the Gospel. Continuing in goodness is not to be understood here to mean, our continuing in a state of integrity, according to Mr.

Stuart. There is no real difficulty in the expression, continuing in God's goodness. We continue in God's goodness, by continuing in the faith.

Ver. 23.—*And they also, if they abide not still in unbelief, shall be graffed in: for God is able to graff them in again.*

The Apostle having, from the beginning of the 17th verse, pressed upon the believing Gentiles the necessity of humility, now reverts to the subject of the future conversion of the Jews. In order to furnish a new proof of this great event, he introduces a fourth argument (see exposition of verse 16), taken from the power of God. *God is able to graff them in again.*—According to the figure which the Apostle had been employing respecting the casting off and the restoration of that part of the Jewish nation that was blinded, comparing them to branches broken off, there might seem to be no probability that they could be restored. When branches are severed from a tree, they wither and cannot be replaced. Paul, therefore, here refers to the power of God. What is not done in nature, and cannot be effected by the power of man, will be done by God, with whom all things are possible. He is able to make the dry bones live, and to restore the severed branches of the Jewish nation. Some argue that, because the graffing of the Jews into the olive tree here spoken of is conditional, it is not promised. But the Apostle's design is evidently, even in this verse, to excite hopes by showing its possibility. There is no other ground of exclusion with respect to them but unbelief. If that sin were subdued, they would be received. God is able to graff them in if they believe, and He is able also to give them faith.

Ver. 24.—*For if thou wert cut out of the olive tree which is wild by nature, and wert graffed contrary to nature into a good olive tree; how much more shall these, which be the natural branches, be graffed into their own olive tree?*

The former argument, drawn from God's power, is here further insisted on. The Jews were so obstinately prejudiced against the Gospel, that it seemed very improbable that they should ever embrace the truth. But the Apostle had declared the possibility of this being accomplished by the mighty power of God. He now shows its probability. If the Gentiles, he says, who were strangers to the covenants of promise, have been graffed into the good olive tree, how much more is it to be expected that the descendants of the patriarchs, to whom the promises were made, and who are therefore the natural branches, shall be graffed into their own olive tree?

Ver. 25.—*For I would not, brethren, that ye should be ignorant of this mystery (lest ye should be wise in your own conceits,) that blindness in part is happened to Israel, until the fulness of the Gentiles be come in.*

Having in the two preceding verses exhibited first the *possibility,* and next the *probability,* of the restoration of the Jews, according to the order of God's providence, the Apostle, in this and the following verses, down to the 28th, goes on to prove the *certainty* of the future conversion and restoration of Israel. He here addresses the Gentiles as his brethren, thus expressing his affection for them, and stimulates their attention, by declaring that he was about to reveal to them a mystery—a thing hitherto hidden or unknown. The restoration of the Jews is called a mystery, for though declared in the Scriptures, it was not understood. And in this mystery there were two parts, both of which are here unfolded,—first, that blindness is happened to Israel in part only; and, secondly, that this blindness should continue till the fulness of the Gentiles be come in. This mystery was opened to prevent the Gentiles from being *wise in their own conceits,* that is, from being puffed up on account of the preference they now enjoyed. Ignorance of the Scriptures is the cause of high-mindedness in Christians. They are often arrogant and contemptuous through want of knowledge. In the absence of real knowledge, they often suppose that they have a true understanding of things with which they are still unacquainted, and are thus vain and conceited.

Blindness in part is happened to Israel.—This does not mean that their blindness was only partial, and limited in degree, for it was total and complete; but that it did not extend to all Israel, but only to a part, though indeed the far greater part. It is a consolation that the Jews are under no exclusion that forbids the preaching of the Gospel to them, and using every effort for their conversion. Though the national rejection will continue till the appointed time, yet individuals from among them may at any period be brought to the knowledge of God. This fact is of great importance. They are excluded only through unbelief, and this unbelief is not affirmed of all, but only of a part.

Until the fulness of the Gentiles be come in.—Here is the clearest attestation that the blindness of the Jews will yet cease, not only as to individuals, but as to the body. It is not stated at what time this will happen, but it is connected with the fulness of the Gentiles. The fulness of the Gentiles is the accession of the Gentiles to the body of Christ. Here we have another glorious truth presented for our consolation. The world has hitherto groaned under heathen and antichristian idolatry, but the time will come when the kingdoms of this world shall become the kingdoms of our Lord and of His Christ; and this will be closely connected with the recovery of the Jews from their unbelief. This declaration of the Apostle coincides with that remarkable prediction of our blessed Lord: 'Jerusalem shall be trodden down of the Gentiles, until the times of the Gentiles be fulfilled.'

Ver. 26.—*And so all Israel shall be saved: as it is written, There shall come out of Sion the Deliverer, and shall turn away ungodliness from Jacob:*

Here the Apostle further unfolds the mystery of which he would not have his brethren to be ignorant. In the foregoing verse he had declared that blindness had come upon Israel—that blindness which he had before shown was inflicted on part of the Jewish nation by the judgment of God, verses 8-10, which would continue till a certain period was accomplished. He now declares that at that period all Israel shall be saved. The rejection of Israel has been general, but at no period universal. This rejection is to continue till the fulness of the Gentiles shall come in. Then the people of Israel, as a body, shall be brought to the faith of the Gospel. Such expressions as that 'all Israel shall be saved,' are no doubt, in certain situations, capable of limitation; but as no Scripture demands any limitation of this expression, and as the opposition here stated is between a *part* and *all,* there is no warrant to make any exception, and with God this, like all other things, is possible.

As it is written.—'Whether Isaiah, in 59.20' says Mr. Stuart, 'had respect to the salvation of Gospel times, has been called in question. But the context seems to me very clearly to indicate this.' But why are we to rest our conviction on this point on our view of the connection? The Apostle's quotation of the words is ground sufficient to bear the conclusion. This method of treating the Apostle's quotations of prophecy should be most strenuously opposed. That it is prophecy ought to be rested on the ground of its being quoted as prophecy. 'And even if he had respect to temporal deliverance,' Mr. Stuart continues, 'there can be no difficulty in the Apostle's using his words as the vehicle of conveying his own thoughts with regard to spiritual deliverance.' There is indeed no difficulty in supposing that the same prophecy may, in its primary sense, refer to a temporal deliverance, and in its secondary, to a spiritual deliverance. But there is a very great difficulty in supposing that the Apostle would cite a prophecy respecting a temporal deliverance, which had no reference to the deliverance of which he was speaking. This would be very puerile. It would be worse than puerile—it would be a perversion of Scripture. It would be employing a false argument.

There shall come out of Sion the Deliverer, and shall turn away ungodliness from Jacob.—Mount Zion was the special residence of the God of Israel; and out of Zion was to go forth the law, and the word of the Lord from Jerusalem, Isa. 2.3. And though Israel has for a long time departed from Him, yet thither at length will the Redeemer return, and make His word and law powerful to restore them unto Himself. 'He shall set up an ensign for the nations, and shall assemble the outcasts of Israel, and gather together the dispersed of Judah from the four corners of the earth,' Isa. 11.12.

The Deliverer, etc.—These words are quoted from Isa. 59.20, 'And the Redeemer shall come to Zion, and unto them that turn from transgression in Jacob.' Here it is said that the Redeemer or

Deliverer shall come to Zion; but if He come out of Zion He must have come to it previously; as it is said, Psa. 14.7, 'Oh that the salvation of Israel were come out of Zion.' Besides, it is added, He shall come, namely, out of Zion, to them who turn from transgression in Jacob; and such must have thus been turned by Him. We may be assured that the Apostle, speaking by the same Spirit as the Prophet, and directed by the Spirit to quote him, has substantially given the meaning of his words. If Jacob be turned away from transgression, it is this Deliverer who will accomplish the object.

In this prophecy, in the fifty-ninth chapter of Isaiah, God is represented as doing two things. One is, to reproach the Jews with the multitude and enormity of their transgressions; and the other, to promise to them the redemption of the Messiah, and by Him an everlasting covenant. When, therefore, all nations shall be given to the Messiah, and submit to His authority, the prophecies concerning Him will be fulfilled in their utmost extent, and His reign over all the earth will be established.

Yours affectionately

A. Saphir

Christ in the Pentateuch

By T. H. Bendor-Samuel

(an address given at the Annual Meeting of the Bible League, October, 1966)

When St. Paul stood before Agrippa, having been accused of teaching things contrary to the law, he replied in defence, 'I have said none other things than those which the prophets and Moses did say should come' (Acts 26.22). In this claim he was but following our Lord Himself for He said that Moses is the accuser of those who reject Him: 'There is one that accuseth you, even Moses, in whom ye trust. For had ye believed Moses, ye would have believed Me: for he wrote of Me. But if ye believe not his writings, how shall ye believe My words?' (John 5.45-47). We may expect, therefore, to find in the five books of Moses things which concern Jesus Christ. Nor should this surprise us, for God is the same in every age and generation. His grace is unchanging. From the very beginning of time there has been only one way of salvation, namely, faith in God's promises. Jesus Christ is the sum and substance of the promises of God. They are all centred in Him, whether apprehended prospectively in the days of a partial revelation, or retrospectively in our times of a completed revelation.

Christ is to be found in the Old Testament and therefore in the Pentateuch, its initial and basic part, not just as a matter of Biblical prophecy, interesting and instructive to us as we read it today, but because He is the sole answer to human spiritual need and the only way to God. God is not acting today in a different way from His dealings in earlier times. The coming of Jesus Christ has indeed ushered in a new age in the advent of the Kingdom of God, but God's rule in the hearts of men is unchanged in character. The new covenant is a new act of God with a new power but it is the same in principle and is based upon the same laws. Revelation, because it is truly divine revelation and not just human discovery, does not falsify itself in being progressive. Twilight has given place to daylight but the Christ who was formerly dimly glimpsed, and the Christ who is now completely revealed, is one and the same. Even in the twilight men came to God by Him. Nothing shows more clearly the divine origin of Scripture than its remarkable inner unity. From Moses to Paul is a gap of many centuries, with vastly different cultures and thought patterns, but the character, requirements and provisions of God are consistently the same.

Christ is to be found in the Pentateuch in three ways, historical action, covenanted promise and modes of worship.

1. Historical Action

In the books of Moses we read repeatedly of God's breaking in upon history and revealing Himself in a person who can surely be no less and no other than Jesus Christ. These historical manifestations are theophanies, divine appearances. Mysterious indeed they were, but they anticipated and foreshadowed an even greater mystery, the incarnation. Here were truly the 'goings forth' of Him who was of old, from everlasting, who yet came forth out of Bethlehem (Micah 5.2). Mankind, however, has not been redeemed by a theophany but by an incarnate Saviour. The Lord Jesus had not just the appearance of man but He 'took part in flesh and blood'. No mere appearance could have made our Lord our Kinsman and our federal Head. No mere theophany could have fulfilled all righteousness and suffered and bled to save us. The atonement rests upon the real and actual identification of the Saviour with the human race, and could not have been accomplished merely by His visiting us in a form which we could understand. Nevertheless, the theophanies revealed the same Person.

Thus, it was Christ who walked in the garden and talked with Adam and Eve in the cool of the evening (Gen. 3.8). Man's Maker was also man's Companion and Friend until the advent of sin made Him Man's Judge. But man's sin transformed Him also into Saviour, as the great words of the

Protevangelion declare, at once condemning evil, pronouncing its doom and promising deliverance (Gen. 3.15). He it was who clothed Adam and Eve when the shame of their nakedness could not be covered by the fading leaves of their own contrivance, and so, in the provision of their covering at the cost of life, we may well have the institution of access to God by sacrifice. It was the same Christ who sought and found poor wandering Hagar when she fled from her mistress. He knew where she had fled to and He appeared to her there. As Luther said, 'we are all God's Onesimi', and He is ever the Good Shepherd who goes after the lost sheep in the wilderness 'until He find it'. Others have said with Hagar, 'Thou God seest me', and have been rescued and brought back to life and duty (Gen. 16.13).

Christ it was who visited Abraham and sat at his tent door and gave him the promise of the covenant seed in spite of his childless age (Gen. 18.10). He it was who shared with Abraham, 'the friend of God', His purposes for Sodom and patiently received his prayer of intercession for that sinful city and for Lot.

It was Christ who met Jacob at Peniel and wrestled with him until the breaking of the day (Gen. 32.24), touching his strength and turning it into dependence, making wrestling Jacob into clinging Israel who thus, as God's warrior, had power with God and with men. Here indeed is the Christ who transforms and renames, and by whose word Simon becomes Cephas, and Saul becomes Paul. He is the One whose name is secret and wonderful.

It was Christ who was Captain of the Host of Jehovah, demanding Joshua's submission (Joshua 5.14); the Angel of God's presence, promised in Exodus 23.20, the One in whom is God's name, an adversary to our adversaries, who leads His people into their inheritance. It was Christ who appeared to Balaam when he set forth to curse God's elect and stood in the way with a sword to protect them, turning the curse into a blessing (Num. 22.23). We have no power at all to speak anything save that which He puts into our mouth.

And so the history goes forward, lit up again and again by His appearing who is the Angel of Jehovah, showing Himself to Israel at Bochim and saying, 'I will never break my covenant with you' (Judges 2.1); to Gideon (Judges 6.12); to Manoah (Judges 13.18); saving and delivering His people.

Placing all these occasions together we see the very Person and character of the Christ of the Gospels, seeking the lost, redeeming the wayward, delivering the perishing, guiding the wanderers, bringing God's name and grace into operation among men. In these records of history Moses, and the writer of Judges wrote of Christ.

2. Covenanted Promises

In His dealings with men, God of His own free love, enters into covenant with them and makes them pledges and promises which He will not and cannot break. These 'exceeding great and precious promises' are all centred in Christ. He is the instrument and fulfilment of them all. Moses pointed to Christ when he wrote of the coming seed of the woman who should bruise the serpent's head (Gen. 3.15). It was of Him that Noah spoke when he said: 'Blessed be Jehovah, God of Shem' (Gen. 9.26). The covenant made by God with Abraham was based upon the promise that 'In thee shall all the families of the earth be blessed' (Gen. 12.3). Abraham believed God and it was counted to him for righteousness and so he became the father of all them that believe (Rom. 4.16). It is through Jesus Christ that the blessing of Abraham has come to us (Gal. 3.14). In Genesis, as in embryo, is found the whole Messianic concept, later to be so richly expanded by the Hebrew prophets and realised in the Christ of the gospels. From Abraham was to come blessing for all mankind. The divine call so freely and undeservedly made to him, and to the nation that by God's power sprang out of him, his response of obedience and faith, these formed the source of a rivulet that was to swell and widen through the ages until, in Jesus Christ, from all mankind would be those who share the call and echo the response. Paul can tell the Galatians that 'the blessing of Abraham is come on the Gentiles through Jesus Christ' (Gal. 3.14), because, from its very inception, the substance of the Abrahamic promise *is* Christ. The work of the Lord Jesus has not altered the character of the covenant promise but revealed that which was contained in it from the very beginning. The New Testament teaching that we are not under law but under grace does not introduce anything new. Abraham was saved by grace long before the law was given. Israel was never offered salvation by law, else why the sacrificial system with its promise of pardon to the worshipper who came by faith? Thus in its deepest significance the covenant and the promise speak of Christ.

This promise given to Abraham was confirmed to Isaac and Jacob. It was seen afar by Balaam when he cried, 'There shall come a Star out of Jacob and a Sceptre shall rise out of Israel' (Num. 24.17); and by Moses when he said, 'The Lord thy God will raise up unto thee a Prophet from the midst of thee, of thy brethren, like unto me; unto Him shall ye hearken' (Deut. 18.15). So the mighty stream of divine promise, assured and guaranteed by the immutable covenant, broadens and swells down through prophet, psalmist and sage, finding its fulness in the advent of the Lord Jesus; it is seen from the very beginning here in the books of Moses himself.

3. Modes of worship

The third way in which the Pentateuch contains Christ is in the system of worship given by the Lord to Israel. Here was a divinely ordered form by which alone men could approach God. Much of it can be seen to have existed from the beginning. Later, it was regulated and expanded in the Levitical order established by Moses, the lawgiver. It was a system that had at its heart, from Eden onwards, atonement by sacrifice.

At its centre was the priest, appointed by God and chosen from among men. His ministry made God available to men and men acceptable to God. Aaron, consecrated by water, blood and oil, pictures our great high Priest who has put away sin by the sacrifice of Himself and who now appears before the presence of God for us. His ministry transcends and supersedes that of the human Aaronic priesthood that typified Him, for His is an unchanging priesthood. 'He is made, not after the law of a carnal commandment, but after the power of an endless life' (Heb. 7.16).

Israel's priest ministered in an earthly sanctuary, a shrine that in every detail speaks of Jesus Christ. Here is our approach to God, the one gate into the courtyard, the altar of burnt offering where sin is judged and the sinner cleansed, and the laver of constant cleansing. Here is our life with God in the holy place with its table of presence bread, its lampstand and its altar of incense. It is in Christ that we shine and feed and worship. Here in the most holy place is the ark of the covenant and the mercy seat shadowed by the cherubim; but veil, ark, mercy seat and sprinkled blood, all tell of Jesus Christ and His work for us.

There was not an activity carried on in that centre of worship that does not point to Jesus Christ. The daily burnt offering made each morning and evening, the meal offering in its perfection, the peace offering (the communion service of the Old Testament), the sin and trespass offerings all adumbrated His one perfect and eternal act of expiation on Calvary. All these things had no intrinsic value or effectiveness in themselves. But their meaning was Christ, the Christ who was so surely to come, and thus the faith of those who brought them was faith in Him, and this was indeed effective.

Year by year the covenant people of God possessed the riches of a calendar that pictured the Lord Jesus. The seven annual festivals from Passover and unleavened bread, to the wave sheaf and Pentecost and then on to Trumpets, Atonement and Tabernacles, all brought, each recurring year, anticipations of God's plan of redemption, from the coming of Christ our Passover on to His giving of the Spirit, and then finally His second advent and the far-reaching ingathering that will accompany it.

In these three distinctive ways—interventions in history, covenanted promises, and a revealed system of worship—Christ is to be seen in the Pentateuch. But there is yet a further feature of the books of Moses which speaks to us of Jesus Christ, one that does not lie on the surface but which we are justified in claiming as being Christological on the analogy of New Testament usage, namely, the types. There are typical people—Adam, the son of God (Luke 3.38); Melchizedek, the royal priest; Isaac, the obedient son; Joseph, rejected by his brethren but eventually their saviour; 'Ye thought it for evil, but God meant it for good'. (Gen. 50.20). There are typical things—Adam's coat, Abel's lamb, Noah's ark, Jacob's ladder, the manna in the wilderness, the smitten rock, Aaron's rod, the brazen serpent, the mysterious Urim and Thummin—all these and more are anticipations of the One who was to come. We view them in the fuller light of a completed revelation and they add to the glory of our blessed Redeemer. The men to whom they were given are included in the great cloud of witnesses to whom testimony is given that they lived by faith (Heb. 12.1). The one great object of their faith is the object of our faith also, seen in fuller glory but essentially the same, the Christ of the everlasting gospel. Our thanksgiving is that, in the fulness of His coming, 'God has provided a better thing for us, that they without us should not be made perfect' (Heb. 11.40).

THE CITY OF REFUGE.

" These six cities shall be a refuge, both for the children of Israel and for the stranger, and for the sojourner among them, that every one that killeth any person unawares may flee thither."—*Num.* xxxv. 15.

THE sun sinks low,
And his crimson glow
Is toning to quiet grey,—
Haste, traveller, fly!
For against the sky
Lies the home thou must gain this day.

The road is fair,
The towers stand there,
All clear in the evening light:
There is danger nigh—
Fly, traveller, fly!
If thou would'st be safe this night.

At those city gates
None ever waits,
And within is a home for thee:—
Fly, traveller, fly!
For against the sky
Lies the refuge where thou would'st be,

Safe from all harm,
Not a rude alarm,
Not a fear when once safe within;
For its long repose
A rest foreshows
For the souls that would flee from sin.

The open door
Is for thousands more,
And the city is strong and fair;—
Fly, sinner, fly!
For it stands hard by,
And the Saviour waiteth there.

Israel the Nation

By Philip Henry Gosse

The people of Israel must ever be regarded with an interest unrivalled by that which attaches to any other of the nations of the earth. Where else shall we look for a people who can not only trace back their lineage with certainty to a single ancestor, but can point to historical records of their fortunes, detailing with indubitable truth, with inimitable pathos, and with minute particularity, their lights and shadows, their glories and their sorrows, during a period which stretches away into an antiquity of nearly four thousand years? And what picture of national history could ever display lights so bright, or shadows so deep and dark as this? No people ever stood on such a pinnacle of moral elevation, none ever fell into such an abyss of crime; no nation ever possessed such true grandeur, none ever groaned in such a depth of misery.

But there is one feature that strongly distinguishes the Jewish history and throws it out in broad relief from every other. It is not so much the history of man's actions, as the history of God's dealings with man. Indeed, this might truly be said of all earthly transactions; that the hand of God is in them all, permitting, overruling, guiding, in His ever-watching Providence. 'The Most High ruleth in the kingdom of men; He doeth according to His will . . . among the inhabitants of the earth' (Dan. 4.32, 35). But this general providential acting is not what we prominently see in the records of the Hebrew nation; but the direct and overt interference of Jehovah in Person. The history of the seed of Abraham is a history of miracle; and that not in the way of rare and startling exception, but in its true and proper character; the absence of miracle was the deviation from the rule.

Cradled in Miracle

The nation was cradled in miracle. Their independent existence was effected amidst the most stupendous supernatural plagues upon their oppressors, and by mighty signs and wonders on their behalf. They marched through a divided sea. God Himself descended in the darkness and thick cloud, 'with the sound of a trumpet and the voice of words' to give them 'the fiery law'; the cleft rock assuaged their thirst and they fed upon the bread of heaven; while their forty years' wandering in the wilderness was guided by the pillar of cloud by day and of fire by night. Jordan rolled back its waters to give them entrance into the promised land, and the sun arrested its course to help them to subdue it. But not to recall the numberless instances of Divine interposition scattered throughout the sacred records, we will mention but these two permanent ones, the oracular responses by Urim and Thummim in the high priest's breastplate; and above all, the constant indwelling of the Shekinah or visible glory, first in the tabernacle, and then in the temple, until the Babylonish captivity.

It is true that in the latter periods of their history this intermingling of the Divine with the human was less marked than in the eras of their glory; their incorrigible rebellion and idolatry more and more alienated their gracious King and God, and compelled Him to hide His face from them. Yet this was slowly done: the glory of God lingered, as loath to depart from the holy house (Ezek. 10.4, 18, 19; 11.23). Some of the darkest of their days witnessed glorious manifestations of Divine power, and that in an oppressor's land. Even the guilt of princes and people afforded occasion for the exercise of a miraculous and extraordinary ministry; and the awful denunciations of inspired prophets were so many proofs of the omniscience as well as of the long-suffering mercy of God. The solemn warnings, the affectionate remonstrances, and the tender appeals of these Divinely-inspired addresses, while they showed the deep-seated sin of Israel, most touchingly declared the grace of God and His loving reluctance to break off His familiar communication with them. Nor was this light of prophecy a transient meteor-gleam, but was protracted through many centuries at least, and resembled the shining of the morning star, which increases in brightness when the other stars are waning, and fades only at the approach of the rising sun. For it does not certainly appear that the gift of prophecy was entirely taken from the Jewish nation until the coming of the Lord Himself, when the mission of the servant merged into the superior mission of the Son.

Christ and Israel

The rejection of the meek and lowly Son of Man filled up the iniquity of Israel. 'Full of grace and truth' He came unto His own, but His own received Him not. 'Full of grace and truth' the glorious Word made flesh dwelt among them, but the proud, bitter and worldly spirit that reigned in them had no sympathy with Him. He went about doing good, healing their sicknesses and carrying their sorrows; but with the suicidal fury of a maniac they trampled upon His love, and outraged His power, attributing both to the energy of Beelzebub. He would have healed the daughter of Zion but she would not be healed. 'How often would I have gathered thy children together, even as a hen gathereth her brood under her wings, but ye would not!' And what remained, but that with weeping eyes and a bleeding heart, with a love that many waters could not quench, the rejected King and Lord should pronounce the ruin which He saw to be now inevitable? (Luke 19.41-44).

But even yet there was long-suffering with God. The door of mercy was not immediately closed. The sin was consummated; that guilty deed at which the sun shrank back aghast, and the course of nature was convulsed, the crime of crimes, was accomplished. Man imbrued his hands in the blood of the Son of God, and killed the Prince of Life! The doom was self-pronounced: 'His blood be upon us and upon our children!' but its execution yet lingered. A glorious exhibition was to be given of that truth, 'Where sin abounded grace did much more abound'; and the risen Jesus, sending forth His disciples upon their blessed errand of preaching repentance and remission of sins in His Name, expressly commanded them *to begin at Jerusalem.* And well did they perform their work! Animated by the Holy Spirit, 'with great power gave the apostles witness of the resurrection of the Lord Jesus'; and the burden of their testimony was this: 'The God of our fathers raised up Jesus, whom ye slew and hanged on a tree. Him hath God exalted with His right hand, to be a Prince and a Saviour, for to give repentance to Israel and forgiveness of sins' (Acts 5.30, 31). Amidst scorn, reproach and blasphemy, in stripes and imprisonments, in stonings and deaths, in hunger and thirst, in cold and nakedness, did the disciples of the crucified and risen Lord pursue their untiring labour of love, preaching peace and forgiveness through that precious blood which Israel's guilty hands had shed. Nor was their mission without success, though they might complain that all day long they stretched out their hands unto a disobedient and gainsaying people. Though the national desolation could not be averted, yet a goodly 'election of grace' was found; many myriads of Jews believed the message of eternal life and were gathered into the fold [in Acts 21.20 the word translated 'thousands' in the A.V. is 'myriads' in the Greek].

The Falling of Judgment

But the nation with its rulers was incorrigible. Their zeal for the law took the form of the bitterest hostility to, and persecution of, their Christian brethren; and the very last incident which the sacred historian has recorded of Jerusalem is strikingly and mournfully characteristic of the moral corruption of the time. More than forty of the Jews, *with the full concurrence of the chief priests and elders,* bound themselves under a great curse that they would neither eat nor drink till they had assassinated Paul.

Thus, if we bring the light of the blessed Word of God to bear upon the history of this people, we cannot fail to discover what was the cause of their deplorable overthrow. 'Righteousness exalteth a nation, but sin is the reproach of any people'; and in Israel we behold the deepest sin, accompanied by the highest aggravations, that had ever yet been witnessed in the world. The corruptions of the heathen, vile as they were, could by no means be compared with the criminality of Israel; 'the times of [Gentile] ignorance God winked at' (Acts 17.30); but it is an established principle in His dealings with His creatures, and one which it behoves *us* to remember, that to whomsoever much is given, of the same shall much be required. 'You only have I known of all the families of the earth; *therefore* I will punish you for all your iniquities' (Amos 3.2).

The Messiah and His Birthplace

By T. H. Bendor-Samuel

The Promise to Bethlehem (Micah 5.2).

The prophet Micah was the contemporary of Isaiah in the days when the kingdom of Judah was approaching its end. He witnessed the captivity of the northern kingdom of Israel, a fate that was to befall Judah some 130 years later. Like Isaiah, he shows that contemporary events had to be understood as being directed by God. The fall of Samaria and Jerusalem was on account of their sin. Zion was doomed to be ploughed like a field and reduced to piles of rubble (3.12). But, all through his denunciation of his people's failure, there occur bright glimpses of mercy yet to follow. The mountain of the Lord was to be exalted and Zion was to become the centre from which God's law was to go out to all the earth (4.1-4). It is in this setting that the promise is given of the birth of the Messiah in Bethlehem. The captivity was indeed to be grievous but the ultimate triumph of God's grace was never in doubt. This grace was to be realized through the birth of the One who was both human and divine.

The place of His birth

'Thou Bethlehem Ephratah' (v. 2). Genesis 35.19 gives the original name of the town as Ephratah ('fruitfulness'), and adds the later name, Bethlehem ('house of bread'). It must have been a fertile and pleasant place indeed to have had this double description. How fitting for the birthplace of Him who is the very bread of life! Though the birthplace and home town of king David and the scene of the beautiful meeting and marriage of Boaz and Ruth, his great-grandparents, it was an insignificant place, *'least among the thousands of Judah,'* that is, not counted as a separate district in the tribal divisions. This may have been because of its proximity to Jerusalem, the capital, which was only six miles distant. Yet, from this little place the Messiah was to come. There is no corner of the world where the name of Bethlehem is not famous, for the mighty God chose this place for the greatest event in history, the advent of His own Son. Dr. Pusey quotes Bernard of Clairvaux as saying, 'O Bethlehem, little, but now made great by the Lord, He hath made thee great, who, being great, was in thee made little. What city, if it heard thereof, would not envy thee that most precious stable and the glory of that crib?' David's greater Son came thus to David's city, as the story of the nativity recounts (Matt. 2.5-6). The chief priests and scribes were able to tell Herod that it was there that the Messiah was to be born, an identification that was to result in our Lord's first deliverance from Satan's malice and, alas, in the slaughter of the innocents.

Christ's coming forth

'Out of thee shall he come forth unto me' (v. 2). 'Unto me' could be rendered 'of me', pointing to the fact that Christ's advent was the work of God. If so, then this indeed is a reference to the great power and grace of God. What greater thing and what more helpful thing has almighty God ever done than to send His Son to save mankind? If we read it as 'to me' then it speaks to us of the equally remarkable fact that Christ came to do the will of God. He came in divine power to perform a divine purpose. He came to do much for us but, in the first place, He came to do something for God. His love demanded that His people should be redeemed and it was for this that the Son came. He was the divine instrument.

Christ's divine nature

'Whose goings forth have been from of old, from everlasting' (v. 2). The Messiah was to be of earthly birth, coming out of little Bethlehem. His being, however, was eternal. He had been active from eternity. Here we see the two natures of the incarnate Son of God. Going forth from everlasting and now, going forth from Bethlehem. *'In the beginning was the Word; the same was in the beginning with*

God' (John 1.1-2). When Jesus said that Abraham had rejoiced to see his day His enemies objected, *'Thou art not yet fifty years old and hast thou seen Abraham?'* Jesus replied, *'Before Abraham was, I am'* (John 8.58). Paul tells the Philippians that Christ subsisted *'in the form of God'* and *'was made in the likeness of men'* (Phil. 2.6-7). He says to the Corinthians that, 'though He was rich, yet for your sakes He became poor' (2 Cor. 8.9). Only in the wonderful person of the Lord Jesus Christ, born of the virgin Mary through the power of the Holy Spirit, at once both God and man, can these words of Micah be fulfilled. The incarnation was no expedient, no afterthought. It was the eternal purpose of God, planned before the beginning of time and here promised in this remarkable prophecy. Looking at the wonder of His person, we worship!

Christ's eternal being

'Whose goings forth have been from of old, from everlasting,' 'from days of eternity' (v. 2). It is the eternal God who is *'from everlasting to everlasting'* (Psa. 90.2). The Son shares the eternity of the Father. Proverbs 8.23-30 says of divine wisdom: *'I was set up from everlasting, or ever the earth was. I was daily his delight.'* We see that divine wisdom personified in the Son. He shared the eternal counsels of God. He was the instrument of creation. *'Without Him was not anything made that was made'* (John 1.3). He was the angel of Jehovah who appeared to the fathers, the angel of God's face who was with Israel. All that He did when He went forth from of old finds its culmination in His incarnation when He went forth out of Bethlehem. The one who walked with our first parents in the cool of the Eden day is the one who walked with the disciples in Galilee and walks with us still. He who sought and found fugitive Hagar in the desert, sought and found the woman at Sychar and still seeks and finds. He who led Joshua victoriously into Canaan still leads His people in conquest. The things He did in ancient days He is doing still.

Christ's future greatness

His position is that of ruler. God's promise to David, the founder of the dynasty, was, *'I have covenanted with David, there shall not fail thee, a man to be ruler in Israel'* (2 Chron. 7.18). In spite of all His people's failure, this covenant still stands. It is realized in the Messiah who is to be ruler in Israel. He was *'born king of the Jews'* (Matt. 2.2), crucified *'king of the Jews'* (Matt. 27.37) and will return as king of the Jews. In that great day He will be welcomed, *'Blessed is He that cometh in the name of the Lord'* (Psa. 118.26). The promise that He shall reign has been realized in the risen Lord's ascension to the heavenly throne. He is the ruler of His church through His Spirit who dwells among us. God has given Him the highest place and we, His people, must give Him no place lower. But the prophets also speak of a time that is to come when, first His people, Israel, and then the whole world will acknowledge His authority and rule. That time has not been reached yet. In Micah's day Israel was under God's judgment. 'Therefore will He give them up,' but this is only for a while. The promised birth is to take place and the scattered remnant is to return (v. 3). Then will be seen the full glory of His rule, *'He shall stand and feed in the strength of the Lord, in the majesty of the name of His God and they shall abide'* (v. 4). This, now hidden from unbelieving Israel, will be seen by them. They are His brethren. No longer given up to captivity, they are to be regathered. This is to be accomplished in His strength and majesty. His greatness, who sprang from little Bethlehem is to be unbounded, reaching *'unto the ends of the earth'* (v. 4). Israel's ruler is to be the world's ruler. We rejoice in His presence in glory where He has sat down on His Father's throne (Rev. 3.21). We rejoice in the ever-widening spread of the gospel so that more and more come under His gracious rule. We look forward with joy to the promised day when, at His return, Israel will acknowledge Him as King and Saviour and when His greatness will extend to the ends of the earth.

Drawn from the life by T. Fry. *Engraved by T. Trotter.*

ALEXANDER CRUDEN, M.A.

ALEXANDER CRUDEN
(1699-1770)
(compiler of the first really comprehensive Bible Concordance)

Section Seven

Articles Against Modernism

Contents: Section Seven

Articles Against Modernism

Why I am an Evangelical Christian, and not a Modernist.*

By Dr. A. C. Dixon

"Ready always to give an answer to every man that asketh you a reason concerning the hope that is in you" (1 Peter 3.15).

I am an Evangelical Christian because I am a thinker; not necessarily a profound thinker, but I have a thinking machine so constructed that, when I think some things, I must think other things. When I think intelligent result, I must think intelligent cause. I cannot help it unless my thinking machine is out of order.

Some time ago I stood in an Arizona desert, and here was a leaf of the grease wood, oiled to prevent evaporation in the dry season. Here was another leaf so poised on its stem that, when the wind blew, it presented its edge rather than its side, evidently to prevent evaporation again. Here was the mesquite tree, sending its roots forty feet down into the ground, that it might find water for its sustenance during the dry season. Here was the cactus conserving water during the rainy season and guarding it with thorns, that there might be ample supply for the dry season. As I stood there among these proofs of design, I was compelled to believe that back of all this was not a thing but a thinker; and that thinker can be none other than God.

I am an evangelical Christian because evangelical Christianity believes that back of the material universe is a personal, intelligent, all-powerful God, who created all things and established the laws that govern them.

Christian Free Thought

I am an evangelical Christian because I am a free thinker. Evangelical Christianity encourages me to think. 'What think ye?' asked Christ of His disciples. I verily believe that a healthy mind, which thinks independently, untrammelled by prejudice, when it has collected the proofs in favour of the inspiration of the Bible, the Deity of Christ and other fundamentals of Christianity, must be convinced that its claims are established. And the freedom of thought which comes from thinking God's thoughts after Him, as expressed in Nature and Revelation, exceeds any other liberty which comes to the mind of man. The Psalmist felt great freedom of soul when he wrote, 'I will walk at liberty, for I seek Thy precepts' (Psa. 119.45). There is a universe of liberty in the precepts of God, and all who do not wish to think falsely or ignobly can revel in this world of liberty. 'If ye continue in My word,' said Jesus, 'ye shall know the truth and the truth shall make you free.' Wherever the Bible has gone it has carried with it civil and religious liberty. Ecclesiasticism has fostered the spirit of persecution, but the Bible never. I am an evangelical Christian, because evangelical Christianity, founded upon the Bible, encourages me to think untrammelled by prejudice.

Christian Agnosticism

I am an evangelical Christian because I am an agnostic. Professor Huxley, the famous British scientist, was asked at a social function one evening, what attitude he bore to religion; and his reply was, 'So far as I can tell, I am an agnostic,' by which he meant that he did not know whether there is a God or not. So he refused to affirm or deny. The word 'agnostic' had such a scholastic, academic flavour about it that it became very popular. If Mr. Huxley had used the Latin equivalent, 'ignoramus,' it would not have been so popular.

In a short time papers, magazines and books were filled with writings on agnosticism; the infidelity, that had been defeated in so many fields, took refuge in this bomb-proof of ignorance, of which it was not at all ashamed, but rather exultant.

* Substance of an Address given under the auspices of the Bible League in Caxton Hall, Westminster, June 22nd, 1923. Dr. Dixon was Pastor at the Metropolitan Tabernacle, London (1911-19).

Professor Huxley, in claiming to be an agnostic, simply meant to say that he could not find God by looking through a telescope or microscope, and therefore refused to affirm or deny that there is a God. And we may stand with him on this common ground. No one can find God by looking through a telescope or microscope. There is, however, a strong presumption that, if there is a God, He will reveal Himself in some other way; and, when I turn to the Bible and find God so fully revealed there, I feel like thanking agnosticism for the despair which has led me to its pages. Agnosticism has thus become a good witness to the importance of the Bible as a revelation.

I am, therefore, an evangelical Christian because I am an agnostic. Evangelical Christianity admits the impossibility of finding God through a telescope or microscope, which turns me to the Bible in which God is fully revealed in the Lord Jesus Christ.

Christian Rationalism

I am an evangelical Christian because I am a rationalist. Modern rationalism claims that reason is a sufficient guide without revelation. But whose reason? Mine? or yours? or some other fellow's? There is no universal reason. What is reasonable to one may appear utterly unreasonable to another. There are grades of reason from the idiot to the philosopher. Which shall be my standard?

And reason is easily influenced by prejudice, passion, ignorance, love, hatred, and sin. Did you ever try to convince a man against his prejudices? It was a difficult undertaking. Have you ever reasoned with men in the grip of passion? It was futile. And unless you know everything in the universe, your healthy reason is apt to lead you astray. For, if you do not know everything, there is apt to be a flaw in your premises; and, if there is a flaw in your premises, it is certain that there will be a flaw in your conclusion. Reason blinded by love and inflamed by hate is often the slave of lust! During the French Revolution the cry was raised, 'Down with the Bible!' 'Down with the Church!' 'Up with Reason!' It was to be an age of reason.

But instead of going to the University of Paris for a broad-browed philosopher as the personification of reason, they went to a low variety theatre and selected a dissolute actress, dressed in gaudy attire, and placing her on a throne in Notre Dame called upon the people to worship before this shrine of reason. And they acted more consistently than they thought. Men who claim to be guided by pure reason are often the slaves of lust.

Reason is also a part of the intellectual craft on which we are sailing. It may be a light on deck serving the useful purpose of showing us where to place our feet next and keeping us from falling overboard. It may be even a light at the prow. But sensible pilots do not guide their vessels by lights on the deck or at the prow. If they do so, it means wreck. They guide their vessels by the Pole Star, to which the needle of the mariner's compass points. To attempt to guide our intellectual vessel by unenlightened reason, which is a part of the vessel, is a very unreasonable proceeding. But reason, if enlightened by a revelation from God, will guide us aright.

I am an evangelical Christian because I am willing to be guided by reason enlightened by revelation; and the man who refuses to accept this enlightenment is irrational. He is unreasonable enough to refuse the light which reason needs to make it trustworthy.

Scientific Christianity

I am an evangelical Christian because I am a scientist. Many unbelievers claim that they are dominated by the scientific spirit of the age and cannot therefore be Christians. But what is science? The best dictionaries agree in this definition: 'Science is knowledge gained and verified by exact observation and correct thinking,' and within the circle of this true definition I am an evangelical Christian because I am a scientist. Before the time of Lord Bacon scientists had their theories and sought to make Nature recognize them. As a result the scientific world was divided into contending factions. Bacon insisted that we sit at the feet of Nature and accept what she teaches. First learn the facts and then draw your deductions from them. There seems to be a trend now back to the Pre-Bacon period. Some scientists have accepted a theory of evolution, and they spend their time seeking proofs of their theory instead of confining themselves to 'Knowledge gained and verified by exact observation and correct thinking.'

Germinal Life not Reproductive

Within this sphere of 'Knowledge gained and verified by exact observation and correct thinking' we find that germinal life develops gradually into the mature product. 'First the blade, then the ear, after that the full corn in the ear' (Mark 4.28). And we find that this development is governed by certain fixed laws. One of them is that germinal life is never reproductive. Only the mature product can reproduce a germ or embryo. Embryos do not multiply into embryos. Eggs do not hatch eggs. Apples do not multiply into apples. It takes a tree to produce an apple. Even babies do not bear babies, though they have passed far beyond the embryonic stage. Now, when you leave the realm of 'Knowledge gained and verified by exact observation,' and go into the abysmal past and insist that germinal life without the power of reproduction, shall evolve through millions of years into the mature product, my scientific spirit revolts against the absurdity. It is not a question as to whether God created at first an egg capable of hatching into an eagle under certain conditions of heat. That is not evolution, but direct creation. Evolution demands that the egg shall have been created millions of years ago, and shall gradually evolve through these million years into the eagle. It is unscientific to believe that this can take place without the power of reproduction. The knowledge I have 'gained by exact observation and correct thinking' forbids my believing this biological absurdity.

Germinal Life not Improvable

I find, again, in the scientific realm of 'Knowledge gained and verified by exact observation and correct thinking' that germinal life is unimprovable, except through the mature product. If you would have better apples, you must make better trees. You cannot improve the quality of an apple by working directly upon it. If you would have better eggs, you must make better hens. To attempt to improve the quality of an egg by working directly upon it is almost certain to vitiate its quality, if not destroy its life. If you claim that germinal life came into existence without the mature product, and evolved through millions of years into the mature product without the power of improvement, you multiply my difficulties, if I am to be governed by the scientific spirit. How can I believe that germinal life came into existence in the abysmal past, and continued to exist through millions of years without the power of reproduction, and continued to improve without the power of improvement? It strikes me as utterly unscientific to accept this two-fold biological absurdity.

Germinal Life not Preservable

I find, also, in the realm of 'Knowledge gained and verified by exact observation and correct thinking,' that germinal life is not preservable, except under favourable conditions, for a limited time. Nature provides for such preservation during a brief period, but under unfavourable conditions germinal life is easily destroyed. A British scientist said to the British Association: 'If embryonic life had come into existence in the chaotic condition under which we claim that it did, it would almost certainly have been destroyed immediately.' It has not, in itself, the power of resistance against unfavourable conditions, and the conditions must be unfavourable, when there is no mature product with the fostering care of motherhood.

If, now, you claim that germinal life came into existence millions of years ago, and continued through long successive ages without the power of reproduction, and continued to improve without the power of improvement, and continued to be preserved without the power of preservation, you have multiplied my difficulties still more. I do not see how a scientific spirit can accept this three-fold biological absurdity.

Germinal Life not Variable

I find, further, that in the realm of 'Knowledge gained and verified by exact observation and correct thinking' one species does not evolve into another species. When two species cross the result is a hyvrid, as in the mule. No reputable scientist claims that one species has ever been seen to evolve into another species. Propagation 'after its kind,' as revealed in the first chapter of Genesis, is universal law. And when you invite me to imagine with you that in the abysmal past this law has somehow been violated by the evolution of one species into another, my scientific spirit revolts against this unscientific procedure. If in this realm of imagination you insist that germinal life continued to exist through long stretches of time without the power of reproduction, continued to be improved without the power of improvement, continued to be preserved without the power of preservation, and that one species has evolved into another contrary to all my 'Knowledge gained and verified by exact observation,' you have multiplied biological absurdities which my scientific spirit cannot accept

The Origin of Evolution

Tracing this evolution to its fountainhead, I find that it originated in an unscientific, speculative age. Between 700 and 300 B.C. there were several schools of evolutionists among the Greek philosophers. Thales, of Miletus, taught that water was the primordial germ. Heraclitus taught that fire was the primordial germ. Pythagoras, the mathematician, taught that number was the primordial germ. Plato, greatest of them all, disagreed with his compeers and insisted that man began equal with the gods and that beasts were degenerate men.

Darwin and Malthus

Charles Darwin in his University course caught the vision of the Greek philosophers and, rejecting the theory of Plato, became an ardent advocate of the hypothesis that everything was evolved from beneath; that life originated with germinal beginnings; that in Nature there is perpetual war, which he called 'the struggle for existence,' the strong and fit destroying the weak and unfit, and thus causing everything to move upward. Darwin did not, so far as I can learn, get his idea of perpetual warfare in Nature from the Greek philosophers, who were more benevolent in their thinking. They believed that all life and form were evolved from beneath by quiet forces, but they did not give the strong the scientific right to destroy the weak. Darwin confesses in his autobiography that he received this suggestion from Rev. Thomas Robert Malthus, an Anglican clergyman, who died in 1834, when Darwin was 25 years of age. I do not know that Darwin ever met Malthus, but he was a careful reader of his books, and in his autobiography acknowledges that he received his suggestion from Malthus, who taught that man increases with geometrical ratio while food supply increases with only arithmetical ratio. Therefore, wars and pestilences are necessary, that the surplus population may be killed off in order that the remainder may survive.

Evolution with its 'struggle for existence' and 'survival of the fittest,' which gives the strong and fit the scientific right to destroy the weak and unfit, is responsible for the destruction and oppression of the weak and unfit by the strong and fit. It has fostered autocratic class distinctions and is no friend to those who stand for the protection of the weak against the oppression of the strong. The greatest war in history, which drenched the world with blood and covered it with human bones, can be traced to this source. If the strong and fit have the scientific right to destroy the weak and unfit, that human progress may be promoted, then Might is Right and Germany should not be criticised for acting upon this principle.

The 'Superman'

Nietzsche, the neurotic German philosopher, hypnotized the German mind with his pagan brute philosophy, 'The weak and botched,' said he, 'shall perish; first principle of humanity. And they ought to be helped to perish. What is more harmful than any vice? Practical sympathy with the botched and weak—Christianity.' 'If what I publish be true,' he wrote to an invalid woman, 'a feeble woman like you would have no right to exist.'

Nietzsche's philosophy of beastliness has its roots in the evolutionary assumption that the strong and fit, in the struggle for existence, have the scientific right to destroy the weak and unfit.

There is only one thing worse than Atheistic evolution and that is the Theistic evolution, which makes God responsible for this infernal method of doing things.

THE MENACE OF EVOLUTION

I tremble for the future of the world if the millions of China are to be moulded and dominated by a philosophy, which gives to the strong and fit the scientific right to destroy the weak and unfit. It is easy for the patriotism of any nation to make its people believe that they are the fittest nation in the world; and if China with that conviction should become conscious of her strength she would become, under masterful military leadership, the menace of the world. Any nation that teaches this pernicious delusion to its youth is now a menace to the peace of the world; and if all nations teach it, war will be the normal method of settling all disputes. Universal peace can never come until nations turn from this voice from the jungle to the song of the angels on the plain of Bethlehem: 'Peace on earth among men of good will.'

If the home is to be preserved as a sacred institution, the evangelical Christianity which teaches that marriage came down from God and not up from the beast is worthy of belief. The jungle theory as to the origin of marriage is to-day keeping busy the divorce courts of the civilized world.

If government came down from God, so that 'the powers that be are ordained of God,' as evangelical Christianity teaches, law will rule in righteousness and courts will mete out justice, but if the basis of government came from the jungle, where brute force prevails, as modernism teaches, the Bolshevist rule by bullet and bayonet is scientific and the scientific mind ought to accept it. This jungle origin of government is to-day a world-wide peril.

If the Bible is a revelation from God through inspired men, as evangelical Christianity believes, its teaching is authoritative and its truths have in them an irresistible dynamic; but if the Bible is a mere record of human experiences, as men have struggled upward from their jungle origin, as modernism insists, its teaching has no authority, and its sayings are to be accepted or rejected by the inner consciousness, which is itself a product of the jungle.

If man came down from God, created in His image, and has been wrecked by sin, as evangelical Christianity teaches, then sin is an intrusion, an enemy that ought to be expelled; but if man came up from the beast through the jungle, as modernism teaches, sin is 'embryonic goodness,' 'righteousness in process of formation,' even a search after good; of course such sin has no guilt and may be condoned if not coddled. Such a delusion makes it easy to believe that sin has no existence, and all things, even theft, falsehood, and murder, are good, because there is no evil in the world.

If the Church has come down from God in the sense that its members are born from above, as evangelical Christianity teaches, we have in this world a unique spiritual organism of which Jesus Christ is the head, endued with an irresistible dynamic 'Power from on high.' But if the Church came up from the beast through the jungle and is the expression of man's struggle out of beastliness into spirituality, as modernism teaches, we have simply one earth-born institution among many, and cannot be optimistic regarding its destiny.

If Christ came down from Heaven, as He says He did, 'the only begotten Son of God' in the sense that He is the only one in the universe begotten of God in a virgin's womb, 'God manifest in the flesh,' as evangelical Christianity teaches, we have in Him a unique personality, God, who is a Spirit, made concrete, thinkable, approachable and lovable; God lowering Himself to our level, that He may lift us to His level. But if Christ is the expression of humanity's struggle up from the beast through the jungle, as modernism teaches, we have in Him simply a combination and culmination of beastliness in body, soul, and spirit, detached from heaven, on the same plane with others, with no power to lift or transfigure except by means of example and influence.

The beast-jungle theory of evolution robs man of his dignity, marriage of its sanctity, government of its authority, the Bible of its trustworthiness, the Church of her power, and Christ of His glory. Such a theory is not based upon 'knowledge gained and verified by exact observation and correct thinking,' but upon unscientific vagaries.

I am an evangelical Christian and not a Modernist because I am an optimist. Of course, I am an optimist because I am an evangelical Christian. But even the natural man loves stars better than darkness, and rainbows better than clouds.

Evangelical Christianity is a religion of hope while Modernism with its denial of the supernatural is a religion of despair, so far as it is a religion at all.

The philosopher Hobbs, one of the most learned men of his day, said while dying, 'I am taking a leap into the dark.' Contrast that with Paul's experience, as he wrote: 'The time of my departure is at hand: I have fought the good fight, I have finished my course, I have kept the faith. Henceforth there is laid up for me a crown of righteousness, and not for me only but for all those who love His appearing.'

In the Greek word translated 'departure' there is a suggestion of lifting anchor, spreading sail and going out of the harbour into the open sea. In Sunday school I used to sing of death as furling sail and casting anchor in the harbour. But to Paul's vision death was not contraction but expansion; not casting anchor in the limitations of time; but lifting anchor and spreading sail for a voyage out of the land-locked harbour of time into the ocean of eternity, with its larger sphere of development and service. When God took Moses into the mount and kissed his soul into heaven, he introduced him into larger knowledge, character, and opportunity. 'To die is gain.' 'When this earthly house of our tabernacle is dissolved, we have a building of God, a house not made with hands, eternal in the heavens.' The house eternal is larger and more substantial than the earthly house. 'Almost well,' said a dying negro Christian; 'a few more breaths and I shall be perfectly well.' 'There is no hope: prepare for the worst,' said an infidel doctor to a dying working man. 'Your "no hope,"' replied the Christian with a radiant face, 'is the brightest hope I ever had. In a short time I will be with Christ and like Him. Hallelujah.' And before we come to death, we can say, 'All things work together for good to them that love God.' 'Your sorrow shall be turned into joy.' 'It is God who said, Light shall shine out of darkness, who shined into our hearts, to give the light of the knowledge of the glory of God in the face of Jesus Christ.' The best the light of the sun can do is to shine away darkness, but God can make light shine out of darkness. Evangelical Christianity makes the path of the Christian shine brighter and brighter till the perfect day, while Modernism without atonement for sin, and the hope of the body based upon the bodily resurrection of Christ, can only grow darker and darker till the perfect night. It is the difference between a bound into the light and a leap into the dark. There is only one thing more to be desired than departing to 'be with Christ which is far better,' and that is His personal return in glory, when 'they that sleep in Jesus will God bring with Him.' 'Come, Lord Jesus, come quickly.'

Lord, Thy Word abideth,
And our footsteps guideth;
Who its truth believeth
Light and joy receiveth.

When our foes are near us,
Then Thy Word doth cheer us,
Word of consolation,
Message of salvation.

When the storms are o'er us,
And dark clouds before us,
Then its light directeth,
And our way protecteth.

Who can tell the pleasure,
Who recount the treasure
By Thy Word imparted
To the simple-hearted?

Word of mercy, giving
Succour to the living;
Word of life, supplying
Comfort to the dying!

O that we discerning
Its most holy learning,
Lord, may love and fear Thee,
Evermore be near Thee.

(Henry W. Baker)

What Modernism Means

By A. H. Finn

An amazing portent has appeared in the Christian world.

There are at the present time teachers and preachers claiming to be Christians—many of them able, thoughtful, earnest, sincere men—who contend even somewhat vehemently that the Christian creeds need to be restated in terms of modern thought. They maintain that these creeds embody an **'outworn theology'** and obsolete philosophy, and that to insist on them means alienating the more thoughtful and educated laity from the Christian religion. Among them there are no doubt differences of degree, some going very much further than others are willing to go, yet inasmuch as all are agreed in demanding that our religious beliefs and teaching should be brought into line with modern thought, it is convenient to designate them as 'modernists' and their system as 'Modernism,' though that word was at first applied to teaching differing somewhat in form from that it has now assumed.

At the outset it has to be noted that they are no mere matters of 'pious opinion' that are called in question. Most of the points at issue are directly concerned with our Lord Himself, His Person and His Word. The Virgin Birth is abandoned, or at the very least considered so doubtful that it ought not to be made an article of faith: the atoning value of the Sacrifice of the Cross is ignored: the bodily Resurrection is interpreted to mean a mere spiritual survival: the Ascension is given a totally different meaning: the Return in Glory dismissed in silence: and, most serious of all, the real Godhead of our Lord is in effect denied.

It is startling to find that these beliefs which for at least 1,500 years have been considered essential to Christianity are now being challenged, denied, or explained away by Christians. Still more ominous is it that these teachings are not confined to any one section or denomination. In the Church of England adherents are found among those who are classed as High and Low, as well as among the Broad Church: there is even an influential body of men calling themselves 'Liberal Evangelicals,' who advocate the modernist views. Adherents are also to be found in Nonconformist denominations that hitherto have prided themselves on being Evangelical. Even in the Church of Rome the somewhat similar teachings of Tyrrell and Loisy have to some extent prevailed.

The assertion made above that the real God-head of Christ is in effect denied may be met by pointing out that those who hold modernist views admit that Christ was Divine and even allow Him the title 'the Son of God'. When, however, they explain what they mean, it becomes evident that these admissions lose all real value. Those who make them assert that the Divine and human natures are **'essentially one,'** and therefore that all men are in some degree divine and all are in a sense sons of God. They consider that Christ possessed this divinity and this sonship in a unique, supreme degree; that in Him we have the fullest revelation of the character of God. In other words they hold that He has shown us what God is because He was like God. That is not at all the same thing as acknowledging that He was Himself God as well as man.

A highly placed dignitary of the Church of England recently published a newspaper article in which he asserted that our Lord was neither omniscient nor omnipotent **'for He was truly man.'**

That sounds logical and reasonable, yet none the less there is a serious flaw in it. Put it in the form of what is called a syllogism, that is making two statements and deducing from them the logical conclusion, and it would run thus:

(a) Man is not omniscient nor omnipotent;
(b) Our Lord was truly man; therefore
(c) Our Lord was neither omniscient nor omnipotent.

A little consideration will show that statement (b) is defective, for it assumes that our Lord was truly man *and nothing more.* That begs the whole question, for the Catholic Faith has ever been that He was truly Man and also truly God.

Compare this with another syllogism:
(a) Animals have not the gift of self-conscious reason;
(b) Man is an animal; therefore
(c) Man has not the gift of self-conscious reason!

Here the conclusion is obviously absurd, and the fallacy is the same as before. Statement (b) is defective, leaving out the very point in which man differs from other animals, and assuming that man is an animal *and nothing more*. If man can be truly an animal, and yet also have a higher nature capable of self-conscious reason, then Christ could be truly man and yet have, united with His manhood, a higher nature capable of omniscience and omnipotence.

But now turn the original syllogism round the other way:
(a) God is omniscient and omnipotent;
(b) Our Lord (it is asserted) was not omniscient and omnipotent; therefore
(c) Our Lord was not God.

The modern teaching, then, although cloaked in seemingly reasonable phrases, does in effect deny the Godhead of our Lord.

'Kenosis'

Here however what is known as the 'Kenosis' theory may be urged. Is it not written that He 'emptied Himself'? and does not that mean that He laid aside His Divine attributes of omniscience and omnipotence?

What does the passage actually say? 'Who being [*Gr.*, being originally, *margin*] in the form of God, counted it not a prize [*Gr.*, a thing to be grasped] to be on an equality with God, but emptied Himself, taking the form of a servant [bond-servant], being made [becoming] in the likeness of men' (Phil. 2.7, R.V. and margins).

The 'emptied Himself,' then, is asserted on the part of One who was originally 'in the form of God.' But that is precisely what the Modernists do not admit. They assert that this is the doctrine of the 'pre-existent Messiah' which was no part of Christ's own teaching, having been borrowed by Paul from non-Christian, Jewish apocalyptic sources. The 'Kenosis' theory, therefore, can only be put forward by those who acknowledge that our Lord was originally in the form of God before He became Man.

Then would come the question what are we to understand by 'emptied Himself.' Is it not clear that it it consisted in taking 'the form of a servant'? He could lay aside His Divine glory and prerogatives as He did. He could not lay aside His Divine nature, and omniscience and omnipotence are essential qualities of that.

In the course of a correspondence which followed the publication of the article above referred to, one writer alleged that our Lord Himself declared that He was not omniscient. That, of course, alludes to the one verse, 'Of that day and that hour knoweth no one, not even the angels in heaven, neither the Son, but the Father' (Mark 13.32), which is often taken to mean that our Lord owned Himself ignorant about the coming of the last day. As against this one isolated passage, there are several recording that our Lord knew the unspoken thoughts of men, was aware of events happening at a distance, and claimed to know the future even to the end of time. Of this last an instance is furnished by the context of the very passage in question. Our Lord had been telling His disciples about the coming of the Son of Man in glory (v. 26), and the signs that should herald His approach (vv. 24, 25), winding up with the emphatic declaration, 'Heaven and earth shall pass away: but My words shall not pass away' (v. 31), which surely implies a knowledge more than human. Is it reasonable to claim the very next verse as a confession of ignorance? Moreover, the wording of the verse itself is significant. Our Lord speaks of 'the Son' absolutely, not here of 'the Son of Man,' and that in close connection with 'the Father.' Now at another time He told His disciples that it was not for them to know the times and seasons 'which the Father hath set within [or, appointed by] His own authority' (Acts 1.7, R.V.). The actual determining of times and seasons is the special prerogative of 'the

Father.' Then it is at least possible to understand the words 'neither the Son but the Father,' as meaning that the Son could only know of that day and hour by reason of His intimate union with the Father.

There is yet another doctrine of the Christian faith impugned by the Modernists, namely, the doctrine of the Trinity. The ancient Creeds do certainly teach us that in the Godhead there are three Persons. Even in the simplest form, that known as the Apostles' Creed, we learn to believe (as the Church Catechism has it) in 'God the Father, who hath made me and all the world; in God the Son, who hath redeemed me and all mankind; and in God the Holy Ghost, who sanctifieth me and all the elect people of God.'

The Trinity

It is evident that this teaching is closely bound up with that other teaching about the Person of Christ. If He was indeed 'the only begotten Son of God,' then there must be more than one Person in the Godhead: there must be God the Son in some way to be distinguished from God the Father. For those who do not believe that our Lord was really God as well as man, the doctrine of the Trinity becomes unnecessary and even mischievous.

On the other hand if the belief in the Three Divine Persons is mistaken, then the belief in the Godhead of Christ becomes impossible. The two teachings must stand or fall together. Therefore the Modernists maintain that the belief in the Trinity is merely a piece of ancient philosophizing now quite discredited and rejected by the more enlightened philosophy of to-day. They do not scruple to assert that to believe in Three Persons in the Godhead is **'Tritheism pure and simple,'** that is a belief in three Gods. So they hold that we must not speak of Persons at all, but only of qualities: that, as one of them has put it, the Father means God's Power; the Son, His Wisdom; and the Holy Ghost, His Love.

The Person of Christ

From all this it is quite clear that what Modernism aims at is not a mere re-stating of Christian belief. It really means substituting an altogether different Creed for the old ones. Yet the views now propounded, so far from being 'modern,' are simply the revival of questions thrashed out and considered to have been settled centuries ago. As to the Person of Christ, it is the old, old difficulty, How can one Person be both God and Man? God is infinite, infallible, all powerful: man is finite, fallible, and frail. How is it possible that these incompatible qualities could be united? As to the Trinity, how can three be one?

Both these problems were eagerly discussed in the first three centuries, and to each of them solutions in two opposite directions were propounded. As to the Person of Christ, some held that He was really God and only seemed to be human: others that He was only a man, but endowed with a Divine Mission, which is really the contention of Modernists (and, it may be added, of Moslems and Unitarians). As to the Trinity, somc held that only the Father is God, the Son and Spirit being either created beings or at least of an inferior nature: others, that Father, Son and Spirit are only different aspects of one and the same Being, which again is not far removed from the Modernist position. Neither the problems involved nor the attempted solutions are in any sense modern. All that is modern is the claim that we are now so much more enlightened, and that our superior knowledge and more accurate philosophic thought reject the answers that have so long been deemed the true ones, namely, those given by the Christian Church.

For the great body of Christians accepted none of the solutions here outlined. As to the Christ it was held that He was both God and Man, the two natures being united indissolubly yet unconfusedly in one Person. As to the Trinity, it was held that each of the three Persons is God and Lord yet 'not three Gods but one God.' No doubt it is difficult to understand how these things can be, yet perhaps not more difficult than to understand how man can have an intellectual and spiritual nature united to a bodily nature, or how anything ever came to exist at all.

It is important, however, to note that the answers embodied in the Creeds were not arrived at by philosophical or metaphysical subtleties. The appeal always was, What do the Scriptures teach? What have Christians believed from the first? That appeal still remains the same.

Article 8 of the Thirty-nine Articles of Religion affirms that the three Creeds 'ought thoroughly to be received and believed: for they may be proved by most certain warrants of Holy Scripture.' How then do those who challenge or explain away fundamental statements of the Creeds deal with the Scriptural warrants on which they are founded? They get rid of them by the simple expedient of declaring that much of what has been received as Scripture is untrustworthy, or rather inherently false.

Two Testaments

For this they have to rely on what is commonly called the Higher Criticism.

So long as that was confined to the Old Testament there were many, both clergy and laity, who seemed to consider that it did not much matter what happened to that so long as we retain the New Testament. The Mosaic law, they thought, is abrogated; the Law and the Prophets have been fulfilled in Christ: we can afford to dispense with these so long as we have the Gospel, which is all that we need.

To argue thus is to lose sight of the organic unity of the Bible as the revelation of God's Will and Ways, and, further, neglects our Lord's own saying, 'These are they which testify of Me.' The saying of Augustine, 'The New Testament is concealed in the Old, and the Old Testament is revealed in the New,' holds good. The New Testament is founded on the Old, springs out of it as a tree from the root, is connected with it by a vital union, and what injures the one must affect the other.

Moreover, those who think the destructive criticism of the Old Testament is of no great importance, fail to perceive that the methods used to disintegrate and depreciate the Old would inevitably be further used to discredit the New. That is exactly what has happened. Modernists claim that what they call '**scientific criticism**' has shown that a very large part of the New Testament is no longer to be relied on. Much of what is contained in the first three Gospels is now said to consist of later additions and accretions which have obscured, or rather supplanted, the real facts of Christ's life and the simplicity of His teaching. In the same way, most of the Apostolic teaching about Christ is set down as not really Christian at all, but derived from Jewish and heathen sources. Especially is the Fourth Gospel the object of attack, as representing the Johannine doctrine of the Incarnate Word (Logos) and not the true Christology. There can be no doubt that the purpose of the author (whoever he may have been) is that declared in ch. 20.31, 'that ye might believe that JESUS is the Christ, the Son of God,' a purpose clearly evident also in the Epistle which is admittedly by the same author. From the solemn affirmation in the Prologue, 'The Word was God,' down to the confession of Thomas, 'My Lord and my God,' that is the belief which the writer strives to instil. More than that, he has supported it by detailed narratives of incidents which the Modernists say never happened, and by sayings and lengthy discourses whichthey declare Christ never uttered. If the author knowingly invented all these, he must have been an unscrupulous liar: if, misled by fanatical enthusiasm, he unconsciously wove this tissue of falsehoods he must have been demented.

A similar indictment of falsity is preferred against much in the Epistles of Paul, those attributed to Peter, the Epistle to the Hebrews, and the Book of the Revelation. It is a very greatly expurgated New Testament which the Modernists accept as genuine, and it is only in this way that they can evade the Scriptural testimony to the Godhead of our Lord, His Virgin Birth, bodily Resurrection, and Ascension.

Here again the Modernists play into the hands of the Moslem. When Mohammedan controversialists are confronted with the testimony that Christ was God found in the New Testament which yet they recognize as the 'Anjeel' (Evangel), part of 'the Book,' i.e., God's Word, they at once reply by asserting, just as the Modernists do, that the true Gospel has been largely adulterated and falsified by the Christians.

How far the criticism relied on by Modernists can fairly be called '**scientific**' may be illustrated by a single example, since to attempt even to outline an examination of the critical methods would take far too long.

It is an essential part of the critical contention that the true account of our Lord's life is to be derived from the passages which are common to the first three Gospels. Yet there are accounts found in all three—the Temptation, Transfiguration, Resurrection, the feeding of 5,000, the Gadarene swine, the cursing of the fig-tree—to which credence is not given. Why is this? They are not rejected on account of deficient evidence, or on grounds of literary criticism, but solely because the critics deem them incredible or inconsistent with the estimate formed of Christ's character. That is not unprejudiced treatment of the evidence, and prejudice is not scientific.

Still the Modernists would claim that their criticism enables them to bring their religious teaching into harmony with the teachings of modern science, and in this sense may be called scientific.

What is Meant by Science?

What then is meant by Science?

It ought to mean the statement of the facts of Nature as far as ascertained in the present state of our knowledge. It is often taken to include the inferences which scientists have drawn from the facts, and those inferences are not necessarily infallible. It may be as well to see how far those inferences might conceivably carry us.

Julian Huxley has recently published a volume in which he asserts that the Christian view, **or any view of God as a personal being, is becoming frankly untenable.** He says, '**A personal creation of the world, in any reasonable sense of that term, is now meaningless except for a hypothetical creation of the original substance of the cosmos in the first instance.**' That would appear to mean that processes of evolution are sufficient to account for all that now exists except possibly for the existence of the original material which somehow or another began to evolve. It would also imply that life has evolved out of lifeless matter, and reason out of unintelligent life. Again he continues, '**Immutability of the fundamental laws of matter and motion . . . and the substitution by science of an orderly for a disorderly conception of nature, makes it impossible to think of occasional interference by God with this world's affairs.**' In other words, because science considers the laws of matter and motion immutable and finds the processes of nature orderly, therefore there cannot be a higher Power to interfere with them. According to that, a man cannot lift a stone from the ground because that would interfere with the 'immutable' law of gravitation! On grounds like these Huxley gives '**the name of God to the sum of the forces acting in the cosmos as perceived and grasped by human mind.**' That goes far beyond the agnosticism of Huxley's illustrious predecessor. It is sheer atheism.

Of course, the Modernists do not go to such lengths as these. They do believe in the existence of a personal God though their conception of Him differs from that presented in the Scriptures and the Creeds. They admit that He has to some extent interfered in the affairs of this world, if only in the mission of Christ. They even allow some sort of Revelation and Inspiration in some parts of Scripture. They do believe in the Power, Wisdom and Love of God. Only they consider that '**Science**' forbids them to accept the Genesis account of the Creation, the Fall and the Deluge, and compels them to reject the miraculous and the supernatural.

At present they seem to occupy a sort of half-way house, a compromise between what they consider that Science requires them to recognize and their own belief in a personal God and in Christ. It is doubtful whether such a precarious position can be permanently held. Suppose, for instance, that Huxley's views should come to be endorsed by practically all scientists as the true teachings of Science, would the Modernists consider themselves bound to bow to scientific teaching so far as to abandon belief in a personal God? That would of necessity mean that all Scripture and the whole of Christianity, including even the residuum to which the Modernists still cling, must be given up as a snare and a delusion.

Science has every right to claim a respectful hearing on matters within its own domain, but we must be very sure that what we are called upon to accept is really Science and not scientific guess-work. With all our wonderful discoveries and laborious research, our scientific knowledge is still very far from being complete and perfect. Some of the greatest scientific men who ever lived have readily owned that what we positively know is but an insignificant fraction of what remains to be learned, and it is rash in the extreme to build theories on partial and incomplete knowledge. What after all do we actually know about matter and motion? How then can we determine their **'fundamental laws'** and pronounce them immutable? All we have a right to say is that so far as human experience goes they behave in an ascertained regular orderly way, but to assert that they never have behaved and never can behave otherwise is to assume that human experience has exhausted all possibilities. In the particular instance of miracles, it also disregards positive testimony that within human experience they have been known to vary from their usual procedure. Very recently indeed we have been informed that the atom, instead of being indivisible as has so long been believed, has been shown by experiment to be exceedingly complex, a sort of solar system in tiniest miniature. If that be so, it may profoundly modify our conception of matter. It has even been suggested that it may show that the transmutation of metals, so long scouted by scientists as an impossible dream of the alchemists, is an actual scientific possibility. At any rate, this should warn us against jumping to the conclusion that Science has said its last word, even in matters that have long been considered definitely settled. When then Modernists claim that we ought to modify our religious beliefs and teaching so as to bring them into agreement with modern thought, modern science and modern philosophy, we do well to remember that human thought, science, philosophy are not immutable. They have varied much in the past and are likely to vary again in the future.

Then too there is the question whether Science is really competent to deal with the matters of religion: whether these come at all within its scope. Scripture and Christianity have from the very first claimed that their teachings have to be received by faith, and that implies that they concern matters beyond our present knowledge and understanding. For instance, a personal God by His very nature must needs be One who far transcends the facts of which our senses can take cognizance. Science properly so called has no right to dogmatize on His existence or non-existence. It has no data to go upon. Creation, too—the bringing into existence of all that now is in the universe—lies far beyond the reach of Science which at the utmost can only tell something of the processes by which the present condition has been reached. To endeavour to clip matters of faith to suit human thought is something like trying to measure infinity with a foot-rule, or to weigh impalpable thought in material balances.

What Modernism Offers

We may now turn to consider what Modernism has to offer in place of the beliefs which have been so long considered the very essence of Christianity.

Its adherents claim as a special merit that it sets before the world a thoroughly human Christ, more reasonable and more acceptable to humanity than the Deified Christ of the Creeds. It is altogether questionable whether the Christ so depicted is one whit more human than the Christ of the Gospels who hungered, thirsted, was wearied, suffered, sorrowed, and wept, and these human traits are as clear in St. John's Gospel as in the other three. So too the Christ of the Creeds was born of a human mother; was possessed of 'a reasonable soul and flesh'; was crucified, dead, and buried. In all this there is no lack of a true humanity.

What does appear, however, is that the Modernists, while representing Christ as **'truly man,'** do not represent him as 'perfect man.' According to them, he was just a Palestinian Jew of nearly 2,000 years ago, with all the limitations of his country, race, and age; ignorant of classical thought and culture as of modern science; ignorant even of the true origin and meaning of his own Hebrew Scriptures, or if not ignorant, then unworthily conforming his teaching to the ignorance of others; fallible in that some of his anticipations of the future have not been justified; not daring to call himself 'good,' and not necessarily sinless though his disciples may have thought him so. What possible claim on our reverence could such an one have? How could we find in him **'the fullest disclosure of the character of God'?** Oh! but he is credited with a **'character of singular beauty,'** and wonderful spiritual insight in his teaching (at least, in as much of the teaching as the critics allow to be genuinely his). As much might be urged for Gautama the Buddha. Why should one be credited more than the other?

The Christ of the Modernists does not even reach the level of an ideal humanity.

What then of the teaching?

The Modernists insist much on the beauty, sublimity, spirituality of Christ's moral teaching. Yet even in the 'Sermon on the Mount,' so often taken to be almost the sum and substance of His teaching, He speaks with an authority which is surely something more than human. He asserts that He came to fulfil the Law and the Prophets: He claims to supersede the received interpretation of a law believed to be Divine by His mere 'I say unto you': He claims that He Himself will reject those who call Him Lord but work iniquity: He ends by declaring that those who hear and do His words are building on a Rock. If He was no more than the Modernists make out, would not all this be inexcusable arrogance?

Again, it is asserted that He preached, not Himself but the Kingdom of Heaven. Yet it was precisely on the charge that He made Himself a King that He was accused to the Roman governor. Unless He had claimed to be the King of the Kingdom, what pretext could there have been for this accusation?

At the very best the Modernist Christ could only be a singularly wise and enlightened teacher, who inculcated a pure and lofty morality, and by his life, compassion, and self-sacrificing martyrdom set a noble example for us to follow. That may be a Christ to appeal to the enlightened, civilized, philosophic few. Of what use would he be to the great mass of mankind, the savage, the ignorant, the down-trodden, the tempted, the sinful, the suffering, the dying? Morality? Ah! the precepts are too high above us. Example? We may admire, but how can we hope to imitate? What men really need is a Saviour to deliver, a Mediator to intercede, a Power to uplift. That the Modernist Christ can never be. He has passed (so they say) into **'a mode of being transcending time and space where men live in the presence of God.'** How then can he give us any help, even if he is aware of our struggles and of our needs? He might as well be in the unruffled calm of a Buddhist Nirvana.

The Modernists are earnest in impressing on us that by insisting on what they call the outworn philosophy and theology of the Creeds, we alienate the thoughtful, the educated, the scientific. That is no new accusation to bring against the Christian Gospel. Long, long ago it was to some, even to the wise with the wisdom of the world, foolishness and a stumbling-block. Yet is it, to the believer, the power of God and the wisdom of God.

Stripped of smooth phrases, then, Modernism really means the following assertions:—

(1) That for the truth we must look to human reasonings, not faith;

(2) that much of Scripture, especially in the New Testament, is untrue;

(3) that all down the ages from the days of the Apostles Christ has been misrepresented and His teachings falsified by His own followers;

(4) that plain statements in the Creeds are false, e.g.;

(a) that our Lord JESUS the Christ was God as well as man; *(b)* that He was born of a Virgin; *(c) that He* rose from the dead; *(d)* that He ascended into heaven; *(e)* that He will return to judge the living and the dead; *(f)* that the Holy Spirit is the Lord and Life-giver.

Conclusions

Modernism strips Christianity of its distinctive doctrines, and turns it into a religion in which many a Moslem, Jew, heathen, or agnostic might acquiesce. It would have us believe in a Christ who was but an imperfect moral Teacher, and robs us of much of the Christian hope. By making Science and modern thought the test of truth it stands on the edge of a very slippery down-grade.

It is difficult to understand how ordained clergy of the Church of England who accept these views can consent to go on using in Divine worship a Book of Common Prayer which is full of the teachings they repudiate, but this is not a matter of the special teachings of one branch of the Church. Modernism strikes at the root of all that Christians in all ages have held sacred.

All therefore should unite to contend earnestly against it: all who believe that Holy Scripture is the true word of God, and that in JESUS the Christ we have indeed 'God with us,' the Lamb of God 'who taketh away the sin of the world,' a Saviour and Redeemer 'mighty to save,' an ever-living Intercessor and Advocate enthroned at the right hand of God, Perfect Man truly, yet also

'Very God of very God.'

Testing the Higher Criticism in the Law Courts

By H. E. Irwin, K.C.

Part One

In the year 1910 there passed away one of the outstanding literary men of the last half of the nineteenth century. Reviewing the history of his times, he expressed his opinion that the writings of the so-called Higher Critics of the Bible constituted the particular blot upon the literature of his day.

Some of us who know that the Bible is the very Word of God, a revelation to men of the wisdom of God and His plan for man's redemption, have longed for the day—which was sure to come—when some one or more of this school of the false prophets would have the temerity to step out into the highways of the world,—equipped with the tools and the rules by which they have, as they vainly imagine, analyzed, dissected, rejected, and reconstructed God's Word to the extinction of all spiritual content,—and demonstrate the wonders of their skill and knowledge by applying them to the books of to-day. And this has now actually happened.

A Canadian woman of accredited literary capacity, Miss Florence Deeks, toiled three or more weary years to write the story of woman's part in the world's history. She called it *The Web.* She took the voluminous manuscript to the MacMillan Company of Canada, the Canadian branch of one of the best known publishing houses of Great Britain and the United States. There it lay for six or eight months; at about the end of which period the Anglo-Saxon world was flooded with the loudly heralded *Outline of History* from the press of the English publishing house whose branch in Toronto had had in their possession the manuscript of *The Web* for practically the identical period during which the author of *The Outline* was writing, at terrific speed, the two volumes of his work.

A Damage Suit against H. G. Wells

When she read *The Outline,* the author of *The Web* was convinced that she recognized so many of her own original ideas, and such frequent repetitions of her own sequence of events in narration, that she felt assured that the author of *The Outline* had not merely fallen upon but into *The Web,* and had actually appropriated many parts of it and incorporated them in his book.

She consulted eminent counsel, and brought action for 500,000 dollars' damages against H. G. Wells, the author of *The Outline of History,* and against the MacMillan Company, the publishing house from which it issued, and other commercial houses engaged in promoting its sale.

On behalf of the defendants (Mr. Wells and his publishers) it was alleged that the manuscript of *The Web* had never been in the hands of the author of *The Outline,* that no copy of it or of any portion of it had ever been made, and that no part of the contents of the manuscript had ever, by any other means, been made available to him. They affirmed that it had never been out of the custody of the Toronto house and that the author of *The Outline,* which was written in England, had not been in Canada during the period when the manuscript of *The Web* was in the hands of MacMillans.

The plaintiff had no evidence wherewith to offset this denial. How, then, was she to prove to the satisfaction of a Court of Justice that her unpublished book had been plagiarized? That was a question to stagger the most optimistic of advocates.

But some person conceived a happy thought. Why not seek out the services of one of those men who can take the books of the Bible and by analysis, dissection, and some wonderful faculty known only to themselves, determine just what portion was written by the alleged author; and not only so, but ascertain how many other authors had any part in the finished product, and assign to each the very chapters, verses, or parts of verses, contributed by each?

Set one of these critics to the task, it was urged, and he will ascertain exactly what pages, paragraphs, phrases, and words in *The Outline of History* were taken by its author from the manuscript of *The Web.*

There was at that time in the University of Toronto an Associate Professor of Ancient and Old Testament Languages and Literature, the Rev. W. A. Irwin, M.A., D.B., Ph.D., who reckons among his Alma Maters both Toronto University and Victoria University of Canada, and the University of Chicago. He had been teaching these languages for ten years, and a year later he was appointed to the professorial chair in the Department of Old Testament Languages and Literature at Chicago University.

To him Miss Deeks took her case. I quote from the professor's signed statement, filed in court at his own request, as a part of the plaintiff's case.

> Miss Deeks called upon me, told me the story of her manuscript and her belief that Mr. H. G. Wells had used it in writing his *Outline of History,* and asked me to undertake a study of the two works for evidence bearing upon this contention. I consented, in considerable measure because this is the sort of task with which my study of ancient literatures repeatedly confronts me, and I was interested to test out in modern works the methods commonly applied to those of the ancient world.

A Laboratory of Biblical Dissection

He wrought, and read, extracted, tabulated, and compared, according to the rules approved by the Bible critics and by which they have reached their assured results.

And now for the trial,—for all things are now ready.

The pleadings have been placed on the records of the court. The plaintiff has charged that, with the connivance of the MacMillan Company, H. G. Wells, author of *The Outline of History,* has had access to her unpublished manuscript of *The Web* and has used considerable portions thereof which he has incorporated in *The Outline.* The defendant Wells has alleged in denial that he had no knowledge of *The Web,* had never seen the manuscript, and had never used any portion of its contents. In like manner the defendant, the MacMillans, pleaded in denial that they had never broken faith with Miss Deeks by permitting anyone to have access to the manuscript of *The Web* while it was in their custody.

It is for the plaintiff to prove to the court by satisfactory evidence the facts she had pleaded. And now comes forth the professor, fresh from the laboratory of Biblical dissection, and upon his oath saith that by his analysis and comparisons, and by the application of the rules of Biblical Criticism, it is established beyond a doubt that:—

1\. . . . the author of *The Outline* had access to the manuscript of *The Web.*

2\. . . . the manuscript was at hand as he wrote.

3\. . . . the manuscript was constantly available, lying close at hand on his work table, and referred to repeatedly if not steadily throughout the course of his writing.

4\. . . . Sometimes it lay open before him and his writing was palpably a disguised copying of a passage from *The Web.*

Moreover, we find a privilege accorded to this witness seldom accorded to any witness in a court of justice. In addition to giving his evidence by way of oral answers to questions of counsel, he was permitted to file with the court a sixty-page statement of his findings, with the reasons therefor. Another witness of the same sort was also sworn and heard in the same behalf.

The Verdict of the Courts

The plaintiff's case rested there. With what result?

Listen to the words of the learned trial Judge, the Honourable Mr. Justice Raney, reported in the Ontario Law Reports, 1931, at page 828:

> If I were to accept Professor Irwin's evidence and argument, there would only remain for my consideration the legal questions involved in the piracy of a non-copyright manuscript. But the extracts I have quoted, and the other scores of pages of Professor Irwin's memorandum, are just solemn nonsense. His comparisons are without significance, and his argument and conclusions are alike puerile. Like Gratiano, Professor Irwin spoke 'an infinite deal of nothing.' His reasons are not even 'two grains of wheat hidden in two bushels of chaff.' They are not reasons at all.

The court dismissed the action of plaintiff and gave defendants their large costs.

But perhaps the trial Judge erred. Let us follow on to the Appellate Division of the Supreme Court of Ontario. Four Appeal Judges sit upon the hearing. All agree in dismissing the appeal. One of these Judges, the Hon. Mr. Justice Riddell, is known both in legal and in literary circles throughout Canada and almost equally well known in the larger cities of the United States. He writes a Judgment covering fourteen pages of the Law Reports. In it he says, at page 840: 'I have no hesitation in agreeing with the learned trial Judge in the utter worthlessness of this kind of evidence—it is almost an insult to common sense.' And again: 'I am wholly in accord with the view of the trial Judge as to the weight to be given to this evidence in this case.'

Thus, the application of the methods of the so-called Higher Critics and religious modernists to the determination of the authorship of various portions of a book *written in our own day* is, by the highest authorities on evidence, adjudged and declared to be:

Fantastic hypotheses.

Solemn nonsense.

Almost an insult to common sense.

Utter worthlessness of *this kind* of evidence.

Comparisons without significance.

Arguments and conclusions alike puerile.

Not even two grains of wheat hidden in two bushels of chaff.

Not reasons at all.

Hard to understand how anyone, party or witness, could imagine that any court could accept or be influenced by it.

The plaintiff, Miss Deeks, was not satisfied with the decision of the Appellate Division of the Supreme Court of Ontario. She had the right to carry an appeal to the Supreme Court of Canada, or to carry it directly to the foot of the Throne, and there be heard by the Lords of the Privy Council, the highest Tribunal of Justice and the Court of last resort in the British Empire. She chose the latter, and the hearing of this appeal was begun on the first day of October last, and continued until the morning of November 3, when, on the conclusion of argument for the appellant (the plaintiff in the action), Lord Atkin, the Presiding Justice, delivered the unanimous judgment of the Court, dismissing the appeal.

The proceedings before the trial and at the trial were such that the plaintiff's case rested solely on the weight to be given to the evidence of Professor Irwin. She had not a tittle of evidence to show that the defendant Wells ever had even the possibility of access to the manuscript of *The Web*.

Speaking of this situation, the learned trial Judge, in the concluding words of his written judgment, says:

> The defendants were not, I think, called upon to offer any evidence to rebut Professor Irwin's fantastic hypotheses, but Mr. Wells and the MacMillan Company of Toronto preferred to offer evidence.

This statement of the trial Judge means that if Mr. Wells and the MacMillan Company had chosen to offer no evidence, he (the Judge) would notwithstanding have found that the plaintiff had failed to prove her charge of plagiarism. Or in other words, that he would have found that the 'assured results' of Professor Irwin's comparison and investigation of the two books, made in the approved methods of the Higher Criticism, was no proof at all, and could not properly be made the basis on which to rest a judgment of the Court.

And this finding of the trial Judge stands to-day, approved unanimously by the full bench of the Appellate Division of the Supreme Court of Ontario, and both these judgments have been unanimously affirmed by the highest Tribunal of Justice and the Court of last resort in the British Empire.

This, then, is the settled law of Canada and all the British Empire, not only for a case which involves a claim of 500,000 dollars' damage, but in every case,—be it a claim for one dollar before a rural justice of the peace: *evidence arrived at by the methods of the so-called Higher Criticism is not sufficient whereon to base a judgment that would transfer a dollar bill from the pocket of one party to an action to the pocket of the other party.*

Is it reasonable, is it right, that any fair-minded man, woman, or child should accept this very same kind of evidence as sufficient whereon to base a rejection or even a doubt as to the truth or genuineness of any portion of God's Word?

What, then, becomes of the 'assured results' of the Higher Critics and the Modernists? But that is a trivial question compared with that of the resultant effect in time and in eternity upon the millions who have been misled and deluded by the persistent presentation of these same 'assured'—but now exploded—'results.'

I cannot conclude this article without saying that, after a thorough examination of Professor Irwin's evidence, it would be unfair for me to leave the impression that he was *wittingly* offering a stone for bread. The Word, Old Testament and New, tells us very plainly of a law which psychology, alas, ignores: that the persistent refusal to receive the truth brings on blindness and results in actually believing a lie.

Then, too, there is a condition of mental servitude to a false system which puts into the hands of its servants tools that never can build true. The professor is that servant, and I propose in a further article to show how faithfully he has used the tools, obeyed the rules, and followed the methods with which the so-called Higher Criticism has equipped him, and that they are the same tools, rules, and methods with which it has always wrought in both the textual and Higher Criticism of God's Word, our Bible.

Part Two

Before we consider further Professor Irwin's higher critical work on the manuscript of *The Web* and on *The Outline of History,* let us take a moment to get his angle of vision. We know that his life training and sphere of study was that of Oriental Languages, especially Old Testament Languages and Literature. Moreover he tells us that the problem of ascertaining whether, and to what extent, one author of a work dealing with world history has borrowed portions, methods, and plans of another author on the same subject, 'is the sort of task with which my study of ancient literatures repeatedly confronts me.'

A Higher Critic at Work

He is accustomed, therefore, to dealing with the problem of the authorship of works in ancient literature, more especially the authorship of the Old Testament books, of the languages of which he is now the professorial chief instructor in the University of Chicago. He will, in working out the problem of authorship in these two modern books, use the methods and proceed upon the lines of Higher Criticism that prevail in the great majority of universities. These methods and lines of procedure are defined in the Encyclopaedia Britannica (Vol. 3, page 506) as an attempt to determine:

(a) The scope of the various books,
(b) The time in and the conditions under which they were written,
(c) Whether they are severally the work of one or more authors,
(d) At what date they reached their present form,
(e) Whether they embody earlier sources, and
(f) If so, to reconstruct these and assign dates to them.

Let us pay a visit now to the professor and watch him at his work in his own laboraory. We are not intruding. He has, himself, hung the picture high before public gaze in his signed statement, which lies to-day upon the records of the court. 'My method,' he says, 'was to place the two works side by side, compare parallel passages, and draw my own conclusions.'

The professor approached this work with no lack of confidence. He had his own familiar tools and methods at his command (his appointment in the University of Chicago is evidence of his recognized skill in the handling of these tools and methods), nor had he to dig in unknown soil, for he admits that he possessed 'advantages . . . for such an investigation,' particularly 'in regard to that field of history with which I am most familiar, viz. the Near East.'

A Floating Cosmic Body

As a Higher Critic, he realized from the outset of his investigation that 'the really conclusive evidence' (of the suspected plagiarism) 'will be found, if at all, in details of related passages, affording minute similarities of ideas, words, literary structure, etc.,' and he proceeds to an examination of the way in which the two authors 'immerse themselves in the measureless ages before the world was.' And this is what he finds:

'Both start with a floating (or spinning) cosmic body, which both describe as a 'speck' comparatively (or as it seems to us) which though vast (or prodigious) is small in the 'greater vastness (or immensity) of space.'

'Now these two sentences are identical. It is quite out of the question that they arose independently There is certainly some common source or suggestion back of their resemblance. But we go on. *Web* is here speaking of the sun; *Outline,* of the earth, but at the foot of page five, it turns to tell of the sun. And there it gives us palpably and identically this same sentence of *Web,* re-shaped, it is true, but retaining an astonishing verbal identity. Note these parallels and resemblances:

Web	Outline
In the beginning.	Vast ages ago.
Floated.	Spinning.
Concentrated into a focus of heat and light.	Concentrated into a compact centre of heat and light.
Masses of cosmic matter.	Mass of matter.

'It is to be observed, then, that both immediately (*Web* in the next sentence, *Outline* in the same one) speak of the formation of the planets by the detachment of certain fragments. Both mention the earth as one of these, and both refer verbally in this same context to a solar system.'

'Now these passages take us a step further. The interrelation here cannot be explained as dependence upon a common mere suggestion; the dependence is documentary. Either, one is dependent upon the other, or, both have used a common written source and followed it closely.'

'The conclusion is inescapable. We have here documentary interdependence; no brushing aside as "common knowledge" will suffice.'

An Unsafe Bridge

Miss Deeks, the author of *The Web,* says that her only source has been Duruy's *General History of the World.* The professor recognizes the possibility that Wells might have drawn from some earlier source from which Duruy had drawn, but he dismisses it as 'a strong improbability.' Any impartial, reasoning mind will at once perceive that, so long as there was even a possibility of Wells having drawn from some source from which Duruy had drawn, the professor's whole argument fails. But the barest and frailest of possibilities is always strong enough to carry the full weight of a Higher Critic, so he steps blithely over the bridge of his insecure hypothesis and proceeds:

'The question then remains of the identification of this documentary authority. Miss Deeks puts forward Duruy's *General History of the World* as her one source. Wells did not use nor even know Duruy. The argument then is simple. The similarities of *Outline* to *Web* are due to some documentary source, which Mr. Wells used. That source was not Duruy. It was not a source of Duruy, it was not some unidentified dependent of Duruy; there is no possibility left, but that it was *Web.* Briefly, these two parallel passages prove conclusively that Mr. Wells used Miss Deeks' works. If that be all the case requires, we need go no further, unless indeed to swell the total of evidence.'

To make sure that the professor was working true to form, let us turn to one of his predecessors in the theological circles of Toronto, Dr. J. E. M'Fadyen, a professor at Knox College. Here is a sample from M'Fadyen's *Introduction to the Old Testament.* The writer argues:

1. There are six unhistorical statements in the first seven chapters of Daniel, and this was the period in which Daniel represents himself as living, about 605-530 B.C.

2. The statements in Chapter 11 are a wonderfully accurate summary of the times of Antiochus Epiphanes, in the third and second centuries B.C.

Therefore the book of Daniel was written by some one who lived in or later than the second century B.C.

But what are the real facts? Some twenty years before M'Fadyen wrote this 'Introduction,' the first four of the statements in Daniel that he calls 'unhistorical' had been established as thoroughly historical by newly discovered facts and evidences, then published. The other two, he admits, are, to his mind, just 'improbabilities.' That is, 'the seven years' insanity of Nebuchadnezzar,' which, he says, 'is extremely improbable'; and 'the equally improbable attitude that Nebuchadnezzar in his decree (III.) and his confession (IV.), and of Darius in his decree (VI.), are represented as having adopted toward the God of the Jews.'

And M'Fadyen concludes: 'Only one conclusion is possible—that the book was written in the later period, not the earlier. It is the product of the period which it so minutely reflects.'

Knowing that Chapter 2 of Daniel is set forth as prophecy, M'Fadyen, without attempting an explanation or a word to justify it, argues and concludes that the author of Daniel was an imposter who actually lived in the times of which he fraudulently pretended to be prophesying.

And Professor Irwin was applying to the book written by Mr. Wells the same Higher Critical methods employed by Professor M'Fadyen in dealing with the book of Daniel.

Mental Broad Jumping

Professor Irwin next compares the accounts of the development of animal life, and he finds similarities, which he sets out as follows:

Web	Outline
Millions of years.	Millions of simian generations.
An animal with a relatively enormous brain case, a skilful hand.	One particular creature small brained by our present standards, but it had clever hands.
Dwelt in caves and trees.	It clambered about the trees and ran, and probably ran well, on its hind legs on the ground.
Feeding on nuts and fruits.	It handled fruits and beat nuts upon the rocks.
Much the same as the man-like apes of Borneo to-day.	It was half ape, half monkey.
Tendency to throw stones, flourish sticks, and in general defeat aggression.	Caught up sticks and stones to smite its fellows.
Emerged from the animal into mankind.	It was our ancestor.

Here the professor admits 'there is the possibility again of the unknown source which has accidentally given the same original features as Miss Deeks'; 'but again this is deemed so remote as to be negligible'; and we find another 'assured result' as follows:

> 'So we find conclusive evidence here again that Mr. Wells has taken a passage from Miss Deeks, only thinly disguising his plagiarism by a few slight alterations. And this is written so immediately from Miss Deeks' passage that he must have turned practically direct from her manuscript to his own writing.'

At length the professor gets on his 'familiar ground,' the Near East, and he finds certain similarities in the two books in speaking of 'Phoenician shipping to India.' In comparing the accounts of this historical fact, as set out by the two authors, he finds not many, but a few, unusual features common to both. And being on familiar ground, he is able to take a run and a jump for another 'assured result.'

> 'Once again our conclusion must be that we have clear proof of documentary interrelation.'

The professor cannot find any authority from which Mr. Wells could have drawn his phrasing, which is found similar to that of Miss Deeks. Then he finds himself confronted by this situation: 'The close identities of the two passages are of brief compass, and the balance of the resemblances shows a rather free reshaping, while on the other hand, the context of the description in the two works is totally different.'

Even the alchemy of modern criticism will not enable him to detect Mr. Wells, in this instance, in the act of copying from the manuscript of *Web*. But, says our professor:

'SUPPOSE he had read *Web's* passage just before starting this chapter; unless his memory is one of almost unusual power, the similarities would be much less close than we actually find. *The situation will, however, be satisfied* BY THIS THEORY: In his reading of *Web,* this passage had attracted him; he had made a note of its character and location—the difficulty of locating passages in this manuscript, unprovided as it is with index or table of contents, implies strongly that his notes on relevant passages were written, not mental. Then coming to this section 7, he realizes that this summary of Phoenician Commerce is just the thing he wants; he turns it up, refreshes his memory with a hasty glance, then pushing the manuscript aside, writes this concluding section of his chapter.' How quickly the supposition begets a theory and the theory becomes a fact! It would seem that any theory which the mind of a Higher Critic can conceive as possible becomes inevitably, *ipso facto,* an 'assured result' or an 'inescapable conclusion.'

'Assured Results' again

Again, the professor finds further evidence in the two stories of the history of Israel. He admits that both authors had a common source in the books of Kings and Chronicles, but he finds certain points where *Outline* and *Web* agree in divergence from the Biblical order and content, and the following 'two passages of striking verbal similarities.'

(1) *Web*

> 'received into his harem a princess of declined Egypt.'

Outline

> 'to receive a Babylonian Princess into his harem . . . the steady decline of Egyptian prestige.'

(2) *Web*

> 'to maintain his outward splendour, he so impoverished his people with taxation and oppression that they rose in rebellion.'

Outline

> 'his kingdom long oppressed by taxation to sustain his splendours, breaks off.'

And another assured result!

'There is not a doubt that here again Mr. Wells has used *Web*; and the features demand that he had it on his desk, framing his treatment by its general form and turning to it under each succeeding head for suggestion and direction.'

And so the signed report of the professor, now on the records of the Court, summarizes his 'assured results' as follows:

'So the conclusion of the entire investigation, my answer to the problem which Miss Deeks set me last November is this:

1. Mr. Wells had read Miss Deeks' manuscript before commencing his work on what we now know as the *Outline of History*.
2. He analyzed her manuscript and made frequent notes of features which attracted him.
3. With but unimportant revision he adopted this analysis as a plan for his own writing. His use of the plan of *Web* was such as to justify the epithet,—slavish.
4. Certain passages in the *Web* he took over in detail. He rewrote them in such fashion as might be hoped to obscure their dependence, but they remain a palpable copying.
5. He kept her manuscript readily available as he wrote, apparently at times it was actually open before him, and he made frequent reference to it.
6. He used the *Web* as his chief source and authority.

The Critic Confounded

All this is quite up to the average level of Higher Critical reasoning and is a fair sample of the critics' plea of evidential values. Presented to a Court of Justice, and tried by the standards and rules of evidence which the experience of forty-five generations of Anglo-Saxons on two continents have proved to be the safest for human life and liberty, they are met with amazement that 'anyone, party or witness, could imagine that any Court could accept or be influenced by it.' Why not safeguard God's Word as we do our chattels, and require its accusers to produce some degree of real evidence?

Not in one hundred years have the destructive methods of the critics received such a setback as they have in this case. It is beside the point to say that Higher Criticism itself was not on trial, or that Professor Irwin was not a leading exponent of this school of the critics. The tools and the methods he employed were exactly the same as those used in the critical schools of Germany, England, or America, and their user is a faithful exponent of the school he represents.

In all the history of Bible study there is no more tragic page than that which passes under the name of Higher Criticism, which repudiates the truth of God's revelation to man, makes Almighty God a liar, and denies the testimony of the Holy Spirit who has set His seal of authentication upon the Word. That the methods employed by the critical school are neither sound, sane, nor scholarly has been contended for generations by evangelical scholars. The critics have laughed, and have hurled their gibes and sneers at the 'reactionary' evangelicals. Here are the statements of three unbiased British Courts of Justice regarding their 'scholarship.' Let them laugh these off if they can!

What are we to think of men who set themselves up as scholars and endeavour to correct the 'mistakes of Moses,' yet who fail so miserably in the application of their methods to a modern work where everything would be in their favour? Has it not demonstrated once again that when men forsake the truth, and endeavour by naturalistic presuppositions to 'correct' God's Word, the very light they had becomes darkness and they believe a lie? There is no other explanation for this strange phenomenon of a highly educated man presenting evidence in a court of law that can only be called by the judge 'solemn nonsense' and puerilities which are an amazement to the judges of the Courts of Justice.

The Emancipation from the 'Higher Criticism.'

By Oxonian

The phenomenon known as The Higher Criticism is comparatively modern. The spirit, which animates it, is as old as the third chapter of Genesis. It is only an expression of the inevitable confusion in which the natural mind of man involves itself by a wrong attitude towards the Word of God. And the essence of the matter is given us in the third chapter of St. John's Gospel. Nicodemus, the teacher of Israel, was baffled by the Word of God. And the explanation is given him. He must be born of the Spirit. In those words lies the explanation of the Hihger Criticism. It is not a science, it is not any kind of knowledge. It is just a record of the various blunders which the natural man makes in attempting to understand the Word of God. No amount of intellectual acumen or sincerity is a sufficient safeguard. Men of outstanding genius and undoubted sincerity of purpose have arrived at conclusions which have only aroused the contempt or pity of the next generation of investigators. More than once the very bases of scientific criticism have had to be relaid. But error exposed can only give place to fresh error in minds which have not experienced the birth of the Spirit. The buildings erected are in turn demolished, but the ground upon which they were reared remains—the incapacity of the natural mind to receive the things of God. It is only the reborn soul that can find its way out of this labyrinth of darkness. Until the miracle of the birth from above has opened our eyes, the study of the Bible must in the end engulf us in the bog of 'The Higher Criticism' in one form or another.

Youthful Experiences

Behind this general statement lies a personal experience. I have been tied all my life by the godliness of my upbringing to an inner consciousness that Christianity must be true and real. But until lately that consciousness has brought not happiness but discomfort, not clearness but perplexity, not holiness but the misery due to sin. And throughout this period, in spite of hearing the Gospel explained with perfect clarity and conviction, I was not able to attain any such understanding of it myself, but was always liable to start aside to some new and faulty presentation of it, and that notwithstanding a full realisation, that the whole critical theory was puerile and inconsistent. I had in fact everything to keep me from falling into the abyss of misunderstanding, and yet I was unable to avoid that abyss. Perhaps I may make each point clearer.

My home was Christian in the real sense, so that it was impossible to doubt that the religion which purified it was true. The effect of my father's belief both upon his parish as a whole and upon individuals, who came under my notice, was so unmistakable, that it never occurred to me to doubt that here was the secret of life and the truth of God. And the impression made upon me was so unquestioned that I have never confused right and wrong, or ceased to fight against evil in myself. That fight was of varying intensity at different periods, but it never ceased, and was responsible for continual and growing discomfort of soul. Confirmation had no effect, beyond a slight disappointment that it made so little difference. But on the whole I should unhesitatingly have called myself a Christian, and tried to conceal from myself the unsatisfactory features of my life. Any hint of Higher Criticism had not so far come into my mind.

University Experiences

Then followed a period of education at Oxford. And here was gained the one conviction which always prevented me in later years from being swept off my feet by the Higher Criticism. The study of philosophy convinced me rapidly that truth at any rate was not to be attained by the exercise of the intellect. No system of philosophy could prove its case against any other. In every matter I found the greatest names ranged against each other in a ceaseless and unprofitable battle. Idealism, Materialism, Pragmatism, even Solipsism, all had their defenders, and each was a respectable theory. Above all it was obvious that conduct did not spring from philosophy. One would naturally have expected the fruits of Idealism and Materialism to have been entirely different. But the conduct of their respective supporters was indistinguishable. At the close of this period I was brought into contact with the Higher Criticism, and rejected it at once, as another instance of this wearisome game of intellect. But throughout all this period I had no clear idea myself of Christianity, or indeed of anything else. I was living upon a convention, and old memories of home-training. But conduct and thought alike were without any real guide or light.

Ordination

It was, I think, the old tradition and the inner belief that Christianity must be true, which led me to be ordained as a Minister of the Church of England at this time. But I can safely say that the various types of preparation which I underwent, did nothing to dispel the accumulated fog in my soul or mind. But I was perplexed to find that men holding the most divergent views on every conceivable point of faith and practice were still thought capable of teaching the same truth. I was myself able to accept the thirty-nine Articles and the Prayer Book as true and agreeable to the Bible, and at this period of my life I came nearest to peace of mind. But I can say unhesitatingly that I was not 'born again.' Rather was it that all that I had learned and tested at home came to the top and carried me on for the time.

Teaching Theology

A short time after my ordination I returned to Oxford to teach theology, and here began my real acquaintance with the Higher Criticism. Before I could teach I had to learn, and before long I came to the old deadlock of philosophy. There was nothing definite to teach. There were theories in plenty, arguments by the score. But there was nothing which was beyond the attack of its opponents. Each new book employed itself, perhaps mainly, certainly in part, in exposing the errors of its predecessors. As in philosophy, theory after theory had arisen only to fall under the assaults of its critics. There was nothing to teach except a confused mass of suggestions, probabilities, and exploded theories. The truth of to-day was the error of to-morrow. And the only definite conclusion possible was that one had better trust nothing in the Bible, since so much could be said against everything.

I can safely say that no period of my life was so miserable and disastrous as this. I had indeed achieved utter contempt for the puerility and dishonesty of the Higher Criticism, but I had nothing better to offer myself. And this intellectual and spiritual chaos was followed, as is invariably the case, by moral weakness. It was perfectly obvious that the discrediting of the Bible left one nothing but the moral opinions of men as a guide. And these were so hopelessly at variance that they were worse than useless. Again one was entangled in the old round of argument and theory. Life lost all definition of purpose and thought and action. One was good by fits and bad by fits, without any clear direction of either condition.

As an Army Chaplain

In some such condition I joined up as an Army Chaplain, when the war broke out. Again I found myself one of a number of men taking very different messages to their fellows. I feel sure that my own work was well-nigh useless, if not entirely so. But the end was near. One cannot go on indefinitely in inward struggle. One side or the other must win. There came a day when I made the decision that at all costs the moral knot must be cut. And I began to turn finally to the practice of the words of the Lord Jesus Christ. He might never have uttered them; they might be wrong. But there they were. They were better than my actions. And from that moment began the process outlined in St. John 7.16-17—'My teaching is not Mine, but His that sent Me. If any man willeth to do His will, he shall know of the teaching, whether it be of God, or whether I speak of Myself.' There was a definite moment in my life, when I faced the truth. 'You must cast out of your life what you know to be wrong now, or sink finally into the abyss.' But the decision did not end matters. Rather it was the beginning of a tremendous struggle lasting three years, in which I reached the depths of despair at times. I had also to face a complete nervous breakdown, brought on by some fault in an anti-typhoid inoculation.

It was not until three years had gone by that God finally opened His Word to my understanding. But the faith of despair was born long before that happened, and the Spirit of God was all the time strengthening and cleansing and repairing.

The Spirit Enlightens Me

Now the point which above all others I wish to emphasise, is that it was no intellectual process which enabled me to understand the Bible. Even utter contempt for the Higher Criticism had not helped me one iota. It was only the Spirit of God after my own entire and despairing surrender to God, as the only possible hope, who could make me understand the Revelation of God. So it is always. Faith in the Lord Jesus Christ as our Saviour, and the determination to obey Him, must precede a true understanding of God's Word. The natural man cannot receive the things of God, even when he reads them and knows them by heart. Until the foolishness of the Cross be accepted the veil remains unlifted. And that veil is only done away in Christ. That is the explanation of the obscurantism of the Higher Critics; that is why they refuse to consider the other side; that is why the fulfilment of prophecy is an offence to them. It is because 'The god of this Age hath blinded the minds of the unbelieving, that the light of the Gospel of the Glory of Christ, who is the image of God, should not dawn upon them.' The only weapon we have against the acceptance of the Higher Criticism is the sword of the Spirit, which alone can convict of sin, of righteousness, of judgment. That weapon is 'sharper than any two-edged sword, and piercing even to the dividing of soul and spirit, of both joints and marrow, and quick to discern the thoughts and intents of the heart.' We must labour to produce conviction, not of intellectual error, but of sin; of spiritual, not mental, bankruptcy. We must first preach the Gospel message of salvation to sinners. Only after that has been accepted can we help to show the wisdom of God to unbelievers. We fight, not the conclusions of science, but the darkness of sin, not the difficulties of spiritual men, but the foolishness of natural men. We are, left to ourselves, as foolish as they. The Holy Spirit, who alone enlightens us, can alone enlighten them and lead them into all truth.

Say, Christian, wouldst thou thrive
In knowledge of thy Lord?
Against no Scripture ever strive,
But tremble at His word.

Revere the sacred page;
To injure any part
Betrays, with blind and feeble rage,
A hard and haughty heart.

If aught there dark appear,
Bewail thy want of sight;
No imperfection can be there,
For all God's words are right.

The Scriptures and the Lord
Bear one tremendous name;
The written and the incarnate Word
In all things are the same.

(Joseph Hart)

Section Eight

‘Things that Accompany Salvation’

Contents: Section Eight

'Things that Accompany Salvation'

The Watchwords of Paul's Ministry

By E. K. Simpson

There is an inexhaustible fascination about the life of the great apostle of the Gentiles. The French critic Sainte-Beuve wrote of Pascal, doubtless in a moment of heightened enthusiasm, that his was 'a royal nature, stamped with the seal of the archangel.' I honour the memory of Blaise Pascal, but the words might have been far more fitly penned concerning Paul. His commanding intellectual gifts none call in question except a few supercilious coxcombs; but it is as a new creature in Christ Jesus that he shines a star of the first magnitude in the bright galaxy of the children of light, a steadfast beacon in the spiritual firmament. By the grace of God he became, and wrought the transcendent work which so much surpasses our lame eulogies. In the brief time at our disposal we can only glance at some of the watchwords, or, if you will, ruling principles, of his wonderful ministry, such as are furnished to our hand in that half-autobiographical chapter, the fourth of second Corinthians.

It is instructive to note how large a portion of the Word of God is occupied with details of biography. That is no accident; for the Bible is designed for the whole human family; and nothing interests the average mind so keenly as a life-history skilfully told. Apart from the thoroughly morbid mania for fiction, no department in our public libraries is so well thumbed as that of biography. I conceive that if an uninspired historian had been left to depict the beginnings of the Christian Church, we should have had plenty of particulars about its organization, plenty of statistics, and a *very* elaborate essay on the moral condition of the ancient world; in short, a mass of accessory details; but a very dim and nebulous portraiture of the chief actors in the blessed enterprise: a great deal more background than foreground! How superior is God's method of drafting history! Instead of a formal chronicle of the infant church as such, we are presented with the acts of the apostles, with a sketch of Peter's foundation-laying and Paul's missionary architecture which fixes our attention on the living stones of the Temple, and interweaves the history of the structure itself with that of the master-builders. And what an arresting tale it is! Why, none of your circumnavigations of the globe or expeditions to the poles can vie in charm for one instant with the career of the Apostle Paul, crowded with toils, chequered with trials and crowned with triumphs alike unparalleled. Here surely the instinct of hero-worship may find lawful scope. But viewed more inwardly as an outpouring of love to the Lord Jesus on the part of an ex-persecutor and blasphemer, there is enough fuel of spiritual heroism in this story to kindle and keep aglow the ideals of a lifetime. While we are musing thereon may the sacred fire burn!

The more we ponder the record of this wondrous devotee, the more we admire his dauntless mettle and the more we magnify the grace of God in him. Here is a gallant soul, if ever there were one, fired with a master-passion which burns up the dross of all baser ambitions. Here is an aspirant to a place in the noble army of martyrs, eager to face any odds in the cause of Jesus Christ. Here is a Christian Sir Galahad, sallying forth to tilt with dragons and chimeras dire, bent on scaling Satan's most impregnable fastnesses, penetrating his foulest dungeons, and striking off his prisoners' fetters in the name of the great Captain of Salvation under whose colours Paul is proud to fight, not counting his life dear unto him, so that he may wage a good warfare and finish his course with joy. Here is a crusader true as steel ready to face the gates of hell without blenching, a volunteer for forlorn hopes, prepared to encounter the serried hosts of darkness, not to win some perishable earthly laurel, but the unfading Victoria Cross of the skies; and firmly resolved, when the trumpet of recall shall have sounded and the spoils of battle have been garnered at the King's appointed rendezvous—resolved to cast down all his trophies, and himself among them, at Emmanuel's feet, an offering far too mean to express his inexpressible love and adoration. Truly this man knew what concentration of aim means. He could avouch with good warrant: 'This one thing I do, forgetting the things that are behind and reaching forward to the things that are before, I press towards the mark for the prize of my high calling in Christ Jesus'! There you have one of his watchwords. But I like best to picture him under the emblem of a general entrusted with the conduct of a critical campaign. He frames his manoeuvres with the eye of a great tactician (for a great tactician he was), using all the data available for his guidance; yet submitting all his plans to the revision of his Commander-in-chief, with whom he is in constant communication; for he tells us that he cannot so much as think a thought aright apart from the presiding mind of Christ. I am aware that it is the fashion nowadays to suppose that Paul was very largely left to his own resources, and that he made a blunder in talking philosophically to the Athenians, or in going up to Jerusalem on that last journey at an unpropitious moment. But that does not tally with his own account of his apostleship. We have Augustine's *Retractions,* but where are Paul's? What though the Holy Ghost witnessed that bonds and afflictions awaited him? Nevertheless his purpose *held;* for no prospect however louring could deter him from pursuing the track chalked out for him on heaven's route-maps. Could he not throw out the bold challenge: 'The things that I purpose, do I purpose them according to the flesh'? Surely the Lord's will could embrace his within its encircling folds without trammeling his proper freedom of action. Surely God was not lacking to His elect servant, instant in prayer for direction; surely the signals he received were not so ambiguous that this greatest of all spiritual pioneers and noblest of all defenders and expounders of the faith mistook his road and stumbled into pitfalls of self-will. There is a special providence in the fall of a sparrow; how much more in the itinerary of a chief apostle charged with despatches of the utmost moment to be published to every creature under heaven for the obedience of faith! I cannot believe that the spiritual athlete who when running the last lap of his long-distance race could exclaim: 'I have finished the course': had run at random, or swerved aside from the track.

(1) Sterling Integrity

Let us scan a few of those ruling convictions that braced Paul's soul for his arduous toils, some of them formulated in the chapter named. The first that meets us there is his claim to *sterling integrity* and rectitude of aim Godward and manward. In common with every faithful preacher he disavows all chicanery and double-dealing, all craft and finesse. 'Not handling the word of God deceitfully, but by exhibition of the truth commending ourselves to every man's conscience in the sight of God.' That disclaimer is borne out by all we know of Paul. He stands before us a model of frankness and honest dealing, without one atom of claptrap or artifice, never 'giving the truth a sprain,' as the French express it, in order to gain over a certain class of hearers. Of course a mind so perspicacious and alert as his could not but adapt itself to the capacity and antecedents of the audience he was addressing. None ever excelled the apostle in varying his manner and method to suit varying occasions. But the written word remained his authoritative textbook as it had been his Master's, and that though he himself was an ordained organ of inspiration; and Christ remained his exhaustless theme. In fact, to study manpleasing was in his eyes perfidy in a preacher of the gospel. He could appeal to the Ephesian elders in witness that he had not shunned to declare the whole counsel of God without faltering, without paltering. His traducers twitted him with being a babbler and a fanatic; but malice itself durst not brand him a hypocrite. This man was no mealy-mouthed trimmer, no time-server, and therein lay one secret of his strength. His yea was yea, not a bundle of negations shrouded under a mask of double meanings or tricked out with pretentious bombast. He had nothing in common with the sleek foxes hooded in lamb's-wool who lie in wait to deceive in so many modern pulpits. He belonged to the noble order of the vertebrates, not the ignoble herd of the molluscs. He did not mistake divination for divinity nor oscillation for progress. The joists of his creed were of seasoned timber, and no pressure could make them start.

Once upon a time he had been a rabid Pharisee; but on the Damascus road he was born again from top to toe, new-created every inch a Christian, and took an oath of whole-hearted allegiance to King Jesus for evermore.Christianity as exemplified in him betrays no curvature of the spine; she stands erect, well-knit, unbending. Nobody can detect any taint of Jesuitical cunning in Paul's moral build, any vestige of affinity with the reptile. The furrows he drove all ran straight as a ruler. O for a phalanx of Pauline Ironsides, sound in wind and limb, in this age of religious rickets, when the Church is pestered with so many clerical corkscrews warranted only to wriggle; when so many supple and oily By-ends abound, whose words may be smoother than butter, but war against the eternal verities rankles in their disaffected hearts! Paul's theology was not a jar of mixed pickles assorted to taste. He was not a parasite of the times, 'servile to all the skyey influences,' nor carried off his feet by the undertow of the current of his age. To keep a conscience void of offence was with him a ruling passion; and nothing roused his ire so strongly as the shameful sight of professed disciples of a crucified Lord dangling after the world's harlot embraces, the spectacle of renegade trucklers to Belial ready to sell their Master dog-cheap for the squalid reward of the sycophant and the seducer. In the 'strong breast-plate of a heart untainted' this doughty warrior of the cross took, ay, and he *kept,* the field. Brother, according to the grace given unto thee, go thou and do likewise! And if

'Men heed thee, love thee, praise thee not,
The Master praises; what are men?'

(2) Staunch Faith

What was the secret of the apostle's holy intrepidity? That is no secret: he believed and therefore spake. Let us note then, secondly, his *staunch faith* in the evangel he preached, *'my* gospel,' as he fondly styles it; that was what spurred him on. It appears in this same chapter. What does he virtually say here? That if men are lost, the Gospel is not to blame, but themselves. There is no flaw in the pure white ray that streams from the face of the uplifted Christ; if men prefer darkness, the fault lies in their bleared optics, to which light is painful. In the Father's house there are no empty cupboards, but bread enough and to spare; if any perish with hunger, it is because they are too proud to be beggars at God's door. Very beautiful is Paul's confidence in the untold worth of the tidings he brings, his serene complacency in the grandeur of the message of redeeming love committed to his trust. Remember that in his day the cross was the symbol of all that was foul and revolting, the most abject indignity to which outcast humanity could be reduced. But no criminal associations could tarnish the glory that irradiates Calvary to his purged and lovelit eyes. That loathsome gibbet, that bleeding victim, that visage more marred than any man's, thrills his capacious soul to its inmost depths. A spiritual beauty invests the dying Lamb of God, more unearthly than ever brooded over the ancient sanctuary in the days of its golden prime, when the Shekinah-glory lit up the holiest of all. He catches fire whenever he gets within hail of it. 'God forbid,' he cries, 'that I should glory save in the cross of our Lord Jesus Christ,' the instrument of my crucifixion to the world. This crown-jewel of the truth as it is in Jesus requires to his thinking no florid embellishment, 'then most adorned when unadorned the most.' Enticing words of man's wisdom serve but to obscure its native lustre. There is, there can be, but one such evangel, and Paul hurls a flaming curse at the angel from heaven fool enough to proclaim another. Fitted for every age and clime, potent to subdue supercilious Athens, to purge licentious Corinth, to sweeten reeking Rome, the gospel of the grace of God has to him a virtue in it capable of disinfecting a plague-stricken world. Faith of that stamp awoke responsive faith wherever its persuasive accents were heard. Even when its advocate pled in chains, it well-nigh took King Agrippa by storm. Ifs and peradventures—what deliverance can they work in the earth? They are not watchwords of victory, but omens of defeat. A church of the doubters is a negative quantity in the field. It may find a corner in the sick-list, but it can never rank in the muster-roll of effective troops of the line. Friends, it is a grand thing when a combatant believes in the trustiness of his arms: that puts strength into his sinews. The apostle was fully persuaded that he held God's Excalibur in his grasp, and he smote accordingly. Moody has well said that a mutilated Bible is like a broken sword. Let me add that a splintered sword may easily gash its wielder. But Paul grasped the true Damascus blade of the Spirit, crying, 'Give me that: that has no fellow'! You know his ultimatum to unbelief: 'Let God be true and every man a liar!' As the Puritan Thomas Adams quaintly says: 'God doth not love a nice dainty maidenly faith; He loves a faith that hath boldness in it.' Such was our apostle's. He did not half believe half the contents of half God's revelation, errors and omissions excepted! That would have crippled all his prowess. Not thus had he learned Christ. No, come fair weather or foul, he had embarked all his goods in the Galilean vessel; and so entire was his confidence in her Skipper that he besought all comers to take passage with him in the gallant brig *Unsinkable* bound for the Fair Havens overseas, and certain to ride out every gale.

(3) Sound Doctrine

We remark further that Paul's staunch faith was embedded in a substratum of *sound doctrine.* On this he lays particular emphasis. He covets for his converts the 'full assurance of understanding.' True, the servant knoweth not always what his Lord doeth, and there are seasons when we are called providentially to tread a pathway lying in the dark. Yet Jesus has been pleased to advance us from the rank of servants to that of friends and confidants, and we are bidden to know the things freely given to us to know. Rome extols a blind faith, but the God of knowledge delights in reasonable service. Paul preached a revealed, settled, articulate, ascertained religion. There was a faith of God's elect to be striven for, there was a doctrine according to godliness which was to determine the bounds of Timothy's communion. The Church is not a caravanserai offering free stable-room to all kinds of opinions and speculations. Our holy faith is not the tentative draft of a religion to be licked into shape by 'modern thought.' It is a finished masterpiece bearing the Artist's signature, and woe to him that tampers with it! We are solemnly warned not to allow any counterfeit to be palmed off upon us in its stead.

The spirit of the age, to be sure, avers that what we believe does not matter, and eagerly quotes Pope's sophism:

> For modes of faith let graceless zealots fight;
> His can't be wrong whose life is in the right!

But its belief *is* a matter of life and death to the soul; for 'as a man thinketh in his heart, so is he.' Our creed about smoking or gymnastics or the virtues of cold baths may not greatly matter; on topics like these we 'think and let think.' But when it comes to a question of our state before God, whether innocent or guilty, of the claims of His moral law upon us, and on what terms (if any) He acquits law-breakers, and restores in them His lost image, it is of infinite moment into what mould of doctrine our souls are infused, for we are shaped thereby. All soul-beliefs are formative. The character of our creed fixes ours; we take its ply. Paul insists that a Christian is not a man wise in his own conceits, nor yet a 'babe in the wood' crying for the light, but a man rooted and grounded in the faith, holding it fast and therefore holding it forth; not one who has pious opinions, not a seeker who can say, 'I guess, I fancy, I imagine,' but 'I have found' and 'I know.' No wonder our retailers of dissolving-views resent his fixity, his positivism, of belief; for if he has the mind of Christ, clearly they have not. Yet what is this finality of conviction but our seal set to that God is true? Granted ascertained truth to be here, then neutrality spells treason. 'Who can be loyal and neutral in one moment? No man,' says Shakespeare; and he is right. We *are* partizans of Christ, whole-hearted, unqualified partizans, or what on earth do we mean by calling ourselves Christians? Then let us pay heed to the heart-stirring trumpet-call sounded in our ears by this closest of reasoners and withal sturdiest of believers, resonant as the famous signal flown by Nelson for his hearts of oak at Trafalgar; 'Stand fast in THE faith: quit you like men; be strong.'

(4) Indefatigable Zeal

Now we understand that *indefatigable zeal* of his. Necessity was laid upon him to preach his gospel. No repulses could daunt nor persecutions dismay convictions so intense as his. Oftentimes he was troubled on every side, often in the enemy's line of fire. Perils multiplied thick and fast; you know his famous inventory of them; how he was 'in deaths oft.' Yet his stout heart did not quail nor his resolution falter; for the Eternal God was his refuge, and if he had not the clue of the devious maze he was threading, he knew who had. He was to be sure and sow the right sort of seed; its fruition rested with the Increase-giver. After all, brethren, we must leave our seedplots in charge of the great Husbandman. His spring-tide and harvest shall not fail, whatever may betide our patch of tillage; and

His springtide is best. Only bear in mind that the kingdom of heaven is not a forcing-house, but a field where crops spring up under storm and sunshine, man knoweth not how. He however that regardeth the clouds and forgetteth Him who sitteth upon them, shall not reap. Faint hearts are *not* promised full cornsacks.

(5) Labour of Love

We must not omit to remark that Paul not only preached sound doctrine, but he *lived the application.* His ministry was one long labour of love. Knowledge, mere head-knowledge, puffeth up, but love breaketh down. It was the tenderness which blended so sweetly with the apostle's robust faith that disarmed hostility and evoked affection. As one has said, 'A Paul too proud for tears would never have turned the world upside down.' But when such a Boanerges as he travails in birth till Christ be formed in his hearers; when he yearns over his brethren after the flesh almost to the disregard of his own salvation; when he exclaims, 'Who is weak and I am not weak? Who is affronted and I burn not?' when he protests that he will very gladly spend and be spent for these wrangling Corinthians, or offered on the sacrifice and service of those obscure Philippians' faith, we perceive how radically the leopard that prowled along the Damascus road of yore has been transformed into a gentle lamb, though still intrepid of spirit, and no longer wonder at the sore weeping that marked that final parting with the Ephesian elders. We are not Stoics, at least I hope not; for Jesus wept, and from their Master Paul and Brainerd and Whitefield and many another learnt the holy art, and their sacred tears are fruitful yet. It was in that school Paul was taught the strains of his anthem of love, and how to become all things to all men that he might win some. But it is the old theology of Emmanuel's passion and compassion, not newfangled rodomontade, that can unseal that fountain of effectual tears.

(6) Counsel of Farsightedness

There is one other watchword found in this chapter which invites remark. We might name it Paul's *counsel of farsightedness.* He bids us 'look not at the things that are seen but at the things that are not seen.' So long as we are lodged in a tabernacle of flesh, we shall have to combat the tyranny of the senses. Visible things thrust themselves perpetually on our notice, and their glamour completely dupes the worldling; nor can anything short of a living faith break their spell. Other-worldliness is rated as a stigma nowadays; yet rightly viewed the imputation conveys high praise. Let us be visionaries! 'Man is a creature of large discourse,' says Hamlet, 'looking before and after'; and he famishes on a diet of mere perishables. The unbeliever's outlook is microscopic. But microscopes do not bring the distant near; contrariwise they shut it out. We need a telescope for that, a *longue vue* as the French term it. Alas! sin has so blurred our sight that till the Spirit opens our eyes the world to come lies out of focus and quite beyond our ken. Only as we climb the mountain-slopes of revelation do we gain a Pisgah-sight of the City of God clear as crystal, and falling in love with the bright vision dote no longer on the trashy wares of this Vanity Fair. How needful Paul's advice to walk by faith, not sight! For what is our present abode but a bivouac? Our tenure of life how insecure, that life itself how fugitive! Some day or other this world shall go up in a puff of smoke. A morning will dawn when the scaffolding of time shall be taken down, and the building of God eternal in the heavens loom in sight, the sole indestructible reality and fixture. Seeing then that the day of the Lord so cometh as a thief in the night, let us not sleep as do others, but, with loin-girt Paul, 'watch and be sober, looking for the glorious appearing of our great God and Saviour Jesus Christ.'

Some features of this full-orbed ministry I must needs skip. What stress Paul lays, for example, on *holy living* and self-discipline, and with what *humility* he serves, punctilious for his Lord's honour, careless of his own, bearing and forbearing with a plasticity limited only by principle! This chief apostle knows how to be abased as well as to abound, nay how to glory in his infirmities, that the excellency of the power resident in him may be seen to be Divine. Frailties he had, no doubt, for he was human, and encounters with indwelling sin; but his strong yet sober spirit was blessedly exempt from self-seeking, and far too catholic in its sympathies to fall a prey to crotchets or to party-spirit.

Signally courteous to men of low estate, Paul stood before princes a much princelier soul than they. Truly he was his own epistle.

'To Live is Christ'

But if you ask me for that watchword of his which includes all the rest, I should point to his well-worn escutcheon, and read emblazoned thereon the immortal motto: 'To me life is Christ,' or call to mind his own declaration to the Colossians: *Christ is all and in all.* This is the very core and marrow of his testimony. 'The life he lived in the flesh he lived by the faith of the Son of God, who loved him and gave Himself for him.' How many layers of self-righteousness the ex-Pharisee stripped off that he might be found in Christ, clad in the righteousness of faith, I cannot say; but this I know, that for that dear Name everywhere spoken against he trod all the world counts precious and all that he had once prized underfoot, that he might put on Christ and grow up into Him in all things, a miniature image of the one perfect fair copy. Christ was his consuming Passion, his vital Element, the very Pivot and Polestar of his being. Call it not lunacy, as Festus did, this rapturous abandonment to his Master; call it sanctified reason in its noblest exercise embracing an infinite treasure at its proper valuation. Paul gave his Lord utter pre-eminence because He was and is and shall be the Alpha and Omega, the beginning and the ending, the Son of the Highest, and the Highest the Son. 'It is beautiful,' says Gilfillan, 'to see Peter and John and Paul like three flames of holy fire climbing higher and higher on the altar of the Crucified, and Paul's pointed column at length outsoaring the rest, chief among the first three.'

Was He not Paul's *Saviour?* Never could he forget that he had been a persecutor of the saints, a noonday sinner, transgressing with a high hand; and that nothing less than all longsuffering and superabounding grace had arrested Saul of Tarsus as he was posting hard to hell. He was not ashamed of the shameful cross; for had it not dyed his crimson stains whiter than snow, his stains who had been the scourge of the saints and the chief of sinners? Great sinners make great preachers when they testify out of melted hearts to the depth of the sinnership from which grace has raised them up, and to the measureless dimensions of that love divine which stood surety for them, and drew down on its own guiltless head the curse which was their due. Paul's was a ministry of reconciliation; he preached Christ crucified, let the Jew rail and the Greek scoff his fill. He could do no other; for that was the keystone of his own faith, and had not the foolishness of God proved wiser than man in his own conversion? Therefore he shut men up under a broken law, and then proclaimed to them God's sovereign remedy, a soul-subduing, sin-expunging, substitutionary Sacrifice appropriated by a living faith.

Moreover, Christ was his *Satisfaction.* To be joined to Him makes heaven on earth, to behold His face adds a heaven to heaven. To the soul coupled with Him losses become gains, obstacles helps, repulses victories. All things are possible through His enabling. He is the staple-ring of all the apostle's chains of reasoning, and the clenching persuasive to all holy living. His was indeed a Christ-ensphered existence; the man was *emmanuelized.*

Lastly: He was Christ's liege *soldier,* subject to his King's behests. Look at Paul the aged, a caged eagle pent in behind Nero's prison-bars. Think of that impassioned nature, inured to hardships and eager for the fray as ever, that glowing soul which no thorn in the flesh could daunt, no growing infirmities chill—think of the old veteran seamed with scars of honour, shut out from the high places of the field where he had trodden down strength, shut in by vacant walls, his free spirit cramped in a Roman dungeon and exposed to the strain of forced inaction and galling suspense; the churches for which he watched and prayed so ardently left meanwhile untended, and he himself, to all seeming, laid aside almost as if he were a 'vessel wherein is no pleasure.' Does the iron enter into his soul? Does he faint or repine or weep *now?* Nay; never did the flame of devotion burn steadier in that generous breast. Nero's prisoner, did I say? I beg Paul's pardon; he is the prisoner of Jesus Christ, and that makes all the difference. Whether it is expedient for him to be bond or free, present in or absent from the body, his Lord knows best; but if he is bound, the Word of God is not. Homesickness for the better country he has long felt; fain would he loose cable and hoist sail for the blessed shore. But he is not his own; he is under law to Christ. May He not do what He will with *His* own? Glancing backward we hear him say calmly: 'I have fought a good fight, I have kept the faith'; and glancing ahead with equal composure: 'There is laid up for me a crown of righteousness which the Righteous Judge shall give me at that day.' What had this earth to tender to a soul like that? Had Nero vacated his imperial throne, and offered him the kingdoms of this world and the glory of them, Paul, like his Master, would have spurned the paltry bribe. Would that have been any equivalent for the inheritance incorruptible, undefiled and that fadeth not away? He needed nothing but death to usher him into his real estate.

'To Die is Gain'

The hour of his disenthralment struck ere long. Somewhere outside the gates of the Seven-hilled City on the Ostian way that grey head, of which the world was not worthy, was severed by the executioner's sword from its body of humiliation, and the best day's work ever done in the Lord's vineyard thus reached its welcome close. Little did the Roman headsman who dealt the blow dream, as the long divorce of steel fell on his unshrinking victim, that he was wreathing the imperishable garland of martyrdom round that furrowed brow. However, it was the witness, not the truth, that made exodus that day. God gives His servants their discharge in due season, but He carries on His work. The proud tyranny that laid its iron grasp on this chosen vessel has long ago bitten the dust; but the blood-stained banner that was dearer to Paul than life has floated over a thousand spiritual battle-fields since the day of his ascension, and it waves over our heads to-day. For him death was swallowed up in victory. He had long practised dying daily, and feared not those who having slain the body had no more that they could attempt. They might sever Paul's head from the trunk; but from the Resurrection and the Life, the Light of his eyes and the Life of his life, they could not part him one half-second. Was not death verily gain to him? For loneliness he gained the best society, for travail rest, for exile home, for broken notes the perfect chord, for scowling looks and hostile tongues the vision of the King in His beauty and the sound of the Master's 'well done'—the only plaudit for which he panted. Thy stroke has glanced aside, O Nero; thy caged eagle has flown! Far beyond the narrow verge of thy jurisdiction lo! he mounts with unflagging pinion upward to the third heaven, his native element and clime, and already he is 'kindling his undazzled eyes at the full midday beam' of that heavenly Sun that knoweth no going down.

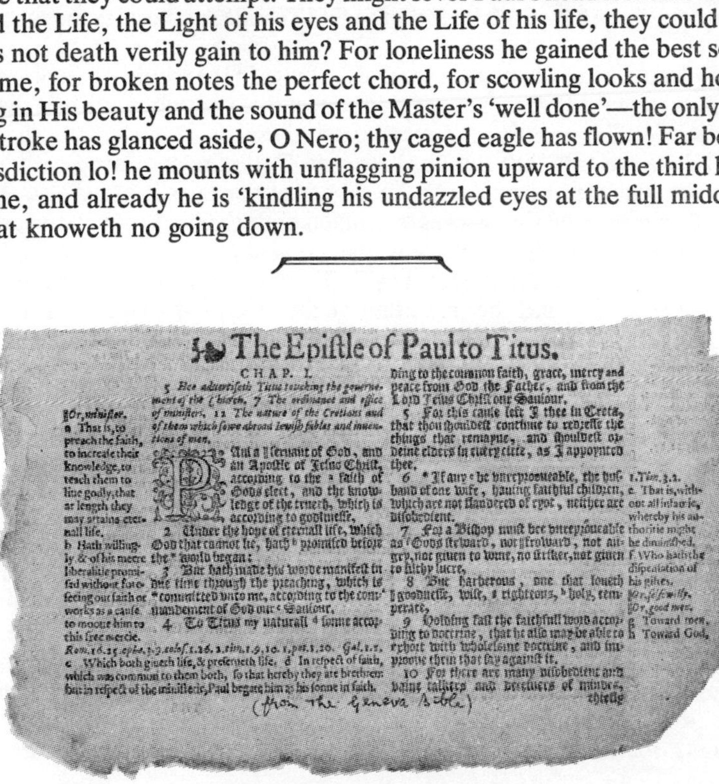
The Epistle of Paul to Titus.

CHAP. I.

5 Hee aduertiseth Titus touching the gouernement of the Church, 7 The ordinance and office of ministers, 11 The nature of the Cretians and of them which sowe abroad Iewish fables and inuentions of men.

Paul a seruant of God, and an Apostle of Iesus Christ, according to the a faith of Gods elect, and the knowledge of the trueth, which is according to godlinesse,

2 Under the hope of eternall life, which God that cannot lie, hath b promised before the world began:

3 But hath made his worde manifest in due time through the preaching, which is committed unto me, according to the commandement of God our Sauiour,

4 To Titus my naturall sonne according to the common faith, grace, mercy and peace from God the Father, and from the Lord Iesus Christ our Sauiour.

5 For this cause left I thee in Creta, that thou shouldest continue to redresse the things that remayne, and shouldest ordeine elders in euery citie, as I appoynted thee.

6 If any be unreproueable, the husband of one wife, hauing faithful children, which are not slandered of ryot, neither are disobedient.

7 For a Bishop must bee unreproueable as Gods steward, not frowarde, not angry, not giuen to wine, no striker, not giuen to filthy lucre,

8 But harberous, one that loueth goodnesse, wise, righteous, holy, temperate,

9 Holding fast the faithfull worde according to doctrine, that he also may be able to exhort with wholesome doctrine, and improoue them that say against it.

10 For there are many disobedient and vaine talkers and deceiuers of mindes,

Or, minister. a That is, to preach the faith, to increase their knowledge, to teach them to liue godly, that at length they may attaine eternall life. b Hath willingly & of his meere liberalitie promised without foreseeing our faith or works as a cause to mooue him to this free mercie.

Rom. 16.25. ephe. 1.9. colos. 1.26. 2. tim. 1.9, 10. 1. pet. 1.20. Gal. 1.1.

c Which both giueth life, & preserueth life. d In respect of faith, which was common to them both, so that hereby they are brethren: but in respect of the ministerie, Paul begate him as his sonne in faith.

1. Tim. 3.2. e That is, without all infamie, whereby his authoritie might be diminished. f Who hath the dispensation of his giftes. Or, good men. g Toward men. h Toward God.

(from the Geneva Bible)

(from The Geneva Bible)

The Epistle to the Hebrews

By William Wileman

Whoever may have been the human agent selected and qualified by the Holy Spirit to write this Epistle, the fact of its Divine authorship is never in doubt to any who have eyes to see 'light in His light.'

The previous thirteen Epistles have for their first word the signature of the writer: 'Paul.' The Hebrew Epistle also has for its first word the signature of the writer: 'God.' The present writer judges that Paul was the human pen that wrote this profound Epistle; and also that there was a divinely-wise reason for its anonymity. He therefore desires to notify some special features of the Epistle that may not be obvious upon the surface.

1. At least three times the Holy Spirit declares Himself to be the Author of the Old Testament Scriptures. 'The Holy Ghost saith' (3.7); 'the Holy Ghost this signifying' (9.8); 'the Holy Ghost is a witness' (10.15). We have herein the three essentials of authorship: stating, making manifest, and witnessing. In addition to this, running entirely through the Epistle, we have the continuous iteration of the phrase, 'He saith,' in each case giving a quotation from the Old Testament. And in the tenth chapter a quotation is given by each of the Three Persons in the Godhead: the Father, in verse 30; the Son, in verse 7; the Holy Spirit, in verse 15. And still further, there is the remarkable word in chapter 2.6: 'But ONE in a certain place testified.' When we consider that David, the human writer of the eighth Psalm, wrote of man, and that the Divine Writer of Hebrews applied the quotation to the Lord Jesus Christ, is it far from the mark to give capital letters to the word ONE? Incidentally, there are thirty-five direct quotations in the Epistle from the Old Testament, besides the numerous allusions to persons and things.

2. In the second place, one of the most remarkable things in the whole Bible occurs in the Epistle to the Hebrews; namely, several statements are made concerning previous writings that are not found in those previous writings. The prominent instances are these:

(*a*) In chapter 5.7 we are told that the Lord Jesus in Gethsemane prayed with 'strong crying *and tears*.' This fact is not recorded by any of the evangelists; nor does it occur elsewhere in Scripture.

(b) In chapter 9.19 we are told that Moses 'sprinkled both *the book* and all the people.' This fact is not recorded in Exodus 24.8, where we only read that he sprinkled the people, not the book.

(c) In chapter 12.21 we are told that Moses said, 'I exceedingly fear and quake.' In Exodus 19 we read that the people trembled and the mountain quaked; but not that Moses did so.

The question therefrom arises: How are we to account for these and some other additions to previous writings? I think the answer is twofold. First, a very complete answer is contained in the fact of Inspiration. A mind breathing the atmosphere of the Bible will realise this intuitively. But, secondly, I would like to make a suggestion that I have never seen or heard expressed by any writer or speaker. What happened to the newly-converted Paul during his three years' retirement into Arabia (Gal. 1.17, 18) before he entered his ministry? It is perfectly clear that here and then he had certain things revealed to him by his Lord. For instance: 'Behold, I show you a mystery' (1 Cor. 15.51); that is, I tell you something never revealed before. 'How that by revelation He made known unto me the mystery' (Eph. 3.3). 'This we say unto you *in* the word of the Lord' (1 Thess. 4.15); in this case a truth is revealed never previously mentioned.

The suggestion I wish to make is simply that this unique fact indicates the Pauline authorship of the Epistle to the Hebrews. When we recognize the principle that all Divine revelations are progressive, and that our reception of them is also progressive, we need not be at any loss to realize that Paul was specially selected and specially fitted to record facts never previously revealed. He lived in communion with his Lord so intimate that he was tenderly susceptible to receive the impression of His mind.

And may I not extend this thought to a practical issue? The more we live in communion with the Author of Scripture, the more capable shall we be to understand His mind. The more vital the Word is in the heart, the more fruitful will it be in the life.

Luke: The Physician and His Writings

By Dr. Howard A. Kelly

'Luke, the beloved physician, and Demas, greet you,' wrote Paul to the Colossians some nineteen hundred years ago when for the first time he, himself, was 'the prisoner of the Lord' nominally under Nero in Rome; in his letter to Philemon, he wrote, 'There salute thee . . . Demas and Lucas, my fellow labourers'; and again, to Timothy, from his Roman prison, shortly before sealing his confession with a martyr's death, 'Demas hath forsaken me . . . only Luke is with me.' These are the only passages in which Luke's name is mentioned in the New Testament, and yet there remains not even a plausible doubt as to his authorship of the Gospel which goes by his name and of the Book of the Acts.

Too many of us of the medical profession, I opine, are neglectful of our distinguished heritage in this Doctor Luke and his writings which form so integral a part of our New Testament, voluntarily classifying ourselves with a man who continues to live in poverty with a large bank account available which, properly invested, would yield him a substantial income.

Luke also has a strong and a wider claim on the vast Gentile world in particular, as the only New Testament non-Jewish writer, evident from his name as well as from his enumeration in the Epistle to the Colossians in a group apart from those 'who are of the circumcision.' He is comparable in this isolation and honourable exception with Job in the older Hebrew Scriptures.

That Luke was a doctor of medicine was not questioned for eight centuries; his doctorate has latterly been securely established by the painstaking life-long comparative studies of the early Greek medical literature by William Kirk Hobart, of Trinity College, Dublin (1882) who has shown that the interests of the author and his invariable viewpoint are those only possible to a trained physician, while the diction throughout all his writings is more replete with medical terms than that of any eminent medical man of our own day who discusses lay matters. His medical sympathies, naturally most manifest in the miracles of healing, become peculiarly evident when contrasted with the parallel passages of his lay brethren, Matthew and Mark. That Nestor of Biblical critics, Adolf Harnack, is emphatic in holding this mooted question as settled beyond any reasonable peradventure.

It is evident in this era of our so-called Christian civilization, when the New Testament narratives are circulated by countless millions in hundreds of tongues, that this ancient physician, Luke, is actually more read, and read in more languages, than any or all subsequent authors, sacred or professional. It would seem, therefore, that we, his colleagues of a later day and generation, owe it to the dignity and reputation of our profession to study attentively the writings, life, and history of this eminent *doctor medicinae* as one who has exercised a more profound influence upon the minds and conduct of men than all the writings of all other physicians who have lived in the last two millenniums.

It was the privilege of Luke in his Gospel to trace the history of the Christ from the announcements to Zacharias the priest and to the virgin mother Mary antecedent to His birth, on down through His childhood and through His manifestation to the world in the years of His ministry, to His sacrificial death on the cross and His resurrection. Following these memorabilia, he has in the Acts depicted the origin and establishment of the orphaned but waiting church, the advent and vicegerency of the Holy Spirit, and the witnessing of the disciples extending out through Judea, Samaria, Asia Minor, Greece, and Rome—the record of a Christian church upon earth in the midst of an often bitterly antagonistic world, producing finally the nearest approach to a true civilization the world has ever seen.

Let us for a moment try to determine what considerable portion of the arch of the Christian faith we owe to our gentile doctor, Luke, in the New Testament Pentateuch, the four Gospels and the Acts. I proceed to count the pages in my Greek Testament in order to estimate the percentage contribution of each—Matthew, Mark, Luke, and John. There are 306 pages in all in the five books; of these Luke in his Gospel contributes 72 and in the Acts, 69, or about 46 per cent. of the whole! The remaining 54 per cent. is divided among the other three writers. Limiting our count to the four Gospels, we find there are 235 pages, of which Luke in his Gospel has written 72, or about 30 per cent.; considering only the three synoptics—182 pages—Luke wrote 40 per cent. Thus from a mere numerical computation, we become aware of the preponderating importance of his writings, and in several senses he is a *primus inter pares.* As to the question of quality, who will be bold enough in a matter so vital to say that one takes precedence over another, where each was commissioned to paint a picture of Him who is both Son of God and Son of Man, our Kinsman Redeemer, the representative Head of the new race of first-born ones.

When read for the first time as a mere record of facts, the four Gospels appear much alike with considerable repetition of sundry familiar scenes, exhibiting but minor differences; a closer study, however, reveals a vast divergence in the scope and purpose of each of the four albeit with a great underlying harmony. Luke's immediate object in his Gospel was to establish his 'most excellent Theophilus' (loved of God or loving God, either or both, possibly an assumed loving Christian name to hide the identity of a Roman official) in the certainty of his Christian faith. Note the remarkable introductory of forty-two words in the Greek. Without the slightest conscious or apparent effort, our doctor simply, directly, and naturally gives us more reasons for the scientific basic solidity of his convictions as to the absolute verity of that which he is about to relate than any other writer, in any age, has ever expressed with a like succinctness and certitude about any important matter whatever commanding his attention. I may perhaps here admit on a parity the impressive, revelatory, opening verses of the First Epistle of John, which contain also in a superlative measure all that is essential to the competency of a trustworthy witness. Let me skeletonize this proemium for emphasis: 'Things most surely believed among us—delivered unto us—from the beginning—eye-witnesses—ministers of the Word—it seemed good having had a perfect understanding—of all things—from the very first—to write in order—that thou mightest know the certainty—of things wherein thou hast been instructed.' Then follow the facts in twenty-four chapters expanding and expatiating upon the fundamental purpose, the evangel, common to each of the gospels, proclaimed by our Lord in His very first sermon (Luke 4.18) and in His final visit in the house of Zacchaeus, at the end of His pilgrimage—'For the Son of Man is come to seek and to save that which was lost.' Luke uses the verb 'to evangelize' twenty-five times, compared to once in the other Gospels.*

The object of the Acts, also dedicated in continuation to the same Theophilus, leaps up to the eye in the first verse, by simply placing emphasis on the word 'began,' thus declaring that Jesus, who had companied with them for three years in person, though now invisible still continues His work through His Vicegerent, the Holy Spirit, working in and through all His true followers, age after age.

Jesus, nearly two thousand years ago, enunciated the basic rule of the laboratory and of all scientific investigation and discovery at the very outset of His career when he said to the inquiring disciples, 'Come and see.' Hippocrates was greater than Plato or Aristotle when he also laid down the law of medical progress in three words, *tribe meta logou:* cultivate living contacts with a matter, develop familiarity, acquire experience, and then do your reasoning and form your judgments. Paul, Spirit-taught, says in a direct, simple, practical way, 'Prove all things, hold fast to that which is good.' On this basic principle acted Doctor Luke, cautious scientist that he was, setting the example ages ago, when he followed up his terse scientific introduction with a record of an angelic visit to Zacharias, and to the Virgin Mary, promising to each a child miraculously born. The heavenly visitant concluded his declaration to Mary with the statement, staggering to our materialists, 'For with God nothing shall be impossible.' An unregenerated world had still to pass through the degenerate Middle Ages and await the advent of Roger Bacon, Tycho Brahe, Galileo, and John Hunter, before it accepted this salutary maxim as its open sesame to the secrets of nature.

As we read the Gospel and marvel at the twenty miracles therein recorded, we must recall Luke's repeated observations of miraculous events as he travelled with Paul, even including the raising of the dead (Eutychus at Troas); a mind so prepared, and believing in the Deity of Jesus, obviously does not balk at but rejoices in the miraculous as necessary evidence.

*The figure 25 here includes Acts as well as Luke's Gospel (Ed.)

In broad outline as noted, the three synoptics—Matthew, Mark, and Luke—are strikingly similar; in each, Jesus, the Son of God, comes among us and takes our human nature upon Himself by an earthly mother, and in each we have the record of His life, His deeds, His teachings and the hostile reactions of the world, the flesh, and the devil, culminating in His death and His resurrection. This simple theme, however, becomes wonderfully varied as related in each of the gospels.

For the sake of my interested medical colleagues, let us analyze Luke's Gospel more closely.

The political world of the great Roman government is in evidence as a mere timekeeper, the dial of the clock as it were, for these far greater events (chap. 2.1-5 and 3.1-3). Luke's first three chapters record our Lord's birth and draw us into the sweet and yet profound intimacies of His home life and His bringing up, concluding with His genealogy traced back to Adam, the fountain head of the human race. Then from chapters 4 to 8, our Lord mingles freely with the Galilean world—Son of God, with power to forgive sins, and Son of Man, accepted by some but rejected by the hierarchy, journeying about with His disciples who are unwittingly at school for two years and a half preparing for their later work. From chapters 9 to 21, at last fully recognized by the disciples as the Christ (Messiah), we have what we might call their six-month, intensive university course, a daily clinic with many spiritually pathological cases brought before them, the material often being furnished by His opponents—Pharisees, lawyers, and Sadducees—our Lord's use of them recalling the declaration of old, 'Surely the wrath of man shall praise Thee, the remainder of wrath shalt Thou restrain.' Chapters 22 and 23 consummate the tragedy of His sacrifice on the cross for our sins, so utterly unexpected by all His followers, but from the first anticipated by Him, for 'Thus it is written and thus it behoved Christ to suffer and to rise from the dead the third day' (chap. 24.46). The concluding act in the great drama in chapter 24 is the conquest of death in His resurrection and His ascension on High. Then follow the book of the Acts of the Spirit-endowed infant church and the fourteen Epistles of Paul, Luke's intimate associate.

Let us now note some special characteristics of this gospel by our proto-evangelist-physician.

Of particular interest to us as doctors are those unavoidable medical traces Luke has naturally left in his writings; so numerous are they that it is at once evident that a doctor of old, of whom but for the gospel we would never have heard, was fully as immersed and interested in his calling as any doctor in our own day and generation. To expatiate in detail upon this important subject would call for a substantial volume; we, therefore, confine ourselves to a few pregnant excerpts.

In Luke, Peter's wife's mother had the great fever, a term distinguishing the more serious and threatening from the group of lesser fevers. Our Lord 'stood over her and rebuked the fever, and it left her, and immediately she arose and ministered unto them.' Mark only tells us that she was in bed with a fever. Luke gives us a clear picture of the leper's condition when he tells us, 'And it came to pass when He was in a certain city, behold a man who was full of leprosy,' much as if we were to say that a small-pox victim had the confluent form, an enlightening diagnosis and prognosis for a doctor. Here Jesus 'put forth His hand and touched him, saying, I will: be thou clean. And immediately the leprosy departed from him.' In the first chapter of Mark, it is simply, 'And there came a leper to Him.' Luke uses the doctors' term for the paralytic who was let down through the roof because of the crowd, which is *paralelumenos,* while Mark uses the term of the lay world, *paralutikos,* which is reflected into English as paralytic. The trained physician notes the associated facts and naturally paints a more striking picture in his fuller details. Luke tells us in chapter 6 of one of the early miracles in the synagogue, which gave offence because it was done on the Sabbath day, that it was the man's right hand that was withered, while Mark simply tells us that the man had 'a withered hand.' Similarly, long after, when the multitude arrested Jesus in the garden, Luke, seeing a remarkable medical (surgical?) miracle, tends more to orient a doctor's mind when he relates that, 'One of them smote the servant of the High Priest and cut off his right ear . . . And Jesus touched his ear and healed him'; Mark only notes that 'One of them that stood by drew a sword and smote a servant of the High Priest and cut off his ear,' and adds no more, and John labels Simon Peter as the impetuous man, as indeed we might have guessed. In the case of the demoniac in the Gergesene country across the Sea of Galilee, Luke adds that for a long time he wore no clothes. Aretaeus, closest in spirit and method, and as a clinician to Hippocrates (F. H. Garrison), notes this as one of the characteristic signs of madness. Of the woman cured of her issue by touching our Lord's garment as He went with Jairus to heal his daughter, Luke writes that, 'Immediately her issue of blood was staunched,' using sharply defined medical terms paralleled by Hippocrates and Dioscorides; Mark only says, 'The fountain of her blood was dried up and she felt in her body that she was healed of that plague.' In the cure of the epileptic after the transfiguration, in Luke, the father cries out, 'Master, I beseech thee look upon my son for he is my only child.' The word for 'look upon' (*epiblepein*) is the medical term for seeing and going carefully into a case.

Harnack, who closely follows Hobart whose lists I consult repeatedly, says in conclusion that the majority of Hobart's some three hundred distinctive references 'plainly reveal the pen of a man who was either a physician himself or had a special interest in medicine,' for in these narratives where they are paralleled in Mark's Gospel, the different words used by Luke 'are most simply and surely explained from the professional interest of a physician. Indeed I cannot see that any other explanation is possible.'

In the miracles peculiar to Luke, the raising of the widow's son at Nain, the healing of the woman who was doubled over for eighteen years, and the man with dropsy, as well as in the parables of the good Samaritan and Dives and Lazarus, in addition to the healing of the lame man at the gate beautiful and of Aeneas, of Tabitha, and Saul's blindness, the lame man at Lystra, and the account of Elymas the sorcerer smitten blind, and the vision of Peter, 'Everywhere in the stories (which are moreover remarkable for their fulness of detail) traits appear which declare the interest or the sharp eye or the language of the physician' (A. Harnack).

In the account of the man who fell among thieves and was left half dead (*hemithane*), the expression is paralleled in Galen. Touching this man's treatment by pouring oil and wine into his wounds, as Harnack notes, the arch critic Wellhausen, in a moment of intensely applied autoschediastic ratiocination, somewhat superciliously indicted this dogma, 'Into a wound one pours oil, but not oil and wine,' a curious lapse of a hypercritical astute mind, for the ancient practice was not uncommon in the treatment of wounds and sores (testibus Hippocrates, Dioscorides, Galen, and Aretaeus).

The story of the lame man in Acts 3 is another instance in the long list, showing indubitably the hand of the physician. Luke says, 'And he took him by the right hand, and lifted him up; and immediately his feet and ankle bones received strength. And he, leaping up, stood, and walked, and entered with them into the temple, walking, and leaping, and praising God.' Elsewhere he supplies the important addenda that the man was lame from his mother's womb, and in 4.22, notes with emphasis, 'For the man was over forty years old' on whom this miracle was shewed. A passage from Galen's "Medicus" serves to illuminate the peculiarly anatomical terms.

For one who would further analyze the Gospel in order to come into closer touch with the writer, I would suggest several lines of study easily carried out. Even those little words we are so prone to pass over without remark, when repeated may become indices of tendencies as straws mark the flow of a current.

For example, the word 'certain' runs through the Gospel from the first to the last chapter. Its slight vagueness and its constant use reveal a Gospel written for one not familiar with the geography of the distant Palestine country. It is also evident by this token that it is for the average person we meet daily on Main Street and wherever we are, at all times, under all circumstances. So it came to pass that it was 'a certain priest,' 'there was a certain Pharisee,' 'a certain creditor,' and 'a certain woman,' our Lord was in 'a certain city,' there was 'a certain Samaritan,' 'a certain lawyer,' 'a certain rich man,' and so on. A certain man and a certain place are any man, every man, anywhere, at all times, so universal is our Gospel.

Note the miracles and the parables which form so large and important a part of the framework of the Gospels. Take first the miracles of healing and note their disposition. After the introductory first three chapters, these miracles are evidently far more abundant in chapters four to eight. This grouping is clearly evidential in character, our Lord appealing to man on the basis of his miraculous works according to prophecy; then after two years and a half of His ministry, the disciples make the great confession that He is indeed the Christ, the Son of God. At once now He begins to teach them by the more profound truths of the parables which as the miracles fade out come more and more into prominence in the narrative, ending with the parable of the fig tree, prophetic of His return to earth to reign. The accompanying chart shows not only the actual miracles but every mention of healing, with the purpose of exhibiting the predominance of the miraculous element. The x marks refer to healing the multitudes.

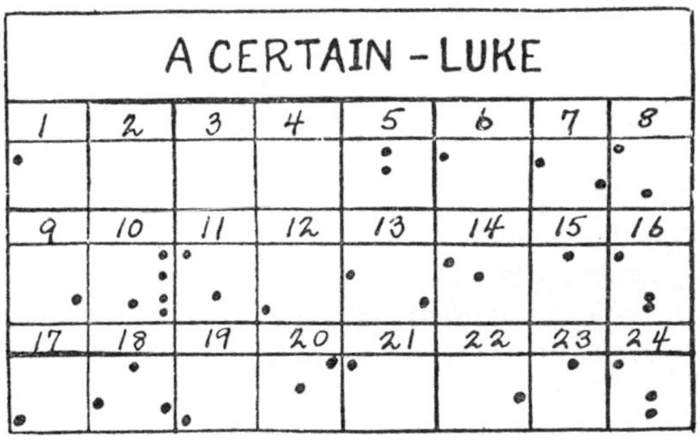

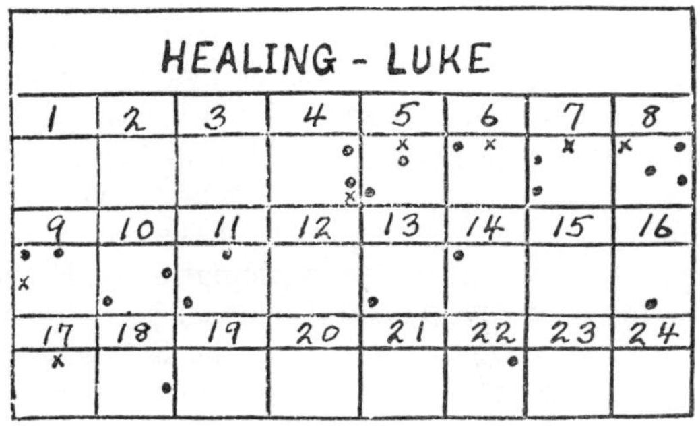

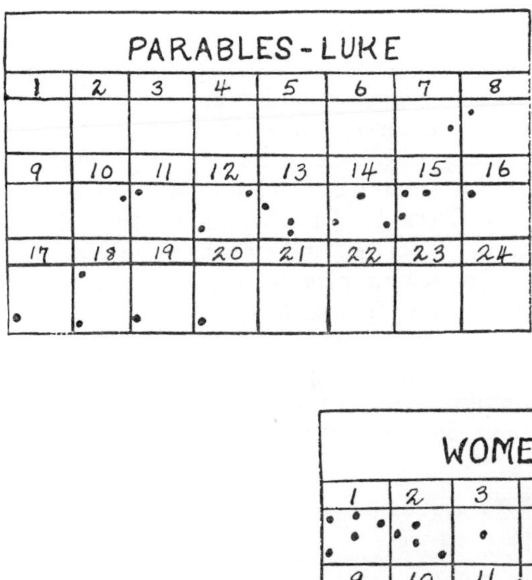

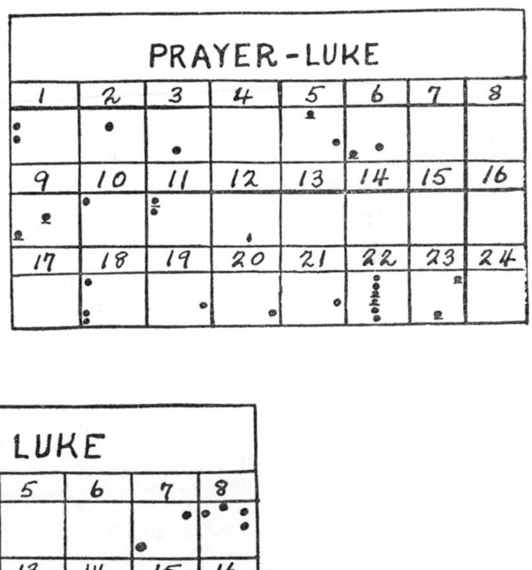

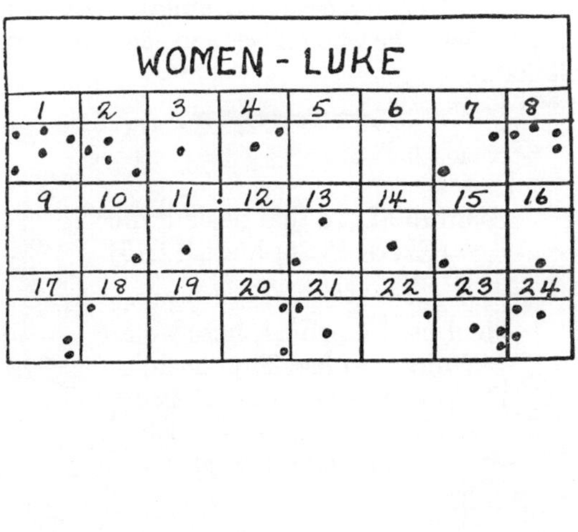

There are some twenty-seven parables in Luke, including as well the briefer ones. Aside from the parable of the two debtors in Simon's house and of the sower, all the more formal parables, some twenty-one, are found in the last chapters. Associate the increasing opposition of the hierarchy determined to destroy Him with the use our Lord made of His enemies to give His disciples some of their most important instruction.

Is not this arrangement that of life? First miracles, then parables; first, come, see, and be convinced, then, sit down and learn like a child. Such, too, is the lesson of Martha and Mary, peculiar to Luke, first hear and learn and then do (chap. 10).

One of Doctor Luke's most striking teachings is that of our Lord as a man of prayer, shown in the accompanying graph which notes every mention of prayer. The underlined dots refer to our Lord's own prayers, seven of which are not mentioned elsewhere than in Luke. If to this list we add those of the other gospels, it becomes evident that His life was passed in an atmosphere of prayer.

Luke's Gospel, more than any other writing ever penned, gives woman her position in a Christian community. The heathen world was ashamed to speak of its women, and the Jew regularly prayed, 'O Lord, I thank Thee that I was not born a woman!' It was common in heathen lands to destroy female infants at birth. On the graph, I have recorded every occasion when woman is mentioned; note the significance of this in the whole narrative. Nowhere is woman obtrusive; her function is not public, executive, or governmental. The one great transgression where a woman takes the initiative is that of Herodias, who murdered John the Baptist (*qui facit per alium, facit per se*). One concludes from careful study of this Gospel that the position of woman here, as in the world at large, is a vitally necessary complement to that of man. If man stands for incessant activity and force, woman represents grace, the virtues of the home life, and the heart. Which shall we call the greater where both are indispensable?

Doctor Luke's graphic pictures have so thrilled the guild of painters that he is accounted their patron saint, and art took its birth in the canvases of the mighty painters of old depicting the Gospel and the Acts. His, too, is the gospel of song as well as of angelic visitation and the triumphant recognition of the new bond uniting heaven and earth. It is important, however, to realize that the purpose of Luke's writing does not lie in all these and many other excellencies, but in his manifest desire to glorify the Christ, the Son of God, and himself to subscribe with Paul, 'Whose I am and whom I serve,' or again, as 'Paul, a servant of Jesus Christ' (Rom. 1.1), and 'James, a servant of God and of the Lord Jesus Christ' (Jas. 1.1), and 'Simon Peter, a servant and an apostle' (2 Pet. 1.1). Luke's is the exposition of 'the gospel of the grace of God' offering a salvation full and free to all men in all ages. Here is the one physician in the heathen world who recognizes the Great Physician (Luke 4.23), yields his life wholly to Him, and is inspired to produce 'the most beautiful book in the world' (Renan). Luke's finding of Christ was no loss of identity or lessening of his personality; on the contrary, both were enriched and enlarged to the utmost. His effective appeal is to all men everywhere—Go thou and do likewise; he who refuses and neglects the opportunity thus offered us in this life suffers incalculable loss.

'I am the Lord that healeth thee'
(Exod. 15.26; Matt. 12.15)

. . . . . .

Heal us, Immanuel, here we are
Waiting to feel Thy touch;
Deep wounded souls to Thee repair,
And, Saviour, we are such.
(William Cowper)

The Scandal of the Cross

(Gal. 5.2)

By E. K. Simpson

'The Scandal of the Cross,': there always has been an offence of the cross. I know it is the fashion with those parties who dislike the preaching of Christ crucified quietly to assume the contrary. They ascribe their settled antipathy to the doctrine of the cross to a superfine moral sense, so refined that it cannot brook the ethical paradox of the substitution of the innocent for the guilty. But, like so many other of their notions, this is a fond delusion. It always has been a stumbling-block since its first announcement. Some of the earliest readers of the roll of the Prophet Isaiah were assuredly no less stumbled by his fifty-third chapter than the Ethiopian eunuch; or what meaneth that Scripture: 'We hid, as it were, our faces from Him; He was despised and we esteemed Him not'? Yet the Messianic reference of this signal prediction of a vicarious Sin-bearer was so unmistakeable that it gave rise among the later rabbis to the fiction of two distinctive Messiahs, the conquering Ben David and the slain Ben Joseph respectively. Even the coming shadow of Calvary projected across the centuries scandalized Israel after the flesh.

That self-same shadow, falling athwart the Saviour's pathway, as the hour of His offering up drew on, so offended Simon Peter that it brought words of rash remonstrance from his impulsive lips. Jesus had just commended him for his grand confession of faith; yet almost at once the future mouthpiece of the Spirit is smitten with the sharp two-edged sword which goes forth from Christ's mouth—smitten hip and thigh with it. *Scandalon ei emou* (not *emoi,* observe). 'Thou art My stumbling-block,' in allusion doubtless to the meaning of Peter's name; as though to the tensely strung spirit of the Eternal Priest whosoever sought to rear a barrier between Him and His predestined sacrifice was a trammeling obstacle in His track. It had been foretold—had it not?—that He Himself should be a rock of offence against which many should stumble and fall and be broken. Here pre-eminently does that pregnant sentence find fulfilment: 'He that is not with Me is against Me.'

So I venture to say that no generation has been brought face to face with Calvary in which the unregenerate heart has not displayed some repugnance thereto. Multitudes of thoughts disclose themselves in the presence of this touchstone. Here is the most potent of all spiritual reagents, the sovereign detector of the inmost trend and bias of a man's life. Few indeed can enter into this awful precinct and remain impassive, stolid, unavowed; and if they do, it argues either a very debauched or a very shallow nature. Let a man once grasp the implications of the mighty tragedy at which he is gazing, and I defy him to remain neuter any longer, any more than to lie unstirred at the summons of the last trump or bide incognito before the Great White Throne! The plain truth is that all the enmity latent in the unyielded breast musters its forces in sullen hostility for the assault of this acropolis of revelation. How should it not constitute a stone of stumbling, disallowed indeed of men, but laid by the hand of Omnipotence to be the irremovable head of the corner?

The cross was, of course, to the ancient world an abomination in another sense than that in which it is a bugbear to the modern. The mere setting up of a malefactor's gibbet as the ensign of a religion aspiring to universal audience must have seemed to the haughty Roman or the fastidious Greek the wildest lunacy conceivable. Infatuation reached its floodmark in their eyes when Paul preached a crucified Saviour. Jew and Gentile, at feud on most points, were heartily agreed here. Israel in the bulk panted for a bond-loosing, not a bleeding Messiah; and we can guess with what concentrated scorn pagan culture would recoil from a message culminating in a death-scene reserved for the riff-raff of its condemned cells, the very dregs and refuse of its slave-marts. 'It is a misdemeanour,' says Cicero in one of his Verrine speeches, 'to bind a Roman citizen, a crime to flog, a kind of parricide to kill him; but to crucify him—how shall I stigmatize that?' Never let us forget that the death that Immanuel died was the lowest indignity to which the most abject social pariah could be doomed.

And no wonder it awakened loathing. For those lingering pangs, that ruthless exposure, the ghastly impotence of the impaled victim, whose racked bones and sinews (as the prophetic Psalm reminds us) feasted the ravenous maw of callous brutality or glutted spite; the spectacle withal of sons of Belial, set on fire of hell, flinging pitiless taunts at the gasping wretch languishing inchmeal before their eyes; these 'horrors on horror's head accumulated' might well brand the accursed tree with an infernal hall-mark all its own. In all the ghastly annals of torture where shall we find its parallel? Not till our gaze lights on some marble-hearted Roman inquisitor, playing the demon in human guise with equal gusto, and devising agonies longer drawn, pangs if possible more excruciating, than even this frightful implement of vengeance wreaked on its quivering victim.

We cannot feel surprise that the scandal of the cross should have so warped the mind of a great Latin historian that he dismisses Christianity curtly from notice as a shocking and abominable superstition. Paul's intrepid glorying in the Crucified must have seemed to his contemporaries the brain-sickness of an arrant madman. Never in sooth has the temptation to set the cross aside in favour of an ethical gospel pressed so urgently on its heralds as in that first century. All hail to the robust faith which refused to tread the primrose path of compromise, and, shouldering the offensive emblem with undaunted resolution, went forth without the camp, bearing the Lord's reproach, with His own lovelight reflected in its radiant eyes.

Yet why is the cross a perpetual stumbling-block, a trap to unwary feet? Something more than its painful associations is requisite to account for this steady aversion. Had the entire cause of scandal lain there, the offence would have vanished when crucifixion ceased to be linked in the public mind with gangs of reprobates and outcasts exiled from common human sympathy. Such a revolution of sentiment did occur, we know, throughout Christendom as to transform a symbol of infamy into a boast and a watchword, the crusader's badge and blazon. Yet the hostility revives in a different shape, because it is deeper-seated than any social opprobrium attaching to the penal code of a bygone civilisation. After all, it is not the material cross but its spiritual significance that stirs antagonism, and keeps it alive. What gives such mortal offence is the *doctrine* of the cross.

Now if I were asked to sum up in a single proposition the essence of that repugnance I should do so by answering that it *outrages the instincts of human pride* in a very galling fashion. Pride, according to Professor Shedd, is the inmost kernel of sin; and Bishop Moule gives us the counterpart truth when he says that humility is the distinctive quality—the *Eigenart,* he calls it—of Christian virtue. I may cite in confirmation the suggestive remark of the Genevan philosopher Amiel, not himself a believer, that Pelagianism makes Christianity a religion of dignity instead of lowliness, whereby (he adds) 'its specific accent is lost.' Exactly! Nothing shows more plainly that the modernist is a réchauffé of the Pelagian than the hauteur with which he mantles his crest of self-assumption. How could such an earnest believer in himself possibly stomach a salvation *all* of grace, to be sued for *in forma pauperis*? He would rather be lost than saved on such humiliating terms!

Yet the very first lesson that the scholar in Christ's school has to learn is the lesson that he cannot save himself. That taxes his docility at once. Plenty of worldlings are nothing loth to acknowledge their dependence on a higher power in smooth generalities. All rebels against heaven are not of the Titanic brood, not defiant Pharaohs or Sennacheribs. But it is one thing to own one's debt to an unseen Benefactor for an outfit in life, and quite another to bow low in the dust as a rank transgressor against the thrice-holy Jehovah, and rest all one's hopes of reconciliation on the effectual mediation of the Lamb of God. That makes the sensibilities of the old Adam wince sorely, that necessitates a positive new creation to bring us down to the Lord's terms of amnesty. O the folds within folds of self-righteousness in these treacherous hearts of ours! 'The arch-flatterer,' says Bacon, 'is a man's self.' Somebody has remarked of the poet Shelley, that he possessed 'unlimited powers of self-acquittal.' So do all of us, apart from the grace of God and the sternly benignant probings and lancings of His Spirit. Men will forgo a thousand sweets and court a thousand sours to save the credit of their darling virtue by some form of meretricious misery. *'L'orgueil ne veut pas devoir,'* says Rochefoucauld; and inasmuch as the very essence of Christ's gospel consists in the being beholden to

Him for everything, eternal life included, no wonder pride takes huff at the doctrine of the substitutionary death of the Just for the unjust, to bring us to God.

Unhappily, we live in an age which, however proficient in mechanical achievements, betrays a seriously relaxed moral fibre, coupled with a tone of self-congratulation that would be perfectly ludicrous were not the outcome of it so grave. The age's material record-breaking has obviously turned its giddy brain. Lack of principle and laxity of practice flaunt themselves in the most unlooked for quarters; yet we swagger as no generation before us has swaggered. Meanwhile, sin is being eagerly petted and palliated within the professing church as well as outside it, and the fatal affinity subsisting between free-and-easy religious views and free-and-easy living receives fresh illustration every day. We are afflicted moreover with paroxysmal chatterings even from the elevation of episcopal thrones not unworthy of a simian pedigree, echoed from a lower platform in the corresponding jabberments from the chairmen of certain denominational unions which have seen better days! *Infantes sumus et senes videmur,** as Martial puts it. But how rare to-day the child's heart within the man's, ready to own its shortsightedness and impotence, and prompt to welcome light from heaven shining in a spiritually squalid place. The artificial life we live, thanks to some of the questionable boons of modern science, does us grievous wrong. The strong simplicities, the grand sublimities, of Holy Writ no longer wake a response in the sophisticated children of self-indulgence, to whom life is not a pilgrimage but a picnic, who gird themselves for no stern battle nor crucial race, but stroll into its highway with madcap gaity, in the spirit of carnival dissipation, like a set of revellers bent on turning all they meet to farce and frolic. Yet if the old Book be true, and true it is, life is not a circus, but an *arena,* where an infinite jewel lies at stake.

Now nothing rebukes more scathingly than the cross of Christ this frivolous chase of baubles pursued in defiance of higher voices sounding ever and anon in the trifler's ear. Cowper knew that when he penned the lines:

> I thirst, but not as once I did
> The vain delights of earth to share;
> Thy wounds, Immanuel, all forbid
> That I should find my pleasure there.
>
> It was the sight of Thy dear cross
> First weaned my soul from earthly things,
> And taught me to despise as dross,
> The mirth of fools, the pomp of kings.

But that cross must needs be a bugbear to the vanity-fair spirit of worldliness mingled with religious cant so shamefully prevalent nowadays, which seems determined to count everything serious as trivial and everything trivial as serious. Even in the Galatian church it was those who wanted to make a fair show in the flesh to whom the cross was most distasteful.

One aspect of the offence of the cross in this connexion is worth particular notice, and that is its *levelling character.* Popery has its sliding-scale of indulgences, adjusted at once to the sinner's lusts and his pocket. But the true evangel deals very unceremoniously with our showiest virtues. It brings in the whole world guilty as perpetual defaulters Godward. Rank and title, culture and good-breeding, confer no premium on their possessors in the quest of God's salvation. Obscurity may inherit glory, whilst universal fame may be destined to everlasting contempt. What a drastic gospel it is on this score! Not a saint shall climb to the skies by a thread of his own spinning; not a guest sit down at the marriage supper of the Lamb in a garment woven on his own loom. How many highly respectable characters have taken umbrage at these provisos! The Duchess of Buckingham wrote to Lady Huntingdon protesting against Whitefield's 'repulsive doctrines,' remarking naively enough that it was

*We think ourselves sages, and are children.

monstrous to be told 'that one has a heart as sinful as the common wretches that crawl in the gutter.' Alas for her comfortable persuasion that she was *la crème de la crème,* while the rank and file were creation's skim-milk! Assuredly when the Son of God bowed His august head on our behalf to the drudgery of Nazareth and the scandal of the cross, He once for all put down the mighty from their seat and exalted the humble and meek. 'All ye are brethren' settles that! No hand save the Pierced can enter names in the peerage-list of the skies, no hand but His confer on the princes of His own creation their amaranthine crowns. By birth we are serfs, sold under sin, and cease to be too low-born for heaven only when we are born again from above.

But enough of the reproach of the cross. It is high time to traverse the indictment by showing in conclusion that the scandal of the cross, rightly read, spells its glory. In so doing we are following inspired guidance; for the Apostle ends his remonstrance with the legalist Galatians by the rapturous declaration, 'God forbid that I should glory save in the cross of our Lord Jesus Christ.' Ever since Paul had lowered his topsails of self-righteousness and run under the lee of divine grace, Calvary had become the fair haven of his soul's anchorage, and he could never weary of chanting its praises. It may be all very well for those who fancy they are launched on a pleasure-cruise, flitting across summer seas beneath azure skies, to deem themselves independent of God's harbour of refuge. But the voyage of life is not all in the Pacific zone. Yonder lurid background of sin is a thunder-breeder, ever ready to surprise the unsheltered barque, and wrap it in a tornado of seething ruin. And so, to every truly awakened soul, the crowning attraction of the death of the Lord Jesus Christ consists in the inviolable shelter it offers from the menace inevitably overhanging the head of every lawbreaker.

Here lies the very gist of the matter. What leads, in the vast majority of cases, to the rejection of the doctrine of atonement? That fatally deficient view of moral evil which treats it, not in Kant's famous definition as 'the thing that ought not to be,' but as a legitimate, albeit regrettable, element in the evolutionary process; or, to change the figure, as a scalpwound incident to the juvenile pranks of a humanity still in its teens, not as a poison working virulently in its blood. One of the most salient traits of the average modernist is his obtuseness to the plague of his own heart. He stands on excellent terms with the old Adam, both in himself and others. But the God of the Bible has sworn truceless war with the Amalek of sin; He can and will give it no quarter; for His is no slipshod rule, tolerant of iniquity as a sort of inevitable mischief. Why, sin affronts His light with its insolent darkness, and, where it bears sway, supplants His holy law by the antagonistic code of hell. Perfect holiness *must* react energetically against sin, or deny its nature. And so we read that 'every transgression shall receive its just recompense of reward,' *somewhere.* 'One day,' said Dr. Guthrie, 'every unpardoned sin will find out its father.' Final impunity for evil-doers there is none. The Lord will not flout any of His own attributes to let off an offender, for all His attributes act in consentient unison.

Once a man is brought face to face with the living and true God, and convinced of his own inward leprosy, no palliatives of priestly magic, no purgative pills of his own prescription, no, nor any idle trust in the molluscous good nature of the Supreme Ruler, will any longer yield him relief. He discerns that either the Lord of all must become his Champion and Shield, or else his case is incurable. Now to that man the truth of the Saviour's substitutionary work ceases to be an academic thesis, and grows into a question of life and death. Brethren, have we not trodden this path? Have we not felt that nothing less than a sacrifice for sin of infinite worth could span the gulf? Offence or no offence, a Divine Sponsor incurring our liabilities was the only adequate remedy for a plight like ours. If the sinner's flesh is ever to come again like that of a little child, a divine Fount must be opened for sin and uncleanness. 'Give me Christ and Him crucified,' he cries, 'or else I die.' Thank God, that gaping chasm has been bridged once for all; redeeming love has espoused our cause and shouldered our responsibilities, and now who shall sever us from the Lover who loves His own to that end which never ends? When shall that glowing heart that broke for our sakes wax cold? 'Christ must forget Himself,' says Calvin, 'ere He forget His people.'

Here is something like a gospel. Those who would rob us of it are bound to furnish an unimpeachable substitute. But creation may be ransacked in vain to find a substitute for our

Substitute. On the other hand, the modernist's pardon is a cheap affair, involving no divine self-sacrifice whatsoever; and being devoid of any firm basis of righteousness, at bottom arbitrary, an exercise of might rather than right, capable therefore of being recalled. But the covenant of Evangelical peace rests on the self-same foundation as the Throne of God. 'The believer's salvation,' said Stewart of Cromarty, 'is indispensable to the glory of God.' *Our* mercy-seat consists not of pinch-beck but of pure gold.

One would have thought that the intrinsic sublimity of the Biblical plan of salvation would have given pause even to those religious Vandals who lift up their axes *con amore* on the carved work of the sanctuary. The German sceptic Lessing honestly confessed the grandeur of the creed he disavowed. He wrote to a friend, 'I agree with you that our old religious system is false, but I cannot agree with you that it forms a patchwork of sciolism or bad philosophy. That description applies to the stuff set up in its stead, but I know of nothing that drew out a fine intellect so effectually as that same old-fashioned theology.' Lessing was right. There is a philosophy in our plan of salvation. Evangelical forgiveness is forgiveness granted on valid and determinate grounds, and linked with a change of heart that prevents it from being abused. The modernist's is an antinomian settlement, made in contempt of the moral law. 'Let bygones be bygones, and behave yourself for the future,' is what it amounts to. Not very lofty ethics after all! Ah, the bed is too short for a man to stretch himself upon, the diet too thin to sustain spiritual life. Not so, brethren, with the fare or the lodging of the Lord's own house of entertainment. Here is bread enough and to spare; here is a place of shelter from all possible storms. Behold a righteousness like the great mountains, not sparing Heaven's Well-beloved that it might justly spare us. Behold an ocean of compassion likewise, a saving deluge spreading out like the consuming flood of old, rescuing the perishing soul by an expedient infinitely wise and gracious. Behold the Second Adam, recapitulating all things in Himself, suffering as the Lamb of God in the nature that sinned, and honouring the outraged law far more by His flawless obedience unto death and voluntary self-oblation than it could have been honoured, had no child of man transgressed. For by every principle of equity the Divine rank of the Mediator enhances the value of His mediation to infinity. *Majestatem res data Datis habet.**

Last, but not least, behold a love unutterable, passing knowledge the more the more it is known, fathomless as its Fountain, everlasting as its Author, a love which comes as near to the laying bare of the heart of the Eternal as aught finite minds can grasp. *That* a figment of human invention? Strange credulity of unbelief! Spiritually stone-blind must he be who cannot see the Divine signature on the hem of this vesture rolled in blood.

Take the practical test. By the matchless story of Jesus and His love received and rested in as the ground and the pledge of a new heavens and a new earth both within and without us, millions of souls, high and low, savage and civilised, have been radically transformed. God forbid that we should not glory in the Church's conquering ensign, in that most comprehensive death for sin which ends its curse for the believer, in that infinite expression of Divine love and wisdom which is set before us in the bleeding Figure on the tree. O friends, let us rally round the cross. Let us make it the centre of our heart's thought and adoration. Let us lift it higher and higher. For here lies the hope of a perishing world, and here rises a spring of joy and peace inexhaustible as the heavenly pleasures, in fact a constituent part of them.

God forbid that we should glory save in the cross of our Lord Jesus Christ, the triumphant solution of that problem of the reconcilement of justice with mercy which baffles every false religion, that union of the titles of King of Righteousness and King of Peace in the Person of Him whose name is above every name, and His work above every work.

*The gift given carries with it the majesty of the giver.

Knowledge Found in the Book of Job

By H. L. Bleby

The Book of Job shows a wide range of knowledge—and an accuracy of knowledge as well as information on certain particular points—which it is impossible to attribute to anyone living at the time and under the circumstances which the Higher Criticism imputes. Incidentally: you cannot bring this book into line with any theory of gradual evolutionary development of human knowledge from savagery to modern attainments. The book is impossible, for any writer of ancient days, apart from the inspiration of the Holy Spirit.

In dealing with the Book of Job we stand in a different position from that which we occupy in considering any of the other Old Testament books. It is not related, as they are, to the history of the Israelites, because it stands out of connection with the history of the Chosen People. But it is crammed full (beyond any other book of the Bible) with natural and physical facts. You may twist history with comparative immunity, but physical facts if maltreated are liable to twist you. He is wiser who avoids disputing the mathematics of momentum with a motor car; its chief argument is such a convincing bump.

Higher Critics assure us that Job and his sufferings, his friends and their discussion, more particularly the scenes in which Satan appears in the high courts of Heaven, are only creations of the vivid imagination of a Hebrew poet who set forth his theological views in the form of a drama. They fail, however, to agree as to when this man can have lived. Various reasons are advanced for advocating a late date. Some suggest Solomon's reign, others the 7th or 8th century B.C. One more advanced writer finds out that Job's view of Satan and the angels could only have been learnt in the exile, and another writer says, 'The main problem of our book grows directly out of the historical situation of post exilic Judaism.' (They seem to have forgotten 'the commercial relations of Solomon's time' and his 'school of Literature,' and much they were so emphatic about.) We read in the Encyclopedia Britannica, 'The tendency among present scholars is to put the book of Job not earlier than the 5th century B.C. There are good reasons for putting it in the 4th century.' With kind condescension, the writer adds, 'The story may have circulated in both oral and written form considerably earlier.' One might enquire: since the views which the story embodies are of the same date as the story itself, what has become of their argument that its philosophy, and so forth, require a later date? However, do you not think that, for gentlemen who claim to date with precision even fragments of verses, with a book of 42 chapters, a range of 7 centuries is just a little wide and vague? To see what this really amounts to, we need to translate it into terms of Anno Domini, and apply it to a known document. It is just exactly as if they told us that Doomsday Book could not have been written before the time of Shakespeare, giving as an alternative the Jacobean period of literature, and then a date in each successive century, until—to parallel their final date—we find that Doomsday Book is not yet written, but will be published sometime next century. Now that is what we may call 'illuminating.' That helps us with our history of literature! Who can doubt the value and accurate precision of the scientific results of the Higher Criticism, after that?

We regard both Job and his friends as real historic characters, referred to as such (Ezek. 14.14 and Jas. 5.11), in Old and New Testaments alike.

The events, both those in heaven and those on earth, as well as the discussion recorded in this book, we believe to have actually taken place. Luther describes the treatise as 'parable founded on fact.' It is a parable, but lived out and recorded for our learning.

The name Uz perhaps attached to more than one locality. Job's home seems to have been on the northern border of the Arabian desert: possibly the North-Eastern (Chaldean) border, but there is more to say in favour of the traditional site of the Hauran (Bashan). Its southern border is not too far from Edom, with which Uz is connected in Lamentations 4.21.

The date of Job's life and of this discussion, we may perhaps place between Abraham and Moses, about the time of the going of Israel into Egypt.

The length of Job's life is patriarchal. The form of religion is patriarchal—the head of the household acting as priest and offering expiatory sacrifice (Job 1.5). Direct communication from God to man is still normal. Nature seems as yet the only open page of God's revelation. We notice the absence of anything connected with the Mosaic law and ritual.

Job and his friends, though Gentiles, retained the knowledge of the true God. They belong with a few other cases—Melchizedek, Balaam (already falling away) and Jethro, to a class of Gentiles that died out with the patriarchal era. It is in Abraham's family that we find the truth held longest amidst universal corruption. Now: Eliphaz (bearing the same name as one of Esau's sons) was a Temanite, and one, Teman, was a great-grandson of Abraham—Gen. 36.11 and 34 and 42 (that brings us to the fourth generation after Abraham). Bildad was a Shuhite, and one, Shuah, was a son of Abraham (Gen. 25.2). Elihu was a Buzite, and one, Buz, was a nephew of Abraham (Gen. 22.21 and Jer. 25.23). So all these were, not improbably, descendants not far removed from Abraham. Job himself, though living in Uz, may quite probably have been the same, perhaps through Esau or Midian (his story was, presumably, handed down in the family of Jethro the Midianite). Job knew religious traditions which we may believe were preserved in the Hebrew line—Creation (Job 38.1-13), Adam and the Fall (Job 31.33), Job uses words (Job 10.9, as does Elihu—Job 34.15), pointing directly to God's sentence, 'Dust thou art and to dust shalt thou return' (Gen. 3.19).

The mutual relationship of these men would account for their acquaintance with each other. It would also throw light upon the language in which the discussion took place. The writer of Job knew of a time when a dweller in Uz, a Temanite, a Naamathite, a Shuhite, and a Buzite, could hold an involved discussion, yet find no difficulty in one another's speech. How could this be realized in the time of Solomon or later? We conclude that they all spoke the pre-Hebrew dialect of the family of Terah. No doubt, it was already beginning to be marked by characteristic peculiarities for each, but as yet sufficiently similar, which points to a time not too long after Abraham.

This dialect could hardly be the Hebrew spoken by the Israelites, over two centuries later after the captivity in Egypt. (We remember how 70 years' captivity so altered Hebrew that it could not be understood when Ezra read to the people—Neh. 8.8). The book as we have it must therefore be in some sense a translation. We need not hesitate to accept the view that Moses came across the story, either oral or memoirs written by Job, when residing with Jethro, and that Moses is the most probable writer—or shall we say 'translator'—of the story. Our Higher Critical friends have asked for a Psalmist, suggesting Asaph or Heman. Well! They may have the writer of Ps. 90. Moses there speaks again of affliction and deliverance. The Talmud attributes the work to Moses, and one can hardly conceive of any Hebrew falsely fathering upon their great Lawgiver a treatise which is fiercely hostile to their universally accepted teaching about suffering.

The poetical form of the rendering must, of course, be owed to the translator, so the objection that it is improbable that Job in his affliction would have spoken poetry, is altogether empty and beside the mark. The faithfulness of the translation (though poetry) may be judged from the care taken, for example, to keep the very term each used for the name of God. In the introductory narrative and in the closing chapters the name Jehovah is freely used. In the speeches of Job's friends it never occurs once throughout, and in Job's speeches it comes in once only (Job 12.9). The favourite term used by these disputants of patriarchal times is the unusual Eloah (found only 56 times in the O.T., 41 of these in Job). This is, however, never used by Bildad; nor does it occur in the introduction. Shaddai—Almighty—also is frequently used, though again not in the introduction (it is an early form found only 6 times after the date of Ruth, only 48 times altogether in the O.T., 31 of these in Job). The ordinary words El and the plural Elohim are fairly frequent. But the late form Elah (peculiar to Ezra and Daniel and once only in Jeremiah) is not found. Most suggestive and instructive! Bildad's personal peculiarity of vocabulary is noteworthy.

The frequent use of 'tabernacle' for dwelling, a description of ostrich hunting, with other indications, shew a clear knowledge of desert life. But we find also city life, with no small degree of civilized amenities.

The book is also thoroughly conversant with Egypt and Egyptian affairs: 'ships of reed' ('swift ships,' A.V.) mentioned in Job 9.26 is—Rawlinson tells us—a correct description of the Nile boats, but not of those that plied on the Euphrates. Again, the method of reaping corn by cutting the ears and leaving the straw standing, described in Job 24.24, is—the same eminent authority assures us—a quite characteristically Egyptian method.

The distribution of knowledge amongst the speakers in this book is significant. It is by no means the ability of one writer coming out all through, but the different speakers shew characteristic differences in their mentality, marking them as real. It is far too subtle to be merely the art of a dramatist.

The man who seems to be least instructed is Zophar the Naamathite. He shows some elementary knowledge of Anatomy (20.25). He speaks of iron weapons and a bow of bronze (20.24) ('steel,' A.V.). His only other ventures are two on Zoology—'a wild ass's colt' (11.12),—the poison of asps and the viper's tongue (20.14 and 16). Even in these he gets one wrong. It is, however, a very fortunate error, since it is one almost impossible to attribute to a late Hebrew writer. Such a man in Solomon's reign or later must have known the stories connected with the Exodus (had they not been written, they would have been nursery tales), and among these the story of the brazen serpent inculcates that it is the serpent's bite that is deadly, but Zophar (following a blunder that has been quite common) puts it down not to the serpent's fangs but to its tongue.

Next in attainments above Zophar comes Bildad, with one mention of armies (25.3), and only 7 other references, all to very simple things, but accurate as far as they go. He was a Shuhite (belonging to a people known in the inscriptions as Tsukhi, who lived on both sides of the Euphrates above Hit). This man, coming from riparian lands, naturally uses the rushes and flags as his illustration. We have already noticed his peculiarity of vocabulary.

Eliphaz seems a man of far greater capabilities. Beside two references to the sword (5.15 and 5.22), natural objects come in ten times, and without blunder. In addition to this he shews a distinguishing cast of mind in an interest in non-material matters. Beside historical knowledge of the repeopling of the earth (15.18, 19)—and an allusion to a legal pledge (22.6)—he brings into prominence dreams and a ghost that makes the flesh creep (4.13-16), and angels (4.18).

Elihu is entirely another type of individual. Like the character of his speeches, the character of his knowledge is pretentious. He makes more mentions of nature than the other three. These are more elaborate than the illustrations used by the others; but he makes the worst blunder, regarding the sky as solid (37.18). Job makes no such mistake. We shall look at an astronomical statement by Job quite incompatible with Elihu's ideas. Knowing that these are two real and distinct men, that is reasonable; but if they were both products of the brain of one and the same dramatist, whence comes this contradiction?

Job is a man of immense knowledge, far beyond all the others put together, and always accurately correct. One mistake has been charged to him, but it is the critics who are wrong. He says, 'he buildeth his house as a moth' (27.18); now, if you look at the rest of the verse you will find betho, 'his house,' is parallel to succah, the booth or temporary shelter which for the passing purpose of watching the crops the keeper or watch-man erects in the field; the meaning of the passage demands an illustration of that which is not for permanent habitation, a temporary dwelling for a temporary purpose. You could not find a better illustration of that than the cocoon which the moth builds for himself.

In two cases attempts are made to tangle the book of Job in references to mere mythology. How the most riotous imagination can read into the description of ostrich hunting in Job 39.18 (in the speech of the Almighty), a reference to the fable of the Phoenix, is hard to conceive. It is sheer perversity. While the expression, 'to rouse leviathan' (R.V., 3.8), is just the practical equivalent of our modern phrase, 'to put your head in the lion's mouth.' Apparently it preserves for us an interesting ancient proverbial saying. There is not the slightest reason to connect it with the old myth of the dragon ready to devour the sun—a myth originated to explain eclipses. There is no inaccuracy or mythology in the speeches of Job or of the Almighty.

There are 22 references that we may describe as Geological in the speeches of Job. Admittedly the writer might have gained some experience of mining operations; but he shows more than a passing acquaintance with these matters to write unhesitatingly, with a discrimination between various methods. He tells of fiery conditions below the earth's surface (28.5). Subterranean heat is surely a startingly advanced knowledge for his day. In the speech of the Almighty we have a vivid picturesque description of the Creation (38.1-11). It is figurative and clearly not an echo of Gen. 1. Yet it does not clash with this, nor introduce mythological elements. Therefore it is certainly His; not a human composition attributed to Him.

We pass on to Astronomical questions. At first sight these are less convincing, for we are aware that a very considerable knowledge of Astronomy was possessed by the ancients. But we know that calculations based on these passages furnish an argument for the early date of Job; and it requires a good deal of credulity to believe that the late writer, postulated by the Higher Criticism, could get his astronomy correct, not for his own time but for 1,500 years or more earlier. However, even if one accepted all that, we are faced with the astounding words of Job, 'He . . . hangeth the earth upon nothing' (26.7). Of course, Job is a poem, and we find such poetical expressions as 'foundations of the earth' and 'pillars of heaven' (26.11; 38.4-6), but here we come across a definite statement that manifests knowledge of the scientific truth. That the earth is a sphere, hanging in space, seems to have been first taught amongst the Greek philosophers by Thales (though it was long enough after him before it was generally accepted). Thales certainly learnt some things from the Chaldean and Egyptian astrologers; probably this fact was known to them earlier. I will quote from a book published by the S.P.C.K.; only a very simple treatise, but by a quite competent authority, Sir Edmund Beckett, Bart. He is in great anxiety lest anyone should think that the astronomy of the book of Psalms can be correct, and that when the Bible says 'the round world' it means the world is round; he writes, 'The tradition that Thales discovered that the earth is a globe about 600 B.C. is therefore erroneous, and Sir G. C. Lewis (author of 'Astronomy of the Ancients') says that there is no foundation for it. It may have been unknown to the Greeks before then, as it was to the Jews; for the Bible was not written to reveal physical philosophy.' (*Astronomy without Mathematics,* p.2.) Notice he says clearly 'unknown to the Jews.' Then how about their Jewish dramatist? 'He hangeth the earth upon nothing' is one of the things that the book of Job knew. One writer (Stanley Leathes) calls it 'a very remarkable instance of anticipation of the discoveries of Science.' Well, well! In a book we are constantly assured is unscientific?

The botanical references need not detain us. There are 14 in the speeches of Job. We are given 4 in the speeches of God.

We turn to Zoology. Beside the list of animals in Job's possessions (1.3), and his sacrifices (42.8), we get 13 mentioned by Job. In the speeches of God we are taught about 14; as well as 3 others, which we must consider in detail:—The 'Reem' (Roaring Animal, the word means), translated in our A.V. 'Unicorn' (39.9-10), is doubtless rightly rendered in the R.V. 'Wild Ox.' Its hunting is shown in Assyrian sculptures; but we cannot suppose this animal would frequent the deserts of Northern Arabia.

Now, Behemoth (40.15). This word, by deivation, simply means 'dumb animal.' It is the word used in Gen. 1.24-25 (translated 'cattle'). It undoubtedly indicates a great pachydermatous beast; by some it is taken as the Elephant, by others as the Hippopotamus. Our point is that either creates difficulty for the Higher Critics' author. Let us look at them separately:—By the time of Solomon, at any rate, they had another name for the Elephant; since ivory is called 'shen-habbim,' elephant's tooth (1 Kings 10.22, 2 Chron. 9.21) The animal was itself new to dwellers in Palestine in Maccabean times, when the Syrians used it in warfare (1 Mac. 1.17, 18 and 6.46). Whence then this knowledge of the habits of this creature in its native haunts? Not a mere report of its existence: that would perhaps have been possible. You avoid nothing of this difficulty by accepting, with the R.V. margin, the more probable translation, Hippopotamus. If you purpose spending your summer vacation hunting our friend the Hippo in the Jordan valley, or around the Arabian deserts, you will return home sadder, poorer, but zoologically wiser: simply because he has not been there within the history of man.

There is a pigmy Hippopotamus found in W. Africa. We are told that a species used to be found in Madagascar; the only other species, the ordinary Hippopotamus, belongs to tropical E. Africa, though anciently it seems to have been found a little lower down the Nile than it is now. Whence then this accurate account of Behemoth? Are not these, as represented, the words of the Lord of all creation? Moreover, a further suggestive point emerges from the mention here of the Jordan. R.V. has it, and A.V. reads, 'He trusteth that he can draw up Jordan into his mouth' (40.23). Some commentators want to change the word and make it into the Nile, since it is a Nilotic animal. Is it not clear that 'Jordan' can only be local colouring? You or I might say of a building 'Higher than the dome of St. Paul's,' merely because St. Paul's is our handiest local standard; though we should not for a moment imply any connection of the building with St. Paul's Cathedral. We see that to the hearers (Job and his companions) the Jordan was a river of local importance, which confirms our view of the geography of Uz.

Who is this alleged dramatist to whom Jordan was a local standard, who, nevertheless, knew intimately the fauna either of India (for the Indian Elephant), or of the upper reaches of the Nile (for the Hippopotamus or African Elephant), as well as all the other lore we are considering? Moses, it is true, might come nearest to satisfying the requirements. But we thoroughly believe the words to have come direct from God, as stated; so we need no appeal to Moses, even though he may be the penman. And the very last thing in the world a Higher Critic is prepared to admit is that Moses wrote anything in the Bible, so they themselves slam the door on that explanation.

We pass on to another creature, mentioned twice in this book, under the name of 'Leviathan.' The Higher Critics make him into a sort of Zoological quick-change artist. He appears in one Psalm, according to them, as a 'whale or other large Cetacean.' In another Psalm (Rub your eyes!) he is 'Pharaoh, King of Egypt.' In Isaiah (hey-presto!) he's 'a symbolical snake or python.' (Wave your wand!) Here in Job he comes out 'a crocodile.' We are told, in summary, 'this word is used . . . in generic sense, to signify any huge monster of the deep or of the rivers.' Evidently one of the 'portmanteau words' described in *Alice through the Looking Glass.* Also, by the way, can anyone enlighten us? Is 'Pharaoh' to be classed as 'a monster of the deep' or 'a monster of the rivers,' and to which category does the 'python' belong? If you can accept that nonsense you may as well believe the transformations of the ogres in childhood's fairy tales. What are the facts? The creature is mentioned in Ps. 74.14 in connection with 'the dragons in the waters.' Again it occurs in Ps. 104.26, described as 'taking its pastime' in the sea. It is also found in Is. 27.1, where the description is (R.V.) a 'swift serpent,' (A.V.) a 'piercing serpent,' also a 'crooked serpent,' and here again it is connected with the 'dragon that is in the sea.' We have already considered the reference to it in Job 3.8. Finally, in Job 41, we have a whole chapter of detailed description of it, where in verses 31 and 32 'the deep' and 'the sea' are again mentioned. Most commentators with the R.V. margin translate it here 'crocodile.' Now it is true that the largest species of crocodile (which has been reported to attain a length of 33 feet) is found in salt water. But (we quote from the 'Encyclopedia Britannica' for this) it is 'found from Bengal to S. China, N. Australia and the Fiji Islands, and this species is the only one which is ever found at sea, the remaining species frequent fresh water only' . . . 'living as a rule in sluggish streams and lakes.' So if Leviathan were the Estuarian or salt-water crocodile you must widen the knowledge shewn by this book to Bengal and the Malay peninsula or beyond. To meet the difficulty, some have said flatly, 'the sea here means the Nile.' (Pulpit Commentary in loc.) Just now we had for Behemoth, Jordan made into the Nile, here it is the deep sea. We think we hear the howl of derision that Modernists would raise if we said such a thing in support of any of our beliefs.

But this is not the only maritime wonder with which our author is conversant. If we turn to his knowledge of Physics and Physical conditions we find, in 38.30, a description of ice-locked seas. It is definitely salt-water ice. No possible example of this could be found nearer than round the Sea of

Azov. But are conditions even there enough to satisfy the beautiful poetic description, 'Ice and the hoary frost of heaven . . . the waters are hidden as with stone, and the face of the deep is frozen'? This seems to set before us rather an Arctic or Antarctic picture. The statement is made with confidence as fact, not tentatively as travellers tales might be. Indeed, what traveller of those days could bring such a tale? The ships of Solomon coasted, creeping from headland to headland, perhaps as far as the coast of Malabar, or it may be to S. E. Africa. The Phoenicians, greatly daring, ventured beyond the pillars of Hercules, to our own Cornish coast—their secret Isles of Tarshish where they traded in tin. One single voyage occupied years, and then they would gain no knowledge of the Frigid Zones. Besides, if any mariner could have brought back voyager's yarns of a Leviathan and of oceans in the grip of ice, what possible human author of the book of Job could have authenticated them and recorded them as solid scientific facts? Is it not again most clear that we have here the very words of the Author of Nature, as they profess to be?

Physics has yet one more witness to bear to this most remarkable book. At the close of the 16th century A.D., Galileo, the greatest scientist of his day, could not help a baffled well-digger with any other explanation than the popular, but to us amusing, saying 'Nature abhors a vacuum, but not above 32 feet.' His pupil, Toricelli, first suggested the pressure of the atmosphere and that air had weight, which Blaise Pascal proved by experiments he performed in 1648 A.D. We know then exactly when this information was added to—shall we say—'the evolutionary progress of' human knowledge? It would be incredible, but that you can verify it for yourselves by a reference to your Bible: this scientific fact was stated in plain terms more than 3,000 years earlier in the book of Job. We are told in 28.25, God 'seeth under the whole heaven to make a weight for the wind, Yea, he meteth out the waters by measure' (R.V.).

It is impossible here to discuss in any detail the theological knowledge shewn in the book.

But in conclusion we must refer to what Job states in 19.25. In spite of all the laboured prevarications to explain away the full meaning of these words, this stands amidst all his overwhelming knowledge something which Job considers worth the emphatic boast 'I know.' The grandest item of all the knowledge that he possessed! A truth which only the Holy Spirit can now reveal to us, or could manifest to him. '*I know* that my Redeemer liveth, and that He shall stand at the latter day upon the earth: and though after my skin worms destroy this body, yet in my flesh shall I see God.'

Parts of Book of Job
(Geneva Bible, 1560)

Gods mercy and power.

32 Canst thou bring forth [r] Mazzaroth in
their time? canst thou also guide [t] Arc-
turus with his sonnes?
33 Knowest thou the course of heauen, or
canst thou set [u] the rule thereof in the
earth?
34 Canst thou lift vp thy voyce to the
cloudes that the abundance of water
may couer thee?
35 Canst thou sende the lightninges that
they may walke, and say vnto thee, Loe,
here we are?
36 Who hath put wisdom in the [x] reines?
or who hath giuen the heart vnderstan-
ding?
37 Who can nomber cloudes by wisdom?
or who can cause to cease the [y] bottels
of heauen,
38 When the earth groweth into hardnes, [z] and the clottes are fast together?

r Certain starres so called: some thinke they were the twelue signes. t The North starre with those that are about him? u Canst thou cause the heauenly bodies to haue any power ouer the earthly bodies? x In the secret partes of man. y That is, the cloudes, wherein the water is contained as in bottels. z For when God doth not open these bottels, the earth commeth to this inconuenience.

CHAP. XLII.

6 *The repentance of Iob. 9 [He] prayeth for his friendes. 12 His goods are restored double vnto him. 13 His children, age and death.*

1 Then Iob answered the Lord, & said,
2 I knowe that thou canst doe all
things, & that there is no [a] thought
hid from thee.
3 Who is he that hideth counsel without
[b] knowledge? therfore haue I spoken y
I vnderstood not, euen things too won-
derfull for me, [c] and which I knewe not.
4 Heare, I beseech thee, & I will speake:
I will demaund of thee, [d] and declare
thou vnto me.

a No thought so secret, but thou doest see it, nor any thing that thou thinkest, but thou canst bring it to passe. b Is there any but I? for this God laid to his charge, Cha. 38. 2 c I confesse herein mine ignorance, and that I spake I wist not what. d Hee sheweth that he will be Gods scholer to learne of him.

The Furniture of the Tabernacle

By 'Epaphras'

The chief feature of the Tabernacle was its being 'the tent of meeting.' It was a place of 'access.' It made answer to the patriarch's cry, and to the impassioned longing of many a heart besides: 'Oh, that I knew where I might find Him, that I might come even to His seat!' The chasm between the seen and the unseen was bridged. Men needed no longer to grope in the dark, stretching the hand to the right and the left if haply they might find God. He came into the midst of His people. His tent was planted in the midst of the tents of His Israel. He became neighbour and guide and friend and saviour and Father unto them. That spot of earth was as the heaven where His voice is heard, His face is seen, and His glory is the light thereof. Into that 'Tent of Meeting' came Israel in darkness, and guilt, and need that could not be uttered; and in it they found light, and peace, and a fulness which human speech was still less able to express. Those who desired to know the secret of Israel's spiritual insight and manhood would have found the whole explanation there. In and from that 'Tent of Meeting' the life of God flowed into the life of Israel.

In all this we have a Divine picture of what is secured for us in the redeeming work of our Lord Jesus. By it we meet God in Him. Our distance vanishes, and our ignorance, and our coldness. God is nigh and known and loved and served. If anyone wishes to know what it is that has made Christian men and women different, not only from other people, but from what they themselves once were, the explanation is there. They are new creatures in Christ Jesus. They have found the Tent of meeting. They have met God in Christ and they dwell with God in Him.

There is another aspect of the type which might well be dwelt upon—the uniqueness of the Tabernacle. It stood utterly alone in Israel. To no other tent was this promise attached. God did not say He would meet with Israel in the tabernacle of Aaron, Israel's High Priest; or in the tabernacle of Moses, Israel's Lawgiver and Guide, and the man with whom God spake face to face. Of none but this did the words hold good: 'There will I meet with the children of Israel and it shall be sanctified by My glory' (Exodus 29.43). Is it possible to avoid thinking of the 'ONE NAME given under heaven among men whereby we must be saved?' Even had Jesus not applied the figure to Himself and spoken of 'the temple of His body,' this mark would have been enough to have explained the symbol.

But so far we have only looked at the purpose for which the Tabernacle was designed. We have given no heed to the structure itself, and have not marked wherein it differs from the tents that encompass it on every side. If the intention which it was to fulfil speaks of Christ, perhaps the arrangements of which it is the scene may bear a still fuller testimony to the Redeemer and His work. Let us, then, approach and scan the picture which the sacred page has still preserved for us, though the structure itself has long since passed away.

There was first of all the outer court, one hundred cubits long and fifty cubits broad. This was surrounded by sixty pillars five cubits high and five cubits apart. Upon these, curtains were hung, except on the eastern side, where an open space was left between the five middle pillars. This was the entrance and was closed by a curtain twenty cubits wide. Within the court, which was itself uncovered, the tent was erected, thirty cubits long by ten cubits broad. The acacia wood of the wilderness had two qualities, which gave it a special fitness for a structure that was to be frequently removed and to be long preserved. These were durability and lightness. Boards of this wood plated with gold formed the framework of the tent. This structure was ten cubits high (the cubit may be taken at about a yard). Four curtains were hung upon the gold-covered acacia boards. The first of fine Egyptian byssus, reckoned among the ancients as worth its weight in gold, was arranged so as to fall upon the inside of the tabernacle. This was woven in different colours and was covered with figures representing the heavenly cherubim, who surround the throne of God on high; for, when He draws nigh to us, His state and greatness must not be forgotten. Three coverings were placed upon the outside. In the front of the Tabernacle were five gold-plated pillars, and from these a curtain was suspended which closed the entrance. Within there was one more division. The holiest of all was separated from the holy place by a second curtain, hung upon four pillars. This was also made of the precious byssus. The innermost sanctuary was ten cubits every way, its length and breadth and height being equal. Into it no one was permitted to enter save the High Priest and even he only once a year, upon the great day of Atonement. The Holy Place, twenty cubits long, ten broad and ten high was the scene of the daily ministration of the priesthood.

Such was the structure: now let us look at what it contains. It is the furniture of the Tabernacle that declares its purpose and that foreshadows the blessings of the gospel time. Everything here arrests and instructs. As we mark and inquire, we are filled and overwhelmed with the sense of the unity and constancy and grandeur of God's purpose. It is not the arrangement, or the structure, or its splendour that strikes us: it is rather the atmosphere into which we now pass. The place is filled with the consciousness of sin; but it is a consciousness of sin which is bathed in the light of the Divine mercy. Facing us as we enter is the altar of burnt-offering. It stands in the court under the open sky. It is a square structure, made of acacia wood covered inside and out with copper. It is five cubits in length and breadth and three cubits high. The hollow in the centre is filled with earth. About half-way up, a bank runs round the altar on which the priests stand when arranging the wood, laying the offering upon it, and performing the other services connected with this part of their duties. At the four corners of the altar there are four horns. Up to this altar the sin offering was led. It was an animal perfect of its kind—condemned to die for no defect or fault of its own, and an image, therefore, not only of innocence, but also of perfectness. The transgressions of the people are confessed upon its head. It is slain. The iniquities are not its own, yet it dies for them. Its blood is smeared upon the horns of the altar, and the body is presented a whole burnt-offering to Jehovah.

Into the meaning of this rite we do not now minutely enter. Let it only be marked that in this 'Tent of meeting' we begin with substitution. The innocent dies for the guilty, the perfect for the imperfect. We have now to note another feature. The substitutionary rite does not begin and end at the altar. No: this substitutionary offering binds the near and the far together. It enclosed the whole. The blood is borne from the altar past what lies between the altar and the Holy Place. It is carried through the Holy Place itself. The sacred curtain is raised. The very presence-chamber of Jehovah is entered. The blood is carried in there and sprinkled on the mercy-seat which is over the Ark. This Ark is the only furniture of the Holiest of all. It is covered within and without with gold. It is two-and-a-half cubits long, and one-and-a-half in breadth and height. Within the Ark were the tables of the law. Over it was a solid plate of fine gold, 'the covering' or mercy-seat, and on each side of the mercy-seat were the cherubim. This was the dwelling-place of Jehovah. The glory of God rested there: 'There will I meet with thee, and will commune with thee from above the mercy-seat.' Now there was still one thing needed after all the work was finished, and after the ark was placed in the Holiest of all. The blood shed at the altar had to be borne in and sprinkled on the mercy-seat. There was no atonement till that was done; but, when the sprinkled blood was there, the guilty were accepted. God was reconciled. The law, that made its demands and lifted up its accusations, was covered over. It no longer separated between God and the people whom He had chosen for His own. Its voice was hushed; it was put out of sight. God had no longer *that* before His eyes—only the blood that speaketh better things than that of Abel, and which tells of mercy where the tables of the law cried for judgment.

These emblems tell their own story. One has died for us in the outer court. His blood has been carried in before God within the veil. We who have looked to Christ crucified and risen shall, each man and woman of us, soon stand there in the light of the eternal glory. We have known the law. It was not hid from us. We have fled to the cross from the fear, the terror, and the despair it raised within us. We shall meet it there, for the judgment will be according to truth. But the blood has gone before us. The sprinkled mercy-seat will cover over demand and accusation. God will speak unto us and commune with us from above the mercy-seat; and He will speak peace to His people and abounding consolation.

I do not know how it is possible for any one to mark these things and not see the Divine seal both on the Old Testament figure and on the New Testament work. How could these things so make answer to each other across the interval of even the three hundred years which the most advanced rationalism is compelled to confess separates them—how could they so fit into each other and explain each other, unless they proceeded from the same mind? This conviction will deepen as we proceed. Between the altar of burnt-offering and the mercy-seat other symbols were embraced. There was first of all the laver, in which the priests washed their hands and feet before they proceeded with their priestly service. It was the symbol of the cleansing that meets us as we pass the cross. Those, whom Christ has washed from guilt in His own blood, He makes a royal priesthood. We are not only forgiven: we are fitted for service. We must not defile the place we tread or the things we touch. 'Thou shalt make a laver of brass . . . and thou shalt put it between the tent of meeting and the altar . . . so they shall wash their hands and their feet that they die not.' Do we, the priests of the most high God, bear in mind that the place we tread is holy ground and the things holy which we handle? Do we remember that a fountain is opened for sin and for uncleanness, and that, as we open our hearts to the Spirit of God and pass into fellowship with Him with whom we have been reconciled, the blood of Jesus Christ God's Son cleanseth us from all sin?

The priest passed from the laver of cleansing to the Holy Place. On his right hand as he entered, that is, on the north side, stood the table of Shew-bread. There were twelve loaves, made of fine flour without leaven and placed there fresh and warm every Sabbath. The table itself was made of acacia wood and plated with gold. It was a cubit and-a-half in height, two cubits long, and one cubit broad. The twelve cakes were placed upon the table in two piles, six cakes in each. The number gives us the key to the interpretation. The twelve cakes represent the twelve tribes. Bread is the outcome of the husbandman's toil. He has ploughed, and sown, and hoped, and waited patiently till it received the early and the latter rain. He has reaped; but, even after that, the labour required that the fruit of his toil might be presented as bread was by no means over. The wheat had to be put on the threshing floor and trodden under foot, that the grain and the chaff might be separated. Even then all was not done. It had to be ground—ground till the fine flour was ready and the fruit of toil might be placed as bread before the face of the husbandman. As bread that strengtheneth man's heart is to us, so is a perfected life to God. The Lord's portion is His people. He rejoices in us. We minister—with reverence be it spoken—to the Divine strength. Do we realise that we are much to God? and that, when we are presented faultless before the presence of His glory, the exceeding joy in heaven will be sympathy with the joy that will fill the heart of God? Let not our Father toil in vain! Let Him humble us even in the dust, if so be the chaff may cease to cling to us! Let Him cast us into tribulation, if so be we may come forth fitted to rejoice Him who hath loved us with an everlasting love!

On the opposite side (the south) was the lamp-stand. It was seven-branched and was formed of the purest gold. It has been reckoned that the material alone was worth more than five thousand pounds. The workmanship was of the most elaborate kind. The lamp was supplied with the purest olive oil. 'Thou shalt command the children of Israel that they bring thee pure olive oil beaten for the light, to cause the lamp to burn always' (Exod. 27.20). It was the only light of the Holy Place. There was no window or other provision by which the light of day could penetrate. The light which reveals the external works of God could not avail to illumine this place of holy service, or to make the way plain which leads into the very presence of God. Lamps, fashioned after the mind of God, and kindled, trimmed, and fed by the hands of the great High Priest, the minister of the inner sanctuary, can alone render this highest of all service. When spiritual men have failed in the churches, the light has died. There has been talk enough about the things of God, but there has been no power. If our work is to be done, we must be light in the Lord, as well as doers of the things that are pleasing in His sight.

We have, last of all, to notice the golden altar of incense. This stood before the veil and, therefore, nearest to the place of God's glory. It was the place of accepted prayer. Our service is much to God. The life that makes answer to God's dealing, as the soil or fruitful vine to the husbandman's toil—that also is much. Not less is the light, which, from a heart filled with the Spirit of God, makes plain the seeker's way and the place where the priests of God may praise and serve. But more than all is the going out of the heart to God in prayer. That is the noblest, sweetest fruit of faith. The altar of incense, though for convenience of daily priestly ministration it stood without the veil, is yet spoken of in Scripture as if it belonged to the Holiest of all. Prayer takes us nearer than any other act. It is access to our Father. It lifts up the gates of our soul, too, that God may enter in. If we but ask Him to bless, He can show His love, and prove His livingness and nearness and power in His marvellous answering. Our love will thus be fed by proofs of the individualizing love of God—the love of God to *me*, and our delight in God will deepen and all our service become full of freshness and devotion. Self will be lost in ever-growing thought of God. And yet, just because prayer is so thorough a test of faith, and because our faith, notwithstanding all our service, is so small, we restrain our prayer. We come to the Altar in the outer court, to the laver of cleansing, to the table of Shew-bread, to the light of the Holy Place. We look onward to the blood-stained mercy-seat making answer to the claims of the law. But how reluctant are we to draw nigh and minister at the Altar of Incense! Let us face our unbelief in this respect. Let us bid the tempter go behind us and keep us no longer from our Father's feet as suppliants and intercessors; and let us pour out our heart to Him who will prove Himself the Father of mercies and the God of all consolation!

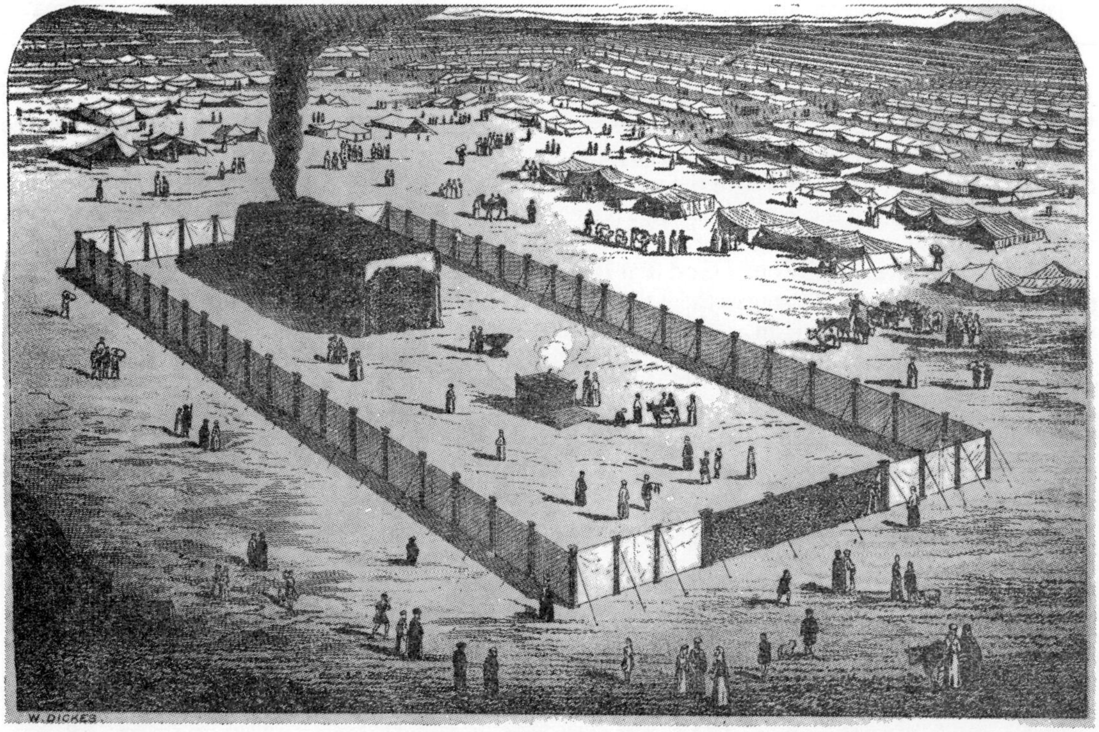

The Tabernacle in the Wilderness

The Deity of Christ

By H. J. Galley

'Uncle, is the other Lord, Jesus?' asked young Marcus Bergmann. The uncle was a Rabbi, and was teaching him to read the Hebrew Scriptures. They had reached Psa. 110.1. 'The LORD said unto my Lord.' The Rabbi was so vexed that he boxed his nephew's ear with a blow that deafened him for the rest of his life. Marcus Bergmann grew to manhood, was called by grace, called to the ministry, ministered to the Jews in East London, and twice translated the New Testament into Yiddish.

Yes, the other Lord is Jesus! The deity of Christ is implicit in the Old Testament, and explicit in the New. In Isaiah 9.6-7 it is written, 'Unto us a child is born.' That refers to the virgin birth of the Child Jesus. 'Unto us a son is given.' That has reference to the Son of God coming out of eternity into time. 'His name shall be called the Mighty God.' That speaks of the omnipotence of God the Son. 'The everlasting Father.' That tells of the eternal being of the eternal Son. Likewise in Micah 5.2. 'But thou, Bethlehem Ephratah, though thou be little among the thousands of Judah, yet out of thee shall he come forth unto me that is to be ruler in Israel, whose goings forth have been from of old, from everlasting.' (Margin: 'From the days of eternity.')

In some mysterious way, far too deep for the best human brains to fathom, our Lord and Saviour Jesus Christ is both God and man. Theologians call it 'Hypostatic Union.' This is but the English form of a Greek word which means essence, nature, substance. It may define, but does not explain the union between the Lord's Godhead, and His Manhood. God the Son is essentially—in essence—the same as God the Father and God the Spirit. He is really and truly God: the same as They are really and truly God.

This is humanly inexplicable as is acknowledged in 1 Tim. 3.16, 'And without controversy great is the mystery of godliness: God was manifest in the flesh.' Faith is not unreasonable; it transcends reason, and believes whatever God has revealed, although it cannot be explained in human terms. Again, in John 1.1-3, 10 and 14. 'In the beginning was the Word, and the Word was with God, and the Word was God.' (In the original the emphasis is on the predicate—GOD—and not on the copulative verb). 'The Word was GOD.' 'All things were made by Him, and without Him was not anything made that was made.' (v.10). 'He was in the world, and the world was made by Him, and the world knew Him not.' (v.14). 'And the Word was made (Greek and R.V. 'became') flesh.' The Lord Jesus was not made flesh involuntarily, but He became flesh voluntarily.

Such was the love of the Son of God that He became the Son of man, to die for the sins of men, to save the sons of men, and to make them the sons of God. Blessed be His holy Name. How this should warm our hearts towards Him.

As a spoken word reveals an invisible thought, so the Incarnate Word reveals the invisible Father. Thus He said, 'He that hath seen Me hath seen the Father.' (John 14.9).

Dr. G. Campbell Morgan used to hint that Luke referred to our beloved Lord when he wrote (ch.1.2) 'They were eye witnesses and ministers of the Word.' That is certainly what John intended in 1 John 1.1, 'That which was from the beginning, which we have heard, which we have seen with our eyes, which we have looked upon, and our hands have handled, of the Word of Life . . .' Whoever saw Jesus of Nazareth looked upon God and man, whether they recognised His Godhead in His Manhood or not.

The devout reader of the New Testament can see both the Deity and humanity of our blessed Lord. Matt. 8.23-27 shows the Lord as man, utterly exhausted, so that the fury of the storm failed to awaken Him; but it reveals Him as God, able to command the weather to obey Him. Small wonder that the astonished disciples called out, 'What manner of man is this, that even the winds and the sea obey Him?' The combination of Deity and humanity is seen again in John 11.33-43. The Master is so truly man that the exquisite words are written, 'Jesus wept'; and yet He is so verily God that He can raise the dead with a word—'Lazarus, come forth.' His almighty voice was immediately effectual, for 'he that was dead came forth.' Once more in Luke 23.34-43, both the humanity and deity of the Saviour are seen. He was so really man that He actually died; and He was so 'very God of very God' that He saved the soul of a poor sinner there and then, and took him to heaven that same day. 'Verily, I say unto thee, Today shalt thou be with Me in paradise.' (Paradise is heaven: 2 Cor. 12.1-4.)

The Lord Himself claimed to be God. Matt. 11.27. 'All things are delivered unto Me of My Father; and no man knoweth the Son but the Father; neither knoweth any man the Father but the Son, and he to whomsoever the Son will reveal Him.' Surely in these words He declares that He has a unique relationship to His Father. (v.28). 'Come unto Me, all ye that labour and are heavy laden, and I will give you rest.' In the Greek the word 'I' here is emphatic, as much as to say, 'I and I alone,' or 'I and I only' will give you rest. The Person who invites all other men to bring their burdens to Him, and promises them rest, and who makes that promised rest to come true, must be God as well as man; for only God could bear all the burdens of all the burdened and give them relief. For further claims to Deity turn to Matt. 12.6. 'But I say unto you, That in this place is one greater than the temple.' (v.8). 'For the Son of Man is Lord even of the Sabbath Day.' (v.42). 'Behold, a greater than Solomon is here.' Matt. 13.41. 'The Son of Man shall send forth His angels, and they shall gather out of His kingdom all things that offend.' Matt. 24.30. 'And then shall appear the sign of the Son of Man in heaven . . . and they shall see the Son of man coming in the clouds of heaven, with power and great glory.' Even when the Lord stood bound before the High Priest, even then He declared that He is God. Matt. 26.64. 'Jesus saith unto him, Thou hast said: nevertheless I say unto you, Hereafter ye shall see the Son of Man sitting on the right hand of power, and coming in the clouds of heaven.' In passing it should be noted that all these claims are from a synoptic source, and not Johannine records; not that we have any sympathy with critics who favour the former rather than the latter. Far from it!

In John 5.23 the Lord said, 'All men should honour the Son, even as they honour the Father. He that honoureth not the Son, honoureth not the Father which hath sent Him.' If this is not a claim to equality with the Father, what is it? (v.25). 'Verily, verily, I say unto you, The hour is coming and now is, when the dead shall hear the voice of the Son of God; and they that hear shall live.' Ch. 10.30. 'I and My Father are one.' As He said this the Jews took up stones to stone Him; and when He demanded to know for what good work they would stone Him, they replied, 'For a good work we stone Thee not; but for blasphemy; because that Thou, being a man, makest Thyself God.' They who heard the tones of His voice, saw the gestures of His person, and felt the impact of His influence, made no mistake when they understood Him to mean that He is God.

Our Lord is either 'very God of very God' or the imposter of imposters. We scarcely dare to write this, but it is written with affection and reverence. Unitarians and others who deny the Deity of the Lord Jesus Christ cannot have it both ways: nor is there any intermediate way. It is one way or the other. When the Lord makes these claims to His Godhead, they are either altogether true, or altogether false.

The other New Testament writers all place the Son on an equality with the Father. Paul in Romans 1.7 says, 'Grace to you and peace from God our Father and the Lord Jesus Christ.' And so in his other epistles, especially in Philippians 2.5, 6. 'Christ Jesus, who being in the form of God, thought it not robbery (Greek—a prize, something to be grasped) to be equal with God.' Titus 2.13 (Greek and R.V.) 'Our great God and Saviour Jesus Christ.' The Lord Jesus is both our God and our Saviour. James 1.1. 'James a servant of God and of the Lord Jesus Christ.' 2 Pet. 1.1 (Margin, R.V. and Greek). 'The righteousness of our God and Saviour Jesus Christ.' Again our Saviour is our God. 2 John 9. 'Whosoever transgresseth and abideth not in the doctrine of Christ, hath not God. He that abideth in the doctrine of Christ, he hath both the Father and the Son.' Once more the Father and the Son are equals. Jude 1. 'Jude, the servant of Jesus Christ and brother of James, to them that are sanctified by God the Father, and preserved in Jesus Christ.' This evidence is cumulative as proof of our Lord's Deity.

It should be borne in mind, that while the Lord Jesus used His power as God for the benefit of others, He never employed it to help Himself. It is true that we pay no heed to the kenosis theory of self-emptying, yet we must believe the fact of self-limitation. He never took advantage of His Godhead to assist His humanity. He voluntarily became dependent upon the Holy Spirit to give Him grace and power and wisdom, although He fully possessed all these and all other divine attributes. He even did not speak His own words and yet He had the right to do so. He spake what the Father gave Him. John 14.10, 'The words that I speak unto you I speak not of myself.' John 17.8, 'For I have given unto them the words which Thou gavest unto me.' As He made Himself dependent upon the Father for the words He spoke, so He made Himself dependent upon the Spirit for the works He wrought. Matt. 12.28, 'I cast out devils by the Spirit of God.' The danger of committing the unpardonable sin by our Lord's traducers was that of seeing Him work miracles by the Holy Spirit, and attributing those wonders to the evil spirit, and thus blaspheming the Holy Ghost.

This voluntary self-limitation of the Lord Jesus explains incidents in His life where He appears to be bound by human limitations. God the Son had all the powers of deity, but chose to make Himself dependent on God the Father and on God the Spirit. This is the explanation of such a passage as Mark 13.32, 'But of that day and of that hour knoweth no man; no, not even the angels which are in heaven, neither the Son, but the Father.' As God, the Son knew that hour, for He is omniscient; but as man, by voluntary self-limitation, He did not know. Possessed of the full Deity, He had all power; and it was only because He was determined to become like ourselves, dependent on the Holy Spirit, that He never drew upon His divine resources to help Himself. He even made Himself dependent upon the Holy Spirit to live a sinless life, and to offer Himself the spotless sacrifice for our sins. Heb. 9.14, 'Christ, who through the eternal Spirit offered Himself without spot to God.' How very near this life of dependence brings Him to us. Oh for grace to love Him more!

The only explanation of the preservation of the church is that the great Head is the almighty Jehovah Jesus, and that He is alive and keeps it alive by His omnipotent, guardian care. Its enemies cannot destroy it either by persecution, ridicule or contempt. It is indestructible because He is invincible. It was when Peter confessed his Lord's deity, by acknowledging Him to be the Messiah, that Jesus said (Matt. 16.18), 'Upon this rock will I build my church (the foundation fact of deity), and the gates of hell shall not prevail against it.'

'On the Rock of Ages founded,
What can shake thy sure repose?
With salvation's walls surrounded,
Thou may'st smile at all thy foes.'

If any one is willing to put it to the test by coming to the Lord Jesus, asking to be saved from sin, seeking help at all times, even praying for impossible things to be done, such things as only God could do, such will have evidence in personal experience of the deity of the Saviour. Those who decline to make such a test would be unscientific in method, and would be put out of court as witnesses. They could not testify, for they do not know. Every reasonable person who is willing, can have the fact of the Lord's Deity confirmed in every day life.

Here is a kind word of advice, especially to our younger readers. All who deny the Deity of Christ are wrong in all else, for this is fundamental. Never waste time in considering other religious ideas which are built on any other foundation than a belief that He is VERY GOD OF VERY GOD. Christadelphians, so-called Jehovah's Witnesses (new name for original Russellites), mis-called Christian Scientists, Mormons, extreme Modernists, Unitarians, or any others who do not believe that Jesus is God, are wrong, because they begin to go wrong there. Hear John Newton:

'What think ye of Christ?' is the test
To try both your state and your scheme.
You cannot be right in the rest
Unless you think rightly of Him.
As Jesus appears in your view,
As He is beloved or not,
So God is disposed to you,
And mercy or wrath is your lot.

Some take Him a creature to be,
  A man, or an angel at most;
Sure these have not feelings like me,
  Nor know themselves wretched and lost.
So guilty, so helpless am I,
  I dare not confide in His blood,
Nor on His protection rely,
  Unless I were sure He is God.

If asked what of Jesus I think
  (Though still my best thoughts are but poor),
I say, He's my meat and my drink,
  My Life, and my Strength, and my Store;
My Shepherd, my Husband, my Friend,
  My Saviour from sin and from thrall,
My hope from beginning to end,
  My Portion, my Lord and my All.'

Oliver Cromwell's Watch and pocket Bible:
the tiny open book above the main title reads:
'John chap. 1, ver. 17: The law was given by Moses
but grace and truth came by Jesus Christ'.

The Divine Initiative*

By H. J. Galley

'In the beginning God' (Gen. 1.1).

There are two kinds of railway time tables: one for public use, and the other for railway officials and workers only. The first contains the times of passenger trains alone, whilst the second gives the times also of goods trains; special trains; empty coaches from termini to carriage sidings, and light engines from stations to engine sheds. Such a compilation requires brains of the finest organizing ability. It must be conceded that even the greatest railway is but a small system contrasted with the abysmal universe: therefore, as Sir James Jeans has suggested, there must be a Master Mathematician at the back of it. If a railway must have someone to plan it, to build it and to run it, the universe must have One to plan it, to build it, and to control it. Common sense and reason demand that there must, of necessity, be a Creator and Controller who guides millions of millions of worlds in their orbits so that they never collide. There is the Divine Initiative—'In the beginning God created the heaven and the earth' (Gen. 1.1).

There is

The Divine Initiative in Providence

as well as in Creation. Wherever man and other creatures are found, whatever they need for protection and provision is there where they are. Such design is evidence of The Designer. People who leave their native lands for other countries find that they enjoy better health if they eat the food that is provided in their new surroundings. The Lord Jesus taught that His Father provides for the wild flowers that have no gardener to tend them, and for the wild birds that have no one to feed them: also that He even carefully notices the commonest of all birds, the perky little sparrow. From these facts of providence the Lord sets up an argument for faith, for since His Father cares for all creatures in general, He is sure to make provision for His children in particular. Thus, we who are children of God, can enjoy the subjective experience of these objective providential promises.

Further, there is

The Divine Initiative in Revelation

Other great world-religions have what they call their sacred books, even as Jews have the Old Testament, and Christians have that and the New. The vital difference between the Bible and these pseudo-sacred books is that it is Divine Revelation, whilst they are human imagination. In this God reveals Himself to man, in them man speculates about God—or gods. This is the one and only holy Revelation. Borrow an English translation from a Public Library of the Mohammedan Koran, read a few pages, and see how far from holy it is. So it is with the so-called sacred books of these other religions. The Bible reveals that the holy Creator created mankind in His own image, placed them on moral probation; they exercised their moral freedom in the wrong direction, by disobeying the Lord God, and falling into sin; God is love and He is just; He provided a Substitute for the sinner in the Person of His Son; the Son of God added humanity to His Deity and became the Son of Man; He died for the sin of man, that man might live and be saved, and that the sons of men could become the sons of God. The Word of God is the only Book of a great religion that contains good news: the Gospel.

In the Gospel God takes the initiative in

Commissioning His Messengers

'Whosoever shall call on the Name of the Lord shall be saved. How then shall they call on Him in whom they have not believed? and how shall they believe in Him of whom they have not heard? and

*Précis of an Address delivered at the Annual Meeting of the Bible League, 1955.

how shall they hear without a preacher? and how shall they preach, except they be sent—*except they be sent.*' (Rom. 10.13-15). Moses and Gideon were hesitant and nervous, and both had to be thrust into service. The prophets needed the same Divine impulse to urge them to serve the Lord. None of the apostles took the initial step of asking the Lord if they could help Him: He gave them an effectual call: that was pre-eminently so in the case of Saul of Tarsus. So it is today: no one really and truly becomes a preacher or a teacher of the Good News unless the Lord takes the initiative in sending him or her forth as one of His heralds.

As in the preaching of His Word, so in

The Hearing of the Same,

the Lord always takes the initiative. The Saviour said, 'No man can come to Me, except the Father which hath sent Me draw him' (John 6-44). There are three stories in the fifteenth chapter of Luke which establish this principle: (1) The Lost Sheep—a lost dog may find its way back home over even hundreds of miles, but a lost sheep never will; the shepherd must take steps to find it, or it will be for ever lost. So must the Good Shepherd seek and find lost souls, or they will never be saved. (2) The Lost Coin; in the nature of things this could never reinstate itself; the good housewife must light a lamp and sweep the room till she finds it. So with lost souls, they will never be saved unless the Holy Spirit enlightens their blind eyes first to see what sinners they are, and then to see what a wonderful Saviour Jesus is. (3) The Lost Son; although he did come to himself and say 'I will arise and go to my father,' he did not take the initiative. His father, every day after he left home, went to the nearest coign of vantage and looked in every direction to see if his lost son were returning: he not only looked, but he loved; he loved and sent out thought waves of love to his wandering boy: it was these that touched the wanderer's heart, and took the initiative in his journey back to his father. There is a Divine initiative by telepathy as well as in human relationships.

The same God who takes the initiative in beginning the work of grace in the human heart takes

Each Initial Gracious Step

in the revival of that wonderful operation. 'Being confident of this very thing, that He which hath begun a good work in you will perform (*margin,* 'finish') it until the day of Jesus Christ' (Phil. 1.6). Although the spiritual life in a believer may die down, it never dies out. John Bunyan, in *Pilgrim's Progress,* leads Christian to the Interpreter's House, where, amongst other marvels, he sees a fire against a wall, with one constantly pouring water on it, notwithstanding which it burns ever brighter. The mystery is explained when the pilgrim is led to the other side of the wall, and sees that there is a hole in it, through which another for ever pours oil on the flames and keeps them burning always hotter. Thus it is taught that, whilst the world, the flesh and the Devil (the world being the worst of the three) constantly throw cold water upon the believer, they can never extinguish the work of the Holy Spirit because He for ever pours His grace into the believer's heart.

As it is the Lord who takes the initiative in reviving His gracious work in the hearts of Christians individually, so it is He who takes the initiative every time in

Revivals in the Church Collectively.

'Not by might, nor by power, but by My Spirit, saith the Lord of Hosts' (Zech. 4.6). The writer visited South Wales during the Revival there in 1904-5. In one church a leader did his utmost to work up revival fervour, but in vain. Real, true revival is not worked up by man, but poured down by God. In another church quite an ordinary Prayer Meeting slowly but surely became an extraordinary Prayer Meeting, hymn books were ultimately discarded, the Holy Spirit inspired such praise and prayer and testimony that the building became too small, and larger premises were soon crowded; sinners were saved, saints were revived, and it so affected a local coal mine where the manager said that, although he was not a religious man, he had to believe in the Revival, for, since it came, the miners gave him no trouble, and sent up more coal and better coal. We should give the Lord no rest until He answers our earnest, fervent and urgent supplication, 'Wilt Thou not revive us again?'

Finally it is the Lord Himself who will take the initiative

In His Second Advent.

Whilst not all Christians see eye to eye as to certain details of the Coming Again of our Blessed Lord, they are all united in believing the great and glorious truth that when He said 'I will come again' (John 14.3) He meant 'I will come again'; therefore He is coming back. The Church was never set the task of helping to bring in the visible Kingdom of God on earth. It is commissioned to preach the Gospel all over the world to everybody. At the end of this Gospel Dispensation the Lord will come again, as He said. He will come 'triumphant down the parting skies' and 'every eye shall see Him.' He will not only come again, but He will come to reign. The Scripture will come true where it is written, 'The kingdoms of this world are become the kingdoms of our Lord and of His Christ, and He shall reign for ever and ever' (Rev. 11.15). 'God also hath highly exalted Him, and given Him a Name which is above every name: that at the Name of Jesus every knee should bow, in heaven, and in the earth, and under the earth, and that every tongue should confess that Jesus Christ is Lord, to the glory of God the Father' (Phil. 2.9-11).

'All hail the power of Jesus' Name;
Let angels prostrate fall;
Bring forth the royal diadem,
And crown Him Lord of all.'

Amazing grace (how sweet the sound)
That saved a wretch like me!
I once was lost, but now am found:
Was blind, but now I see.

'Twas grace that taught my heart to fear,
And grace my fears relieved;
How precious did that grace appear
The hour I first believed!

Through many dangers, toils, and snares
I have already come;
'Tis grace has brought me safe thus far,
And grace will lead me home.

The Lord has promised good to me,
His Word my hope secures;
He will my Shield and Portion be,
As long as life endures.

Yes, when this flesh and heart shall fail,
And mortal life shall cease,
I shall possess within the veil
A life of joy and peace.

The earth shall soon dissolve like snow,
The sun forbear to shine;
But God, who called me here below,
Will be for ever mine. *(John Newton)*

The Authorship of the Fourth Gospel

By E. J. Poole-Connor

Did John, the son of Zebedee—John the apostle, of whom we read so much in the early pages of the New Testament—write the Gospel that bears his name?

From the last quarter of the second century to the last quarter of the eighteenth century, the answer, with almost complete unanimity, was 'Yes.'

But with the rise of what is commonly known as the higher critical school—emanating largely from Germany, and marked by a strong bias against the supernatural—John's authorship of the Fourth Gospel began to be called in question. The various alternatives to the traditional view which were then and later advanced to account for its origin need not now concern us. All that is here necessary to bear in mind is that the same rationalistic school which sought to explain away the miraculous element in Scripture in general, and which leaned so strongly toward the Unitarian view of our Lord's Person, was that which was foremost in searching out reasons for discrediting the Johannine authorship of the last of our Lord's biographies.

A Disquieting Tendency

It is, therefore, not without disquiet that we have observed a tendency in certain Evangelical quarters to make concession to the modernistic view. We cannot admit, as some appear inclined to do, that the question of the apostolic authorship of the Fourth Gospel is a minor consideration; nor can we feel happy at the reasons which have been advanced in support of such a plea. It has been said by some whose general orthodoxy is unquestioned that it does not greatly matter whether John the Apostle wrote the Gospel that bears his name, or not; the fact that the Christian church has accepted it as an inspired and authoritative document is sufficient warrant for giving it a place in the sacred canon.

This statement appears to us to cut at the very root of Biblical authority.—The case for the sovereignty of the Scriptures in the Christian church, as we see it, stands thus: Our Lord called out a body of men whom He appointed as His apostles; their function being two-fold. They were to be trustees of His teaching and witnesses of His resurrection; the latter event being 'the sign from heaven' which should authenticate all His claims. (Luke 11.15, 16, 29, 30; Matt. 12.39, 40). Hence when in the Divine purpose Paul was later called to be the Apostle to the Gentiles, it was necessary for Him to be similarly qualified for his office. He must receive our Lord's personal instruction, and be granted the sight of His resurrection body (Gal. 1.12, with 1 Cor. 15.8).

The teaching committed to the Eleven by Christ was conveyed partly by word of mouth; and after His ascension to heaven, by the Holy Spirit. There were also in the apostolic church certain prophets through whom, in the assembly, the Holy Spirit spoke. (1 Cor. 14.29-31). Such utterances were necessarily in harmony with the apostles' doctrine and were, in a certain sense, subordinate to it; and they ceased with the closing of the canon of Scripture.

For the Christian church therefore, the teaching of Christ is now contained in the New Testament, wherein alone is to be found the writing of the apostles, and of those who wrote with their approval; the whole being under the direction and inspiration of the Holy Spirit.—In other words, the New Testament derives its authority from that of the apostles, even as they in turn derived it from Christ.

Roman and Modernistic Teaching

This great Evangelical doctrine is controverted or weakened alike by the teaching of the Church of Rome and by the modernistic or Barthian theology now prevalent in the various sections of Protestantism. The former declares that *Tradition* (which is a somewhat formless and elusive body of patristic and papal pronouncements) is of equal authority with the Scripture; it also asserts that it is the Church which authorises the Scriptures, and not the Scriptures the Church. Speaking broadly, Modernism claims that Divine revelation is confined neither to tbe Bible nor to Tradition.

It is evident, therefore, that when any Evangelical states that it does not greatly matter who wrote the Gospel of John, since *the Church* has authenticated it, he is verging on dangerous ground. For, on the one hand, he is departing from a doctrine which is essential to Protestantism, and, on the other, he is raising bewildering questions as to who or what is that body which possesses this power of authorisation. If by 'the Church' he means Christendom he does but create confusion; for while one section of it holds John's Gospel to be an integral portion of the Word of God, another wholly refuses to accept it as such.

To the present writer, the authority of the Fourth Gospel lies wholly in the belief that its author was John, the son of Zebedee, the apostle of Jesus Christ. Could it be shown that it was a post-apostolic work by another presbyter of the same name, or was a composite production reflecting Hellenistic influences, its value as a Divine revelation would, in his view, be destroyed; nor would any subsequent acceptance of it by a vague entity called 'the Church' serve to restore to it the trustworthiness with which it had formerly been credited.

In view of these things it is important that Evangelicals should be reminded that the grounds for believing in the Johannine authorship of the Fourth Gospel are both clear and cogent.—The subject is an extremely large one; we must therefore confine ourselves, with a single exception, to one line of evidence. This will be found in the contents of the Gospel itself; but it would be unfair to our subject to omit one powerful item of external proof, to which almost all Evangelical commentators call attention. It is this:—

The Testimony of Irenaeus

One of the early Christian bishops, whose name was Irenaeus, was born in Asia Minor, where the apostle John spent the last twenty or thirty years of his life, and while still a young man he came in contact with Polycarp (70-156 A.D.), who had been a disciple of John the apostle. In a letter addressed to his friend Florinus in the year 177, Irenaeus thus writes: 'I can describe the very place where the blessed Polycarp used to sit when he discoursed . . . and his manner of life and personal appearance . . . and how he would describe his intercourse with John, and with the rest who had seen the Lord, and how he would relate their words. And whatsoever things he had heard from them about the Lord and about His miracles, Polycarp, as having received them from eye-witnesses of the life of the Word, would relate altogether in accordance with the Scriptures.' Upon this extract Dr. McClymont, author of the Commentary on John's Gospel in the "Century Bible," makes the following cogent remark: 'It is beyond dispute that this Irenaeus had accepted the Fourth Gospel as a genuine work of the Apostle John. Is it creditable that he would have done so, if it had not been acknowledged by his teacher Polycarp, who had been a disciple of John? And if it was accepted by Polycarp as a genuine writing, notwithstanding its marked dissimilarity to the other Gospels, what better evidence could we have that John was really its author, and that it was accepted as his, from the very first, by the leaders of the Church in Asia Minor?' (*The New Testament and its Writers,* p. 42).

Internal Evidence

In summarising the internal evidence of the Johannine authorship of the Gospel, we shall avail ourselves of the line of argument followed by the late scholarly Brooke Foss Westcott, Bishop of Durham (1825-1901), in the Introduction to his Commentary on the Gospel in question. It may thus be summed up. It can be shown, says the Bishop, that the writer was (i) a Jew, (ii) a Jew of Palestine, (iii) an eye-witness of the events he describes, (iv) an Apostle, and consequently (v) the Apostle John.

I. *The author of the Fourth Gospel was a Jew.* This is demonstrated by his marked familiarity with the current Jewish thought and outlook. (*a*) He was, for example, fully acquainted with the contemporary Messianic expectations. He refers to the Pharisees' question to John Baptist 'Art thou that Prophet?' (see chap. 1.21, with Deut. 18.15), and to the Samaritan woman's saying 'I know that Messias cometh, which is called the Christ' (4.25). He reports the common talk concerning our Lord: 'Many said . . . Of a truth this is that Prophet . . . But some said, Shall Christ come out of Galilee?'

(7.40-42). Also in 12.34 'We have heard out of the law that Christ abideth for ever; how sayest thou then that the Son of Man must be lifted up?' The constant conflict of our Lord with the Jews' expectation of a temporal sovereignty, then and there to be set up, is indicated in such Scriptures as chap. 6.15—'When Jesus therefore perceived that they would come and take him by force to make him a King, he departed again into a mountain alone'; and in the record of Pilate's question 'Art thou the King of the Jews?' and our Lord's answer 'My Kingdom is not of this world . . . (else) would my servants fight' (18.33-37).

(*b*) The writer of the Gospel was equally well aware of the other religious ideas common to the people and the time, such as the hostility between the Jews and the Samaritans (4.9); the contempt of the rulers for the untrained masses: 'This people that knoweth not the law are cursed' (7.49); and the general belief in the transmitted punishment for sin: 'His disciples asked him, saying, Master, who did sin, this man or his parents, that he was born blind?' (9.2). Where the writer refers to Jewish ceremonial, too, he does so with precision. He relates accurately our Lord's reminder to the Jews that punctilious as they were in regard to the Sabbath, they yet did not hesitate to circumcise a man on the sabbath-day (7.22, 23); and with equal accuracy records that the accusers of our Lord would not enter a Gentile court, for fear of being ceremonially defiled (18.28). It has been sometimes thought that the writer tripped in speaking of Caiaphas as being 'high priest that same year' (11.49), the elevation to the high-priesthood not being, in fact, an annual appointment. But there was no slip here. What the writer was noting was the remarkable fact that in that same year in which our Lord's life or death was in question, such a ruthless man as Caiaphas should control the Jewish policy, and yet should utter so remarkable a prophecy. Neither here nor elsewhere does the author fall into error.

'A Hebrew Soul in a Greek Body'

(*c*) That the writer of the Gospel was clearly a Jew is also shown, the Bishop says, by the style in which the book is written. 'The vocabulary, the structure of sentences, the symmetry, the numerical symbolism of the composition,' he says, 'the expression and the arrangement of the thoughts, are all essentially Hebrew . . . The words are Greek words, but the spirit that animates them is Hebrew.' The author's personal outlook, as the Bishop shows, is Jewish. The Old Testament is the basis of his religion. Judaism, he constantly insists, is the starting-point of Christianity. His eye is ever upon the fulfilment of the ancient prophecies. As he relates the story of the crucifixion, he sees their presence; the parting of the garments, the casting of the lots, our Lord's thirst, His unbroken limbs, His pierced side, are all 'that the Scripture might be fulfilled'—Much more could be quoted under this head, but this must suffice.

II. *The author of the Fourth Gospel was not only a Jew, but a Jew of Palestine.* This is the second point on which Bishop Westcott lays stress. It is shown (*a*) by the fact that he manifestly lived in the midst of the events he described, and had an intimate knowledge of the local topography. 'These things were done in Bethabara beyond Jordan, where John was baptising' he says, locating the sphere of the Baptist's earlier ministry (1.28); later he says of him, 'And John was baptising in Aenon near to Salim, because there was much water there.' (3.23). Of our Lord's journey through Samaria he writes 'Then cometh he to . . . Sychar; now Jacob's well was there' (4.5). Of Bethany, the home of Lazarus and his sisters, he says that it was about fifteen furlongs from Jerusalem (11.54). He gives similar information concerning the lake of Galilee; he speaks of 'going down' to this place or that. He knew Jerusalem well, before its destruction by the Romans; all the details given of events taking place within or without its walls are from one who is clearly standing on his own ground.

III. The Bishop's third point is that *the writer of the Fourth Gospel was an eye-witness of the events that he relates.* This is shown, he says, by the intimate particulars found in his narrative. (*a*) It is noticeable, for example, in his references to the *time* at which events took place. It was at 'about the tenth hour' when John's two disciples came to see where Jesus dwelt (1.39). It was at 'about the sixth hour' (presumably according to Roman time, in the evening) when our Lord reached Jacob's well (4.6); at 'the seventh hour' the nobleman's son recovered from his fever (4.52); and again it was at 'about the sixth hour' (on this occasion almost certainly in the morning), when Jesus stood before Pilate, on the day of His crucifixion (19.14).

(*b*) The writer observed details concerning *numbers*, also. There were 'six waterpots' at the marriage at Cana (2.6); it was a lad who gave up to our Lord his 'five loaves and his two fishes' (6.9); the disciples had rowed 'five and twenty or thirty furlongs' before they saw Him walking on the water (6.19); there were 'one hundred and fifty and three' great fishes caught on the morning of the day on which they met their risen Lord on the shore.

The Author of the Fourth Gospel an Apostle

IV. Further, *the writer of the Gospel was evidently an apostle;* so says the Bishop, and he adduces the following details to substantiate his claim. (*a*) The emotions and reactions of the disciples, he says, were evidently well known to him. He observes the effect of the miracle at Cana upon them: 'his disciples believed on him' he tells us (2.11), and, he quotes the Scripture which was brought to their mind when they saw Him driving out the traffickers in the Temple (2.17); also their remembrance after His resurrection of this word concerning the raising up of 'the temple of His body' spoken during His earlier ministry (2.22). He relates that though they marvelled at His holding speech with the Samaritan woman 'yet no man said . . . Why talkest thou with her?' (4.27); he remarks on their fear at the sight of Jesus walking on the sea (6.19) and the reaction of some of them to His promise of eternal life if they fed upon Him as the bread which came down from heaven: 'this is a hard saying' they said (6.60).

(*b*) Not only so; the writer of the Gospel possessed a knowledge of our Lord's emotions also: 'When Jesus saw (Mary) weeping, and the Jews also weeping . . . he groaned in the spirit and was troubled' (11.33), he tells us; and it is he who notes the agitation of our Lord as He announced that one of His disciples should betray Him (13.21). Many similar instances show clearly that the author was one of the inner circle that gathered around their Lord.

Here, then, was a Gospel written by a Jew, cognisant of Jewish customs, ideals, and aspirations; a Jew to whom the land of Israel was wholly familiar; one whose detailed narrative shows him to be an eye-witness of the events that he records; a person who was one of our Lord's intimate followers—who else could he be but John the son of Zebedee, 'the disciple whom Jesus loved'?

Heinrich Ewald's Strong Conclusion

Such, very scantily outlined, is Bishop Westcott's argument (so far as internal evidence was concerned) for the Johannine authorship of the last of the four Gospels; and so cogent has it been felt to be that almost all later commentaries and handbooks on John's Gospel have laid it under contribution.—One singular fact is associated with it. The German professor Heinrich Ewald (1803-1875) though opposed to the great extremes of what was known as the Tübingen School of Theology, was almost equally antagonistic to the views of his more conservative brethren; yet the Bishop was able to quote from him the following somewhat startling statement: 'Those who since the first discussion of this question have been really conversant with it, never could have, and never have had, a moment's doubt. As the attack on St. John has become fiercer and fiercer, the truth during the last ten or twelve years has been more solidly established, error has been pursued into its last hiding-place, and at this moment the facts before us are such that no man, who does not determine knowingly to choose error and reject truth, can dare to say that the Fourth Gospel is not the work of the Apostle John.' 'These,' says the Bishop, 'are calm and decisive words, which are simply true'; and with them our summary may fittingly close.

The Place of The Holy Spirit in Preaching*

By Paul Tucker

In dealing with my theme I can but offer a few thoughts for consideration. Knowing something of the testimony of the Bible League I am encouraged to believe that the subject to be brought under review is not without meaning. If there were more preaching in the power of God's Spirit there would be less expression of man's vacillating subjective reasoning, which is so often contrary to the categorical statements of Holy Scripture. Would that every preacher could say with Paul, 'My speech and my preaching was not with enticing words of man's wisdom, but in demonstration of the Spirit and of power; that your faith should not stand in the wisdom of men, but in the power of God' (1 Cor. 2.4, 5).

The Human and the Divine

There are two elements in the preaching of the Word. There is, first, the human element. Paul speaks of '*my* preaching.' Preaching is a ministry which God has committed to men. Frail creatures, reclaimed by the grace of God are the instruments used by Him for proclaiming the Gospel. God could have employed heavenly intelligences, but He did not do so. When Peter and John were imprisoned by order of the Sanhedrin, an angel was sent to release them and to bid them to 'stand and speak in the temple to the people all the words of this life' (Acts 5.20). When Cornelius, the Roman centurion, was seeking fuller spiritual light, an angelic vision was granted him, with the command 'Send men to Joppa and call for one Simon . . . he shall tell thee what thou oughtest to do' (Acts 10.5, 6). In each case an angel had come from the heavenly glory to give men direction concerning preaching—why did not they themselves preach? They had come a long way! Someone has said that if the angelic host were commissioned to proclaim the gospel heaven would be empty of them in five minutes. Yet the amazing ministry of declaring 'all the words of this life' is entrusted to men, and not to angels.

Apart from the fact that man has experienced the grace of God, in a unique way, so that he is qualified to speak the divine message out of a full heart, there would seem to be a deeper reason for his thus being commissioned. It was through the spoken word that man fell. Satan did some very effective preaching in the garden of Eden! His sermon was one of duplicity, instilling doubt; and the word proved mightier than the sword. I incline to the idea that as man's ruin was brought about by the preaching of a lie, it was God's purpose that his recovery should be achieved by the preaching of 'the word of the truth of the gospel'; and that, by members of a race whom Satan had sought to destroy. Here surely is seen what has been called 'poetic justice' in the means by which moral equilibrium is restored. In any case, to employ man is God's method. As Phillips Brooks has said, 'Preaching is . . . truth through personality.' Not personality apart from truth, nor yet truth independent of personality; both are combined.

The Place of the Holy Spirit

So, then, there is the human element in preaching. The mind, the emotions, the individuality—all are to be used to God's glory; nor can this aspect of the ministry of the Word be ignored. But there is also the divine element; there is the place of the Holy Spirit in preaching; and it is with His place and His activity that we are now mainly concerned. For the sake of clarity we may deal with our theme in three phases:— (1) The PREPARATION for preaching; (2) the MOMENT of preaching; and (3) the RESPONSE to preaching.

First, then, the act of PREPARATION. I am personally convinced that before the sermon is made ready, the preacher himself needs to be prepared. Ere Peter could preach to Cornelius and his household, he

*An address delivered at the Annual Meeting of the Bible League, 1956.

himself required spiritual adjustment. On this occasion the seeker was more ready than the messenger. The 'hold-up' was not with Cornelius; but with Simon; the delay was until the moment when the latter could say 'The Spirit bade me go, nothing doubting' (Acts 11.12). Are we concerned that the Holy Spirit should prepare us ere we set about constructing our sermon? The prophet Ezekiel, 'as a sign,' is most helpful here. Note his self-abnegation by reason of 'the appearance of the likeness of the glory of the Lord' (Ezek. 1.28); and observe what follows: 'The Spirit entered into me . . . and set me upon my feet . . . and the Spirit said unto me . . . thou shalt speak my words unto them' (Ezek. 2.2, 3, 7). When the man is ready, help is assured in the preparation of the material—'the Spirit spread it before me, and it was written within and without' (verse 10). When the Word is thus opened to us, when the Spirit of God arrests our attention until the Scripture becomes life to us, we may indeed greatly rejoice. Do we not too often rack our brains for a subject instead of seeking that the Spirit should search and illumine our hearts? 'He spread it before me'—blessed assurance it is when the Lord gives the Word, and the preacher enters the pulpit fortified by such a conviction! Ezekiel was told to 'eat' (3.3) and 'speak' (3.4). The suggestion is that of sympathy with the truth itself. The Spirit must make the message real in the experience of the messenger. Too much preaching lacks this identification of life. Too many addresses are like the announcements at a great railway station—they speak of places that have never been visited by the speaker. Oh, the tragedy of preaching a truth that has never become operative in the preacher's own heart and life! Nor must we forget the implication of verse 24: 'Go and shut thyself within thine own house.' No sermon is complete in its preparation until we have dealt with it in prayer before God, and turned our study into a sanctuary.

Memory, Mind and Motive

I pass from the preparation to the actual MOMENT of preaching. How intimately the Holy Spirit is associated with the delivery of the Gospel! The Apostle Peter speaks of the gospel preached 'with the Holy Ghost sent down from heaven' (1 Peter 1.12). Paul congratulates the Thessalonians on the way that they had received the truth, and adds, 'For our gospel came not to you in word only, but also in power and in the Holy Ghost.'—Notice, then, some of the ways in which the Spirit of God is associated with preaching (*a*) He can aid the memory. 'The Holy Ghost,' said our Lord, ' . . . shall bring all things to your remembrance, whatsoever I have said unto you' (John 14.26). This Scripture primarily applies to the inspiration of the New Testament. The apostles were safeguarded from mistake or exaggeration in what they recorded because the Holy Spirit brought back accurately to their memory that which the Lord Jesus had taught them. But there is also a principle here. The Holy Ghost is the Spirit of Remembrance; and what preacher has not experienced His faithfulness in bringing to mind some truth hidden away in the subconsciousness? Sometimes He brings back thoughts of earlier days or years which the speaker had no idea of mentioning. It is His ministry, that no flesh should glory in His presence.

But further (*b*), God's Spirit can make us scriptural in our preaching. He can mould our thinking. 'To be carnally minded is death; but to have the mind of the Spirit [margin] is life and peace.' How carnal a man can be in the pulpit! Some utterances would never fall from a preacher's lips, some jests would remain unspoken, if the Spirit were mastering his mind. He alone enables us to fulfil a scriptural ministry. 'Which things we speak,' says the Apostle Paul, 'not in words which man's wisdom teacheth, but which the Holy Spirit teacheth, comparing spiritual things with spiritual' (1 Cor. 2.13).

(*c*) God's Spirit, too, will give to us the right motive in preaching. Everything that has its origin in the Holy Spirit has its culmination in the Person of Christ. Jesus said, 'He shall glorify me.' The Spirit-filled messenger will exalt the Saviour—he cannot do otherwise. Every man, message, or movement may be judged by the place given to Christ. The great question is not, Is He present, or even prominent? but, Is He pre-eminent? To be influenced by the Holy Spirit in our preaching is to have a Christo-centric motive.

God's Spirit (*d*) will also ensure freedom; 'Where the Spirit of the Lord is, there is liberty' (2 Cor. 3.7). How we need to be liberated from the fear of man, the oppression of the Adversary, the bane of circumstances, and the bondage of sin. There is an emancipating activity when we preach in the power of the Holy Spirit.

Fearlessness and Graciousness

There are two revealing terms in Scripture which set forth the Holy Spirit's relation to the moment of preaching. The first is 'fulness.' In Acts 4.31 this is linked with fearlessness in preaching. 'They were all filled with the Holy Ghost, and spake the word of God with boldness.' In Acts 6.10 the 'fulness' is associated with preaching that is irresistible: 'They were not able to resist the wisdom and the spirit by which he (Stephen) spake.' Elsewhere we read that the speaker was 'full of the Spirit'; thus his ministry, though unacceptable, was mighty in its impact and could not be gainsaid. So compelling was the force of truth that the audience put fingers in their ears (verse 57). A church with a ministry such as this would be as 'terrible as an army with banners.'

Another relationship of the Holy Spirit to preaching is that of His anointing. This is used of our Lord's own ministry. Applying Isaiah 61 to Himself He declared in the synagogue at Nazareth, 'The Spirit of the Lord is upon me, because he hath anointed me to preach . . . the gospel' (Luke 4.18). This anointing is here linked with graciousness. 'They wondered at the gracious words that proceeded out of his mouth' (verse 22). It differs from the 'fulness' in that the latter is within the believer, while the former is upon him. There seems a veiled reference to this in Acts 4.33: 'With great power gave the apostles witness of the resurrection of the Lord Jesus, and great grace was upon them all.' How greatly we need this quality! Many a messenger has been limited by an absence of grace in voice, or tone, or manner. Let us remember that we cannot whip our hearers into belief or spirituality; that we need to be, like our Lord, 'full of grace and truth.'

Enlightenment and Life

A final word concerning the RESPONSE of the listeners. Here again God's Spirit is active. He who aids in preparation and delivery is also at work while the message is proclaimed. Observe the importance and indispensability of His work in this regard. (*a*) He alone can convict of sin (John 16.7-9). A jury may convict of crime; conscience may convict of sins; the Holy Spirit alone can convict of *sin*; that is, of the refusal to believe in the Lord Jesus Christ. This is regarded as negligible by the worldly man. There are many sins, in his opinion, far worse than that. But when the Holy Spirit begins to work in his heart he sees that the crowning and condemning sin is unbelief. Who but He can bring this about?

(*b*) The Spirit, too, enlightens the mind. Spiritual truth, however clearly and logically presented, cannot be received by the natural man. He has not the capacity. The understanding is darkened. So the Apostle Paul declares in his great statement, based on words found in Isaiah, 'Eye hath not seen (it is not by observation), nor ear heard (it is not by information), neither hath it entered into the heart of man (it is not by imagination) the things which God hath prepared for them that love Him. But God hath revealed them unto us by His Spirit; for the Spirit searcheth all things, yea, the deep things of God.' Nothing could be clearer. Divine truth is apprehended by revelation; the unveiling of the truth preached is by the Holy Ghost.

The Life Giver

Further, (*c*) the Spirit only can give life; and that is what dead men need. 'You hath He quickened,' says the Apostle. It is the Spirit alone that imparts life. All our preaching and persuading will not do this. Ezekiel saw in vision a valley of bones, relics of the ravages of war; they were 'very many' and 'very dry.' What a depressing congregation! Ezekiel preached and there was some response: bones came together; articulated skeletons assumed flesh, sinew, and skin; but a fatal deficiency remained: 'There was no breath in them.' It was not until the wind of God entered into them—until God breathed upon the slain—that they rose to their feet animated and powerful, 'an exceeding great army.'

Preaching may produce some results. There may be a 'noise'; there may be a display of organization; there may be a measure of transformation in behaviour. Yet only the Spirit of God can quicken hearts into newness of life. Only He can send revival, aptly described as 'the inrush of the Spirit into a body that threatens to become a corpse.'

Thus while in all our preaching the human element will necessarily be present, may the divine element be paramount; for it is 'not by might, nor by power, but by my Spirit, saith the Lord of Hosts' (Zech. 4.6).

'A safe stronghold', in Luther's hand

The Man that was Born Blind

John 9.1-41

A short consideration by an Ophthalmic Surgeon

Dr. J. E. Shelley

One does not need to be a specialist to be struck by the terrible prevalence of blindness in Palestine at the time of our Lord. Evidence of this is to be found in the great number of miraculous healings of the blind, recorded in the Gospels. Indeed, when John the Baptist's disciples asked for the signs of Christ's Messiahship, He placed first on the list, 'The blind receive their sight' (Matt. 11.5). This miracle of restoration of sight is almost, if not quite, the most common wonder of Christ's works, *and in some ways the most remarkable.*

When, as a soldier, I was stationed in Egypt, and later rode through Palestine and Syria, the appalling condition of the eyes of the population was instantly obvious. Later, when working at the Ophthalmic Hospital of St. John, at Jerusalem, I learned that the proportion of *totally* blind persons per 100,000 in Egypt was 890! In Southern Palestine it was nearly as bad. There were villages in which a person with two sound eyes was the exception and one village near Bethlehem (Beit Sahhur) was known as the Village of the Blind. To enforce this it might be added that the corresponding figure in Great Britain was 50 per 100,000. With all the appliances and advances of modern science, we could do little for the people in those days, 1919 to 1936. Indeed, before the Sulphanamides, we saw literally hundreds of children, mostly Arabs, lose both eyes from Acute Conjunctivitis, in spite of everything that we could do. Thank God, owing to improved social conditions and the fact that the Sulpha drugs have almost wiped out that terrible disease, Acute Conjunctivitis, a marked improvement has taken place.

But there is one miracle that strikes an Ophthalmic Surgeon with especial force. This is the 'Healing of the man blind from his birth' and who in this state of blindness had lived to become an adult. We notice that in verse 2 of our chapter, the disciples attribute his condition either to the sin of his parents or to his own sin. Our Lord says his condition was NOT due to his parents' sin, or his own. It was *not* due to disease, therefore. It was NOT a case of congenital Syphilis, for example. The condition existed 'that the works of God should be made manifest in him'. This phrase immediately reminds us of God's works of creation recorded in Genesis 1 and 2. More than this, our Lord Himself reminds us of these days of Creation when He says, 'I must work the works of Him that sent Me, while it is day, The night cometh when no man can work. As long as I am in the world, I am the Light of the World'.

We must remember that it was Christ who *spoke* these words, of whom it is written in John 1. 'In the beginning was the Word, and the Word was with God, and the Word *was* God . . . *all things were made by Him; and without Him was not anything made that was made.'* So that when we read in Genesis 2.7 that 'the Lord formed man (Adam) out of *the dust of the ground,* and breathed into his nostrils the *breath of life,* and man became a living soul', it was the same Christ who had created Adam before whom the blind man stood.

This gives point to the words of verse 6 in John 9. 'When He had thus spoken, He spat on the ground and made clay', for spittle is what comes from a man's mouth just as words do, and breath does, and clay is that with which the Word is mixed; or on which the Word operated, and man was formed on the sixth day. But, before dealing with this wonderful work of creation at the Pool of Siloam, we might ask ourselves, to what was this man's condition of blindness due?

It was NOT due to disease. It WAS most certainly developmental, for he was born thus. Ida Mann, in her book, *Developmental Abnormalities of the Eye,* says 'a developmental abnormality of the eye is called congenital when it appears before birth'. So, this was a Congenital Abnormality of both eyes, causing blindness. Since it was NOT due to disease, it must have been due to *arrest* of the normal development of the eyes. It was a case of Anophthalmia (absence of eyes) or possibly,

Microphthalsnia, in which extremely minute rudiments of the globe are found. In these cases, which are rare, 64 Bilateral and 12 Unilateral had been reported in 1900. 'There is no vestige of an eye' (Ida Mann). The condition is generally divided into Primary and Secondary Anophthalmia. The Secondary need not trouble us for it is associated with the gross abnormalities of the face and brain (the children seldom survive), which was evidently not present in this case. This man was a case of Primary Anophthalmia. Ida Mann quotes authorities saying that in a typical case *no other defect is present.* She quotes Collins as stating that 'with regard to the rest of the individual, in most cases, there were no other abnormalities'. I give these extracts because this man displayed a mental alertness and penetration which were conspicuously absent in the case of the Pharisees!

But what I wish to stress is that this is not a miracle of healing. It is a CREATION of two organs, previously absent from this man's body. Not only so, it was the creation of the most wonderful sense organs found in man. This is not the place to dilate on the marvels of the human eye, of the photo-sensitive tissue in the retina or the wonderful mechanism for focussing the light upon it, but we must not overlook the teaching which is contained in the words 'He made clay and anointed the eyes of the blind man'. In Romans 9.20-21 we read, 'Nay but, O man, who art thou that repliest against God? Shall the thing formed say to Him that formed it, Why hast thou made me thus? *Hath not the potter power over the clay,* of the same lump to make one vessel unto honour and another unto dishonour?' In this miracle, we have the Great Potter finishing the 'vessel', this man's body. He had not completed it at birth. He had *arrested* the development of the eyes for the very grand purpose that 'the works of God might be made manifest in him'.

This is a demonstration of 'the works of God': the work of God in making man, in this instance (Genesis 2.7). From it we learn that God and Christ made man directly from the clay without ancestors! exactly as Christ created these most marvellous organs in this case.

In verse 32, the Holy Spirit records the words of the once blind man: 'SINCE THE WORLD BEGAN was it not heard that any man opened the eyes of one who was born blind'. How right he was, any opthalmic surgeon will testify!

But notice the words, 'Since the world began'. It was at the beginning of the world that God created Adam and his eyes *directly* from the clay. Ever since then, the bodies of countless millions of the human race have been built up indirectly during gestation by nutriment supplied by the mother, and afterwards by nutriment supplied by the digestion of food taken in by the mouth.

But here was a case where God had returned to the method used 'WHEN THE WORLD BEGAN'—CREATION FROM THE DUST OF THE EARTH. We cannot say whether the Lord Jesus used the atoms of the sixteen elements present in that lump of clay as the material basis of the living cells of the man's eyes. But, if He did not, He created them from nothing and thus formed instantaneously these two marvellous organs. When subsequently Jesus found him, He asked the man, 'Dost thou believe on the Son of God?' Then the man says, 'Who is He, Lord, that I might believe on Him? And Jesus said unto him, Thou hast both seen Him and it is He that talketh with thee. And he said, Lord, I believe. And he worshipped him'. Notice that Jesus asked him, 'Dost thou believe on the SON OF GOD?' He does not here designate Himself as the Messiah or the Christ, nor as the Son of Man, but as *one with God,* as the second Person in the Trinity. He uses this Name because in this case He had made manifest a work of God in creation. He had acted here as the ONE 'without whom was not anything made that was made'. The once blind man instantly perceived the force of this claim, for he was himself the living demonstration of its truth, and he at once bestowed on *Christ the worship justly due to Him as* GOD THE SON.

The Holy Spirit in God's Word has given us this example of the way God created man at the beginning, 'when the world began'. To attempt to thrust into God's Word the brutal and cruel theory of evolution is to contradict flatly the plain teaching of God's Word in this and many other passages. It dishonours God, degrades man, and grieves the Holy Spirit.

'Earth to Earth'

CONSIDERATIONS ON THE PRACTICE OF CREMATION

By S. M. Houghton

'In the sweat of thy face shalt thou eat bread, till thou return unto the ground; for out of it wast thou taken: for dust thou art, and unto dust shalt thou return' (Gen. 3.19).

'It is sown a natural body; it is raised a spiritual body' (1 Cor. 15.44).

The obituary columns of our newspapers make it abundantly clear that, in many quarters, cremation rather than burial is rapidly becoming the normal mode of disposing of the bodies of the dead, and the evangelical Christian comes, willy-nilly, face to face with the issues involved in the practice. It is urged upon him by some that hygienic considerations in lands of ever-increasing population make cremation highly desirable, if not absolutely essential, and by others that there is nothing in biblical teaching and Christian theology that conflicts with it. Some would argue that the evangelical tends to be a hidebound conservative, inimical by temperament to all new ideas, both theoretical and practical, and averse to change even if it be change for the better. Accordingly some are bewildered; they look into the Word of God and seemingly they find little to guide them; they look to the pulpit and find it normally silent. Is it, they wonder, a case of 'Please yourself'? As they survey the contemporary scene they find some evangelical ministers willing to take part in funeral services in which cremation has a part, and they ask themselves whether their difficulties in accepting cremation are due to prejudices which cannot find support in the Word of their counsel, or on the other hand whether the acceptance by so many of this form of disposal of the bodies of the dead is, after all, acceptable to God and in keeping with a conscience which seeks to remain void of offence in the sight of God and men.

Historically considered, it is certainly the case that cremation dates from ancient times. It has been the practice of Hinduism from times out of mind. It was common among the aboriginal peoples of India, and it is common among Buddhists. It was once widely practised among some of the 'Indian' tribes of North America. In Europe it finds ample illustration in the tombs of the Stone and Bronze Ages and down to the beginnings of the Christian era. Among ancient Greeks and Romans it was fashionable, particularly among the official and wealthier classes, although—and here we quote from the Oxford Classical Dictionary (Article on Disposal of the Dead: 1950 edition)—'it does not appear that these two methods (cremation and inhumation) corresponded to different eschatological beliefs . . . In the Roman Empire considerations of economy or convenience had a good deal to do with the choice'. The Dictionary gives a clear and fairly detailed account of the disposal of the dead in the classical world.

Certain anthropologists tell us that among some uncivilized peoples the idea prevailed that the spirits of the departed would return to the buried bodies to plague the living, and that cremation must be practised to prevent this. There was also the notion that cremation set free the spirit of man for ever from the ties of this life and enabled it to enjoy unfettered bliss in the life beyond death. Clearly, however, such beliefs bear no relation to biblical revelation, and they have no bearing upon our inquiry.

The great national exceptions to cremation in the old world were Egypt, China and Israel (Judah). In the first-named the practice of embalming and then burying was observed, as we find illustrated in the Book of Genesis and in the vast number of tomb pictures and papyrus records, some of which can be seen in our museums and investigated in our libraries. Jacob was embalmed by order of Joseph (Gen. 50.2). Joseph himself was later embalmed and 'put in a coffin in Egypt', until his descendants could give him sepulture in the land of his fathers. The oath which he had caused them to swear was the outcome of his faith in the God of Abraham, Isaac and Jacob (Gen. 50.24-26). By faith he gave commandment concerning his bones (Heb. 11.22).

The Chinese held it as part of their moral code that the bodies of the dead should be buried in China's earth, whence arose the practice of returning to China for interment such as died outside their native land. The Chinese custom was evil so far as it was associated with the worship of one's ancestors. Some critics have also remarked that it penalized the living because a deep veneration caused the best spots of land to be reserved for the burial of the dead. It was an aspect, too, of China's intense conservatism. But the Christian cannot rightly call China's national custom in question.

It is the practice of the Jews that lies at the root of Christian custom. John's Gospel includes the phrase, 'as the manner of the Jews is to bury' (19.40), and the entire mass of Old and New Testament witness constitutes the strength of the argument for Christian burial as against the modern plea for cremation. It was the spread of belief in the Gospel throughout Europe that ended the practice of cremation as it was found among Greeks, Romans, and 'barbarians'. The doctrines of redemption (including that of the body) and of resurrection, backed by age-old Jewish custom, caused all who confessed Christ and embraced His teachings to desire interment at death, and this became universal in Christendom. In the early centuries of the Christian era, 'it was to outrage this well-known Christian sentiment that persecutors sometimes burned the bodies of the martyrs and scattered their ashes in mockery of the resurrection' (A. Plummer).

We may well ask when and why the idea of cremation of the dead reappeared, and we shall virtually confine our attention to Britain although progress was rapid on the Continent of Europe. It was in the middle of the 19th century that cremation found its advocates. A few Italian chemists and physicians appear to have ventilated the idea in their own country, and it was in Italy that progress was first made, a major landmark being the legalization of the practice in 1877. Garibaldi, the best-known Italian of his age, was himself cremated when he died in 1882. His will had arranged for this. In England, Sir Henry Thompson, a professor of surgery of London University, was chiefly responsible for founding the first cremation society in the land in 1874, and he became its first president. Land was purchased for a crematorium, but the Home Office was hostile to the scheme and for a time it remained in abeyance. In 1884 a father was indicted for attempting to burn the body of his child instead of having it buried. The legal judgment that resulted laid it down that the father's act was not an offence against English law, unless it could be proved that a public nuisance had been committed. The decision greatly encouraged the Cremation Society to go ahead with its plans. Its propaganda found support in some quarters and in 1902 an Act of Parliament gave definite legalization to the practice of cremation, while at the same time guaranteeing exemption from participation for any minister who found it repugnant to his convictions. Since then progress has been steady.

We may well note the fact that in Britain support for cremation began and increased at a time when a liberal theology had invaded the churches. It would certainly be a difficult matter to prove that the progress and practice of cremation was directly due to the departure from a biblical theology. But it undeniably ran parallel to it, and particularly to a weakening in the belief in the resurrection of the body and in the physical resurrection of Christ Himself. Practice hinges on doctrine, and if the latter is denied or doubted, it is no wonder if practice undergoes a corresponding change for the worse. The man who denies the literality of the physical resurrection of the Lord is he who is also prepared to deny that the dead of all the ages will in God's time experience a resurrection. No matter then what becomes of his earthly tabernacle when his soul vacates it!

It is not unworthy of note that Sir Henry Thompson, who championed the cause of cremation until his death in 1904, was himself an agnostic of a most pronounced kind. Two years before his death he wrote a short book entitled 'The unknown God', the title being taken from Acts 17.23. A London minister of the period, speaking about the matter, told his congregation: 'The altar which St. Paul saw in Athens had on it the inscription, "Agnosto Theo", which might without any great violence be rendered, "To the Unknown God"; and here, after these many centuries, that same altar is still raised, and a man in the heart of the Christian civilization, a distinguished man who has passed his life in scientific and beneficent labour, bows down before that altar'. The preacher went on to say that, to the writer of the book, God was nothing more than Infinite and Eternal Energy; truth could only be learned from the study of phenomena; man could only discover truth by his own unaided efforts; no revelation had ever been given to man; the Bible has no divine authority, and Christ, though treated with respect as a remarkable person and even a remarkable teacher, is dismissed as a young Jewish enthusiast. And Sir Henry believed that all educated persons would, in no distant time, accept the position of the agnostic and discard completely the belief that man had received a supernatural revelation.

But we turn to consider the biblical position. To what extent is the Christian bound by a practice, undeniably Christian as it was formerly Jewish, which has remained unchanged through nearly a score of centuries? If he can travel by air without stirrings of conscience, and discard the pedestrian modes of travel of his forefathers, is he also entitled to discard inhumation and take up with cremation? Is any Christian doctrine denied or compromised in cremation? We do well to ask ourselves these and similar questions, and to seek biblical answers. In this, as in all else, we must seek 'to the law and to the testimony: if they speak not according to this word, it is because there is no light in them' (Isaiah 8.20). We are not to cleave to a practice simply and solely because it is ancient. An innovation may be for the better. Is it so in this case? We shall confine our attention to religious considerations as these are, with us, paramount.

We again emphasize the fact, plain to all, that burial has been the age-old practice of Jews and Christians. Old and New Testaments alike know nothing else. The few Old Testament exceptions are not difficult of explanation. In several cases men were burned with (supernatural) fire as a token of divine displeasure, just as at sundry times, both biblical and post-biblical, the wrath of men has been vented upon their kind in such events as the 'burning fiery furnace' (Daniel 3), and the fires of martyrdom in more modern times. Hatred for Wycliffe and his doctrine led to his exhumation and the burning of his bones long after he had died. To Marian martyrs was given the signal honour of manifesting their faith at the stake.

In Numbers 11.1-3 the 'fire of Taberah' burnt and consumed the complainers among Israel. In Numbers 16.35, 250 men who offered incense in the Korah, Dathan and Abiram rebellion were destroyed by fire from the Lord. Leviticus 20.14 shows the awful end of a man, his wife and his mother-in-law, who violated divine laws governing human relationships; while 21.9 in the same book decrees death by burning for the daughter of a priest who profaned herself and her father by playing the whore (cf. Gen. 38.24). In Joshua's day the death of Achan and his family, the troubler of Israel, was by stoning followed by the burning of the bodies with fire, after which, we read, 'so the Lord turned from the fierceness of His anger' (7.25-26). We are accustomed to being told that these various cases reflect merely the mental and religious outlook of long ago, and that our thoughts of God do not run along such lines. We think not so. All things written aforetime, by divine inspiration, were written for our learning, for our encouragement and for our admonition 'upon whom the ends of the world are come' (1 Cor. 10.11).

Centuries later, when Jeroboam I commenced golden-calf worship in Bethel and Dan, the 'man of God out of Judah' denounced his act and prophesied that men's bones would be burned upon the idolatrous altar at Bethel; this would render it an abomination indeed to all pious persons, and even to the ungodly worshippers. Fire from heaven burned up the two companies of fifty which were sent by the ungodly Ahaziah to take the prophet Elijah (2 Kings 1.10-12). Amos records special divine indignation against Moab because its king had 'burned the bones of the king of Edom into lime' (2.1), an act comparable to that recorded in 2 Kings 3.27. As recompence, Amos prophesied that God would send a fire upon Moab and its palaces. In other words, from a nation which did not own the God of Israel, Jehovah required behaviour befitting His moral law written in the consciences of men at large. And that law ran contrary to the burning of an enemy's corpse, rendering honourable interment impossible.

The teaching of the Old Testament, clearly enough, is that the burning of a human body is only right when a sin peculiar for its hideousness is awarded a penalty designed to show the hatred with which it is regarded by God. The burning of the bodies of King Saul and his sons by the men of Jabesh-gilead, after they had taken them from the Philistines, seems to have been occasioned by the desire to prevent the further desecration of the bodies by the enemy if, perchance, they recovered them. Dr. Robert Jamieson remarks, in his comments on this passage (1 Sam. 31.11-13): 'This was not a Hebrew custom. It was probably resorted to on this occasion to prevent all risk of the Bethshanites coming to disinter the royal remains for further insult'. Hence it is a 'neutral' passage on which no teaching can be based. Amos 6.10 records the burning of a human body. Ten men die in one house, probably of plague and starvation, during a siege; an uncle, as the next of kin, comes to dispose of the dead by burning, the highly unusual practice only being resorted to through dire necessity, and possibly to prevent contagion. 'Here', says A. R. Fausset, 'it heightened the sadness of the picture that there was not admissible the decent mode of interment, but that a mode had to be adopted most alien to their feelings and religion—viz. burning, and this by the one who loved the dead most, the uncle, now that father and brothers were gone.'

The references to burnings accompanying royal entombments (*e.g.* 2 Chron. 16.14—the burial of Asa) do not indicate cremation, but nothing more than the burning of spices and possibly furniture in the king's honour. Jeremiah 34.5 makes reference to the same practice. It was common also in the Greek and Roman world to present 'grave-gifts' to be burned with the body (if cremated) and these might be large and costly. It seems to have been a widespread custom throughout the ancient world, particularly followed in the case of distinguished persons. There is no suggestion of burning the dead belonging to the hosts of Gog and Magog in Ezekiel 39. After the tremendous slaughter which this chapter indicates, it takes the victors seven months to deal with the bodies of the slain, but it is burying, not burning, which is mentioned.

Again, whereas we have in the Old Testament two cases of translation, those of Enoch and Elijah, we learn that it was not the will of God to translate Moses when his work was done. His prayer (Psa. 90) speaks of man 'flying away' (v.10), but not in the sense of a translation including the body. Moses himself was to die by the hand of God. Mount Nebo became his death chamber, and from its window he looked upon the land which he was not to enter. 'So Moses the servant of the Lord died there in the land of Moab, according to the word of the Lord; and He buried him in a valley in the land of Moab . . . but no man knoweth of his sepulchre' (Deut. 34.5-6). Where God is Himself the undertaker—we speak reverently—there is no thought of cremation.

'And no man knows that sepulchre,
And no man saw it e'er,
For the angels of God upturned the sod
And laid the dead man there.'

We may well agree with the famed poetess: 'That was the grandest funeral that ever passed on earth.'

The only New Testament reference to the burning of the human body occurs in 1 Corinthians 13.3, and obviously it has no relevance to the relationship of cremation to the death of the Christian. The apostle was undoubtedly aware of the Greek practice and uses it as if to say, 'If a man (a Greek) is prepared to lay down his life for a cause in which he believes, it profits him nothing unless love is the motive of his action'.

But the New Testament, and Christian doctrine based upon it, certainly include indications, if not precepts, that burial, not cremation, is the mind of the Lord. We have already made reference to the replacement of cremation by burial in Christendom when the Gospel had spread abroad. The change calls for explanation, and it cannot be doubted that, in chief, the practice of the Jews, the facts of the Gospel of Christ, the belief in the resurrection of the body, and the theological tenet that the Christian's body was the redeemed temple of the Holy Spirit of God, combined to bring it about. The practice of the Jews needs no further comment, the further points do.

That Christ was buried is an essential part of the Gospel. He was the corn of wheat which fell into the ground and died, that it might bring forth much fruit. Loving hands anointed Him for His burial (John 12.24; 12.7; Matt. 26.12). When Paul summarizes the Gospel which he preached—and he had first received it from heaven—he says that 'Christ died for our sins according to the Scriptures, and that He was buried, and that He rose again the third day according to the Scriptures' (1 Cor. 15.3-4). That Christ was to be buried was prophesied by Isaiah in his 53rd chapter: 'They appointed His grave with the wicked, but He was with the rich in His death' (v.9), and the fact is wonderfully sacred to Christian hearts. For Christians' sake the Lord of life experienced death. He

'bowed to the grave, destroyed it so,
And death by dying slew.'

If, when we ourselves come to die, we wish to follow His steps (1 Pet. 2.21), it is supremely fitting that we should seek honourable burial. Those who, in God's providence, have been called through faith to meet death in the fires of martyrdom have honoured their Lord indeed. But the many who through faith have escaped sword and fire and scaffold have honoured the Lord equally in their 'sleep in Jesus'. The delightful apostolic phrase suggests the provision of a bed in which the blessed of the Lord thus sleep, and the bed is the grave, whether it be rocky cave or excavated earth. The word 'cemetery' itself simply means 'a place of sleeping'. It is the body alone which sleeps. The soul and spirit depart to be with Christ, which is far better (Phil. 1.23). The inferior part, redeemed together with the soul by the precious blood of Christ, remains on earth until the trump of resurrection 'awakes the chorus, from desert and field, of the blessed dead'.

'Alone and safe in the holy keeping
Of Him who holdeth the grave's cold key,
They have laid thee down for the blessed sleeping,
The quiet rest which His dear ones see.'
(Horatius Bonar).

C. H. Spurgeon, speaking in the Metropolitan Tabernacle, once said that if he were presented with a choice between living until the Lord's second advent, or dying before the advent, he would choose the latter, so that he might have fellowship with the Lord in burial and bodily resurrection. Perhaps we cannot echo the desire, but it is a permissible one. And certainly the whole tenor of the New Testament favours the burial of the body of the believer, not its burning.

Again, the fact of a bodily resurrection yet to come suggests the congruence of burial with the 'blessed hope'. The apostle in 1 Corinthians 15 takes it for granted that the bodies of believers who die are buried. There is nothing to suggest otherwise. His own emphatic and repetitive word is 'sown'. His analogy is drawn from agriculture. The seed, 'it may chance of wheat or of some other grain', is sown in the earth and bears after its kind. 'God gives it a body (in that which follows the sowing) as it has pleased Him'. 'So also is the resurrection of the dead.

IT IS SOWN in corruption; it is raised in incorruption:
IT IS SOWN in dishonour; it is raised in glory:
IT IS SOWN in weakness; it is raised in power:
IT IS SOWN a natural body; it is raised a spiritual body.'

Repetition of the expression indicates the emphatic character of the apostolic teaching. Cremation cannot fit into the analogy. The farmer does not burn his seed in order to procure a harvest. The Christian is not, in this sense, to give his body to be burned. Burning, if it takes place, does not and cannot defeat the will and purpose of God. There is assuredly to be a resurrection both of the just and of the unjust (Acts 24.15). The human body may have been burned in fire, may have been eaten of beasts or of cannibals, may have become mingled as dust with the dust of earth and scattered to the four winds. In the day of resurrection, by a display of stupendous power—the power which raised the body of Christ from Joseph's tomb in Jerusalem and rendered it a glorious body—the believer's body will be raised again and fashioned like Christ's body of glory. The bodies of unbelievers will be raised to shame and everlasting contempt (Daniel 12.2). Daniel speaks of 'sleepers in the dust of the earth' and, as in much else, the New Testament carries on the same thought.

We remark in passing that burial, as that which befits a so-called Christian land and nation, is embedded in English literature, and not only in Christian literature. One or two examples must suffice. The most famous poem in our language includes the lines,

'Beneath those rugged elms, that yew-tree's shade,
Where heaves the turf in many a mouldering heap,
Each in his narrow cell for ever laid,
The rude forefathers of the hamlet sleep.

'The breezy call of incense-breathing morn,
The swallow twittering from the straw-built shed,
The cock's shrill clarion, or the echoing horn,
No more shall rouse them from their lowly bed.'

But the trump of God will avail when call, twittering, clarion and horn fail. The voice of the Son of God will be heard by 'all that are in the graves' and resurrection to life or to damnation will be the immediate and inevitable consequence (John 5.28-29).

Or again, when an English poet laments 'the brave who sink to rest, by all their country's wishes blest', he imagines that

'Honour comes, a pilgrim grey,
To bless the turf that wraps their clay:
And Freedom shall awhile repair
To dwell, a weeping hermit, there.'

But it is when we turn to our 'more sure word of prophecy' that we find the endorsement which comforts truly Christian hearts. Believers sleep, not only in the grave, but in Jesus. 'My flesh also shall rest in hope' (Psa. 16.9; Acts 2.26). Unlike the Lord's body, the bodies of believers certainly see corruption. But if, in a spiritual sense, they are 'buried with Christ by baptism into death' (Rom. 6.4), they may know too that the very sepulture which they receive at the hands of their kindred and friends sees them following according to the pattern shown to them in Scripture's mount (for mount it is). In the grave for a while they find a silent fellowship with the Lord, of whose body it was said by the angelic visitor to earth, 'Come, see the place where the Lord lay'. The grave's dishonour is removed by the burial of Christ, even as death's sting is removed by His death and its power is snatched from it by His resurrection. The lifeless body which lay for three days in the garden-tomb is described by the angel as 'the Lord'. In occupying a similar resting place, do we not demonstrate our soul's rest in the Lordship of Jesus Christ? 'Be it so; and Thine, Lord, all the glory!'

To honour the Lord thus is a part of blessedness. Death has lost its sting; the grave does not have the victory. 'Thanks be to God who giveth us the victory through our Lord Jesus Christ.' Let us, like the 'beloved brethren' of the Epistle, follow in the steps of the 'blessed of the Lord'. Let us imitate them in their steadfastness and unmovability, and repudiate firmly and graciously the teaching and belief that cremation is a 'more excellent way' than that which its adherents wish to displace. If we die, let devout men carry us to our burial. Let us honour the Lord in death as in life. Certainly, in another sense, the body's honour is not yet, for 'it is sown in dishonour'; but when the body is raised in glory, then we shall see and share the glory of the Lord and know the excellency of our God.

'I shall sleep sound in Jesus,
Filled with His likeness rise,
To love and to adore Him,
To see Him with these eyes—
'Tween me and resurrection
But Paradise doth stand,
Then, then, for glory dwelling
In Immanuel's land.'

The Singular Care and Providence of God, and the Textus Receptus

By Bishop D. A. Thompson

In the unhappy reign of King Charles I what became known as the Long Parliament first met on the third of November 1640. Its members were burdened not only by the unconstitutional policy of the monarch but also by the anti-evangelical administration of Dr. William Laud, Archbishop of Canterbury. This prelate was virtually destroying the reformed character of the Church of England. His tyrannical and cruel ways were begetting in the minds of many faithful ministers the thought that the solution of their problems lay in presbyterianism or independency (*i.e.* in what afterwards were called the Baptist and Congregational Church systems).

At this time the majority of the Members of Parliament wished to see the Established Church cleansed of Laudianism and a revival of pure religion throughout Great Britain. With this end in view they nominated a body of 121 divines with 30 lay assessors, to assist Parliament, when requested, in religious matters. This company first met on July 1st, 1643 in the Henry VII Chapel of Westminster Abbey. Hence it is known as the Westminster Assembly. When the cold weather set in the members moved to the adjoining Jerusalem Chamber, which has a large fire-place, by which means they could meet, debate and work in a comfortable temperature.

Parliament directed this august assembly to revise the Thirty-nine Articles of Religion. But this was soon countermanded, as relations between London and Edinburgh became more cordial, and eight Scottish Commissioners were welcomed as additional members of this body. The request was then made for a new and fuller credal statement, for a Longer and a Shorter Catechism, and other ecclesiastical documents.

Richard Baxter affirmed, 'The divines there congregated were men of eminent learning and godliness, ministerial ability and fidelity'. Amongst their number were some of the greatest scholars, preachers and theologians of Christendom. They reflected the mind of the Puritans throughout England, Scotland, Ireland and Wales. They were united on the great doctrines of the historic Christian and Reformed Faith but differed on such matters as Church order and ministry, the sacrament of baptism and events connected with the return of our Lord from Heaven.

These divines fell into five groups. There was a small band of learned, pious Episcopalians, of whom the most outstanding was Dr. James Ussher, Archbishop of Armagh. He was so respected for his great scholarship, tolerance and sincerity, that when he died in 1656, (in England), by order of the Protector, Oliver Cromwell, he was given a state funeral and buried in Westminster Abbey.

The most numerous group consisted of those of presbyterian outlook. Of these the minority were convinced adherents of that form of Church polity advocated by John Calvin. The majority were incumbents of the Church of England who had little quarrel with the Prayer Book, provided it was interpreted in accordance with the Thirty-nine Articles of Religion. They were perfectly happy with the episcopal form of Church government, provided it was of the primitive type, and functioned so as to comprehend some of the principles of presbyterianism and independency (as in the Church of Ireland and other Provinces of the Anglican Communion today), and was divorced from the monstrous error of sacerdotal apostolic succession. They had been driven into the arms of the minority by the intolerance and ritualism of Archbishop Laud as well as by his claim that episcopacy was of divine right. Of the former were Matthew Poole, the scholarly commentator on Holy Scripture, and Edmund Calamy. Of the latter were Dr. William Twisse—who was chosen by the Assembly to be its prolocutor—most learned yet most humble, and Dr. E. Reynolds, who at the Restoration was consecrated Bishop of Norwich, and contributed the General Thanksgiving Prayer to the 1662 Prayer Book.

Amongst the small group of Independents were Thomas Goodwin, Jeremiah Burroughs and Philip Nye. Amongst the Erastians was the great Hebrew scholar Dr. John Lightfoot. Of the Scottish Commissioners, the name of Samuel Rutherford is almost a Christian household word.

The King frowned upon the Assembly and as a consequence the Episcopalians rarely attended, though in another but very true sense Archbishop Ussher was present all through! In 1615 he had drawn up the One Hundred and Four Articles of the Church of Ireland (which eventually, under royal pressure, had to be abandoned for the Thirty-nine Articles of the sister Church in England). The Westminster Assembly took the One Hundred and Four Articles almost word for word and rearranged them so as to form the Westminster Confession, only adding by direction of Parliament, the proof texts. From the Archbishop's *Body of Divinity,* the Catechisms were woven. These great theological works, with slight changes, were approved by Parliament and adopted by the General Assembly at Edinburgh (1648). They became the subordinate standards of Presbyterians throughout the English-speaking world. Before the close of that century they had been adapted for use by the Baptists and Congregationalists. How great is the debt of these three Christian Communions to the erudite Archbishop of Armagh!

The Westminster Confession and the Hebrew and Greek Texts of Scripture

The Westminster Confession consists of thirty-three chapters, each on some special doctrine of the Christian Faith, and each divided into numbered paragraphs. The first chapter is entitled, **Of the Holy Scripture,** and paragraph eight begins:

> 'The Old Testament in Hebrew (which was the native language of the people of God of old), and the New Testament in Greek (which, at the time of the writing of it, was most generally known to the nations), being immediately inspired by God, and by His singular care and providence, kept pure in all ages, are therefore authentical; so as, in all controversies of religion, the Church is finally to appeal unto them.'

Here it is to be noted that the members of this famous Assembly—godly, learned men, 'mighty in the Scriptures' (Acts 18.24), after discussion and debate, unhesitatingly declared that Holy Writ (*a*) was 'inspired by God', and (*b*) its text, 'by His singular care and providence, kept pure in all ages'.

These scholarly theologians recognized that there was a Providence of God and that its operations are sometimes clearly seen as the past is reviewed (see 2 Chron. 16.9 and Westminster Confession, Chapter 5). For instance, taking the life of Joseph in retrospect, it is evident that Divine Providence ruled and overruled in all his vicissitudes, so that his being sold and taken into Egypt, and his unjust imprisonment there, were links in a chain which led to his becoming the powerful minister of Pharaoh, in which capacity he was able to succour his father and his brethren in their necessity. The same over-ruling Providence is seen in the life of Moses, in that he was wondrously rescued from a watery grave as an infant, brought up as the son of Pharaoh's daughter, received the best education and training that Egypt could give, and thus qualified, later, to be God's ambassador to Pharaoh, and to lead the children of Israel out of Egypt and through the wilderness.

So these learned men, as they turned over the pages of history, felt convinced that the overruling Providence of God had been exercised for the preservation, and that too in its purity, of the Written Word. Doubtless they called to mind, that when Jehoiakim, king of Judah, cut the leaves out of the book of the prophecies that Jeremiah had dictated to Baruch the scribe, and cast them into the fire that was on the hearth, so that they were burnt, the Lord in 'His singular care and providence' ordered the prophet to commit the Divine messages a second time to writing (Jeremiah, chapter 36).

Again, when the forces of the Syrian king Antiochus Epiphanes (d. 164 B.C.) had overrun the Holy Land, and were bent on destroying the Jewish religion, the very existence of the Old Testament was at stake. Not only was the Temple desecrated, the Levitical sacrifices proscribed, the performance of the rite of circumcision forbidden, but the possession of any of the Holy Scriptures was punished with death. Yet God in 'His singular care and providence' raised up Judas the Maccabee and endued him and his patriotic followers with such courage that again and again they inflicted decisive defeats upon the oppressors, drove them out of Jerusalem and cleansed the Temple. This from the human angle saved the Holy Oracles from perishing from off the earth.

The Temple Standard Old Testament

Just before our Lord Jesus Christ was born at Bethlehem the humble Temple of Zerubbabel was replaced by the magnificent Fane of Herod (John 2.20). In it, in a special chamber, were deposited and preserved several standard codices of the entire Old Testament from which copies of the whole or parts of it could be made, or existing copies checked and if necessary corrected (cf. Deut. 17.18; 31.9 and 24-26; 1 Sam. 10.25; 2 Kings 22.8, The expression, 'To the Chief Musician' attached to so many of the Psalms (*e.g.* 4, 5, 6, etc.), Prov. 25.1 and Josephus' *Antiquities of the Jews,* Book 3, Chapter 1, Section 7 and Book 5, Chapter 1, Section 17).

Thus when our Lord said, 'It is written' (Matt. 4.4, 6, 7, 10; 21.13; 26.24, 31, etc.), or 'Have ye not read?', or others used the same or a similar expression (Matt. 2.5; 12.3 and 5; 19.4; 21.16 and 42; 22.31; 24.15, etc.), it meant that the text quoted was to be found in that Temple Standard Scripture and in accurate copies of it. No one ever disputed the purity and accuracy of those sacred writings and objected that the text was 'corrupt', 'hopelessly corrupt', or that the original text was 'irretrievably lost' (as do many critics today).

In A.D. 70 Jerusalem was besieged by the Romans and destroyed. In that conflict the Temple was set on fire. The Legionaries rushed into the burning courts and removed (*a*) The Table of Shewbread, (*b*) The Golden Candlestick or Lampstand, (*c*) One of the priestly silver trumpets, and (*d*) One of the standard copies of the Law (definitely the Pentateuch, but it may have been the entire Old Testament). The visitor passing through the Arch of Titus, Rome, can see, sculptured on the inside, Roman soldiers bearing some of these trophies on their triumphal return to the capital. This has been a silent witness for almost nineteen hundred years to the accuracy of the record that Josephus wrote concerning that pathetic event (*The Wars of the Jews,* Book 7, Chapter 5, Sections 5 and 7).

Some of these spoils were deposited in the Temple of Peace shortly afterwards erected, but the Standard Old Testament Codex was kept in the Imperial Palace. Here it remained for rather more than one hundred and fifty years. Then a sincerely religious Emperor, especially friendly to Jews and Christians, Alexander Severus, ascended the throne (A.D. 222-235). He took as his motto, 'Do unto others as thou wouldst have them do unto thee'. He was accustomed to pray every morning in his private chapel where he had images of Apollonius and Orpheus and effigies of Abraham and Jesus Christ! His mother, an artful, ambitious and cruel woman, when passing through Antioch, called for Origen to visit her, and conversed with him (Gibbon's *Decline and Fall of the Roman Empire,* Chapter XVI). But little impression was made on the Queen Mother.

This emperor seems to have been deeply grateful to the Jewish merchants in Rome for never failing to keep his armies supplied with food in their long and arduous campaigns. To mark his appreciation he built them a synagogue (like a certain centurion in the Gospel story—Luke 7.1-10). When the day came for it to be opened, he showed still further his good pleasure by presenting the Temple Scripture to this Jewish community. (See *Introduction to Massoretico—Critical Edition of the Hebrew Bible,* by Dr. C. D. Ginsburg, pp. 408-421, Dr. E. W. Bullinger's *The Massorah* (being a popular summary of Dr. C. D. Ginsburg's work), also *How to read the Bible,* by the Rev. J. Urquhart, Volume 1, pp. 132-134).

It is evident that this Standard Scripture taken from the Temple was used by the Jews during the 3rd and 4th centuries for making fresh copies of their Holy Oracles, for references to it are found in the Massorah. These were the notes made in the upper, lower and side margins as well as between the columns in the Hebrew manuscripts, to aid the scribes in preserving and reproducing the original text in its purity.

It is very striking that Josephus states in his autobiography that the other Temple Scriptures ('the holy books') were given to him by the express concession of Titus (Autobiography, paragraph 75). Nothing is known of their subsequent history but it cannot be doubted that they were specially treasured. From these Temple Scriptures all the Hebrew manuscripts of the Old Testament are derived—either directly or indirectly. This text was first printed by the Jewish Soncino Press (in Italy), 1482-1488, and is the Hebrew Textus Receptus.

In the 4th and 5th centuries there was the irruption of the Barbarians. The Imperial City was sacked, first by the Goths under Alaric in 410 and again by the Vandals under Genseric in 455. Many important buildings were destroyed by these intruders. It seems that the aforementioned synagogue and its priceless Scripture were amongst those that thus suffered, for they disappear from history at this time.

Those who drew up the Westminster Confession, and those who afterwards most warmly and gratefully endorsed it, and also followed the history of that Temple Codex rescued from the flames in A.D. 70, have seen in it another instance of God's 'singular care and providence' operating for the preservation in its purity of the text of that inspired and inerrant literature to which the Lord Jesus referred whenever He used the expression, 'It is written' or a similar phrase.

The New Testament

Until about one hundred years ago most evangelical Protestants had the same convictions with respect to the Greek New Testament. They felt that in the Textus Receptus they had substantially the reproductions of the autographs of the New Testament writers. They saw the hand of God in the warnings uttered by the early Church Fathers when heretics began deliberately to corrupt the New Testament text. It enabled the scribes, when the persecutions ceased, to weed out these corruptions. They gave attention also to every place where there were variant readings and uncertainties, so much so that before the close of the 4th century the text had become uniform, in the type known as the Byzantine.

These Protestants considered that the Reformation was the greatest blessing the Lord had sent to the Visible Church since Pentecost, and that it largely centred around the work of Erasmus, Ximenez, Stephens and Beza, whose labours led to the printing of the text common to the great majority of the Greek New Testament manuscripts. In all this they could see nothing less than the 'singular care and providence of God' giving them substantially the text of the autographs.

The work of collecting manuscripts of the New Testament and of studying them did not, however, end with the death of Beza. It was continued by a succession of scholars. Their devotion to this branch of sacred learning has been touched on in an earlier study but a reminder of the salient features of their researches and of the emergence of two schools of thought therefrom becomes necessary here.

The Textual Critics

Amongst those who so laboured was Brian Walton (1600-1661), Bishop of Chester, whose Polyglot New Testament consisted of the Greek Text of Stephens (1550) with variants from the recently acquired Codex Alexandrinus (which had arrived in London in 1627) and sixteen other manuscripts collated by Archbishop James Ussher, together with the Syriac, Latin, Ethiopian and Persian versions. He was followed by John Fell (1625-1686), Dean of Christ Church and afterwards Bishop of Oxford, who added the readings of eighteen more manuscripts (mostly in the Bodleian) and of the Coptic or Bohairic and Gothic versions. His disciple, Dr. John Mill (1645-1707), Fellow of Queen's College, Oxford, and Principal of St. Edmund Hall, extended these researches and included the evidence of patristic quotations. This work was carried still further by Richard Bentley (1662-1742), Master of Trinity College, Cambridge.

Although these scholars noted variant readings, this in no wise undermined their confidence in the general accuracy of the Textus Receptus. But during this period Religious Rationalism had grown apace in Germany, and the unbelief it generated was to have most sad and serious spiritual repercussions in that land and in Britain. It created an atmosphere which facilitated attacks upon the Reformation Text. Strange as it may seem, it was a devout evangelical, the German Lutheran, J. A. Bengel (1687-1752) who was one of the first to turn from this text. He declared that he preferred the most ancient authorities, and on the strength of such convictions altered the Textus Receptus. Yet his knowledge of the texts of the oldest manuscripts was very meagre, for their publication for the use of scholars did not, and indeed could not, appear until the period of from fifty to one hundred years and more, after his death! He must be held largely responsible for making so fashionable, in this connection, the slogan, that the older the manuscript the greater its weight. He, and those carried away by this adage, never seem to have paused and reflected, that a document can be written in a very great hurry and under very difficult or dangerous circumstances, as in times of persecution, and consequently be marked by great carelessness and many mistakes. In other words an ancient manuscript is not necessarily an accurate copy of an exemplar: it can be the very reverse.

J. J. Wettstein, of Basle, who had been an assistant of Richard Bentley, of Cambridge, and was experienced in such matters, lost no time in pointing out that the manuscripts on which Bengel placed such great reliance and used to 'correct' and 'improve' the Textus Receptus were characterized by many careless mistakes and omissions and hence could only be regarded as untrustworthy.

This most regrettable example set by the otherwise excellent Bengel was followed by another German, J. S. Semler (1725-1791), a thorough-going religious Rationalist, and he by his disciple J. J. Griesbach (1745-1812), a foe of orthodox Christianity. Griesbach had a distinct animus against the historic Christian Faith. He declared, 'Among the several readings of one place, that must deservedly be regarded as suspect which more than the others manifestly favours the dogmas of the orthodox.' Surely it is incomprehensible that born-again believers should give any wieght to the judgment of such a textual critic. Karl Lachmann (1793-1851) also rejected the Textus Receptus. On the other hand C. F. Matthaei (1744-1811), although a German, became a professor at Moscow, and collated a large number of Russian manuscripts. He upheld the Textus Receptus and regarded the early manuscripts with their many differences and omissions as unreliable. The Roman Catholic scholar, J. M. A. Scholz (1794-1852), travelled through Europe, examining all the manuscripts he could find. He considered that the Textus Receptus was authentic, and he was one of the first, if not the first, to pronounce that the oldest manuscripts have only survived because, being erroneous, they had been less used.

Thus by the early 19th century there had emerged two schools of thought with respect to the text of the Greek New Testament. The first was convinced that by 'the singular care and providence of God', the text of the writers of the New Testament was preserved in that which was common to the great majority of the manuscripts. When these scholars were charged with lightly esteeming the few most ancient manuscripts, their reply was, that there was sufficient evidence from their many omissions, additions and mistakes to stamp them as being carelessly copied from bad, perhaps even corrupted copies of still earlier manuscripts. When it was objected that this textual school had few manuscripts of a really early date, the reply was, that this was only to be expected. Copies of the Bible would chiefly be found in churches or in the buildings of religious communities. In these, several services would be conducted every week and in many cases several every day. Consequently, within fifty to one hundred years, the Codex would be so much the worse for wear that it would have to be discarded and perhaps reverently destroyed, and a new transcription take its place.

The other school of textual critics felt strongly that the text of the few most ancient codices of the 4th, 5th and 6th centuries must over-ride the readings of later copies. They took it for granted that the most ancient must be the most accurate, without any qualifying clause. It must be pointed out that towards the close of the century, these critics, especially their leader, Dr. Hort, were so carried away by their theory, that they could not see the unsatisfactory nature of the principles, or lack of principles, upon which they built up their new and revolutionary text.

But at the beginning of the 19th century both sides to this controversy were handicapped by the inability to be sure of the readings of some of the most ancient manuscripts. How and when those disabilities were removed must now be briefly explained.

The Five Most Ancient Manuscripts

By common consent the oldest Codex of the Bible is that in the Vatican Library known as Vaticanus (designated B). It was first listed in the catalogue of 1481 and its previous history is unknown. Certain facts concerning it should be noted. First, neither Cardinal Ximenez nor Eramus considered that its text should override that of others. On the contrary these first two editors of the earliest printed Greek and Latin New Testaments preferred manuscripts of a later date. Again, a number of attempts to collate, and to have facsimiles printed of this venerable Codex proved either unsatisfactory or abortive. Napoleon had it transported (with other treasures) from Rome to Paris, where the Roman Catholic scholar J. L. Hug (1765-1846) examined it and stressed its great age. From that time it has generally been accepted as having been written about 340.

In 1815 the Codex was returned to Rome. Then the Vatican authorities showed a most strange indisposition to allow scholars to inspect it. Sir Frederic Kenyon records that in 1843 Tischendorf, after waiting for several months, was allowed to see it for six hours. Next year De Muralt was permitted to study it for nine hours. In 1845 Dr. S. P. Tregelles was allowed to see it but not to copy a word. His pockets were searched before he might open it, and all writing materials were taken away. Two clerics stood beside him and snatched away the volume if he looked too long at any passage! Deans Alford and Burgon had similar experiences.

At long last the opinion of scholars throughout the world forced the hands of the papal authorities, and a worthy copy of the Vaticanus New Testament was printed in 1868 (followed in due course by the rest of the sacred volume). In 1889-1890 a complete photographic facsimile of the whole manuscript made its contents the common property of all scholars.

Dr. F. H. A. Scrivener states: 'One marked feature, characteristic of this copy, is the great number of its omissions, which has induced Dr. Dobbin to speak of it as presenting "an abbreviated text of the New Testament"; and certainly the facts he states on this point are startling enough. He calculates that Codex B leaves out words or whole clauses no less than . . . 2,556 times in all. That no small proportion of these are mere oversights of the scribe seems evident from the circumstance that this same scribe has repeatedly written words and clauses **twice over**' (*Introduction to the Criticism of the New Testament,* Volume 1, p. 120).

The reference to the large number of omissions refers to words and clauses found in the vast majority of other manuscripts and in the Textus Receptus. That most of these were found in manuscripts which are no longer extant but were written much earlier than the Vaticanus is evident from a study of the works of the Fathers who quote them.

It would be well for the reader to pause and consider these figures and facts. Do they suggest to his mind that the readings of this oldest Codex, the Vaticanus, must be the most accurate, and used to correct all others? Or would the assessment be that although the most ancient of the manuscripts, the Vaticanus bears evidence that it is a carelessly written copy of a still earlier copy, which may well have been hastily transcribed during those difficult times of persecution and marred by defects including the omissions?

The next oldest manuscript is that which Dr. L. F. C. Tischendorf (1815-74) found in the year 1844 in the monastery of St. Catherine near to what is called Mount Sinai. Hence, it is known as the Codex Sinaiticus and designated by the first letter of the Hebrew alphabet, Aleph. It is thought that it was written about ten years after Codex Vaticanus. Through the influence of Czar Alexander II of Russia, it was sent to St. Petersburg in 1859 and through his munificence and the indefatigable labours of the discoverer copies were available to scholars in 1862.

By 1871 Dean Burgon had thoroughly studied the printed copies of these two oldest codices and wrote: 'Ought it not sensibly to detract from our opinion of the value of their evidence to discover that it is easier to find two consecutive verses in which the two MSS differ, the one from the other, than two consecutive verses in which they entirely agree? . . . On every such occasion only one of them can possibly be speaking the truth. Shall I be thought unreasonable if I confess that these perpetual inconsistencies between Codex Vaticanus and Codex Aleph—grave inconsistencies, and occasionally even gross ones—altogether destroy my confidence in either?' (Last Twelve Verses of the Gospel of Mark, pp. 77-78; in Sovereign Grace Book Club reprint, pp. 155-6).

The Codex Alexandrinus (Codex A) is that which was presented by Cyril Lucar, the evangelical Patriarch of Constantinople, to the King of England in 1627. Thus it arrived in this land sixteen years too late for use to be made of it in preparing the Authorized Version. Later King George II handed it over to the care of the British Museum. Scholars consider that it was written in the first half of the 5th century.

A collation of the New Testament was prepared for Walton's Polyglot (1657), and another by C. G. Woide, a distinguished Coptic scholar and Assistant Librarian in the British Museum (1786). A photographic reproduction of the whole was published in 1879-83.

Different parts of the New Testament have been copied from different originals. The text of the Gospels approximates to the Byzantine, but that of the Acts and of the Epistles is nearer to the Vaticanus. Dr. Scrivener states that the Codex has been judged to be carelessly written. Some words have been written twice over by mistake.

The next manuscript in respect to age and importance in this connection is Codex Ephraemi (Codex C). It once belonged to the Italian Medici family but has long been housed in the National Library of Paris. The original manuscript contained the whole Greek Bible. But a scribe appropriated about two-thirds of the leaves of the Old and New Testament, washed or scraped off the ink giving the text of Scripture, and wrote over the first faded writing the works of Ephraem the Syrian. This is known as a 'palimpsest' (*i.e.* a manuscript the original writing of which has been effaced to make room for a second). This is what can be seen in the Paris Library. The most diligent searches have failed to discover the other leaves. The application of chemicals has sufficiently restored the original writing to enable the text to be deciphered, although often not without great difficulty.

Thus there are portions of every book of the New Testament except 2 Thessalonians and 2 John. Various scholars had worked at this palimpsest with partial success, but after the device of applying chemicals had been tried, the tireless and enthusiastic Dr. Tischendorf in 1843 printed all that it held of the New Testament. The text is partly Byzantine, partly Vaticanus and other types.

The last manuscript to call for attention is one which was rescued from a monastery in Lyons when the city was sacked in 1562. It passed into the hands of Theodore Beza (the assistant of Calvin) and hence is called Codex Bezae (denoted Codex D). It contains little more than the Gospels and the Acts of the Apostles. Beza presented it to the University of Cambridge in 1581, but expressed the hope that it would not be printed, as it appeared to be so faulty. Neverthcless, it was collated by scholars from time to time. By order of the University it was published in full by Dr. Kipling in 1793. A new edition was issued by Dr. Scrivener in 1864, and a photographic facsimile was published in 1889. It is reckoned to be of the early 6th century.

Dr. Scrivener states: 'No known manuscript contains so many bold and extensive interpolations (six hundred, it is said, in the Acts alone) . . . Its variations from the sacred text are beyond all other examples'. Two of the least offensive, out of those listed by Sir Frederic Kenyon, shall be given. In this manuscript in Acts 19.9, the detail is added that Paul preached daily in the school of Tyrannus 'from the fifth hour to the tenth'. In the first verse of this same chapter, the Bezae text runs very differently from that found in our Bibles: 'Now when Paul desired in his own mind to journey to Jerusalem, the Spirit spake unto him that he should turn back to Ephesus; and passing through the upper parts he cometh to Ephesus, and finding certain disciples he said unto them'.

The Controversy

This can now be summarized. Since the days of Bengel there had been a call, feeble at first, but steadily growing stronger with the passing of over a hundred years, for the discarding of the Textus Receptus (the old Byzantine or Traditional Text), and the construction of a new New Testament text, based on the readings of the oldest manuscripts. These scholars, well-intentioned but most misguided, were obsessed with their slogan that 'the older the manuscript, the closer must its text be to the autographs'. While in general, other factors being equal, this would be true, these textual critics blinded themselves to the fact that it was possible for an old manuscript to be a bad copy of an earlier bad copy, in which case there might be many omissions or additions of words and clauses, and other careless mistakes.

From the facts just given, the reader will note that from 1786, when reliable copies of the Codex Alexandrinus became available to scholars, well-edited copies of the other oldest codices followed in fairly rapid succession. The Ephraemi appeared in 1843, the Sinaiticus in 1862, the Bezae in 1864, and finally the Vaticanus in 1868. This no doubt gave more force to the call of the liberal theologians for a revision of the Greek New Testament Text. The wise of both schools of thought urged that the time was not yet, for ample opportunities must be given to the scholars of Christendom to study, to debate and if possible to resolve the problems of the many and great diversities of readings in the oldest manuscripts.

Yet on February 10th, 1870, the Convocation of Canterbury decided that the Authorized Version of the Bible should be revised and 'clear and plain errors', whether in the Greek Text or the English translation, rectified. Translation companies, one for the Old Testament and another for the New were appointed. Their membership was very mixed—learned conservatives had to work with those of the rising English school of German neology. There could not have been happy team work.

The Chairman of the New Testament Company was Bishop Samuel Wilberforce, of Winchester. He was the son of that great philanthropist who had worked both inside and outside of Parliament for the suppression of the slave trade and the liberation of its victims. At its first meeting two discordant notes were struck. First, it was proposed that a Unitarian (Dr. Vance Smith) should be co-opted on to the Translation Panel. Professor B. F. Westcott (later Bishop of Durham), Dr. (later Professor) F. J. A. Hort and Dean Stanley, of Westminster, probably the three most influential members of the Company, let it be known that they would resign if the Unitarian was excluded. The proposal was passed on a majority vote. This started a chain of incidents and acute controversy. Bishop Wilberforce registered his abhorrence by never again attending the meetings of the Company. (He met with a fatal accident on July 19th, 1873.) His place was taken by Bishop C. J. Ellicott of the then united sees of Gloucester and Bristol.

The New Text of Prof. B. F. Westcott and Dr. F. J. A. Hort

The second divisive matter related to the Greek Text. Dr. Hort, a most studious but very aggressive and dominating personality, had worked with his close friend Prof. Westcott for nearly twenty years on the Greek Text of the New Testament. Neither of these scholars had been evangelical and as the influence of the German neology increased they moved slowly and discreetly with the times. Dr. Hort, in particular, held the Textus Receptus in the utmost reproach. With the publication of the text of the Vaticanus in 1868 these two Cambridge dons lost no time in correcting, as they considered it, the Textus Receptus by means of the purer(?) texts of the Vaticanus, first and foremost, and then of the other four oldest codices. As these five manuscripts differed considerably, Dr. Hort used his 'intuitive power' to decide which of the alternatives was 'intrinsically probable'.

At the first meeting of the Revisers, Dr. Hort and Prof. Westcott distributed the page-proofs of their new text, on the pledge of secrecy, and with the evident design that it should replace the Textus Receptus. This embarrassed many of the members. They felt that their commission to rectify only 'plain and clear errors' did not envisage the construction of a new Greek text, which had not been known to Christendom for, quite definitely, about fifteen hundred years, and for which there was no proof that it was generally accepted as the genuine reproduction of the autographs in the period preceding the close of the 4th century.

Moreover, while all members were first-class Greek scholars, only one other amongst them was at home in textual criticism—Prebendary F. H. A. Scrivener. He, like Westcott and Hort, had graduated from Trinity College, Cambridge, and was considered by many to be equal, if not superior, to the two dons. It was agreed that at each meeting Dr. Scrivener should first state the case for the Textus Receptus, and be followed by Dr. Hort, who was determined that the Revised Version should go forth to the world based on his new text.

Most of the members were out of their depth in this controversy, and it would appear that usually about one third of those present stood by Dr. Scrivener while the rest deferred to the dons mainly because of their standing in the academic world.

There is evidence that there was not a little dissatisfaction on these grounds. Dean Merivale, after attending nineteen meetings, withdrew in disgust. Other scholars, for example Bishop Moberly, of Salisbury, and Archbishop Trench, of Dublin, showed their unhappiness by their rare attendances. Bishop Wordsworth, of St. Andrews, and the learned Archdeacon Lee, of Dublin, openly expressed their disillusionment (see *Revision Revised,* by Dean Burgon, pp. 228-232).

The work was completed by the end of 1880. On May 12th, 1881, the 'Westcott and Hort' (designated WH) New Testament in Greek was published, followed a few months later by Dr. Hort's Introduction, justifying his (approximately) six thousand departures from the traditional Greek text on the ground that his corrections were based on the Vaticanus or one of the four other ancient manuscripts. On May 17th the English Revised Version New Testament came from the press. Both books met with a storm of criticism. Canon F. C. Cook, the editor of the *Speaker's Commentary* (reputed to be familiar with fifty-two ancient and modern languages) opposed the WH text in his *Revised Version of the first three Gospels considered,* while Dean J. W. Burgon wrote a series of articles in the *Quarterly Review,* afterwards published as *Revision Revised.* Most regrettably both books are now out of print and only obtainable from libraries.

The WH Text, the restoration, or the adulteration, of the autographs?

Common sense asserts that if the texts of these five manuscripts, being the most ancient, are therefore pure and reliable reproductions of the writings of the New Testament pen-men, then there will be no, or at the most very little, difference between them. Dean Burgon subjected them to this test. He, as all textual critics had done before him, took the Textus Receptus as the most convenient standard of comparison (but not as the absolute standard of excellence). The figures have been given before, but as it is so rare to come across them and they are of such importance, they will bear repetition. In the four Gospels alone, the Dean found that the deflections from this standard, and therefore the extent to which they stood apart from one another were in the following proportions: Alexandrinus, 842; Ephraemi Rescript, Paris, 1798; Vaticanus, 2370; Sinaiticus, 3392; Bezae, 4697. The first conclusion he drew from these figures registering differences was, that four out of the five must be, while all five may be outrageously faulty copies. Further, he noted the readings in the Gospels peculiar to each codex. Those peculiar to the Alexandrinus number 133; to the Parisian Rescript 170; to the Vaticanus 197; while Sinaiticus exhibits 443; and the Bezae no fewer than 1829. Yet again, within the same limits, the Vaticanus is found to omit at least 2877 words; to add 536; to substitute 935; to transpose 2098; to modify 1132—in all 7578. The corresponding figures for Sinaiticus are respectively 3455, 839, 1114, 2299, 1265—in all 8972. Moreover the omissions, additions, substitutions, transpositions and modifications, are by no means the same in both. These five old uncials, the Dean asserted, are never once found to be in accord in respect of any single variant reading. The Vaticanus, the Sinaiticus and the Bezae codices were on this account, he considered, the depositories of the largest amount of fabricated readings, ancient blunders, and intentional perversions of truth, which are discoverable in any known copies of The Word of God (*Revision Revised,* XIX, 14, 16).

This great textual scholar concludes his survey with these words: 'Will anyone, after a candid survey of these premisses, deem us unreasonable, if we avow that such a specimen of the *concordia discors* which everywhere prevails between these oldest uncials (but which especially characterizes the Vaticanus, the Sinaiticus and the Bezae), indisposes us greatly to suffer their unsupported authority to determine for us the text of Scripture?' (*Revision Revised,* 17).

These particular manuscripts must ever be venerable on account of their age and also by their history. But they are certainly not the best, and because of the persistent use of that inaccurate term, we must in future refer to them as what they really are.

The WH text (together with its many modifications) represents the erosion of some of the outer defences of the 'Impregnable Rock of Holy Scripture'. It repudiates and casts doubt upon many passages and clauses which the Church as a whole has always regarded as part and parcel of Holy Scripture. It cannot be considered as promoted bythe 'singular care and Providence of God' but rather has been the subtle and undermining work of Satan, preparing the way for a succession of translations which are not accurate versions but painful perversions of Holy Writ.

This tampering with the Greek New Testament Text has many features similar to another grievous error let loose upon Christendom and the world about the same time—the theory of evolution. As Darwin's work undermined the belief of many in the biblical Doctrine of Divine Creation, so Westcott and Hort's theories have led to the disparagement of the Textus Receptus and the craze for a new Greek text and fresh translations of the Bible. As Darwin's followers generally ignore the objections to the theory of evolution, so the new textual critics never attempt to answer the classic works of a scholar like Dean Burgon in defence of the Reformation Text. As evolutionists have captured most of the key positions in the universities, colleges and schools, it has become common to exclude those who still believe in the Genesis account of Creation from teaching positions, and to regard them as behind the times. Very often those who from deep conviction uphold the Traditional Text and the Authorized Version of the Bible, are considered a nuisance, incomprehensible and cranks. But those who stand in the 'old paths' (Jer. 6.16) of morality and of evangelical religion are content to bear reproach, confident that the Protestant Reformed theology, built upon the Textus Receptus and the King James Version, will be vindicated before the throne of God.

When quiet in my house I sit,
  Thy Book be my companion still,
My joy Thy sayings to repeat,
  Talk o'er the records of Thy will,
And search the oracles divine,
Till every heartfelt word be mine.

O may the gracious words divine
  Subject of all my converse be!
So will the Lord His follower join,
  And walk and talk Himself with me;
So shall my heart His presence prove,
And burn with everlasting love.

Oft as I lay me down to rest,
  O may the reconciling word
Sweetly compose my weary breast!
  While, on the bosom of my Lord,
I sink in blissful dreams away,
And visions of eternal day.

Rising to sing my Saviour's praise,
  Thee may I publish all day long;
And let Thy precious word of grace
  Flow from my heart, and fill my tongue;
Fill all my life with purest love,
And join me to the church above.

(Charles Wesley)

Seven Aspects of Revival

By Malcolm H. Watts (Salisbury)

(1) It is generally true that a *brokenness of heart* has characterized the beginnings of Revivals. The church of the area affected, under the growing pressure of God the Holy Ghost, has begun to yield and give in to God. It is a most singular manifestation of God's power. Space will not permit me to give illustration of this from each of the great Revivals of the past, so for the moment we shall confine ourselves to one particular revival—that of 1859. On October 3rd, 1858 Humphrey Jones was ministering in Wales in a place called Ysbyty Ystwyth and, although he preached with great fervour from Amos 6.1, a coldness and deadness seemed to be in the church. After the meeting the preacher made complaint to the elders: 'Not one of you helped me with so much as an "Amen".' Then one of them, a godly brother, rose and said: 'It is very difficult with a man, when the ministry condemns him, to cry "Amen" with it'. With that he burst into tears and fell back into his seat. An eye-witness tells us that immediately the entire church was struck and 'every face was bowed low and bathed in tears'. Officers of the church must never think that they are beyond rebuke, nor must they ever think that they have no need for a new work of grace. 'Take heed therefore unto yourselves' is an exhortation to such (Acts 20.28), for if church-leaders are hardened, all in their care will suffer loss: 'The *house* of the proud shall be destroyed' (Prov. 15.25). Now that must also happen to the members. An account of the same revival in Ireland will help us here. William Campbell, leader of the revival in Islandmagee, traced the history of the revival there to its origin: 'The first manifestation was on Wednesday, the 8th June (1859), *the day of humiliation* prior to the communion . . . Many came up to the house of God that day—they could not tell how it was—with more than an ordinary feeling of godly fear . . . From that day until the present time, God has been walking in mercy throughout the length and breadth of the parish.' The whole church had first to be humbled. Believers must be brought low and be truly humbled for sin before there is hope (Lam. 3.29). It is when we are made to see our weakness and cease from our striving, that we can really lay hold upon God for our strength (Is. 27.5); for not until all wrong attitudes and hard prejudices are smashed before God will the church see its desperate need for pardoning and restoring power; and not until such a time will God grant it.

(2) A more constant and diligent *attendance at the means of grace* is also a promising feature: in barns, schools and private houses people begin to gather in ever-increasing numbers. That could have been observed in the early days of the Protestant Revival of the fifteenth and sixteenth centuries. Take Scotland as an example. When John Knox returned to Edinburgh towards the end of 1555, he little realized that Scotland was soon to be won by grace, but there were indications of the divine purpose. 'His whispered name ran like magic through the tall 'lands'—the towering tenements of the Royal Mile: and still they came and still they listened' (Elizabeth Whitley). 'Their fervency doth ravish me,' wrote Knox in high spiritual delight. In Edinburgh he was able to preach to 'a greater audience than ever before he had done in that town'. 'The trumpet blew the old sound three days together,' wrote Knox to his mother, 'till private houses of indifferent largeness could not contain the voice of it'. At the sight of it, he abounded more and more in hope: 'Rejoice . . . the time of our deliverance approacheth'. That has always been the case in Revival. This matter of church-attendance may be seen in the light of God's sovereignty and it may be seen in the light of man's responsibility: God's sovereignty, for when people begin to frequent the house of God as they should it is because they are of them 'whose spirit God hath raised, to go up to build the house of the Lord' (Ezra. 1.5); but man's responsibility, for faithful and regular attendance is clearly a duty, and God acts according to this principle: 'them that honour me I will honour, but they that despise me shall be lightly esteemed' (1 Sam. 2.30). Believers (and this applies particularly to church-members should never be absent from the Lord's Day services or from the mid-week service, unless it proves to be impossible, for God responds to the worship when *all* His people gather, by filling the place with His glory (Exod. 40.34; 1 Kgs. 8.11).

(3) It is a hopeful sign when *God raises up preachers* and there is an evident desire to hear them. There was no better proof of a work beginning in the sixteenth century than when Luther, Calvin, Zwingli, Farel, Beza and a host of others raised their voices in the cause of truth. A generation or so later witnessed the emergence of a remarkable company of devout scholars and preachers. These were 'stalwarts of evangelicalism,' 'they lived in the presence of the Eternal' and even now they are 'names that cannot die'. Puritan preachers proclaimed the advent of the Puritan Revival.

But general decline set in again. It was time for God to revive His work and as the hour of grace struck for England, John and Charles Wesley, together with George Whitefield, began their journeyings which led them throughout the British Isles. By 1744 forty powerful preachers were aiding the Wesleys as they ranged the country. When the Archbishop of Armagh complained about the using of these men, many of whom could not boast of the world's learning, Charles Wesley replied: 'You hold your peace and the stones cry out!' This was of God. Revival had begun. Today we are seeing a resurgence of sound doctrine. We thank God for it. But now we want to see the raising up of great preachers. May God raise them up in answer to our prayers! (Matt. 9.38 Note: the thrusting out of preachers will precede the harvest).

(4) At such times there always is, at a very early period, the *rousing of the church to the holy work of prayer*. By this means the way of the Lord is prepared. Earnest desires in the hearts of God's chosen to take unto themselves the burden of the work and pray, as never before, promises revival as sure as any oracle of prophecy (Ps. 102.13). Further biblical support for this may be found in many other passages of God's Word (Jud. 3.9, 10; 2 Chron. 15.15; Acts 4.31). Let us illustrate from the 1904 Revival. 'The Carmarthenshire Presbytery urged,' wrote Eifion Evans, 'that the week of prayer in January, 1900, should be earnestly concerned with 'a more extensive outpouring of the Holy Spirit'. In North Wales, too, the same urgency was emphasized in several presbyteries . . . Apart from such collective evidences there were those who longed for a personal as well as a national quickening . . . The people of God should be praying in these days for Revival in our time. So often no prayer is offered for it in the Prayer-Meeting. Months pass and not one soul prays for an outpouring of the Holy Spirit. 'Ye have not, because ye ask not' (James 4.2). The presence of believers at their appointed Prayer-Meetings is demanded by the God of Heaven in view of the desperate state of things at the present time.

(5) *Real soul-concern* is one of the most hopeful signs. Charles H. Spurgeon, who saw something of Revival here in England and also in Ireland, preached on this very subject: 'When some begin to be impressed, when you find in the after-meeting, some in tears who do not know much about the Gospel yet, but who want to know; and when, here and there, you see signs of deep repentance for sin, and a humble trembling . . . all these are tokens for good.' The biographies of men used of God in Revivals all lend support to Spurgeon's observation. John Wesley first visited Cornwall in 1743 and, preaching at Treswithen Downs near St. Ives, he saw the beginnings of something which was destined to affect the whole country: 'It was here first,' he wrote in his journal, '(that) I observed a little impression made on two or three of the hearers'. When Daniel Rowlands began to preach in Wales about the year 1738, according to his biographer the Rev. E. Morgan, 'The impression on the hearts of most people, was that of awe and distress'. Rowland Hill, a remarkable man indeed, preached with unwearied diligence as he travelled with the gospel and one wrote to him from Bideford informing him of the success of his labours: 'Indeed, sir, there seems to be a lasting impression left on the minds of many.' What are these 'impressions'? They are the strange and wonderful effects of the preached Word making men in earnest about their soul's state. How careless we are about our own souls! We never seek spiritual counsel. Decline sets in and we refuse to attend to the matter. Things sadly grow worse. It is not so in Revival (Acts 2.37; Jn. 16.8-11; Zech. 12.10).

(6) The *desire to testify to God's saving grace* is also one of the early evidences of a Revival. In the Spring of 1859 Aberdeen was witnessing great things: 'The simplest utterances of even babes in Christ were instrumental in converting sinners. In fact, the testifying of believers and its effect was a marked feature of the work' (Macpherson). The origin of the Revival which flooded Ulster with blessing may

be traced to the word of testimony which a certain Mrs. Coville gave to a dying woman in Ballymena, for it led to the conversion of James McQuilkin, who had heard it and who had been deeply affected by it. 'Her words were overheard,' wrote Dr. Paisley in his History of the Revival, 'and the barbed arrows from this bow drawn at a venture fastened with a mighty pricking upon his conscience'. McQuilkin was to be God's man in a Revival about to break over Ireland.

Man cannot effect Revival. The sovereignty of God is involved. But I do call the reader's attention to the fact of such testimonies. God ordained that these should be the sparks of the blessed fire. Many of us are very reluctant to tell anyone of the Saviour's love and yet we long and pray for blessing. Friend, be faithful in this matter, and who knows but that God will be gracious? (Isa. 2.3; Psa.66.16; Mk. 5.19).

(7) A *solemnity* is also apparent. One man, visiting a revival area, was impressed with something unusual. He did not know exactly what it was. 'What has happened here?' was his question. 'Something is in the air. Things seem like the day of judgment.' He was near the truth. The destinies of souls were being made known. God was there. 'An unusual solemnity'; 'intense earnestness'; 'consideration and seriousness'; 'deep silence, broken only by a sigh or a sob'; 'the atmosphere of eternity'; these are the expressions used in the various histories of Revivals. In these grand and impressive scenes the Lord God appeared on behalf of His fainting church. Souls were first gripped by the powers of the world to come: then all heaven seemed to break upon them. Surely, it was this solemnity which elevated the souls of men to a high and holy state and surely it was in that state that God met with them. Every church should think on these things. A diviner element must pervade our services. All meetings of God's people must be so conducted as to meet the approval of the Majesty on High, so that, in His time, He may be moved to appear in the midst to save and sanctify His own (Josh. 3.5; Joel 2.15-21; Acts 9.31).

Revive Thy work, O Lord,
Thy mighty arm make bare;
Speak with the voice that wakes the dead,
And make Thy people hear!

Revive Thy work, O Lord,
Create soul-thirst for Thee;
And hungering for the Bread of Life,
O may our spirits be!

Revive Thy work, O Lord:
Give power unto Thy Word;
Grant that Thy blessèd Gospel may
In living faith be heard.

Revive Thy work, O Lord,
Disturb the sleep of death;
Quicken the smouldering embers now
By Thine almighty breath!

Revive Thy work, O Lord,
Exalt Thy precious Name;
And, by the Holy Ghost, our love
For Thee and Thine inflame!

Revive Thy work, O Lord,
And give refreshing showers;
Thy glory shall be all Thine own,
The blessing, Lord, be ours!

(Albert Midlane)

The Keeping of the Lord's Day

By S. M. Houghton

In this brief article it will be taken as axiomatic that man as an individual and man in society needs one day's rest in seven, neither more nor less; that such a day has been appointed for him by a merciful and all-wise Creator; that man as a fallen creature tends to kick (and often violently) against the barriers by which the day is marked off from its fellows; and that perpetual vigilance on the part of those who fear God and are resolved to keep His commands is essential to maintain the sacred day in being and prevent it from being filched openly or surreptitiously from mankind. Many, if not all, of our readers will be well aware that in February, 1983, a Sunday Trading Bill was debated for five hours in the House of Commons. It proposed the abolition of all laws which restrict Sunday Trading hours and, in effect, would have rendered the Lord's Day no different from any other day of the week. Shops would have been left free to open 24 hours a day for seven days a week. In the mercy of God the Bill was defeated by 106 votes to 205. Had it been otherwise, and had the Bill become law, it would have marked a significant step in the downward march of the nation to defiant ungodliness.

Not all who voted against the Bill did so from Christian principles. Some were merely concerned to defend employees against any extension of the hours of work in general; others, to keep in check the doubling of wages for Sunday work, for this would bear heavily on the owners of shops; still others were keen to prevent ill effects on the social life of the community. The few, the true God-fearers, argued against the Bill from a biblical standpoint. The Member of Parliament for Devon West, for example, spoke as follows:

'Christians naturally believe in the Fourth Commandment, which provides that the seventh day be kept as a day of rest and worship. I believe that to be right and wise. It is wise and common sense for the individual, for the family, and for the nation. I believe that it is common sense as well as a Christian standpoint that we should preserve one day in the week that is set aside for rest, relaxation and complete change. For those who have a faith and for those who believe in the Christian way of life, people should be allowed to worship with complete freedom. The Fourth Commandment, which should not be put on one side, is sensible if we wish to live in a civilised society. We live in a mad enough rush for six days of the week and it is important that one day should be set aside for complete change'. The Member of Parliament for Belfast (South) reminded his fellows that 'The Sabbath was made for man and not man for the Sabbath. The Sabbath is a creation ordinance for men, who need that tempo of change and relaxation. When we respect the law of God, people will respect the laws of the land and there will be no arguments about enforcement'.

The Lord's Day in Today's World

The Lord's Day question is intimately bound up with relations which exist between the believer in God and His incarnate Son on the one hand, and the unbeliever or the merely nominal Christian on the other. Both are represented in our public bodies, national and local, both have their peculiar interests, both are involved in the application of the principles underlying the sacred Day. For evangelical Christians the question presents itself, How far is a national Parliament, in a state which remains professedly Christian, entitled to legislate in this matter for a people who are increasingly casting aside the 'bands' and 'cords' of God. At one time all members of the legislature were not only professedly Christian but also professedly Protestant. The taking of their seats was conditioned by an oath taken 'on the true faith of a Protestant'. In 1829 came Roman Catholic Emancipation (bitterly opposed by a minority of the House of Commons), not the giving to Romanists of the right to vote, as some erroneously suppose, but the extension to them of permission to sit in Parliament. Yet the oath still included the phrase, 'on the true faith of a Christian', which members of the Church of Rome, of course, felt free to use. Later in the century this phrase was dropped, but the phrase 'so help me God' remained, excluding men who claimed to disbelieve altogether in Deity. So it came about that Jews as well as Christians could belong to the legislature, and indeed men of any religion who professed belief in God.

Towards the end of the 19th Century came the controversy linked with the name of Charles Bradlaugh, freethinker and atheist, who was elected M.P. for Northampton in 1880. His claim to affirm instead of swearing on the Bible was refused by both government and legislature and he was thereby unseated. Re-elected the following year, he was ejected from the House of Commons by force. In 1885 Northampton claimed that its sovereign will to have Bradlaugh as its M.P. was superior to the will of Parliament to reject him. A new Speaker in the House of Commons then allowed him to take his seat. In 1888 Parliament legalised the substitution of an affirmation for an oath both in the House of Commons and the law courts. Men of any or no religious belief then became eligible to occupy seats in Parliament. Hence it comes about that 20th-Century Parliaments are composed of men of much diversity of opinion, Christian and non-Christian. Yet this is the body which deals with matters affecting the sanctity of the day of days.

The Day's Origin and Pattern

The evangelical Christian cannot but experience soul concern over the matter. The right keeping of the Lord's Day is part and parcel of his faith in God. His earthly nationality (which does not forsake him on account of his profession of Christianity), his love of country, his deep-seated reverence for all that is of God, and his quickened conscience, demand of him a God-centred outlook on matters which, at national level, pertain to the spiritual and temporal welfare of neighbours and friends and fellow-countrymen. Certainly his own personal testimony and influence cannot but converge upon the principles laid down by God Himself in His Word for the right observance of His day. For His day it was and remains, let men think what they will. His own divine testimony assures us that upon it He rested and was Himself refreshed (Exod. 31.17), a declaration which is almost startling in its implications and its assurance of blessing. Many of our fellow-men seek to convince us that Sunday-keeping emanates rather from Puritanism, which they hate, than from God, and claim that it is a 17th-century creation, reinvigorated by Victorianism, but now effete, outdated, only fit for discardment, a grotesque caricature of God's true intention.

We think not so. In its essential character it dates from the divine rest following upon the six days' work. Its pattern was fixed by God. Not that it was made by God for Himself; He faints not, as does man, neither is weary. It was ordained for man, a truth restated and confirmed by Christ Jesus in the words, 'The Sabbath was made for man'. It was given renewed authority by its incorporation in the 'ten words' of Sinai, confirmed by the prophets, clarified by the Lord in the days of His flesh, emphasized by His resurrection appearances and by Pentecost, and (with the transference of the day from the seventh to the first, thus stressing a *new* work wrought by God) glimpsed at in Epistles and Apocalypse. It is the connecting link between the two tables of the law. In gospel days its keeping is a vivid testimony to an unbelieving world of the blessedness of the consecrated Christian life. It sets forth the Christian's ambition to seek first God's kingdom and God's righteousness. In its keeping is great reward.

In the New Testament the Lord's Day is not dealt with in legalistic fashion, as if on the first day of the week the Christian is deprived of his liberty and put as it were into a strait-jacket. It may surprise some that, along with the preaching of the gospel in a Gentile world which kept no such day, there is no particular mention, from the Acts of the Apostles onwards, of its obligatory character. The Council at Jerusalem (Acts 15) which sent to the Gentile churches such decrees as seemed good to the Holy Ghost and to it, made no mention in them of the Lord's Day. Yet it is clear that the apostles gave teaching about the keeping of the day wherever churches were planted. There is a strong probability that the absence of a stronger approach to the subject stems from the fact that many of the early believers were slaves, required by their masters to work without any regard to the keeping of a sacred day, and a refusal to work would have involved the direst consequences. The Christian conscience is not subjected to intolerable burdens. There were dangers enough in the situation on other counts. Countless early martyrdoms testify to that; blood was shed in fearful abundance in the early Christian centuries. And the Lord, in gentleness to His own, as it were says on this issue, 'I will put upon you none other burden'. And so it has remained. The New Testament does not legislate upon the subject of the Lord's Day as does the Old Testament upon the seventh-day Sabbath. There is a carrying on from one Testament to the other of certain principles, and the Four Gospels certainly show us the true spirit of the day in contrast with the strait-jacket attitude of scribes and Pharisees, but fresh legislation there is none. Yet the Holy Spirit in His gracious operations quickens mind and conscience in regard to the matter, reveals the mind of the Lord, 'shows thee, O man, what is good', renders tender the believer's inmost convictions, and shows him how, in the context of time and opportunity, the first day of the week, the day of resurrection, may be kept and used to the divine glory and to his own and others' good.

It is not so much a question of, May I do this? or, Is it right to do that? The exercised Christian, seeking to know and to follow the mind of the Lord in the Word, and listening prayerfully to the promptings of the Spirit, intuitively perceives the will of God. The very fact that he keeps the first day and not the seventh is eloquent private testimony to himself that he has already entered into rest in Christ, and that, by a marvellous act of divine imputation, the righteousness which justifies him is not his own but Another's. The day itself announces to him that he is 'in Christ' beyond the reach of condemnation, and 'accepted in the Beloved'. He is enabled to rejoice and be glad in it. He embraces it as 'the day which the Lord has made'.

'O Day of Rest and Gladness . . . Joy and Light'

How then in the use of the day can he (or she) glorify the Redeemer whose Name the day bears? Both negatively and positively! He will gladly lay aside the normal business of life, the mundane occupation allocated to him by an all-wise Father. The writer remembers vividly after many years the words of Sir Thomas Inskip (later Viscount Caldecote), at the time Solicitor General, who, addressing a public meeting, assured his hearers that, even when greatly pressed by legal business, at twelve midnight on a Saturday, he would willingly and joyfully lay down secular involvements and consecrate the ensuing 24 hours to the Lord. For the believer in a less exalted calling, and making very little 'noise' in the world, the same principle holds good. Necessary domestic cares will be kept to a minimum. Essential preparation for eating and drinking, and keeping warm, will be undertaken, as far as is humanly possible, before the sacred hours begin, so that attendance upon the means of grace and the worship of God in fellowship with others is not hindered. Children will from the cradle upwards be taught that there is 'something different' about the Lord's day. The usual run of toys will be replaced by other attractions and employs, more in keeping with the day's character. Family joys should be at their height. It is sad testimony to godliness when gladness is banished in favour of gloom on the week's opening day. True Christianity will heighten true joy rather than take from it. 'The voice of rejoicing and salvation is in the tabernacles of the righteous' (Psa. 118.15).

Then, too, the Christian learns in a multitude of unobtrusive ways that such observance and use of the day is for his highest good. His body is rested, his mind is refreshed, his soul is fed as with marrow and fatness (Psa. 63.5), his companions are helped, not to say edified. As he seeks to be 'in the Spirit on the Lord's day' (Rev. 1.10), his meditation becomes sweet, with the inescapable consequence that he is 'glad in the Lord' (Psa. 104.34). Our last phrase significantly comes from the ending of a psalm devoted to the celebration of God's works in nature—light, the atmosphere, seas and waters, mountains and valleys, beasts and birds, grass and trees, sun and moon, leviathan and creeping things, and much else—all find mention in the ascription of praise by the psalmist to God; whereby we may learn that blessedness is to be found in the contemplation of God's works as well as of His words. In the works of His hands as well as in the words of His mouth we may exult.

But for the most part it will be the Word itself that normally furnishes food for thought and theme for praise. As that Word is read at home, or received in ministry in Christian gatherings, or found in Christian writings, it becomes a 'found' Word, a word 'eaten', the 'joy and rejoicing of the heart' (Jer. 15.16). To hide the Word in one's heart is one chief way of giving glory to God.

Sweet is the work, my God, my King,
To praise Thy Name, give thanks
and sing,
To show Thy love by morning light,
And talk of all Thy truth at night.

My heart shall triumph in the Lord,
And bless His works and bless His
word:
Thy works of grace, how bright they
shine!
How deep Thy counsels! how divine!

Sin, my worst enemy before,
Shall vex my eyes and ears no more;
My inward foes shall all be slain,
Nor Satan break my peace again.

Sweet is the day of sacred rest,
No mortal care shall seize my breast;
Oh, may my heart in tune be found,
Like David's harp of solemn sound.

Then shall I share a glorious part,
When grace hath well refined my
heart,
And fresh supplies of joy are shed
Like holy oil to cheer my head.

Then shall I see and hear and know
All I desired or wished below;
And every power find sweet employ
In that eternal world of joy.

(*Isaac Watts,* 1719.)

O day of rest and gladness,
O day of joy and light,
O balm of care and sadness,
Most beautiful, most bright!
On thee the high and lowly,
Through ages joined in tune,
Sing, 'Holy, Holy, Holy,'
To the great God Triune.

Thou art a port protected
From storms that round us rise;
A garden intersected
With streams of Paradise;
Thou art a cooling fountain
In life's dry, dreary sand;
From thee, like Pisgah's mountain,
We view our promised land.

On thee, at the creation,
The light first had its birth;
On thee, for our salvation,
Christ rose from depths of earth;
On thee our Lord victorious
The Spirit sent from heaven:
And thus on thee most glorious
A triple light was given.

To-day on weary nations
The heavenly manna falls;
To holy convocations
The silver trumpet calls,
Where gospel-light is glowing
With pure and radiant beams,
And living water flowing
With soul-refreshing streams.

New graces ever gaining
From this our day of rest,
We reach the rest remaining
To spirits of the blest,
To Holy Ghost be praises,
To Father and to Son;
The church her voice upraises
To Thee, blest Three in One.

(*Christopher Wordsworth,* 1862.)